THE SANSKRIT LANGUAGE

THE GREAT LANGUAGES

General Editor

L. R. PALMER, M.A., D.PHIL., PH.D.
formerly Professor of Comparative Philology
in the University of Oxford

PUBLISHED

THE FRENCH LANGUAGE
By A. EWERT, M.A., LITT.D.

THE SPANISH LANGUAGE, TOGETHER WITH PORTUGUESE, CATALAN, BASQUE
By WILLIAM F. ENTWISTLE, M.A., LITT.D., LL.D.

THE CHINESE LANGUAGE
By R. A. D. FORREST, M.A.

RUSSIAN AND THE SLAVONIC LANGUAGES
By WILLIAM F. ENTWISTLE, M.A., LITT.D., and
W. A. MORRISON, B.A., PH.D.

THE LATIN LANGUAGE
By L. R. PALMER, M.A., D.PHIL., PH.D.

THE SCANDINAVIAN LANGUAGES
By EINAR HAUGEN, M.A., PH.D., LITT.D., L.H.D.

THE ROMANCE LANGUAGES
By W. D. ELCOCK, M.A., L.ÈS.L., D. DE L'U. TOULOUSE
(revised with a new introduction by JOHN N. GREEN. M.A., D.PHIL.

THE ITALIAN LANGUAGE
By BRUNO MIGLIORINI, DOTT. IN LETTERE
(abridged and re-cast by T. G. GRIFFITH. M.A., B.LITT.)

In Preparation

THE GREEK LANGUAGE
By L. R. PALMER, M.A., D.PHIL., PH.D.

To be published in Spring 1978

THE GERMAN LANGUAGE
By R. E. KELLER, D.PHIL., M.A.

THE SANSKRIT LANGUAGE

by

T. BURROW

FABER AND FABER
3 Queen Square
London

First published in 1955
by Faber and Faber Limited
3 Queen Square London W.C. 1
Second impression 1959
Second edition 1965
New and revised edition 1973
Reprinted 1977
Printed in Great Britain by
Robert MacLehose and Company Limited
Printers to the University of Glasgow

ISBN 0 571 04819 6

PREFACE

The discovery of the Sanskrit language by European scholars at the end of the eighteenth century was the starting point from which developed the study of the comparative philology of the Indo-European languages and eventually the whole science of modern linguistics. In spite of this there does not exist in English any book presenting a systematic account of Sanskrit in its relation to the other Indo-European languages. One may even go further and say that there is no work in any language which adequately fulfils this purpose. Wackernagel's great work, begun sixty years ago, still remains to be completed, although, with the recent appearance of a further instalment, its completion has been brought nearer. Thumb's *Handbuch des Sanskrit* which was of service to many generations of students is now very much dated, and always fell between the two stools of trying to be an elementary text-book of Sanskrit and a treatise on its comparative grammar at the same time.

On account of its antiquity and well-preserved structure Sanskrit is of unique importance for the study of Indo-European, and an up-to-date account of its comparative grammar is necessary, not only to students of Sanskrit itself, but also to those interested in any branch of Indo-European philology. Consequently when I was asked to contribute a book on Sanskrit to the series *The Great Languages*, it was clear that by concentrating on the study of Sanskrit from this point of view the greatest need would be met. This is particularly true since for the history of Indo-Aryan inside India, from Sanskrit down to modern times, students already have at their disposal the excellent work of Jules Bloch.

Providing a reliable account of Sanskrit in its relation to Indo-European is at the present moment not altogether a simple matter. Forty years ago there existed a generally agreed doctrine of Indo-European theory which had been systematically presented in the early years of the century in Brugmann's *Grundriss*. At that time it would merely have been a question of adopting this corpus of agreed doctrine to the needs of the student and general reader, and of the particular language described. Since then the discovery of Hittite has revolutionised Indo-European studies and a considerable part of the older theory has been unable to stand up to the new evidence. Consequently Indo-European studies can now be said to be in a state of flux. New theories have appeared, and are clearly necessary, but the process is not yet completed. There is no generally received body of doctrine replacing the old, and many of the fundamental points at issue remain disputed. Furthermore attention has tended to be largely concentrated on phonetic questions raised by Hittite, and matters of morphology, on which its evidence is also of fundamental importance, have been less exhaustively studied.

In these circumstances I have attempted to present a reasonably consistent account of the comparative grammar of Sanskrit based on the evaluation of the new evidence. A work like this is not the place to enter into discussion of the various conflicting theories that are in the field, if only for reasons of space, and bibliographical references have been systematically omitted. What has been written in recent years on these problems has been taken into account, and such theories as appear acceptable are incorporated in this exposition. It is hoped that it will go some way to providing an up-to-date synthesis of a subject which in its present state is hardly accessible outside the widely scattered specialist literature.

The study of Sanskrit has advanced recently in another direction also. Investigation of the influence of the pre-Aryan languages of India on Sanskrit and on Indo-Aryan in its later stages, has shown that this is considerable and solid results have been achieved. As far as the structure of the language is concerned, particularly in its early stage, which is the only one relevant to the comparative study of Indo-European, this influence hardly counts at all. On the other hand in the field of vocabulary it is very important that the Indo-European and non-Indo-European elements should be separated. The last chapter of the book contains a summary of the main findings on the part of the subject so far as established at the present stage. Future work will no doubt add more.

T. Burrow

PREFACE TO THE THIRD EDITION

A number of alterations to the text of the *The Sanskrit Language* have been made in this edition, the principal ones being as follows. In Chapter I the latter part of Section 6 has been rewritten to conform with the now prevailing opinion that the Aryan vestiges of the ancient Near East are to be connected specifically with Indo-Aryan. Also rewritten are Section 11 and (in part) Section 17 of Chapter III to take account of the conclusions reached on those topics in the articles of mine which are quoted in the Appendix. Chapter VIII has been renamed Loanwords in Sanskrit, so that loanwords from Greek and Iranian (Section 2) can be dealt with in it as well as loanwords from Austro-Asiatic and Dravidian (Section 1). The list of loanwords from Dravidian in this chapter has been shortened by the omission of some items now considered to be false or dubious.

At the end an Appendix has been added containing references to the most important contributions to the subject which have appeared since 1955, and also some supplementary notes.

September 1972 T. BURROW

CONTENTS

CHAPTER I

SANSKRIT AND INDO-EUROPEAN

§1. Indo-Aryan and Indo-Iranian

In the greater part of India today languages are spoken which are derived from a single form of speech which was introduced into India by invaders from the north-west more than three thousand years ago. The invading peoples were known in their own language as *ā́rya-*, a word which is also commonly used as an adjective meaning ' noble, honourable '. Behind them in Central Asia remained kindred peoples who eventually occupied the plateau of Iran, as well as large tracts of Central Asia. These peoples used the same name of themselves, in Avestan *airya-*, and from the genitive plural of this word the modern name Īrān is ultimately derived. In conformance with this usage the term *Aryan* is now used as the common name of these peoples and their languages ; alternatively the term Indo-Iranian is commonly used. To distinguish the Indian branch from the Iranian, the term *Indo-Aryan* has been coined, and as applied to language, it covers the totality of languages and dialects derived from this source from the earliest times to the present day. It is practical to distinguish three periods, Old, Middle and Modern Indo-Aryan. The classical form of Old Indo-Aryan eventually came to be designated by the term *Saṃskṛta-* meaning ' polished, cultivated, correct (according to the rules of grammar) ', in contradistinction to *Prākṛta* the speech of the uneducated masses, which was the same Indo-Aryan in origin, but was subject to a process of steady change and evolution. As a term to distinguish Indo-Aryan from the non-Aryan languages the adjective *ā́rya-* was used in opposition to *mlecchá-* ' barbarian '. In addition we may note that one of the terms for ' speech ', *bhāratī* (sc. *vāk*) had originally an ethnic sense, meaning ' language of the Bharatas '.[1]

[1] At an early period the most prominent of the Indo-Aryan tribes, whence also the indigenous name of India *bhārata(-varṣa)*.

Sanskrit in its narrower sense applies to standard classical Sanskrit as regulated by the grammarians but may be conveniently used more widely as equivalent to Old Indo-Aryan. In this sense it covers both classical Sanskrit and the pre-classical or Vedic language. Middle Indo-Aryan, that is Prakrit in the widest sense of the term, comprises three successive stages of development: (1) The earliest stage is represented in literature by Pāli, the language of the canonical writings of the *Thera-vāda* school of Buddhism. This is a language of the centuries immediately preceding the Christian era. On the same level of development are the various dialects recorded in the inscriptions of Aśoka (*c.* 250 B.C.), and also the language of other early inscriptions. (2) Prakrit in the narrower sense of the word, or Standard Literary Prakrit, represents the stage of development reached some centuries after the Christian era. It is found mainly in the Drama and in the religious writings of the Jains. The various literary forms of Prakrit were stabilised by grammarians at this period and, as a written language, it remains essentially unchanged during the succeeding centuries. (3) Apabhraṃśa is known from texts of the tenth century A.D. but as a literary language it was formed some centuries earlier. It represents the final stage of Middle Indo-Aryan, the one immediately preceding the emergence of the Modern Indo-Aryan languages. The Modern languages, Bengali, Hindi, Gujarati, Marathi, etc., begin to be recorded from about the end of the first millennium A.D., and from then their development can be followed as they gradually acquire their present-day form.

Thus we have before us in India three thousand years of continuous linguistic history, recorded in literary documents. During the course of this period a single, and originally alien idiom has spread over the greater part of the country, and, evolving by slow degrees, has resulted in the various languages now spoken in Northern and Central India. Enormous changes have taken place during this time, and the languages we meet today are very different indeed from the ancient speech spoken by the invading Aryan tribes. Nevertheless the documentation available enables us to follow in detail the various intermediate stages of development and to observe how, by changes hardly noticeable from generation to generation, an original language has altered into descendant languages which superficially at any rate, are now barely recognisable as the same.

The earliest document of the linguistic history of Indo-Aryan is the *Ṛgveda*, which, by rough guess-work, is placed in the region of 1000 B.C. The language we find there is the source from which all later developments in India have arisen. But this language itself had evolved out of a yet earlier form of speech, by precisely the same kind of slow change and alteration which caused it to evolve later into something else. This earlier evolution is unrecorded by any direct documentation, but it can be reconstructed in considerable detail by means of comparison with related languages. By this method two stages in the prehistory of the language can be established: (1) By comparison of early Indo-Aryan with the very closely related Iranian, it is possible to form a fairly accurate idea of the original Indo-Iranian or Aryan language from which both have evolved. (2) By comparing Indo-Aryan and Iranian with the other Indo-European languages (enumerated below) it is possible also to go beyond this, and to reconstruct in general outline the characteristics of the original language from which all these are derived.

Since Iranian in view of its very close relationship with Indo-Aryan is of the first importance for the study of Indo-Aryan philology, a short account of its distribution and documentation is desirable. The migration of the Indo-Aryans to India brought about, or perhaps was the final stage of, the separation of the primitive Aryan community into two distinct divisions which henceforth evolved separately in linguistic as in other respects. The Iranians left behind in the region of the Oxus valley[1] proceeded to expand rapidly in various directions, occupying not only the Iranian plateau which remained their centre of gravity, but also large tracts of Central Asia, extending on the one hand to the confines of China and on the other hand to the plains of South Russia. From an early period Iranian showed a much stronger tendency to differentiation into separate dialects which soon became independent languages than was the case with Indo-Aryan, which for geographical and other reasons maintained a comparative unity over most of North India for a very long period.

For the old period Iranian is represented by documents in Avestan and Old Persian, and it is these texts which are of

[1] A recollection of Chorasmia as their original home is preserved in the traditions of the ancient Iranians.

prime importance for comparison with Vedic Sanskrit. *Avesta* is the name given to the ancient collection of sacred writings preserved by the adherents of the Zoroastrian religion, and it is after this that the language is named. It is an eastern Iranian dialect, the exact location of which has not been precisely determined. The oldest section of the Avesta, the *Gāθās* are attributed to Zoroaster himself. Concerning his date there has been much dispute, and it seems that the traditional date of the Zoroastrians themselves, which places him around 600 B.C. can hardly be correct. The language of the *Gāθās* is no less ancient than that of the *Ṛgveda,* and for this and other reasons the composition of the two texts must belong roughly to the same period. Old Persian, a south-western dialect, and one showing tendencies to modernisation in comparison with the earliest Avestan, is preserved in inscriptions of the Achaemenian kings in a special cuneiform alphabet invented for the purpose.

The relations between this ancient Iranian and the language of the Veda are so close that it is not possible satisfactorily to study one without the other. Grammatically the differences are very small ; the chief differentiation in the earliest period lies in certain characteristic and well-defined phonetic changes which have affected Iranian on the one hand and Indo-Aryan on the other. It is quite possible to find verses in the oldest portion of the *Avesta,* which simply by phonetic substitutions according to established laws can be turned into intelligible Sanskrit. The greater part of the vocabulary is held in common and a large list could be provided of words shared between the two which are absent from the rest of Indo-European. This resemblance is particularly striking in the field of culture and religion, and may be illustrated by a few examples: Skt. *híraṇya-*, Av. *zaranya-* 'gold', Skt. *sénā*, Av. *haēnā*, O. Pers. *hainā* 'army', Skt. *ṛṣṭí-*, Av., O. Pers. *aršti-* 'spear', Skt. *kṣatrá-*, Av. *xšaθra-* 'sovereignty', Skt. *ásura-*, Av. *ahura-* 'lord', Skt. *yajñá-*, Av. *yasna-* 'sacrifice', Skt. *hótar-*, Av. *zaotar-* 'sacrificing priest', Skt. *sóma-*, Av. *haoma-* 'the sacred drink Soma', Skt. *átharvan-* 'a class of priest', Av. *aθaurvan-*, *āθravan-* 'fire-priest', Skt. *aryamán-*, Av. *airyaman-* 'member of a religious sodality'. In the same way we find the names of divinities and mythological personages held in common, e.g., Skt. *Mitrá-*, Av. *miθra-*, Skt. *Yamá-*, son of *Vivásvant-*, Av. *Yima*, son of *Vīvahvant-*, Skt. *Apā́ṃ Nápāt*, Av. *apąm napāt*

'Grandson of the waters' (a divinity), etc. In this field, however, movements of religious reform with which the name of Zarathuštra is associated have tended to alter the picture from the Iranian side. For instance Av. *daēva-*, O. Pers. *daiva-*, corresponding to Sanskrit *devá-* 'god' has acquired the meaning of 'devil'. In the same way some Vedic divinities appear in the *Avesta* as evil spirits: Skt. *Índra-*, *Nā́satya-*: Av. *Indra*, *Nåŋhaiθya-*.

The material for Old Iranian is somewhat restricted both as to quantity and as regards the number of dialects represented. For the Middle Iranian period, thanks mainly to discoveries of the present century, the documentation is much wider. We now have, in addition to Middle Persian proper (Pahlavi) extensive documents in two important East Iranian languages which are not represented in the early period, namely Sogdian and Saka (mainly in the dialect of Khotan, but with a few texts in a neighbouring dialect). The publication and interpretation of the material in these languages has progressed rapidly and successfully, but the results are not yet in the main available in a form easily accessible to students of general Indo-Aryan or Indo-European philology. Eventually a considerable contribution should be available from this source, because, although they cannot compete in antiquity with the Avestan and Old Persian texts, they constitute independent branches of Iranian which were not previously known and therefore have preserved things which were lost elsewhere from an early period.[1]

In the mediaeval period the domain of Iranian became very much restricted, mainly on account of Turkish expansion. Over large tracts of Central Asia Iranian has long since died out. It has remained principally in Iran or Persia proper, where modern Persian can look back to a continuous literary tradition of over a thousand years. On the periphery of this area, particularly on the Indo-Iranian frontier, there are still many minor languages surviving in small areas, and one which is still important, namely Paštō, the official language of Afghanistan. At the other side of the territory in the Northern Caucasus Ossetic still survives from one of the numerous Iranian invasions of South Russia.

[1] For instance the IE word for '(young) pig', Lat. *porcus*, Lith. *paršas*, was not previously known in Indo-Iranian, but has now turned up in Khotanese: *pā'sa-*.

§2. Primitive Indo-European

The Indo-Iranian languages which have been briefly outlined form together one branch of the Indo-European family. The discovery of the historical relationship of the members of the Indo-European family was a direct result of the discovery of the Sanskrit language and literature by European scholars towards the close of the eighteenth century. The similarity of the Sanskrit language, both in grammar and vocabulary to the classical languages of Europe is so far-reaching that scholars familiar with Latin and Greek could not fail to be struck by the resemblance. Since up to this time there had existed no clear idea of the real nature of the development of languages and of their relations with each other, the explanation of this unexpected but quite undeniable affinity could not be provided without a completely new and scientific approach to the study of language. In his famous address to the Royal Asiatic Society of Bengal in 1786, Sir William Jones indicated in broad outlines the significance of the new discovery :

'The Sanscrit language, whatever be its antiquity, is of wonderful structure ; more perfect than the Greek, more copious than the Latin, and more exquisitely refined than either ; yet bearing to both of them a stronger affinity both in the roots of verbs and the forms of grammar, than could possibly have been produced by accident ; so strong indeed that no philologer could examine them at all without believing them to have sprung from *some common source*, which perhaps no longer exists. There is a similar reason though not quite so forcible, for supposing that both the Gothick and the Celtick, though blended with a different idiom, had the same origin with the Sanscrit ; and the old Persian might be added to the same family.'

The truth of these remarks has been adequately demonstrated by the subsequent development of the science of Comparative Philology, which dates from this time. During the past century and a half the languages of the Indo-European family have been the subject of intensive scientific study. The main features of the parent language have been reliably reconstructed, and the historical and prehistorical development of the several branches has been worked out in detail. The methods and principles employed have been subject to progressive improvement and refinement, and new discoveries have continued and still continue to produce a wider and deeper understanding of the subject. The methods first evolved in the study of the Indo-European languages have further been successfully employed in the study of independent linguistic families (Semitic, Finno-ugrian, Bantu, etc.). The whole science of linguistics has come into existence as a result of the stimulus provided by the discovery of Sanskrit.

The Indo-European languages are divided into ten major branches, in addition to which there are known to have been other branches which have died out without leaving adequate record. The ten major branches are as follows :

I. Aryan or Indo-Iranian, summarised above.

II. Baltic (Lithuanian, Lettish and the extinct Old Prussian) and Slavonic (Old Church Slavonic or Old Bulgarian, Russian, Polish, Czech, Serbo-Croatian, Bulgarian, etc.). These two groups are very closely related to each other, though not as closely as Indo-Aryan and Iranian. There are some ancient divergencies between them which make it impossible to reconstruct a primitive Balto-Slavonic language, intermediate between Indo-European and the existing languages in the same way as Indo-Iranian can be reconstructed. Nevertheless in view of their many close resemblances it is convenient to group them together under a common name, Balto-Slavonic. The earliest recorded Slavonic is the Old Bulgarian of the ninth century ; Lithuanian is known only from the sixteenth century.

III. Armenian, known from the fifth century A.D.

IV. Albanian, known only from modern times.

These four groups are collectively known as the *satəm*-languages for reasons which will be explained below. Opposed to them are the *centum*-languages, which are as follows :

V. Greek, with numerous dialects. The literature begins with the Homeric poems, *c.* 800 B.C., but during the last twenty-five years the decipherment of documents in the linear B script and Mycenean dialect has pushed back the history of the language by 500 years.

VI. Latin, which has developed into the various Romance Languages (French, Italian, Spanish, Portuguese, Rumanian, etc.). It is known in literature from *c.* 200 B.C., and there are scanty inscriptional remains from an earlier date.

VII. Celtic, consisting of Continental Celtic or Gallic,

which is extinct, and Insular Celtic which is divided into Irish (Gaelic) and Brittanic (Welsh, Cornish, Breton). Literary records of Celtic begin with the Old Irish glosses of the eighth century.

VIII. Germanic, which may be divided into East Germanic or Gothic (extinct), Nordic or Scandinavian, and West Germanic, to which belong the English and German languages. The earliest literary monument of Germanic is the Gothic translation of the Bible by Ulfila (A.D. fourth cent.).

The two major members of the family which remain to be mentioned are known from discoveries made in the present century. They are :

IX. The so-called 'Tocharian' preserved in Buddhist manuscripts discovered in Chinese Turkestan, dating from the sixth to the tenth centuries A.D. It is divided into two dialects which are for convenience termed A and B.

X. Hittite, which is preserved in cuneiform tablets recovered from Boghaz-köi in Anatolia, the site of the capital of the ancient Hittite kingdom. The time covered by these records is the period from *c.* 1700 to *c.* 1200 B.C., the bulk of them being dated towards the end of this period. It is the oldest recorded IE language, and at the same time in many ways aberrant from the usual type. Its discovery has raised many new and interesting problems.

In addition to the major languages listed above, there existed in antiquity a considerable number of other IE languages which have become extinct and are known only from scanty remains in the form of inscriptions, proper names and occasional glosses. To put the Indo-European family into proper perspective the more important of these are enumerated below.

In the first place there are certain ancient languages of Asia Minor which together with Hittite form a special group. The cuneiform texts from Boghaz-köi include texts in two such languages, Luwian and Palaean, which show close relationship with Hittite. The so-called Hittite Hieroglyphic inscriptions which have now been partially deciphered, have revealed a language which is closely related to the Luwian of the cuneiform texts. Later the Lycian language, in which there are inscriptions in alphabetic script, has been shown to have relationship with Luwian. Most recently the Lydian language, known from inscriptions from Sardis, has been shown to belong with the above languages in the Anatolian group.

Fragmentary records of other Indo-European languages have been preserved from the Italian and Balkan peninsulas, and, resulting from a later movement of peoples, and separate from the above Anatolian group, in Western Asia Minor. In Italy Oscan and Umbrian are known from a fair number of inscriptions, and together with Latin they are classed as the Italic group. The language of the Siculi in Sicily is also considered to belong with Italic. In the south-east corner of Italy, Messapian is held to be a later introduction from across the Adriatic, possibly related to Illyrian. Venetic in North East Italy is classed as a separate Indo-European language, though showing some signs of relationship with Italic. In the Balkan peninsula the Illyrian language is known only from proper names, and there is an unsettled debate as to whether or not it is the ancestor of Albanian. The information of Thracian, the other main Balkan language in ancient times is equally scanty, and its position remains obscure. In Asia Minor fresh invasions from the Balkans brought to an end the Hittite empire (*c.* 1200 B.C.) and introduced new Indo-European languages into the area. Of these Phrygian is scantily preserved in inscriptions.

The languages of the Indo-European family have become more widely diffused over the world than those of any other linguistic family. They also form the majority of the cultivated languages of mankind. It is not surprising therefore that the question of the original home of Indo-European has been the subject of much speculation. In the early days it was usually held that this lay in Central Asia, and that from there successive waves of emigration had carried the various members of the family to Europe. This was mainly due to the exaggerated importance attached to Sanskrit and to confusion between the primitive Aryans of whom we have spoken with the much earlier Indo-Europeans. It is as we have seen reasonably certain that it was from Central Asia, more specifically the Oxus valley, that the Indians and Iranians set out to occupy their respective domains. But there is not the slightest trace of evidence or probability that the ancestors of the Germans, Celts, Greeks and other European members of the family were ever near this area. Consequently it is now usually held that the original home lay somewhere in Europe. The main argument for this is the simple but effective one that it is in Europe that the greatest number of Indo-European languages, and the greatest diversity of them is to be found, and this from the earliest recorded times. At an ancient period we find enormous stretches of Asia in the occupation of Indo-Iranian, a single member of the family, and as yet little differentiated; in Europe on the other hand a concentration of many languages occupying comparatively restricted areas, and already markedly different from each other. It follows of necessity that the presence of Indo-European in the Indo-Iranian area is the result of late colonial expansion on a vast scale, while in Europe the existence of such great diversity at the earliest recorded period indicates the presence there of Indo-European from remote antiquity.

It is true that the discovery of the two Tocharian dialects in Chinese Turkestan has slightly modified this picture, and it has led some to think again of an Asiatic home. But the addition of one new branch only in Asia is obviously insufficient to turn the balance. Moreover the nature of Tocharian, which has undergone profound and far-reaching phonetic changes strongly suggestive of alien influence, makes it clear that this language has travelled far from its original home. Somewhat similar changes have taken place in Hittite and the allied languages of Asia Minor, and this is held to have been due to the influence of the pre-Indo-European languages which existed in that area (Proto-Hittite, Churrian, Urartean, etc.). So we may conclude that these languages also have been brought in by invaders, and since in ancient times the distribution of languages in this area was such that the non-Indo-European languages mentioned lay to the East and the Indo-European languages to the West, it becomes clear that the direction of the invasions must have been from the West, that is to say from Europe, across the Hellespont. Further it has been pointed out that the characteristics of this Asianic branch of Indo-European are such as can only be explained by the assumption that it was separated from the main branch of Indo-European at a period very much earlier than the movements which lead to the final break-up of IE linguistic unity. This means that the earliest of all the Indo-European migrations which can be deduced from our evidence, and one that must have antedated the migration of the Indo-Iranians by a very long period of time, already points to the existence in Europe of the Indo-European tongue.

Within Europe it is possible to narrow down considerably the territorial limits within which the cradle of the Indo-European languages is to be sought. It is known with reasonable certainty that the Italian and Greek peninsulas were colonised from the North. The occupation of France and the British Isles by Celts from Central Europe occurred at a comparatively late date (*c.* 500 B.C.). The Iberian peninsula remained predominantly non-Indo-European till Roman times, and in modern Basque there still exists a survival of pre-Indo-European speech. The Eastern limit is indicated by the fact that before the two Asiatic migrations (Tocharian and Indo-Iranian) Indo-European must have been bounded to the East by an early form of Finno-ugrian, and there is some evidence of contact between these two families in the primitive period. There is reason to believe that the original centre of Finno-ugrian expansion lay between the Volga and the Urals and this forms the extreme limit beyond which Indo-European was not to be found in the early stages of its history. This leaves the central portion of Europe extending from the Rhine to Central and Southern Russia, and it is probable that by the time of the Indo-Iranian migrations the larger part of this area had long been occupied by various Indo-European dialects.

It is not possible to define the original Indo-European homeland in terms any narrower than these, nor is it desirable to try, since those who have attempted to do so have usually suffered from misconceptions about the nature of ' Primitive Indo-European ' and about the time when the earliest divisions began. The evolution of the Indo-European should not be regarded as being on a par with that of the Romance languages from Latin. In the latter case the various languages are derived from a single unitary language, the language to begin with of one city. But in the case of Indo-European it is certain that there was no such unitary language which can be reached by means of comparison. It would be easy to produce, more or less *ad infinitum* a list of forms like Skt. *nā̆bhi-*, Gk. *ὀμφαλός* ' navel ', which although inherited directly from the primitive IE period, and radically related are irreducible to a single original. In fact detailed comparison makes it clear that the Indo-European that we can reach by this means was already deeply split up into a series of varying dialects.

It is from this point of view that the question of the ' splitting ' of Indo-European should be regarded. It has not been uncommon to find in works of general history or linguistics a conception that somewhere about the second half of the third millennium B.C. a single undivided Indo-European occupying a comparatively restricted area being taken by a series of migrations to the various countries where IE languages are later found, after which migrations the various individual languages were evolved. But it is now becoming clear that by this period the various members of the family must have already begun to assume their historic form. For instance when the Indo-Iranians first set off on their migrations from Europe, very likely about 2000 B.C. as is often suggested, they took with them not Indo-European which they subsequently proceeded to change into Indo-Iranian, but the Indo-Iranian which we can reconstruct, which had already assumed its essential features in the original European homeland. It is clear that once the migrations began over such wide territories all opportunities for unitary development of Indo-Iranian must have ceased, and since, as we have observed there quite undoubtedly was at one time a unitary development of Indo-Iranian, this must have taken place before any migrations began.

What applies to Indo-Iranian must apply with equal force to the other members of the family. We have already remarked on the deep divergencies between the various European members of the family, and this can only be accounted for by pushing back the period of original division to a period much earlier than is usually assumed. If there ever existed a unitary Indo-European which spread from a restricted area, this lies long behind the earliest period which can be reached by any comparison. ' Primitive Indo-European ' must be regarded as a continuum of related dialects occupying an extensive territory in Europe (very likely the major part of the area indicated above), dialects which already before the period of the great migrations had begun to assume the character of separate languages.

§ 3. Divisions of Indo-European

The question of the early Indo-European dialects has been the subject of considerable study and some useful results have been acquired. It is possible to form a fair idea of their distribution in the period preceding the emergence of the individual languages. The most striking and important early dialect distinction is that which separates the *satəm*-languages from the *centum*-languages. These two groups are so named from the way they treat IE *k̂* in the word for 'hundred' (IE **k̂m̥tóm*). The *centum*-languages preserve it as such (Lat. *centum*, Gk. *ἑκατόν*, Ir. *cēt*, Toch. A. *känt*); in the *satəm*-languages it is changed to some kind of sibilant (Skt. *śatám*, Av. *satəm*, Lith. *šim̃tas*, O. Sl. *sŭto*). Similar changes occur in the case of IE *ĝ* and *ĝh*. The languages participating in this change are Indo-Iranian, Balto-Slavonic, Armenian, Albanian. Since this feature is so wide-spread, and since it occurs without any variation of the conditions in all the languages concerned, it must be assumed that the change took place in the Indo-European period, before the dispersal of the several languages, and that it affected a group of contiguous dialects within the Indo-European area. The unity of these dialects, and of the languages derived from them is further confirmed by the fact that the loss of the labial element in the IE series k^w, g^w, g^wh (e.g. Skt. *ká-* 'who?', Lith. *kàs* as opposed to Gk. *πο-θεν*, Lat. *quo-d*, Goth. *ƕas*) is characteristic of precisely this same group of languages.

Before the discovery of Tocharian and Hittite it was common to regard the *centum-satəm* division as a division between Western and Eastern Indo-European, and it was customary to regard the *centum*-languages as a united group like the *satəm*-languages. This was never altogether satisfactory, since not only is Greek cut off from the Western IE languages by the intervening *satəm*-language Albanian, but also because apart from this it displays no special similarities with them, but rather with the *satəm*-languages. The discovery of the new languages, which were unmistakeably *centum*-languages, made it quite impossible to speak of an East-West division any longer, and also made it clear that there was no unitary *centum*-group. The *centum*-languages are alike only in preserving original *k̂*, *ĝ*, *ĝh* as occlusives, and it is a commonplace of linguistics that common preservations are not necessarily a sign that dialects or languages are closely related. We may therefore substitute a division of the Indo-European dialects into:

I. A central group which can be equated with the *satəm*-languages, and is characterised by the innovations mentioned above.

II. Four peripheral dialect groups surrounding the central group, namely (1) West Indo-European comprising Italic, Celtic and Germanic ; (2) Greek, which however has special relations with the central group ; (3) Eastern Indo-European which has survived as 'Tocharian' ; (4) Hittite and other IE languages of Asia Minor which separated earliest from the original IE stock.

The historical distribution of the IE languages corresponds on the whole to this, but in the case of Sanskrit migrations at a comparatively late date took it to the extreme East of the Indo-European domain. Before this period its ancestor, primitive Indo-Iranian must have held a fairly central position, being directly in contact with the other dialects of the *satəm*-group, and having to the East of it that form of Indo-European which eventually turned into the dialects A and B of Chinese Turkestan. Its position can further be determined by the specially close relations which are found to exist between it and Balto-Slavonic. Since the Balts and the Slavs are not likely to have moved far from the positions in which they are to be found in their earliest recorded history, the original location of Indo-Iranian towards the South-East of this area becomes highly probable.

The Western group of Indo-European languages consisting of Italic, Celtic and Germanic, is distinguished by certain common features in grammar and vocabulary, which indicate a fairly close mutual connection in prehistoric times. These ties are particularly close in the case of Italic and Celtic, even though they are not sufficient to justify the theory of common Italo-celtic. The connections of Germanic with the other two groups are less close, but they are quite definite. At the same time it has some special affinities with Slavonic, and further with the central group in general (e.g. absence of the medio-passive terminations in *-r*).

There is an almost complete absence of special features common to Indo-Iranian and Western Indo-European. All that has been pointed out so far consists of certain common elements of vocabulary which have been largely eliminated in the rest of Indo-European. These words are in many respects highly interesting and important, but they consist entirely of ancient Indo-European words which have been preserved independently by two groups which otherwise have no special connection. Such words are: Lat. *credo*, Ir. *cretim*, Skt. *śrad-dhā-* 'believe'; Lat. *rēx*, Ir. *rí* 'king'; Skt. *rā́j-*, *rā́jan-*, Ir. *rígain* 'queen'; Skt. *rā́jñī*, Ir. *ríge* 'kingdom'; Skt. *rā́jya-*; Lat. *ius* 'justice', *iustus*, Ir. *uisse* 'just, righteous', Skt. *yós*, Av. *yaoš* 'rightness, purity'; Lat. *ensis* 'sword', Skt. *así-*; Lat. *rēs* 'property'; Skt. *raí-*; Ir. *bró* 'millstone'; Skt. *grā́van-* (also, differently formed Goth. *qairnus*, etc.); Ir. *gert* 'milk', Skt. *ghṛtá-* 'ghee'; Ir. *aire* (gen. s. *airech*) 'chief, noble'; Skt. *aryá-*, *ā́rya-* 'master, lord, noble, Aryan'. More dubious is the old equation Lat. *flamen*, Skt. *brahmán-* 'priest'. Many of these words are connected with religion, law, etc., and the fact that they are preserved in these two branches alone is due to the highly conservative tendencies which characterised the societies concerned. They do not imply any close connection between the original dialects on which the languages are based.

Greek shows little sign of close connection with any of the other *centum*-groups. On the contrary its closest connection appears to be with the *satəm*-languages, particularly with Indo-Iranian and Armenian. It is sufficient to glance through a comparative grammar of Sanskrit to see that the correspondences between Sanskrit and Greek are much more numerous than those between Sanskrit and any other language of the family outside Indo-Iranian. This is particularly so in the case of verbal inflection. The fact that the two languages are recorded from such an early period is partly responsible for this state of affairs, but it is by no means entirely so. Some of the common features involved are of late Indo-European origin, and must be regarded as common innovations, and not as cases of the common preservation of ancient forms. For instance the Indo-European languages have no common form of the genitive singular of *o*-stems. The form *-osyo* which is common to Greek (*-οιο, ου*), Armenian (*-oy*) and Indo-Iranian (Skt. *-asya*, Av. *-ahya*) has no more claim to antiquity than Italo-Celtic *-ī* or the Hittite form (*-aš*, <*os*) which appears to be identical with the nominative. In fact the great variations in case suggest that the various forms have developed in the late Indo-European period when the language was already widely divided into dialects. It is therefore important evidence of close prehistoric connection. Likewise the augment is found only in Greek (*ἔφερε*), Indo-Iranian (Skt. *ábharat*) and Armenian (*eber*), with traces of Phyrgian. Since there is no reason to believe that it ever existed as a regular component of the verbal inflection in those languages in which it is not recorded, its development in Indo-Iranian, Greek and Armenian must be regarded as a common innovation of the closely related dialects on which they are based. The elimination of the *r*- endings of the medio- passive in Sanskrit and Greek is a significant common characteristic. Phonetically Sanskrit and Greek show a common treatment of the sonant nasals (IE *n̥*, *m̥*), replacing them by the vowel *a*. In view of the close connection that exists between them in other respects this is unlikely to be a matter of chance. In other respects, e.g. in the matter of prothetic vowels Greek seems to be closest to Armenian, and there are also some remarkable coincidences of vocabulary between them.

The fact that Greek shows more signs of close connection with the *satəm*-languages Armenian and Indo-Iranian than with any other is in striking contrast to the absence in it of the distinctive sound changes of the *satəm* group. We must assume that the IE dialect on which Greek is based was originally in the closest contact with the central dialect group, but that this contact was severed at a period preceding the *satəm* sound changes.

The most striking thing about the two Tocharian languages is that they have no special connections whatever with Indo-Iranian, the only other Asiatic family. They are no closer to Indo-Iranian—in some respects they appear more different—than to languages far to the West like Italic and Celtic. This is in accordance with the fact that the parent dialect of Indo-Iranian was originally a central dialect, and as such would have with a dialect on the Eastern periphery, from which Tocharian is descended, no more in common than with the percursors of Italic and Celtic on the extreme West. Neither have they any special relations with any other of the individual groups of Indo-European. The prevalence of the middle terminations in *r* in Tocharian does not indicate any close relationship with Italo-Celtic on the one hand or with Hittite on the other, but merely a type of inflection that was characteristic of early Indo-European, but was tending to be reduced or eliminated in the later period in dialects of the central area. Attempts to find other evidence of connection with one group or another have been singularly lacking in results. The two languages have become much altered from the original Indo-European. The old system of nominal inflection has to a large extent broken down, and the percentage of words in the vocabulary for which it is possible to find satisfactory etymologies is comparatively small. At the same time some features of the two languages have an ancient aspect which suggests that they are derived from a comparatively early form of Indo-European. This would imply a comparatively early migration in the case of Tocharian, and such an assumption accounts best for the great difference between Tocharian and Indo-Iranian. We must assume that an Eastern Indo-European dialect group had for centuries existed in isolation before the comparatively late migration which took Indo-Iranian to Asia from the central Indo-European area.

The separation of Hittite and the languages allied to it from the main body of Indo-European must have taken place earliest of all. This is the only way to explain the great differences which exist between it and the type of Indo-European that has been reconstructed from the previously known members of the family. The most striking feature of Hittite is the preservation of *ḫ*, which has elsewhere disappeared. In addition to this the language deviates from the usual type in many other respects. In the formation of nouns the percentage of consonantal stems, and in particular the old neuter types in *l* and *r* alternating with *n*, is much greater than in the standard types of Indo-European. The feminine gender is undeveloped. The inflection of nouns is much simpler than in the type of Indo-European represented by Sanskrit, and there is no reason to believe that this is due to losses on the part of Hittite. Above all, the conjugation of the verb differs widely from the system reconstructed largely by the comparison of Sanskrit and Greek, which at one time passed for primitive Indo-European. Consideration of these facts has led some scholars, notably E. Sturtevant, to separate Hittite from the Indo-European family proper, and to postulate an earlier Indo-Hittite from which Hittite on the one hand and Indo-European on the other are separately descended. The majority of opinion is against this extreme view and it seems more satisfactory to speak of Early and Late Indo-European, rather than of Indo-Hittite and Indo-European. It has already been pointed out that the dialect divisions of Indo-European go back to a period long antedating the migration of Indo-Iranian. Even though the separation of

Hittite must have been very early indeed, it need not have preceded the beginning of these dialectal divergences of Indo-European. Certainly there was no united Indo-European in the late period, which the Indo-Hittite theory demands. It is true that much of the evolution which has taken place in Indo-European outside Hittite, and which must be placed in the period following the separation of Hittite, is evolution common to all the branches (e.g. the development of the feminine), but this is easily understandable as long as the various dialects remained in contiguity. The important difference now is that instead of thinking simply in the terms of Primitive Indo-European we may now distinguish Early Indo-European of the time previous to the separation of Hittite, and Late Indo-European characterised by certain developments which can be determined, in which different dialects evolving in common were gradually beginning to assume the character of different languages.

§4. Indo-Iranian and Balto-Slavonic

The *satəm*-languages, apart from Indo-Iranian are only known from times much more recent than most of the *centum*-languages. Further there is the possibility that some ancient members of this group, notably in the Balkan and Danubian regions, have disappeared without record. It is therefore not possible to form a precise idea of the position of Indo-Iranian within the *satəm* group as a whole at an early period. The only thing that emerges clearly is that there did at one time exist a special relationship between early Indo-Iranian and those dialects of Indo-European which developed eventually into the Baltic and Slavonic languages. Since this is important for the location of the early home of Indo-Iranian, the evidence may be given in some detail.

Phonetically the most noteworthy common feature is the change of *s* to *š* (>Slav. *ch*) after *k*, *r*, *i* and *u* in Indo-Iranian and Slavonic, and after *r* also in Lithuanian.[1] This is unlikely to be a matter of chance, since the conditions under which the change takes place are so closely parallel. The conclusion which must be drawn is that at one time the two branches were in close geographical proximity, and that this innovation affecting IE *s*

[1] For examples see p. 79.

established itself over a limited area comprising Slavonic and Indo-Iranian, but excluding the rest of Indo-European. The fact that the change appears only to a very small extent in Baltic demonstrates that the Baltic group was to a certain extent autonomous of Slavonic even at this early date.

Another change which has occurred in both groups is that of *k* to *č* before the vowels *ĕ, ĭ*.[1] This however seems to be a case of parallel independent development. In Old Slavonic the paradigmatic alternation occasioned by this change, and by the second Slavonic palatalisation, remains in full force (e.g. Nom. S. *vlŭkŭ*, Voc. *vluče*, Loc. *vlŭcě*). Such alternation has been eliminated in Sanskrit even at the earliest period, and it is unlikely that it could have maintained itself in Slavonic over the very long period that it would be necessary to assume if the change in Slavonic had been so ancient.

In grammar a fair number of special features common to both groups can be enumerated, though there are also some notable divergences. The most important of these latter is the existence in Balto-Slavonic in common with Germanic of an element *-m-* which appears regularly in place of the *-bh-* which is familiar from Sanskrit and other IE languages (e.g. Dat. abl. Pl. Lith. *vilkáms*, Sl. *vlŭkomŭ*, Goth *wulfam* : Skt. *vṛ́kebhyas*). This is an ancient Indo-European divergence cutting across the usual dialect divisions. Another idiosyncrasy of Balto-Slavonic is the use of the old ablative to form the genitive singular of *o*-stems : Lith. *vil̃ko*, O. Sl. *vlŭka*.

In spite of these divergences there are many special grammatical features uniting the two groups. The more important of these may be briefly enumerated :

A. *Nominal Inflection :* (1) Nominative without *r* of *r*- stems, Skt. *mātā́* 'mother', *svásā* 'sister' : O. Sl. *mati*, Lith. *motė̃*, *sesuõ*. (2) The locative plural in *-su* (as opposed to *-σι* in Greek) is found only in these two groups : Skt. *vṛ́keṣu*, O. Sl. *vlŭcěchŭ*. (3) The Dual inflection is closely similar, containing a good deal that is not found elsewhere, e.g. Skt. Nom. D. *bāle*, *yugé*, *nā́manī*, *mánasī*, *akṣī́*, *sūnū́* : O. Sl. *ženě*, *ižě*, *imeni*, *tělesi*, *oči* (Lith. *akì*), *syny* (Lith. *sū́nu*), Gen. D. Skt. *tayos*, *dvayos* : O. Sl. *toju*, *dvoju*. (4) A similar development in the singular stem of feminine nouns in *-ā* : e. g. Instr. Skt. *táyā*, *sēnayā* : O. Sl. *tojǫ*, *rǫkojǫ*, Loc. Skt. *sénāyām*, Av. *haēnaya* : Lith. *rañkoje*. (5)

[1] For examples see p. 76.

Close similarity in the declension of *i-* and *u-* stems, as illustrated by equations like Dat. S. Skt. *sūnáve* : O. Sl. *synovi.*

B. *Pronouns and Adverbs :* (1) Common characteristics in the form of the personal pronouns, e.g. Nom. S. in *-om*, Skt. *ahám*, O. Sl. *azu*, nasalised accusative, Skt. *mā́m*, O. Sl. *mę*, Gen. S. Av. *mana*, O. Sl. *mene* (as opposed to Skt. *máma*). (2) The extended stem of the demonstrative pronoun, etc., in certain cases, e.g. Dat. S. Masc. Skt. *tásmai*, O. Pruss. *kasmu stesmu*, O. Sl. *tomu*, Fem. Skt. *tásyai*, O. Pruss. *stessiei*. (3) Preference for the interrogative stem *kʷo-* as opposed to the stem *kʷi-*, Skt. *ká-*, Lith. *kàs*. (4) The possession of certain common pronominal stems, e.g. Av. *ava-*, O. Sl. *ovŭ*, Skt. Av. *ana-*, Lith. *anàs*, O. Sl. *onŭ*. (5) Various adverbs, Skt. *kúha*, Av. *kudā* 'where', O. Sl. *kŭde*, Skt. *kadā́* 'when ?', *tadā́* 'then', Lith. *kadà*, *tadà*, Skt. *ná* 'like', Lith. *neĩ*, Skt. *bahís* 'outside', O. Sl. *bezŭ* 'without', Skt. *vinā*, O. Sl. *vŭnĕ* 'outside', O. Pers. (*avahya*) *rādi* 'on account of (that)', O. Sl. (*togo*) *radĭ*.

C. *The Verb*. In the conjugation of the verb features special to Indo-Iranian and Balto-Slavonic are not remarkably common. This may partly be due to the fact that Slavonic (and to a greater extent, Baltic) is only recorded late, and in the verbal inflection is less conservative than it is in the nominal inflection (e.g. loss of the perfect and the middle). Points of note are (1) similarities in the *s-* aorist, e.g. vṛddhi of root (Sl. *vesti : vĕsu*, Skt. *váhati ávākṣam*) and termination *-om* of 1sg. (as opposed to Gk. *α*) ; (2) The future in *-syo-* is found with certainty only in Indo-Aryan and Lithuanian : Skt. *dā́syāmi* 'I will give', Lith. *dúosiu* ; (3) The causative is well developed in both groups, and many identical forms can be quoted, e.g. Skt. *bodháyati* 'he awakens', O. Sl. *buždǫ*, *buditi*.

In the sphere of vocabulary Indo-Iranian shares with Baltic and Slavonic a considerable number of words which are not found in the other Indo-European languages. These correspondences are much more numerous than those which can be discovered between Indo-Iranian and any other member of the family, and they supply important evidence for the early connection of the two families. There is for instance no common Indo-European word for 'goat'. Sanskrit *ajá-* is connected with Lith. *ožỹs*, but parallels are absent in other IE languages. Greek and Armenian which go together in this case, as frequently have a similar word (*αἴξ*, *aiç*), but one that cannot be united with it according to the laws of IE phonology. Another word is peculiar to the Western IE languages (Lat. *haedus*, Engl. *goat*, etc.). The distribution of these words corresponds roughly to the dialectal division sketched above, and illustrates the importance of vocabulary in the study of this question. The derivative *ajína-* ' skin ' corresponds to O. Sl. *azĭnu, jazĭno*, and in both languages an original meaning ' goat's skin ' has been widened to the meaning ' skin ' in general. There is also a class of words in which the root is common to many IE languages, but the particular suffix found in Indo-Iranian is found elsewhere only in Slavonic and Baltic. Examples of these are: Skt. *phéna-* ' foam ', O. Pr. *spoayno*, Lith. *spáinė*, as opposed to the Western IE words with *m*-suffix (Lat. *spūma*, Engl. *foam*). Skt. *dákṣiṇa-* ' right(-hand) ' corresponds exactly to O. Sl. *desinŭ*, Lith. *dešinẽ*, whereas various different suffixes appear in other languages (Gk. δεξιός, δεξιτερός, Lat. *dexter*, Goth. *taíhswa*). Similarly Skt. *grīvā́* ' neck ' and O. Sl. *griva* ' mane ' correspond exactly in formation, but can be compared only as far as the root is concerned with Gk. δέρη ' neck ' (√*gʷer*). The *n*- suffix of Skt. *majján-* reappears only in Slavonic (O. Sl. *moždanŭ*) and Baltic (O. Pruss. *muzgeno*). A form corresponding precisely to Skt. *miśrá-* ' mixed ' appears only in Lith. *mìšras*.

Another feature which deserves consideration is the existence of special meanings common to the two groups. The meaning ' wake ' is common to Skt. *budh-* and the related Balto-Slavonic words, but is not found in other languages. The meaning ' write ' of Iranian (*ni-*)*pis-* recurs in O. Sl. *pĭsati*.

Of the remaining words which are peculiar to Indo-Iranian and Balto-Slavonic the following are the most important: Av. *spənta-* ' holy ', O. Sl. *svętŭ*, Lith. *šventas*; Skt. *savyá-* ' left ', Av. *haoya-*, O. Sl. *šujĭ*; Skt. *barhís* ' bed of Kuśa grass ', Av. *barəziš* ' cushion, pillow ', O. Sl. *blazina* ' cushion '; Skt. *kṛṣṇá-* 'black ', O. Sl. *črŭnŭ*, O. Pruss. *kirsnan*; Skt. *bhára-* ' fight, battle ', cf. O. Sl. *borjo* ' fight '; Skt. *óṣṭha-* ' lip ', O. Sl. *usta*, O. Pruss. *austin* ' mouth '; Skt. *avatá-* ' spring, well ', Lett. *avuots*; Av. *varəsa-* ' hair ', O. Sl. *vlasŭ*, Russ. *vólos*; Skt. *girí-* ' mountain ', Av. *gairi-*, O. Sl. *gora* ' id ', Lith. *gìria, gìrė* ' forest '; Skt. *tūṣṇī́m* ' silently ', Av. *tušni-* ' silent ', O. Pruss. *tusnan*; Skt. *tucchyá-* ' empty ', Khotanese *ttuśśaa-*, O. Sl. *tŭštĭ*, Lith. *tùščias* ' id '; Skt. *dádhi* (gen. *dadhnás*) ' curds ', O. Pruss. *dadan*; Skt. *páyas* ' milk ', Av.

paēma, Lith. *pēnas* (with varying suffixes); Av. *xšvid-* 'milk', cf. Lith. *svíestas* 'butter'; Skt. *áṅgāra-* 'coal', O. Sl. *ǫglĭ*, Russ. *ugol'*; Skt. *bradhná-* 'yellowish, light-coloured', O. Sl. *bronŭ* 'white'; Skt. *árbha-* 'small, child', cf. Russ. *rebënok* 'child'; Skt. *vratá-* 'vow', Av. *urvata-*, O. Sl. *rota* 'oath'; Skt. *āṇḍá-* 'egg, testicle' (Kalaša *ondrak* 'egg'), O. Sl. *jędro* 'testicle'; Skt. *pāṃsú-* 'dust' Av. *pąsnu-*, O. Sl. *pěsŭkŭ* 'sand'; Skt. *dhānā́* 'corn, grain', Pers. *dāna*, Lith. *dúona* 'bread'; Skt. *śyāmá-*, *śyāvá-* 'dark-coloured', Lith. *šē̃mas* 'grey', Skt. *sāndra-* 'thick, viscid', cf. O.Sl. *sedry krĭvĭnyje*, *sjadry krovnyja* 'thickened, congealed blood'; Pers. *raz* 'vine, vine-tendril', O. Sl. *loza*; Av. *fšarəma-*, Pers. *šarm* 'shame', O. Sl. *sramŭ*; Skt. *srāmá-* 'lame', O. Sl. *chromŭ*; Av. *hāma-* 'the same', Pali *sāmaṃ* adv. 'self, of oneself', O. Sl. *samŭ* 'self'; Skt. *viśpáti-* 'head of settlement or clan', Av. *vīspaiti-*, Lith. *viẽšpats* 'lord'; Av. *sarəta-* 'cold', Lith. *šáltas*; Skt. *śāka-* 'vegetables, greens', Lith. *šẽkas* 'green fodder'; Skt. *śaphara-* 'Cyprinus sophore', Lith. *šãpalas* 'Cyprinus dobula'; Skt. *śakuná-* '(large) bird', O. Sl. *sokolŭ* 'falcon'; Skt. *śā́pa-* 'drift wood', Lith. *šapai*; Skt. *bhaṅga-* 'wave', Lith. *bangà*. Among verbs which are common to the two groups we may mention Skt. *hávate* 'calls', Av. *zavaiti*, O. Sl. *zovetŭ*; Skt. *śvit-* 'to be bright, white', Lith. *šviẽti*, O. Sl. *svitěti*; Skt. *bhī-*, *bháyate* 'fear', O. Sl. *bojǫ sę*, Lith. *bijaũs*; Skt. *pruṣ-*, *pruṣṇā́ti* 'sprinkle', O. Sl. *prysnǫti*; Skt. *dham-*, *dhmā-* 'to blow', O. Sl. *dŭmǫ*, *dǫti*, Lith. *dumiù*, *dùmti*; Skt. *bṛṃh-*, *bṛṃhate* '(elephant) trumpets', Lith. *brenzgu*, *branzgu* 'to sound, make a noise'; Skt. *muc-* 'to release, Lith. *munkù*, *mùkti* 'to get loose'; Skt. *gṝ-*, *gṛṇā́ti* 'praises', O. Pruss. *girtwei* 'to praise', Lith. *giriù*, *gìrti*.

The list of common words and other features which are special to the two groups is clearly impressive, and the whole of the material must be referred to the period of Primitive Indo-Iranian. When on the contrary we look for signs of special contact between Iranian itself and Slavonic (or Baltic) we find that there are practically none. It is true that some of the words that are listed above are found only in Iranian and not in Sanskrit, but it is equally possible to point out others in which the reverse is the case. Furthermore if we take such a word, e.g. Av. *spənta-*, O. Sl. *svętŭ*, Lith. *šveñtas*, it is immediately clear that the form of the Baltic and Slavonic words is such that they cannot be derived either from the Primitive Iranian form (**svanta-*) or the Primitive Indo-Iranian (**śvanta-*), but that all the words must be referred to an earlier *satəm* form (**śvento-*).

Attempts to find examples of Iranian loanwords in Slavonic have been singularly unsuccessful. There is a Russian word *sobáka* ' dog ' which is plausibly derived from Median σπάκα (Herod.) but the word is not pan-Slavonic, and it remains quite obscure by what means the word has reached Russian. In the case of Russ. *topór* ' axe', Pers. *tabar*, we are dealing with a migratory word of uncertain origin. Iranian origin has been assumed for Sl. *sŭto* ' 100 ' because the form of the word does not agree with Slavonic phonology, but neither is it the form we would expect to be derived from Iranian *satəm* (which should give *sot-*). There is a remarkable coincidence between the Slavonic word for ' god ' (O. Sl. *bogŭ*) and O. Pers. *baga-*, but in view of the complete absence of other loanwords it is better to see in these words a case of common inheritance.

This absence of Iranian influence on Slavonic is surprising in view of the repeated incursions of Scythian tribes into Europe, and the prolonged occupation by them of extensive territories reaching to the Danube. Clearly at this later period the Slavs must have remained almost completely uninfluenced politically and culturally by the Iranians. On the other hand at a much earlier period (*c.* 2000 B.C.) before the primitive Aryans left their European homeland, Indo-Iranian and the prototypes of Baltic and Slavonic must have existed as close neighbours for a considerable period of time. Practically all the contacts which can be found between the two groups are to be referred to this period and this period alone.

§5. Indo-Iranian and Finno-ugrian

During the same period there is conclusive evidence of contact between Indo-Iranian and Finno-ugrian, a neighbouring family of non-Indo-European languages. This latter family consists of three European languages which have attained the status of literary languages, Finnish, Esthonian and Hungarian, and a number of now minor languages which are spoken by a small number: Lapp, Mordwin, Čeremis, Zyryan, Votyak, Vogul, Ostyak. Of these Vogul and Ostyak are now found to the East of the Urals, but are considered to have moved there from the West. These two, with Hungarian form the Ugrian sub-group, and are distinguished from the rest by certain common features. The Hungarians moved from the region of the Volga to the territory they now occupy in the ninth century. In Siberia there are several Samoyede languages which as a group are related to Finno-Ugrian. The two families are classed together as the Uralian languages.

Even before the Indo-Iranian period there is evidence of contact between Indo-European and Finno-ugrian. Certain remarkable coincidences (e.g. Lat. *sal* 'salt', Finn. *suola*; Skt. *mádhu* 'honey', Gk. *μέθυ*: Finn. *mete-*; Skt. *nāman-*, Gk. *ὄνομα* 'name': Finn. *nime-*, Goth. *watō* 'water', etc.: Fi. *vete-*) have long since attracted attention, but there is lack of agreement as to how exactly they are to be interpreted. One theory is that the two families are ultimately related, but the available evidence is not sufficient to establish this with any certainty. On the whole it seems more probable that the coincidences, insofar as they are not due to chance, are the result of mutual contact and influence in the early prehistoric period.[1]

Evidence is both more abundant and easier to interpret when it comes to early Indo-Iranian contacts with Finno-ugrian. Here it is possible to point out a considerable number of words in Finno-ugrian which can be shown to have been borrowed from Indo-Iranian at this stage. The most important of the Finno-ugrian words which have been ascribed to Indo-Iranian are as follows:

(1) Finn. *sata* '100', Lapp. *cuotte*, Mordv. *śado*, Čer. *šüδö*, Zyry. *śo*, Voty. *śu*, Vog. *sāt*, *šāt*, Osty. *sȯt*, *sȧt*, Hung. *száz*: Skt. *śatám*, Av. *satəm*. (2) Mordv. *azoro*, *azor* 'lord', Voty. *uzïr*, Zyry. *ozïr* 'rich'; Vog. *ōter*, *ā̊ter* 'hero': Skt. *ásura*, 'lord', Av. *ahura-* 'id'. (3) Finn. *vasara* 'hammer', Lapp. *væčer*, Mordv. *vižir*, *užer*: Skt. *vájra-* 'Indra's weapon', Av. *vazra-* 'club, mace'. (4) Finn. *porsas*, Zyry. *porś*, *poryś*,

[1] Borrowings are likely to have occurred in both directions, and usually it is difficult to decide which family has been the borrower. As an example of a probable loan from Finno-ugrian we may quote Engl. *whale*, O.N. *hvalr*, O. Pruss. *kalis*: Av. *kara-* 'mythical fish living in the Raŋhā (=Volga): Finn. *kala* 'fish' etc. The restriction of the meaning indicates that the IE languages are the borrowers, and it is likely that Iranian and the northern IE languages have done so separately.

Voty. *parś, pariś* 'pig' was ascribed to an Aryan **parśa-* (=Lat. *porcus*) and this is now attested by Khotanese *pā'sa-*. (5) Finn. *oras* '(castrated) boar', Mordv. *urëś* 'id': Skt. *varāhá-*, Av. *varāza-* 'boar'. (6) Finn. *utar*, Mordv. *odar*, Čer. *vodar* 'udder': Skt. *ū́dhar* 'id'; (7) Finn. *ora*, Mordv. *uro*, Hung. *ár* 'awl': Skt. *ā́rā* 'id' (= OHG *āla*, etc.); (8) Hung. *ostor* 'whip', Vog. *ošter*, Čer. *woštyr*: Skt. *áṣṭrā*, Av. *aštrā* 'whip' (√*aj-* 'to drive'); (9) Hung. *arany* 'gold', Vog. *sureń, sareń*, Mordv. *sirńe*, Zyry. Voty. *zarńi*: Skt. *híraṇya-*, Av. *zaranya-*; (10) Finn. *arvo* 'value, price', Hung. *ár*, etc.: Skt. *arghá-*, Osset. *arγ* 'id' (Lith. *algà*, etc.); (11) Finn. *sisar* 'sister', Mordv. *sazor*, Čer. *šužar*: Skt. *svásar-*, Av. *x^vaŋhar-*; (12) Hung. *sör* 'beer', Voty. *sur*, Vog. *sor*, Osty. *sar*: Skt. *súrā* 'strong drink', Av. *hurā*; (13) Finn. *sarvi* 'horn', Mordv. *śuro*, Čer. *šur*, Lapp *čoarvve*, Hung. *szarv*: Av. *srū-, srvā* 'horn' (=Gk. κέρας, etc.); (14) Vog. *šuorp, šōrp* 'elk': Skt. *śarabhá-* 'a kind of deer' (from the root of the last); (15) Mordv. *sed'* 'bridge': Skt. *sétu-*, Av. *haētu-*; (16) Mordv. *vərgas* 'wolf', Zyry. *vörkaś*: Skt. *vṛ́ka-*, Av. *vəhrka-*; (17) Zyry. Voty. *turïn* 'grass': Skt. *tṛ́ṇa-*; (18) Zyry. *vörk* 'kidney': Skt. *vṛkká-*, Av. *vərəδka-* 'id'; (19) Vog. *tas* 'stranger': Skt. *dāsá-* 'non-Aryan, slave'; (20) Hung. *vászon* 'linen': Skt. *vásana-* 'garment, cloth'. (21) Fi. *mehiläinen* 'bee', Mordv. *mekš*, Čer. *mükš*, Zyry. Voty. *muš*, Hung. *méh*: Skt. *mákṣ-, mákṣā, mákṣikā* 'bee, fly', Av. *maxšī* 'fly'; (22) Fi. *siika-nen* 'beard of grain, etc.', Mordv. *śuva*, Čer. *šu*, Zyry. *śu*: Skt. *śū́ka-* 'id'; (23) Mordv. *śava, śeja* 'goat': Skt. *chā́ga-*.

The detailed problems raised by these and other comparisons are not without complications, but certain general conclusions emerge clearly. Most important of all is the fact that, taking the words as a whole, the primitive forms which have to be assumed after a comparison of the Finno-ugrian forms, are identical with those which have been reconstructed for primitive Indo-Iranian, and are free of any of the later sound changes which are characteristic of Iranian on the one hand and Indo-Aryan on the other. This is quite well illustrated by the first word which represents a primitive form *śata-* (the Indo-Iranian and Sanskrit form) and not *sata-* (the Iranian form). The characteristic Iranian change of *s* to *h* is uniformly absent (3 Mordv. *azoro*, 11 Mordv. *sazor*, 15 Mordv. *sed'*, etc.). Likewise characteristic Indo-Aryan changes such as of *źh*, *jh* to *h* are not to be found (5 Finn, *oras*, etc.). There is therefore not the slightest doubt that the period when these borrowings took place was the primitive Indo-Iranian period, and it appears probable that the seat of this primitive Indo-Iranian must have been in the region of the middle Volga and the Urals for this contact to have been possible.

One point that is noticeable when looking at a few of these words is that the change of Indo-European *l*, *l̥* to Aryan *r*, *r̥* has already taken place (7 Finn. *ora*, 9. Vog. *sareń*, etc., 16. Mordv. *vargas*). This is a change which is complete in Iranian, but incomplete in Indo-Aryan. That is to say that there were dialects in early Indo-Aryan which preserved IE *l* (not *l̥*), as well as those (the Rigvedic) which agreed with Iranian in this respect. The Finno-ugrian forms show that this feature must have already been widespread in the earlier, Indo-Aryan period, and the existence of *r*-forms in the Aryan of the Near East corroborates this. It cannot however have been universal, for in that case no *l*-forms would have been found in Sanskrit at all.

It is usually quite clear that these words have been borrowed by Finno-ugrian from Indo-Iranian and not vice versa. We have equivalents of the words in other IE languages, and before being borrowed into Finno-ugrian they have undergone the changes characteristic of the Aryan branch. Even where an Indo-Iranian word has no actual equivalent in the other IE languages, its structure and the possibility of deriving it from a known IE root will often show it to be an old inherited word. For instance Skt. *vájra-*, Av. *vazra-*, is formed with the well-known suffix *-ra* (IE *-ro*), and can be derived from the IE root which appears in Gk. (Ϝ)ἄγνυμι 'break, smash'. There are however a few words in the above list where it is not possible to be certain in this way. Nothing like the Indo-Iranian word for 'bee' (No. 21) is found in any other IE language, and this makes it more likely on the whole that in this case the Indo-Iranians have adopted a Finno-ugrian word. Similar considerations apply to Nos. 22 (Skt. *śūka-*) and 23 (Skt. *chā̆ga-*). There may be further examples of Finno-ugrian words in Indo-Iranian, but the matter has never been investigated from this point of view. As plausible equations we may mention: Skt. *kapha-* 'phlegm', Av. *kafa-*, Pers. *kaf* 'foam, scum:

Hung. *hăb* 'foam, froth, cream', Veps. *kobe* 'wave, foam', Sam. (Kam.) *khòwü* 'foam'; Skt. *kū́pa* 'pit, well': Fi. *kuoppa* 'pit', Lapp *guöppe*, Čer. *kup*, Voty. *gop*, etc.; Skt. *śalākā* 'splinter, etc.': Hung. *szilank* 'chip, splinter', Fi. *sale*, 3. *saleen* 'id', etc. In cases like these, and others could be added, no IE etymology has been found for the Sanskrit words. Since it is certain that we must assume long contact between the early Indo-Iranians and the neighbouring Finno-ugrians, and since there is no reason why the movement of words should have been entirely one way, we should consider Finno-ugrian to be a likely source of Aryan words in cases like the above where striking similarity in form and meaning is found.

§6. Aryans in the Near East

The earliest recorded traces of the Aryan peoples come neither from India nor from Iran, but from the Near East. The presence of Aryans in this area is recorded principally in documents of the Mitanni kingdom of North Mesopotamia during the period 1500-1300 B.C. The list of royal names preserved in a variety of cuneiform documents has a distinctly Aryan appearance, even though their interpretation is not absolutely certain in all cases. The names of these kings are as follows: *Sutarna, Paršasatar, Sauššatar, Artadāma, Artašumara, Tušratha, Matiwāza*, i.e. in Indo-Aryan form *Sutaraṇa-* (cf. Ved. *sutárman-*), *Praśāstár-* 'director, ruler', **Saukṣatra-* 'son of *Sukṣatra-* (?)', *Ṛtadhāman-* (nom. *Ṛtádhāmā*) V.S., *Ṛtasmara-* 'mindful of right', **Tviṣratha-*, cf. V. *tveṣáratha-* 'having rushing chariots', **Mativāja-* 'victorious through prayer'. In addition there are found in private documents from this area written in Assyrian a number of proper names of local notables which can be interpreted as Aryan, e.g. *Artamna, Bardašva, Biryašura, Puruša, Šaimašura, Satawaza*, i.e. *Ṛtamna-* 'mindful of the law', *Vārddhāśva-* 'son of *Vṛddhāśva-*', *Vīryaśūra-* 'hero of valour', *Púruṣa-* 'man, male', *Kṣemaśūra-* 'hero of peace or security', *Sātavāja-* 'who has won prizes' (Bvr. cf. v. *Vā́jasāti-*).

This was a period of the expansion of Mitanni influence in the surrounding territories. Consequently we come across rulers of neighbouring principalities having similar Aryan names, and this extends as far as Syria and Palestine. The clearest examples of Aryan names among these are *Šuvardata*:

**svardāta-* 'given by heaven', *Šatuara*: **Satvara-*, a stem bearing the same relation to Skt. *sátvan-* 'powerful, victorious: a warrior', as does Skt. *īśvará-* 'lord' to Av. *isvan-*; *Artamanya*: *Ṛtamanya-* 'thinking on the law', *Biridašva*: *Vṛddhāśva-* 'possessing large horses', *Biryawāza*: *Vīryavāja-* 'having the prize of valour', *Indarota*: *Indrotá-* (RV) 'helped by Indra', *Šubandu*: *Subandhu-*.

The contemporary Hittite kingdom had close relations both of peace and war with the Mitanni kingdom, and some of the documents from the Hittite capital provide important evidence for the presence of Aryans in the Mitanni country. The most interesting of these documents is a treaty concluded between the Hittite king Suppiluliuma and the Mitanni king Matiwāza (*c.* 1350 B.C.). Among the divinities sworn by in this document there occur four well known Vedic divine names. They are *Indara, Mitraš(il), Našatia(nna), Uruvanašš(il)*, which stripped of their non-Aryan terminations are unmistakeably Ved. *Indra-, Mitra-, Nāsatya* and *Varuṇa-*. It is clear that not only Aryan language, but also Aryan religion in a form closely resembling that known from the Ṛgveda, was current in this region of the Near East during this period.

The introduction of the horse to the countries of the Near East which took place during the early part of the second millenium B.C. seems to have been due mainly to these Aryans. The usefulness of this animal in war soon made it popular in the neighbouring kingdoms, among them the Hittites. Among the archives of the Hittite capital there exists a treatise on the care and training of horses. This is written in the Hittite language, but the author, who had charge of the royal horses was a Mitannian called Kikkuli. Furthermore some of the technical terms used in the work are Aryan words. These are *aika vartanna, tera v°, panza v°, satta v°* and *navartanna* (hapl. for *nava-v°*) = Skt. *eka-vartana-* 'one turn (of the course)', and likewise for the numbers 3, 5, 7 and 9. The existence of these loanwords in the Hittite text shows clearly the priority of the Aryans in this field.

In addition to the above evidence there are a few Aryan traces among the documents of the Kassite dynasty of Babylon (*c.* 1750-1170 B.C.). The Kassites themselves were invaders from the East, from the Iranian plateau, and their language, of which something is known, has no connection whatever with

Aryan or Indo-European. Nevertheless in a list of names of gods with Babylonian equivalents we find a sun god *Šuriaš* (rendered *Šamaš*) which must clearly be identified with Skt. *sū́rya-*. In addition *Maruttaš* the war god (rendered *En-urta*) has been compared with Skt. *marút-*, though here some difficulty is caused by the fact that the Skt. word always occurs in the plural. Among the kings of this dynasty one has a name which can be interpreted as Aryan: *Abirattaš*: *abhi-ratha-* 'facing chariots (in battle)'.

The existence of Aryans in this area was unsuspected until the discovery of these Aryan names in cuneiform documents, and a long discussion has proceeded for many years concerning them. Even though the material is small, it can nevertheless be concluded that a significant migration of Aryans in this direction had taken place at this early period. Although the chief centre of the Aryan influence, as far as our records go is the Hurrian state of Mitanni, what we find there is an Aryan dynasty ruling over a Hurrian population, with no evidence of any sizeable Aryan settlement. The kings of the Mitanni belonging to the dynasty with the Aryan names use Hurrian as their official language, and it is considered unlikely that in this situation they would have retained their original Aryan speech for long. The question that then arises is to decide from what base the conquest of the Mitanni state had proceeded, since such a base, with an Aryan population, is necessary to account for it. A clue to the answer to this problem is probably to be found in the fact that Aryan influence is found not only among the Hurrians, but also among the Kassites, a people originating in the mountainous regions of Western Iran. A settlement of Aryans in North-Western Iran, to the East of the Hurrian country, and to the North of the Kassites, would account for both of these developments.

Since the first discovery of Aryan traces in the ancient Near East discussion has proceeded as to whether these Aryans are to be connected with the Indo-Aryans or the Iranians, whether they are to be identified with the Proto-Aryans from which those two branches are descended, or whether they are to be regarded as a third branch of Aryans beside the other two. The predominant opinion at present is that they are to be connected specifically with the Indo-Aryans. This conclusion is founded partly on linguistic grounds, and partly on the fact that the Aryan gods mentioned in the above mentioned treaty are specifically Vedic gods. The linguistic argument for this conclusion is illustrated by the word *aika-* ' one ' which corresponds to Sanskrit *eka-* wehereas Iranian has *aiva-* with a different suffix (cf. p. 258). Likewise the name of the sungod Šuriyaš corresponds to Sanskrit *Sū́ryas*, whereas Iranian shows no such form, but only the base (*hvar* = Vedic *svàr*) form which *sū́rya-* is derived. As far as the treaty gods are concerned, they are prominent in the Ṛgveda, and are indeed all mentioned together in one hymn (RV. 10.125.1), but they cannot be shown to be all Proto-Aryan or Proto-Iranian, and there are in fact some reasons for believing that they were not so.

If the Aryans of the ancient Near East are to be connected specifically with the Indo-Aryans, then we must assume that they were two migrations proceeding from the same source, a massive one into North-West India and a smaller one in the direction of North-Western Iran. Since the Vedic Aryans certainly entered India across the mountain barrier separating the subcontinent from North-Eastern Iran, we must conclude that the closely related section of the Aryans who appear in the Near East started from the same source, taking a route which was to be followed early in the next millennium by the Medes and Persians.

The chronology of these two movements corresponds very closely. The Aryan invasion of N.W. India can be dated by the end of the Indus civilisation, for which no doubt they were largely responsible, and it may be assumed to have taken place in successive waves over a considerable period of time. In the ancient Near East their presence is established by 1500 B.C. at latest, and the process of migration and settlement must have occupied a considerable period before that.

§7. The Emergence of Indo-Aryan

The pre-history of the Aryan language of India takes us far from the North-West India of the Vedic period both in space and time. Comparison with other languages renders possible a reconstruction of linguistic history which is nowhere directly recorded, and establishes as a fact important migrations and movements of peoples which otherwise would be unknown to history. It has also been possible to say something definite, though naturally within fairly wide limits, about the origin of these movements, and about their chronology. The distribution of the IE languages suggests that their origin is to be sought in Central and Eastern Europe. The special relations of Indo-Iranian with the *satəm*-group of languages, and with Balto-Slavonic in particular, together with evidence of contact between it and Finno-ugrian in the Primitive Indo-Iranian period, point to its original location in Central Russia. From there the movement was eastward and southward, with the result that Central Asia became for a time the home of the Aryans. There is evidence that the division into the two branches, Indo-Aryan and Iranian, had already commenced at this early period. The Indo-Aryan group was the first to move south, first into eastern Iran, and then into India on the one hand, and into western Iran on the other. The second wave of migration was that of the Iranians, who established themselves first in eastern Iran, thereby cutting off the Indo-Aryans to the east from the Proto-Indoaryans to the west. Later the advance of the Iranians westwards resulted in the submergence of the latter, but their original presence there is attested by these documents from the Near East.

Chronologically there is not much direct information to rely on. The earliest and most important data are those relating to the presence of Aryans in the Near East from 1500 B.C. onwards. This is an important pointer to the period of the migrations, which to judge by historical analogies are likely to have taken place during a limited period of time. The first half of the second millennium B.C. which would seem to be indicated by this evidence as the general period of the migrations is one which agrees comfortably with all the general considerations which can be adduced. The next direct information about the Aryans refers to the Iranians. The presence of Medes and Persians in Iran proper is attested in the Assyrian annals from the ninth century B.C. onwards, and it is unlikely that they had occupied this area in any force for very long before this period. For the Indo-Aryan invasion of India no direct evidence is available. Nevertheless the very great similarity between the Vedic language and the earliest Iranian precludes any long period of separation between the two, and makes it impossible that the age of the Vedic hymns can be pushed back to the third or fourth millennium B.C. The average rough guess which places the period of the Indo-Aryan invasions *c.* 1700-1400 B.C. and the period of the composition of the *Ṛgveda* *c.* 1200-1000 B.C. is not likely to be many centuries out, either one way or the other.

There is some linguistic evidence to show that the Indo-Aryan invasion took place in successive phases, and not in one simultaneous movement. There are dialectal differences between the Vedic language of the North West and the later classical language of Madhyadeśa. The most striking of these is that the Vedic language turns *l* into *r* whereas the classical language, to a large extent, preserves the distinction between *r* and *l*. This Vedic feature is characteristic of the whole of Iranian, and furthermore it can be traced in the Aryan of the Near East and in some Aryan words in Finno-ugrian. Clearly the fact that the more easterly dialects of early Indo-Aryan have avoided this change indicates a comparatively early separation from the main body, in comparison with the Vedic dialect which has undergone this change in common with the rest of Aryan before being introduced into India.

Certain features of the Kafiri languages of the North West indicate important dialectal divergencies of ancient Aryan at a time preceding the invasion of India. In some ways these languages stand half way between Indo-Aryan and Iranian. They agree with Indo-Aryan in retaining *s* which Iranian changes to *h*, but with Iranian in the treatment of the two palatal series (e.g. *zim* 'snow': Skt. *himá-*, *ǰā̄-* 'kill': Skt. *han*). In this respect they form simply an intermediate dialect group, as might be expected from their position between the two main groups. On the other hand in their treatment of the sound which appears in Sanskrit as *ś* they have preserved a form which is more archaic than anything found elsewhere in Indian and Iranian (*ċ* in *ċuna-* 'dog', *duċ* '10', etc.). This can only be satisfactorily explained as the isolated preservation of a very ancient dialectal feature within Indo-Iranian. The same considerations apply to the absence of cerebralisation of *s* after *u* in words like *dōs* 'yesterday' and *mūsə* 'mouse'. The change of *s* to *š* (>Skt. *ṣ*) under specified conditions is, as we have seen, so ancient as to be shared by both Indo-Aryan and Slavonic, but it seems that some peripheral dialect of Indo-Aryan must have escaped it in connection with *ŭ*, and it is from this source that the Kafiri forms are derived. The evidence would suggest that the Aryan dialect which preserved these archaisms was the very first to reach the borders of India, and that later successive waves of Indo-Aryan invaders confined it into a narrow space in the mountain valleys of the North-West frontier, where it has survived in isolation to this day.

The history of Indo-Aryan begins with the first introduction of Aryan speech into India, but between this event and the composition of the first recorded document of Indo-Aryan, the hymns of the *Ṛgveda*, a considerable period must have elapsed. This is clear from the fact that in the text of the *Ṛgveda* itself, although historical allusions are not uncommon, there is no reference anywhere to the fact of the migration, nor any definite indication that it was still remembered. Linguistic reasons also compel us to assume such a period, since the number of linguistic (mainly phonetic) changes that have taken place since the common Indo-Iranian stage is considerable. No doubt the beginnings of dialectal cleavage go back to the Indo-Aryan period, but there is no doubt that the bulk of the characteristic changes of Indo-Aryan and Iranian respectively have taken place after the complete separation of the two groups, that is to say, after the Aryan invasion of India.

Some of the more important changes that affected Indo-Aryan during this period may be briefly listed: (1) *ǰh* and *źh* become *h* (= Ir. *ǰ* and *z*), (2) *ǰ* and *ź* are confused as *j* (= Ir. *ǰ* and *z*), (3) a single group *kṣ* results from the two combinations *k* + *s* and *ś* + *s*; these are kept apart in Iranian, (4) Aryan voiced groups of the type *gžh*, *bžh* are replaced by unvoiced *kṣ*, *ps* (Skt. *dipsa-* : Av. *diwža-*), (5) Aryan *z* is elided in all positions (Skt. *medhā́-*, cf. Av. *mazdā̊*), (6) Elision of Aryan *ž* before *d* gives rise to cerebral *ḍ* (*nīḍá-*) and this, in conjunction with other combinatory changes (*aṣṭau*, *viṭ*, *kāraṇa-*) is the beginning of a new series of consonants previously foreign to Aryan, as well as to the rest of Indo-European. (7) *s* (*ṣ*) is elided between two consonants (*ábhakta*, *s*-aor.). (8) All final consonant groups are simplified and only the first remains (Skt. *vāk* : Av. *vāxš*). (9) A tendency begins to weaken the aspirates *dh* and *bh* to *h* (*ihá* 'here' : Av. *iδa*, but Pa. *idha* has retained the older form). (10) The Aryan diphthongs *ai*, *au* are turned into the simple vowels *ē*, *ō*.

This list of changes is impressive enough, and of great importance for the future history of Indo-Aryan, and a reasonable length of time must be assumed for their completion. At the same time we have the impression that the period of fairly rapid linguistic change preceded the Vedic period. With the establishment of a recognised literary language, and a tradition of education associated with it, this rapid evolution was stopped as far as classical Sanskrit is concerned. The phonetic changes that distinguish Classical Sanskrit from the Vedic language are negligible in comparison with those that took place in the immediate pre-Vedic period. On the other hand the popular language, developing soon into the Prakrits, continued to show this tendency to rapid change. In particular it is interesting to note that the type of change seen in the examples listed above is similar to that of the later Middle Indo-Aryan changes. The assimilation of consonant groups in final position is the beginning of a process that affects all consonant groups. The development of voiced aspirates to *h*, which is general in the case of *ǰh*, *źh* and sporadic elsewhere, is continued in Pali and Prakrit. The cerebral consonants once created become more and more prevalent. From the first Indo-Aryan is affected by certain characteristic tendencies to change which continue to be influential in later periods. These changes which set in from the beginning were rapid, and in the language of the people continued to be rapid. It was only the standardisation of Sanskrit at a very early period by organisers of Brahman civilisation, that arrested this development, in the case of the classical language, before it had proceeded too long, and thereby preserved for us a form of language which in most respects is more archaic and less altered from original Indo-European than any other member of the family.

CHAPTER II

OUTLINES OF THE HISTORY OF SANSKRIT

§ 1. The Vedic Language and the Classical Language

About the pre-history of Indo-Aryan, both in India where it emerged as an independent form of speech, and outside India through the successive stages of Indo-Iranian and Indo-European, much can be deduced, and deduced with certainty with the help of comparative philology. But of all these stages of the language no direct record is preserved. The historical period of the language begins—probably, as we have seen, round about the period 1200-1000 B.C.—with the composition and compilation of the *Ṛgveda*. From this time the literary tradition is continuous and uninterrupted, and the gradual development of Indo-Aryan, through the various stages until the period of the modern languages is reached, can be followed in detail.

During this period great changes have taken place, and their operation has been continuous throughout the whole period. By all this change and development Sanskrit has been affected only to a small extent. From the beginning, from the time of the composition of the Vedic hymns and the establishment thereby of a recognised literary language, there was a strong tendency among the Brahmins, the guardians of this literature and of the religious and social system that went with it, to preserve the language against change. This applied not only to the preservation of the sacred texts themselves, which have been handed down with scrupulous accuracy by oral tradition, or to the composition of literary works on ancient models, but also to the language of everyday speech among the Brahmins, and in the royal courts with which they were always closely associated. This led to a growing divergence between the language of the educated classes and that of the people, which was subject to a fairly rapid alteration in the direction of Middle Indo-Aryan from an early period.

At the same time the language of the élite did not remain without change, in spite of all the influence of conscious conservatism. The classical language as fixed by Pāṇini (fourth cent. B.C.) is a noticeably younger form of language than that found in the Vedic texts, though much less altered from it than the spoken language of the masses, which is known slightly later from the inscriptions of Aśoka. We have in fact up to this period two parallel developments of Indo-Aryan occurring side by side in different strata of the community, slow and gradual change in the dominant Brahman community restrained by education and a literary tradition, and beside it a rapid evolution among the mass of the population unhindered by education and tradition. With Pāṇini's work Sanskrit in its external form became finally stabilised and no more change was allowed. From then on the history of Indo-Aryan is the history of Middle Indo-Aryan in its various phases (Pali, Prakrit, Apabhraṃśa) and then of Modern Indo-Aryan. In this evolution Sanskrit took no part, but remained as it was fixed by Pāṇini at a period long antedating the bulk of the classical literature.

The differences between Vedic and Classical Sanskrit affect to a very small extent the phonetic structure of the language, and in this respect the contrast between Classical Sanskrit and Early Middle Indo-Aryan is most striking. They are more noticeable in the field of vocabulary and grammar, though here also they are comparatively restricted in scope.

Phonetically, apart from some dialectal phenomena such as *ḍ, ḍh* for *ḷ, ḷh*, and the replacement of *r* by *l* in certain words, the differences are mainly concerned with innovations of Sandhi. This is noticeable for instance in the case of *-iy- -uv-* of the Veda which are normally replaced by *y, v*. The rule has been applied to the accepted text of the *Ṛgveda*, so that for instance what is written *tanvàs* is, from the evidence of the metre, to be pronounced *tanúvas*. Among Vedic peculiarities of final Sandhi we may note that *s* is only inserted between final *n* and initial *t* when it is etymologically justified (*sarvāṃs tān*, but *varṣman tasthau, maghavan tava, ajagmiran te*), and that before vowels the terminations of the acc. pl. *-ān, īn, ūn* appear as *-ām̐, īm̐r* and *ūm̐r* (*sargām̐ iva, paridhīm̐r ati*). In such cases later Sanskrit has regularised the Sandhi by the analogical extension of a form that was originally justified only in a certain context (e.g. *-ān, -īn, -ūn* was the regular phonetic development before voiced consonants and in final position, and from there its use was extended to cases where a vowel followed). Apart from such comparatively minor changes Classical Sanskrit preserves the basic phonetic structure of the Vedic language intact.

The tendency to change is a good deal more noticeable in the morphology, and in Classical Sanskrit the wealth of forms prevalent in the earlier language is considerably reduced.

Nominal stem-formation shows a reduction in variety in the classical language, and with the disuse of certain suffixes whole classes of words so formed tend to become obsolete. For instance, the suffix *-yu* is productive in the Vedic language producing not only primary derivatives (*yájyu-* 'pious') but also a number of secondary formations connected with denominative verbal stems (*devayú-* 'devoted to the gods', *vājayú-* 'eager to win'). After the early Vedic period it ceases to be productive, and in consequence most of the words so formed went out of use. Only those that were common enough to survive as individual words remained: *manyú-* 'anger', *dasyú-* 'robber', etc. Examples could be given of the same tendency over the whole field of nominal stem formation.

In nominal composition the Vedic type of governing compound seen in examples like *bharádvāja-* 'carrying off the prize', etc., became early obsolete. In other respects we see not a diminution in nominal composition, but a steady extension in its use. The members of a compound are rarely more than two in number in the Veda, and the conditions under which they may be formed are limited. As the language advances greater freedom is observed both as to the number of members in a compound, and as to the type of syntactical construction allowed to be so expressed. Finally the stage is reached where compounds of any length may be formed almost without restriction, the whole character of the literary language being thereby changed. In this respect the later classical language goes far beyond anything that would have been countenanced by Pāṇini.

There is considerable simplification and modernisation in nominal declension. Older forms of inflection in *a*-stems such as instr. sg. in *-ā* (*vīryà* beside *vīryèṇa*) and nom. pl. nt. in *-ā* (*bhúvanā* beside *bhúvanāni*) are given up in favour of the new formations. At the same time some innovations of the Vedic language (nom. pl. m. *-āsas*, instr. pl. *-ebhis* beside *-ās*, *-ais*) are discarded. One type of inflection of *i-* and *u-* stems (*ávyas*, *krátvas*) is abandoned, though one type of special neuter inflection is preserved (*vā́riṇas, mádhunas*) and a new type of feminine inflection is introduced from the *ī-* stems (*gátyās, dhenvā́s*). Of the two types of inflection of *ī́-* stems, the *vṛkī́* type is abandoned in favour of the *devī́* type with some influence of the former on the latter (nom. pl. *devyàs* as opposed to *devī́s* of the Vedic language), and some isolated survivals (nom. sg. *lakṣmī́s*). The irregular vocatives in *-s* of the *van-* and *vant-* stems (*bhagavas*, etc.) are abandoned. Endingless locatives of the type *akṣán* are abandoned in favour of the fully inflected forms (*akṣáṇi* or *akṣṇí*). The Vedic locative formations from the personal pronouns in *-é* (*asmé*, etc.) disappear. In the dual the number of cases that can be formed from these pronouns is reduced from five to three by the elimination of the nominative and ablative forms (*āvám, yuvám* ; *āvát, yuvát*). In the conjugation of the verb the classical language simplifies considerably the complicated morphology of the earlier language. The alternative termination *-masi* of the 1st pers. plural is abandoned, and likewise the long forms of the 2nd plural in *-tana, -thana*. That form of conjugation in the middle which is characterised by the absence of *t* in the 3rd singular and the termination *r* in the 3rd plural (*duhé, duhré*, impf. *áduha, áduhra*) is abandoned. The old imperatives in *-si* disappear. The *s-* aorist is enlarged in the 2nd and 3rd singular to produce forms more easily recognisable (*ánaiṣīt* for *ánais*). The root aorist is confined to roots in long *ā* and the root *bhū*. Pluperfect forms are eliminated. The most important loss in the verbal structure is that of the subjunctive. This mood is very common indeed in the Veda, and also later till the close of the Brāhmaṇa period, but by Pāṇini's time, apart from forms of the first person incorporated in the Imperative, it had fallen quite out of use. The use of the unaugmented forms classed as Injunctive is confined to constructions with the prohibitive *mā́*. Modal forms outside the present system cease to be used, as also participles from aorist bases. In place of the great variety of infinitive forms in the Veda, only one, that in *-tum* is used in the classical language. Similarly old variant forms of the gerund (e.g. in *-tvī, -tvāya*) and gerundive (e.g. in *-tva, -enya*) disappear.

An important difference between the Vedic and the classical language lies in the treatment of the prepositional prefixes attached to verbal roots. In the classical language the prefix stands immediately before the verbal form with which it is compounded. On the other hand in the Vedic language its position is quite free, and it may be separated from the verb by several words, or, on occasion, come after it. This freedom was characteristic of Indo-European, and elsewhere the tendency has generally been to associate the prefix more closely with the verb as time went on. There is the same difference in this respect between Homeric and classical Greek as between Vedic and classical Sanskrit.

Finally there are changes in vocabulary. This has already been noticed in connection with disuse of certain types of nominal stem formation, but it applies equally to the whole field of vocabulary. A number of old Indo-European words which are current in the Veda are no longer used in the classical period. Such are *átka-* 'garment' (Av. *aδka-*), *ápas* 'work' (Lat. *opus*), *ándhas* 'juice of soma plant' (cf. Gk. *ἄνθος* 'flower'?), *áma-* 'strength' (Av. *ama-*), *árvant-* 'steed' (Av. *aurvant-* 'swift'), *avatá-* 'spring' (Lett. *avuots*), *ādhrá-* 'mean, lowly' (Av. *ādra-*), *āpí-* 'friend, ally' (cf. Gk. *ἤπιος* 'kind'), *iṣirá-* 'vigorous, strong' (cf. Gk. *ἱερός* 'sacred'), *īrmá-* 'foreleg' (Lat. *armus*, etc.), *uśíj-* 'a kind of priest' (Av. *usig-*), *ṛṣvá-* 'high' (Av. *ərəšva-*), *kravíṣ-* 'raw flesh' (cf. Gk. *κρέας*), *gātú-* 'way, course; abode' (Av. *gātu-*), *gnā́* 'wife of god' (Av. *gənā* 'wife', Gk. *γυνή*. etc.), *cánas-* 'pleasure, satisfaction' (Av. *čanah-*), *cyautná-* 'deed, enterprise' (Av. *šyaoθna-*), *jánas* 'race' (Gk. *γένος*, Lat. *genus*), *jáni-* 'woman' (Av. *jaini-*), *jénya-* 'under the care of, entrusted to' (Sogd. *zynyh*, Khotanese *ysīnīya-*, whence Central Asian Prakrit *jheniǵa* 'id'), *jráyas-* 'expanse, flat surface' (Av. *zrayah-* 'lake'), *títaü-* 'sieve' (for **títaнu-*, cf. Gk. *διαττάω* 'sift', etc.), *toká-* 'offspring', *tókman-* 'offshoot' (Av. *taoxman-* 'seed'), *tvakṣ-* 'to be active, energetic' (Av. *θwaxš-*), *dasmá-*, *dasrá-* 'accomplished, clever', *dáṃsas-* 'wonderful deed' (cf. Av. *dahma-* 'instructed', *daŋra-* 'accomplished', *daŋhah-* 'cleverness', Gk. *δέδαε* 'taught', *ἀδαής* 'uninstructed', *δαήμων* 'instructed', etc.), *dáma-* 'house' (Lat. *domus*, etc.), *dā́nu-* 'moisture' (Av. *dānu* 'stream', Osset. *don*), *dāśvás-* 'worshipper', *drapsá-* 'banner' (Av. *drafša-*), *nákt-* 'night' RV 7. 71, 1 (Lat. *nox*, etc.; adverbial *náktam* remains), *náhuṣ-* 'neighbour', *néma-* 'half' (Av. *naēma-*), *pan-* 'to praise, extol', *pastyā̀* 'habitation', *pitú-* 'nourishment, food' (Av. *pitu-* 'id', Lith. *pẽtūs* 'midday meal', etc.), *bhṛṣṭí-* 'spike' (Av. *°barəšti-*, cf. Engl. *bristle*, etc.), *pā́jas-* 'surface' (Khot. *pāysa-*, Sogd. *p'z* 'face'), *mṛḍīka-* 'mercy' and related words (Av. *mərəždīka-*), *márya-* 'young man' (cf. Gk. *μεῖραξ* 'lad' and the *Marianni* of the Mitanni documents), *miyédha-* 'sacrificial offering' (Av. *myazda-*), *mīḍhá-* 'reward, prize' (Av. *mižda-*, Gk. *μισθός*, etc.), *yáhu-*, *yahvá-* 'young, youngest, latest' (Av. *yazu-*, f. *yezivī* 'id'), *yós* 'welfare, rightness' (Av. *yaoš*, Lat. *iūs*), *ródasī* 'the two surfaces (of heaven and earth) (Av. *raodah-*, *raoda-* 'face', Pers. *rōy* 'id'), *vádhri-* 'castrated' (Gk. *ἐθρίς* 'castrated ram'), *vasná-* 'price, value' (cf. Lat. *vēnum*, Gk. *ὦνος*, etc., Hitt. *uššania-* 'to sell'), *vā́ja-* 'prize, booty', *vīḍú-* 'strong, firm', *ven-* 'to long for', *śáma-* 'hornless' (cf. Gk. *κεμάς* 'young deer', Lith. *šmúlas* 'without horns'), *śíprā* 'moustache', *śuná-* 'welfare', *śyetá-* 'orphan' RV. 1. 71. 4 (cf. Av. *saē*, O. Sl. *sirŭ*, etc.), *sap-*, *sáparya-* 'to attend to religious ceremonies' (Gk. *ἕπω* 'attend to', Lat. *sepeliō* 'bury'), *sas-* 'to sleep' (Hitt. *šeš-*) *stigh-* 'to step, stride' (Gk. *στείχω*, Goth. *steigan*, etc.), *syoná-* 'soft, gentle', *háras-* 'heat' (Gk. *θέρος* 'summer', Arm. *ǰer* 'warm weather'), *hary-* 'to be pleased, exhilarated' (Gk. *χαίρω* 'rejoice').

The existence of homonyms frequently results in the suppression of one of such pairs. The early Vedic language possessed *ásura-*[1] 'lord' (Av. *ahura-*) and *ásura-*[2] 'demon'. Only the latter is in use from the later Vedic period onwards. Similarly of the pair *arí-*[1] 'devoted, trustworthy' (whence *árya-*, *ā́rya-*, cf. Hitt. *ara-* 'friend, ally', etc.) and *arí-*[2] 'enemy' (<**ali-*, cf. Lat. *alius*, etc.), only the latter is preserved. Vedic *kārú-*[1] 'singer' (*kṝ-* 'to celebrate', cf. Gk. *κῆρυξ*, *κᾱ́ρυξ* 'herald') yields to classical *kāru-*[2] 'artisan' (*kṛ-* 'to do, make), and Vedic *rájas*[1] 'space' (*raj-* 'to stretch out', cf. Lat. *regiō*, etc.) is abandoned on account of the competition of *rájas*[2] 'dust, dirt'. Similarly of the pairs *paruṣá-*[1] 'light grey' (Av. *pouruša-*, cf. Engl. *fallow*, etc.) and *paruṣá-*[2] 'knotty, rough' (*páruṣ-*, *párvan-* 'knot'), *pāyú-*[1] 'protector' and *pāyú-*[2] 'anus', *phalgú-*[1] 'reddish, pink', *phalgú-*[2] 'hollow, without substance', the homonym listed first ceases to be used in the later language.

Changes of meaning naturally occurred over so long a period. Many of these occurred in the natural growth of the language. For instance *váhni-* in the Veda means simply 'carrier' and it is applied to Agni in his capacity of carrying the oblations to the gods. Later it means 'fire' in general by a perfectly natural extension of meaning. The term *dásyu-* is primarily ethnological, meaning the non-Aryan inhabitants of India; later it acquires the meaning 'robber, brigand'. Similarly *dāsá-* 'slave' was originally a tribal name (cf. the *Dahae* of Central Asia), and the same may apply to *śūdrá-* 'member of the fourth caste', since a tribe with this name is known to have existed in N.W. India from both Indian and Classical sources.

In other cases the change of meaning in the later language is due simply to a misunderstanding of the Vedic word. This is the case with *kratu-* 'sacrifice' as opposed to Vedic *krátu-* 'wisdom, insight'. Here there is no change of meaning, but simply a failure to understand properly the meaning of the Vedic texts. In classical Sanskrit *mātariśvan-* means 'wind'; originally it meant the divine being who discovered fire by the method of rubbing two sticks, and also Agni himself (from **mātariś-* 'fire-stick', etymologically equivalent to Lat. *mātrix*); the change of meaning can only be due to the fading of the old mythology in the popular mind. Vedic *kīlā́la-* meant a certain milk preparation (cf. Khowar *kiḷāḷ* 'a kind of cheese'); its use in classical Sanskrit to mean 'blood' is due to a misunderstanding of the old texts.

False popular etymology in the case of the old words *ásura-* 'demon' and *ásita-* 'black' led to the creation of two new words. Since the initial *a-* in these words was falsely interpreted as the negative *a-*, *sura-* 'god' and *sita-* 'white' were created as their opposites.

The above examples show that the losses in vocabulary during this period of the history of the language were considerable. As elsewhere the Indo-European heritage of Indo-Aryan was steadily reduced with the passage of time. One result was that many of the old words of the Veda ceased to be understood in later times. The difficulties that ensued gave rise at an early period to a special school of interpretation (*nirukta-*) of the Veda. Collections of difficult vocables were made and attempts to explain them on an etymological basis were made. These labours were summed up in the work of Yāska, who may be roughly contemporary with Pāṇini. These attempts at interpretation were successful to only a limited degree, and it emerges quite clearly there existed no reliable tradition as to the meaning of many Vedic words, with the result that the authors were frequently reduced to guessing. The same applies to the later commentatorial works culminating in the great Bhāṣya of Sāyaṇa. In modern times the labours of scholars, equipped with greater resources than the ancients, have done much to reduce the field of uncertainty, but even now there remains over a considerable amount of material which defies certain interpretation.

In contrast to the losses of the old vocabulary, classical Sanskrit has acquired a large number of new words from various sources. These gains far more than counterbalance the losses, and the vocabulary of classical Sanskrit is one of the richest known. Of course there are many words which appear first in the later language and at the same time belong to the most ancient layer of Indo-Aryan. The absence of such words from the older texts is partly accidental, since, extensive though they are, the Vedic texts do not contain the whole linguistic material of pre-classical Sanskrit. Partly also it is a question of dialect; the widening of the horizon in the case of later as opposed to Vedic Sanskrit led to the inclusion of Old Indo-Aryan material which may not have been current in the dialects which underlay the early standard language. For instance the adverb *parut* 'last year' is not recorded before Pāṇini, but it is an ancient IE word as is shown by the Greek equivalent πέρυσι. Similarly the related *parāri* 'year before last' is, we may be sure, absent from the early texts only by accident. There are many words which must be ancient because their formation is of an ancient type, e.g. *vipula-* 'abundant' from the root *pṝ-* 'to fill'. In this case the preservation of IE *l*, elsewhere not found with this root, suggests that its absence from the early Vedic texts is a matter of dialect.

A large number of the new words are fresh formations based on the existing stock of roots and formatives. As long as the suffixes of derivation retained their living character, there was ample scope for the creation of new terms as occasion demanded. This was particularly so since it was combined with the facility of compounding verbal roots with prepositional prefixes, and in this way terms could be created at will for any conceivable need. From the root *kṛ-* 'to do' alone, by means of the suffixes of derivation, and with the help of some score of prepositional prefixes, many hundreds of words were manufactured, whose meanings cover every field of practical and theoretical expression.

The vocabulary was further enriched from outside Indo-Aryan itself. The pre-existing vernaculars made a sizeable contribution to the Sanskrit vocabulary. This influence is strongest, it seems, in the case of Dravidian words and that can be identified with certainty as Dravidian run into several hundred. Though a few are found already in the Vedic language, the majority do not become current before the classical language. A smaller proportion was provided by the Kolarian languages. Some words were introduced from outside India, e.g. from Iranian (*vārabāṇa-*, 'breast plate') or from Greek (*horā* 'hour'). See further Chapter VIII.

Even when all these new words have been accounted for there remains a considerable number of words in classical Sanskrit whose origin is unknown. Most were no doubt originally *deśī* words in the Indian terminology, and since the linguistic complexity of pre-Aryan India must have been greater than anything that now appears, we should not be surprised to find so many words whose origin remains unexplained.

Such in brief are the main changes which took place in Sanskrit between the early Vedic and the classical period. In the pre-classical literature this evolution can be traced in its succeeding stages. This literature, which is devoted entirely to religion and ritual, falls into three main sections.

I. The Saṃhitās of the Ṛgveda, Sāmaveda, Yajurveda and Atharvaveda.

II. The Brāhmaṇas, prose texts devoted to the mystical interpretation of the ritual.

III. The Sūtras, containing detailed instructions for performing the ritual, of which the Śrautasūtras deal with the great public sacrifices, and the Gṛhyasūtras with household ritual.

The periods which are conventionally assumed for the composition of this literature are (1) Saṃhitās 1200-800 B.C., (2) Brāhmaṇas, 800-500 B.C., (3) Sūtras 600-300 B.C.

In the absence of any definite information, such chronology rests mainly on guess-work. On the other hand, the relative chronology of the succeeding strata can be established beyond all doubt by means of linguistic data contained in the texts themselves. The linguistic changes summarised above took place gradually and the language of the succeeding phases of the literature becomes steadily more and more similar to the classical norm. The gulf that separates the language of the

Ṛgveda from classical Sanskrit is very much greater than that separating the language of even the earliest prose texts from it. The later Saṃhitās can be shown on the basis of language to be later in date than the Ṛgveda, and within that work itself the tenth book is known to be the latest for the same reason. In the same way a chronological distinction can be made between earlier and later Brāhmaṇas.

Since the Brāhmaṇas are in prose, their language may be taken as reasonably representative of the spoken language of the upper classes in the later Vedic period. It still retains pre-classical features, such as the use of the old subjunctive, but already the majority of the old Vedic forms have fallen into disuse. By the time of the composition of the Sūtras the language has reached in all essentials the stage at which it was codified by Pāṇini. In all the Sūtras it is possible to find grammatical forms which do not conform strictly to the Pāṇinean rules. But in contrast to the earlier literature these forms are not as a rule archaisms. The difference is rather that their usage is somewhat more lax and careless than that allowed by the strict formulation of the grammarians, and in this respect they accurately reflect the spoken usage of the period of Pāṇini himself and of the period immediately preceding. Their language is based, not like the later classical Sanskrit on an established and traditional grammatical system, but on that same spoken language of the educated Brahmins, which is the source of the grammatical system of Pāṇini. These texts are very important in linguistic history: they stand side by side with Pāṇini as an independent authority on the living Sanskrit language during the period immediately preceding its final codification. It is here, and not in the later literature, that we must look for a living illustration of the language that Pāṇini established in its final form.

§ 2. Old Indo-Aryan

The Sanskrit language, in its Vedic and Classical form, had, as already observed, a definite geographical location. In the very earliest period this lay in the Punjab, but the centre soon moved eastward to the countries of Kuru and Pañcāla, and there it remained during the whole later Vedic period. Certain dialectal divergencies between the language of the Ṛgveda and that of the later literature—notably the use of *l* instead of Vedic *r*—can be ascribed to this. In addition there existed dialect areas containing features which find no place in Sanskrit. Quite early in the Vedic period there were extensive settlements of Indo-Aryans to the East (Kosala, etc.) and to the South (Avanti, etc.). The spoken language outside the area which was the home of classical Sanskrit differed in certain respects from the spoken language of this area. The term Old Indo-Aryan is sometimes used as alternative to Sanskrit, but this is incorrect, since there were other dialects of Indo-Aryan in addition to those on which Sanskrit is founded. The term Old Indo-Aryan should be used for the whole body of Indo-Aryan during the early period, and Sanskrit is not co-extensive with this.

Of the non-Sanskritic dialects of Old Indo-Aryan no direct remains are preserved, and there would not be much to be said about it, if it were not for the fact that in the later Middle Indo-Aryan dialects a fair amount of material exists which cannot be explained out of Sanskrit, Vedic or Classical, but only out of equally ancient, but different forms of Indo-Aryan such as have been referred to above. A complete collection of such material has never been put together, but enough evidence is available to demonstrate the one-time existence of non-Sanskritic dialects of Old Indo-Aryan. The differences involved were not very great (as compared for instance with the early dialects of Iranian), but they are sufficient to be worth taking into account.

Among the phonetic features we may note primarily the change of final *-as* to *-e* in contrast to its treatment as *-o* in Sanskrit and the later Prakrit dialects of the central area. This was a distinguishing feature of Eastern Indo-Aryan, but examples are also found in the extreme North-West. In *sū́re duhitā́* ' daughter of the sun ' one dialectal form of this type is preserved in the Ṛgveda. In place of Sanskrit *kṣ* Middle Indo-Aryan forms sometimes show *jh-*, *jjh-*, *ggh* in cases where Iranian has the sonant combination *γž* (Pkt. *jharaï* ' flows ', Pa. *paggharati*, Skt. *kṣar-*, Av. *γžar-*, etc.). There are dialectal variations in the treatment of ancient *ṛ*H (*ṝ*) ; OIA *ūr* in place of Skt. *īr* is attested in some cases : Pkt. *juṇṇa-* ' old '<**jūrṇá-* (: Skt. *jīrṇá-*), *tūha-* ' ford '<**tūrtha-* (: Skt. *tīrthá-*). In some dialects ancient *-žd-* was replaced by *-ḍḍ-* instead of by single *-ḍ-* with compensatory lengthening as in Sanskrit, e.g. Pa. *niḍḍa-* : Skt. *nīḍá-* ' nest '. In Pa. *idha* ' here ' a more ancient form of the word is preserved than in Skt. *ihá*, Pkt. *siḍhila-*

'slack' (out of **śiṭhila-*) and Skt. *śithirá-* (°*la-*) are parallel independent developments from earlier **śṛthirá-* (*śrath-* 'to loosen').

A number of grammatical differences can be observed, though the loss of so much of the old inflection in Middle Indo-Aryan has eliminated much of this. Forms of the third plural ātmanepada like Pa. *vijjare* 'are seen' (>**vidyare*) indicate that such *r-* endings were more extensively used in some Old Indo-Aryan dialects than in Sanskrit. Pa. *jigucchati* 'is disgusted' (Skt. *júgupsate*) shows *i-* reduplication of the desiderative in the case of roots containing the vowel *-u-* which is absent in Sanskrit but known to Old Iranian (Av. *cixšnuša-* 'desire to please') Pa. *harāyati* 'is angry' continues an Old Indo-Aryan form bearing the same relation to Skt. *hṛṇīte* as Vedic *gṛbhāyáti* to *gṛhṇā́ti*. In *viheseti* 'injures', *vihesā* 'injury' (<**viheṣayati*, **viheṣā*, √*hiṃs-*) Old Indo-Aryan forms unknown to Sanskrit are represented. In Pa. *sabbadhi* 'everywhere' an old adverbial termination is preserved which has a parallel in Gk. -θι. Pa. *kāhāmi* 'I will do' represents an Old Indo-Aryan *aniṭ* future **karṣyāmi* as opposed to Skt. *kariṣyā́mi*. Pa. *sāmaṃ* 'oneself', which is unknown to Sanskrit, is the equivalent of Av. *hāma-*, O. Sl. *samŭ*. Participial forms like *mukka-* 'released', *ruṇṇa-* 'weeping' continue old formations in *-na*, as opposed to the Skt. formations in *-ta*. The Ardha-Māgadhī participles in *-mīṇa* seem to represent an ancient Indo-Aryan variant of Skt. *-māna*. The participle *dinna-* 'given' implies an old formation reduplicating with *i* as in Greek (**didāmi* : Gk. δίδωμι). The participles in *-tāvin* (*vijitāvin-* 'who has conquered') are an ancient formation equivalent to the *-tavant-* participles of Sanskrit. In *etase* 'to go' we have a Vedic type of infinitive not elsewhere found. The absolutives in *-tūna* (Pkt. °*ūna*), *gantūna*, etc., differ in apophony from the Vedic forms in *-tvāna*. Difference in apophony is frequently observable in stem formations: e.g. *supina-* 'dream' = Gk. ὕπνος as opposed to Skt. *svápna-* with guṇa; *garu-* 'heavy' has guṇa of the root as opposed to Skt. *gurú-*; compare in the same way *turita-* 'hastening', *thīna-* 'slothful' (<**stīna-*) with Skt. *tvarita-*, *styāna-*. Nominal stem formations unrepresented in Sanskrit are not uncommon, e.g. Pa. *nahāru-* 'sinew', *theta-* 'firm' *theva-* 'drop' <**snāru-*, **stheta-*, **stepa-* (*stip-* 'to drip'); Pkt. *māhaṇa-* 'brahmin' (lit. 'great one'), cf. V. *mā́hina-* 'great'.

A number of words with IE etymology appear first in the later stages of Indo-Aryan: e.g. Kharoṣṭhī Prakrit *aṭa* ' flour ', Hindī *āṭā* ' id ', cf. Pers. *ārd* from the root in Gk. ἀλέω ' to grind '; Pa. *lāmaka-* ' inferior, wretched ', Pj. *lāvā̃* ' maimed ', cf. Engl. *lame,* Russ. *lom,* etc., Pkt. (Apabhraṃśa) *tūra-* ' cheese ', cf. Gk. τῡρός.

From evidence such as this we can form some idea, fragmentary though it is, of the dialectal variety of Old Indo-Aryan. It is necessary to bear this in mind so that the evolution of Sanskrit can be seen in its proper perspective. The formation of a standard language implies a rigorous process of selection and exclusion. In all spoken language there is continuous variation from area to area and from class to class. Sanskrit was based on the spoken language of the higher classes of Madhyadeśa, influenced by the older sacred language of the Ṛgveda which had originated further West. This was the centre of propagation of Brahmin religion, in its orthodox form, and of a fixed standard language which was the property of the Brahmin community in whatever part of Āryāvarta they resided. Pāṇini speaks occasionally of differences in speech between the Easterners and the Northerners. But these are always trivialities. Sanskrit as a spoken language was essentially the same over the whole of North India, and from an early period also in the Deccan. Under the surface there were dialectal differences which for the earliest period can be dimly perceived, and which come out into the light of day during the next stage of the language, Middle Indo-Aryan.

§ 3. The Grammarians

The importance of the grammarians in the history of Sanskrit is unequalled anywhere in the world. Also the accuracy of their linguistic analysis is unequalled until comparatively modern times. The whole of the classical literature of Sanskrit is written in a form of language which is regulated to the last detail by the work of Pāṇini and his successors.

Grammatical interest in India arose in the first place in connection with the necessity of preserving intact the sacred texts of the Veda. It was of the utmost ritual significance that every word used in the recitals at the sacrifices should be pronounced absolutely correctly. Among the means by which the correct transmission of the Vedic texts was achieved was the *Padapāṭha*, in which each word of the text was repeated separately. To do this correctly, as it is done in the main, involved the beginning of grammatical analysis and, since it involved the resolution of Sandhi, phonetic analysis.

The phonetic teaching necessary for the correct recitation of the Vedas is embodied in the *Prātiśākhyas*. There are several of these attached to various Vedic schools, and they deal with the subject in great detail and with accuracy. They are a very important source for our knowledge of ancient pronunciation. It is disputed whether any of these texts in their present form are earlier than Pāṇini, but in some form or other instruction of this sort must be as old as the Vedic schools themselves. Later works dealing with phonetics are the *Śikṣās* which exist in large numbers and contain valuable observations.

Difficulties in the interpretation of the Vedic texts owing to the obsolescence of words led to the beginnings of lexicography. The earliest work of this kind, the Nighaṇṭu consists of lists of difficult Vedic words, of divinities, etc., drawn up for the use of teachers. The commentary on these by Yāska, who is probably not far removed from Pāṇini in time, contains the earliest systematic discussions on questions of grammar. Here we find the parts of speech already distinguished as *nāman* 'noun', *sarvanāman-* 'pronoun', *ākhyāta-* 'verb', *upasarga-* 'preposition' and *nipāta-* 'particle'. The derivation of nouns by means of *kṛt* and *taddhita* affixes has become a well established theory, and an interesting argument between Śākaṭāyana and Gārgya is reported as to whether all nouns can be derived in this way from verbal roots. The former maintained that they could, and in spite of the cogent arguments on the other side advanced by Gārgya, this was the theory that generally held the field in Sanskrit grammatical theory. It is a fact that a larger proportion of the Sanskrit vocabulary is capable of such analysis than is the case in most languages.

The date of Pāṇini is most commonly fixed in the fourth century B.C. which is in accordance with the native tradition which connects him with the Nanda king of Magadha. Nothing is known of his life except the fact that he was born in the extreme North-West of India at Śālātura. His *Aṣṭādhyāyī* which fixed the form of Sanskrit grammar once and for all, consists of some 4,000 aphorisms of the greatest brevity. This brevity is achieved by the invention of an algebraical system of notation of a kind not found outside the grammatical schools. The system is so idiosyncratic that it could not possibly have been invented there and then by one man and imposed immediately on all his colleagues. It is clearly the growth of many centuries and Pāṇini is to be regarded as the final redactor of a traditional *Vyākaraṇa* who superseded all others on account of his superior comprehensiveness and accuracy. Many of the predecessors of Pāṇini are in fact cited in the text, but the merits of his own work condemned theirs to early oblivion.

The brevity which the Sūtra style aimed at and achieved was due to the fact that all instruction was still oral and dependent on memory. It implies also from the very beginning the existence of a commentary (*vṛtti*), also oral, in which the examples were contained. When this was first written down is not known, but the earliest existing commentary on Pāṇini, the *Kāśikā*, dates from a thousand years after his time (*c.* A.D. 700). A *gaṇapāṭha* containing lists of words referred to in the Sūtra by citation of the first word in them followed by *-ādi*, and a *dhātupāṭha*, containing a list of verbal roots, formed essential parts of his system.

The Sūtras of Pāṇini were supplemented and to some extent corrected by Kātyāyana at a date not long after the composition of the *Aṣṭādhyāyī* itself. These notes (*Vārttika-*) are of the same brevity as the original work, but were fortunately soon made the subject of an extensive commentary (*Mahābhāṣya*) by Patañjali. His date is fortunately known through contemporary references, notably to the Śuṅga king Puṣyamitra and to an invasion of the Bactrian Greeks, which fix him definitely in the second century B.C.

Later grammatical works exist in abundance, and many diverse schools arose, but none of them have any independent authority, being completely derivative from Pāṇini. The earliest is the *Kātantra* which arose about the Christian era, and whose author Śarvavarman is said by tradition to have been connected with the Sātavāhana dynasty of the Deccan. The work aimed at introducing the study of correct Sanskrit to a wider public than the educated Brahmins for whom Pāṇini and his immediate successors had written. Of later works mention may be made of the Grammar of Candra (A.D. sixth century) which achieved great popularity among the Buddists, and the

Jainendra Vyākaraṇa (c. 678) which was composed on behalf of the Jains. Later the polymath Hemacandra produced also for the Jains the *Haima Vyākaraṇa*. In addition, a number of minor systems are known which were popular in various localities, but which have nothing original to contribute.

The object of all these later grammars was to present the material contained in Pāṇini in a form comparatively easy to assimilate, and in this respect they performed a service to very many who were not equal to the arduous task of mastering the original text itself. How useful they were is shown by their continuous popularity. They contain little that is original since for them there existed no other source from which they could draw except the work of their illustrious predecessor. To Pāṇini the main source of his work was the living speech of himself and his contemporaries. It is the merit of his grammatical system that by means of the Sūtra and commentary, and by such subsidiary compilations as *Dhātupāṭha*, *Gaṇapāṭha*, etc., the vast bulk of the contemporary linguistic usage was incorporated, analysed and codified in the teachings transmitted from teacher to pupil in the schools of the Grammarians. The rapid process of linguistic change that took the vernaculars through the various stages of Middle Indo-Aryan enhanced progressively the value of this codification. It is characteristic of Ancient India that the founders of schools and doctrines should be exalted to semi-divine status and regarded as omniscient. In the case of Pāṇini this was more justified than in other cases since he had direct knowledge of the living Sanskrit language of the fourth century B.C. which is the source of all his statements. As a result of his labours and the labours of his school this form of language was accepted as a standard throughout the long period that remained of the classical civilisation of India. As the gap between this and the vernaculars grew continually wider, the usage of the speakers and writers of Sanskrit grew more dependent on Pāṇini, and his authority more absolute. Pāṇini's grammar was based on the language of his contemporaries, and conversely the language of Kālidāsa and his successors is based on the grammar of Pāṇini. The Sanskrit of the classical literature was a living language in the sense that it was written and spoken by the educated in preference to any other, but at the same time it was a language that had to be learnt in schools by means of an arduous discipline. It was a prerequisite for all men of letters of the period that they should know by heart the *Aṣṭādhyāyī*, and evidence of this dependence appears continually in their works.

As time went on, the cultivation of classical Sanskrit also came to depend on the *Kośas* or lexica. Apart from the Vedic *nighaṇṭus* lexicography is a later growth in India than grammar. The extant lexica are mostly late and are compilations out of earlier works. *Amarakośa*, the earliest existing, has not been accurately dated, but it is put approximately in the period A.D. 600-800. Earlier works are known and sometimes quoted, but not preserved. These works are in metre and intended to be learnt by heart, a practice which in the traditional schools has continued to this day. When this first became an essential requirement of a literary education is not clearly known, but certainly for the later period of Sanskrit literature we may assume that the writers were so equipped.

In spite of their late date and, in general, unscientific method, the lexica are of considerable value, since they preserve a large number of words which are not recorded in available texts. At the same time careless copying and inaccurate transmission has created some ghost words, which careful comparison of the various lexica may remove.

§4. Epic Sanskrit

The bulk of the classical Sanskrit literature was composed at a period very much later than the fixing of the language by Pāṇini. An earlier period in literary and linguistic history is represented by the two great popular epics, the Mahābhārata and the Rāmāyaṇa. It does not seem that either of these two works reached its final form until well after the Christian era, but the tradition of epic recitation goes back into the Vedic age. The Mahābhārata in particular was a long time in forming, and a good deal of what is incorporated in the final recension may claim an earlier date.

We have therefore in the Epics extensive documents of Sanskrit belonging to a period nearer to Pāṇini than the classical literature in the narrow sense. They provide also evidence of the wide popularity of one type of Sanskrit literature among the masses of the people, since these works were reserved for no special or cultivated audience, but intended for public recital to the population in general. Their popular character is evidenced by their language. This is Sanskrit definitely enough as opposed to the contemporary Middle Indo-Aryan, but it is a Sanskrit which frequently violates the rules which Pāṇini had laid down and which were always observed in the more orthodox literary circles. Among the common deviations of the Epic language a few characteristic types may be quoted. The distinction between the active and middle forms of the verb, which was still fully alive in Pāṇini's time, and for which he caters in some detail, is beginning to be blurred in the Epic. Active forms are used for middle and vice-versa, and even the passive verb sometimes takes active endings (*śrūyanti* 'are heard', etc.). There is some confusion between the gerunds in *-tvā* and *-ya*, and the rule of Pāṇini which restricts the former to uncompounded and the latter to compounded verbs is not always observed. Unaugmented preterites occur, a characteristic which is also found in the Veda, as well as in early middle Indo-Aryan. Conversely the augmented forms are occasionally found with the prohibitive particle (*mā . . . agamaḥ* 'do not go'). The particle *mā* is not used exclusively with the unaugmented aorist according to rule but indifferently with imperative (*mā bhava*) optative (*mā brūyāḥ*) future (*mā drakṣyasi*) and so on. The tenth class and causative verbs make a middle participle in *-ayāna* (*codayāna-* as opposed to correct *codayamāna-*) a usage to which metrical convenience has contributed. The careful rules of Pāṇini concerning the use of the alternative forms *-atī* and *-antī* in forming the feminine of present participles are not strictly observed. The distribution of *seṭ* and *aniṭ* forms frequently does not conform to rule.

These and other irregular forms correspond to what is found in early middle Indo-Aryan, indicating that Epic Sanskrit is a later form of Sanskrit than that of Pāṇini. No pre-Pāṇinean forms are found in the Epic, which means that although the epic tradition goes back to the Vedic period, and although the Mahabhārata story was familiar to people before Pāṇini's time, even the earliest portions of the present text must be distinctly later than him. Since for centuries the transmission of the epic stories depended on oral tradition, and not a fixed oral tradition like that of the Vedic schools, it is not surprising that a circle of stories originating in the Vedic period should in their final form appear in a language of a much later date with no archaic forms preserved.

The recitation and transmission of the Epic legends was not the business of the Brahmans, but of the Sūtas, a class of royal servants whose duties had originally included that of charioteer. It was natural that their language should be of a more popular nature than that of the educated classes *par excellence*, the Brāhmans. At the same time it is interesting that all along, in spite of the competition of Prakrit, Sanskrit was cultivated in much wider circles than in the priestly schools for whom Pāṇini's work was intended. Outside the brahmanical schools the knowledge of grammatical theory must have been elementary to say the least, and in the early period at least the knowledge of Sanskrit on the part of the epic reciters must have depended primarily on usage and not on formal instruction. From this arose the tendency to approximate the language to some extent to the prevailing type of Middle Indo-Aryan. Later when the gulf between the two became greater formal instruction in Sanskrit became a universal necessity, but by this period the epic style and the epic language had already established itself in its own right, and linguistic features such as those mentioned above were accepted and retained.

The language of the Epics served also as a model for the language of the Purāṇas, of which the earliest core dates to the same period. It is continued in the numerous later compilations, and further in a variety of sectarian *āgamas*, etc. Linguistically these compilations are not of great interest, except occasionally in the matter of vocabulary, and many, particularly the later ones, testify to the deficient education of their authors in grammar.

§5. The Sanskrit of the Classical Literature

The special characteristics of classical Sanskrit arise from the fact that most of the literature dates from a period very much later than the period in which the form of the language was fixed. If Kālidāsa is to be dated *c.* A.D. 450 a period of no less than eight hundred years separates him from the grammarian Pāṇini. The work of Kālidāsa stands almost at the beginning of the body of classical literature which is preserved, and the greater part of this is separated by more than a millennium from the regulator of the language. This accounts largely for the artificiality of style and language which is not absent from the best authors, and which in some is exaggerated beyond reason.

The literary gap in the period immediately preceding and succeeding the Christian era is due to the loss of the bulk of the pre-Kalidāsan literature, since it is known that *kāvya* in all its forms was actively practised during all this time. The earliest Sanskrit inscriptions (e.g. of Rudradāman, A.D. 150) show the existence of a developed Sanskrit Kāvya. Patañjali (*c.* 150 B.C.) quotes some *kāvya* fragments and mentions by name a poet Vararuci. His own work is a valuable example of the prose style of the period, and it enables us to form a picture of early Pāṇinean Sanskrit at a time when it was still a fully living language. The works of Aśvaghoṣa who flourished under Kaniṣka (A.D. 78+) preserved in Nepal (and fragmentarily in Central Asia), though long forgotten in India, have survived by fortunate chance, as the sole examples of Sanskrit Kāvya literature in its earlier phase.

The gap, only partially to be filled, between Pāṇini and the classical literature, is responsible for certain changes in style and usage, which have affected the language of the latter, in spite of strict adherence to the rules of grammar. These changes comprise certain losses and also a number of innovations. Of the losses the most important was that of the old system of accentuation. This was still in full force in the time of Patañjali and it must have continued in being for some time after that, but by the time the bulk of the classical literature was composed it had certainly disappeared from ordinary use. Certain of Pāṇini's grammatical forms though recognised were not in practice used. Already Patañjali remarks that forms of the second plural of the perfect like *ūṣa, tera, cakra* are no longer in use, their place being taken by the participial forms *uṣitāḥ, tīrṇāḥ, kṛtavantaḥ*. Later a good deal else was tacitly ignored. There are many constructions and idioms taught by Pāṇini which are not recorded in the later literature (*anvāje-* or *upāje-kṛ* 'to strengthen', *nivacane-kṛ* 'to be silent', etc.), and many others which have obviously been employed by the later authors as evidence of their grammatical learning (e.g. in *Naiṣadhacarita, darśayitāhe*, first person of the periphrastic future middle). There are losses in vocabulary and such words as *anvavasarga-* 'allowing one his own way', *niravasita-* 'excommunicated' and *abhreṣa-* 'fitness, propriety' are no longer used. In particular the *Gaṇapāṭha* contains numerous terms which are found nowhere else, and since this text was handed down without meanings for a long time, it is often impossible now to discover the meaning of such words. The old distinction in meaning between the three past tenses (Imperfect, Aorist, Perfect) was not normally observed. The Aorist, though cultivated by the learned, seems to have gone out of common use.[1] The middle perfect participles in *-āna* are entirely disused, and the active participles in *-vas* appear only rarely.

The innovations of the later classical Sanskrit affect mainly syntax and vocabulary. The most striking syntactical development is the increasing tendency to use compound words and the increasing length and complexity of the compounds used. In the earliest Sanskrit the use of compounds is not noticeably more predominant than in the Greek of Homer. In the language of Pāṇini's day there were still strict rules and limitations in the formation of compound words, as is clearly evident from his own statements and examples. In the later language they are formed without restriction (e.g. any adjective may be so construed with any noun, as opposed to the original arrangement by which this could only be done when the term had a special significance, *kṛṣṇasarpa-* ' cobra ', etc.), and not infrequently in direct contradiction to Pāṇini's rules (e.g. *jagatkartar-* ' world-creator ' against P. 2. 2. 15-16). But the main thing is that there ceases to be any limitation to the number of members a compound may contain, since compound words treated as units may be compounded with further words, and by a process of accumulation long complexes are built up in which the syntactical relation of the members is expressed without recourse to inflection. This practice is not only at variance with the earlier usage and with Indo-European usage in general, but is also obviously incompatible with any form of popular speech which can have prevailed in India during the period This linguistic development is a purely literary development, and it is a sign of the growing artificiality of the Sanskrit language as the difference between it and the vernacular Middle Indo-Aryan grew wider.

[1] The hero of the drama *Padmaprābhṛtaka* (*c.* second or third cent. A.D.) asks a grammarian who speaks pedantically to use ordinary Sanskrit (*vyāvahārikā bhāṣā*). The pedantry which is illustrated consists in the liberal use of aorists and desideratives.

Another syntactical development affects the verb, but this is based on popular usage. Of the past tenses the aorist, with the amalgamation of some imperfect forms, survived in Early Middle Indo-Aryan, but by the time of the later Prakrit all traces of the old preterites have disappeared. Their place was taken by passive constructions with the past participle passive, and it is from this usage that the preterites of modern Indo-Aryan derive. The tendency is also reflected in Sanskrit literature, and the passive construction becomes gradually more predominant. It had obviously the advantage of simplicity, since the complicated verbal inflection of Sanskrit could be dispensed with, and in works of deliberately simple style like the *Hitopadeśa* it is evidently chosen for this purpose. For active use the participle in *-tavant* is adapted to serve as an alternative to the past tense: *kṛtavān* 'he did'. The nominal phrase in which the meaning is expressed by the juxtaposition of subject and predicate, without any verb becomes increasingly popular. This is particularly so in the philosophic literature, and since that language also favours long compounds, we may find long passages of exposition in which the only grammar consists of a few case inflections of abstract nouns.

The vocabulary of Sanskrit was on the whole remarkably stable. Nevertheless it is possible to collect from the later literature a considerable body of words which do not appear in the earlier period. In some cases it may be an accident that they are not recorded earlier, but even making this allowance, there must remain a fair number of new words. Increases in vocabulary derive from the following sources:

(1) They could be created, when required, on the basis of existing Sanskrit roots, prefixes and suffixes, and by the formation of new compounds with special senses.

(2) In the course of time some Prakrit words were adopted into Sanskrit, though proportionally the number is never very large. No certain examples of this kind appear in the Vedic language, but they begin to appear in small numbers in the Epic and classical period. Words of this type are *bhaṭṭa-*, *bhaṭṭāra- bhaṭṭāraka-* 'master, lord' (Skt. *bhartar-*), *naṭa-* 'actor' (Skt. *nṛt-* 'to dance') and *dohada-*, *dohala-* 'morbid desire of a pregnant woman' which occur (more commonly) beside the regular Sanskrit *daurhṛda-*. Skt. *uḍu-* 'star' derives from a Prakrit *uḍuvai-* 'moon' misinterpreted as meaning 'lord of

the stars ' though it is actually derived from a Skt. *ṛtupati-* ' lord of the seasons '. In the medical texts *koṭha-* ' a form of leprosy ' occurs beside *kuṣṭha-* ' leprosy ' of which it is a Prakrit development. Among other words originating in Prakrit we may mention *kola* ' breast, lap ' beside the original *kroḍa-* ' id ', *khuḍḍaka-* ' small ' beside *kṣudraka-*, *vaiyāvṛtya-* with Prakritic -v-, more commonly used than the original *vaiyāpṛtya-* ' business or commission entrusted to one ', *vicchitti-* ' carelessness in dress or decoration ' which probably derives from *vikṣipti-*, and *oja-* ' odd (of numbers) ' which in later texts tends to replace the original *ayujá-*. In the case of some words taken over from Prakrit there are no Sanskrit originals, e.g. *avahittha-* ' dissimulation ', *chaṭā* ' heap, mass ' (Pkt. *chaḍā*) etc. Some words are disguised by false Sanskritisation; e.g. *karpaṭa-* ' ragged cloth ' is taken from Pkt. *kappaḍa-* which itself represents **kat-paṭa-* ' inferior cloth '. Likewise Pkt. *ludda-* ' hunter ' (ultimately identical with the name of the god *Rudrá-*) is Sanskritised as *lubdhaka-* as if derived from *lubh-* ' to be greedy', and Pkt. *pāraddhi-* ' hunting ' (from *rabh-* ' to attack ') is Sanskritised as *pāparddhi-* meaning literally ' evil gain '.

(3) The Greek and Iranian invasions of India from the North-West resulted in a limited number of loanwords from these sources being admitted into Sanskrit. These are dealt with in Chapter VIII.

(4) Sanskrit received a considerable number of words from the substrate languages, Austro-Asiatic and Dravidian, particularly from the latter. These are also dealt with in Chapter VIII.

(5) The term *deśī* is applied to those words in Prakrit which are derived from no Sanskrit equivalent. The number of such words which can be explained out of Dravidian or some other source is comparatively small and will probably always remain so. They become still more abundant in the Modern Indo-Aryan period and present a philological problem which is not easy to solve. On the whole classical Sanskrit avoids such words, but a number are incorporated, and in particular the Jain writers have adopted a fair number.

§6. Sanskrit and Prakrit

During the whole period of its existence Classical Sanskrit had beside it as competitor Middle Indo-Aryan in its various forms, not only as a spoken language but also as a language of literature. In the early period this competition was much more important than it was later ; though it appears paradoxical at first sight, the Sanskrit language only reached its full development as a language of culture and administration at a time when it had ceased to be a mother tongue.

The rise of Middle Indo-Aryan as a literary language coincided with the foundation of the new religions of Buddhism and Jainism round about 500 B.C. The founders of these religions deliberately chose the vernacular—the dialect of Magadha in the first instance—as the vehicle of their teaching. In the third century B.C. Aśoka had his inscriptions engraved in various local dialects and ignored Sanskrit. It follows that the language of administration of the Mauryan empire was also in Middle Indo-Aryan, and not as universally the case later, in Sanskrit. If this process had not been reversed Sanskrit might have yielded place to the younger language, but quite the reverse happened and from the end of the Maurya period a steady process set in which resulted in Sanskrit becoming the predominant language of literature, culture and administration.

The epigraphical tradition established by Aśoka continued for some centuries. Until after the Christian era the vernacular language alone was used for epigraphical purposes, and this means that business and administrative documents—all of which were written on perishable materials and have not survived—were composed in the same language. After the Christian era Sanskrit too begins to appear in inscriptions, at first in competition with Prakrit, and finally in exclusive use. The inscription of Rudradāman (A.D. 150) marks the victory of Sanskrit in one part of India. In the South Prakrit remained in use longer and was not finally ousted by Sanskrit until the fourth or fifth century A.D. Eventually the use of Prakrit was discontinued entirely and from the Gupta period to the Mahommedan invasions Sanskrit—admittedly often incorrect Sanskrit—remained in exclusive use.

The linguistic revolution in epigraphy is paralleled in other fields. The early Buddhist scriptures were exclusively in Middle Indo-Aryan. Towards the beginning of the Christian era a change took place, and the northern Buddhists adopted Sanskrit instead. Aśvaghoṣa (*c.* A.D. 100) is a master of polished Sanskrit, and that he should choose this language as a vehicle of propaganda is an indication of the ascendancy which Sanskrit had achieved at this time. Here also we may observe that Sanskrit established its ascendancy first in the north. The Theravādins of South India and Ceylon remained faithful to Pāli.

The Jains were slower in making a change than the Buddhists. They were the most conservative of Indian sects and up to the time of the final constitution of the present canon of the Śvetambaras (at the council of Valabhī in A.D. 526) they used Prakrit exclusively. But even they turned to the use of Sanskrit in the succeeding period. At the same time they continued to cultivate Prakrit seriously, beside Sanskrit, at a time when in other literary circles the traditional Prakrit was being employed as little more than a literary exercise.

In these fields we may observe the transition which led to the predominance of Sanskrit. Elsewhere lack of material makes a clear picture more difficult. In poetic literature there was under the Sātavāhanas and their successors an active tradition of lyrical poetry in Mahārāṣṭrī of which fragments are preserved in the anthology of Hāla. At the same time the major poetic works of the early period were in Sanskrit. The Mahābhārata and the Rāmāyaṇa have an importance in the literary history of India which nothing in Prakrit could even remotely approach, and they were the productions of a period when to judge by inscriptions Prakrit had almost superseded Sanskrit in everyday use. Thus it is obvious that the inscriptional evidence gives a very one-sided picture of contemporary linguistic conditions. Outside the sectarian religions Sanskrit was always, even when the use of Prakrit was most flourishing, the primary literary language of India.

The growing predominance of Sanskrit as opposed to Prakrit in the period succeeding the Christian era can be attributed to two reasons, one ideological and one practical. In the Maurya period the heterodox religions of Buddhism and Jainism had attained such influence as to threaten the existence of the old Brahmanical order. In the succeeding period, beginning with the usurpation of Puṣyamitra (*c.* 188 B.C.), a reaction set in and there began a gradual decline of these systems in the face of victorious orthodoxy. This change in the religious atmosphere was reflected in language, and Sanskrit, associated with the traditional Vedic religion gained ground at the expense of Prakrit, whose cultivation was mainly due to the activities of the unorthodox sects.

The practical reason was that Sanskrit offered a united language for the whole of India. In the early Middle Indian period the differences between the various local vernaculars were not so great as to preclude mutual understanding, but even at this period Aśoka found it necessary to engrave his edicts in three different dialects. With the progress of time the differences between the local dialects grew greater, so that Sanskrit became a necessary bond for the cultural unity of India. Furthermore the Prakrits were unstable and subject to continual change through the centuries. Any literary language established on the basis of a vernacular rapidly became obsolete. The traditional Prakrits in the later period were as artificial as Sanskrit, and did not have the advantage of its universal appeal and utility. For such reasons alone Sanskrit was the only form of language which could serve as a national language in Ancient India, whose cultural unity, far more influential and important than its political disunity, rendered such a language essential. The relation between Sanskrit and Prakrit in the classical period is admirably illustrated by the Sanskrit Drama. Here it is the convention that certain characters speak Sanskrit and others speak Prakrit, and the usage of the drama no doubt accurately represents the actual practice at the time. The use of Sanskrit is fairly narrowly limited to the highest classes of society, namely kings, ministers, learned Brahmans and so on. Women, with few exceptions, speak Prakrit, and also children, showing that it was everybody's first language. Furthermore, Prakrit is spoken not only by all the lower classes, but also predominantly by the wealthy and influential class of merchants and bankers. The comic figure of the *vidūṣaka*, an unlearned Prakrit-speaking Brahman, shows that not all members of this class were capable of mastering the strenuous discipline necessary for the acquisition of Sanskrit.

Only the earliest dramas, of which *Mṛcchakaṭika* is the best surviving example, reflect living usage in this way. In the greater number of extant dramas which belong to a later period (A.D. 500-1000), the composition is according to tradition, and the Prakrit becomes merely a transmogrified Sanskrit composed according to the rules of the grammarians learned by rote. In this period the vernacular had advanced much further on the road to Modern Indo-Aryan.

§7. THE SANSKRIT OF THE BUDDHISTS AND JAINS

The adoption of Sanskrit by the Buddhists, and later the Jains, widened the field of Sanskrit literature, and the Sanskrit language which was thus adapted to new needs did not remain unaltered in the hands of these authors. The Sanskritisation of Buddhist literature is particularly complicated since it took place gradually and beginning by a compromise between Sanskrit and the Middle-Indian dialects of early Buddhism ended in the adoption of pure classical Sanskrit. We may distinguish between the following types of Buddhist Sanskrit :

(1) Mixed Sanskrit. This language was used by the Mahāsaṅghika school. In it the original Prakrit appears half Sanskritised, the words being in the main restored to their Sanskrit phonetic form while the Prakrit grammar is largely retained. For instance Pa. *bhikkhussa*, gen. sg. of *bhikkhu* 'monk' (Skt. *bhikṣu-*) is not replaced by a regular Sanskrit *bhikṣos*, but is mechanically changed to *bhikṣusya*. It may be assumed that for a period, in certain circles, such a hybrid language was actually employed by those who wished to employ the superior Sanskrit language but were not able to master its grammar.

(2) The Sarvastivādins of the north-west adopted proper Sanskrit from an early period. The old canonical works were translated into Sanskrit, and fragments of them are preserved in this form. The language of these works has of necessity incorporated wholesale the vocabulary and syntax of the original Māgadhī, but allowing for this, and for some false Sanskritisations which are to be expected, it is free from the barbarisms of (1).

(3) We must distinguish from (2) works of the same school which were not translations but which were independently composed at a period much later than the canonical literature. The stories which were inserted to enliven the matter of the Vinaya-piṭaka, and which are collected in the Divyāvadāna, Illustrate best this type of Sanskrit. Though it fails often enough to satisfy the canons of Pāṇinean grammar, the style is admirably clear and lucid and not an unwelcome change to the laboured artificiality of some of the classical prose. The vocabulary is characterised by the use of many vernacular and provincial words, many of which turn up again in Modern Indo-Aryan (e.g. *lardaya-* 'to load' : Hi. *lāḍnā*), and which are not found in the older types of Buddhist language (e.g. Pali).

(4) The use of pure classical Sanskrit, associated with all the characteristics of the Kāvya style, is seen in the works of Aśvaghoṣa and his successors. Such works are distinguished from other works of classical Sanskrit literature only by the use of Buddhist technical terms. Likewise the works of the logicians and philosophers follows the style of similar orthodox works in Sanskrit, with the addition of the terminology peculiar to the Buddhists.

The Jains resisted longest the use of Sanskrit, and only began to take to it in the second half of the first millennium A.D. During this period Prakrit only gradually gives way to Sanskrit, but in the end Sanskrit establishes itself here as elsewhere. The Sanskrit of the Jains is influenced by the language of the earlier Prakrit literature in the same way as the Sanskrit of the Buddhists. In vocabulary it draws more extensively than contemporary classical Sanskrit on vernacular sources, and words familiar later in Modern Indo-Aryan are often first recorded here.

§ 8. Sanskrit in Greater India

The expansion of Indo-Aryan was halted in South India by the native Dravidian languages (Tamil, Telugu, Kanarese) which in course of time established themselves as literary languages. Nevertheless the influence of Indo-Aryan in this region was at all times powerful, and it is evident in the vocabulary of these languages from the earliest records. They were earliest influenced by Prakrit, which was the administrative language of the Sātavāhanas and their immediate successors. Inscriptions extending as far south as Kāñcī show that all the Telugu-Kanarese area was governed by Aryan dynasties whose mother tongue was Prakrit. The intruding Indo-Aryans were not numerous enough to impose Indo-Aryan as the spoken language of the area and after about A.D. 400 the Prakrit inscriptions cease. Sanskrit replaced Prakrit, as elsewhere, for purposes of administration and culture, and as a spoken language it was replaced by the native Dravidian. At the same time the native Dravidian began to be cultivated, Kanarese from *c.* A.D. 450 and Telugu from *c.* A.D. 650. The Prakrit influence in these languages, dating from the earlier period, is rapidly overlaid by extensive borrowings from the Sanskrit vocabulary. In their early classical form these languages draw on Sanskrit wholesale, and the process was continued in the succeeding periods. At the present time a considerable and essential part of the vocabulary of these languages is Sanskrit.

In the Tamil country of the extreme South Indo-Aryan influence was weakest. Tamil was the earliest Dravidian language to be used for literary purposes, and it was to begin with comparatively free from Aryan influence. In the later period the influence of Sanskrit increases, but never on the scale that is found in its two northern neighbours.

Ceylon received its Aryan language through colonisation from Northern India. In addition Buddhism established Pāli as a literary language. At a later period still the cultivation of Sanskrit was introduced, at some periods on quite an extensive scale.

The spread of Buddhism was responsible for the introduction of Indo-Aryan linguistic influence into large regions of Central Asia. At one time a form of Prakrit served as the administrative language of the kingdom of Kroraina in Chinese Turkestan. Buddhist Sanskrit texts were current over a wide area, and works long lost in India have been recovered in recent years in Central Asia. Under Buddhist influence the native languages of this area began to be cultivated, notably the Iranian Khotanese, and the two closely related Indo-European languages which go by the name of Tocharian. The vocabulary of these draws abundantly on Sanskrit or Prakrit sources. On the other hand Tibetan which became Buddhist from the seventh century onwards resisted foreign linguistic influence, and by what must have been a considerable *tour de force,* the whole Buddhist vocabulary was rendered into native Tibetan. This had been done at an earlier period by the Chinese where differences of script and language rendered any other course impracticable.

The influence of Sanskrit was equally extensive in countries to the East and South-East. In Burma there is early evidence of the influence of Sanskrit Buddhism. This was replaced (A.D. eleventh cent.) by a religious reformation which established Theravāda Buddhism as the official religion and with it Pāli as the language of religion. Further East there were Hindu colonies in South Siam (Dvārāvatī), Cambodia (Kambuja) and Annam (Campā). Abundant Sanskrit inscriptions dating from the third century A.D. onwards remain to show the importance of Sanskrit in these areas, and its influence was felt on the native languages when they came to be cultivated. Even today Siamese is drawing on Sanskrit for its technical vocabulary. At the same time Hindu culture spread to Indonesia and in Java, Sumatra and Bali Sanskrit literature was cultivated.

The native languages came strongly under the influence of Sanskrit and Sanskrit culture-words remain widely current in the area today. The classical language of Java abounds in Sanskrit words, just as it's literature draws its inspiration from Sanskrit models. The Mahommedan conquest of Java (A.D. sixteenth cent.) put an end to Hindu dominion in the area, but the influence of the preceding centuries was too deep to be eradicated.

§9. Writing in India

The art of writing was late in making its appearance in Aryan India. It had existed before the Aryan invasion in the Indus civilisation, but it perished along with this civilisation. During the period when the Vedic civilisation was being built up no form of writing was employed in India, and in its absence the technique was evolved of preserving intact the Vedic literature by means of oral tradition. Even when writing was introduced this oral tradition persisted in the various departments of knowledge and it continued as a basic feature of Indian education and culture down to modern times.

It is not known when the alphabet was first introduced into India. So far as preserved records go it is only attested from the third century B.C. when the two alphabets, Kharoṣṭhī and Brāhmī, appear fully developed in the Aśokan inscriptions. The Kharoṣṭhī alphabet, which is written from right to left, is confined to the extreme North-West of India, to that part of the country which in preceding centuries had been part of the Persian dominions. It is an adaptation of the Aramaic alphabet which was employed in this region in the Achaemenid period, and it was probably evolved towards the close of this period. It continued in use in the same area, and in some adjoining parts of central Asia down to the fourth century A.D., after which records in it cease.

The Brāhmī alphabet, which differs from Kharoṣṭhī in being written from left to right, is the source of all later Indian alphabets, as well as of those in countries abroad which formed part of the area of Indian cultural expansion (Burmese, Siamese, Javanese, etc.). It is also derived from some form of the

Semitic alphabet, but the exact source from which it is adapted and also the period remain uncertain. It is suggested that it may have been introduced from the South Semitic area by means of the trade routes to the ports of Western India, and the period most commonly assumed is about 500 B.C.

The work of adaptation was considerable since it involved not only the addition of vowel signs, but also the changes and additions necessary to express adequately the Indian consonantal system. The perfection with which the task was accomplished was consequent on the labours of the ancient Indian phoneticians whose achievements have already been mentioned. In spite of this, use of writing was only slowly adopted in the Brahmin schools, and in the early period its function lay primarily in business and administration and only secondarily as an instrument of literature. For this reason all the earliest records preserved are in Prakrit, and Sanskrit documents only appear later. It is unlikely that much literature existed in manuscript form before the second century B.C.

The early Brāhmī alphabet was comparatively uniform and served for the whole of India outside the small area where Kharoṣṭhī was in use. After the Christian era local variations were intensified and Brāhmī developed into a variety of regional alphabets differing from each other as much as they had changed from the original form. The structural principles of the alphabets always remained the same but the individual shapes of the letters were subject to endless variation. In North India the alphabet gradually evolved into what is now known as Devanāgarī. With the introduction of printing this alphabet was adopted generally for Sanskrit, but before this period Sanskrit manuscripts were written in the various regional alphabets of the localities where they were produced, e.g. Śāradā in Kashmir, Bengali, Oriya, Telugu-Kanarese, Malayalam and, in the Tamil country, Grantha.

The commonest material used for writing in India was palm-leaf. The exclusive use of this prevailed in South India down to modern times. The characters were incised on this material by means of a stylus and the ink rubbed in afterwards. In the North, particularly in Kashmir, the inner bark of the birch was used on which the letters were written in ink. This method was also used in the North for palm-leaf manuscripts, and the differences between the Northern and Southern alphabets is largely occasioned by different methods of writing. As a result of the perishable nature of these materials really ancient Indian manuscripts are rare. The oldest are those that have been discovered, in a more or less fragmentary condition, in the dry soil of Central Asia. The bulk of Sanskrit literature is preserved only in manuscripts belonging to the last few centuries.

CHAPTER III

PHONOLOGY

§ 1. Indo-European Consonant System

The comparative study of the phonetic systems of the existing IE languages makes it possible to reconstruct, with a reasonable degree of certainty, the phonetics of the parent language. On this basis a systematic historical account of the Sanskrit phonetic system can be provided in which the various stages of development in the prehistoric period can be distinguished in respect of their relative chronology. Developments may be severally characterised as: (1) Changes in the Indo-European period; (2) Changes common to Indo-Aryan and Iranian only; (3) Changes peculiar to Indo-Aryan, which have occurred after its separation from Iranian. In sketching the phonetic development of Sanskrit we shall indicate, as far as possible to which of these three periods the various changes belong.

The following reconstruction of the IE consonantal system has been generally adopted by comparative philologists:

		Surd	Surd Aspirate	Sonant	Sonant Aspirate
Occlusives (Stops, Plosives)	Labio-velar	k^w	k^wh	g^w	g^wh
	Velar	*k*	*kh*	*g*	*gh*
	Palatal	*k̂*	*k̂h*	*ĝ*	*ĝh*
	Dental	*t*	*th*	*d*	*dh*
	Labial	*p*	*ph*	*b*	*bh*

Nasals: *m*, *n*, *ŋ*; Liquids: *l*, *r*; Semivowels: *y*, *v*; Sibilants: *s*, *z*; Doubtful *þ*: , *đ*.

The reconstructions are of two kinds. In the first and commonest case the phoneme postulated for Indo-European occurs in a number of the existing languages in which it has continued unchanged; in the second and rarer case the phoneme assumed for Indo-European is nowhere preserved as such, but it is deduced by comparison of the forms derived from it. Naturally there is the greatest certainty in the case of the first class, but even the pure reconstructions of the second class are, with few exceptions, established beyond reasonable doubt.

In the following cases an Indo-European consonant is preserved unchanged in Sanskrit and in other languages :

p : *páñca* ' 5 ' : Gk. πέντε ; *pátati* ' flies ' : Gk. πέτεται ; *ápa* ' away, from ' : Gk. ἀπό : *sárpati* ' crawls ' : Gk. ἕρπει Lat. *serpit.*

t : *tanú-* ' thin ', Gk. τανυ-, Lat. *tenuis* ; *tráyas* ' 3 ', Gk. τρεῖς, Lat. *trēs* ; *vártate* ' turns ' ; Lat. *verto.*

d : *dáśa* ' 10 ', Gk. δέκα, Lat. *decem* ; *dīrghá-* ' long ' ; Gk. δολιχός, O. Sl. *dlŭgŭ* ; *véda,* ' I know ', Gk. οἶδα, Lat. *video.*

k : *kravíṣ-* ' raw flesh ', Gk. κρέας ; *kákṣa-* ' armpit ', cf. Lat. *coxa.*

g : *yugám* ' yoke ', Gk. ζυγόν, Lat. *iugum* ; *sthag-* ' to cover ', Gk. στέγω.

n : *nā́ma* ' name ', Lat. *nōmen* ; *náva-* ' new ', Gk. νέος, Lat. *novus* ; *nábhas* ' cloud ', Gk. νέφος ; *dā́nam* ' gift ', Lat. *dōnum,* O. Sl. *danŭ.*

m : *mātár-* ' mother ', Lat. *māter* ; *mā* ' me', Lat. *mē* ; *mū́ṣ-* ' mouse ', Lat. *mūs,* O. Sl. *myšĭ* ; *dáma-* ' house ', Gk. δόμος, Lat. *domus.*

l : *lubh-, lúbhyati* ' desire, covet ', Lat. *lubet,* Goth. *liufs,* O. Sl. *ljubŭ* ' dear ', *laghú-* ' light, swift ', Gk. ἐλαχύς, Lat. *levis.*

r : *rudhirá-* ' red, blood ', Gk. ἐρυθρός, Lat. *ruber* ; *rā́j-, rā́jan-* ' king ', Lat. *rēx,* Gallic °*rīx* ; *bhárati* ' bears ', Gk. φέρω, Lat. *fero,* Goth. *baíra.*

y : *yúvan-* ' young man ', Lat. *iuvenis* ; *yákṛt* ' liver ', Lat. *iecur* ; *yū́ṣ-* ' broth, soup ', Lat. *iūs,* O. Sl. *jucha.*

w (*v*) : *vā́c-* ' speech ', Lat. *vōx* ; *váhati* ' carries ', Lat. *vehit* ; *náva-* ' new ', Lat. *novus* ; *ávi-* ' sheep ', Lat. *ovis.*

s : *sána-* ' old ', Lat. *senex,* Ir. *sen* ; *sánti* ' they are', Lat. *sunt* ; *sūnú-* ' son ', Lith. *sūnùs,* Goth. *sunus* ; *áṃsa-* 'shoulder', Goth. *ams* ; *ásthi* ' bone ', Gk. ὀστέον, Lat. *os, ossis.*

In cases like the above the reconstruction of the IE forms presents a minimum of problems ; reconstruction in the full sense is not necessary since the phonemes in question are widely preserved. They are not preserved in all languages (e.g. Engl. *thin* : Lat. *tenuis* ; Welsh *hen,* Ir. *sen*), but a study of all the available evidence leaves little doubt as to which languages preserve the original sound. In other cases change has been more widespread. There are instances where the original IE sound is preserved only in one language, others in which the sound, which theory demands for the parent language, is preserved nowhere at all. Even in these cases it is possible to fix the original sound with reasonable certainty.

§2. The Sonant Aspirates

The sonant aspirates which it is normally believed Indo-European possessed are preserved as a class by Sanskrit alone. Elsewhere they are changed in various ways ; in Iranian, Slavonic, etc., the aspiration is lost ; in Greek they are changed into the corresponding surd aspirates, in Latin (and the other Italic dialects) into fricatives. Examples of this series are as follows :

bh : Skt. *bhrū́-* 'brow', Gk. ὀφρῦς, O. Sl. *brŭvĭ* ; *bhrā́tā* 'brother', Gk. φρᾱ́τηρ 'member of a phratry', Lat. *frater*, O. Sl. *bratrŭ*, O. Ir. *brāthir* ; *bhárati* 'bears', Av. *baraiti*, Gk. φέρω, Lat. *fero*, Arm. *berem*, O. Sl. *berǫ*, Goth. *baíra*, O. Ir. *berim* ; *nábhas* 'cloud, sky', Gk. νέφος, O. Sl. *nebo*, Hitt. *nepiš*.

dh : *dhā-*, *dádhāti* 'to place', Av. *daδāiti*, Gk. τίθημι, Lith. *dėti* ; *dhūmá-* 'smoke', O. Sl. *dymŭ*, Lat. *fūmus* ; *mádhu* 'honey, mead', Av. *maδu*, Gk. μέθυ, O. Sl. *medŭ*, A.S. *medu*, O. Ir. *mid* ; *vidhávā* 'widow', cf. Gk. ἠίθεος 'young (unmarried) man', O. Sl. *vĭdova* 'widow', Lat. *vidua*, O. Ir. *fedb*.

gh : *stigh-* 'to stride', Gk. στείχω, Goth. *steiga* ; *meghá-* 'cloud', cf. Gk. ὀμίχλη, O. Sl. *mĭgla*, Alb. *mjégulë*. In the case of the guttural series the sonant aspirates have undergone changes in Sanskrit in common with the other members of the series. These will be detailed below.

Although the sonant aspirates are preserved in Indo-Aryan alone among the IE languages, there is little doubt that they should be attributed to the parent language, since no other type of phoneme can account so simply for the various developments that appear. The theory, prevalent in some quarters, that in these cases we are dealing with a series of original IE fricatives, has nothing to recommend it.

Although Sanskrit preserves the sonant aspirates as a class, it does not preserve them all unchanged. The special developments of the sonant aspirates belonging to the two guttural series will be treated below. The dental and labial sonant aspirates are normally preserved as in the examples given above, but in some cases, even in the earliest period *dh* and *bh* are weakened to *h*, an anticipation of their later fate in Middle Indo-Aryan.

dh : *hitá-* 'placed' (*dhā-*), also *-dhita-* in the Veda; *-hi*, termination of the 2 sg. impv., also *-dhi*, Av. *-δi*; the verbal terminations of the 1st dual and plural ātmanepada, *-vahe*, *-vahi*, *-vahai*; *-mahe*, *-mahi*, *-mahai*, cf. Av. *-maide*, *-maidī*; *ihá* 'here', Pa. *idha*, Av. *iδa*; *sahá* 'with', Vedic also *sadha-* in cpds., Av. *haδa*; *lóhita-*, *róhita-* 'red', cf. *rudhirá-*; *róhati* 'climbs', Vedic also *ródhati*; *nah-* 'to bind', cf. ppt. *naddhá-*; *snuh-* 'to drip', cf. Av. *snaod-*.

bh : *grah-* 'to seize', Vedic also *grabh-*; *kakuhá-* 'high' beside *kakubhá-* 'id', *kakúbh-* 'peak'.

An aspirate was not allowed to remain in Sanskrit when an aspirate followed. The effect of this rule in grammar is seen in reduplication where the corresponding unaspirated sonant is used—*dhā-*, *dadhaú*, *bhā-*, *babhaú*, *han-* : *jaghā́na*. The same rule is observable in Greek (θνήσκω : τέθνηκα); it is not however an Indo-European feature inherited in common, but a phenomenon that has occurred independently in each language. In Greek this de-aspiration did not take place until the sonant aspirates had been turned into surds, and consequently the unaspirated surd is the result. We find therefore in these cases an initial surd of Greek corresponding to an initial sonant of Sanskrit. Thus the IE root *bheudh-* 'to perceive' produces on the one hand Gk. πεύθομαι (through *φευθ-) and on the other hand Skt. *budh-*. The same correspondence is seen between Gk. τεῖχος 'wall' and Skt. *dih-* 'smear, cement with earth', *dehī́* 'rampart'; similarly Gk. πενθερός 'father-in-law': cf. Skt. *bandhu-* 'relation', *bandh-* 'to bind', Gk. πῆχυς 'arm': Skt. *bāhú-*, Gk. πυθμήν 'bottom': Skt. *budhná-*. In other Indo-European languages no dissimilation of this kind took place, and whatever phoneme corresponds regularly to an IE sonant aspirate appears also in this position: e.g. from IE *dheiĝh-* (Skt. *dih-*) Goth. *deigan* 'knead', Lat. *fingo*, Osc. *feihúss* 'muros'.

When a sonant aspirate came immediately before final *s* or *t* the aspiration was lost at an early period, e.g. in Skt. *ádhok*, 2 and 3 sg. impf. of *duh-* 'to milk' for earlier **ádhokṣ*, **adhokt*, *ádhāk*, 3 sg. s-aor. of *dah-* ' to burn ', for **adhākšt* ; likewise in the nom. sg. of root stems °*dhuk* ' milking ', °*dhruk* ' injuring ' from °*dhukṣ*, °*dhrukṣ*. In their earlier form these roots had two aspirates, **dhugh-*, **dhagh-*, **dhrugh-*. In the above combinations the second aspirate was lost before the rule of aspirate dissimilation set in, and consequently the aspiration of the initial consonant was preserved in these cases. An exactly parallel development took place in Greek : *θρίξ* ' hair ', pl. *τρίχες*, *τρέφω* ' I nourish ', fut. *θρέψω*. From the standpoint of the individual languages it appears that in such cases the aspirate of the final is thrown back, but it becomes clear from comparative study that there were originally two aspirates of which the first was preserved from dissimilation in these circumstances.

The treatment of internal combinations of sonant aspirate + *t* or *s* was different, and will be described below (§ 14, 16). Here we may note only that the aspiration in class. *dhipsati*, etc., as opposed to Ved. *dípsati* is an innovation due to analogy.

§ 3. The Surd Aspirates

The surd aspirates appear only in Indo-Iranian with any frequency, and even there they are much less common than the corresponding sonants. Of these very few indeed can be established as Indo-European by direct comparison. Such comparisons are available only in Greek where there appear a few aspirates corresponding to the surd aspirates of Sanskrit, and in Armenian. Elsewhere, apart from a few traces in Latin (e.g. *funda* ' sling ' : Gk. *σφενδόνη*) this series has been confounded with that of the unaspirated surds.

The following examples will serve for illustration :

ph : Skt. *sphūrj-*, Gk. *σφαραγέομαι* ; *sphyá-* ' wooden ladle ', cf. Gk. *σφήν* ; *phā́la-* ' ploughshare ', Pers. *supār* ; *sphuráti* ' throbs, quivers ', Lith. *spiriù*, Gk. *σπαίρω*, Lat. *sperno*, cf. also Gk. *σφαῖρα* ' ball ' ; *phéna-* ' foam ', Osset. *fing*, O. Sl. *pěna*, O. Pruss. *spoayno* ; *śaphá-* ' hoof ', Av. *safa-*.

th : *véttha* ' thou knowest ', Gk. *οἶσθα* ; *sthā-* ' stand ', Gk. *ἵστημι* ; *sthag-* ' to cover ', Gk. *στέγω* ; *rátha-* ' chariot ', Av. *raθa-*, cf. Lat. *rota* ' wheel ' ; *pṛthú-* ' broad ', Av. *pərəθu-*, Gk. *πλατύς*, without aspiration, but cf. *πλάθανος* ' flat board for making cakes ' ; *pṛthuka-* ' young animal ', Arm. *orth* ' calf ', Gk. *πόρτις*, *πόρταξ* ' heifer ', without aspiration, but cf. *παρθένος* ' maiden ' with aspiration.

kh: *śaṅkhá-* 'shell', Gk. κόγχος; *śā́khā* 'branch', Arm. *çax*, Lith. *šakà*; *khā́-* 'well', Av. *xå*.

In contradistinction to the sonant aspirates which constitute an ancient and primary element of the IE phonetic system, the surd aspirates are a late creation, and recent advances in IE theory have made it possible to show how they came into existence. Apart from some possible cases of spontaneous aspiration in combinations with *s* (Skt. *sthag-*, etc.), their origin can be attributed to a combination of IE H with a preceding unaspirated surd. The nature of this H which has lately figured largely in IE studies will be examined below. For the present it will be sufficient to remark that it has disappeared in all IE languages except Hittite, but when immediately preceded by *p*, *t*, *k*, it has had the effect of aspirating these consonants. Thus the aspiration which in Skt. *sthā-* 'stand' (IE *stā*, i.e. *sta*H-, i.e. *ste*H_2) arises in the first instance from the reduced form of the root, IE *st*H- (Skt. *tiṣṭha*<*titi-st*H-*eti*), and is generalised from there. In Greek on the other hand (ἵστημι) the unaspirated *t* proper to the strong form of the root has prevailed. In Sanskrit *path-* 'road' (Instr. *pathā́*, etc.)<*pat*H-, H is a suffix which appears in its guṇa grade as *ā* (<*a*H) in nom. s. *pánthās*. In the latter case *th* appears only by analogy from the weak cases, as is confirmed by the Av. form *pantå* (original alternation *panta*H-*pat*H-). The root *prath-* 'to extend' and its derivatives (*pṛthú-* 'broad', etc.) contains two incorporated suffixes (IE *pl-et-*H-), the combination producing the surd aspirate in Sanskrit. This H- suffix, without the intervening *t-* suffix appears in Hitt. *palḫiš* 'broad', and in Lat. *plānus*. In Gk. πλατύς, no H- suffix is present, and there is therefore no aspiration. In Skt. *rátha-* 'chariot' we have a nominalised adjective (**rat*H-*á* 'wheeled' with a common change of accent) based on the *ā* (-*a*H) stem which appears in Lat. *rota* 'wheel' (*rota*H).

A corresponding aspiration of sonants by H is possibly a factor to be considered, but not many examples have been found. Such an instance may appear in Skt. *síndhu-* 'river' as compared with the root *syand-* 'to flow', where the form of the noun may be easily explained by the presence of an H-suffix before the final *u-* suffix.

It is believed that one type of IE H (H_3) affected a preceding surd differently, by voicing it, in Skt. *píbati*=O. Ir. *ibid* 'drinks' (√*pō-*, i.e. *pe*H_3, pres. **pi-p*H_3*-eti*), but this appears to be the only example. Incidentally it may be observed that *b*, apart from a case like this, or as an allophone of *p* (Skt. *upabdá-*: cf. *pad-* 'foot', etc.) was of extreme rarity, if not altogether absent in Indo-European.

§4. The First Palatalisation

When we come to the so-called guttural series (Labio-velar, Velar, Palatal, see above), we find that these sounds have been very considerably altered in Sanskrit. To begin with the Palatal series, the treatment is illustrated by the following equations:

k̂: Skt. *śván-* 'dog', Av. *span-*; Gk. *κύων*, Lat. *canis*; *śatám* '100', Av. *satəm*, Lith. *šim̃tas*: Gk. *ἑκατόν*, Lat. *centum*, O. Ir. *cēt*, Goth. *hund*; *śéte* 'lies': Gk: *κεῖται*; *śáṅkate* 'hesitates, doubts': Lat. *cunctor*; *víś-* 'clan, settlement', Av. *vis-*, O. Pers. *viθ-*, O. Sl. *vĭsĭ* 'village', Alb. *vis* 'place': cf. Gk. *οἶκος* 'house', Lat. *vīcus*; *śróṇi-* 'buttock', Av. *sraoni-*, Lith. *šlaunìs*: Lat. *clūnis*, O. Ic. *hlaun*; *śru-* 'to hear', *śrávas-* 'fame', Av. *sru-*, *sravah-*, O. Sl. *slovo* 'word': Gk. *κλέος*, *κλύω*, Lat. *clueor*, etc.; *dadárśa* 3rd sg. pf. 'he saw': Gk. *δέδορκε*; *diś-* 'to point out': Gk. *δείκνυμι*, Lat. *dīco*, etc.

ĝ: Skt. *jā́nu* 'knee', Av. *zānu*; Gk. *γόνυ*, Lat. *genu*; *járant-* 'old', Arm. *cer* 'old man': Gk. *γέρων*; *jámbha-* 'tooth', O. Sl. *zǫbu*, Alb. *δemp* 'id': Gk. *γόμφος* 'nail', Engl. *comb*, Toch. A *kam*, B *keme* 'tooth'; *juṣ-* 'to enjoy', *jóṣa-* 'enjoyment', Av. *zaoša-* 'id': Gk. *γεύομαι* 'taste', Lat. *gustus*, Goth. *kiusan* 'chose'; *rajatá-* 'silver'; Av. *ərəzata-*, Gk. *ἄργυρος*, Lat. *argentum*, Ir. *argat* 'id'; *ájati* 'drives', Av. *azaiti*; Gk. *ἄγω*, Lat. *ago*; *bhū́rja-* 'birch', Lith. *béržas*, O. Sl. *brěza*: AS. *beorc*.

ĝh: Skt. *himá-* 'snow', *hemantá-* 'winter', Av. *zima-*, Arm. *jiun* 'snow', Alb. *dimɛn*, Lith. *žiẽmà*, O. Sl. *zima* 'winter': Gk. *χείμων*, Lat. *hiems*, O. Ir. *gim-red* 'winter'; *aṃhú-* 'narrow', *áṃhas-* 'distress, difficulty', O. Sl. *ązŭkŭ* 'narrow': Gk. *ἄγχω* 'throttle', Lat. *ango*, *angustus*, O. Ir. *cum-ung*, Goth. *aggwus* 'narrow'; *lih-* 'to lick', Arm. *lizum*, Lith. *lëžiù*, O. Sl. *lizati*: Gk. *λείχω*, Lat. *lingo*, O. Ir. *ligim*, Goth. *bi-laígōn* 'to lick'.

It will be observed that ultimate Indo-Aryan and Iranian developments differ from each other (Skt. *ś, j, h*=Av. *s, z, z*). This is because the changes that have occurred have taken place in two phases: (1) a previous common Indo-Iranian development *ś, ź, źh*, (2) the change of these to the actual forms in Indo-Aryan and Iranian after the separation of the two groups. The first change is common to Indo-Iranian and the languages of the *satəm* group (see Chapter I) and took place within the Indo-European period. Later there were various special developments in other languages too, which in the case of Slavonic happen to be identical with those of Iranian.

The intermediate forms *ś, ź, źh* will explain most of the Indo-Iranian developments, as they will the Balto-Slavonic, but it is likely that before complete assibilation there was an affricate stage. Evidence of this is preserved in the Kafiri dialects, which occupy an intermediate position between Indian and Iranian. The treatment that occurs in Kati *duċ* '10' and *ċuī̃* 'empty' for instance (Skt. *dáśa, śūnyá-*) seems clearly to reflect a form more ancient than that of Sanskrit. We may therefore postulate an earlier Indo-Iranian (and the same will apply to the *satəm* languages generally) series *ć, ʃ, ʃh* (or *t′, d′, d′h* to be distinguished from *č, ǰ, ǰh* of the second palatalisation). This being so it becomes possible that (1) Skt. *j* of this series, with its affricate pronunciation, has developed directly out of *ʃ*, through confusion with the other affricate *ǰ*; without a sibilant stage *ź*, and (2) that Old Persian *θ, d* which appear in place of *s, z* in the rest of Iranian (*θard-* 'year', Av. *sarəd-*, Skt. *śarád-*; *dauštar-* 'friend', Av. *zaoša-* 'enjoyment', Skt. *jóṣa-, joṣṭár-*; *dasta-* 'hand', Av. *zasta-*, Skt. *hásta-*) have developed directly out of such affricates and that there is therefore no common Iranian treatment.

§5. Treatment of the Labio-velars

The languages of the *satəm* group all agree in another feature, namely in the loss of the labial element in the IE series k^w, g^w, g^wh. In the *centum* languages the series was to begin with preserved, but later subject to various developments, of which the commonest is the substitution of pure labial occlusives. Leaving aside cases which have been affected by the second palatalisation, the treatment of the labio-velars may be illustrated by the following examples:

kʷ : Skt. *ká-* 'who ?' *kím* 'what', Lith. *kàs*, O. Sl. *kŭ-to* : Gk. τίς 'who', πόθεν 'whence', Lat. *quis* ; *yákr̥t* 'liver', Av. *yākarə* ; Gk. ἧπαρ, Lat. *iecur* ; *krīṇā́mi* 'I buy', O. Russ. *krĭnuti* ; Gk. ἐπριάμην 'I bought', Ir. *crenim*, Welsh *prynaf* ; *kŕ̥mi-* 'worm', Lith. *kirmėlė̃* : Ir. *cruim*, Welsh *pryf* ; *riṇákti* 'leaves', *riktá-* 'left', Arm. *lk'anem* 'I leave', *elik'* 'he left', Lith. *lĕkù* 'I leave' : Gk. λείπω, Lat. *linquo*, etc.

gʷ : Skt. *gam- gácchati* 'go' : Gk. βάσκω, Lat. *venio*, Goth. *qiman* ; *gó-* (nom. s. *gaús*) 'cow', Arm. *kov*, O. Sl. *govędo* : Gk. βοῦς, Lat. *bōs*, O. Ir. *bō* ; Skt. *gnā́* '(divine) woman, wife', Av. *gənā*, O. Pruss. *genna*, Arm. *kin*, pl. *kanaik'* : Gk. γυνή, βανά, Ir. *ben*, Goth. *qinō* ; *gurú-* 'heavy' Gk. βαρύς ; *gur-* 'to lift up, heave', Av. *gar-* 'to throw' : Gk. βάλλω ; *grā́van-* 'pressing stone' : Ir. *brō*, gen. *broon* Welsh *breuan* 'mill-stone'.

gʷh : Skt. *jaghā́na* 'slew' : O. Ir. *geguin*, cf. Gk. ἔπεφνον, φόνος ; *arghá-* 'value, price' ; Lith. *algà* : Gk. ἀλφάνω 'earn' ; *gharmá-* 'heat', Av. *garəma-*, O. Pruss. *gorme* : Gk. θερμός 'hot', Lat. *formus* ; *laghú-* 'light, swift' : Gk. ἐλαχύς, ἐλαφρός, Lat. *levis*.

As can be seen from these examples the *satəm* languages have uniformly abandoned all trace of the labial element in these constants, and this, in conjunction with their sharing in the first palatalisation, provides strong evidence that they are derived from a single dialect group within Indo-European. Both changes belong to the late Indo-European period and not to the separate evolution of the various languages of this group.

The element ʷ which is attached to these velars differs from full IE *w* in that it is not convertible to the vowel *u* when the succeeding vowel is elided : e.g. Skt. *hánti* 'slays' : *ghnánti* 'they slay' from IE *gʷhenti* : *gʷhnonti* ; similarly Gk. ἔπεφνον, etc., as opposed to usual treatment of *w* as seen in such cases as *svápna-* 'sleep' : *suptá-* 'asleep'. It is possible, however, that this applies only to the late Indo-European stage. There exist some survivals, particularly in Hittite, in which this element is seen to be vocalised, after the manner of *w* proper. Corresponding to the Sanskrit verbal forms above Hittite has 3 s. *kuenzi* : 3 pl. *kunanzi* and corresponding to Skt. *nakt-*, Gk. νύξ, Lat. *nox* 'night' (IE **nokʷt-*) it has *nekuz meḫur* 'night time'. Other instances of this treatment are seen in Toch. A. *kuryär* 'commerce': Skt. *krī-* 'to buy' (IE **k^wrī*), in Toch. A. *kukäl* 'chariot', Gk. κύκλος 'wheel': Skt. *cakrá-*, Engl. *wheel* (**k^wek^wlos*) and in Gk. γυνή 'woman': Skt. *gnā́* (**g^wnā*). Examples like these seem to reflect an earlier stage of Indo-European, when the labial element in connection with these velars was equivalent to ordinary *w*.

§ 6. The Pure Velar Series

This series has been invented to account for those cases in which *k, g,* etc., of the *centum-* languages are not palatalised in the *satəm*-languages, and they are devoid of the labial element whose influence is so marked in the case of the labio-velars. Examples quoted are such as the following:

k: Skt. *kákṣa-* 'armpit', cf. Lat. *coxa*, OHG. *hahsa*; Skt. *kravíṣ-* 'raw flesh', Lith. *kraũjas*, O. Sl. *krŭvĭ* 'blood', Gk. κρέας, Lat. *cruor*; Skt. *kṛntáti* 'cuts' (√*ker-t-*), Gk. κείρω; *karkaṭa-* 'crab', Gk. καρκίνος, Lat. *cancer*; *kṛnátti* 'spins', cf. Gk. κλώθω 'spin', Lat. *colus* 'distaff'; *aṅká-* 'bending, lap', cf. Lat. *uncus*, Gk. ὄγκος; °*kulva-* 'bald', Lat. *calvus*; *kaví-* 'a wise man', Gk. κοέω 'take notice of', Lat. *caveo*.

g: Skt. *sthag-* 'to cover', Gk. στέγω, Lat. *tego*; *tigmá-* 'sharp', Gk. στιγμή 'puncture'; *ā́gas-* 'guilt', Gk. ἄγος; *ugrá-* 'strong', Av. *aogarə*; 'strength', Lat. *augeo, augustus*.

gh: *stigh-* 'to stride', Gk. στείχω Goth. *steiga*; *dīrghá-* 'long', O. Sl. *dlŭgŭ*, Gk. δολιχός, Hitt. *dalugaš*; *meghá-* 'cloud', Lith. *miglà*, Gk. ὀμίχλη.

The difficulty that arises from postulating a third series in the parent language, is that no more than two series (Lat. *quis* : *canis*, Skt. *kás* : *śvan-*) are found in any of the existing languages. In view of this it is exceedingly doubtful whether three distinct series existed in Indo-European. The assumption of the third series has been a convenience for the theoreticians, but it is unlikely to correspond to historical fact. Furthermore, on examination, this assumption does not turn out to be as convenient as would be wished. While it accounts in a way for correspondences like the above which otherwise would appear irregular, it still leaves over a considerable number of forms in the *satəm*-languages which do not fit into the framework. Such are Skt. *klam-* 'to be tired' beside *śram-* 'id', cf. Gk. κλαμαρός 'weak, slack', and *ruc-/ruk-* 'to shine' beside *ruśánt* 'bright', cf. Gk. λευκός 'white', etc. Examples of this kind are particularly common in the Balto-Slavonic languages: Lith. *akmũ* 'stone', Skt. *áśman-*, cf. Gk. ἄκμων; *klaušyti* 'to hear', cf. Skt. *śróṣamāṇa-*, Toch. A. *klyos-*; Lith. *pekus*, O. Pruss. *pecku*, Skt. *páśu* 'domestic animal', Lat. *pecu*; O. Sl. *svekrŭ* 'father-in-law', Skt. *śváśura-*, Lat. *socer*; O. Sl. *črěda* 'collection, herd', Skt. *śárdha-*; Lith. *smakrà* 'chin', Alb. *mjekrε*, Skt. *śmáśru-* 'beard', Ir. *smech* 'chin'. Clearly a theory which leaves almost as many irregularities as it clears away is not very soundly established, and since these cases have to be explained as examples of dialect mixture in early Indo-European, it would appear simplest to apply the same theory to the rest. The case for this is particularly strong when we remember that when false etymologies are removed,[1] when allowance is made for suffix alternation, and when the possibility of loss of labialisation in the vicinity of the vowel *u* is considered (e.g. *kravíṣ-*, *ugrá-*), not many examples remain for the foundation of the theory.

§7. The Second Palatalisation

After the completion of the changes characteristic of the *satəm-* languages the parent dialect of Indo-Iranian possessed the two series *k, g, gh* and *ś, ź, źh* (or *ć, ȷ́, ȷ́h*). The latter remained essentially unchanged till the end of the Indo-Iranian period. The former underwent the following alteration. Before the vowels *ĕ* (later changed to *ă* in Indo-Iranian) and *ĭ* and before the semivowel *y*, *k*, *g* and *gh* developed respectively into the affricates *č*, *ǰ* and *ǰh*, of which the last was later altered into Iranian *ǰ* and Sanskrit *h* respectively.

k: Skt. *ca* 'and', Gk. τε, Lat. *que*; *catvāras* 'four', O. Sl. *četyre*, Lith. *keturì*, Gk. τέσσαρες, Lat. *quattuor-*; *sácate* 'associates with', Av. *hačaiti*, Gk. ἕπεται 'follows', Lat. *sequitur*, Ir. *sechithir*; *páñca* 'five', Lith. *penkì*, Gk. πέντε, Lat. *quinque*; *pácati* 'cooks', O. Sl. *pečetŭ*, but 1 sg. *pekǫ*; *cakrá-* 'wheel', A.S. *hweohl*, cf. Gk. κύκλος, Toch. A. *kukäl*; *cáru-* 'a particular vessel', A.S. *hwer* 'kettle', cf. O. Ir. *coire*, Welsh *pair* 'id.'

g: Skt. *jīvá-* 'alive, life', *jīvati* 'lives', Av. *ǰvaiti*, O. Sl. *živŭ* 'alive', Lat. *vīvus*, Gk. βίος; *jyā́* 'bowstring', Lith. *gijà*

[1] For instance Skt. *kāla-* 'black' is from Dravidian and not connected with Lat. *cāligō*, etc.; the Aryan root *kan-* (Skt. *kanyā́* 'girl', etc.) cannot be connected with Gk. καινός 'new', because its primary meaning is quite certainly 'little' and not 'new'.

'thread', Gk. *βιός* 'bow'; *játu* 'gum, lac', A.S. *cwidu*, cf. Lat. *bitūmen*; °*jāni-* 'wife', Goth. *qēns*; *rajanī́* 'night', Gk. *ἐρεμνός, ἐρεβεννός* 'dark'.

gh: Skt. *hánti* 'slays', Av. *ǰainti*, as opposed to Skt. *jaghána* 'slew', O. Ir. *geguin*, Hitt. *kuenzi* 'slays'; *árhati* 'is worth', Av. *arəǰaiti*, as opposed to Skt. *arghá-* 'price', Lith. *algà* 'reward', Gk. *ἀλφάνω*; *háras-* 'heat', Gk. *θέρος* 'summer' (: *gharmá-*, etc. above); *dáhati* 'burns', Av. *dažaiti* : *nidāghá-* 'heat of summer', Lith. *degù* 'I burn'.

The second palatalisation took place fairly early in the development of Indo-Iranian, before the change of *ĕ* to *a* which distinguishes this branch from the rest of Indo-European. Similar changes appear in some other languages of the *satəm* group, e.g. Slavonic (*četyre* '4', *živŭ* 'alive') and Armenian (*ǰerm* 'warm') but these appear to have occurred independently and later.

§ 8. The Two Palatal Series in Indo-Aryan

In Indo-Aryan the distinction between the two palatal series, which is fully preserved in Iranian (*s, z, z* : *č, ǰ, ǰ*) is retained only in the case of the surds (*ś* : *c*). On the other hand the sonants, both unaspirated and aspirated, are confused with each other as *j* (= *ź* and *ǰ*) and *h* (= *źh* and *ǰh*) respectively. But the distinction between the two remains effective in many ways in the grammatical system, because according to their origin both *j* and *h* are treated in two different ways in various contexts. In declension and inflection the rules of sandhi operate differently according to the different origins of *j* and *h*. This may be illustrated from the formation of the participle in *-ta* from the two types of root respectively.

j: (a) *yaj-* 'sacrifice' (Av. *yaz-*) : *iṣṭá-*, *sṛj-* 'to let go' (Av. *harəz-*) : *sṛṣṭá-*, *mṛj-* 'to wipe' (Av. *marəz-*) : *mṛṣṭá-*.

(b) *nij-* 'to wash' (Av. *naēǰ-*) : *niktá-*; *bhaj-* 'to distribute' (Av. *baǰ-*) : *bhaktá-*; *yuj-* 'to join' (Av. *yaoǰ-*) : *yuktá-*.

h: (a) *vah-* 'to carry' (Av. *vaz-*) : *ūḍhá-*, *lih-* 'to lick' (Av. *raēz-*) : *līḍhá-*; *sah-* 'to overcome' (Av. *haz-*) : *sāḍhá-*, *soḍhá-*.

(b) *dah-* 'to burn' (Ir. *daǰ-*, Av. *dažaiti*) : *dagdhá-*, *druh-* 'to injure, betray' (Av. *druǰ-*) : *drugdhá-*. In this, as in many other respects the distinction between the two series remains active in Sanskrit grammar.

In the case of the second palatalisation, as opposed to the

first which operated in all conditions, there exists an alternation in the roots affected between palatalised and non-palatalised forms, depending on whether the vowel following was originally *ĕ* or *ŏ*. This is seen in perfects like *jaghā́na* 'slew' and *jigā́ya* 'conquered', as contrasted with the present tense forms *hánti* and *jáyati*. Similar alternation is not permissible in the case of roots whose *j* and *h* belong to the first palatal series, e.g. *jajā́na* 'begat' (*jan-* : Av. *zan-*) and *juhā́va* 'called' (*hū* : Av. *zav-*).

To begin with the distribution of palatalised and non-palatalised forms must have depended entirely on the nature of the succeeding vowel, and consequently an alternation between the two must have been active in the paradigms of noun and verb. In the parallel palatalisation of Slavonic such alternation exists, e.g. between *vlŭkŭ* 'wolf' nom. s. and *vluče* voc. s., and between *pekǫ* 'I cook' and *pečetŭ* 'he cooks'. Since the natural tendency of linguistic evolution is to smooth out such irregularities (as is done later in Russian, etc.) it is likely that the Slavonic palatalisation did not long precede the beginning of the literary tradition. On the other hand in the case of Indo-Iranian the change had taken place early enough for the working of analogy to become widely effective. Variation in the paradigms of noun and verb after the Slavonic style has been eliminated, except as between vocalic and consonantal suffixes (loc. s. *vācí*, loc. pl. *vākṣú*). On the other hand the alternation remains active between different nominal derivatives (*bhoga-* : *bhoja-*, etc.). At the beginning of a root alternation between palatal and guttural remains active only in the case of a few roots as those quoted above. Mostly it is eliminated, and in this respect Sanskrit shows a greater tendency to innovation than Old Iranian; cf. Skt. *akar* 3rd sg. root aor., Av. *čōrət̰* (early Aryan *ačart*<*ekert*), and *agamat*, *a*-aor. Av. *ǰimat̰*. In the latter case the proper name *Jamadagni-* ('who goes to the fire') preserves the earlier, pre-Vedic form. In the reduplication of the perfect, etc., the alternation always remains, based on the fact that the vowel of the reduplicating syllable was originally *e* (*jagā́ma*<*gʷegʷōme*, etc.).

There are a few instances in Sanskrit where *j* of the older palatal series alternates with *g* in the formation of nominal derivatives, e.g. *sárga-* 'emission' (*sṛj-*, Av. *harəz-*) *yāga-* 'sacrifice' (*yaj-*, Av. *yaz-*). The guttural here cannot be original, and it is due to the analogy of the palatals of the later series operating after the two had fallen together in pronunciation.

§ 9. Developments of *s* in Indo-Iranian and Slavonic

In Sanskrit it is the rule that the dental sibilant must be replaced by the cerebral after *k, r, ṛ, i* and *u*. By a similar rule in Iranian *s* (>Ir. *h*) is replaced by *š*. Further in the Slavonic languages *s* is usually replaced by *ch* in these conditions, and this *ch* represents an earlier *š*. In Lithuanian a similar change is found, but only after *r*. Examples are :

After *k* : (Skt. *kṣ*, Ir. *xš*, Slav. *ch*<*kx*<*kš*) Skt. *vakṣyā́mi*, Av. *vaxšyā* ; Skt. *kṣudrá-* 'small', cf. O. Sl. *chudŭ* 'id'; Skt. *áraikṣam*, *s*-aor. of *ric-* 'to leave' (IE *leikʷ-*), Gk. ἔλειψα ; cf. O. Sl. *těchŭ*, *s*-aor. of *tekǫ* 'I run'.

After *k̑* : Skt. *ś* : (Skt. *kṣ*, Ir. *š*, Slav. *s*), Skt. *ákṣa-* 'axle', Av. *aša-*, O. Sl. *osĭ*, Lith. *ašìs*, Gk. ἄξων, Lat. *axis* ; Skt. *dákṣiṇa-* 'right (hand)', Av. *dašina-*, O. Sl. *desinŭ*, Lith. *dešinẽ*, Gk. δεξιός, Lat. *dexter*, etc. ; Skt. *takṣ-* 'to construct in wood (as a carpenter), Av. *taš-*, O. Sl. *tesati*, Lith. *tašýti*, Gk. τέχνη 'art' (**téksnā*), τέκτων 'carpenter' (**tékstōn*), Hitt. *takš-* 'to join', Lat. *texo* 'weave'; Skt. *makṣū́* 'quickly', Av. *mošu*, Lat. *mox*.

After *r* (and *ṛ*) : Skt. *várṣman-* 'summit', *várṣīyas-* 'higher', O. Sl. *vrĭchŭ* 'summit', Lith. *viršùs* 'upper part'; *mṛṣ-* 'to overlook, forgive', *márṣa-* 'forbearance', Lith. *miršti* 'to forget', *maȓšas* 'forgetfulness', Toch. A. *märs-* 'to forget'; *dhṛṣṇóti* 'dares', O. Pers. *adaršnauš* 'he dared', cf. Gk. θάρσος 'boldness', Goth. *gadars* 'dare', Engl. *durst*, etc.

After *i* : Skt. *piṣ-* 'to pound', O. Slav. *pichati* 'to knock, strike', Lat. *pinso* ; *triṣú*, loc. pl. of *tri-* 'three', O. Sl. *trĭchŭ*; *áśveṣu*, loc. pl. of *áśva-* 'horse', Av. *aspaēšu*, cf. O. Sl. *vlŭcěchŭ* (*vlŭkŭ* 'wolf') ; *víṣa-* 'poison', Av. *vīša-*, Lat. *vīrus*, Gk. ἰός.

After *u* : *juṣ-* 'to enjoy', *jóṣa-* 'enjoyment', Av. *zaoš-*, cf. Lat. *gustūs*, etc. ; *mū́ṣ-* 'mouse', O. Sl. *myšĭ*, Lat. *mūs*, etc. ; *śúṣka-* 'dry', *śóṣa-* 'drying up', Av. *huška-* 'dry', O. Sl. *suchŭ*, Lith. *saũsas*, Gk. αὖος 'id'.

As can be seen, the parallelism between Indo-Iranian and Slavonic is not absolutely complete, because they differ in the treatment of that *s* which follows IE *k̑* (>Skt. *ś*, Slav. *s*). But in all other respects they agree, and the correspondence is too close for such changes to have taken place independently. In Lithuanian the same kind of development is observed, but only in connection with *r*, which points to a remoter contact than was the case between Indo-Iranian and Slavonic.

Cerebralisation of *s* does not take place in Sanskrit when *r* or *ṛ* immediately follows: e.g. *visra-* 'bad-smelling (meat)', cf. *víṣa-*, etc., Av. *vaēša-* 'corruption'; *tisrás, tisṛ́bhis, tisṝṇā́m*, from *tri-* 'three'; gen. s. *usrás* from *uṣar-* 'dawn', *sisrate* from *sar-* 'to go'. In Avestan there is no such restriction, e.g. *tišrō*, nom. pl. fem. cf. *θri-* 'three'.

§ 10. The So-Called Mobile *s*

Indo-European *s* when it formed the first member of an initial consonant group, was an unstable sound, and liable to disappear under conditions which it has not been possible accurately to define. Forms with and without *s* are found side by side in the various languages, as illustrated by the following examples:

Skt. *tányati* 'thunders', Lat. *tonāre*: Skt. *stanayitnú-* 'thunder', cf. Gk. *στένω*, O. Sl. *stenją*, etc.; Skt. *tāyú-* 'thief', O. Sl. *tatŭ* 'id', Gk. *τητάω*, Hitt. *tāya-* 'steal': Skt. *stená-* 'thief', *stāyú-, stāyánt-*, etc.; Skt. *tṛ́-, tārā́* 'star': Skt. *stṛ́-*, Av. *star-*, Gk. *ἀστηρ*, etc. 'id'; Skt. *tij-* 'to sharpen', *tigmá-* 'sharp': Gk. *στίζω, στιγμή*, etc.; Skt. *tud-* 'to push', Lat. *tundo*: Goth. *stautan* 'id'; Skt. *phéna-* 'foam', O. Sl. *pěna*: O. Pruss. *spoayno*, with variant suffix Lat. *spūma*: Engl. *foam*; Skt. *plīhán-* 'spleen': Av. *spərəzan-*, Gk. *σπλήν*, etc.; Skt. *páśyati* 'sees': *spaś-* 'spy', Lat. *specio*; Skt. *khañj-* 'to be lame': Gk. *σκάζω*; Skt. *phā́la-* 'plough-share': Pers. *supār*; Pers. *fih* 'oar': Skt. *sphyá-* 'wooden ladle'; Av. (*vī-*) *xad-* 'to break up (earth)': Skt. *skhad-* 'to smash to pieces', cf. Gk. *σκεδάννυμι*; Skt. *nava-* 'sneeze': Germ. *niesen*: Engl. *sneeze* (*neu-s-*: *sneu-s-*); Skt. *lavaṇá-* 'salty, salt': cf. Lat. *sal, nihākā́* 'fog', *nīhā́ra-* 'mist, dew': *snih-* 'to be moist', etc. There is no perfectly satisfactory theory to account for this variation which affects all Indo-European languages. Most probably it is the result of some kind of external sandhi affecting initial *s-* in the Indo-European period. It seems fairly clear that the phenomenon is due to loss of initial *s*, and if this is so the theory that would regard the *s* as the remains of some kind of prefix is out of the question.

§ 11. The Reconstructions *þ*, *þh*, *đh*

In a certain number of words etymologically connected, chiefly between Indo-Aryan and Greek, an *s* (*ś*) in the former appears to correspond to τ or θ in the latter. The commonest examples of this interchange, which has caused considerable difficulty, are the following: Skt. *tákṣan* -' carpenter ' : Gk. τέκτων ; Skt. *ŕkṣa-* ' bear ', Lat. *ursus* : Gk. ἄρκτος, Ir. *art* ; Skt. *kṣan-* ' to wound ' : Gk. κτείνω ' kill ' ; Skt. *kṣi-* ' to dwell ', Av. *šay-* : Gk. κτίζω, κτίμενος ; *kṣi-* ' to possess ' : Gk. κτάομαι ; *rakṣ-* ' to injure ' : Gk. ἐρέχθω ; *kṣám-* ' earth ' : Gk. χθών ; *kṣar-* ' flow ' : Gk. φθείρω ' perish ' ; *kṣi-* ' to destroy ' : Gk. φθίνω. It has been customary to assume a set of IE fricatives to account for these correspondences, namely *þ*, *þh*, *đh*, but it is certain that these creations are without serious foundation, since in the case of some of them Hittite evidence has shown that a quite different kind of explanation is necessary, and in view of this the rest are naturally suspect. Corresponding to the Greek and Sanskrit words for ' earth ' Hittite has *tekan-* and Toch. A *tkaṃ* from which it may be deduced that the original form of this word was **dheĝhom-*, or, with elision of the radical vowel, **dhĝhom-*. In Greek there has been metathesis of the initial consonant group; elsewhere we find elision of the first member of the group: Lat. *humus*, OIr. *zam-*, etc. Likewise for ' bear ' Hittite has (in all probability) *ḫartagaš*, from which it can be seen that there has been the same transposition in Gk. ἄρκτος. The Sanskrit forms of these words have developed from original unmetathesised form changed according to the rules of Sanskrit historical phonology. An original Hr̥tk̑os ' bear ', with loss of H; *r̥tk̑os*, develops through the stages *r̥tśa-* > *r̥tṣa-* to *ŕkṣa-*. The development of the word for ' earth ', though more complicated as containing a voiced aspirated group, follows the same line in principal: *dhĝhom-* > *dźham-* > *ḍẓham-* *ṭṣam-* > *kṣam-*. In the case of Skt. *kṣi*, Gk. φθίνω the original root *dhg^ωhi-* produced Indo-Iranian *dǰhi-* which was modified to *dźhi-* and then treated as the initial group of the word for ' earth '. In the case of some words Sanskrit has elided the first member in such groups, so that an original **dhĝhyes* ' yesterday ' (cf. Gk. χθές, transposed) appears as *hyas* (<*ĝhyes*). The correspondence of Skt. *śyená-* ' hawk ' and Gk. ἰκτῖνος is of the same nature.

Not all the examples are to be accounted for in this way. In some cases there is suffix variation. Skt. *ákṣi* ' eye ' contains original *-s-* which is not to be compared with Gk. τ in ὀκταλλος on the assumption of original *þ*. Suffix variation should probably also be seen in Gk. τέκτων ' carpenter ' (**teks-lōn*) as opposed to Skt. *tákṣan-*.

§ 12. Treatment of *r* and *l*

In Iranian IE *r* and *l* appear indiscriminately as *r*.[1] In the language of the *Ṛgveda* this is predominantly the case. In Classical Sanskrit both *l* and *r* are found, but their distribution does not correspond exactly with that of Indo-European. In certain Eastern dialects of Indo-Aryan (notably in the inscriptions of Aśoka and in the Māgadhī of the Drama) only *l* is found. The treatment of IE *l* in Sanskrit is illustrated by the following examples :

(a) *l* becomes *r* : *riṇákti* ' leaves ' : Lat. *linquit* ; *śróṇi-* ' buttock ' : Lat. *clūnis*, Lith. *šlaunìs* ; *sarpís* ' butter ', Toch. A. *ṣälyp*, cf. Engl. *salve* ; *aratní-* ' elbow ' : Gk. ὠλένη, Lat. *ulna* ; *śrávas* ' fame ' : Gk. κλέος, O. Sl. *slovo* ' word ' ; *gárbha-* ' embryo ' : Gk. δελφύς ' id ', ἀδελφός ' brother ' (cf. *sodara-*) ; *cakrá-* ' wheel ' : Gk. κύκλος ; *paraśú-* ' axe ' : Gk. πέλεκυς ; *píparti* ' fills ' : Gk. πίμπλημι ; *pur-* ' city ' : Lith. *pilìs*, Gk. πόλις ; *śri-* ' to lean ' : Gk. κλίνω ; *sū́rya-* ' sun ', Lat. *sōl*.

(b) *l* remains : *lúbhyati* ' covets ' : Lat. *lubet* ; *palitá-* ' grey-haired ' : cf. Gk. πολιός, πελιτνός, etc. ; °*kulva-* ' bald ' : Lat. *calvus* ; *palā́va-* ' chaff ' : O. Sl. *plěva*, Lat. *palea* ; *palvala-* ' pond ' : cf. Lat. *palus* ' swamp ' ; *plīhán-* ' spleen ' : Gk. σπλήν, Lat. *lien* ; *dala-* ' portion ' : Lith. *dãlìs* ; *klóman-* ' lung ' : Gk. πλεύμων.

In comparing the Vedic with the Classical language we notice : (i) that in a number of words the latter has *l* where the former has *r*, and this normally in cases where *l* appears in other IE languages, e.g. *laghú-* ' light ' v. *raghú-*, Gk. ἐλαχύς, Lat. *levis* ; *plu-* ' to float ', v. *pru-*, Gk. πλέω ; *lip-* ' to smear ', v. *rip-*, Gk. ἀλείφω ; *lih-* ' to lick ', v. *rih-*, Gk. λείχω ; (ii) that a considerable proportion of the classical words which preserve IE *l*

[1] There are a few exceptions in Modern Persian and occasionally elsewhere : Pers. *lištan* ' to lick ', Skt. *rih-*, *lik*, Gk. λείχω ; *lašin* ' soft ', Skt. *ślakṣṇá-* : *lab* ' lip ' : Lat. *labium* ; Oss. *sald* ' cold ' : Lith. *šáltas*.

are not found in the text of the *Ṛgveda*, either by accident, or because their meaning was of such a nature that they were not likely to appear in a text of sacred hymns (e.g. *plúṣi-* ' flea ' : Arm. *lu*, Alb. *pl'ešt*, cf. Lith. *blusà*) ; (iii) that some derivatives which have become isolated from their roots preserve IE *l* even when it is normally replaced by *r* in the corresponding roots : *ślóka-* ' verse ' (*śru-*), *vipula-* ' great, extensive ' (*pṝ-*, *píparti* ' fill ').

The explanation of this apparently complicated treatment is fairly simple. The dialect at the basis of the Ṛgvedic language lay to the north-west, while the classical language was formed in Madhyadeśa. The original division must have been such that the Western dialect turned *l* into *r* in the same way as Iranian (being contiguous to Iranian, and at the same time probably representing a later wave of invasion), while the more easterly dialect retained the original distinction. It was in this latter area that Classical Sanskrit was elaborated, but it was not evolved as a separate literary language, distinct from that of the Veda ; on the contrary it developed as a modification of the old sacred language of the Vedic hymns. The latter was always the foundation of the literary language, but since after the earliest period (and this excludes most of the later tenth book of the *Ṛgveda*), the centre of its cultivation shifted eastward to Madhyadeśa, in its further development it was subject to the continuous influence of the dialectal forms of this region. So in the case of the distribution of *r* and *l* many of the basic words of the vocabulary retain always the form established by the Vedic literature, but in other cases *l*-forms based on the dialect of Madhyadeśa replace them. In cases where the word in question is not found in the Vedic text, and where therefore there existed no established literary tradition, the Eastern form with original *l* almost universally appears.

The treatment of IE *r* is different in that in the vast majority of cases it continues to be represented by *r* in all periods of the language, e.g. *rudhirá-* ' red, blood ', Gk. ἐρυθρός ; *járant-* ' old ', Gk. γέρων ' old man ' ; *raí-* ' property ', Lat. *rēs*, *pári* ' round ', Gk. περί ; *vártate* ' turns ', Lat. *vertitur*, *párdate* ' breaks wind ', Gk. πέρδεται ; *pā́rṣṇi-* ' heel ', Gk. πτέρνα, Goth. *faírzna* ; *sru-* ' to flow ', Gk. ῥέω ; *náras* n. pl. ' men ', Gk. ἀνέρες, ἄνδρες ; *sárpati* ' crawls ', Gk. ἕρπω, Lat. *serpō* ; *rā́j-*, *rā́jan-* ' king ', Lat. *rēx* ; *rátha-* ' chariot ', Lith. *rãtas* 'wheel', Lat. *rota* 'id'; *vīrá-* 'man, hero', Lith. *výras*, Lat. *vir*, etc.

On the other hand instances of *l* in place of IE *r* are comparatively rare: *lóhita-* 'red' (also *róhita-*, Av. *raoiδita-*, cf. *rudhirá-*); *álam* 'suitable, enough', v. *áram*, cf. Gk. ἀραρίσκω; *palāyate* 'flees' (*parā* with *i-* 'to go'). The number of such examples is too small to justify the assumption of an *l*-dialect to account for them. Such an *l*-dialect does in fact occur later in the Magadhan Prakrit, but it was limited to a small area, and this Prakrit cannot account for forms with *l* out of *r* which occur in the later Vedic literature. It is also to be noted that in some cases where a change *l*>*r* has been assumed (e.g. *lup-* compared with Lat. *rumpo*) it is more likely that *l* is original.

§ 13. Indo-European h

Of late a new phonetic element has entered into accounts of Indo-European as a result of the discovery of Hittite. In this language there appears a sound *ḫ* which was unaccounted for in the normally prevailing conception of IE phonetics. It is found in basic IE words and must therefore be attributed to Indo-European. Since it is absent in the corresponding words in all the other languages, they must be presumed to share a common change by which it has been lost, and to represent, in this respect, a more advanced state of Indo-European than that preserved in Hittite. Common examples of *ḫ* are: Hitt. *ešḫar* 'blood': Skt. *ásṛk*, Lat. *aser*, Gk. ἔαρ, Toch. A. *ysār*; *ḫaštai* 'bone': Skt. *ásthi*, Gk. ὀστέον, Lat. *os*; *ḫant-* 'front': Skt., *ánti* '(in front of), near', Gk. ἀντί, Lat. *ante*; *ḫarki-* 'white': Toch. *ārki*, Gk. ἀργός, Skt. *árjuna-*, etc.; *paḫḫur* 'fire': Gk. πῦρ; *paḫš-* 'to protect': cf. Skt. *pā-* 'id', etc.; *išḫai-*, *išḫiya-* 'bind': Skt. *syáti* 'binds'; *newaḫḫ-* 'renew': Lat. *novāre*; *palḫiš* 'broad': cf. Lat. *plānus*, etc. For Indo-European the symbol h, used by H. Pedersen is the most convenient (IE **pel*h- etc.).

In some instances h disappears without trace (*ásṛk* 'blood') but in others its effects survive. It is clear that the long vowel in Lat. *novāre* results from the combination of a short vowel + h, a combination which remains in Hittite, and the same can be assumed in the case of Lat. *plānus* (*pla*h-, varying in apophony from Hitt. *palḫ-*). Skt. *syáti* 'binds', from the Hittite evidence, stands for *sh*yáti*, of which sh- is the root in its weak form, and *yá* the suffix of the fourth class. The simple root with guṇa appears in the aorist (*ásāt*) showing the same development of *a*H to *ā*. Hitt. *paḫš*- ' to protect ' is enlarged by an *s*- suffix, and when this is removed we see the same correspondence *aḫ* : *ā* between this and Sanskrit *pā*-. Since the nominal and verbal suffixes *ā* are identical, the same development *a*H>*ā* (as in *novāre*) is to be assumed in the case of the feminine suffix *ā* (Lat. *nova*, Gk. *νέā*, Skt. *návā*), and this implies a similar development in the case of the long vowels *ī* and *ū* in nominal and verbal derivation, since the compound suffixes *yā* and *vā* must in the same way be derived from *i*+*a*H and *u*+*a*H, and the corresponding weak grades are for *i*-H and *u*-H.

Another effect of H, observable in languages other than Sanskrit, is the coloration of a succeeding vowel by H, producing notably a change from *e* to *a*. For instance the root which appears in Sanskrit as *krī*- ' to buy ' is to be set up for Indo-European as *kʷri*H-, and in Greek an original aorist form *ekʷri*H-*eto* appears as *ἐπρίατο*, the original presence of H being indicated by the *a* instead of *e* of the termination. Similarly from the root *kru*H- (Skt. *krū*- in *krūrá*-, etc.) an original *es*/*os* stem **kreú*H*os* appears in Greek as an -*ας*- stem, *κρέας*. The confusion of the vowel qualities has eliminated such variation in Sanskrit, but there remain a number of other circumstances in which the presence of H can be detected, notably :

(1) The older theory assumed a vocalic *r* and *l* (written *r̥ʳ*, *l̥ˡ* and in other ways) before a following vowel in certain cases to account for correspondences like Gk. *βαρύς* ' heavy ', Skt. *gurú*-, Goth. *kaúrus* ' id '. But there was no clear reason why the rule that these phonemes appear as vowels in interconsonantal position, but as consonants before and after vowels, should not be valid in this case. A restoration *gʷr̥*H*ú*- showing that the *r̥* originally occupied an interconsonantal position, accounts for all these developments. In most IE languages where *r̥* develops into a vowel (varying from language to language) +*r*, this combination remains before a vowel when H disappears, and similarly in the case of *l*. In Sanskrit the process is somewhat different, since here vocalic *r̥* normally remains, but when the loss of H would leave it before a vowel, its place is taken by the combinations *ir* and *ur*. Iranian, which is usually so close to Indo-Aryan, differs markedly on this point, showing *ar* where Sanskrit has *ir* or *ur*. Examples of such words

are Skt. *tirás* ' across ' : Av. *tarō* ; *śíras-* ' head ', Av. *sarah-*, cf. Gk. κάρᾱ, κάρηνον ; *purás* ' in front ', Av. *parō*, Gk. πάρος ; *púras* n. pl. ' cities ', cf. Lith. *pilìs* ' fort ' (guṇa in Gk. πόλις) ; *purú-* ' much ', Av. *pouru-* (Ir. *paru-*) ; *híraṇya-* ' gold ', Av. *zaranya-* ; *girí-* ' mountain ', Av. *gairi-*, cf. Lith. *gìria* ' forest ' (guṇa in O. Sl. *gora* ' mountain ') ; *giráti*, *giláti* ' swallows ', *tiráti* ' crosses, overcomes ', *kiráti* ' scatters ', etc. The variation between *i* and *u* in these cases depends on the preceding consonant ; preceded by a labial, or in some cases by an old labio-velar, *u* appears, elsewhere *i* is normal.

(2) The combination *ṛ*H also gave rise to a special development when followed by a consonant. In this case *īr*, *ūr* appears in Sanskrit, but in Iranian predominantly *ar*. So we have *śīrṣán-* ' head ' beside *śíras* (*k̂ṛ*H*sen-* : *k̂ṛ*H*es-*), *tīrṇá-* and *kīrṇá-* beside *tiráti*, *kiráti*, etc., and with *ū*, *pūrṇá-* ' full ' (after labial). Other words with *īr*, *ūr* of this origin are : *īrmá-* ' arm, foreleg ', Av. *arəma-*, O. Pruss. *irmo*, Lat. *armus*, Engl. *arm* ; *ūrdhvá-* ' upright, high ', Av. *ərəδwa-*, Lat. *arduus* ; *ū́rṇā* ' wool ', Av. *varənā*, Lith. *vìlna* ; *ūrmí-* ' wave ', Av. *varəmi-*, A.S. *wielm* ; *ŭ̄rvárā* ' cultivated land ', Av. *urvarā* ' cultivated plant ' < **ṛ*H*varā*, cf. Lat. *arāre* ' plough ', Gk. ἄρουρα 'ploughed field ', etc. ; *dīrghá-* ' long ', Av. *darəγa-*, O. Sl. *dlŭgŭ* ; *pū́rva-* ' former ', Av. *paurva-*, O. Sl. *prŭvŭ* ; *bhū́rja-* ' birch ' (Lith. *béržas*, etc., with different grade). To account for these developments original long sonant liquids were set up (*ṝ*, *ḹ*), and these could have conceivably existed at an intermediate stage (*ṛ*H > *ṝ* > *īr*, *ūr*), the development being parallel to that of *i*H, *u*H to *ī*, *ū*.

In the same fashion the long sonant nasals which were postulated may be replaced by *n̥*H and *m̥*H. From the root *san*(H) ' to win ' the Skt. participle *sātá-* develops regularly through **sa*H*tó-* from *sn̥*H*tó-*, with regular weak form of root. In the case of *m̥*H the nasalisation is preserved (or reintroduced), but the original presence of H is clearly enough indicated by the long vowel : *dāntá-* ' tamed ', *śāntá-* ' appeased ', from *dam*(H)-, *śam*(H)-.

(3) In the Vedic language *-ya-* after a light syllable is pronounced as one syllable if it is simply a combination of *y* + *a* : *ávya-* ' belonging to a sheep ', *kavyá-* ' wise ', *ványa-* ' of the forest ', *havyá-* ' oblation '. When on the other hand it goes back to *-i*H*a* (a suffix parallel to *-ira*, *-iṣa*, etc.) *ya* is pronounced *-iya* : *dámiya-* ' belonging to the house ', *ráthiya-* ' relating to a

chariot', *jániya-* 'relating to the people', *udaníya-* 'watery' The two types are of course confused in the later language, and the difference revealed by the Vedic metre, is simply explained when it is realised that there are two different suffixes, (1) *i*+*a*, (2) *i*+H+*a*. The declension of the stems in *ī* and *ū* (<*i*H, *u*H) where the suffix always retains its syllabic value before a vocalic ending (gen. s. *vṛkíyas, tanúvas*<°*i*H*as*, °*u*H*as*) confirms this quite clearly, since the corresponding genitives of *ávi-* 'sheep' and *mádhu* 'honey' (*ávyas, mádhvas*) show always the consonantal value of *y* and *v*.

(4) Most significant of all, traces of the original nature of H are preserved in Sanskrit in cases where it was immediately preceded by an occlusive. Here the combination occlusive + H may produce an aspirated occlusive. As already stated, it was in this way that the whole category of surd aspirates arose in late Indo-European. Examples of this have already been given. Examples of sonant aspirates arising in this way are seen when an aspirate in Sanskrit appears to correspond to a non-aspirate in other languages, or when a final non-aspirated occlusive of a root appears with aspiration in a derivative. In these cases original suffixal H is responsible for the aspiration; e.g. *máhā-* 'great': Gk. μέγας. Here the root is followed by the suffix *a*H(>*ā*), which appears in its weak form (-H-) in the gen. sg., and this H being in immediate contact with the preceding *g* causes aspiration (*meĝ*-H-*és*>*meĝhés*>*mahás*), and from such forms the aspiration is extended to the whole declension. The same thing has taken place in *duhitár-* 'daughter' (*dhug*-H-*itár-*): Gk. θυγάτηρ, *ahám* 'I' (*eg*H-*óm*): Gk. ἐγώ (*egó*H), *sadhástha-* 'seat, abode' (*sed*-H-*es-*): *sad-* 'to sit', *síndhu-* 'river': *syand-* 'to flow'.

Before the discovery of Hittite there existed in Indo-European studies a 'Laryngeal Theory', which, since it received partial confirmation from the new Hittite evidence, has come to be generally adopted in recent years. Briefly stated in its most popular form the theory maintains that there existed three laryngeals, which in this notation would be represented by H_1, H_2, H_3. The original long vowels of Indo-European (as opposed to those long by vṛddhi), result from a combination of a single guṇa vowel *e* with the several laryngeals, so that from eH_1, eH_2 and eH_3, *ē* (e.g. *dhē-* 'to put'), *ā* (e.g. *stā* 'to stand') and *ō* (e.g. *dō* 'to give') are respectively derived (i.e. the roots are originally *dhe*H$_1$, *ste*H$_2$, *de*H$_3$). The theory further maintains that when preceded by these three laryngeals this same guṇa vowel takes the form *e*, *a* and *o* respectively (*es-* 'to be': H$_1$*es-*; *anti* 'in front': H$_2$*enti*; *ost(h)i-* 'bone': H$_3$*esti*).

Hittite provides some positive evidence in support of this theory, but it is incomplete, and in certain respects contradictory. We have already quoted instances showing the development of the guṇa vowel + H to *ā* and of the change of *e* to *a* when preceded by H. On the other hand there are difficulties: although *ḫ* appears where the theory demands it in *ḫant-*: Gk. ἀντὶ it is absent in *appa*: Gk. ἀπό where the theory equally demands it. In Hittite there is only one *ḫ* and it is a long way from this three or even four demanded by the theory. It is not therefore surprising that the theoreticians differ considerably in the details of their exposition. For the purposes of Sanskrit grammar the question of the plurality of H is fortunately of little significance, because the variation of vowel quality (*a*, *e*, *o*), with which it is bound up, has ceased to exist in Sanskrit. For all practical purposes it is possible to operate with a single, undifferentiated H, and that will usually prove sufficient.

Another aspect of the Laryngeal theory should be briefly mentioned. From the beginning it has been involved in the theory of Indo-European 'Shwa' (ə). In the Laryngeal theory it is replaced by a vocalic version of the laryngeals (H̥ with three varieties). As a result of this the laryngeals themselves commonly receive the notation $ə_1$, $ə_2$, $ə_3$. It will be pointed out below that the hypothesis of an Indo-European *ə* is without justification either in the framework of the laryngeal theory or of any other. Indo-European H is not capable of vocalic function and when left in interconsonantal position through loss of the associated guṇa vowel it is in Sanskrit elided: e.g. Skt. *dadmás*, *dadhmás* from *dā*, *dhā*.

§ 14. Combinations of Occlusives

The following changes in combination are inherited from Indo-European:

(1) A sonant is changed into a surd when immediately followed by a surd: *yuktá-* 'joined': *yuj-* 'to join', *yugám* 'yoke', cf. Gk. ζευκτός: ζεύγνυμι; *patsú*, loc. pl. of *pád-* 'foot', cf. Gk. ποσσί, ποσί. Conversely a surd becomes sonant when fol-

lowed by a sonant: Skt. *upabdá-* 'trampling on': *pád-* 'foot', cf. Av. *frabda-* 'fore part of the foot', Gk. ἐπίβδαι 'day after a festival'; *dadbhís* instr. pl. of *dant-*, *dat-* 'tooth'; *abjít-* 'conquering the water': *áp-* 'water'.

(2) In the case of the combination sonant aspirate followed by *-t-* the whole group is voiced and the aspiration attached to the second consonant; thus from *dah-* 'to burn' (from *dagh-* by the second palatalisation), *budh-* 'to understand' and *labh-* 'to receive', the participles in *-tá* are *dagdhá-*, *buddhá-* and *labdhá-*. In the older Avestan language a similar development is observed, though the aspiration as always in Iranian has been lost: *aogədā* 'said' from **augdha*, i.e. Aryan *augh-* (Av. *aog-*) + *ta*, cf. Gk. εὔχομαι; *ubdaēna-* 'woven' from Aryan *vabh-*. The later Avestan substitutes combinations of type (1) above even in the case of the original sonant aspirates: *aoxta* 'said', *druxta-* 'betrayed' (*draog-*: Skt. *druh-*) *dapta-* 'deceived' (*dab-*: Skt. *dabh-*). In the same way in Sanskrit *dhatté* 'places' has been substituted for **daddhe* (= Av. *dazdē*) which would be the regular combination of *dadh-* + *te*. Elsewhere in Indo-European innovating forms of this type have completely replaced the old type of combination: e.g. Gk. ἐκτός: ἔχω; πύστις, cf. Av. *apaitibusti* 'not noticing', as opposed to Sanskrit *buddhí-*.

(3) Dental combinations in Sanskrit normally conform to the above rules: *vétti* 'he knows' from *vid-*, *ruddhá-* 'obstructed' from *rudh-* + *tá*, etc. On the other hand Iranian substitutes the sibilant *s* or *z* in these positions: *vōistā* 'thou knowest': Skt. *véttha*; *hastra-* 'session': Skt. *sattrá-*; *ni-uruzda-* 'locked up': Skt. *ruddhá-*. The Greek treatment agrees with Iranian: οἶσθα 'thou knowest', πύστις 'information', cf. Av. *apaitibusti*: Skt. *buddhí-*. In the Western IE language *-ss-* results from the combination: Lat. *ob-sessus* (*sedeo*), O. Ic. *sess* 'seat'. A tendency to modify the dental combinations is therefore wide-spread. It is assumed that in Indo-European a sibilant was inserted in these cases (t^st, t^sth, d^zd, d^zdh). Since all interconsonantal sibilants are elided in Sanskrit an IE *voít*^{s}*tha* would produce Skt. *véttha*, and at the same time it accounts for the Iranian and Greek forms. In the case of the voiced combination we find two kinds of treatment in Sanskrit, on the one hand the usual type *ruddhá-*, *vṛddha-*, etc., and on the other hand some ancient

forms testifying to the existence of *z* instead of *d* as in Iranian : *dehí* impv. 'give' beside *daddhí*, cf. Av. *dazdi*, and *dhehí* 'put', both with *e* out of earlier *az* according to the rule below. Either this is a case of dialectal divergence, or the type *dehí* (<*dazdhí*) represents the regular phonetical treatment which has been replaced in the majority of cases by new analogical formations.

§ 15. Combinations Involving the Palatal Series

The second palatal series is simple in the matter of consonant combination, since all that is involved is the retention of the original guttural before a consonant, which then combines according to the rules given above : *vac-* 'to speak' : *uktá-*, *yuj-* 'to join' : *yuktá-*, *yokṣyā́mi*, *dah-* 'to burn' : *dagdhá-*.

Combinations of the old palatal series are much more complicated. In the early Indo-Iranian period *ś*, *ź* and *źh* were changed to *š* and *ž* before dental occlusives (with aspiration and voicing of the occlusive in the case of *źh* according to the rule given above for *dagdhá-*, etc.) : the resulting sibilants were identical with those that arose from Indo-European *s*, *z* after *i*, *u*, etc., and their subsequent history is the same. In Sanskrit *š* became cerebral *ṣ* and cerebralised the following dental and *ž*, after undergoing the same process, was elided leaving cerebral *ḍ* : e.g. *váṣṭi* 'he wishes' (*vaś-*) Av. *vašti*, Hitt. *wekzi*, cf. Gk. ἑκών etc. 'willing' ; *aṣṭaú* '8' (cf. *aśītí-* '80'), Av. *ašta*, Lat. *octo*, etc. ; Skt. *mṛḍīká-* 'pardon', Av. *mərəždīka-* (*mṛĝ-d*, cf. Skt. *mṛj-* 'to wipe away' and Pers. *āmurzīdan* 'to pardon') ; Skt. *ūḍhá* 'carried' for **uẓḍha-*<*uždha-* (*vah-* 'to carry' from *vaźh-*<IE *veĝh-*) ; Av. *gərəždā* 'complained', 3 sg. aor. mid. from *garəz-* = Skt. *garh-* ; Skt. *léḍhi* 'licks' (*lih-*), etc.

The same change was liable to take place in contact with other consonants : cf. Av. *fšumant-* 'possessing flocks' (*pasu-*, Skt. *paśú-*) ; Av. *frašna-* 'question', Skt. *praśná-* ; Av. *vīžibyō*, Skt. *viḍbhyás* (*viś-*). In these combinations there is not complete agreement between Indo-Aryan and Iranian, but in the case of the latter example at any rate an Aryan **vižbhyas* is attested. The Sanskrit development through *viẓbhyas* to *viḍbhyás* is exactly the same as that seen when *ẓ* (*ž*) was out of IE *s*, e.g. in *viprúḍbhyas* for **vipruẓbhyas* (*viprúṣ-* 'drop').

When immediately followed by *s* these palatals appear as *k* in Sanskrit in intervocalic position ; and the treatment is therefore the same as that of the second palatal series : *vákṣi* ' you wish ' (*vaś-*) like *vakṣyā́mi* ' I will speak ' (*vac-*). This is not a case of preservation of IE *k̂* (cf. Hitt. *wek-* ' wish ') but of its restoration. This is known for the following reasons :

(1) Iranian continues to distinguish the two types of combination derived from IE guttural + *s* and from IE palatal + *s* :

(a) *vakṣyāmi*, Av. *vaxšyā* (*wekʷ-*) ; *kṣatrá-* ' sovereignty ' : Av. *xšaθra-* ; *kṣáp-* ' night ' : Av. *xšap-*, cf. Gk. *ψέφας* ; *bhakṣ-* ' partake of, eat ' : Av. *baxš-* ' distribute ' ; *tvakṣ-* ' to be active ' : Av. *θwaxš-*.

(b) *kákṣa-* ' armpit ' : Av. *kaša* ; *ṛ́kṣa-* ' bear ' : Av. *arəša-* ; *dákṣiṇa-* ' right ' : Av. *dašina-*, cf. Gk. *δεξιός*, etc. ; *makṣū́* ' quickly ' : Av. *mošu*, cf. Lat. *mox* ; *rákṣas-* ' injury ' : Av. *rašah-* ; *takṣ-* ' to construct in wood ' : Av. *taš-*, cf. Hitt. *takš-* ' join ', etc. ; *kṣúdh-* ' hunger ' : Av. *šuδa* ; *kṣi-* ' to dwell ', *kṣétra-* ' field ' : Av. *ši-*, *šōiθra-* ' settlement '.

(2) The evidence from Iranian that there were two combinations in early Indo-Iranian both represented in Sanskrit by *kṣ* is further confirmed by evidence provided by Sanskrit itself, In cases where the group is followed by *t* it gives *k* or *ṣ* according to its origin : (a) *ábhakta* 3 sg. mid. *s*-aor. of *bhaj-*, cf. 1 sg. *ábhakṣ-i* ; cf. also *bhaktá-* ' food ' : *bhakṣ-* ' to eat ' ; (b) 3 sg. *tāṣṭi*, *caṣṭe* from *takṣ-*, *cakṣ-* ; *níraṣṭa-* ' castrated ' from *nirakṣ-*, etc. When the group is final the sibilant is elided according to the general rule. When the *k* goes back to the guttural series it invariably remains : *vāk* nom. s. from **vākṣ*, cf. Av. *vāxš*. When on the other hand the old palatal series is involved, although there are some instances of *k* (°*dṛk*, °*spṛk*, nom. sg. to °*dṛś-*, °*spṛś-*) the normal and regular treatment is *-ṭ* : *víṭ* ' settlement ' : *viś-* ; *vipāṭ* ' the river Beas ' : *vipāś-* ; *spáṭ* ' spy ' : *spáś-* ; *rā́ṭ* ' king ' : *rā́j-*, cf. Lat. *rēx* ; °*vāṭ* ' carrying ' : *vah-* ' to carry ', etc. Here the anomaly of the *k*-forms is explained by the dissimilatory influence of *ṛ* in the vicinity.

It is clear from this evidence that, where Sanskrit has a single combination *kṣ*, there were originally two different combinations. What immediately preceded *kṣ* in the prehistoric period of Indo-Aryan where the palatal series is involved is made clear by the forms of the nom. sg. quoted above. Just as nom. sg. *vā́k* is derived from earlier **vākṣ* by regular loss of the final sibilant, in the same way *víṭ* is derived from **viṭṣ*. At a period which probably did not very long precede the beginning of the recorded tradition this *ṭṣ* was changed into *kṣ* and thus confounded with original *kṣ*. The change is seen in the loc. pl. *vikṣú* (later supplanted by an analogical *viṭsu*) as opposed to the nom. *viṭ*(*ṣ*). Since the simplification of final consonant groups preceded this change, the cerebral, that is to say half the original combination, is preserved in the nom. sg.

It is necessary also to go beyond this *ṭṣ* since even from the point of view of Sanskrit this will not explain *caṣṭé*, etc. (**caṭṭe* would have resulted). In this connection the sandhi of two sibilants should be compared. There are instances of *s* + *s* becoming *ts* : *vatsyā́mi*, *ávātsīt* from *vas-* ' to dwell ', and of *ṣ* + *s* becoming *kṣ* : *dvékṣi* ' you hate ' from *dviṣ-*. Here again forms of the nom. sg.—*dviṭ vipruṭ*—show that there was an intermediate stage *ṭṣ* (which is obviously what would be expected in the case of this combination).

In both cases *ṭṣ* (>*kṣ*) may be derived from *ṣṣ* (Aryan *šš*). The treatment of the palatals before *s* is on the lines of their treatment before dental occlusives. Just as palatal *ś* + dental *t* produce the cerebral group *ṣṭ*, so palatal *ś* + dental *s* produced *ṣṣ* which then, in precisely the same way as the original sibilant combinations, became *ṭṣ* and finally *kṣ*.

In Iranian the development was somewhat different. Here *š* + *š* out of Aryan *ś* + *s* result in single *š*. This is in accordance with another rule for the sandhi of sibilants by which one can stand for two when they come together : cf. Skt. *ási* for *as* + *si*.

When palatal *c* is preceded by *s* the latter is changed to the palatal sibilant *ś* : e.g. *saścati* 3 pl. reduplicated present of *sac-* ' to associate with '. When *s* is followed by *ś* the two lose their identity and are merged as *cch* : *ducchúnā* ' misfortune ' from *dus* + *śuná-* ' prosperity '. Since the same sandhi results when *ś* is preceded by a dental (*pacchás* from *pad-* ' foot ' + suffix *-śas*) we may see here the same tendency to occlusion as in the other sibilant combinations noted above. In *tuccha-* ' empty ' (for **tuśya-*, cf. Khot. *tuśśa-*<**tusya-*) and *kacchapa-* ' tortoise ' (cf. the proper name *Kaśyapa-*) we have the same development of a group *-śś-* which has resulted from an early ' prakritic ' assimilation.

From the standpoint of Indo-European Skt. *ch* (*cch*) results from an original combination *sk̑* (*sk̑h*) ; and in these cases Iranian has *s* : *chid-* ' to cut ', Av. *saēd-*, Gk. σχίζω, Lat. *scindo* ; *chāyā́* ' shade ', Pers. *sāyah*, Gk. σκία ; *gácchati* ' goes ', Av.

jasaiti, Gk. *βάσκω* ; *pṛccháti* 'asks', Av. *pərəsaiti*, Lat. *poscit*. We must assume that in these cases Aryan *s* and *ś* were assimilated to *śś* which was then treated as above. It should be noted that Skt. *ch* is different from the other consonants among which it is classified in that it is always a long or double consonant. It is a matter of indifference whether *ch* or *cch* is written, though it is customary to use the former at the beginning of a word and the latter in the middle.

§ 16. Combinations Involving Sibilants

Indo-European *s* became *z* when followed by a sonant occlusive. This *z* became *ž* in primitive Indo-Iranian under the same conditions that *s* became *š* (Skt. *ṣ*). In Iranian *z* and *ž* are preserved : Av. *hazdyāt̰* 'would sit down' (*sad-*, Ir. *had-*), *mižda-* 'reward', Goth. *mizdō*. In Sanskrit they are eliminated in the following ways :

(a) Before unlike consonants *z* and *ẓ* (Aryan *ž*) are replaced by *d* and *ḍ* respectively : *ádga-* 'branch' : Pahl. *azg* ; *madgú-* 'a water bird', *majj-* 'to dive' (<**madj-*<**mazj-*) : Lith. *mazgóti* 'dive' ; instr. pl. *uṣádbhis*, *mādbhís* from *uṣás-* 'dawn', *mā́s-* 'month' ; *viprúḍbhis*, instr. pl. of *viprúṣ-* 'drop'.

(b) Followed by dental *d*, *dh*, *z* is elided and a preceding vowel *a* is changed to *e* : *edhí* 2 sg. impv. 'be' : Av. *zdī* (*as-*) ; *sedúr* for **sazdur* 3 pl. perf. of *sad-* 'to sit' : cf. Av. *hazdyāt̰* ; *nédiṣṭha-* 'nearest' : Av. *nazdišta-* ; *medhā́* 'wisdom' : cf. Av. *mazdå* 'wise' ; *miyédha-* 'food offered to the gods' : Av. *myazda-* ; *ādhvam* 'sit' 2 pl. impv. from *ās-* ; *śaśādhi* from *śās-* etc. This applies also to cases where *z* developed from original *d* : cf. *dehí*, *dhehí* above. A different treatment is seen in *addhā́* adv. 'certainly' : Av. O. Pers. *azdā*.

(c) Before *d*, *dh*, *ẓ* (which may be derived from IE *s* or from the old palatals, § 15) is elided with cerebralisation of the following consonant, and compensatory lengthening of a short vowel : *nīḍá-* 'nest', Lat. *nīdus*, Engl. *nest* (**nizdo-* from *ni* + *sed-*) ; *mīḍhá-* 'reward', Av. *mižda-*, O. Sl. *mĭzda*, Gk. *μισθός*, Goth. *mizdō* ; *dūḷábha-* 'difficult to deceive' (*dus* + *dabh-*, Vedic *ḷ* for *ḍ*) ; *pīḍ-* 'to press' (cf. *piṣ-* 'to pound'), *hīḍ-* 'to injure' (cf. *hiṃs-* 'id') *krīḍ-* 'to play' (cf. ON *hrista* 'shake') for *piẓḍ-*, *hiẓḍ-*, *kriẓḍ-* ; *astoḍhvam* 2 pl. mid. *s*-aor. of *stu-* 'to praise' ; *mṛḍīká-* 'mercy' (first syllable metrically long in the Veda): Av. *mərəždīka-*; *ūḍhá-* 'carried': *vah-* (<*uẓḍha-*, i.e. *uźh+ta*), *léḍhi* 'licks' (<*leẓḍhi*, i.e. *leźh+ti*). A preceding short *a* may be either lengthened (*tāḍhi*<*taẓḍhi* for *takṣ+dhi*, *áṣāḍha-*: *sah-*), turned into *o* (*vóḍhum* 'to carry': *vah-*; *ṣoḍhā́* 'sixfold': *ṣáṣ*) or turned into *e*: *tṛṇéḍhi* 'shatters' from the present base *tṛṇáh-* of *tṛh-*.

Occasionally *ẓ* is represented by *ḍ* even in this position: *didiḍḍhi*, *mimiḍḍhi*, *ririḍḍhi* from *diś-* 'to point', *mih-* 'to urinate', *rih-* 'to lick'; *ṣaḍḍhā́* beside *ṣoḍhā*. The same variation is seen in Pa. *niḍḍa-*, *kiḍḍā* which reflect a different dialectal treatment in Old Indo-Aryan.

Between consonants *z* disappeared without trace: *jagdhá-* 'eaten'<**jagzdha-* (*ja-ghs-ta-*), as also did *s* (cf. *ábhakta* above).

The combination sonant aspirate + *s* was in the Indo-Iranian period treated in the same way as the combinations of sonant aspirate + *t* noted above. That is to say, in intervocalic position *gh+s* gave *gžh*, and so on. Avestan preserves such voiced combinations though the aspiration as elsewhere is dropped: *aoγžā* 'you said' (<*augžha*, i.e. *augh+sa*), *diwžaiδyāi* 'to injure' (<*dibžha-*, i.e. *di(d)bh+sa*). Sanskrit has the surd combinations *kṣ*, *ts*, *ps* in these cases, but these have replaced original *gžh*, *džh*, *bžh*. The absence of aspiration in Vedic *adukṣat* 'milked', *dípsati* 'desires to injure', coming under the general rule (§ 2) of the dissimilation of aspirates, presupposes forms like *dhugžha-*, *dhi(d)bžha-* where the rule could operate. On the other hand in final position, where these groups were surd and de-aspirated from the beginning (Aryan °*dhukš* nom. sg.), there is never any loss of aspiration in Sanskrit.

Furthermore there are a few cases in Sanskrit where *jh*, *jjh* appear instead of *kṣ* where such a voiced combination is involved: *jájjhat-* 'laughing' (reduplicated formation from *has-*), *nirjhara-* 'waterfall', containing the root which normally appears as *kṣar-* (= Av. *γžar-*). These are Prakritisms, and further examples are quotable from Middle Indo-Aryan: Pa. Pkt. *jhāma-* 'emaciated': Skt. *kṣāmá-*; *jhāy-* 'to burn': Skt. *kṣāy-*; *jhīna-* 'exhausted': Skt. *kṣīṇá-*. Pali has also *jagghati* 'laughs' with *ggh* instead of the more usual treatment *-jjh-*. In all these cases voiced combinations of the type preserved in Av. *γžar-*, etc., are to be assumed, and the difference between these forms and the normal *kṣ* of Sanskrit is indicative of dialect variation in Old Indo-Aryan.

Something has already been said about combinations of sibilant + sibilant. There are three types involved which differ in respect of the date of their operation :

(1) By an old IE rule *s* + *s* could be represented by a single *s* : *ási* ' you are ', Av. *ahi*, Gk. εἶ (IE *esi* out of *es* + *si*) ; *áṃhasu* loc. plur., Av. *ązahu* (*áṃhas* ' distress ' + *su*).

(2) By a rule specific to Indo-Aryan, but one whose operation lay mainly in the prehistoric period, *s* + *s* became *ts* and *ṣ* + *s* became *kṣ* (through **ṭṣ*) : *vatsyáti*, *ávātsīt* from *vas-* ' to dwell ' ; *jighatsú-* ' hungry ' from *ghas-* ' to eat ' ; *dvekṣi* ' you hate ' from *dviṣ* ' to hate '. When these combinations are final only the first element remains, and in the case of the cerebral combinations, since the loss of the final sibilant took place during the stage **ṭṣ*, this appears as *ṭ* : nom. sg. *ukhāsrat* ' dropping from the pot ' (*sraṃs-*), *parṇadhvat* ' shedding leaves ' (*dhva*(*ṃ*)*s-*) ; °*dviṭ* ' hating ', *vipruṭ* ' drop '.

(3) Neuter nouns in *-as*, *-is*, *-us* make their loc. pl. in *-aḥsu*, *-iḥṣu*, *-uḥṣu* (optionally *-assu*, *-iṣṣu*, *-uṣṣu*). This is the latest type, and it is patently imitated from the external sandhi of the nom. sg., as has happened also in the *bh-* cases (*mánobhis*, *havírbhis*, etc.).

§ 17. The Cerebrals

In the cerebral series (*ṭ*, *ṭh*, *ḍ*, *ḍh*, *ṇ*, *ṣ*) Indo-Aryan presents an innovation as opposed to the rest of Indo-European. This somewhat infelicitous name, a mistranslation of Skt. *mūrdhanya-*, dates from the very earliest days of Indo-Aryan philology, and has stuck through long habit. Phonetically ' retroflex ' or ' retroverted ' more adequately describes these sounds which are distinguished from the dentals in that the tip of the tongue is turned back to the roof of the mouth. They are characteristically Indian sounds, and were certainly acquired by the Indo-Aryans after their entry into India. At the same time their use spread to the more easterly of the Iranian languages, those bordering on the Indo-Aryan area (Paštō, Khotanese, etc.). Cerebrals are also found abundantly in Dravidian, and they are certainly ancient in that family. They are also found prevalently in the Muṇḍa languages, but since they appear to be absent in Savara, a member of the family less affected by external influences than any other, they may not be original in that family. Since it is only in India and the immediate vicinity that an Indo-European language has developed such sounds, and since it may be safely assumed that an early form of Dravidian possessing such sounds was spoken over large portions of India prior to the advent of the Aryans, the influence of Dravidian may be held to be responsible to some extent for their emergence. At the same time, in native Indo-Aryan words they are explicable entirely out of the combinatory changes that affected certain consonant groups.

Most of these have been mentioned and can be classified quite simply : (1) Originally dental *t*, *th* became cerebral when preceded by *ṣ* (Aryan *š*) which in this position may either represent IE *s* (§ 9), or be a modification of Aryan palatals *ś*, *ź* (>Skt. *j* : IE *k̂*, *ĝ*) : *vṛṣṭí-* ' rain ' (*vṛṣ-* : cf. Gk. ἔρση, ἐέρση ' dew ', Ir. *frass* ' rain shower '), *váṣṭi* ' wishes ' (*vaś-*, cf. Hitt. *wekzi*), *áṣṭrā* ' goad ' (*aj-* ' to drive ' : Lat. *ago*, etc.) ; (2) Originally dental *d*, *dh*, became cerebral when preceded by *ẓ* (Aryan *ž* of the same twofold origin as *š*) ; since in this case the sibilant was elided the resulting cerebrals *ḍ*, *ḍh* (*ḷ*, *ḷh* in the *Ṛgveda*) came to stand alone in intervocalic position : exx. *nīḍá-*, *ūḍhá-*, etc., see above ; (3) The occlusion of the first part of the group *ṣṣ* (which may be for *ṣ* + *s* or *ś* + *s*) produced *ṭṣ* ; finally the *ṭ* came to stand alone, the simplification of the consonant group in this position (*dviṭ*, *viṭ*, above), while intervocalically the group developed further to *kṣ* ; (4) Originally dental *n* became cerebral *ṇ* under wider conditions, namely when preceded in the same word by *ṣ*, *r* or *ṛ*, except when a palatal or dental intervened : *kāraṇa-* ' cause ', etc.

In addition to these rules by which cerebrals developed there are others which have been more controversial, but which can now be regarded as established. A notable case is the change of IE *l* followed by dental to cerebral, commonly referred to as Fortunatov's law. Though long opposed, this rule is to be accepted. Examples of this phonetic change are as follows: *paṭa-* ' cloth ' <**palta-*: Arm. (<Ir.) *partak* ' veil ', Npers. *pardah*, OSlav. *platĭno* ' linen cloth ', etc.; *paṭala-* ' fold, layer, stratum ', *puṭa-* ' fold, thing folded ' <**paltala-*, **pulta-*: cf. the IE root *pel-* ' to fold ' in Gk. διπλός ' twofold ', Lat. *duplus*, *duplex*, Eng. *fold*, etc.; *sphaṭika-* ' crystal ', *sphuṭa-* ' clear ': cf. the IE root *sp*(*h*)*el-* ' to be bright ' appearing in Sanskrit also in *sphul-*/*sphur-* ' to glitter ', *sphuliṅga-* ' spark '; *hāṭaka-* ' gold ': OSl. *zlato*, Russ. *zoloto*; *jaṭhára-* ' belly ': Goth.

kilpei 'womb'; *kuṭhāra-* 'axe': cf. *kúliśa-* 'id' and Lat. *culter* 'knife', etc.; *jaḍa-* 'cold, stiff, numb, dull' <**jalda-*: cf. Lat. *gelidus*, etc.; *āḍhyá-* 'rich': cf. *ṛdh-* 'to prosper', a root which originally had *l* (Gk. ἀλθομαι etc.); *paṇa-* 'stake, stipulation, hire, wages': Lith. *pel̃nas* 'gain, profit, earnings'; *kuṇi-* 'lame in the arm' <**kulni-*: cf. Gk. κυλλός (<*kulnos*); *pāṣāṇa-* 'stone, rock': Germ *Fels*, etc.; *bhaṣ-* 'to bark', *bhāṣ-* 'to speak': Lith. *bal̃sas* 'voice', Germ. *bellan*, etc.[1]

In addition to these types of combinatory change, there has also been a considerable amount of spontaneous cerebralisation in Sanskrit, and it is possible to list a fair number of words in which a cerebral represents an original dental without any combinatory change being involved. Some instances of this kind have long been recognised, particularly where later Sanskrit has cerebral as opposed to dental in the Veda: e.g. *aṭ-* 'to wander', *ḍī-* 'to fly', *naḍá-* 'reed', as opposed to Vedic *at-*, *dī-*, *nadá-*. Other cases such as *maṇí-* 'jewel' (Lat. *monile*) and *sthū́ṇā* 'column' were also early recognised, and the cerebral was put down to Prakritic influence. Recently, however, it has become clear that this process has occurred in Sanskrit to a much greater extent than previously admitted, and that it is in most cases a genuine Sanskrit and not a Prakrit phenomenon. The following further examples illustrate the spontaneous change to cerebral: *avaṭá-* 'hole in the ground' as opposed to Vedic *avatá-* 'well'; *kuṇṭha-* 'blunt': NPers. *kund*, Bal. *kunt*; *piṇḍa-* 'lump, mass': Arm. (<Ir.) *pind* 'compact'; *paṇḍita-* 'wise', *paṇḍā* 'wisdom': NPers. *pand* 'good advice'; *kūṭa-* 'hammer' from **kūta-*, cf. the root in Engl. *hew*, Lith. *káuju* 'strike', OSl. *kovati* 'forge, hammer', etc.; *koṭi-* 'tip, point': Lat. *cautes*, *cautis* 'sharp, jagged rock'; *kaḍevara-* (>*kalevara-*) 'corpse': Lat. *cadaver*.

A small number of Sanskrit cerebrals are of Prakrit origin, e.g. *bhaṭa-* 'soldier' (<*bhṛta-*), *naṭa-* 'actor', cf. *nṛt-* 'to dance', *bhaṭṭāraka-* 'lord', cf. *bhartṛ-*, and *aṭani-* 'tip of bow' beside earlier *ā́rtnī*. There are some which occur in Dravidian loanwords: *eḍa-* 'goat', *kuṭi-* 'hut, house', *kaṭhina-* 'hard', *guḍa-* 'ball', for which see Chapter VIII. In late Sanskrit some words with initial cerebral appear, which cannot be explained out of either Indo-Aryan or Dravidian: such are

[1] The change did not take place in words in which *l* was changed to *r*: e.g. *ū́rṇā* 'wool' (Lilt *vìlna*, ch.), *jartu-* 'womb' as opposed to *jáṭhára-* etc.

ṭīkā ' commentary ', *ḍamara-* ' uproar ' and *ḍhakkā* ' a large drum '.

§ 18. Miscellaneous Changes

The phonetic changes undergone by a language are for the most part subject to general laws, but when all has been done to elucidate these some exceptions will remain. For instance one can hardly doubt that Skt. *kéśa-* ' hair ' is the equivalent of Av. *gaēsa-* ' id ', since an associated *u-* stem is available in both cases (Av. *gaēsav-* : cf. Skt. *keśav-a-*). Contamination with *kesara-* ' mane ' (cf. Lat. *caesaries*) may explain the change in Sanskrit. Such sporadic changes are found more abundantly in the case of certain consonant combinations. The combination *pl* normally remains when *l* does not become *r* (*plu-* ' swim, float ') but it is changed to *kl* in *klóman-* ' lung ' as opposed to Gk. πλεύμων, Lat. *pulmō* ' id ' (the original meaning was ' swimmer, that which floats '), and in *viklava-* ' distressed ' as opposed to *viplava-*, *vipluta-*. In the case of *tṛp-* ' to steal ' IE *klep* (Gk. κλέπτω, Goth. *hlifan*, etc.) has been altered to *tlep* : a confusion of the groups *kl* and *tl* is common the world over. A similar change of the occlusive, also sporadic, is found in the case of the group *-tn-*. It remains normally (*rátna-*, *pátnī*) but in the feminines of certain adjectives in *-ita* it appears changed to *-kn-* : *ásiknī*, *páliknī* (*ásita-* ' black ', *palitá-* ' grey-haired ') Later examples of this tendency are seen in Pkt. *savakkī* (beside *savattī*) ' co-wife ', Panj. *saukkan*, and in Panj. *arak* ' elbow ' (*aratní-*).

The sibilants are liable to certain changes when in proximity to one another. Initial *s* was changed to *ś* in Sanskrit when *ś* followed in the next syllable : *śváśura-* ' father-in-law ' : Av. *xᵛasura-*, Gk. ἑκυρός, Lat. *socer* ; *śmáśru-* ' beard ' ; cf. Lith. *smakrà*, Ir. *smech* ' chin '. The same assimilation in the reverse order is seen in *śaśá-* ' hare ' for **śasa-* : cf. Khotanese *saha-*, Germ. *Hase*, Engl. *hare*. On the other hand *s* is preserved in the roots *śās-* and *śas-* because the change was impossible in forms like *śā́sti*, *śastá-* (but cf. *śaśana-* for *śāsana-* in the N.W. Prakrit). There is also a change of *s* to *ś* when *ṣ* follows : *śúṣka-* ' dry ' : Av. *huṣka-*, *ślakṣṇá-* ' soft ', Pers. *lašin*, cf. Gk. λαγνός, λαγαρός, Lat. *laxus*, Engl. *slack* ; *śliṣ-* ' to adhere ', *śleṣmán-* ' phlegm ', cf. Engl. *slime*, etc.

Since in cases where a final *ṣ* has disappeared an initial *s* is replaced by *ṣ*, e.g. *ṣaṭ* ' six ' (**ṣaṭṣ*<**saṭṣ*) and *virā-ṣā́ṭ* ' overcoming men ', it is likely that *śúṣka-*, etc., are the result of secondary dissimilation of an intermediate **ṣúṣka-*. This rule does not apply where the system of related forms is strong enough to prevent it, e.g. *vásu-*, *vásīyas-*, *vásiṣṭha-*, though even here isolated forms with *ś* are handed down.

In Vedic *kṣumánt*=Av. *fšumant-* (:*paśu-*) we have an isolated example of a change which has parallels in Iranian (cf. Khot. *kṣārma-* ' shame '=*fšarəma-*).

More or less isolated cases of the reduction of three consonant groups in Sanskrit appear in *stána-* ' breast ' : Av. *fštāna-*, Pers. *pistān* Toch. B *pëścane*; *hradá-* ' lake ' : cf. Av. *γzrād-* ' to flow ; and *tváṣṭar-* ' n. of the divine architect '=Av. *θwōrəštar-*.

From the Indo-European period there was a certain instability about *r, v, y* as the second members of initial consonant groups. This accounts for equations like Skt. *bhañj-* ' to break ', Ir. *bongaim*, Skt. *bhuj-* ' to enjoy ', Lat. *fungor* on the one hand and Lat. *frango, fruor* on the other. Similarly in the case of *v* Skt. *ṣaṣ*, Lat. *sex*, etc., are opposed Av. *xšvaš*, etc., and Skt. *kṣip-* ' throw ' to Av. *xšvaēw-*.

§ 19. Final Consonants

In final position consonants and consonant groups receive in many respects special treatment. This was true also in the prehistoric period ; for instance the aspiration in nom. sg. °*dhuk* as opposed to its absence in *adukṣata* is due to the fact that at an early period the combination *gh* + *s* became -*kš* in final position, whereas intervocalically it became *gžh*. But the tendency to special development in final position has become much stronger by the historical period, and its features anticipate in some respects the later Prakritic developments of Indo-Aryan.

Of the occlusives only the unvoiced series *p, t, ṭ, k* are allowed to stand in absolutely final position, and in their place the corresponding voiced series *b, d, ḍ, g* are substituted before voiced consonants and vowels. The sonantisation before initial vowel is a special characteristic of Sanskrit, and it anticipates the voicing of all intervocalic surds in later times.

Consonant groups were drastically reduced during the period immediately preceding the historical record, and in this respect Vedic contrasts remarkably with early Iranian. Here too the same general tendency was at work which later resulted in the assimilation of all consonant groups. With few exceptions (e.g. nom. sg. *ū́rk* from *ū́rj-* ' vitality ') not more than one consonant may stand at the end of a word, however many were there to begin with. This had serious results in some aspects of the morphology, and led to some grammatical innovations. Thus the terminations are lost in the case of the second and third persons singular of the root and *s*-aorists, and the *s* of the *s*-aorist suffers the same fate in these persons when preceded by a consonant, so that the formations lose their grammatical clarity. On account of this the root aorist comes to be abandoned in Classical Sanskrit except in the case of roots in long *ā*, and new extended formations are provided in the case of the *s*-aorist (*ánaiṣīt* for *ánais*).

The weakest of the final consonants was *s*. In final position this is weakened to the breathing *ḥ* (*visarga*). In sandhi the same change occurs before *k, p* and the sibilants. Preceded by *ā* it is elided before voiced consonants and vowels. The same thing happens when it is preceded by *a*, but here the *-as* is in most contexts replaced by *o*. In the non-Sanskritic dialects of Old Indo-Aryan there was an alternative development of *-as* to *-e*. An example of this is found even in the *Ṛgveda* (*sūre duhitā* ' daughter of the sun ') ; later it is a characteristic of the Eastern (Māgadhī) Prakrits, and examples are also found in some of the Kharoṣṭhī inscriptions of the North-West. These developments of final *-as* began in the Indo-Iranian period, and in Avestan likewise *-ō* is the common representative of final *-as*, beside which there is a dialectal variant *-ə̄* corresponding to the *-e* of Māgadhī, etc. Final *s* is preserved only before *t, th*, while before *c, ch* it exists in the modified form *ś*.

When preceded by *i, u, s* became originally *š* (§ 9) which would normally become Sanskrit *ṣ*. In place of this *ṣ*, before voiced consonants and vowels *r* is substituted. The intermediate stage was presumably *z* and in this case there is complete difference of treatment of a phoneme at the end of a word from its treatment internally. This external sandhi was extended to the sandhi of compounds (*durdama-*, etc.) but old forms like *dūḷábha-* (*dūḍ°-*<*duẓḍ°-*) and *kárūḷatī* show that this is not original but analogical. Likewise the sandhi of neuter *s-* stems in declension (*havírbhis, havíḥṣu* ; . *mánobhis, manaḥsu*) is in imitation of the external sandhi.

Final *r* was weakened in much the same way as *s*. Finally it is represented by visarga (*punaḥ*), but it is retained when preceded by *a* and followed by a vowel (*punar āgacchati*). Elsewhere it behaves in sandhi exactly like *s*. It even becomes *s* before *t* (*punas tam*) a development which is certainly analogical rather than phonetic. In the case of uninflected forms with final *r* preceded by *i* or *u* it is impossible to tell from any sandhi context whether the word originally ended in *s* or *r*; thus though we may conclude that the original form of the adverb meaning 'outside' was *bahír* because of Pa. Pkt. *bāhira-* 'external' (: Skt. *bā́hya-*) derived from it, its form cannot be phonetically determined from Sanskrit itself, and the stem is usually given as *bahís*. This weakening of final *r* had no doubt a good deal to do with the abandonment of a large number of the old neuters in *r*. They were already in decline, but the phonetic weakness of final *r* no doubt hastened the process (the stem *ū́dhas* 'udder' beside *ū́dhar* is due to the tendency to confuse *s* and *r* in final position).

VOWELS

§20. Correspondences

The correspondences between the vowels of Sanskrit and those of other IE languages may be gathered from the following table, in which the examples are quoted after the presumed IE original vowel:

a: Skt. *ájra-* 'plain', Gk. *ἀγρός* 'field', Lat. *ager*, Engl. *acre*; *ápa* 'away, from', Gk. *ἄπο*, Lat. *ab*; *ánti* 'opposite, near', Gk. *ἀντί*, Lat. *ante* 'before'; *ániti* 'breathes', cf. Gk. *ἄνεμος* 'wind', Lat. *animus*; *áyas* 'metal', Lat. *aes*; *nas-* 'nose' (instr. *nasā́*, etc.), OHG *nasa*, O. Sl. *nosŭ*; *haṃsá-* 'goose', Gk. *χᾱ́ν*, *χήν*, Lat. *anser*, Germ. *gans*; *yaj-* 'to sacrifice, worship', *yajñá-* 'sacrifice', Gk. *ἅγιος*, *ἁγνός* 'holy'; *śad-* 'fall', Lat. *cadit*.

e: Skt. *bhárati* 'bears', Gk. *φέρει*, Lat. *fert*, O. Ir. *berid*; *asti* 'is', Gk. *ἔστι*, Lat. *est*; *áśva-* 'horse', Lat. *equus*; *sána-* 'old', Lat. *senex*, O. Ir. *sen*; *sádas* 'seat', Gk. *ἕδος*; *paśú-* 'domestic animal', Lat. *pecu*, O. Pruss. *pecku*, Lith. *pekus*, Goth. *faíhu*; *mádhu* 'honey, mead', Gk. *μέθυ*, AS. *medu*; *mádhya-* 'middle', Lat. *medius*, Gk. *μέσσος*.

o: Skt. *ávi-* 'sheep', Gk. *ὄις*, Lat. *ovis*; *páti-* 'husband, lord', Gk. πόσις, Lat. *potis* 'able'; *ápas-* 'work', Lat. *opus*; *ánas-* 'wagon', Lat. *onus* 'burden'; *ásthi* 'bone', Gk. ὄστεον, Lat. *os*; *dáma-* 'house', Gk. δόμος, Lat. *domus*, O. Sl. *domŭ*; *dadárśa* 'saw', Gk. δέδορκε; *vṛ́kas* nom. sg. 'wolf', Gk. λύκος.

ā: *mātár-* 'mother', Lat. *māter*; *bhrā́tar-* 'brother', Lat. *frater*; *svādú-* 'sweet', Gk. ἁδύς, ἡδύς, Lat. *suāvis*; *ásthāt* 'stood', Gk. ἔστᾱ, ἔστη; *bāhú-* 'arm', Gk. πῆχυς; *snā-* 'to bathe', Lat. *nāre*; *áśvā* 'mare', Lat. *equa*.

ē: Skt. *rā́j-*, *rā́jan-* 'king', Lat. *rēx*; *mā́s-* 'month', Gk. μήν, Lat. *mensis*; *sāmi-* 'half-', Gk. ἡμι-, Lat. *sēmi-*; *mā́* 'not' (prohibitive), Gk. μή, Arm. *mi*; *pitā́* 'father', Gk. πατήρ.

ō: *ā́s-* 'mouth', Lat. *ōs*; *vāk* nom. sg. 'speech', Av. *vāxš*, Lat. *vōx*; *āśú-* 'swift', Gk. ὠκύς, Lat. *ōcior* 'swifter'; *pā-* 'to drink', Gk. πώνω, Lat. *pōtus*; *nápāt* 'grandson', Lat. *nepōs*; *pā́t* nom. sg. 'foot', Gk. (Dor.) πώς; *vṛ́kās* nom. pl. 'wolves', Goth. *wulfōs*.

i: Skt. *imás* 'we go', Gk. ἴμεν; *vidmá* 'we know', Gk. ἴδμεν; cf. Lat. *video*; *tiṣṭhāmi* 'I stand', Gk. ἵστημι; *diví* 'in heaven', Gk. ΔιϜί; *riñcánti* 'they leave', Lat. *linquunt*.

ī: Skt. *jīvá-* 'alive', Lat. *vīvus*; *vīrá-* 'man, hero', Lith. *výras*; *pī́van-* 'fat', Gk. πίων.

u: Skt. *śrutá-* 'heard', Gk. κλυτός; *rudhirá-* 'red', Gk. ἐρυθρός, Lat. *ruber*; *snuṣā́* 'daughter-in-law', O. Sl. *snŭcha*, Gk. νυός, Lat. *nurus*; *udán-* 'water', Gk. ὕδωρ, °ατος, Lat. *unda* 'wave'.

ū: Skt. *dhūmá-* 'smoke', O. Sl. *dymŭ*, Lat. *fūmus*; *bhrū́-* 'brow', Gk. ὀφρῦς, AS. *brū*; *pū-* 'to be rotten', *pū́ti-* 'putrefaction', Gk. πῡ́θω, Lat. *pūs*, *pūteo*, Goth. *fūls*.

ai: Skt. *édhas* 'fuel', Av. *aēsma-*, Gk. αἴθω 'burn', *devár-* 'brother-in-law', Gk. δᾱήρ (<δαιϜήρ), Arm. *taigr*, Lat. *lēvir*.

ei: Skt. *éti* 'he goes', Lith. *eĩti*, Gk. εἶσι; *héman* 'in winter', *hemantá-* 'winter', Gk. χείμων, Alb. *dimεn*; *devá-* 'god', Lith. *dẽvas*, Lat. *dīvus*, Osc. *deivai* 'divae'; *dehī́* 'embankment, wall', Gk. τεῖχος, Osc. *feihúís* 'muris'.

oi: Skt. *véda* 'I know', Av. *vaēδa*, Gk. οἶδα, Goth. *wait*; *té* 'those', Gk. τοί; *bhares* 'you should bear', Gk. φέροις.

au: Skt. *ójas-* 'strength', Av. *aogarə* 'id', cf. Lat. *augustus*; *śoṣa-* 'drying up', Lith. *saũsas* 'dry', Gk. αὖος 'id', AS. *sēar*.

eu: Skt. *bódhāmi* 'I observe', Gk. πεύθομαι 'find out, learn'; *oṣati* 'burns', Gk. εὕω 'burn, singe', Lat. *ūro*; *jóṣati* 'enjoys', Gk. γεύομαι 'taste', Goth. *kiusan* 'choose'.

ou : Skt. *loká-* ' space, room, world ', Lith. *laũkas* ' plain ', Lat. *lūcus* ' grove ' ; *bodháyati* ' he awakes ' (trans.), Lith. *pa-si-baudyti* ' to awake oneself ', O. Sl. *buditi* ' to wake, rouse ' ; *sūnós* gen. sg. of *sūnú-* ' son ', Goth. *sunaus*, Lith. *sūnaũs*.

āi : Skt. dat. sg. fem. *sénāyai*, *devyaí*, Gk. χωρᾳ, Lat. *equae*, etc.

ēi : Skt. *áraikṣam*, *s*-aor. of *ric-* ' to leave ', cf. Gk. ἔλειψα.

ōi : Skt. instr. pl. *vŕ̥kais*, etc., Av. *daēvaiš*, Gk. λύκοις ; dat. sg. *tásmai* ' to him ', Av. *aētahmai*, cf. Gk. ἵππῳ, etc.

āu : Skt. *naús* ' ship ', Gk. ναῦς, cf. Lat. *nāvis*.

ēu : Skt. *dyaús* ' sky ', Gk. Ζεύς ; *áyaukṣam* ' I joined ', cf. Gk. ἔζευξα.

ōu : *gaús* ' cow ', Gk. βοῦς ; *aṣṭaú* ' 8 ', Goth. *ahtau*.

Sonant Liquids and Nasals :

r̥ : Skt. *pr̥ccháti* ' asks ', Lat. *poscit* (<**porscit*), OHG *forscōn* ; *pitŕ̥ṣu* loc. pl. of *pitár-* ' father ', Gk. πατράσι ; *vr̥ttá-* ' turned ', Lat. *versus*, *vorsus* ; *mr̥tá-* ' dead ', cf. Lat. *mortuus*, *mors*, Lith. *mir̃ti* ' to die ', O. Sl. *sŭmrĭtĭ* ' death '.

l̥ : Skt. *mr̥dú-* ' soft ', Lat. *mollis*, cf. Gk. ἀμαλδύνω ' soften, weaken ' ; *pr̥thú-* ' broad ', Gk. πλατύς ' flat ' ; *vŕ̥ka-* ' wolf ', Av. *vəhrka-*, Lith. *vil̃kas*, Goth. *wulfs*.

n̥ : Skt. *matá-* ' thought, considered ', *matí-* ' thought, idea ' (*man-*), Gk. αὐτόματος ' of one's own accord ', Lat. *commentus*, *mens*, *mentio*, etc. ; *hatá-* ' slain ' (*han-*), Gk. φατός (: φόνος, etc.) ; *así-* ' sword ', Lat. *ensis* ; *nā́ma* ' name ', Gk. ὄνομα, Lat. *nōmen*, Hitt. *lāman* ; *a-* ' not ' in *ájñāta-* ' unknown ', Gk. ἄγνωτος, Lat. *ignōtus*, O. Ir. *ingnad*.

m̥ : Skt. *śatám* ' hundred ', Gk. ἑκατόν, Lat. *centum*, Goth. *hund*, Welsh *cant*, Lith. *šim̃tas* ; *gáti-* ' going ', Gk. βάσις, Lat. *in-ventiō*, Goth. *gaqumþs* ; *abhrá-* ' cloud ', Av. *awra-*, Lat. *imber* ; *saptá* ' seven ', Gk. ἑπτά, Lat. *septem*.

§21. Notes on the Vowels

The most characteristic distinguishing feature of Indo-Iranian as opposed to the remaining IE languages is the possession of only a single vowel *a* corresponding to the three vowels *a*, *e*, *o* elsewhere, and likewise in the case of the long vowels, *ā* corresponding to *ā*, *ē*, *ō*. It is clear that this uniformity is due to a special Indo-Iranian development, since the other languages are in substantial agreement with each other in the distribution of the vowels *a, e, o*. Furthermore the palatalisation of the velar series which occurs in Indo-Iranian before *a* only when it corresponds to *e* in the other languages (*ca* = Lat. *que*, etc.) testifies to its existence in these positions in the prehistoric period of Indo-Iranian. The confusion of *a* and *o* is found also outside Indo-Iranian, in Germanic, Slavonic and Hittite. It is not possible to say for certain whether we have here independent parallel development in the various language groups, or whether this fusion of *o* and *a* is an ancient dialectal feature of Indo-European. Certainly in the case of Indo-Iranian and Slavonic, which show other signs of special affinity, the possibility of an ancient common change is deserving of consideration. The change *e* to *a* on the other hand is found only in Indo-Iranian, and it is one of the most characteristic features distinguishing this family from the rest of Indo-European.

The Indo-Iranian development of the sonant nasals (to *a*) is the same as that of Greek, and it is one of the several features that links these two branches. Sonant nasals as such are found nowhere, but have been reconstructed for Indo-European from theoretical considerations. The sonant liquids have in the same way been replaced in most languages by combinations of vowel +*r* or *l*. Only Indo-Iranian preserved the vocalic *r̥*, which represents also original vocalic *l*. In Sanskrit there exists only one case of vocalic *l*, namely the root *kl̥p-* ' to arrange '. Because of Vedic *kl̥p-*, Av. *kəhrp-* ' form, body ', which are usually compared with Lat. *corpus* it is generally considered that this *l̥* is of secondary origin, but this is not altogether certain. Nevertheless as a general rule Sanskrit is much more consistent in turning *l* into *r* in its vocalic form than in its consonantal form. On the basis of sonant *r̥* (which is attested in Indo-Iranian) and *l̥* the sonant nasals can be safely reconstructed. They occur in the same conditions, that is to say by the suppression of the associated guṇa vowel which leaves them to function as vowels, and their treatment in various languages is similar. Thus we have for *r̥* in Gk. αρ(ρα), in Balto-Slavonic *ir* and in Germanic *ur* similarly for *n̥* Gk. *a*, B. Sl. *in*, Germ. *un*. It is clear that the assumption of original sonant nasals is as much necessary to account for the variation in the associated vowel in the various languages as it is by the principles of apophony which are briefly noted below.

Among the vowels of Primitive Indo-European it has been customary to postulate the so-called ' shwa ' (ə̥). This is based on such comparisons as Skt. *pitár-* ' father ' : Gk. πατήρ, etc. Skt. *sthitá-* ' stood ' : Gk. στατός, etc. In such cases the ə was considered to represent the reduced grade of the original long vowels, corresponding to the zero grade of the short vowels *e*, *a*, *o*. It was supposed to have become *i* in Indo-Iranian, and *a* in all the other IE languages. I have shown elsewhere [1] that this reconstruction is without justification, and that it was due to a faulty analysis of the Sanskrit words concerned. In these words the *i* is IE *i* and it is part of the suffix, not part of the root. Skt. *sthitá-* should be analysed *sth-itá* and its formation therefore differs from that of the related words, so that the phonetic reconstructions based on these comparisons become void. The same analysis is to be adopted in all the relevant forms: *sth-íti-* ' standing ' (cf. *sníh-iti-*) *sth-irá-* ' firm ' (cf. *sthéyān*, *sthéman*, Pa. *theta-*), aor. 3 sg. *ásth-ita* ' stood ' (cf. *avād-i-ran*, etc.), perf. 1 pl. *dad-ima* (contrast pres. *dadmás*), *stan-i-hi* ' roar ' (cf. *stanayitnú-*, etc.), *s-itá-* ' bound ' (cf. *sinā́ti*, *siṣāya*, etc.), *ś-itá-* ' sharp ' (cf. Ved. *śiśayá-*, Av. *saēni*, etc.), *krav-íṣ-* ' raw flesh ' (cf. *roc-íṣ-*, etc., and Lith. *kraũjas*, etc.). It is also clear, and established by many examples in Sanskrit that in the zero grade the original long vowels are completely elided: e.g. in the present tense of *dā* and *dhā*, *dadvás*, *dadmás*, *datté*, *datsé*, *dadhvás*, *dadhmás*, *dhatse*, *dhatsva*, etc. (likewise in Iranian. Av. *dadəmahi*, *dasta*, *daste*, *dazde*, *dadəmaide*, etc.); the same elision is found in the participles *dattá* ' given ' and °*tta* (*devátta-* ' given by the gods ', etc.) and in Av. *ptar-* ' father ' beside *p-itár*.

If this ə had been confined to the comparatively few words in which Sanskrit *i* appeared to correspond to *a* in the other languages, it would never have acquired very great importance in Indo-European theory. It was due to its becoming a basic element in the early theories of apophony that it acquired such importance in the traditional theory of Indo-European. In the comparative dictionaries this ə, so insecurely founded, appears in the utmost profusion in IE reconstructions, particularly in the case of the so-called disyllabic roots. Skt. *i* is also suffixal when it appears after such roots and the H which constituted the final element of the root is elided (*táritum*<**tar*H-*itum*). The

[1] *TPS.* 1949, pp. 22–61.

theory of apophony was further complicated by the invention of original long diphthongs, possessing a weak grade *əi* which was held to have developed into *ī* (sometimes into *-ay-*), but there is nothing in the facts to justify the assumption of such long diphthongs or of the weak grades which are supposed to be derived from them. In addition a second 'shwa', supposed to be a reduced grade of the short vowels was introduced by certain authorities. As a result the theory of apophony, which, as will be seen below, is really of the utmost simplicity, became extraordinarily complicated. With the discovery of Hittite *ḫ*, and the subsequent rise to popularity of the laryngeal theory, the main features of the old theory were transferred to the new. IE H was identified with the old shwa (*ə*), and it was believed that all its varieties could function in a vocalic as well as a consonantal function like the liquids and nasals. It has even been common to use the sign *ə* to indicate IE H in its consonantal function ($ə_1$, $ə_2$, $ə_3$), and the whole presentation of the laryngeal theory has continued to be vitiated by the original error of the invention of 'shwa'. Needless to say the objections that apply to 'shwa' in the old form of the theory apply to it with equal force in the new. There is no satisfactory evidence to show that H in any of its varieties could function as a vowel and it is certainly never represented in Sanskrit by *i*.

The effects of IE H on the vowels have already been noticed. By the restoration of H a very considerable simplification of the vowel system is achieved.

(i) The long vowels *ā*, *ē*, *ō* (>Skt. *ā*) may be long through vṛddhi, in which case they have developed out of the short vowels *a*, *e*, *o*. But there is another series of long vowels which are long by nature, e.g. the *ā*, *ē*, *ō* in *stā-* 'to stand', *dhē-* 'to place' and *dō-* 'to give' (Skt. *sthā-*, *dhā-*, *dā-*). In such cases the laryngeal theory analyses the long vowel into short vowel + several varieties of H (*dhe*H_1, *ste*H_2, *de*H_3) the quality of the vowel being determined by the following laryngeal. Thus in all cases long vowels are of secondary origin.

(ii) The varieties of guṇa vowel are partly due to qualitative alternation in Indo-European. This was particularly so in the case of the alternation *e/o* (φέρω : φόρος). But some cases of *o* are left over which have been considered to be original (ὀστέον 'bone') and *a* can only rarely be put down to vocalic alternation (Lat. *quater*, etc.). Cases of 'original' *a*, and *o* according to the laryngeal theory go back to H_2 and H_3 followed by the guṇa vowel which was in itself undifferentiated (H_2*ent-* ' front ', Hitt. *ḫant-*, Gk. ἀντί, etc., H_3*est-* ' bone ', Hitt. *ḫaštai*, Gk. ὀστέον, etc.). Thus we are reduced to a single original guṇa vowel, conventionally written *e*, which is the state of affairs to which Indo-Iranian again returned at a later period as a result of special developments of its own.

A few words of caution should be added in illustration of the fact that the laryngeal theory has not yet acquired a completely satisfactory form. It is never possible to be certain for instance that the vowel *o* is original, since alternating *e*- forms may be missing by accident. Furthermore there exist some *o*/*a* alternations which the theory does not altogether account for. As regards original *a* the absence of any *ḫ* in forms like Hitt. *appa* ' away ' can only be explained away by making the theory uncomfortably complicated. It must be admitted in such a case that the actual evidence available does not allow us to go any further than IE *apo*.

(iii) IE *ī*, *ū* have in all cases developed out of *i*H, *u*H. The special developments of *r̥*, *l̥*, *n̥*, *m̥* followed by H have already been outlined. In this way the old reconstructions of long sonant liquids and nasals can be dispensed with.

These simplifications effected, the IE vowel system is reduced to very few primitive elements. There is only one purely vocalic element to begin with, which may be written *e*. The development of three varieties (*e*, *a*, *o*) and of the corresponding long vowels can be explained on the basis of the effect of laryngeals and of vocalic alternation. In addition there are six elements which may under certain conditions (between consonants, initially before, and finally after consonants) function as vowels—*i*, *u*, *r̥*, *l̥*, *n̥*, *m̥*—but elsewhere (between vowels, etc.) function as consonants—*y*, *v*, *r*, *l* ,*n*, *m*. As regards diphthongs it should be noted that the second element is consonantal, and that from the point of view of Indo-European it would be more consistent to write *éyti* ' goes ', *gews*- ' taste ', etc.

§ 22. Quantitative Alternation: Apophony

The purely vocalic element (Skt. *a*, IE *a*, *e*, *o*) was subject to a quantitative gradation of the following type. It could be elided in any syllable, radical or suffixal, or alternatively it could be lengthened. In other words any syllable may appear in the normal grade (*a*), the strengthened grade (*ā*), or the zero grade. This gradation is of fundamental importance in Sanskrit grammar, and its importance was fully recognised by the Indian grammarians. They gave the name *vṛddhi* to the strengthened grade and *guṇa* to the normal grade. The weak or zero grade they did not name because they constructed their grammatical system in such a way that they started from the zero grade as the basic grade and from this they derived the guṇa and vṛddhi grades by two successive processes of strengthening. The comparative philologists differ from the Indian grammarians in that they regard the guṇa as the normal grade and from it derive the vṛddhi and zero grades by the opposite processes of strengthening and weakening.

The operation of this gradation may be illustrated by a few examples :

(1) Normal grade : *sádas* ' seat ', *sácate* ' associates with ', *padás*, gen. sg. of *pád-* ' foot ', *ghas-* ' to eat ', *dabhnóti* ' injures ', *hásati* ' laughs '.

(2) Extended grade : *sādáyati* ' causes to sit ', *rātiṣā́cas* nom. pl. ' associating with liberality ', *pā́dam* acc. sg. ' foot ', *ghāsá-* ' fodder ', *ádābhya-* ' that cannot be injured ', *hāsa-* ' laughter '.

(3) Zero grade : *sedúr* ' they sat ' < **sazdur*, cf. Av. *hazdyāṯ* ' would sit ', *sáścati* 3 plur. ' they associate ', *upabdá-* ' trampling under foot ', *á-dbh-uta-* ' wonderful ' (literally ' that cannot be harmed, impregnable ', of divine beings), *jákṣiti* ' eats ' (i.e. *ja-ghs-i-ti*), *jákṣati* ' laughs ' (*ja-hs-ati*, cf. Vedic *jájjhatī* and Pa. *jagghati* for different treatments of $h+s$).

The same three grades apply to all suffixal elements. Thus in the case of the *n*-suffix we normal grade (guṇa) in voc. *rā́jan*, loc. *rā́jani*, zero grade in gen. sg. *rā́jñas*, extended grade in acc. sg. *rā́jānam* from the stem *rā́jan-* ' king '. The same gradation applies to all suffixal elements.

Fundamentally this alternation *a*/*ā*/zero is all there is to the system of apophony. Some complications are caused by the combinations of *a* with semivowels, etc., and by some phonetic changes. These may be briefly summarised as follows :

(1) When *a* is lost the semivowels (*y*, *v*) assume their vocalic form in the appropriate phonetic context : *yájati* ' sacrifices ' ; *ijyā́* ' sacrifice ' ; *vápati* ' sows ' ; *uptá-* ' sown '. When the semivocalic element comes second, i.e. in the diphthongs, the

original Indo-Iranian alternation *āi*, *ai*, *i*, *āu*, *au*, *u* is modified in Sanskrit to *ai*, *e*, *i*; *au*, *o*, *u* of which *e* and *o* ceased to be diphthongs in pronunciation. The guṇa and vṛddhi grades acquire the alternate forms *ai*, *au*, *e*, *o*/*āy*, *āv*, *ay*, *av* according as a consonant or vowel follows.

Exx. Normal grade; *jétum* 'to conquer', *jáyati* 'conquers', *śrótum* 'to hear', *śrávaṇa-* 'hearing'.

Strengthened grade: *ájaiṣam* 'I conquered' (*s*.aor.), *jigā́ya* 'he conquered' (perf.), *áśrauṣam* 'I heard', *śuśrā́va* 'he heard'.

Zero grade: *jitá-* 'conquered', *śrutá-* 'heard'.

(2) The liquids *r*, *l* were vocalised under the same conditions. Though *ḷ* has been mostly merged with *ṛ* Indo-Iranian preserves the original sonant pronunciation, so the apophony remains simple. Guṇa: *kártum* 'to do'; Vṛddhi: *cakā́ra* 'did'; Zero: *kṛtá* 'done'/*cakré* 3 sg. perf. atm. 'did'.

(3) The nasals were likewise capable of functioning as vowels, but here the situation is complicated by the change, in Indo-Iranian as in Greek, of the sonant nasals to *a*. The series is therefore (1) *an*, *am*, (2) *ān*, *ām*, (3) *a*/*n*, *a*/*m*, e.g. (1) *gámana-* 'going', *hánti* 'slays', (2) *jagā́ma* 'went', *jaghā́na* 'slew', (3) (a) *hatá-* 'slain', *gatá-* 'gone', (b) *ghnánti* 'they slay', *jagmúr* 'they went'.

(4) Long *ā* is sometimes original, that is to say it appears in the guṇa position, e.g. in the roots *dhā* 'to place', *dā* 'to give', and *sthā* 'to stand'. It is elided in the zero grade like the ordinary guṇa vowel, e.g. *dadhmás*, *dadmás*. We have seen that this *ā* is for *a*H (or in the IE system *ē*, *ā*, *ō* are for $e\text{H}_1$, $e\text{H}_2$, $e\text{H}_3$). Thus we are dealing with the ordinary guṇa vowel in this apophony, and H which cannot function as a vowel but is elided in such positions.

(5) The combinations *i*H, *u*H resulted in *ī*, *ū*, while in combination with corresponding diphthongs (-*ei*H-, -*eu*H-) the H disappeared without trace. So there arises an apophony *e*/*ī*, *o*/*ū*, etc., beside the normal diphthongal apophony: (1) *nétum* 'to lead'/*náyati* 'leads'; *hóman* 'invocation'/*hávana-* 'id'. (2) *anaiṣam* 'I led'/*nāyaka-* 'leader'; *juhā́va* 'called'. (3) *nītá-* 'lead', *hūtá-* 'called'.

(6) Sonant *ṛ* followed by H resulted in *īr*, *ūr*, while in the corresponding guṇa grades it disappeared. In these cases we have the weak grade *īr*, *ūr* in apophony with *ar*, *ār*: (1) *tártum*

'to cross', *pipárti* 'fills'; (2) *tā́rayati* 'causes to cross'; (3) *tīrṇá-* 'crossed', *pūrṇá-* 'filled'.

(7) When *n̥* and *m̥* were followed by H the result in Sanskrit is in the first case *ā*, in the second case *-ān-* (examples occur only before *t*). Hence the apophony *sanóti* : *sātá-* ; *dā́myati*, *damáyati*, *dāntá-*.

(8) There are some deceptive cases where no real apophony is involved. An example is *pā́-tum* 'to drink' : *p-ītá-* 'drunk'. Here the *ī* of the second form is suffixal and therefore cannot be in apophonic relationship to the radical *ā* of the first form.

(9) Roots consisting of more than two consonants admit of two types of guṇa grade : (1) *vártate* 'turns', etc., (2) *trásati* 'is afraid', etc. Usually roots belong to one or the other type and keep to this in the guṇa grade (and in vṛddhi which follows the guṇa in this respect) but double forms occur in some cases, e.g. from *dṛś-* 'to see' we have the series : Weak grade *dṛṣṭá-*, guṇa 1 *darśáyati*, guṇa 2 *drakṣyā́mi*, vṛddhi 1 *dārśanika-*, vṛddhi 2 *ádrākṣam*.

(10) Final vṛddhied forms terminating in semivowel, liquid or nasal may lose this final element : *sákhā* 'friend' (acc. *sákhāyam*, stem *sákhi-*), *áśmā* 'stone' (acc. *áśmānam*, stem *áśman-*), *dātā́* 'giver' (acc. *dātā́ram*, voc. *dātar*, dat. *dātré*, etc.). The tendency is found elsewhere in Indo-European (Lat. *sermō*, etc.) but nowhere as consistently as in Sanskrit (e.g. Gk. πατήρ, Lat. *pater* beside Skt. *pitā́*).

This vocalic gradation was connected with the Indo-European accent. In Sanskrit the connection between alternation of grade and alternation of accent is clear from many examples : *émi* 'I go' : *imás* 'we go' ; *śrótum* 'to hear' : *śrutá-* 'heard' ; *ásti* 'is' : *sánti* 'are' (Lat. *est*, *sunt*) ; *hánti* 'slays' : *ghnánti* 'they slay' (Hitt. *kuenzi* : *kunanzi*) ; *átti* 'eats' (*ád-ti*) : *dánt-* 'tooth' ('eater'). From such examples it is clear that the zero grade is due to the unaccented position of the syllable, and that the guṇa grade is properly the grade of the accented syllable. There are of course many examples in Sanskrit, as in other languages where accent and apophony do not agree, e.g. Skt. *vṛ́ka-* 'wolf', *ṛ́kṣa-* 'bear', *tṛ́ṇa-* 'grass', *vípra-* 'sage, brahmin'. These however create no difficulty since it is known that in many cases the position of the accent has changed in course of time. This is obviously the case in the examples quoted since they are all in origin adjectival formations (e.g.

tṛ́ṇa- (<**tṛṇá-*) is ' what pierces ', cf. *tṛṇátti*) and it was the rule that such formations were suffixally accented. It is also very common in Sanskrit for nominalised adjectives to throw back the accent on to the first syllable.

The application of the above accent rule in its full rigidity would allow only one guṇa syllable in any word. The words quoted are of that type, but the majority of Indo-European words, in any language, are not so. This is mainly due to two reasons. Firstly, when inconvenient or grammatically less clear forms would result, the elimination of the unaccented guṇa vowel was resisted, or if eliminated it was quickly restored. So we have as the gen. sg. of *pad-* ' foot ' not **bdás* which would have resulted from the rule, but *padás* with guṇa vowel in unaccented position. The existence of *dánt-* ' tooth ' (' eater ', cf. *sánt-* ' being ' : *as-*) beside *adánt-* ' eating ' gives us one clear case where a guṇa vowel in unaccented position has been restored by analogy. Secondly the nature of the Indo-European accent underwent a change during the later Indo-European period. It had the power to reduce neighbouring unaccented syllables for a certain period of time, and then, in later Indo-European it ceased to have this effect. Consequently forms like those quoted above which show the full effects of apophony must be considered as belonging to the most ancient stratum of Indo-European. But after the accent ceased to have the effect of reducing adjacent syllables, Indo-European was creating new formations in abundance, a faculty retained by the individual languages particularly in their early stages. The very numerous formations of the type *yajatá-* ' adorable ', *darśatá-* ' worth seeing ', *devásya* ' of the god ', etc., etc., had their origin in this later period when the accent had ceased to have the power to influence the vocalism of the surrounding syllables.

§23. Qualitative Alternation: Metaphony

There existed in Indo-European also a qualitative alternation of the guṇa vowel, and this is well preserved in most branches of the family : e.g. Gk. λέγω ' I say ' : λόγος ' word ' ; Lat. *tego* ' I cover ' : *toga* ' gown ' ; Russ. *vezú* ' I carry ' : *vóz* ' cart, load ' ; Engl. *sing* : *sang*. The alternation affects both the guṇa vowel, as in the examples above and its vṛddhied extension (Gk. δοτήρ : δώτωρ ' giver '). In Indo-Iranian this alternation has entirely disappeared owing to the confusion of the vowel qualities *a, e, o* in *a*. Consequently this Indo-European alternation has no significance for Sanskrit grammar, and it deserves brief mention only because the student of the comparative grammar of Sanskrit will meet it in the material cited from the related languages.

This alternation, like the quantitative alternation is clearly connected with the Indo-European accent. This is evident from the juxtaposition of such forms as Gk. *δαίμων, δαίμονος* on the one hand and *ποιμήν, ποιμένος* on the other. The rule is clear that *e* is the normal grade of a syllable which bears the accent and has always borne the accent (Gk. *ἔστι, ἔπος, νέος*, etc.). Accentual changes and the workings of analogy have to some extent contrived to obscure the picture but this central fact remains beyond doubt. An example of the working of analogy may be mentioned; the termination of the genitive singular appears in some languages in a form that represents IE *-es*, in others in a form that represents IE *-os*. Since this termination was sometimes accented and sometimes unaccented, we may reasonably assume that the two forms were originally differentiated according to accent. Later in the individual languages one form was generalised, sometimes the *-es* form and sometimes the *-os* form being chosen.

The fact that the IE accent should have two quite different effects is bound up with what has been said above about the accent. The elision of the guṇa vowel was frequently resisted for morphological reasons, or if eliminated it was restored. Such retained or restored guṇa vowels were then, possibly at a later period, affected in a different way by the accent, so that *o* appears in place of *e*. Or again the main accent of a word may have changed with the result that the vocalism of the syllable which lost the accent was altered. For instance the numerous words of the type represented by Gk. *δαίμων* belong to a class (agent-nouns) which was originally suffixally accented. The type of formative *-τωρ, -μων*, etc., beside older *-τήρ, -μήν* seems to have come into existence as the result of such an accent shift.

§24. Sanskrit and Indo-European Accent

The last two sections illustrate the importance of the part played by accent in Indo-European. In dealing with the morphology the accent is an indispensable element, without which no proper grammatical analysis can be made. For this reason the accent will be continually under discussion during the succeeding chapters. Here a few general remarks will suffice.

The full technical details of the Vedic and early classical accent of Sanskrit, and of the various methods used to denote them, are somewhat complicated but the main principles are as follows. Each word had normally one accent whose position varies from word to word. Any syllable from the first to the last may bear the accent (e.g. *ápaciti* ' retribution ', *dhāráyati* ' holds ', *namasyáti* ' respects ' and *aparāhṇá-* ' afternoon ' are accented on the first, second, third and last syllable respectively). No simple set of rules can be given to determine on which syllable of a word the accent will fall.

Certain words were enclitic by nature and never bore the accent. These are such particles and pronominal forms as *ca* ' and ', *mā* ' me ', *me* ' of me ', etc. Elsewhere the accent might be dropped in certain circumstances. (1) In the vocative a noun lost its accent except at the beginning of a sentence, when it was accented on the first syllable regardless of its natural accent. (2) The finite verb in the main clause of a sentence is unaccented unless it appears at the beginning of a sentence, in which case it retains its natural accent. In dependent clauses it retained its accent whatever its position. In this case a verbal preposition is most commonly compounded with the verb and loses its accent, e.g. *prá gacchati* ' he goes forward ', *yadi pragácchati* ' if he goes forward '.

The accent so indicated is termed by Pāṇini *udātta-* ' raised ' and the rise was one of pitch or musical tone. The main accent affected also the pronunciation of the following syllable, since the return of the voice to the normal level was effected during the enunciation of this syllable. The accent of the syllable immediately following the udātta is termed *svarita-* and it is described by Pāṇini as a combination (*samāhāra-*) of udātta and anudātta. That is to say it begins at the high pitch of udātta and descends in the process of utterance. There exists also an independent svarita which arises secondarily out of the contraction of *íya* to *yà*, etc., in which case the main accent of the word is the svarita. This is a post-Vedic development since the metre of the earlier texts shows that the contraction had not yet taken place.

The main accent affected the pronunciation of the preceding syllable. This was pronounced lower than normal and it is termed by Pāṇini *sannatara-*. The remaining unaccented syllables were termed *anudātta-*. Thus out of one main accent of a word there arose four different varieties of pitch : *udātta-*, *anudātta-*, *svarita-*, *sannatara-*. Since however all this variation is dependent entirely on the main accent, only that needs to be noted, as above. A separate notation is needed for the independent svarita (*vṛkyàs*, *tanvàs*, etc.) but even that may be dispensed with for the Veda if the words are transcribed according to the pronunciation (*vṛkíyas*, *tanúvas*).

The complications of the accent detailed above were responsible for an unnecessarily complicated system of notation adopted by the Vedic schools. According to the usual system, that adopted in the *Ṛgveda* for instance, the principle is to mark the syllable preceding the udātta, the sannatara, with a subscript line, and the dependent svarita following the udātta by a vertical stroke above. The udātta itself is left unmarked. This achieves the same purpose in a less convenient manner than the method adopted in modern transcription, and by some Vedic schools. The modern recitation of the *Ṛgveda* follows the notational system to the extent of pronouncing the sannatara lowest and the svarita highest musically of syllables and ignoring the udātta altogether. This is a secondary development although it may be old, and at variance with the teachings of Pāṇini which are in complete agreement with the findings of comparative philology.

The system of accentuation described above has for centuries been totally extinct in spoken Sanskrit as it has in all forms of Indo-Aryan derived from it. When exactly the accent died out in ordinary spoken use it is impossible to say with certainty. It was certainly a living thing in the time of Patanjali and even later than Patanjali, Śāntanava treated of the subject in his *Phiṭsūtra*. According to the author of the *Kāśikā* commentary (*c.* A.D. 700) the use of accentuation was optional in the spoken language, which probably means that in practice it was no longer used at this time. On the whole it is unlikely that the use of accentuation survived long after the Christian era. In Middle Indo-Aryan we may take it that the change occurred much earlier, at the very beginning of anything that could be called Middle Indo-Aryan.

The old Indo-European accent was lost, at some time or other in most Indo-European languages just as in Indo-Aryan. Accentual systems derived directly from Indo-European are found only in Greek and Balto-Slavonic. They may also be deduced from the phonetic developments classified as Verner's law for an early stage of Germanic. The existence of accurate information about the accentuation of two of the oldest members of the family, Sanskrit and Greek, is of the utmost value for the understanding of Indo-European.

A comparison of the accentuation in those languages in which it is preserved reveals basic agreement, though to a greater or lesser extent all languages have innovated in detail. The position of the accent in Indo-European for instance is frequently established by the correspondence of Sanskrit and Greek: e.g. *bhárati* 'bears': Gk. φέρει; *śrutá-* 'heard': Gk. κλυτός; *gurú-* 'heavy': Gk. βαρύς; *vácas* 'word': Gk. ἔπος, etc., etc. In other cases they differ showing innovation on one side or the other: *mātár-* 'mother': Gk. μήτηρ; *bāhú-* 'arm': Gk. πῆχυς, etc. The tendency to innovate is also evident from the frequent disagreements between accent and apophony, whether in individual languages (Gk. ἴδμεν 'we know' as opposed to the more original accentuation of Skt. *vidmá*) or in all (Skt. *vṛ́ka-*, Gk. λύκος, etc.). In the latter case the innovation is of the Indo-European period. By means of comparison of the individual languages, by the study of apophony so intimately bound up with accent, and by the proper understanding of the part played by accent in the morphology, it is possible to form a clear and accurate idea of the Indo-European accent. The details are part of the morphology and will be found in the chapters concerned.

The nature of the old accent in Sanskrit and Greek is known from the technical descriptions handed down and partly in the case of Sanskrit from the traditional recitation of the Veda. It was in both languages predominantly musical, and not a matter of stress. This is confirmed by the fact that in both languages metre is completely independent of accent, depending solely on the length of syllables. From this agreement it is deduced that the same kind of accent prevailed in late Indo-European. But, as we have already seen, there must have been a change between early and late Indo-European in this respect. Earlier the accent had the power to reduce the neighbouring syllables, indicating a strong stress element. In the later period this power was certainly lost and this agrees with what is known about the accent of Sanskrit and Greek.

Beside the normal acute accent Indo-European possessed under certain circumstances a circumflex accent. This is clear from the agreement between Greek and Lithuanian, e. g. circumflex accent in gen. sg. fem. Gk. *θεᾶς*, Lith. *gerõs*, gen. pl. masc. Gk. *θεῶν*, Lith. *gerų̃*, instr. pl. masc. Gk. *θεοῖς*, Lith, *vilkaĩs*, as opposed to acute accent in nom. sg. fem. Gk. *θεά*. Lith. *geró-ji* (*gerà*). In such cases Sanskrit has the ordinary udātta accent as elsewhere, and it does not, as Indo-European did, distinguish between the two types of accent. The independent svarita which came to exist in Sanskrit as a separate type of main accent is, as we have seen, a post-Vedic creation and unconnected with differences of accent type in Indo-European.

Nevertheless traces of the old circumflex have revealed themselves in the Veda from a study of the metre. In certain cases the metre makes it clear that a long *ā* is to be pronounced disyllabically, e.g. *gām*, *dyām* as *gaam*, *dyaam*, and the termination of the genitive plural *-ām* as *-aam*. In such cases the corresponding Greek forms frequently have the circumflex accent, and this gives reason to believe that metrical peculiarity of the Veda is the effect of the circumflex accent of Indo-European.

CHAPTER IV

THE FORMATION OF NOUNS

§ 1. General Remarks

The Sanskrit nominal stem may coincide with the root, as happens in a minority of cases, but usually it is derived from it by the addition of a suffix. These suffixes are very numerous and are inherited from Indo-European. They are not, as occurs in some languages (e.g. Engl. *man-ly, man-hood*) derived from what were originally independent words, but are in every case analysable into their component parts, that is to say the individual consonants or semivowels of which they are composed. These primary elements include nearly all the available phonemes, but the ones most commonly used are *r, n, s, t, y/i, v/u, m,* H and *k*. They may appear either with guṇa, i.e. preceded by the thematic vowel (*-ar, -an, -as,* IE *er-, en-, es-,* etc.) or in their weak form (*-r, -n, -s*). The thematic vowel itself may appear as a suffix but naturally, since elsewhere it is always a question of the guṇa grade of a consonantal suffix, only in final position (*bhav-an-a-, udr-á,* etc.). The IE primary suffixes could be added either to roots or to words already ending in another suffix : e.g. the suffix *-as* is added to the root in *vácas-* 'speech', to a base having the suffix *n* in *réknas-* 'inheritance, property', the suffix *t* in *srótas-* 'stream' and the suffix *v* in *pī́vas-* 'fat'. Since the root itself could originally function freely as a noun, that is to say was a word in the full sense, there is no difference in principle between primary and secondary derivation of this kind. A suffix could be added to any word, whether it already had a suffix or not, and the nature of the process was precisely the same. The result was that owing to the very large number of possible combinations of the primary elements, the number of these compound suffixes in all IE languages is very large, and the complexity of nominal stem formation in Sanskrit and the allied languages is entirely a matter of the multifarious combination of a comparatively small number of primitive elements.

In the descriptive and synchronistic grammar of Sanskrit the various suffixal combinations are treated as units, which is what they have in fact become in the course of the development of the language. For the historical and comparative treatment of the subject a more radical approach is needed. Here it is necessary, as is done in the following pages, to start from the single, primitive elements, and in the exposition to build up the whole suffixal system from them in the way that it had developed in the prehistory of the language.

Between the original simple suffixes, as so analysed, no discernible distinction of meaning or function can be found. In some ways they have no meaning. Thus an ancient IE word *wet* 'year' appears in Hittite as such (also in Sanskrit reduced to *-ut* in *parut* 'last year'); in Greek it appears with the suffix *-os* as (F)έτος, without anything being added to the meaning. Likewise in Sanskrit neuter action nouns with suffixes (*-as*, etc.) do not differ fundamentally in meaning from roots used in the same sense: *dvíṣ-* 'hatred': *dvéṣas* 'id.', etc. Of course when several words derived from the same root with different suffixes appear side by side, differences of meaning between these words usually develop, but this is a matter of idiom and nothing to do with the ultimate nature of the suffixes as such. What applies to the simple suffixes applies equally to the compound suffixes. In the examples quoted above the suffixes *-tas*, *-nas* and *-vas* are used in precisely the same way as the simple suffix *-as*. Hittite has a series of suffixes *-sar*, *-tar*, *-mar*, *-var* (with variant *n*-stems) making neuter action nouns of exactly the same nature, and this accurately reflects Indo-European usage. In the course of time specialisation of usage in the case of various suffixes has developed in all languages, but this is secondary and it is possible in some cases to show how it has come about.[1] The most important distinction in nominal derivation in early Indo-European was not between the different suffixes simple or compound, but in a difference of accentuation according to which a word formed with the same suffix functioned either as an action noun or agent noun/adjective. Accented on the root it was an action noun and neuter, accented on the suffix it was an agent noun or adjective and originally of the so-called 'common gender'. The system is preserved to some extent in Sanskrit and is exemplified by such doublets as *bráhma* n.

[1] E.g. in the case of the comparative suffix- *tara*, see p. 149.

'prayer': *brahmā́* m. 'priest', *yáśas* n. 'glory': *yaśás-* m. 'glorious'. The Sanskrit examples are not very numerous, and are only found in the case of a small number of suffixes; they are in fact the last remnants of a system dying out. In earlier Indo-European on the other hand the system was of very great extension and importance, and it is fundamental to the understanding not only of the formation of nouns but also of their declension.

The thematic vowel stands apart from the other suffixes in many ways. Its original function seems to have been to produce agent nouns or adjectives from the various primitive neuter nouns, e.g. *udr-á* 'otter': Gk. *ὕδωρ* 'water'. It was in fact an alternative method to the above in the formation of such nouns. This is its normal use in Hittite, which indeed ignores the method indicated above. The numerous neuter thematic stems which are only enlargements of simple consonantal stems (Skt. *añjan-a-* n.: Lat. *unguen*, etc.) appear to be a later development and are ignored by Hittite.

In the descriptive grammar of Sanskrit nominal derivatives are divided into two major classes, primary and secondary, in the terminology of the Indian grammarians *kṛt* and *taddhita*. The former comprises all those formations which are derived directly from a root by means of a suffix (e.g. *vácas* 'speech' from *vac-*) and the second those which are derived from the basis of nouns already made (e.g. *áśvavant-* 'possessing horses' from *áśva-* 'horse'). Convenient as this twofold classification is from the point of view of Sanskrit itself, it has no fundamental or ancient significance from the point of view of Indo-European. For one thing the same suffix is found functioning in both ways, and when a suffix is found to function predominantly or even exclusively in secondary derivation, it is historically a case of secondary specialisation. The suffix *-vant* is normally a secondary suffix in Sanskrit, but it is primary in such examples as *árvant-* 'steed', *yahvánt-* 'young', also in Av. *bəzvant-* 'abundant', *ərəzvant-* 'straight', and in Hitt. *daššuwant-* 'strong'. It was as a primary suffix that this, like other suffixes which have become predominantly secondary in Sanskrit, first came into being. A historical account of nominal stem formation must therefore be arranged entirely according to the external form of the suffixes concerned.

Secondly many formations which from the point of view of

Sanskrit are primary, are in origin secondary formation. Thus *udrá-* ' otter ' which counts as a primary derivative (*ud-rá-*) is clearly in origin a secondary derivative meaning ' connected with water, water-animal ' (*udr-á-*, cf. Gk. ὕδωρ n. ' water ', etc.). In origin all types of such thematic adjectival derivation are secondary, but owing to the obsolescence of the old neuter action nouns on which they were based they acquired the nature of primary derivatives. In so far as such suffixes remained living suffixes, they were employed as units in the later period in a primary way. Not all formations in *-rá* have the same history as *udr-á-*, etc., but the type of derivation came into existence in this way.

Again in the old IE dichotomy of the types *bráhma* : *brahmā́* we have in the second of these pairs a type of secondary derivation. Logically and presumably historically the neuter action noun precedes the agent noun. The form *brahmā́* ' one connected with *bráhma* ' presupposes by its meaning the existence of the more primitive neuter. In the Sanskrit system such agent noun formations count as primary formations, and this is what the majority have become owing to the disappearance of the corresponding neuter types. This is illustrated very well by the agent nouns in *-tár* (*dātár-* ' giver ', etc.). Hittite has nouns in *-tar* but only neuter action nouns. It is clear that the relation between the two types is the same as that between *bráhma* and *brahmā́* and that *dātár-* was originally ' one connected with giving ' corresponding to an obsolete **dā́tar* n. ' giving '. When the neuter type went out of use it became a primary formation connected directly to the verbal root.

In the development of the system of nominal stem formation in the prehistoric period, certain general tendencies will be observed, notably :

(1) The decline of the neuters. Whole categories of neuter nouns with ancient IE suffixes such as *-er* and *-el* have become almost extinct in most IE languages except Hittite ; but the letters *r* and *l* play a great part in IE nominal derivation, so that although the original types have disappeared, they have left great masses of further derivatives which cannot be explained without them. In other cases the old neuter nouns have not disappeared, but have been transferred bodily to the masculine and feminine classes. This is particularly the case with stems in *i* and *u*, and the action nouns in *-ā*, but it occurs frequently elsewhere.

(2) The growth of grammatical gender. In the earliest period the threefold classification did not exist. There was no feminine and nouns were divided into two types, 'neuters' and 'common gender', the latter so called because the masculine and feminine developed out of it. This is the state of affairs actually found in Hittite, and it is further confirmed by many survivals in other languages (Lat. *ferens* masc. and fem., Skt. *suvā́sās* nom. sg. m. and fem., etc., etc.). The feminine gender arose in the later period of Indo-European, and strictly speaking only then is it possible to speak of gender in the proper sense of the term

(3) The great variety of possible suffixes that could arise from the various combinations of the primitive suffixal elements led necessarily to a process of selection, so that many combinations which are known to have existed have not survived to the Vedic period. Thus out of a series of suffixes forming neuter nouns, and based on the primitive suffixes *-er* and *-en*, namely IE *-er/r̥*, *-mer/mr̥*, *-wer/ur*, *-yer/ir*, *-ter/tr̥*, *ser/sr̥* and *-en/n*, *men/mn/*, *wen/un*, *-yen/in*, *-ten/tn*, *-sen/sn*, only *-men/mn* remains as a living suffix in Vedic in the formation of neuter nouns. The others are better represented in agent-noun and adjectival derivatives which is in accordance with what has been said above about the decline of the neuter formations.

(4) Another feature of great importance is the growing use and extension of the thematic vowel (Skt. *a*, IE *e/o*) as a final suffix. It has been said above that the original use of this vowel as a suffix was probably to form adjectival derivatives, in which case it was accented. Later its use spread as an extension of consonantal stems. This tendency is well known in the further development of Indo-Aryan (Class. Skt. *pāda-* 'foot' replacing *pād-/pad-*, etc.), but it had been actively at work for long in the prehistoric period. Thus Skt. *áñjana-* n. 'ointment' replaces an older consonantal stem which is preserved in Lat. *unguen*. As a result of this development thematic stems became by far the most numerous type both in Sanskrit,[1] and in other languages which reflect the late IE stage. In Hittite, on the other hand, which reflects an earlier stage of Indo-European there is not such a great preponderance of *a*-stems.

[1] In the *R̥gveda* 45 per cent of all nominal stems end in *-a*.

§2. Root Nouns

Root nouns are an ancient type very much in decline in the earliest recorded Indo-European languages. In Sanskrit they are preserved better, on the whole, than elsewhere. Such are *pā́d-/pad-* 'foot': Lat. *pēs, pedis, vā́c-* 'speech': Lat. *vōx, rā́j-* 'king': Lat. *rēx*. They are usually either masculine or feminine, but in the case of verbal roots functioning as action nouns they are normally feminine (*dyút-* f. 'brilliance', etc.). The old neuter type of root noun (cf. Lat. *mel, fel*, etc.) is practically extinct. Of the few examples mention may be made of *śám* 'welfare' which is indeclinable, *ván-* 'wood, tree' which is probably neuter (like its extension *vána-* n.) and *ā́s* 'mouth': Lat. *ōs*.

This type of stem was originally subject to the laws of apophony: Vṛddhi or Guṇa in the Nom. Sg., Guṇa in Acc. Sg. and Nom. Pl. and the weakened form of the root in the other cases. This system is partially preserved in the case of some common nouns (n. sg. *pā́t*, gen. sg. *padás*) but the general tendency is for it to be levelled out. In this levelling out any of the three grades may come to function throughout the declension, the weak form of the stem being normal in the case of verbal roots used as nouns: (1) *vā́c-* 'speech', gen. sg. *vācás*, (2) *spáś-* 'spy', nom. sg. *spáṭ*, (3) *ṛ́c-* 'hymn', nom. sg. *ṛ́k*, gen. sg. *ṛcás*.

Roots functioning as nouns may be used either as action or agent nouns (in the latter case they are feminine): *drúh-* (1) 'injuring, injurer', (2) 'injury'; *dvíṣ* (1) 'hatred', (2) 'enemy'; *bhúj-* (1) 'enjoyment', (2) 'enjoyer'. When used as the second member of compounds they have the latter function only.

This type which has a moderate extension in the Vedic language, becomes more restricted later in accordance with the pre-existing tendency. That is to say with one exception—when such stems are used as the last member of compounds. In this case both in the Vedic and Classical language roots may be freely used as nominal stems. They are also used more widely in the Vedic language as infinitives of the type *dṛśé* 'to see' than otherwise independently. Elsewhere as we shall see the Vedic infinitive tends to preserve old nominal stems which have otherwise become extinct.

Roots ending in short *-u, -i, -ṛ* cannot function as nominal stems. In circumstances where other roots do so they take the suffix *-t*: *°jit-* 'conquering', *mít-* 'pillar', *stút-* 'praise', *°bhṛt* 'bearing', etc.

§ 3. Thematic Stems based on the Root

Stems with the thematic suffix *-a* can be formed on the basis of stems ending in all the other suffixes, and these are best treated in connection with the various types of stem to which the thematic suffix is added. The most simple type of thematic stem is that formed directly from the root. These stems may be divided into two classes according to the usual scheme: action nouns and the like with accent on the root, and agent nouns, etc., with accent on the suffix, final accented *-á* having here as elsewhere an adjectival function. Certain pairs are quotable where both types occur in connection with the same root: *códa-* 'goad': *codá-* 'instigator'; *éṣa-* 'speed': *eṣá-* 'speeding'; *vára-* 'choice': *vará-* 'suitor'; *śóka-* 'glow': *śoká-* 'glowing'. The same type of alternation is familiar also in Greek, *τόμος* 'a cut': *τομός* 'cutting', etc.

In Greek and in other languages which distinguish the vowels *o* and *e* the vowel of both root and suffix is *o*. Original *o* is attested by Sanskrit in some cases where a guttural has not been palatalised: *kéta-* 'intention', *gáya-* 'property', *ghaná-* 'striker, solid'. Such an arrangement can hardly be original since normally *e* would be expected in the accented and *o* in the unaccented syllable. It is likely therefore that we have here a phonetic compromise between the nominal and adjectival types. In Sanskrit there are distinct traces of a variation *o/e* between the two types in the suffixal vowel in the case of roots ending originally in gutturals. The final guttural in these cases is usually preserved in the case of action nouns with radical accent and palatalised in the other type: e.g. *bhóga-* 'enjoyment': *bhojá-* 'bountiful'; *róga-* 'disease': *rujá-* 'breaking, destroying'; *śóka-* 'glow, heat; grief': *śucá-* 'bright'; *yóga-* 'union': *a-yujá-* 'without an associate'; *árgha-* 'value': *arha-* 'worth, valuable' (accent not quoted). The distinction is found in some cases where the accent is on the suffix in both types: *arká-* 'ray': *arcá-* 'brilliant'; *roká-* 'lustre': *rocá-* 'radiant'. Here the accent of the action nouns has been secondarily transferred to the suffix. The variation between the palatalised and non-palatalised form indicates an original variation in the quality of the suffixal vowel according to the position of the accent.

In action nouns the radical syllable commonly has guṇa in agreement with the related languages: *dáma-* 'house', Gk. *δόμος*, Lat. *domus*, Russ. *dom* (IE *dem-* 'to build'). Nouns of this type are *áya-* 'going, course', *háva-* 'invocation', *tára-* 'crossing', *véda-* 'knowledge', *jóṣa-* 'enjoyment' and so forth. There is however another type, for which it is difficult to find parallels outside Indo-Iranian, with vṛddhi of root and, paradoxically, usually having the accent on the suffix. These appear to have been formed on the basis of the vṛddhied nom. sg. of root nouns, just as later Vedic *pāt* nom. sg. 'foot' is extended to *pā́da-*. Typical instances are: *bhārá-* 'burden' (cf. the vṛddhi in Gk. *φώρ* 'thief'), *dāvá-* 'fire', *tārá-* 'crossing', *sādá-* 'sitting', *sāvá-* 'libation', *vāsá-* 'residence'; with radical accent, *vā́ra-* 'choice', *mā́na-* 'opinion'.

Irregular accent is found in the whole class of such nouns which are formed from verbal roots combined with a prefix: *saṃgamá-* 'coming together, union', *abhidrohá-* 'injury', etc.; and in a minority of cases elsewhere: *bhogá-* 'bend', *jayá-* 'victory', *javá-* 'speed'. These irregularities show that a tendency to confuse the two types was beginning; *jayá-* and *javá-* for instance also mean 'victorious' and 'speeding' which is their original significance, but at a time when the importance of the old distinction was diminishing, they came to be used indiscriminately in both functions. Here, as elsewhere throughout the formation of nouns, the Vedic accent is not original, but in spite of such exceptions the old system remains predominant enough for its principles to be clearly seen.

The oldest type of apophony among agent noun/adjectives of this class is that which has the weak grade of the root due to the accented suffix: *vṛdhá-* 'increaser' (: *várdha-* 'increase'), *budhá-* 'intelligent' (: *bódha-* 'understanding'), *śucá-* 'bright' (*śóka-* 'glow'), *turá-* 'victorious' (*tára-*, *tā́ra-* 'crossing'), *priyá-* 'dear', *kṛśá-* 'thin', *rucá-* 'brilliant', etc. More frequently the restored guṇa vowel appears: *arcá-* 'shining', *dravá-* 'running', *yodhá-* 'fighter', *nadá-* 'roarer', *vadhá-* 'slayer', etc. Like the action nouns they may also appear with vṛddhi, and this is connected with the vṛddhi of the nom. sg of the corresponding root stems: *vāhá-* 'beast of burden' (cf the root stem *°vāh-*, nom. sg. *°vāṭ*, acc. sg. *°vā́ham*) *sāha-* 'victorious' (cf. *°sāh-*), *nāyá-* 'leader', *grābhá-* 'seizer', etc.

The agent nouns of this type are on the decline, and as happens elsewhere in the same circumstances, many such stems are no longer used as independent nouns, but only as the last members of compounds: e.g. *°adá-* 'eater' (*annādá-* 'eater of food'), *°gamá-* 'going' (*dūraṃgamá-* 'going far'), *°gará-* 'swallower' (*ajagará-* 'goat swallower', i.e. python), *°ghná-* 'slaying' (*goghná-* 'slayer of cows'). This is because the formation which came to be normally used in making agent nouns was that in *-tár*, and this tended to oust other formations in ordinary free use. In contrast the *tár-* formations were not capable of being used in composition, so there is a dichotomy of the type *ánnasya attā́* : *annādá-* 'eater of food'. In a small number of nouns of this type the accent has been secondarily transferred to the root. Such are *vṛ́ka-* 'wolf', *víṣa-* 'server'. Such transference is common in nominalised adjectives throughout the system.

The adjectives *sána-* 'old' and *náva-* 'new' can be fitted into neither of the above classes. From the corresponding forms in other languages (Gk. *νέος* 'new', Lith. *sẽnas* 'old', etc.) it can be seen that they are distinguished from other thematic stems by having the radical *e*-grade and from the adjectival type by having radical accentuation. This is because they are based on old root stems *new-*, *sen-*, which were adjectives by meaning from the beginning, and consequently the thematic vowel here is merely an extension of the stem, as in the action nouns, and not meaningful as in the usual oxytone thematic adjectival type. In Latin the root stem *sen-* is still used outside the nom. sg. (*senex, senem, senis*).

Both types of the above nouns are masculines. Feminine agent nouns such as are found in Greek (*ἡ ὁδός* 'way', *ἡ τροφός* 'nurse') are non-existent in Sanskrit, which in this respect is less archaic than Greek. The masculine gender of these action-nouns is in contrast to the neuter gender of the various thematic action nouns derived by extension from the various neuter suffixes to be mentioned later. This is because the root nouns, at least those ending in occlusives developed early the distinction between nom. and acc. and used *-s* in the nom. sg. That is to say they were 'common gender', and the thematic derivatives based on them automatically acquired the same gender.

Later they were specialised as masculines owing to their external form. In contradistinction there are a couple of neuter nouns *vána-* ' forest ' and *tána-* ' offspring ' which are extensions of root stems (*ván-*, *tán-*) which had retained their neuter gender.

Old neuter formations are found in *yugám* ' yoke ' (: Gk. *ζυγόν*, Lat. *iugum*) and *padám* ' step ' (: Gk. *πέδον*, Hitt. *pedan*). These are old formations, among the very few simple thematic neuters that can be traced to Indo-European. They will be discussed in connection with the suffix *m* (p. 172 ff.).

§4. Neuter Formations with Alternating *r/n* Suffix

The suffixes *r* (which in Sanskrit may also represent IE *l*) and *n* must be studied together since they early became associated in a common paradigm in which the nom. acc. was formed by the *r*-stem, while the oblique cases were formed on the basis of an *n*-stem. This ancient type of neuter noun is tending to obsolescence in the earliest Sanskrit, as it is in Greek and most of the other languages. In Hittite on the other hand, which presents here, as so often, a more archaic stage of Indo-European, the system is unimpaired. The system as found in Hittite contains simple *r/n* stems with this alternation, e.g. *ešḫar* ' blood ', gen. sg. *ešnaš*, also a series of compound suffixes formed by the addition of these suffixes to stems in *u*, *m*, *s*, *t*, namely *-war*, *-mar*, *-sar*, *tar*. Examples are *partawar* ' wing ', gen. sg. *partaunaš*, *tarnummar* ' letting go, to let go ', gen. sg. *tarnummaš* (*mm*<*mn*), *ḫanneššar* ' law, law suit ', gen. sg. *ḫannešnaš*, *paprātar* ' uncleanness ', gen. sg. *paprannaš* (*nn*<*tn*). This early system of neuter nouns exists only in fragments in other IE languages, but an abundance of suffixes containing *r* and *n* have these primitive neuter types as their ultimate source.

There are a few simple neuter stems in *r* with alternating *n*-stem in Sanskrit. Such are *áhar* ' day ', gen. sg. *áhnas* (Av. *azan-* ' id '), *ū́dhar* ' udder ' gen. sg. *ū́dhnas* (Gk. *οὖθαρ*, *οὔθατος*, Engl. *udder*, etc. ; there also appears to be in the Veda a second *ū́dhar* ' cold ' = Av. *aodar-* ' id.'). In these the suffix has the guṇa grade, but it may also appear in the weak grade, in which case it is strengthened by a further suffix. This is usually *t* : *yákṛt* ' liver ', gen. sg. *yaknás* (Av. *yākar-*, Lat. *iecur*, Gk. *ἧπαρ*, all without any *t*), *śákṛt* ' dung ', gen. sg. *śaknás*, with a variant *-th* in *káprth-* ' penis '. This additional *t* may be compared with additional *t* which in Greek strengthens the alternating *n*-suffix in these nouns: *οὔθατος* compared with Skt. *ū́dhnas*, etc. We may also compare the fact that final radical *-ṛ* is avoided and *-t* added in *lokakṛ́t*, etc. A suffix *j* (<*g*) is found in *ásṛk* ' blood ' (nom. sg., stem *ásṛj-*), gen. sg. *asnás* (: Hitt. *esḫar, ešnaš*, Toch. *ysār*, Gk. *ἔαρ*, Lat. *assir*). This *g* also appears in Lat. *san-g-uis* ' blood ' which like *saniēs* ' gore ' is derived from the *n*-stem of this word with loss of initial vowel through apophony.

Since this type is becoming obsolete we have occasionally defective nouns like *vádhar* ' weapon ' (Av. *vadar-*) not used outside nom. acc. sg. The old alternating *n*-stem appears in the extension *vadhánā* fem. ' id '. Some stems even more obsolescent occur only as the first members of compounds : *uṣar-* (*uṣarbúdh-* ' waking at dawn '), *anar-* (*anarvíś-* ' seated on a chariot '), *vasar-*, (*vasarhán-* ' smiting in the morning '), *vanar-* (*vanargú-* ' going in the woods ', cf. the deriv. *vānara-* ' monkey ' ; *n*-stem in *vánan-vat*), *sabar-* (*sabardhúk* : for *savar-*, cf. *sávana* ' milked at the soma-pressing '). The stems *máhar* ' greatness ' and *bhúvar* ' abundance ' appear only in liturgical formulas and in the compounds *maharloka-* and *bhuvarloka-*, but the instrumentals of the corresponding *n*-stems, *mahnā́* (cf. Av. *mazan-* n.) and *bhūnā́* are common in the *Ṛgveda*. The *n*-stem *gámbhan* ' depth ' appears only as endingless loc. sg., but a corresponding *r*-stem **gámbhar* is implied by the extension *gambhára-* n. ' id.'. Corresponding to Vedic loc. sg. *rājáni* ' under the direction of ' Avestan has nom. acc. sg. *rāzarə* ' rule, regulation '. The instr. *dānā́* implies an old nom. sg. **dār* ' gift ', and from these alternating stems the two extensions Gk. *δῶρον*, O. Sl. *darŭ* and Lat. *dōnum*, Skt. *dā́nam* are derived. These instrumental forms, and also *áśnā́* ' with a stone ' (Av. *asan-*) and *preṇā́* ' with affection ' being isolated, have come to function as the instrumentals of the corresponding *man-* stems.

The adverb *avár* ' down, downwards ' has the same formation as the above neuter nouns, but differs in its accent which corresponds to that in the endingless loc. sg. The same adverbial accent is found in *prātár*, etc. below. Such adverbs also resemble the locatives without ending in that they may optionally add the termination *-i* : Just as we have *akṣáṇi* ' in the eye ' beside *akṣán*, so we have Skt. *upári* ' above ' beside Gk. *ὕπερ* and Av. *aδairi* 'below' beside the **adhar* adv. which is implied by the adjectival derivative *ádhara-* 'lower'.

Neuter stems in *-ar* not otherwise preserved form the basis of a small class of denominative verbs in the Vedic language: *ratharyáti* 'rides in a chariot', *śratharyáti* 'becomes loose', implying **ráthar* nt. 'riding in a chariot' and **śrathar* nt. 'looseness'; cf. *vadharyáti* 'smites with a weapon' beside *vádhar*. There are parallel denominative verbs from the corresponding *n*-stems: *vipanyá-* 'to be wise, inspired' (cf. also *vipanyā́*, *vipanyú-*, and with *-r-* *vípra-* 'inspired, wise'), *bhuraṇyá-* 'be turbulent, agitated' (*r*-stem in Lat. *furor*), etc. There are various secondary formations testifying to the existence of old neuter *r*-stems. The curious formations *dhaurita-* n. 'horse's trot' and *ādhoraṇa-* m. 'elephant driver', which turn up in later Sanskrit can be explained as denominative formations on the basis of an old neuter noun **dhāvar* 'running'. The Vedic vṛddhied derivative *jā́marya-* 'earthly' is based on a **jámar* 'earth' corresponding to Av. *zəmar-* 'id.' (*j-* as in *jmā́*, *jmás*, etc.). A neuter **śvétar* 'whiteness, white spot' is implied by the derivatives *śvaítarī* 'having an (auspicious) white mark' (a cow) and *śvetra-* nt. 'white leprosy', and the alternating *n*-stem appears in the extension *śvetanā́* fem. 'dawn'.

Since Skt. *r* represents both *r* and *l* of Indo-European, IE stems in *-l*, which functioned precisely as *r*-stems, cannot be distinguished from *r*-stems in Sanskrit, except by comparison with other languages. Such a stem is found in *svàr* (*súvar*) 'sun', gen. sg. *sū́ras* (cf. Lat. *sōl*, Goth. *sauil*, etc.). The heteroclitic declension which is absent in Sanskrit appears in other languages (Av. *x^və̄ng*<**svans*, gen. sg., etc.). Some of the *r*-stems mentioned above appear by comparison with other languages to have been originally *l*-stems: *máhar-*: Gk. μεγαλο-; Av. *zəmar-*: cf. Gk. χθαμαλός, Lat. *humilis*, etc.; Av. *rāzarə*: Lat. *rēgula*. The denominative verb *saparyáti* 'serves, honours, worships' is like Latin *sepelio* 'bury' ('honour with funeral rites') derived from an old IE neuter **sepel* 'honouring, worshipping' derived from the root *sep-*, Skt. *sap-* 'honour, serve.'

The *t*-extension to the suffix *n*, which appears in Greek (οὔθατος), etc., is absent in Sanskrit (*ū́dhnas*, etc.), but in some derivative forms an additional *t*-suffix is found which may be connected with the extension *t* of the Greek neuters: *vasantá-* 'spring', cf. *vasar*°, *veśantá-* 'pond' (√*viś-*), *bhuvanti* 'causing abundance', cf. *bhúvar, bhūnā́*. Another example is *sīmánta-* 'parting of the hair' as opposed to *sīmán-* 'id', and the lexica give a word *aśmanta-* 'fireplace' which is related in the same way to *áśman-* 'stone'. Compare also the pair *śakuni-* and *śakúnti-* 'bord'. The *t*-extension appears regularly in the participles in *-ant* which will be discussed later.

§ 5. Compound Neuter Suffixes in *r/n*

By adding the simple suffixes *r* and *n* to stems in *u, m, s* and *t* the suffixes *-war/n, mar/n*, etc., which were so productive in Hittite in the formation of neuter nouns, were produced. In addition they could be added to *i*-stems, and this ancient neuter type is preserved in the Latin passive infinitives, *ūtier, scrībier*, etc. Outside Hittite the compound neuter *r*-stems have become comparatively rare; the corresponding *n*-stems are better represented, and have tended to replace the *r*-formations in the nom. acc. sg.

A neuter suffix *-wer, -war* is found outside Hittite in such examples as Gk. εἶδαρ 'food' (*ἔδϝαρ), δέλεαρ 'bait', Lat. *cadāver* 'corpse', Toch. B *malkwer* 'milk' and the like. They are not uncommon in Avestan: *snāvar-* 'sinew', *θanvar-* 'bow', *karšvar-* 'region of the earth', *dasvar-* 'health', *sāxᵛar-* 'design, plan', *vazdvar-* 'firmness'. The Iranian evidence shows that they had survived in reasonable abundance to the Indo-Iranian period, but in Indo-Aryan they had already become extinct by the earliest period. This was because the *n*-stem was generalised in all cases: nom. acc. sg. *snā́va* 'sinew', etc. Only the adverb *sasvár* 'secretly, stealthily' preserves the suffix in this form, with the usual adverbial (=locatival) shift of accent. It implies a neuter noun **sásvar* which we may compare with Hitt. *šešuvar* 'sleep' (*šešzi* 'sleeps', Skt. *sásti*), the original meaning being 'while people sleep'. In its weak form the suffix is preserved in the adverb *múhur* 'suddenly, in a moment' (whence *muhūrtá-* 'moment'; also *múhu* with simple *u*-suffix, for **mṛhu-*, cf. Av. *mərəzu-* 'short (of life)', Gk. βραχύς). Neuter nouns in *-van* are 1 *dhánvan* 'bow', 2 *dhánvan* 'desert', *snā́van-* 'sinew', *párvan-* 'joint' (cf. Av. *paourvainya-* 'linked'), *sṛ́kvan-* 'corner of the mouth', and some sporadic occurrences in the *Ṛgveda*, *pátvan-* 'flight', *sanítvan-* 'acquisition' and *vivásvan-* 'illumination'. In addition a small number of dative infinitives are formed with this suffix: *dāváne* 'to give' (Gk. δοϝεναι, δοῦναι) *tūrváṇe* 'to overcome', *dhūrvaṇe* 'to injure'; similarly in Av. *vīdvanōi* 'to know'.

A suffix compounded of *i* and *r* appears only in the adverb *báhir* 'outside'. A few defective *in*-stems appear in the *Ṛgveda* in the instrum. sg., namely *prathinā́, mahinā́, variṇā́.* These forms, in origin old neuter *in*-stems, have been attracted to the paradigm of the masc. *man*-stems *prathimán-* 'width', *mahimán-* 'greatness' and *varimán-* 'width', and so preserved. The neuter suffix *-in* further compounded with *v* appears in *sṛ́kvin-* nt. 'corner of the mouth'.

The compound suffixes *m-er, m-en* alternated in the same way, but outside Hittite, *mer* (*mṛ*) is rare and obsolescent. A fair number of examples can be collected from Greek (λῦμαρ, λύματος 'impurity', etc.) but they exist only as survivals. No examples are found in Sanskrit but their one time existence in Indo-Iranian is shown by adjectival derivatives like *admar-á* 'gluttonous' based on an old **ádmar* 'eating, food'. Such forms have been entirely replaced by the extension of the *man*-stem to the nom. acc. sg.

The neuter suffix *man* is the only one of the *r/n* suffixes that remained fully productive in languages other than Hittite. Examples are: (nom. acc. sg.) *ájma* 'career, march' (: Lat. *agmen*), *kárma* 'deed', *cárma* 'skin', *pákṣma* 'eyelash', *pátma* 'flight', *bráhma* 'prayer', *bhárma* 'maintaining, supporting; load' (: O. Sl. *bremę* 'burden', Gk. φέρμα), *vásma* 'garment' (: Gk. εἶμα 'id', Lesb. ϝέμμα), *lóma, róma* 'hair' (<√*lū-*: cf. *lava-* 'fleece, wool, hair'), *mánma* 'thought' (: O. Ir. *menme* 'mind, understanding'), *várma* 'protective armour', *vártma* 'course, way' (O. Sl. *vremę* 'time'), *sádma* 'seat', *syū́ma* 'thong, rein', *svā́dma* 'sweetness'.

A small number of dative infinitives are formed on the basis of this suffix: *trā́maṇe* 'to protect', *dā́mane* 'to give', *dhármaṇe* 'to support', *bhármaṇe* 'to maintain', *vidmáne* 'to know'. In Greek infinitives are also made with this suffix, much more abundantly, and including an archaic type without termination; ἴμεν 'to go', δόμεν 'to give'; ἔδμεναι 'to eat', ἴμεναι 'to go', δόμεναι 'to give', etc.

The nouns of this class are primarily verbal abstracts (action nouns), but they show a strong tendency to acquire concrete meanings, as happens with other neuter abstracts: e.g. *hánma* 'weapon' as well as 'blow', *tárdma* 'hole', *márma* 'a mortal place, vital organ', *cárma* 'skin', *vásma* 'garment', etc.

Like other neuter suffixes in *-n* this suffix is extended by *t* in Greek (gen. sg. *σώματος*, etc.). A case of such extension is found in Skt. *varimát-* 'breadth' (inst. sg. *varimátā* RV. 1. 108. 2).

The neuter suffix *-t-er* alternating with *-t-en*, which is so well represented in Hittite, has become exceedingly rare in other IE languages. Only isolated examples such as Lat. *iter*, Toch. *ytār* 'way' are quotable. In Sanskrit a solitary example of this kind appears to be preserved in RV. 6. 49. 6.: *jágataḥ sthātar jágad ā́ kṛṇudhvam*, 'may ye bring stability to the moving world'. Misunderstood by the redactors the form has been handed down without accent as if vocative of *sthātár-* 'stander', and the passage has been rendered unintelligible. A restoration *sthā́tar* n. 'stability' gives meaning to the line. Apart from this the neuter suffix *-tar-* appears in a small number of locative infinitives, e.g. *dhartári* 'to hold', *vidhartári* 'to bestow'. In Avestan some dative infinitives are made with the same suffix: *vīdōiθre* 'to look at' *barəθre* 'to support'. These forms are interesting as showing that the neuter *r*-stems were capable to some extent of being inflected throughout the declension instead of being replaced by *n*-stems. Under what precise conditions this happened originally it is not now possible to say.

Some adverbs appear with this suffix, having the usual change of accent: *antár* 'inside' (: Lat. *inter*), *prātár* 'early' (: Osc. *pruter*), *sanutár* 'aside, apart' (cf. Engl. *a-sunder*). These imply old neuter nouns **ántar* 'the interior', etc. This type of adverb became very productive in Latin, *aliter* 'otherwise' (cf. *anyátr-a*), *breviter, leviter*, etc. With additional suffix *-ā* we get adverbs in *-trā́*, e.g. *śayutrā́* 'in bed, abed', and this suffix may, and normally does later, appear with a short vowel, *anyátra* 'elsewhere', *átra* 'here', etc. Among the adverbs the Veda has some interesting collective formations: *devatrā́* 'among the gods', *puruṣatrā́* 'among men'. They may be explained by comparing Hittite forms like *antuḫšatar* 'the population, mankind' (*antuḫšaš* 'man'). Similar neuter collectives **devatar*, etc., lie behind these adverbial forms.

A neuter suffix *-tan* is found only in *naktán-* 'night' (instr. pl. *naktábhis*). Alternating *-r* appears in Gk. *νύκτωρ* 'by night' and Lat. *nocturnus*. This neuter suffix is found sporadically elsewhere (Lat. *glūten* ' glue ', etc.) and in Old Persian it is used to make dative infinitives (*čartanaiy* ' to do ', etc.).

The compound suffix *sar/sn*, which is very common in Hittite, is more or less obsolete elsewhere. It is an extension of the neuter *s*-stems, and in Hittite the *-ar/n* has been added so consistently that the simple *s*-stems have practically disappeared. In other languages the simple *s*-stems are well preserved so that it is unlikely that the *sar/sn* formation ever had the same extension elsewhere as appears in Hittite. Nevertheless there are considerable traces of it. Adjectival derivatives of the type *matsar-á* ' exhilarated ' are based on such formations, and the coexistence of *mandasānā́-* ' id.' shows that there was the old *r/n* alternation. Similarly *pūṣaryà-* ' well-nourished ' implies **pū́ṣar* nt. ' fatness, prosperity ', equivalent to Gk. πῦαρ ' beest milk ', and the alternative *n*-stem is used in the masc. derivative *Pūṣán-* ' nourisher (name of a god) '.[1]

A few neuter stems in *-sn-* are preserved in the oblique cases of nouns which appear in the nom. sg. as simple *s*-stems, e.g., gen. sg. *śīrṣṇás*, *doṣṇás*, nom. acc. sg. *śíras* ' head ', *dós* ' arm '. A small class of locative infinitives is made on the basis of neuter stems in *-san-*: *neṣáṇi* 'to lead ', *parṣáṇi* ' to pass ', *gṛṇīṣáṇi* ' to sing ', *iṣáṇi* ' to emit ' (for *iṣ-ṣani* with the old sandhi, p. 95). In Greek also this suffix forms infinitives. The common type φέρειν is best explained in this way (*φερεσεν, **bheresen*, the simple base without ending being used as in ἴδμεν, etc.).

§ 6. Action Nouns transferred to the Masculine

It has been remarked above that the major distinction in Indo-European was between neuter action nouns accented on the root and masculine, originally common gender, agent nouns accented on the suffix. But in Sanskrit as in other languages not all nouns fit into this simple classification ; among the *n*-stems for instance with which we are dealing there are quite a number of masculine formations which cannot be classed as agent nouns, and which from the point of view of their meaning go rather with the neuter action nouns of the above type. Such

[1] Originally **py-ūsar* (√*pī*) as is seen by comparing πῦαρ and Skt. *pīyū́ṣa-*. Similarly *puṣ-* ' to thrive, prosper ' is for **pyuṣ-*, originally a denominative formation like *uruṣyáti*, etc. (**pyuṣyáti*).

are: (*-an-*) *mūrdhán-* 'head' (AS. *molda*), *plīhán-* 'spleen' (Av. *spərəzan-* m., Gk. *σπλήν* m.),[1] *majján-* 'marrow' (cf. O. Pruss. *musgeno*); (*-van-*) *ádhvan-* 'way' (Av. *advan-*), *grā́van-* 'pressing stone' (O. Ir. *brō*, Welsh *breuan*); (*-man-*) *ūṣmán-* 'breath, vapour', *ojmán-* 'strength' (Lith. *augmũ*), *omán-* 'favour, assistance', *takmán-* 'a particular disease', *ātmán-* 'soul, self', *pāpmán-* 'sin' (also adj. 'wicked'), *pāmán-* 'scabies', *premán-* 'love', *bhūmán-* 'abundance', *raśmán-* 'rein', *reṣmán-* 'whirlwind', *sīmán-* 'parting of the hair', *svādmán-* 'sweetness'; (*-iman-*) *jarimán-* 'old age', *mahimán-* 'greatness', *harimán-* 'yellow colour', etc. The question naturally arises as to why such words should have a form which is properly a characteristic of agent nouns. There is no apparent reason why words meaning 'liver' and 'udder' should be neuter and words meaning 'marrow' and 'spleen' masculine; nor is there any immediately apparent cause why verbal abstracts like *omán-* 'assistance' should differ in formation from the normal neuters in *-man*.

In the case of a few of such words we may be dealing with disguised agent nouns. A good example of this kind is seen in Skt. *klóman-* Gk. *πλεύμων* 'lung', so named because it floats on water ('swimmer, floater' √*pleu-*). Likewise we may interpret *raśmán-* as 'that which binds, binder' and *reṣmán-* as 'destroyer'.

When these have been explained away there still remain a number of pure action nouns or abstracts constructed after the manner of agent nouns. In these cases we have to do with a transfer of action nouns from the neuter to the masculine class. The following facts speak for this: (1) A number of words appear in both classes in Sanskrit, *várṣman-* n., *varṣmán-* m. 'height, top, surface', *svā́dman-* n., *svādmán-* m. 'sweetness', *dā́man-* nt. 'giving' (inf.), *dāmán-* m. 'gift, liberality'. Here the neuter may be taken to be the older formation as conforming to old rule. In the case of *dhánvan-* nt. and *dhánvan-* masc. 'desert' the latter is unknown to the earlier language. (2) The same alternation is found as between different languages: Skt. *ojmán-*, Lith. *augmuõ*: Lat. *augmen* nt. (with extension *augmentum*); Skt. *syū́man-* nt. 'thread, suture': Gk. *ὑμήν*.

[1] This word appears in the different languages with a varying arrangement of suffixes in each case: Skt. *plīhán-*: (*s*)*pl-i-*H*-ĝh-én-*; Av. *spərəzan-*: *spl̥-ĝh-en-*; O. Sl. *slězena*: *s*(*p*)*el-ĝh-en-ā*; Gk. *σπλην*: *spl-én*, cf. *σπλάγχνον*; *spl̥-n-ĝh-no-*; Lat. *liēn*: (*sp*)*l-i-ēn* or (*sp*)*l-i-*H*-ēn*), O.Ir. *selg*: *s*(*p*)*el-ĝh-ā*.

(3) The two adjectival forms *pāmar-á-* and *pāman-á-* ' affected with scabies ' show that there was an old neuter *r/n* stem which has given way to the masc. *pāmán-*, and *aśmarī* ' gall stone ' attests an old neut. **áśmar* as opposed to the masculine *n*-stem which is always found elsewhere (Skt. *áśman-*, Lith. *akmuõ*; Gk. ἄκμων ' anvil '). The same relationship exists between the Gk. adjective ἥμερος ' gentle, tame ' and Skt. *sāmaná-* ' quiet '.

The general tendency of the neuter to decline, and with it the decline of the old antithesis marked by accent and gender between action noun and agent noun made it easy for a type of masculine (and feminine) action noun to develop. To a certain extent also personification is responsible for the gender. Terms like *dāmán-* ' liberality ', *omán-* ' favour (of the gods) ' and *bhūmán-* ' abundance ' are regarded in the Vedic hymns as divine powers in their own right. Disease (*takmán-*) and sin (*dhvasmán-*, *pāpmán-*) are likewise regarded as active evil powers. At the same time there are some more mechanical transfers. The abstract formations in *-imán-* (*prathimán-* ' width ', *varimán* ' id ', etc.) take the masculine gender as a class, and there is probably a rhythmical reason behind this because the formations in *-man-* preceded by long *ī* remain neuter (*várīman-* ' width ', *hávīman-* ' call ', etc.).

Masculine action nouns of the same type are common in Greek: τέρμων ' boundary ' beside τέρμα nt. ' id ' (Lat. *termen*), χειμών ' winter ' beside χεῖμα nt., θημών ' heap ' beside θῆμα nt. (Skt. *dhā́man-* nt. with different sense), λειμών ' meadow ', λιμήν ' harbour ', ἀδήν ' gland ' (Lat. *inguen* nt.). In Latin there are both masculine (*ordō*, *sermō*) and feminine (*margo*, *legio*, *cupido*) *n*-stems of this type.

Owing to their early obsolescence the neuter *r*-stems have not undergone this transference with the exception of a single example. The defective stem *uṣar-* (*usṛ-*) ' dawn ' is feminine (acc. pl. *usrás*) but was originally a neuter *r*-stem (cf. *uṣarbúdh* § 4).

§ 7. Thematic Extension of Neuter Stems in *r* and *n*

The original function of the thematic suffix was adjectival and in this case it was accented: *karaṇ-á* ' doing ', etc. This conclusion is indicated by Hittite which possesses such stems (*veštaraš* ' herdsman , etc.) but no thematic neuters like the other languages. When we compare the thematic type of neuter, e.g. Skt. *sánara-* 'acquisition', *kárvara-* 'act' with the non-thematic stems in *-ar, -var,* etc., illustrated above, it is clear that the thematic suffix here has no grammatical function. This, coupled with the absence of such formations in Hittite is an argument for the secondary origin of this type; clearly as between Lat. *unguen* and Skt. *añjana-* the former is the older formation. It is not difficult to see how such forms arose. There were agent nouns of the type *brahmán-* beside *bráhman-* nt. but also from the earliest period another type of agent noun/adjective made by the addition of the accented thematic vowel (Gk. *ἰατρός* beside *ἰατήρ,* Hitt. *veštaraš* beside Av. *vāstar-*). It was then natural and easy to create a neuter thematic type balancing the thematic adjectival type (*káraṇa-* nt. after *karaṇá-*, etc.).

Thematic neuter stems corresponding to the various *r-* and *n*-stems listed above may appear either with the guṇa of this suffix (*kárvara-* 'deed') or with the reduced grade (*dhártra-* 'support'). Both types occur from simple *r*-stems: (1) *sánara-* 'gain', *tásara-* 'shuttle', *pañjara-* 'cage'; framework of the ribs (cf. *pajrá-* adj. 'fixed, firm', Lat. *pango*, etc.), *gambhára-* 'depth', *udára-* 'belly'. It will be noticed, here and below, that there is a certain fluctuation in the accent of the trisyllabic forms. Final accentuation, the characteristic of adjectives, is avoided, but the accent may fall on the penultimate syllable instead of on the root. (2) *ágra-* 'point', *rándhra-* 'hole', *śvábhra-* 'pit'. There are a few substantives with final accentuation but these are adjectival in origin, e.g. *kṛcchrá-* nt. 'difficulty', but also *kṛcchrá-* adj. 'difficult', *riprá-* nt. 'defilement', but cf. Gk. *λιπαρός* 'greasy', *abhrá* nt. 'cloud', cf. Gk. *ἀφρός* 'foam' masc. (nt. *ámbhas-* 'moisture' beside which there must have been **ámbhar,* cf. Lat. *imber*), *kṣīrá-* nt. 'milk' of uncertain etymology but from its accent of adjectival origin.

In *sth-ála-* 'place, ground' there is a thematic neuter formation involving the *l*-suffix.

A few old neuters in *-var* have been extended by the thematic vowel: *kárvara-* 'deed', replacing earlier **kárvar, gáhvara-* 'hiding place', *phárvara-* 'sowing, sowed field' (*(*s*)*phar-*: Gk. *σπείρω*), *catvara-* 'quadrangle, cross-roads' (from a neuter **catvar* on which the adjectival *catvāras* 'four' is based).

With the *tar*-suffix we have a neuter formation in *-tara* in *srastara-* 'bed of grass' (√*sraṃs-*) and a fairly abundant series of neuters in *-tra*: *átra-* 'food' (: *atrá-* m. 'eater'), *kártra-* 'spell', *kṣétra-* 'field' (: Av. *šōiθra-* 'habitation'), *vástra-* 'garment', *śrótra-* 'hearing, ear' (: AS. *hleoþor* 'noise'), *sūtra-* 'thread' (cf. the Lat. agent noun *sūtor*). In addition to such words which can be explained quite simply out of primitive neuter *tar*-stems, there is another series of neuters with the suffix *-tra* less easy to explain since they have paradoxically accent on the final syllable. Such are *antrá-*, *āntrá-* (: Gk. ἔντερα pl.), *astrá-*, *deṣṭrá-* 'direction', *netrá-* 'guidance', *rāṣṭrá-* 'rule, kingdom', *śastrá-* 'invocation', *sattrá-* 'sacrificial session', *śāstrá-* 'command', *stotrá-* 'praise, hymn of praise', *sthātrá-* 'station', *hotrá-* 'office ot *hótar-*, oblation', *potrá-* 'office of *pótar-*', *neṣṭrá-* 'office or vessel of *néṣṭar-*'. A few of these forms may be explained as originally adjectival, e.g. *antrá-* 'what is inside', *astrá-* 'what is thrown', but the majority clearly cannot be explained in this way. They must be explained from a different point of view. There is a series of agent nouns in *-tar* denoting holders of professions and priestly offices, e.g. *śáṃstar-* 'reciter' *hótar-* 'sacrificial priest', *pótar-* 'purifier' and closely associated the *néṣṭar-* (prob. 'sifter', cf. Gk. νεικητήρ λικμητήρ Hes.). Such nouns as a class have the nominal accent, i.e. on the root. The above neuters, *hotrá-* 'office of *hótar-*', etc., have become, as far as their meaning is concerned, secondary derivatives from these agent nouns, thus reversing the position originally prevailing between neuters and agent nouns. In ordinary taddhita derivation there is a special rule in Sanskrit whereby the taddhita derivative is accented on the final *-á* if the primary formation from which it is derived is accented on a previous syllable: *nairhastá-* 'handlessness', *ātithyá-* 'hospitality', *saumanasá-* 'friendliness' from *nírhasta-*, *átithi-*, *sumánas-* (and vice versa, *pā́litya-* from *palitá-* 'grey-haired'). There are also examples from non-vṛddhied formations, e.g. *sakhyá-* 'friendship' from *sákhi-*. This is a new way of using accent in derivation which Sanskrit has developed, and it is this system which accounts for the final accentuation in *hotrá-*, etc. These formations are however not from the beginning taddhitas, but a subdivision of the old simple neuters in *-tra* which have been adapted for a special purpose and have had their accent altered accordingly.

There are a fair number of neuters with the gradation *-atra*, e.g. *nákṣatra-* 'lunar mansion' (*nakṣ-* 'to reach'), *pátatra-* 'wing', *vádhatra-* 'weapon'; with penultimate accentuation, *kṛntátra-* 'piece cut off', *d-átra-* 'gift'; with taddhita accent, *kṣatrá-* 'sovereignty'; post-Vedic *kalatra-* 'wife'.

A thematic extension of an old neuter *sar*-stem appears in *támisra-* 'darkness' (cf. Av. *tąθra-*); with *l pátsala-* 'way' Uṇ.

In Hittite there is a neuter suffix in *-an* (not alternating with *-ar*) making primary verbal abstracts, *ḫenkan* 'death', etc. The same suffix appears in the Greek infinitives in *-εν* and sporadically elsewhere (Lat. *unguen*). In Sanskrit the thematic extension of this suffix has become exceedingly productive in the formation of neuter action nouns from verbal roots. They frequently stand in opposition to agent nouns having the same suffix but accented on the last syllable: *káraṇa-* nt. 'deed', *karaṇá-* masc. 'doing'. Examples with radical accent are *áñjana-* 'anointing, ointment', *cáyana-* 'heaping up', *dárśana-* 'vision', *pátana-* 'fall', *bhójana-* 'enjoyment', *sádana-* 'seat', etc., etc.; from a non-verbal root, *sámana-* 'assembly'. Such words sometimes appear with weak form of root, e.g. *bhúvana-* 'world', and, when the root-vowel is *a*, sometimes with vṛddhi *bhā́jana-* 'vessel'. There is a tendency in the later language to associate these latter formations with the causative of the verb, e.g. *táraṇa-* 'crossing', *tā́raṇa-* 'getting (somebody) across, delivering'. Penultimate accent is sometimes found: *vṛjána-* 'enclosure, settlement' (also *vṛ́jana-*), *kṛpáṇa-* 'misery' (: *kṛpaṇá-* 'miserable'), *daṃsána-* 'wondrous deed', *veṣáṇa-* 'service', *dh-ána-* 'wealth', *r-áṇa-* 'battle' (cf. Av. *arənu-* 'id'.).

Similar neuter formations are found occasionally from the compound *n*-stems: *vayúna-* 'delimitation, appointed time' (: *vélā* 'limit, time, etc.'), *karúṇa-* 'deed'; *dráviṇa-* 'property', *vā́jina-* 'race, contest'; *vétana-* 'wage' (√ *vī*), *r-átna-* 'treasure' (*rā-* 'to bestow'); *mátasna-* 'lung'.

The neuter suffix *men/mn* could be extended by the suffix *-t* (Gk. *σώματος* gen. sg., etc., cf. the Hittite infinitive forms in *-manzi*, *-wanzi*). This complex could also receive the thematic extension, Lat. *augmentum*, *strāmentum*, etc. There is one such example in Sanskrit, *śrómata-* nt. 'fame' (*-mat-*<**-mn̥t-*), cf. OHG *hliumunt*, Germ. *Leumund*.

§ 8. Masculine Formations of the Type *brahmán*—from *r*- and *n*-stems

The essential feature of this type is the suffixal accent as opposed to the radical accent of the neuters, and vṛddhi in the nominative singular. There is some evidence that originally they were themselves capable of being used as adjectives without any change of form. Examples of this are found in many languages, e.g. Gk. *μάκαρ* ' blessed ', *μάρτυρ* ' witness ', Lat. *ūber* in the sense of ' rich ', Hitt. *kurur* meaning both ' enmity ' and ' inimical, enemy '. In Sanskrit there are two formations which may be compared with Gk. *μάρτυρ*, although they have accent on the suffix, namely *aptúr*- ' active in holy works ' and *yantúr*- ' controller '. With the suffix *-uṣ* we have forms like *náhuṣ*- ' neighbour ' and *mánuṣ*- ' man ' which are not in any way distinguished from the corresponding neuter types. Such formations are, however, very much in the minority, because Indo-European early developed this method of indicating the adjectival function of a stem by switching the accent.

In some cases in Sanskrit the two types exist side by side, notably in the case of the suffixes *-man*- and *-as*-, but more often the old system has broken down. This is mainly due to the elimination of the old neuter types, which has left important classes of masculine agent nouns standing isolated. In Sanskrit there is an abundant class of agent nouns in *-tár*, *kartár*- ' doer ', etc. The nature of this formation only became clear with the discovery in Hittite of an archaic class of neuters in *-tar*. We have seen above that this, like similar formations, has left many traces in other languages and therefore must at one time have been widely prevalent. This means that the two types **kártar* nt. ' doing, action ' and *kartár*- masc. ' doer, agent ' must at one time have existed side by side, and this being so it becomes immediately clear that the relationship of the two types is exactly the same as that between *bráhman*- and *brahmán*- Skt. *kartár* ' doer ' is one connected with **kártar* ' doing ' and *sthātár*- ' one who stands ' is similarly related to that *sthā́tar* nt. which, as we have seen, is preserved in a somewhat disguised form in one passage of the *Ṛgveda*.

Since this is one of the commonest formations in Sanskrit the citation of further examples may be dispensed with. A few words are necessary about the accent. Suffixal accent is proper to this type and occurs most frequently in Sanskrit, but there is also a type with retracted accent associated with a curious syntactic distinction: *dātā́ vásūnām* but *dā́tā vasūni*. It has been noticed above that specialist words with this suffix (*hótar-*, etc.) have also as a rule accent on the root. In Greek also there are two sets of forms, with suffixal accent, δοτήρ 'giver', βατήρ 'goer', θετήρ 'establisher', and with radical accent, δώτωρ 'giver', etc. The first of these preserves the most ancient form, with reduction of the root consequent on the accentuation of the suffix. In Sanskrit the suffixal accent is preserved to a large extent, but apart from very few exceptions, e.g. *dṛṃhitár-* 'one who makes firm', guṇa is universal in the agent nouns. Its maintenance or reintroduction in spite of the basic law of apophony may be ascribed to the influence of the related neuters.

This suffix is prominent in the formation of nouns of family relationship: *pitár-* 'father' (cf. Lat. *pater*, etc.), *duhitár-* 'daughter' (cf. Gk. θυγάτηρ, etc.), *mātár-* 'mother' (Gk. μήτηρ, Dor. μᾱ́τηρ, OHG *muoter*, etc.); *bhrā́tar-* 'brother' (Gk. φρᾱ́τωρ, φρᾱ́τηρ, φρᾱτήρ 'member of a phratry', Goth. *brōþar*, OHG *bruoder*, etc.), *jā́mātar-* 'son-in-law' (Av. *zāmātar-*, Alb. *δender*), *yā́tar-* 'wife of husband's brother' (Gk. εἰνατέρες, Lat. *ianitrīces* plur., O. Sl. *jętry*, Lith. *jéntė*); *náptar-* 'grandson' (secondary substitute for *nápāt* = Lat. *nepōs*). Of these it is probable that the word for 'father' is an old agent noun (*p-i-tár-* 'protector' from *pā-(y)-* 'to protect'), but in the majority of cases the etymology is too obscure for it to be possible to say much with certainty. Its gradation is of the old type (cf. Gk. δοτήρ, etc.) as is to be expected in such a word. Only *duhitár-* agrees with *pitár-* in accent and apophony; the rest have both accent and guṇa of root with the exception of *mātár-*, and even here Greek has radical accent, which may easily be original in spite of the agreement between Sanskrit and Germanic. It is not unlikely that these contain some old neuters (**mā́ter*, etc.: Lat. *māteriēs* would be an extension of such a neuter) which were adapted when the gender-system developed. There is also the possibility of the analogical extension of the suffix. This has certainly happened in Skt. *náptar-* and probably in the unusually formed *jā́mātar-* (cf. Gk. γαμβρός son-in-law' differently formed.

The defective noun *stár-* (instr. pl. *stṛ́bhis*), *tár-* (nom. pl.

tā́ras) = Gk. ἀστήρ is formed with this masculine suffix ; the word has become so reduced that in the latter form only the suffix is left.

The suffix *-tar* is the only one of the *r*-suffixes that has become prolific in the formation of agent nouns. But both the simple *r*-suffix and the various compound suffixes which have been enumerated were capable of being used in this way and a small number of examples have survived.

An example with the simple *r*-suffix is seen in *nár-* ' man, warrior ' (Gk. ἀνήρ, Umbrian *ner-*, etc.). A corresponding neuter **ā́ner* is deduced from certain derivatives (Gk. ἠνορέη, εὐήνωρ, etc.).

The suffix *-var* is so used in *catvā́ras* masc. pl. ' four '. The corresponding neuter **cátvar* ' square ' is not preserved, but there is a thematic extension of it in *catvara-* nt. ' quadrangle, cross-roads '. Another example is *devár-* ' husband's brother ', cf. Gk. δᾱήρ (for δαιϝήρ), Lat. *lēvir*, etc. There is no example of such a formation with the *mar*-suffix, but it will be noted below that *karmā́ra-* ' smith ' implies an earlier *karmā́(r)*.

The suffix *-sar* appears in this class in the word *svásar-* ' sister ' (*sva-* ' one's own ') with retracted accent, and in the numerals *tisrás, cátasras* ' three, four ' (fem.). Here the accusative form has come to be used for the nominative ; the old nominatives **tisores, kʷetesores* are represented in Celtic (O. Ir. *teòir, cetheoir*). Lat. *uxōr* ' wife ' is a noun of this class, being based on an *r*-extension of the *s*-stem which appears in Skt. *ókas-* nt. ' home '. There seems to have been a tendency for this suffix, when used adjectivally, to be specialised in the formation of feminine nouns, and with the above we may compare the thematic derivative in Hittite *išḫaššaraš* ' lady ' (*išḫaš* ' lord ').

Similarly agent nouns and adjectives are formed with the accented *n*-suffixes, related in the same way to the neuter *n*-stems : *tákṣan-* ' carpenter ' (: Hitt. *takšan* nt. ' joining '), *rā́jan-* ' king ' (: *rājáni* nt. ' under the guidance of ', alternating *r*-stem in Av. *rāzar-* nt.), *pratidī́van-* ' opponent at play ', *víbhvan-*, *vibhván-* ' powerful '. There are a few old masculines of this formation no longer referable to verbal roots, *yúvan-* ' young man ' (cf. Lat. *iuvenis*, etc. ; *yo-ṣ-ít* ' young woman, woman '), *śván-* ' dog ' (Gk. κύων), Examples from other languages are Av. *spasan-* ' scout, spy ', *vindan-* ' one who acquires ', Gk. πευθήν ' spy ', ἀρηγών ' helper ', Lat. *edō* ' one given to eating', etc. In addition this formation has provided in Greek the nom. sg. of active participles of the thematic type (φέρων, λιπών, alternating with -οντ- in other cases, as opposed to διδούς, etc.) and in Germanic it forms the basis of an adjectival declension. The accent is generally retracted in Sanskrit. It has already been remarked that this is usual in the case of words of adjectival origin which have become completely nominalised (e.g. *rā́jan-*).

The accent is likewise retracted in the adjectival formations in *-van*, but here the weak grade of the root shows that this is not original. Examples are *ṛ́kvan-* 'worshipping, praising' (: Hitt. *arkuwar* nt. 'prayer'), *drúhvan-* 'injurious', *yúdhvan-* 'fighting', *śúbhvan-* 'beautiful', *stúbhvan-* 'praising', *pátvan-* 'flying' (: nt. *pátvan-* 'flight'), *mádvan-* 'exhilarating, exhilarated', *jásvan-* 'famished'. Suffixal accentuation appears only in *muṣīván-* 'thief'. Roots ending in *i*, *u*, *ṛ* take the additional suffix *t* before this suffix: *kṛ́tvan-* 'active', *sútvan-* 'pressing', *sṛ́tvan-* 'moving'. That these are based on an old set of neuters with alternating *r/n* stem is shown by the feminine. This is based on the *r*-stem of the neuters, e.g. *pī́varī* fem. 'fat' is derived directly from the neuter stem which appears in Greek as πῖαρ, whereas the masculines are derived from the associated *n*-stem. Exactly the same distinction between masculine and feminine is found in Greek: πίων masc., πιεῖρα fem. 'fat'. Similar feminine formations in Sanskrit are *yájvarī* 'pious', *śárvarī* 'night', °*śīvarī* 'lying', °*yāvarī* 'going', °*dāvarī* 'giving' (e.g. *Godāvarī* 'cow-giving', name of the river). The suffix forms both primary derivatives, as above, and secondary derivatives. Such are *ṛtā́van-* 'righteous', *satyā́van-* 'truthful', *maghávan-* 'bountiful', and *svadhā́van-* 'powerful'. A fair proportion of the secondary formations retain the adjectival accent: *amatīván-* 'indigent', *arātīván-* 'hostile', *ṛṇāván-* 'indebted', *śruṣṭīván-* 'obedient'. Their feminine is likewise in *-varī* (*ṛtā́varī*, etc.), indicating that there existed at one time also secondary neuter formations in *var/n* of the type **ṛtāvar* 'righteousness'.

In the case of the suffix *-man* a number of pairs are found in the Vedic language with varying accent and meaning illustrating the general principle of noun-formation in Indo-European: *bráhman-*: *brahmán-*; *sádman-* 'sitting, seat': *sadmán-* 'sitter'; *dhárman-* 'ordinance': *dharmán-* 'ordainer';

dắman- ' gift ' : *dāmán-* ' giver '. Other masculine agent nouns of this type are *darmán-* ' breaker ', *bhujmán-* ' fertile ', *somán-* ' soma-presser '. There is one secondary formation in *-mán*, *aryamán-* ' friendly, allied '. In Avestan there is the same antithesis between neuter and masculine *man*-stems in *cinman-* nt. ' care ' : *činman-* masc. ' caring for ' ; *zaēman-* nt. ' wakefulness ' : *zaēman-* masc. ' wakeful '. Formations of this masculine type in Greek are *ἴδμων* ' one who knows ' (: *ἴδμεν-αι* inf.), *τλήμων* ' enduring ', *ἡγεμών* ' leader ', etc. ; in Latin an *alimōnes* nom. pl. (>*alimōnia*) is quoted.

Masculines with the suffix *-san-* are very few : *Pūṣán-*, name of a god (cf. *pūṣaryà-* above, § 5), *vṛ́ṣaṇ-* 'male ', *ukṣáṇ-* ' ox ' (Engl. *ox*, *oxen*, Welsh *ych*, pl. *ychen*, Toch. *okso*). The last two involve extended roots with incorporated *s*-suffix (*vakṣ-*, *vṛṣ-*) and from that point of view may be classed as *an*-stems. A feminine *san*-stem appears in *yóṣan-* ' woman '.

Masculine *tan*-stems are not found in Sanskrit, but appear occasionally in other languages : Av. *marətan-* ' mortal ', *aiwixšaētan-* ' dweller, occupier ', Gk. *τέκτων*, *γείτων* ' neighbour '.

The compound suffix *-in-* is one of the most productive adjectival suffixes in the language. It may appear in primary formations, *arcín-* ' shining ', but it is used much more frequently in secondary formations with a possessive sense, *aśvín-* ' possessing horses ', *dhanín-* ' wealthy ', *pakṣín-* ' winged ', etc., etc. Such adjectives may be formed in any number from stems in *-a* and *-ā*, in which case the final vowel of the stem is replaced by *-in-*, and less frequently from other stems, e.g. *śvanín-* ' keeping dogs ', *śavasín-* ' strong '. The suffix has invariably the accent, which is proper to these adjectival types, but it is invariably in the weak grade, which cannot be original, and this is associated with the formation of a new analogical form of nom. sg. in *ī*. Originally there must have been vṛddhi in the nom. sg. and vṛddhied forms of this formation are found in other languages (Gk. *οὐρανίωνες*, etc.). In Latin there are some feminine action nouns which use the same formation (just as *bhūmán-* ' abundance ', etc., have taken on the form proper to action nouns, see above, § 6), *legiō*, *legiōnis*, etc. These have likewise generalised the strong form. The original system with alternation of strong form in nom. sg. and weak form in gen. sg., etc., is preserved in Oscan which uses a weak form of the stem in the oblique cases : dat. sg. *leginei*, etc. The use of this suffix in a specifically possessive sense is found also in Iranian, e.g. Av. *parənin-* ' having wings ', but examples are comparatively few.

A fair number of adjectives are formed with the accented suffix *-vín* : *sragvín-* ' wearing a garland ', *tapasvín-* ' heated ', *tejasvín-* ' brilliant ', etc. This complicated suffix which is unknown outside Indo-Aryan, seems to be a contamination of the suffixes *-van-* and *-in-*. Beside it there is a rarer suffix *-min* (like *-mant* beside *-vant*), e.g. *vāgmín-* ' eloquent ', *gomin-* ' possessing cows ', *svāmin-* ' owner, master ' (*sva-* ' one's own ').

§ 9. Adjectival Formations in *-nt-*

It has been noted above that *-n* as a neuter suffix could in Indo-European take the extension *-t*. This appears regularly in Greek (*ὕδωρ, ὕδατος* etc.), and elsewhere there are traces of it, though not many (Skt. *várimat-*, etc.). The *-t* could also be added to the adjectival *n*-suffix, and the compound suffix so produced has proved more productive than the neuter *-nt-*. In Sanskrit it appears in the suffixes *-ant*, *-vant* and *-mant*, all of which are highly productive.

The suffix *-ant-* appears in a small number of adjectives, namely *bṛhánt-* ' great ', *mahánt-* ' great ', *ṛhánt-* ' small ', *pṛ́ṣant-* ' speckled ' and *rúśant-* ' bright ', to which may be added the pronominal adjectives *íyant-* ' so much ' and *kíyant-* ' how much '. The first three have the proper adjectival accent, and in *pṛ́ṣant-*, *rúśant-* the apophony shows that the radical accent is unoriginal. Similar adjectives in Iranian are seen in *bərəzant-* ' high ' and *mazant-* ' big '. These are related to neuters in the usual way (Av. *barəzan-* ' height ', *mazan-* ' greatness ') but in this case the adjectival forms have received the *t* extension whereas the neuters have not.

These adjectives are sometimes referred to as being of participial origin. This is obviously not so, since the specialisation of this suffix in participial use, though ancient, is nevertheless a secondary development. The common usage of the suffix in active participles had not been fixed at the time of the separation of Hittite, because there the participles in *-ant* have a passive sense as opposed to the active sense which prevails in the rest of Indo-European : *kunant-* ' slain ' as opposed to Skt. *ghnánt-* ' slaying '. Both are specialisations out of a more general sense 'one connected with slaying'. Such a general meaning is all that is inherent to begin with in any adjectival formation, and it is by adaptation that the special functions of the various suffixes arise.

The non-thematic participles and those from thematic verbs which are accentuated on the suffix keep the suffixal accent: *adánt-* 'eating', *tudánt-* 'pushing', etc. Elsewhere it conforms to the regular accentuation of the verbal stem: *bhárant-* 'bearing', *jíghāṃsant-* 'desiring to slay', etc. This accent is shifted to the suffix in the weakest cases, an ancient feature which has often been levelled out, and the same applies to the suffixally accented adjectives: gen. sg. *adatás, bṛhatás*. In the nom. sg. the stems in *-ant* differ from the adjectival types in simple *-n* in that the case is denoted by the termination *s* and not by vṛddhi. This is so also in Hittite and it seems that from the earliest period of Indo-European that can be reached the nom. sg. was normally expressed in this way in the case of stems ending in occlusives.

The suffix *-vant* occurs in a number of primary formations which illustrate its origin from the compounding of simpler suffixes. Primary formations are: *vívasvant-* also *vivásvant-* 'brilliant' (: simple *n*-stem in *vivasvan-* nt. 'brilliance' and in the Av. derivative *Vīvaŋhana-*), *śáśvant-* 'numerous, all' (cf. *śáśīyas-* 'more numerous' and *śaśayá-* 'abundant'), *árvant-* 'swift, steed' (: *árvan-* 'id'), *ṛ́kvant-* 'hymning, worshipping' (: *ṛ́kvan-* 'id'), *satvánt-* 'name of a tribe of warriors' (: *sátvan-* 'warrior'), *yahvánt* 'young, youngest' (: *yahú-* 'id'), *vivakvánt-* 'eloquent'. The existence of pairs like *ṛ́kvan-*: *ṛ́kvant*; *árvan-*: *arvánt* illustrates the fact that this suffix is a *t*-extension of a simpler *van*-stem. In *yahú*: *yahvánt* the analysis goes further and a simple *u*-stem is left. In Avestan we find *drəgvant-* 'wicked', as opposed to Skt. *drúhvan-* 'id', and an interesting treble series, *ərəzu-*, *ərəzvan-*, *ərəzvant-* 'straight' which shows how the compound suffix is built up step by step. Av. *bəzvant-* 'abundant' bears the same relation to Skt. *bahú-*, as Skt. *yahvánt-* to *yahú-*. Such pairs are found also in Hittite: *daššu-*: *daššuwant-* 'strong, healthy'.

It is as a secondary suffix that *-vant* is most frequently used in Sanskrit: *áśvavant-* 'possessing horses', *kéśavant-* 'hairy', *putrávant* 'having a son' and so on in unlimited number. The usage also occurs widely in Iranian, Av. *zastavant-* 'having hands ', *amavant-* ' strong ', etc., and, outside Indo-Iranian, in Greek : *χαρίεις, χαρίεντα* (for ° *Fεις*, °*Fεντα*) ' having grace, graceful ', *ἰχθυόεις* ' abounding in fish ', etc.

In the *Ṛgveda* there are occasional examples of non-adjectival formations in *-vant* ; for instance *áśvavant-* sometimes appears not as an adjective, but as an abstract-collective noun, e.g. I. 83. I, *áśvāvati prathamó góṣu gacchati* ' he goes first in (the possession of) horses and cows ', where the singular collective corresponds to the plural *góṣu*. Such traces are valuable in that there was originally an old class of neuters in *-vant* related to the adjectives in *-vant* according to the usual principle. Secondary formations with the neuter suffixes are known in Hittite (*antuḫšatar* ' mankind ', from *antuḫšaš*, ' man ', etc.), and such are to be ascribed to Indo-European. We may construct on these lines a neuter **áśvavar* ' collectivity of horses, property in horses ' alternating in the way usual in the case of neuters with **áśvavan-*, or with extension *áśvavant-*, on the basis of which **aśvavánt* ' possessor of horses would be derived in the usual way. Another piece of evidence is got by comparing Av. *karšivant-* ' cultivator ' with Skt. *kṛṣīvalá-* and *kā́rṣīvaṇa-* ' id '. The alternation of suffix between the last two words can only be explained by the existence of an old alternating neuter **kā́rṣivar/n*, and from this Av. *karšivant-* has been derived in the same way as *áśvavant-*.

According to the usual system one would expect the original accent of the adjectives in *-vant* to have been on the suffix. In the secondary formations in Sanskrit this accentuation appears in *nṛvánt-* ' manly ', *padvánt-* ' having feet ' and *nasvánt-* ' having a nose ', where the primitive stems are monosyllabic, and in some cases where the primitive stem is accented on the suffix (but never when this stem ends in *-a* or *-ā*), *agnivánt-* ' having a fire ', *āsanvánt-* ' having a mouth ', etc. The primary formations have the accent only in a minority of cases. The same tendency to throw back the accent was observed in the adjectives in *-van*.

The suffix *-mant* appears in very few primary derivatives, namely *virúkmant-* ' shining ', *dyumánt-* ' bright ' (cf. *dyumná* nt. ' brightness ', *suṣumánt-* ' kind ' (cf. *suṣumná-* nt. ' kind. ness '), *dasmánt-* ' glorious ' (only *dasmát* nt. sg. used adverbially). The relation of *āśumánt-* ' swift ' (*āśumát* adv.) to *āśu-* recalls that of *yahvánt-* to *yahú-*, etc. Elsewhere it is used as a secondary suffix in exactly the same sense as *-vant*. Occasionally the two suffixes are used after the same word, e.g. *agnimánt-* beside *agnivánt-*, but usually one only of the two suffixes is used in connection with each word. There are no absolute rules to say when each suffix will be used, except that *-mant* is regularly employed after stems in *-u*, *paśumánt-* 'possessing cattle', etc. (frequently also to avoid repetition of *v*, *yávamant-* 'rich in barley', etc.). This rule is interesting because much the same kind of rule is found in Hittite both in the case of suffixes related to this (Inf. *arnummar* 'to bring', Supine *waḫnumanzi* 'to turn (trans.)' as opposed to *ešuwar*, *ašuwanzi* from *eš-* 'to be', etc.), and in the 1st person plur. of the verb (*arnummeni* 'we bring' as opposed to *epweni* 'we hold', etc.). The accent of the adjectives in *-mant* follows the same rules that apply to the formations in *-vant*.

§ 10. Thematic Adjectival Formations from *r-* and *n-* Stems

There was an alternative way in Indo-European of making adjectives and agent nouns from the primitive neuter formations, and it was equally commonly used. This was the addition of the accented thematic vowel. These derivatives have the same meaning as those just described, and the two types of formation often exist side by side, e.g. Skt. *atrá-* 'eater': *attár-* 'id'; Hitt. *veštaraš* 'herdsman': Av. *vāstar-* 'id'; Gk. ἰατρός, ἰāτήρ 'physician'; Gk. ζητρός 'executioner': Skt. *yātár-* 'avenger, punisher' (cf. *yātanā* 'punishment, torment' with *-n-* indicating an old alternating neuter). The accent is normally on the suffix, but it is occasionally transferred to the radical syllable: *dáṃṣṭra-* 'fang'. The type has prospered, and with the dying out of the bulk of the old neuter types, the suffixes *-rá*, etc., have come to have the appearance of primary suffixes. Formations of this kind are made on the basis both of the simple neuter suffixes -(*a*)*r*, -(*a*)*n* and of the compound suffixes.

(i) Examples of formations in *-rá* are: *ugrá-* 'powerful' (: Av. *aogar-* 'strength'), *usrá-* 'matutinal, shining like dawn' (*vasar°*, *uṣar-* 'dawn'), *udrá-* 'water-animal, otter' (Gk. ὕδωρ, etc.), *a-vadhrá-* 'not injuring' (*vádhar* 'smiting; weapon'), *kṣudrá-* 'small', *kṣiprá-* 'swift', *vakrá-* 'crooked', *hasrá-* 'laughing', etc. An old neuter alternating *r*/*n* stem is often indicated by the existence of derivatives from the *n*-stem side by side with these formations in *-rá*, e.g. beside *vípra-* ' inspired ' (with retracted accent), *vipanyā́*, etc. ; cf. also *kṣiprá-* ' quick ' : *kṣepnú-*, *kṣipaṇú-* ; *gṛdhrá-* ' greedy ' : *gṛdhnú-* ' id ' ; *dhvasrá-* ' dusty ' : *dhvasáni-* ' sprinkler (a cloud) ' ; *śvitrá-* ' white ' : *śvetanā́* ' dawn ', etc. The accent is thrown back in only a minority of cases and these are mainly substantivised adjectives : *śū́ra-* ' strong man, hero ' (Gk. ἄκυρος ' powerless '), *ájra-* ' field ' (√*aj-* ; original accent in Gk. ἀγρός ; Gk. ἀγείρω ' gather, collect ', is formed from a primary neuter **ager*, cf. the type *ratharyáti*), *vájra-* ' club, thunderbolt ' (' smasher, crusher ', cf. Gk. ἄγνυμι) *vápra-* ' mound, earthwork ' (Av. *vafra-* ' snow '), *túmra-* ' humped ', of the Indian bull (cf. Lat. *tumeō, tumōr*, etc.).

In this, the oldest type, the thematic vowel preceding the *r* is eliminated on account of the following accent. There are also a smaller number of adjectives in which the *-á* is added without any such reduction : *dravará-* ' running ', *patará-* ' flying ', *nyòcara-* ' suitable, agreeable ', *ávara-* ' lower ' (: *avár*), *úpara-* ' nearer ' ; with vṛddhi, *vānara-* ' monkey ' (*vanar°* ' forest '), *vāsará-* ' matutinal ' (*vasar°* ' early morning '). The same type with full vowel before the *r* appears also in other languages, Av. *aδara-* ' lower ', *urvīsara-* ' fugitive ' (*urvaēs-*), Gk. ἐλεύθερος ' free ', etc. Such forms must have originated at a time when the accent had ceased to have the effect of reducing unaccented syllables.

A parallel series in *-ló* was formed in Indo-European. In the Vedic language this suffix would also appear as *-rá*. Instances of *-lá* occur in Sanskrit, e.g. *śuklá-* ' white ' (also *śukrá-*), *sthūlá-* ' thick ' (also *sthūrá-*), *gopālá-* ' cowherd ', but it is never possible to be sure about the origin of *l* in Sanskrit.

(ii) From the base *-var/ur* : With strong form of suffix, *bhāsvará-* ' brilliant ' (**bhāsvar* nt. ' brilliance '), *īśvará-* ' lord ', *śākvará-* ' strong ', *adhvará-* ' sacrifice ' (of adjectival origin from its accent ; cf. *adhván-* ' way '), *sthāvará-* ' stable ' (also *sthāvaná-* showing old alternating neuter), *naśvara-* ' perishable ', *vyadvará-* ' a gnawing animal ' (: Gk. εἶδαρ nt.), *niṣadvará-* ' mud ' ; with *t*-suffix inserted, *itvará-* ' going ', *sṛtvara-* ' id ', *jitvara* ' victorious '. The variant *-vala* appears in *vidvalá* ' clever ' (cf. Gk. εἰδυλίς ' id '), *palvalá-* ' pond ' (cf. Lat. *palūs* ' marsh '), and in a number of secondary formations, *kṛṣīvala-*

'cultivator' (: *kā́rṣīvaṇa-* 'id'), *ūrjasvala-* 'strong', *pariṣad-valá-* 'having a pariṣad, king', *āsutīvalá-* 'priest who presses soma'. A vṛddhied formation is seen in *bhārvará-* 'impetuous' (cf. *bhurváṇi-* 'id.' and Lat. *fervor*, etc.). These formations often exist side by side with adjectives in *-van* : *īśvará-* 'lord' : Av. *isvan-* ; *itvará-* 'going' ; °*itvan-* ; *sthāvará-* 'standing, stable', *sasthā́van-* 'standing together' ; *pīvara-* 'fat' : *pī́van-* 'id': This relationship is based on old alternating neuters, **ī́śvar/n* 'authority', etc.

The weak form of the suffix appears in *bhāsurá-* 'shining', *chidurá-* 'tearing', *bhaṅgurá-* 'breaking', *bhidurá-* 'splitting', *vidurá-* 'wise', *medurá-* 'fat', *aṅkura-* 'bud, shoot ; swelling tumour' (: Gk. ὀγκύλος 'swollen, proud'), *kṣurá-* 'razor' (Gk. ξυρόν nt., cf. O. Sl. *česati* 'to comb', etc.). In the nominalised *śvásura-* the accent is retracted, as commonly ; the accent of Gk. ἑκυρός is more original. Beside *pāṃsurá-* 'dusty', and *madhurá-* 'sweet' forms with *l* appear, *pāṃsulá-*, *madhulá-*, without it being possible to say which is original. Beside *śmaśrula-* 'bearded' there is *śmaśruṇá-*. The weak form of the suffix appears as *-vr-* in *tīvrá-* 'intense'.

(iii) A parallel suffix *-irá* appears in *rudhirá-* 'red' (as opposed to simple *-ra-* suffix in Gk. ἐρυθρός, etc.), *badhirá-* 'deaf' (√*ba(n)dh-* 'to bind, obstruct'), *madirá-* 'intoxicating', *iṣirá-* 'vigorous' (: Gk. ἱερός from simple *r*-stem), *śithirá-* 'loose', *rathirá-* 'charioteer', *médhira-* 'wise' (with retracted accent), *sth-irá-* 'firm', *sph-irá-* 'fat', *rucira-* 'bright' ; more rarely *-ila*, *tṛdilá-* 'porous', *salilá* 'flowing', nt. 'water' beside *sarirá-*, *śithilá-* 'loose' beside *śithirá-* ; with guṇa of suffix (like *-vara-*, *valá*) *samuṣyalá-* 'cohabiting' (*sam* + *vas-*).

(iv) From the neuter suffix *-mar* there are a few such derivatives : *admará-* 'gluttonous' (implying **admar* nt. 'eating'), *ghasmará* 'id', *sṛmará-* 'a swift moving animal' (cf. Gk. ὁρμαίνω, denom. vb. from *n*-stem), *pāmara-* 'scabby ; miserable' (also *pāmaná-* from *n*-stem), *aśmará-* 'stony' (cf. *aśmán* above, § 6) ; with weak form of suffix *dhūmrá-* 'grey' ; with *l* *pakṣmalá-* 'having (long) eyelashes' (*pákṣman-* nt. 'eyelash'), *śleṣmalá-* alternating with *śleṣmaṇá-* 'afflicted with phlegm' (*śleṣmán-* masc. 'phlegm'), *bhīmalá-* 'fearful'.

It was observed in dealing with the simple *r*-neuters that they might either appear with guṇa (*ū́dhar*) or by the weak form of the suffix followed by the extension *t* (*yákṛt*). Forms of the latter type can be deduced from certain derivatives of *mar*-stems: *karmaṭha*- 'workman' from **karmṛthá*- (**karmṛt(h)*- 'work' + *á*; aspiration as in *káprth*-), likewise *narmaṭha*- 'jester' and *harmuṭa* 'tortoise' (**harmṛt-á*- 'an animal possessing a **harmṛt*, i.e. 'roof or shell', cf. *harmyá* 'roof').

(v) A few such adjectives are formed from *sar*-stems: *sapsará*- 'attending on' (√*sap*-), *matsará*- 'exhilarating; exhilarated' (cf. *mandasāná*- from the corresponding *san*-stem), °*ṛkṣará*- 'hurting; thorn' (related to *arśasāná*- 'injuring' in the same way as *matsará*- to *mandasāná*-), *saṃvatsará*- 'year', *dhūsara*- 'grey', *kṛsara*- 'a confection of sesamum, rice, etc.', *kṛcchrá*- 'painful, difficult' (if for **kṛpsrá*-), *usrá*- 'bull' (for **ursrá*-, i.e. **vṛsrá*-, -*sr*- alternating with the *san* of *vṛ́ṣan*-).

(vi) Based on the old neuters in -*tar* there are adjectival formations in -*tará* and -*trá*. By a secondary development the suffix -*tara* has come to be specialised in the formation of comparatives, but there are a few old formations where this is not so, and where the original, more general function of the suffix is apparent. For instance *aśvatará*- 'mule' is an animal which partakes of the nature of a horse (**aśvatar* nt.) and in the same way Iranian *kapautara*- 'pigeon' (Mod. Pers. *kabūtar*) is a bird characterised by bluish-grey colour (**kapautar* nt.). In *kārotará* 'filter, sieve' there is a vṛddhied formation based on neuter action noun **karotar* 'sifting'. This root most commonly appears with *i*- extension (Gk. κρίνω, etc., Ir. *crīathar* 'sieve') but a *u*-extension, as here, is found in Goth. *and-hruskan* 'ἀνακρίνειν'. Other examples of this type are *vatsatará*- 'yearling calf', and with retracted accent *sánutara*- 'clandestine' (: *sanutár* adv.) and *dívātara*- 'diurnal'. The adjective *ántara*- 'interior' is derived from *antár* 'inside (Lat. *inter*, etc.) and this in its turn from IE *en* 'in' + the neuter suffix -*ter*. In the same way Skt. *pratará*- (only in the adv. *pratarám*), Av. *fratara*- 'being in the front', Gk. πρότερος 'former' are derived from *pró*- through an intermediate **próter* 'the front' (adv. **protér*). In this way there arises a class of adjectives based on prepositions, such as Skt. *avatará*- 'lower' (only in the adv. *avatarám*), *úttara*- 'upper', Av. *ništara*- 'being outside', Gk. πρότερος 'former', ὑπέρτερος 'higher', etc. These prepositional formations have a comparative meaning ('higher, lower', etc.) but this does not come from the suffix but from the nature of the base to which it is attached. On the basis of these formations, and from similar cases like Lat. *dexter*, Gk. *δεξιτερός* ' right, being on the right ' there was evolved for this suffix a special comparative meaning, with which it is added as a secondary suffix to adjectives in Indo-Iranian and Greek (rarely elsewhere : O. Ir. *librither*, comp. of *lebor* ' long ') : *āmátara-* ' rawer ', *cā́rutara-* ' dearer ', *tavástara-* ' stronger ', etc. : Gk. *ὠμότερος* ' rawer ', *κουφότερος* ' lighter ', etc. The fact that it is not widespread in Indo-European shows that this use of the suffix is comparatively late.

There are a few adjectives and nouns of adjectival origin in *-trá* : *atrá-* ' eater ' (for *at-trá-* from *ad-*), *vṛtrá-* ' enemy ; n. of a demon ', *mitrá-* ' friend ; n. of a god ', *putrá-* ' son ' (cf. Oscan *puklum* ' puerum ', Paelignian *puclois*, with *-kl-* <*-tl-* ; Lat. *puer* with simpler *r-* suffix) ; with retracted accent, *dáṃṣṭra-* ' fang ', *tárutra-* ' victorious ', *víbhṛtra-* ' who is carried about (Agni) ', *johū́tra-* ' calling aloud ', *úṣṭra-* ' draught-animal, camel ' (apparently from *vah-* with irregular sandhi, cf. Av. *vaštar-* ' drought animal ' = *voḍhár-*) ; with vṛddhi, *jaítra-* ' victorious ' ; with gradation *-atra*, *ámatra-* ' violent ', *yájatra-* ' worthy of worship '.

(vii) With *-ná-* there are a number of nouns and adjectives, e.g. *stená-* ' thief ', *yajñá-* ' sacrifice ' (Gk. *ἁγνός* ' holy, pure '), *ghṛṇá-* ' heat ', *nagná-* ' naked ', *uṣṇá-* ' hot ' ; with radical accent *śvítna-* ' white '. The most common use of the suffix is to make participles from certain verbal roots (about seventy) : *bhinná-* ' broken ', *bhugná-* ' bent ', *pūrṇá* ' full ', *mlāná-* ' withered ', etc.

With the gradation *-aná* there are formed a certain number of agent nouns : *karaṇá-* ' active ', *tvaraṇá* ' hastening ', *krośaná-* ' shouting ', *vacaná-* ' speaking ', *svapaná-* ' sleeping ', etc. These are distinguished by their accent in the usual way from the corresponding class of neuter action nouns : cf. *káraṇa-* ' deed ', *vácana-* ' word '. In Germanic and Slavonic this formation makes passive participles (O. Sl. *nesenŭ* ' carried ', Goth. *fulgins* ' hidden '). The contrast in accent between *káraṇa-* nt. and *karaṇá-* masc. is also found in Germanic, where the infinitive is the equivalent of this neuter type : Goth. *filhan* ' to hide ', *fulgins* ' hidden '.

Though the old type of accentuation is preserved frequently in these adjectives (as above), the system was breaking down, and radically accented forms occur, particularly from verbs of the first class with fixed radical accent: *jávana-* 'hastening' (*jávati*), *dyótana-* 'shining' (*dyótate*), etc.

(viii) Corresponding to *-vará* and *-urá* thematic adjectival stems are made on the basis of the neuter *van-* suffix, with two gradations, *-vana* and *-una*. (a) *vagvaná-* 'talkative', *śuśukvaná-* 'shining', *satvaná-* 'warrior'; from prepositional bases *pravaṇá-* 'sloping forward, inclined', *udvaṇa-* 'elevated'. (b) *mithuná-* 'paired' (Av. *miθwara-* from alternating *r*-stem), *śakuná-* 'bird' (√*śak*, as prophesying the future), *aruṇá-* 'red', *dāruṇá-* 'terrible'; with radical accent *árjuna-* 'white' (Gk. ἄργυρος 'silver' from *r*-stem; cf. also Skt. *ṛjrá-* from uncompounded *r*-stem), *píśuna-* 'slanderous, treacherous' (cf. Gk. πικρός 'bitter, inimical', from simple *r*-stem), *táruṇa-* 'tender' (cf. Gk. τερήν with uncompounded *n*-stem, τέρυς, uncompounded *u*-stem), *víṣuṇa-* 'various'; with penultimate accent, *dharúṇa-* 'holding', *yatúna-* 'energetic'.

Fuller types of gradation are found in occasional forms: *-avana* in *śrávaṇa-* 'lame' (Lat. *cl-au-dus*, etc.), *lavaṇá* 'salty'; nt. salt (**slavana-*: Lat. *sal*); *-ona* in *śroṇá-*, *śloṇá-* 'lame', *syoná-* 'soft, agreeable', *duroṇá-* 'house'.

(ix) The suffix *-iná* parallel to *-uná* appears in a few words: *vṛjiná-* 'crooked', *hariṇá* 'yellowish: deer', *aminá-* 'overpowering', *āśiná-* 'old' (√*aś-*), *śākiná-* 'strong'; with radical accent, *dákṣiṇa-* 'right'. With guṇa of the first element the combination appears as *ena* only in the feminine *sāmidhenī́* (*ṛ́k*) 'connected with lighting the fire'. In Iranian the combination *-aina* is common: Av. *izaēna-* 'made of leather', *drvaēna-* 'wooden', etc. In Sanskrit there are certain further derivatives from such a suffix, namely the gerundives in *-enya*: *váreṇya-* 'desirable', *īkṣéṇya-* 'worthy to behold', etc. The gradation *-yana* (cf. *-vaná*, etc.) is not found in Sanskrit, but it appears in Av. *airyana-* 'Aryan'. The full grade of both suffixes (*-ayana*) is not found but certain patronymics with double vṛddhi (*Dākṣāyaṇa-*, etc.) appear to be based on such a formation. The corresponding forms in Avestan (e.g. *Vaŋhudātayana-*) are without vṛddhi.

(x) Adjectival formations from neuter *man*-stems are rare: *nimná-* 'low; nt. depth'. The neuters *nṛmṇá-* 'manliness', *sumná-* 'kindness' and *dyumná-* 'brightness' appear from their accentuation to be of adjectival origin. Formations of this type are commoner in other languages, e.g. Lat. *alumnus* 'nursling' (cf. *alimōnes, alimōnia*), Gk. στέρεμνος 'hard', the Avestan middle participles in *-mna, yazəmna-*, etc., and the corresponding Greek participles with guṇa (φερόμενος, etc.). The two types differ in the same way as *-vana/-una, -vara/-ura*, etc. The corresponding Sanskrit participles with vṛddhi will be treated below.

(xi) There are a few thematic adjectives based on the suffix *-san*: *kṛṣṇá-* 'black' (: O. Pruss. *kirsna-*, O. Sl. *črŭnŭ*), *ślakṣṇá-* 'smooth', *akṣṇa-* 'oblique' (adv. *akṣṇayā́*), *tīkṣṇá-* 'sharp', *kṛtsná-* 'all'; also a few substantives of adjectival origin: *pyúkṣṇa-* 'covering for a bow', *hálikṣṇa-* 'a kind of animal; a particular part of the intestines', *mṛtsna-* masc. nt. 'dust, powder', *deṣṇá-* nt. 'gift' ('what is given'). With different gradations of suffix *karásna-* 'arm', *vadhasná-* masc. or nt. 'deadly weapon'; *Pūṣaṇá-* beside *Pūṣán-* (cf. *satvaná-* and *sátvan-*), *duvasaná-* 'going far (or the like)'.

(xii) Apart from *cyautná-* 'stirring', nt. 'exploit' (: Av. *šyaoθna-*) the suffixes *-tna* and *-tana* are specialised in connection with adverbs of time (cf. the similar use of *-tara* in *dívātara-*): *nū́tana-*, *nū́tna-* 'belonging to the present time', *pratná-* 'old', *sanātána-* 'eternal', *adyatana* 'of today', *hyastana-* 'of yesterday', etc.

In the above examples we have a series of adjectives all formed in the same way by the addition of the accented thematic vowel to the various *r-* and *n-* suffixes. It has been pointed out that these suffixes were capable of taking the extension *-t*, and there are a few adjectival forms which are based on such an extension. An example from an *r*-stem is *muhūrtá-* 'moment' from *muhur* (: Av. *mərəzu-* 'short', of time). Reference has already been made to certain formations showing Prakritic tendencies, *karmaṭha-*, *harmuṭa*. From the *n*-suffix extended by *t* there are a number of thematic formations which to judge by their accent were originally adjectival, *vasantá-* 'spring' (cf. *vasar°*), *veśantá-* 'pond' (√*viś* 'where rainwater settles') and with weak grade of suffix *avatá-* 'well'. Based on the *man-* suffix there are *hemantá-* 'winter', *sīmánta-* 'parting of the hair' (: *sīman-* 'id. boundary') and *aśmanta-* 'fireplace'; on *van/un*, *śakúnta-* 'bird' beside *śakúna-* (also *śakúni-*, *śakúnti-* with *i*-suffix, cf. *śákvan-*, etc.). In *párvata-* 'mountain', which we may compare with Hitt. *peruna-*, *perunant-* 'rock', there is another variant of the weak form of this suffix (-*wn̥*-), and, as often elsewhere, retraction of the accent. These formations are not very common and some of them from quite an early period were misunderstood as if they were compounds with *anta-* 'end' as second member. For this reason the variant forms, *veśānta-*, *sīmānta-* occur. It is not unlikely that some other apparent compounds of this type, e.g. *karmānta-* 'work, business' (Pa. *kammanta-*), which only occur in the latter form, are corruptions of this type.

§ 11. Thematic Formations with Vṛddhi of Suffix

We have seen above that there exist two quite distinct ways of making adjectives and agent nouns on the basis of the primitive neuter suffixes. In addition there is a series of formations which must be classified by themselves, since they participate in the characteristics of both the above types. They are thematic formations, frequently accented on the final syllable, but at the same time the suffix to which the thematic vowel is attached, has vṛddhi, like the agent nouns of the type *brahmán-* in the nom. sg. In this respect they represent a cross between the two systems, and they appear to be thematic extensions of formations of the *brahmán-* type, based on the nom. sg. For instance we may explain Vedic *karmā́ra-* 'smith' as follows. From the evidence of Hittite and Greek it is clear, as shown above, that the neuter *man-* stems were originally alternating stems with nom. acc. sg. in *-mar*. We have also seen that on the basis of all these neuter suffixes in *r* and *n*, simple and compound, adjectives and agent nouns could be made by the method illustrated by *brahmán-*. Instances in connection with most of the suffixes were quoted. On this analogy we might expect on the basis of **kármar* nt. (obl. base *kárman-*) an agent noun **karmā́r*. Vedic *karmā́ra-* is a thematic extension of such a form, and it has been already pointed out above that this tendency to thematisation, which is familiar from the later history of Indo-Aryan, had already been operating in the prehistoric period. Another formation of this type appears to be *mārjārá-* 'cat', but they are exceedingly rare from *r*-stems. On the other hand such formations are common in the case of the *n*-suffixes, and in particular they have given rise to a series of middle participles in Sanskrit to which nothing exactly corresponds in the other languages.

From the simple *n*-suffix we have the suffix *-ānā́* which is used in the formation of middle participles of the type *adānā́-* 'eating', *duhānā́-* 'milking, etc.' Skt. *adānā́-* is a thematic formation corresponding to the non-thematic Lat. *edō-ōnis*. A formation of exactly the same kind is Lat. *colōnus*, but such are exceedingly rare. There is final accent in the above examples, and in the perfect participles, *bubudhānā́-* 'waking', etc.; but in the reduplicating presents and in the desiderative, initial accent.

Other formations of this type are rare: *samānā́-* 'same, common', a thematic extension of a masculine *n*-stem such as appears in Goth. *sama* (as *sámana-* nt. is an extension of a corresponding neuter *n*-stem) and *purāṇā́-* 'ancient'.

On the basis of the *man*-suffix there are middle participles in *-amāna*, *yájamāna-* 'sacrificing', etc. It is based on that form of the neuter *men*-stem which is attached to the root with the thematic vowel: Gk. φέρεμεν inf., etc. The vṛddhied masculines corresponding to this type are represented by such forms as Gk. ἡγεμών 'leader', κηδεμών 'one who cares for'. Thematic extension of such a type produces the Skt. type *yájamāna-*. In the thematic conjugations to which this type of participle is attached, the stable verbal accent prevails. This type of participial formation is peculiar to Sanskrit, since the most closely related types of participle (Av. *yazəmna-*, Gk. φερόμενος) are differently formed, in the manner indicated above. As has happened in other cases it was by adaptation that such formations acquired the status of middle participles, and this adaptation seems to have been comparatively late, since such participles are known from only a small section of Indo-European.

There is a parallel series of formations in *-asānā́*, most of which have the character of pseudo-participles. Such are: *jrayasānā́* 'far-extending', *namasānā́-* 'rendering homage', *bhiyásāna-* 'fearing', *mandasānā́-* 'rejoicing', *vṛdhasānā́-* 'growing', *śavasānā́-* 'strong', *arśasānā́-* 'injuring', *sahasānā́-* 'overpowering'. In many cases there exists a neuter *-as-* stem beside these formations (*jráyas-*, *námas-*, *śávas-*, *sáhas-*). We have seen that the neuter *as*-stems were capable of taking the extension *r/n*. On the basis of the *san*-stem produced by such an extension (**námasan-*, etc.) these adjectives have been produced by the combined method of vṛddhi of the suffix and addition of the accented thematic vowel. It will also be observed that they bear the same relation to the infinitives in *-sen* (Gk. φέρειν, i.e. *φερεσεν, **bheresen*) as exists between *bháramāna-* and φέρεμεν. To some extent they have acquired the character of participles, but the process of adaptation is incomplete. Unlike the participles in *-māna* they are not integrated with any tense stem, and the practice of classifying them with the participles of the *s*-aorist was more of an emergency measure than a serious attempt at their analysis.

In *ūrdhvasānā́-* ' erect ' we find *-sānā́* used purely as an adjectival suffix. In Pa. *rakkhitamānasāna-* ' whose mind is guarded ', a formation of this type is used to provide an adjectival termination for a bahuvrīhi compound.

Suffixes of the same type are made on the basis of the other compound *n*-suffixes : *-avāna-* in *bhṛ́gavāna-* ' shining ', *vásavāna-* ' possessing riches ', and in the proper names *Ápnavāna-* and *Pṛ́thavāna-* ; *-ayāna-* in *tū́rvayāṇa-* ' victorious ' and *Hárayāṇa-* n. pr. Here belong the middle participles in *-ayāna-*, made in the Epic language from tenth class and causative verbs : *cintayāna-*, *pālayāna-*, etc. Though not used in the Vedic language, nor allowed in the Classical, this formation could be an ancient dialectal feature.

§ 12. Various Extensions of the *r* and *n* Suffixes

The suffix *-ā* is regularly used to make the feminine of the thematic adjectives classified above. In addition it appears in a number of independent formations. In *yóṣaṇā* (once *yoṣáṇā*) ' woman ' and *kanyánā* ' girl ' it appears as an extension of feminine *n*-stems (*yóṣan-* ' woman ', Av. *kainīn-* ' girl '). The formation *kanyálā* which is also found shows that the fem. **kanyan-* on which *kanyánā* is based was originally an alternating neuter. There are also words which may be of adjectival type though no corresponding masculine occurs, e.g. *áṣṭrā* ' goad ' (' driver '). In addition there are a number in which *-ā* is simply an extension of old neuter *r* and *n* stems, adding nothing to the meaning, e.g. *mā́trā* ' measure ' (**mātar* + *ā*). Others are *súrā* ' intoxicating liquor ', *dhā́rā* ' cutting edge ', *urvárā* ' cultivated land ' (Av. *urvarā* ' crop ' : an old *r*/*n* neut. of Indo-European is attested by Ir. *arbor*, nom. acc. pl. *arbann*), *vāgurā́* ' net ', *támisrā* ' darkness ', *hótrā* ' oblation '. The same type is formed on the basis of the *n*-suffix : *tṛ́ṣṇā* ' thirst ', *sénā* ' army ', *sthū́ṇā* ' post ', *dhénā* ' milk-cow '. The gradation *-anā* is common, the words being accented either on the last syllable or the penultimate (for accent of *ā*-stems see below, p. 191) : *arháṇā* ' worth ', *barháṇā* ' might ', *vadhánā* ' slaughter ', *vanánā* ' desire ' ; *asanā́* ' missile ', *jaraṇā́* ' old age', *dyotanā́* ' brilliance ', *raśanā́* ' rein ', *hasanā́*. With these action nouns in *-anā* compare the Greek type ἡδονή ' pleasure '.

There are a few such formations in *-ī* and *-ū* : *rā́trī-* ' night ', *tandrī́-* ' sloth ', *nabhanū́-* ' spring '.

Stems are frequently made by the addition of *i* and *u* to the *r* and *n* suffixes.

(a) The suffix *-i* serves as an enlargement of *r*-stems in *áṅgh-r-i* masc. ' foot ' (cf. O. Sl. *noga* ' foot ' from different gradation of root) *ábhri-* fem. ' hoe ', *áśri-* fem. ' edge, point ', *aṅgúri* fem. ' finger '. Adjectives are *arcátri-* ' singing hymns ', *átri-* ' devouring ', *bhū́ri-* ' abundant ', *śubhrí-* ' beautiful ', *jásuri-* ' exhausted ', *dā́śuri-* ' pious ', *sáhuri-* ' mighty ' (cf. Gk. ἐχυρός, ὀχυρός ' firm ' with thematic suffix) ; nouns of adjectival origin, *sūrí-* ' patron ' (√*sū-*, as the instigator of the sacrifice), *vádhri-* ' a castrated animal ' (: *vadhar* ; Gk. ἔθρις ' id.').

The suffix *-i* is in the same way added to the *n*-suffix in (fem.) *śréṇi-* ' row ', *śróṇi-* ' hip ', *sṛ́ṇi-* (*sṛṇí-*) ' sickle ', *jūrṇí-* ' heat ', *jyānī́-* ' loss ', *glānī́-* ' fading ' ; (masc.) *ghṛ́ṇi-* ' heat ', *yóni* ' womb '. The suffix *-ni* is used to form a number of adjectives and nouns of adjectival origin. Such are *aśni-* ' eating ', *váhni-* ' carrying ' (later ' fire '), *tū́rṇi-* ' speeding ', *dharṇí-* ' sustaining ', *preṇí-* ' loving ', *pṛ́śni-* ' speckled ' (cf. Gk. περκνός with thematic suffix) ; of adjectival origin, *agní-* ' fire '. With the gradation *-ani* there are such nouns as (fem.) *dyotaní-* ' brilliance ', *vartaní* ' track ', *aráṇi-* ' firestick ' (*ar-* ' to fit ', alternating *r* in *arari-* ' door-leaf '). Adjectives are *taráṇi-* ' swift ', *caráṇi-* ' moving ', etc. Similar formations from the compound *n*-suffixes are : *hrādúni-* fem. ' hail ', *tuviṣváṇi-* ' powerful ' (*-vani* as secondary suffix), *aratní-* masc. ' elbow, cubit ', *iṣṭáni*, epithet of Agni, *turváṇi-* ' overcoming ', *bhurváṇi-* ' agitated ', *śusukváni-* ' shining ', *parṣáṇi-* ' carrying across ', *sakṣáṇi-* ' overcoming ', *carṣaṇí-* ' active ' ; no longer of clear derivation, *vṛṣṇí-* ' ram ', *pā́rṣṇi-* fem. ' heel ' (Gk. πτέρνα, etc.).

(b) The *u*-suffix in combination with *r* produces occasional neuter nouns, *áśru* ' tear ' (Toch. A. *ākär*, plur. *ākru-nt*), *śmaśru* ' beard ', and some adjectives, *dhārú* ' suckling ' (Gk. θῆλυς 'female'), *bhīrú-* 'timid', *patáru-* 'flying'; in combination with *n* some adjectives and nouns of adjectival origin: *dhṛṣṇú-* 'bold', *gṛdhnú-* 'greedy', *sūnú-* 'son', *dhenú-* fem. 'cow,' *bhānú-* masc. 'light'. The combinations *-tnú* and *-snú* were fairly productive in the formation of adjectives: *kṛtnú-* 'active', *dartnú-* 'breaking', *dravitnú-* 'running', *pīyatnú-* 'reviling', *stanayitnú-* 'thunder', *kavatnú-* 'stingy, mean'; *vadhasnú-* 'murderous', *jiṣṇú-* 'victorious', *cariṣṇú-* 'wandering', etc. The combination *-vanu* appears in *vagvanú-* 'noise'.

§ 13. The Suffix *s*

The neuter suffix *-as* is better preserved than any of the other old neuter suffixes, and a larger number of words of this type have directly corresponding words in other IE languages than is the case with any other suffix. Such are: *śrávas-* 'fame' (Gk. κλέος, Ir. *clú* 'id.', O. Sl *slovo* 'word'), *jánas-* 'race' (Gk. γένος, Lat. *genus*), *mánas-* 'mind' (Gk. μένος 'spirit'), *háras-* 'heat' (Gk. θέρος 'summer'), *nábhas-* 'cloud, sky' (O. Sl. *nebo*, Hitt. *nepiš-*), *árśas-* 'piles' (Gk. ἕλκος, Lat. *ulcus* 'ulcer'), *vácas-* 'word' (Gk. Ϝεπος, ἔπος), *sádas-* 'seat' (Gk. ἕδος), *pásas-* 'male organ' (Gk. πέος), *édhas-* 'fuel' (Gk. αἶθος 'burning'), *sáhas-* 'strength' (Goth. *sigis* 'victory'), *ápas-* 'work' (Lat. *opus*), *ánas-* 'waggon' (Lat. *onus* 'burden'), *vánas-* 'charm, desire' (Lat. *venus*). Other examples of this very frequent suffix are *tápas-* 'warmth', *práyas-* 'pleasure', *téjas-* 'splendour', *dóhas-* 'milking', *káras-* 'deed', *héṣas* 'injury' (*hiṃs-*), etc.

The normal type has the regular radical accent of neuters, also guṇa of suffix. Accent shift in declension (type *yákṛt*, *yaknás*) has been abandoned, and the accent remains on the root throughout the declension. There are some variant types of gradation, namely (i) vṛddhi of root in *ā́gas-* 'sin' (Gk. ἅγος), *ā́pas-* 'work' (usually *ápas-*), *vā́sas-* 'garment', *vā́has-* 'offering', *pā́jas-* 'side, surface'; (ii) weak grade of root in *úras-* 'breast', *śíras-* 'head', *júvas-* 'speed' (also *jávas-*), *mṛ́dhas-* 'contempt', *dúvas-* 'offering'; (iii) reduction of suffix in *yós-* 'welfare' (Av. *yaoš-*, Lat. *iūs*), *dós-* 'arm'. These variants show that the working of apophony was at one time active in these formations, although in most cases it has been levelled out. The type with weakened grade of root is interesting since it can only be explained out of original terminational accent in the oblique cases. There are rare examples of this switch of accent in declension, e.g. *bhiyás-* 'fear' (transfer to fem.) instr. sg. *bhīṣā́* (beside *bhiyásā*).

Some twenty-five dative infinitives are formed with this suffix. These are sometimes accented on the root, *áyase* 'to go', *cákṣase* 'to see', *dhā́yase* 'to cherish', but much more commonly on the suffix, *ṛcáse* 'to praise', *caráse* 'to fare', *jīváse* 'to live', *doháse* 'to milk', *bhojáse* 'to enjoy', *śobháse* 'to shine', *spūrdháse* 'to strive', etc. The origin of this anomalous accentuation, which is in contrast both with usual fixed radical accent of *as-* stems and with the original terminational accent of the oblique cases, is not at all clear. It may be noted that it recurs in other types of infinitive: *dāváne* 'to give', *vidmáne* 'to know'. In a very few dative infinitives based on the *s*-suffix terminational accent is found with reduction both of root and suffix: *jiṣé* 'to conquer', *stuṣé* 'to praise'.

The normal locatival accent appears in *upási* 'in the lap' (only this form), cf. *akṣáṇi*, etc. The related adverbial accent appears in *purás* 'in front', *tirás* 'across' and *mithás* 'mutually'; cf. *avár*, etc.

There are a few instances of transference of gender in the case of action nouns in *-as*. Such are, (masc.) *tavás-* 'strength' (as well as 'strong' adj.), fem. *jarás-* 'old age', *bhiyás-* 'fear' and *uṣás-* 'dawn' (cf. Gk. ἠώς). These appear mainly to be due to personification. The transference involves the adoption of the adjectival accent (as in *bhūmán-* 'abundance', etc., above).

This neuter suffix was capable from an early period of being extended by the addition of the neuter *r-* and *n*-suffixes. Examples of this (*śīrṣṇás, doṣṇás*, gen. sg., etc.) have been given above, together with derivatives from such stems (*matsará-*, *mandasāná-*, etc.). It could also be added to other suffixes, producing a variety of compound suffixes, e.g.: *-tas* in *rétas* 'seed', *srótas* 'stream' (simple *t*-stem in *sravat*); *-nas* in *rékṇas-* 'inheritance, property', *ápnas-* 'wealth', *árṇas-* 'flood', and, preceded by *i* and *ī*, *dráviṇas-* 'property', *párīṇas-* 'abundance'; *-sas* (repetition of the suffix) in *dákṣas-* 'ability, dexterity' (simple *-as* in *daśas-yáti*) and *pákṣas-* 'side' (simple *-as* in *pā́jas*); *-vas* in *pī́vas-* 'fat', *várivas-* 'expanse'. This latter combination normally appears in the weak form *-uṣ*:

áruṣ- 'wound', *ā́yuṣ-* 'length of life', *tápuṣ-* 'heat', *táruṣ-* 'victory', *yájuṣ-* 'sacrificial formula', *vápuṣ-* 'beauty', *páruṣ-* 'knot (of plants)', *dhánuṣ-* 'bow'. An alternative *n*-extension appears in *dhánvan-* 'bow' and *párvan-* 'joint', and the simple *u*-stem *ā́yu* nt. appears as well as *ā́yu-ṣ-* (cf. also *aru-* in *aruntuda-*). In the same way *s* is added to the *i*-suffix to produce the compound suffix *-iṣ*. Of these neuter nouns *jyótiṣ-* 'light', and *vyáthiṣ-* 'perturbation' are accented on the root according to the general rule. In the rest the original accent system has been disturbed, and they appear with accent on the suffix: *arcíṣ-* 'flame' (also transferred to feminine), *chardíṣ-* 'protection, cover', *barhíṣ-* 'bedding, straw' (Av. *barəziš-*), *rocíṣ-* 'light', *vartíṣ-* 'track', *śocíṣ-* 'flame', *sarpíṣ-* 'butter' (Gk. ἔλπος with simple *s*-stem), *havíṣ-* 'oblation', *kravíṣ-* 'raw flesh' (simple *i*-stem in *ákravihasta-* 'whose hands are not bloody', cf. also *kravyá-*, Lith. *kraũjas*, etc.).

The neuters in *-as* can be turned into adjectives and agent nouns by the usual process of suffixal accentuation associated with vṛddhi of the nom. sg. The neuter and adjectival types appear side by side in the case of *ápas-* 'work': *apás-* 'active'; *táras-* 'energy, force': *tarás-* 'forceful'; *yáśas-* 'beauty, glory': *yaśás-* 'beautiful'; *tyájas-* 'leaving, something let go of': *tyajás-* 'offspring'; *máhas-* 'greatness': *mahás-* 'great'; *rákṣas-* 'injury, damage': *rakṣás-* 'demon'; *dúvas-* 'worship': *duvás-* 'worshipping'. Other examples of the adjectival formation are *tavás-* 'strong', *tośás-* 'bestowing', *dhvarás-* 'deceiving', *yajás-* 'worshipping' and *veśás-* 'neighbour'. The same antithetic types appear in Greek: ψεῦδος 'falsehood': ψευδής 'false', etc.

From the compound suffix *-vas* there are some adjectival formations. The usual antithesis of the two types is seen by comparing *várivas-* nt. 'expanse' on the one hand, and *okivás-* masc. 'accustomed to, familiar' on the other. Formations of the same type are seen in *mīḍhvás-* 'liberal', *dāsvás-* 'worshipping' and *sāhvás-* 'overcoming', which inflect like perfect participles. On the other hand in *ṛ́bhvas-* 'skilful' and *śíkvas-* 'id.' are influenced in form and accentuation by the coexisting *van*-stems. There is a special connection between the adjectival suffixes *-van* and *-vas* in Sanskrit, because the latter is used to make the vocative singular of stems in the former (*ṛtāvas*, *vibhāvas*, etc.; likewise of *vant*-stems: *rayivas*, *bhagavas*, *śacīvas*, etc.). In Avestan we find this suffix used to form the nom. sg. of *vant*-stems, *amavå* nom. sg. of *amavant*- ' strong '.

Apart from the above examples the adjectival -*vás* has been specialised in the formation of perfect participles : *cakṛvás*- ' having done ', *jigīvás*- ' having conquered ', *tasthivás*- ' having stood ', *babhūvás*- ' having been ', *śuśruvás*- ' having heard ', etc. These stems show an ancient apophony in declension, even though the original terminational accent in the oblique cases which caused it has been given up (gen. sg. *tasthúsas* for **tasthuṣás*).

The adjectival *vas*-suffix was capable of taking the enlargement -*u* (cf. *vagvanú*- above, a parallel extension of -*van*). Examples are *vibhávasu*- ' brilliant ' and *śacīvasu*- ' powerful ' based on the *vas*- stems which occur in the vocatives noted above. Compare also Pa. *viddasu*- ' wise ' for **viḍvasu*-.

The specialisation of the adjectival -*vas* in the formation of these participles has resulted in its being separated completely from the corresponding compound neuter suffix which, as we have seen, usually takes the form -*uṣ*. Consequently when adjectives are needed from these, it is done simply by adapting the neuters without change of form. As noted above (p. 138) this practice has parallels elsewhere and is old, although rare through the prevalence of the normal system. Examples are *cákṣuṣ*- ' eye ; seeing ', *vápuṣ*- ' marvel ; wondrous ', *tápuṣ*- ' heat ; glowing ' ; without corresponding neuters, *náhuṣ*- ' neighbour ', *mánuṣ*- ' man ', and with suffixal accent but not the corresponding gradation, *vanúṣ*- ' eager ', *jayúṣ*- ' victorious ' and *dakṣúṣ*- ' flaming '.

There is an adjectival suffix -*yás* which likewise underwent early specialisation and became totally divorced from the neuter suffix -*iṣ*. This is used in Sanskrit, and in other languages for making comparative adjectives. Examples are : *návyas*- ' newer ', *pányas*- ' more wonderful ', *bhúyas*- ' more ', *rábhyas*- ' more violent ', *vásyas*- ' better ', *sáhyas*- ' more powerful ', *sányas*- ' older ', *távyas*- ' stronger '. Similarly Avestan has *spanyah*- ' more holy ', *tąśyah*- ' stronger ', *āsyah*- ' swifter ', etc. This formation is the regular one in Avestan, but in Sanskrit it is much less common than a formation in which the -*yas*- is added not directly to the root, but to the root plus suffix -*ī* : *kánīyas*- younger ' (cf. gen. pl. *kanī-n-ām*), *návīyas*- ' newer ', *mrádīyas*- ' softer ', *práthīyas*- ' broader ', *várīyas*- ' wider ' (cf. *vár-ī-man* 'width'), *tárīyas-* 'very swift' (cf. *tarī-ṣáṇi* inf.), *rághīyas-* 'swifter', *máhīyas-* 'greater', *sthávīyas-* 'stouter' (cf. Av. *ranjyah-*, *mázyah-*, *staoyah-*). In both accent and apophony all these forms (excepting *bhū́yas-* with weak grade of root) are reminiscent more of the neuter types (cf. *várīman-*, *várivas-* : *várīyas*). The reason for this is not clear, though it must have some significance in the question of their origin.

Corresponding forms of the comparative exist in Italic and Celtic: Lat. *seniōr*, O. Ir. *siniu* (IE **sényōs*) 'older'. The *e*-grade of the root and the *o*-grade of the suffix indicate an accent identical with that of Sanskrit (*sányas-*). In Greek the same suffix appears in some cases: ἐλάσσω (*ελαχ-yoς-α) acc. sg., ἐλάσσους (*ἐλαχ-yoσ-ες) nom. pl., but in other cases a *-yon-* suffix with similar function appears: ἐλάσσων, ἐλάσσονος, etc. In Greek, as in Sanskrit, a suffixal *ī* may be inserted before the comparative suffix: ἡδίων 'sweeter'. In Germanic a compound suffix *-is-on-* is utilised: Goth. *batiza* 'better', etc.

The weak form of the suffix (*-is-*) could make adverbs with comparative sense, e.g. Lat. *magis* 'more'. It also forms the basis of superlatives which are made by the addition of the further suffix *-tha* (elsewhere *-to*): *kániṣṭha-* 'smallest, youngest', *jáviṣṭha-* 'most speedy', *nédiṣṭha-* 'nearest' (Av. *nazdišta-*), *ā́śiṣṭha-* 'swiftest' (Av. *āsišta-*), *ójiṣṭha-* 'strongest' (Av. *aojišta-*), *gáriṣṭha-* 'heaviest', etc. As with the comparative the accent of the superlatives is invariably on the root and the apophony is according. Superlatives of the same formation are found also in Greek (ἥδιστος = *svā́diṣṭha-* 'sweetest') and in Germanic (Goth. *frumists* 'first', etc.).

As with the other neuter suffixes, adjectives and nouns of adjectival type can be made by the addition of the accented thematic vowel to the neuter *s*-suffix. These are of the usual two types, an older type in *-sá* with reduction of the suffix on account of the following accent, and a more recent type in *-asá* formed from the neuter *as*-stems with guṇa of suffix. Unlike some other suffixes of similar structure, *-sá* never became very productive or developed independently to any extent.

sá: *rukṣá-* 'shining' (*rócas-* 'light'), *dyukṣá-* 'bright' (for **dyutsá-* after *rukṣá-*; cf. also *ávākṣam* for *ávātsam*, etc.), *pṛkṣá-* 'nourishment' (*pṛ́kṣ-* 'nourishment', a reduced *s*-stem which has been adapted as a fem. root noun), *ghraṃsá-* 'heat of the sun', *vatsá-* 'calf' (Gk. Ϝέτος 'year'), *vṛkṣá-* 'tree' (*válśa-* 'foliage'), *yakṣá-* 'supernatural being' (*yáśas-* 'beauty'), *śūṣá-* 'strong' (*śávas-* 'strength'), *pakṣá-* 'side' (*pā́jas-* 'side, surface'), *rūkṣá-* 'rough, dry' (√*rūṣ-*), *drapsá-* 'banner' (Av. *drafša-*; cf. *drāpí-* 'mantle'), *drapsá-* 'drop' (for **drabžha-*, cf. Gk. τρέφω, etc.), *grapsa-* and *glapsa-* 'bunch' (**grabžha-*, √*grabh-*), *sakṣa-* 'overpowering' (*sáhas-* 'strength'), *haṃsá-* 'goose' (Gk. χήν, etc.). In a smaller number of words, chiefly substantives, the accent appears on the root, *áṃsa-* 'shoulder' (Lat. *umerus* with guṇa of suffix), *útsa-* 'spring' (Gk. ὕδος nt.), *ṛkṣá-* 'star' (*arc-* 'to shine'), *dákṣa-* 'clever' (cf. *daśasyáti*), *gṛ́tsa-* 'dexterous, able'.

-asá: *vacasá-* 'eloquent', *añjasá-* 'straight', *arṇasá-* 'flowing', *tamasá-* 'dark-coloured', *nabhasá-* 'cloudy', *rajasá-* 'dusty', *rabhasá-* 'wild', *manasá-* 'wise', *upānasá-* 'being near a waggon', *vetasá-* 'reed', *camasá-* 'cup', *pīvasá-* 'fat', *divasá-* 'day', *prapyasá-* 'swelling (with milk)'.

Thematic extensions of neuter *as*-stems, such as are common in the case of the suffixes *r* and *n*, are rare if they exist at all. It is possible that *yávasa-* (masc. and nt.) might be of this origin, but otherwise such neuter nouns in *-asa* as occur are oxytone, a fact which indicates their adjectival origin: *aṅkasá-* 'flank', *avasá-* 'refreshment', *atasá-* 'bush', *parīṇasá-* 'abundance'.

Adjectival derivations with vṛddhi are *āyasá-* 'made of metal', *vāyasá-* 'bird', *mānasá-* 'belonging to the mind' and so forth.

Similar adjectival formations from the *is-* and *us-* stems occur: *taviṣá-* 'strong', *bhariṣá-* 'rapacious', *mahiṣá-* 'great; buffalo'; *paruṣá-* 'knotty (as reed); rough', *paruṣá-* 'grey, speckled white' (Av. *pouruša-*; cf. Engl. *fallow*, etc.), *aruṣá-* 'red'; with vṛddhi, *vāpuṣá-* 'wonderful'. The radical accent of *náhuṣa-* 'neighbour', *mánuṣa-* 'man' and *vápuṣa-* 'wondrous' is connected with the fact that the corresponding *us*-stems are themselves used adjectivally without change of accent. Similar accent is found in *táruṣa-* 'overcoming' and *pū́ruṣa-*, *púruṣa-* 'man' (related to *pūrú-* 'man; n. of a tribe' as *mánuṣa-* is related to *mánu-*).

There are a few closely related formations in *-īṣa* and *-ūṣa* (*ī/ū+s+a*), *ṛjīṣá-* epithet of Indra, *āṅgūṣá-* 'hymn' and the neuters *púrīṣa-* 'rubbish', *kárīṣa-* 'dry cow-dung' and *pīyū́ṣa-* 'beest milk' (cf. *pipyúṣī* and Gk. πῦος <**pyūsos*).

There are a number of miscellaneous stems made by the addition of various suffixes to *s*-stems. Such are : *bhīṣā́* ' fear ', *manīṣā́* ' understanding ', *śavasī́* ' strength ', *táviṣī* ' id ', *sarasī́-* ' lake ' ; *plúṣi* ' flea ' (√*plu-*), *dhāsí-* ' abode ', *sānasí-* ' victorious ', *dharṇasí-* ' strong ', *atasí-* ' beggar ' ; *dákṣu-*, *dhákṣu-* ' burning ' ; *bhujiṣyà-* ' free ' ; the rare infinitival forms *avyathiṣyai* ' not to tremble ' and *rohiṣyai* ; *mastíṣka-* ' brain ' ; *naríṣṭā* ' joking ' ; *upástha-* ' lap ' (cf. *upási*), *vaniṣṭhú-* ' entrails ' (cf. Germ. *wanst* ; different suffix in Lat. *venter*). Enlargement with the suffix *-ti* appears in a fair number of examples : *gábhasti-* ' hand ', *palasti-* ' grey-haired ' (cf. *palitá-* ' id '), *pulastí-* ' having straight hair ' (cf. *pulaka-* ' bristling of the hairs of the body '), *Agásti* n. of a ṛṣi. This suffixal combination is well developed in Slavonic, where, however, it makes abstract nouns (O. Sl. *dlŭgostĭ* ' length ', etc.). It appears also in Hittite with the same function : *dalugašti* ' length '. On the other hand it appears occasionally in Latin in adjectival use, as in Sanskrit : *agrestis* ' rural ', *caelestis* ' celestial '. From *iṣ-* and *uṣ-* stems there appear formations of the same kind : *náviṣṭi-* ' hymn of praise ', *pániṣṭi-* ' admiration ', *tatanúṣṭi-* ' spreading out '.

§ 14. The Suffix *t*

The suffix *t* existed with functions like the above simple suffixes, but as an independent suffix it has become much rarer. It also very rarely provides neuters, since the tendency was from a very early period to incorporate the stems ending in occlusives into the common gender system. Its original function as one of the primary neuter suffixes is seen most clearly when it serves as an extension of the neuter *r-* and *n-* stems, e.g. in Skt. *śákṛt*, *yákṛt* and in Gk. χεῖμα, gen. sg. χείματος ' winter ' (but the corresponding *-nt-* stem in Hittite, *gimmant-* ' winter ', is common gender). Similarly the primitive suffix *t* on which the suffix *-t-ar* has been built may be presumed to have been neuter. Apart from this there remain in the various languages a few sporadic instances of a neuter suffix *t* : Skt. *pṛ́ṣat-* ' drop ', *upatápat-* ' fever ' ; Gk. μέλι (for *μέλιτ), Hitt. *milit* ' honey ' ; Gk. γάλα, γάλακτος, Lat. *lac, lactis* ' milk ', Lat. *caput* ' head '.

The use of the simple suffix *t*, in the common gender, to make action nouns and abstracts, is fairly well developed in Hittite, e.g. *kartimmiatt-* ' anger ', *duškaratt-* ' joy '. They are rare elsewhere, but where they occur such nouns have normally acquired the feminine gender : Skt. *nákt-* ' night ', Lat. *nox*, Gk. *νύξ* ; Lat. *quiēs*, *salūs*, etc. Gk. *θέμις*, *χάρις*.

The reason that such formations are so rare is that as a general rule they have been supplanted by extensions of the simple *t*-suffix, namely by *ti* in the case of action nouns, and by *tā* in the case of abstracts. In Skt. *daśát* ' decade ' beside *daśatí-* ' id.' we have an example of the unextended and extended form side by side. An isolated *avīrat-* ' absence of heroes ' (*avīrate* dat. sg. RV. 7.1.19) represents a type that has otherwise been universally supplanted by the compound suffix *tā*.

A very small number of feminine nouns in *-t* appear in Sanskrit : *sravát-*, *vahát-*, both meaning ' stream ', *saścát* ' obstacle', *vehát-* ' cow which miscarries '. Of these the last is presumably adjectival and the others could be. A masc. adjectival form appears in *vāghát-* ' worshipper '. This adjectival suffix appears elsewhere, cf. Lat. *pedes* ' footman ', *eques* ' horseman '.

In *nápāt-* ' grandson ' there is a formation with vṛddhied suffix which may be compared with the similar formations analysed above. This stem is also interesting because it retains an ancient type of declensional apophony. A reduced grade appears in Skt. *nádbhyas* dat. abl. pl., Av. *naptō* abl. sg., *nafšu* loc. pl. (with reduction of the three consonant groups). There are other examples of the vṛddhied suffix in adjectival formations in other languages : Av. *ravas-čarāt-* ' moving in the open country ', Gk. *ἀργής* ' shining ' (*ἀργῆτ-* or *ἀργέτ-* in the oblique cases, cf. the two types *δοτῆρα* and *ποιμένα*), *πένης* ' poor ', *γυμνής* ' lightly armed soldier ', Lat. *ariēs* ' ram ' (gen. *-ĕtis*), AS. *hæle* ' hero ' (*χalēþ*). They differ from the vṛddhied formations involving the other suffixes only in that they take the nominative *-s*, which is the normal practice with stems in occlusives. Skt. *padāti-* ' foot soldier ' and *pattí-* ' id.' are both *i-* extensions of a *t*-stem ; the two different forms derive from the declensional apophony of the primitive stem.

In one special case the suffix *t* remains a living formative in Sanskrit. It has been noted above (§ 2) that roots ending in the vowels *i*, *u* and *ṛ* cannot, like other roots, function without any addition as nominal stems. Where other roots do so they invariably add the suffix *t* : *stút-* ' praise ', *samít-* ' battle ', *niyút-* ' team ', *vṛ́t-* ' army, host ', *rít-* ' stream ', *mít-* ' post ', *hrút-* ' treachery ; foe '. These stems, like the root stems, may be used either as action nouns (in which case they are feminine) or agent nouns ; in the latter use they also appear most frequently as the latter members of compounds : *devastút-* 'praising the gods', *viśvajít-* 'all-conquering', *jyotiṣkṛ́t-* 'making light', etc., etc. Like the root stems they have generalised the weak grade in declension.

In this way the *t-* formations have come to form one system with the root nouns, since they are used in identical circumstances and with exactly the same function as the root stems in the case of other roots. For this reason the Indian grammarians do not class the *t* which appears here as an ordinary suffix (*pratyaya-*), but consider it to be a special addition or augment (*āgama-*). The suffix *t* has acquired this character of augment in a number of other formations, notably in the gerunds in *-ya* (°*jitya* 'having conquered', etc., as opposed to °*dṛśya* 'having seen'), and in the adjectival formations in *van* (*kṛ́tvan-* 'active' as opposed to *yájvan-* 'worshipping'). In these cases too it appears to strengthen the roots ending in *i*, *u* and *ṛ*. We shall see below that the same kind of development has taken place, and to a greater degree, with the suffix *i*.

The compound suffix *-it* appears in a few examples, *yoṣít-* 'woman', *divít-* 'brilliance' (whence *divítmant-* 'brilliant') *sarít-* 'river', *harít-* 'green, yellow', *rohít-* 'red'. These are accented on the suffix, but this does not agree with the apophony ; cf. the type *śocíṣ-*. The adjectives *harít-* and *rohít-*, which must originally have been accented on the root, were at one time stems which could be used indifferently as nouns or adjectives. Of these the adjectives *hárita-* and *róhita-* are thematic extensions, and they preserve the original accent of the simpler forms, because they belong to that small class of adjectives which do not take the normal adjectival accent owing to the adjectival character of the stems on which they are based (cf. *vápuṣ-*, *vápuṣa-* above).

A suffix *-ut* appears in *Marút-* n. of the storm gods (**mar-* 'to shine' : cf. *márīci-* 'ray' and Gk. μαρμαίρω, ἀμαρύσσω), also in *garmút-* fem. 'a kind of grass', and *garut*°- which is found only in the derivative *garútmant* 'winged'. The guṇa grade of this suffix *-vat* is employed in the middle cases of the perfect participles (*vidvádbhyas*, etc.) and the nom. acc. sg. nt. (*vidvát*). In Greek it is used throughout the masculine (εἰδώς, εἰδότος, etc.).

A few adverbs are made with this suffix : *sanat* 'of old', *pradakṣiṇít* 'moving to the right', *cikitvít* 'carefully'. Similarly Av. *paityaogəṯ* ' backwards ', etc. An adverbial suffix *-tas* has been abstracted from the ablative singular of *t*-stems. Originally the type *dakṣiṇatás* ' from the right ' was to be analysed *dakṣiṇat-ás* (cf. *pradakṣiṇít* for the *t*-suffix in connection with this word). With the growing obsolescence of the *t*-suffix, formations of this type came to be analysed *dakṣiṇa-tás*, etc., and the *-tas* thus abstracted became very productive in the formation of adverbs with ablatival meaning : *mukhatás* ' from the mouth ', *agratás* ' in front ', *sarvátas* ' on all sides ', *tátas* ' from there ', *parítas* ' around ', etc.

Adjectives in *-tá* arose in the usual way from the addition of the accented thematic vowel to *t*-stems ; so, *pṛṣatá-* ' speckled ' from *pṛ́ṣat-* ' spot, drop '. Since *t*-stems have mostly disappeared, such adjectives appear normally as independent formations. Some have the suffix in the form *-atá*, e.g. *darśatá-* ' visible ' (Gk. °δέρκετος), *yajatá-* ' to be adored ', *bharatá*, ' (to be maintained), epith. of Agni, n. of a tribe ', *rajatá-* ' silver ' (cf. Av. *ərəzata-*), others in the form *-tá*, *tṛṣṭá-* ' rough '-*śyetá-* ' white ', *ánapta-* ' not wet ' (Av. *napta-* wet), *dūtá-* ' messenger ', *sūtá-* ' charioteer ', *nāpitá-* ' barber ' (for **snāpitá-*, cf. Pa. *nahāpita-*) ; in other cases it is preceded by some other suffix (*i*, *u*, etc.) : *tigitá-* ' sharp ', *palitá-* ' grey-haired ', *ámanyuta-* ' free from anger ', *ádbhuta-* ' wonderful ', *kapóta-* ' bluish-grey ; pigeon '. Mention has already been made of its addition to the suffixes *n* and *r* (*vasantá-*, *muhūrtá-*). The colour words *hárita-* and *róhita-* have radical accent due to the original use of the simple *t*-stems as adjectives. Radical accent appears in some other examples, *ásita-* ' black ', *éta-* ' speckled ', *márta-* ' mortal '.

The colour adjectives either substitute an *n*-suffix in the feminine : *énī*, *śyénī*, *háriṇī*, or add *n* with change of *t* to *k* : *ásiknī*, *páliknī*. Here there are apparently traces of an old alternation corresponding to that of *r*- and *n*- stems.

Apart from these adjectives the suffix *-tá* is specialised in the formation of past passive participles, a function which appears also in the other IE languages. There is a reduction both of root and suffix before the final accented *á* (*bhṛtá-*, as opposed to *bharatá-*) which is characteristic of the most ancient formations. These participles are very numerous and are formed from all roots except a small number which take *-ná* : *śrutá-* ' heard ' (Gk. κλυτός, Lat. *in-clutus*, Ir. *cloth*), *srutá-* ' having flowed ' (Gk. ῥυτός), *tatá-* ' stretched ', (Gk. τατός, Lat. *tentus*), *hatá-*

'slain' (Av. O. Pers. *jata-*, Gk. *φατός*), *gatá-* 'gone' (Gk. *βατός* 'that can be traversed'), *niktá-* 'washed' (Gk. *ἄνιπτος* 'unwashed'), *uṣṭa-* 'burnt' (Lat. *ustus*), *vṛttá-* 'turned' (Lat. *vorsus, versus*), *dṛṣṭá-* 'seen' (AS. *torht* 'clear'), *miṣṭa-* savoury (of food)<*mikṣ-*, cf. Lat. *mixtus*.

As elsewhere the specific function of this suffix is not inherent in it from the beginning but acquired by adaptation. The fundamental meaning of *k̂lutó-* for instance, like that of any other adjectival form of the same type, is no more than 'one connected with hearing'. In Greek the specialisation of meaning has not gone so far, since beside a passive sense, an active sense is frequently found: *δυνατός* 'possible' and 'able', *συνετός* 'intelligible' and 'intelligent', etc. In Sanskrit an active sense is seen in *sūtá-* 'charioteer' ('driver', i.e. 'one connected with **sū-t-* 'driving', from *sū-*, *suváti*) and in *nāpitá-* 'barber'.

The reason for the rarity of the simple suffix *-t* is that it has normally been replaced by compound formations in which a further suffixal element is added to the *t*. The commonest of these, which makes verbal abstracts is *-ti*. This is the commonest of all the suffixes making verbal abstracts or action nouns, and words formed with this suffix show less tendency to develop a concrete sense than is the case with other suffixes. These words are feminine, in contradistinction to the action nouns formed with the suffixes previously discussed, which are neuter. In this respect they follow the simple *t*-stems which in most IE languages are feminine, and in Hittite common gender. The only traces of neuter *ti*-stems that can be found are the pronominal forms *káti* 'how many', *táti* 'so many', *yáti* 'as many' which are such in form though they function differently. It is clear that those stems were among the earliest to break away from the neuter system proper to action nouns as the gender system developed.

The process of the enlargement of *t*-stems by the addition of the suffix *-i* is seen in such pairs as *samít-*, *sámiti-* 'assembly'; *nákt-*, *nákti-* 'night'; *daśát-*, *daśáti-* 'decade'.

The accentuation of these action nouns is subject to no rule. It may appear on the root as in *ṛ́ddhi-* 'prosperity', *gáti-* 'going', *júṣṭi-* 'satisfaction', *dhṛ́ti-* 'firmness', *ráti-* 'enjoyment', *vṛ́ddhi-* 'growth', *śákti-* 'power', *śā́nti-* 'peace', or somewhat more frequently on the suffix: *ūtí-* 'helping', *kṣití-* 'abode', *jūtí-* ' speed ', *dhītí-* ' thought ', *puṣṭí-* ' prosperity ', *bhaktí-* ' sharing ', *bhṛtí-* ' maintenance ', *matí-* ' thought ', *stutí-* ' praise '. This lack of rule in the accentuation is characteristic also of the simple *-i* stems, as will be noted below. In Greek the accent is normally on the root, but since the radical vowel in these formations, in Greek as in Sanskrit, appears always in the weak grade, it cannot have been there unchanged from the beginning. Compared with the general system—accent and guna of root for action nouns and vice versa for agent nouns—these formations present a striking anomaly, and it is not now possible to say what particular developments in early Indo-European were responsible for this state of affairs.

Examples of this formation are abundant also in Greek and a number of parallel forms can be quoted: *ápaciti-* ' retribution ', Gk. ἀπότισις ' id '; *kṣití-* ' dwelling ', Av. *šiti-*, Gk. κτίσις ' settlement '; *kṣíti-* ' destruction ', Gk. φθίσις; *ā́-huti-* ' oblation ', Gk. χύσις ' pouring out '; *srutí-* ' flowing ', Gk. ῥύσις; *pluti-* ' floating ', Gk. πλύσις; *gáti-* ' going ', Gk. βάσις, cf. Goth. *ga-qumþs*; *tati-* ' stretching, row ', Gk. τάσις. In Latin they have been replaced by a still further developed suffix *-tiōn-*, made by adding the vṛddhied *n*-suffix to the *-ti*. These are feminines because the *ti-* abstracts on which they are based were feminine: *mentiō* (Skt. *matí-*) *iunctiō* (Skt. *yukti-*, Gk. ζεῦξις), etc.

The gradation *-atí* appears in a number of examples: *aṃhatí-* ' distress ', *dṛśatí-* ' appearance ', *mithatí-* ' conflict ', *vasatí-* ' abode ', *pakṣatí-* ' root of the wing '.

A few datives of *ti*-stems are classed as infinitives: *iṣṭáye* ' to refresh ', *pītáye* ' to drink ', *vītáye* ' to enjoy ', *sātáye* ' to win ', *ūtáye* ' to help '.

There are also a number of *ti*- stems functioning as agent nouns, mainly in the early language: *jñātí-* 'relation ', (: Lith. *gentìs* ' id '), *pattí-*, *padā́ti-* ' footsoldier ', *addhātí* ' sage ', *rātí-* ' liberal ', *dhū́ti-* ' shaker ', *sápti-* ' steed ', *dhṛ́ṣṭi-* ' bold ', *pū́ti-* ' putrid ', *váṣṭi-* ' eager '; *ámati-* ' poor ', *sthapáti* ' governor; architect ', *vṛkáti-* ' robber ', *rámati-* ' liking to stay ', *p-áti-* ' master '.[1] The position of the accent is subject to no rule, as is the case with the action nouns, and the two classes are not distinguished in the usual way.

[1] From *pā-* ' to protect, govern '. That the *t* in this word is suffixal is evident from its absence in Gk. δέσποινα. Therefore *páti-* is to °*pá-* (*nṛpa-*, etc.) as *vṛkáti-* to *vṛ́ka-*.

The adjectival formations are occasionally extended by the addition of suffixal *n*, *abhimātín-* ' insidious ' (*abhimātí-* ' id '), *rātín* ' liberal ' (*rātí* ' id '). Compare the similar extension in Latin in the action nouns.

A suffix *-tu* is produced in the same way by the addition of *u* to the simple *t*-suffix. These are less numerous than the *ti*-stems, and morphologically less altered from the ancient system. There are for instance still a number of neuters preserved: *dā́tu* ' division ', *vā́stu* ' abode ' (Gk. (Ϝ)ἄστυ ' city '), *vástu* ' thing ', *mástu* ' sour cream ' (cf. Gallo-Lat. *mesga*, Ir. *medg* with different suffix). A neuter formation in *-tu* used adverbially appears in *jā́tu* ' at all, ever '. These neuters have the regular radical accent, associated with guṇa, which is the characteristic of neuter action nouns. The same accent and guṇa appears also in the following masculines (this is the gender which the non-neuter action nouns in *-tu* normally adopt; contrast the feminine *ti*-stems): *ótu-* ' weft ', *tántu-* ' thread ', *dhā́tu-* ' element ', *sáktu-* ' groats ', *sétu-* ' bund, dam ', *sótu-* ' libation '. Occasionally suffixal accent appears: *gātú-* ' way ', *hetú-* (but with guṇa of root), *pitú-* ' nourishment '. Guṇa of the first element of the suffix appears in *edhatú-* ' welfare ', *vahatú-* ' wedding ' and *kr-átu-* ' intelligence ' (*kṝ-* ' to think, commemorate '). There are very few feminines: *vástu-* ' morning ', *sū́tu-* ' giving birth ', *jīvā́tu-* ' life '.

Agent nouns and adjectives are rare: *mántu-* ' councillor ' and *dhā́tu-* ' suitable for sucking ' do not have the proper adjectival accent, which contrasts with the formations in simple *-u*. Regular suffixal accent appears in *tapyatú-* ' glowing ' and *siṣāsatú-* ' desirous of obtaining '.

The suffix *-tu* is a rich source of infinitives. These are regularly accented on the root which normally takes guṇa. They appear in the accusative, dative and genitive.

(1) The accusative infinitive in *-tum* is the only one used in the classical language: *kártum* ' to do ', *gántum* ' to go ', *dā́tum* ' to give ', *śrótum* ' to hear ', *nétum* ' to lead ', *móktum* ' to release ', etc., etc. In the Vedic language which is rich in other kinds of infinitives, this formation is exceedingly rare, appearing in some five examples in the *Ṛgveda*, and in five others in the *Atharvaveda*. It is equivalent in form to the Latin supine, *factum*, *itum*, etc.

(2) Over thirty dative infinitives formed with this suffix are

found in the Vedic language. They are invariably accented on the root which takes guṇa (except *sū́tave* ' to bring forth ' beside *sávitave*) : *étave* ' to go ', *kártave* ' to do ', *dā́tave* ' to give ', *mántave* ' to think ', *yáṣṭave* ' to sacrifice ', etc.

(3) The ablatives occur less frequently : *hántos* ' from being struck ', *étos* ' from going ', etc. The formation appears occasionally also in a genitive sense, *kártos* ' doing ' (with *madhyā́*), *dā́tos* ' giving ' (with *īśe*).

In addition to these three types there also occurs occasionally in the Veda a type in *-tavaí* : *étavaí* ' to go ', *hántavaí* ' to slay '. It has the anomaly of a double accent which has not been explained, and it is always followed by the particle *-u*. It appears to be based on a thematic extension of the guṇated *tu*-suffix (**étava-* nt.) with the old form of the dative singular (Av. *-āi*).

The neuter suffix *-tvá* which must in origin be a thematic formation based on the *tu*-suffix, is frequent, and is used exclusively in the formation of secondary abstract nouns : *amṛtatvá-* ' immortality ', *devatvá-* ' divinity ', *śucitvá-* ' purity ', *śatrutvá-* ' enmity ', etc. The accent of these secondary formations has nothing to do with the old system, but comes from the tendency to evolve a special taddhita accent for secondary neuters which has been noticed above. Avestan has such formations, though not abundantly (*ratuθwa-* ' office of *ratu-* ', etc.), also a number of primary formations with this suffix, *vąθwa-* ' herd ', *staoθwa-* ' prayer '. Primary formations with this suffix are represented in Sanskrit by only a few forms and these are confined to Vedic, namely *pétva-* ' ram, wether ', and a series of words in which *-pitvá* is combined with various prefixes. The commonest of these are *prapitvá-* ' going forth, time of going forth, morning ' and *abhipitvá-* ' coming in, coming home in the evening, evening time '.

The further extended suffix *-tvaná* appears in the Veda in the same sense : *mahitvaná-* ' greatness ', *sakhitvaná-* 'friendship ', etc. Though ignored by classical Sanskrit it turns up again in Middle Indo-Aryan (*-ttana-*), and has been preserved even to the modern period (Hi. *-pan*).

There are some thematic adjectives based on the suffix *-tu* which are used as gerundives in the Vedic language : *kártva-* 'to be done ', *jétva-* ' to be won ', *váktva-* ' to be said ', *sánitva-* ' to be gained ', *hántva-* ' to be slain '. Likewise in Avestan, *ǰąθwa-* ' to be slain '. These are all accented on the root contrary to the general rule for adjectives. The classical type in *-tavya* (*kartávya-*, alternatively *kartavyà-* ' to be done ', etc.) is made from the guṇated *tu*-suffix with addition of the adjectival suffix *-ya*. In Greek yet another variant (*-tewos*) occurs, ποιητέος, etc.

By yet another enlargement of the *-tu* suffix the gerunds in *-tvā́* are provided which are used with uncompounded verbs. These appear with the root normally in its weakened form, and with the accent on the suffix : *iṣṭvā́* ' having sacrificed ', *kṛtvā́* ' having made ', *gatvā́* ' having gone ', *tīrtvā́* ' having crossed ', *dṛṣṭvā́* ' having seen ', *pītvā́* ' having drunk ', *snātvā́* ' having bathed ', etc., etc.

These formations have at first sight the appearance of being instrumentals of action nouns in *-tu*. As such their form would be in order, assuming they are ancient forms, since originally the accent was on the termination in the weak cases and this caused reduction of the root. The chief difficulty against such an explanation is the co-existence in the Veda of a gerund in *-tvī*. This formation is actually more frequent in the *Ṛgveda* than the gerund in *-tvā́-* : *kṛtvī́* ' having done ', *gatvī́* ' having gone ', *bhūtvī́* ' having become ', etc. The latter formation cannot be explained as an instrumental or any other case ending of a verbal noun in *-tu*. Since the explanation of both forms must run on parallel lines, it follows that the forms in *-tvā́* are also not case endings. The only explanation possible is that these are the suffixes *ā* and *ī*, and the fact that they function here in the same manner is in accordance with the close relation between them elsewhere. So we must have here two compound suffixes used adverbially with the final accent that usually appears in the adverbial use of nominal stems (*prātár*, etc.).

The suffix *-tā*, an extension with the *ā*-suffix of the simple *t*-suffix, is specialised in the making of abstract nouns from adjectives. As a primary suffix it is very rare, e.g. *citā* ' layer ', more common in Greek, γενετή, etc. The usual type is represented in the Veda by such examples as *devátā* ' divinity ', *puruṣátā* ' humanity ', *bandhútā* ' relationship ', *vasútā* ' wealthiness ', etc. In classical Sanskrit they are made freely from all adjectival stems : *kṛṣṇatā* ' blackness ', *pūrṇatā* ' fullness ', *dīrghatā* ' longness ', etc. The suffix appears with the same function in other IE languages : Russ. *polnota* ' fullness ' O. Sl.

čr̆nota ' blackness ', *dlŭgota* ' length ', OHG. *fullida* ' fullness ', Goth. *diupiþa* ' depth ', Lat. *iuventa* ' youth '.

This suffix could be strengthened by the further addition of suffixal *t*, producing the suffix *-tāt*. Examples (found only in the *Ṛgveda*) are *upárātāt-* ' proximity ', *devátāt-* ' godliness ', *vṛkátāt-* ' wolfishness, murderousness ', *sarvátāt-* ' completeness '. The same suffix appears in Avestan (*haurvatāt-* ' wholeness,' etc.), Greek (*βαρύτης* ' heaviness ', etc.), where it completely replaces *-tā* as a secondary suffix, and Latin (*civitās*, etc.).

Just as the simple suffix *-t* could be extended by the addition of suffixal *-i* (*daśát-*, *daśatí-*), so the compound could be extended to *-tāti*. Examples are *jyeṣṭhátāti-* ' superiority ', *devátāti-* ' divinity ', *sarvátāti-* ' completeness ', *vasútāti-* 'wealth', *satyátāti-* ' truth ', *śántāti-* ' good fortune '. The last two may also be used as adjectives (like certain formations in *-ti*).

§ 15. The Suffix *m*

The suffix *m* plays an important part in nominal derivation in Sanskrit and the other IE languages. It has already appeared in the groups *-mar*, *-man*, *-mant*, *-min*. It is also productive of thematic adjectives in *-má*, and occasionally appears in other formations. The problem with this suffix is that, in contradistinction to all the others, it is hardly ever found as a simple, uncompounded suffix, although the various compound suffixes mentioned must have been formed, like other compound suffixes, by additions to just such a simple suffix. The only surviving examples appear to be the numeral stems *saptá* and *dáśa*, Lat. *septem*, *decem*, IE **septḿ̥* (earlier *séptm̥* on account of apophony), *dékm̥*. Here the suffix appears in its weak form like the *n*-suffix in *nā́ma* (Lat. *nōmen*), etc., and these numerals are of exactly the type as the primary neuter nouns.

The frequency of *m* in various derivative suffixes shows that it must have originally been common as a primary neuter suffix. The reason that it does not appear as such, is that it has been replaced by other formations, and this has come about in two ways. The first process is illustrated by the juxtaposition of *yugáṁ* nom. acc. sg. nt. ' yoke ' and *yugmá-* ' paired '. Like other thematic adjectival suffixes *yugmá-* is to be analysed *yugm-á* and the consonantal *m*-stem on which it is based is none other than the neuter *yugám*. The *m* in the neuter *yugám* was originally the *m*-suffix, but owing to similarity with the accusative singular of thematic stems (originally all adjectival and of common gender), it came, by an easy process of adaptation, to be treated as a termination, with the consequence that formations of this kind were turned into neuter thematic stems and declined accordingly. The neuter thematic type then became productive, particularly in forming extensions of neuter consonantal stems (*-ana*, *-atra*, etc., above).

The relation that exists between *yugám* and *yugmá* appears also between *bhayám* ' fear ' : *bhīmá-* ' fearful ' and *mádhyam* nt. middle : *madhyam-á-* adj. ' being in the middle '. The adv. *sádam* can be explained as a neuter *m*-stem in view of the derivative *sádman-* ' seat ' ; likewise *áram, álam* ' fittingly, suitably ' from the IE root *ar-* ' to fit ' by comparison with derivatives like Gk. ἁρμός.

Ancient thematic neuters in IE are very rare. Skt. *yugám* is shown to be ancient by the correspondence of Gk. ζυγόν, Lat. *iugum*, etc. Another ancient word is Skt. *padám* ' step ', Gk. πέδον, Hitt. *pedan*, which may be presumed to have originated in the same way, though direct evidence is lacking in this case. Gk. ἔργον ' work ' with the same rare and no doubt ancient apophony as πέδον is to be classed with it. It should be noted that such primitive thematic neuters, which according to this theory are transformed *m*-stems, are not only exceedingly rare, but they are the only class which provide certain word equations between different IE languages. Thus the thematic neuters of secondary origin, namely (1) extensions of neuter consonantal stems and (2) the still later though numerous taddhita formations, are of later origin. It would be difficult otherwise to explain the absence of detailed agreement among these formations between the various languages. In this connection also we must note the complete absence of the latter two formations in Hittite.

The rarity of the thematic neuter formations of the type *padám, yugám* shows that, although this was one way by which the primitive *m*-stems were removed, and although it provides the only plausible explanation for the existence of neuter thematic stems at all, this was not the only, or indeed the main way by which this was done. The other process which operated and which accounted for many was the extension of *m*-stems by the addition of the *r*- and *n*-suffixes. Just as in Hittite the primary *s*-stems were almost entirely replaced by formations of the type *ḫannešar/-ešnaš*, so over the whole of Indo-European with the exception of a few stems that were turned into a new type, the thematic neuters, the *m*-stems were replaced by the *mar/man* stems. Later in most languages the *mar*-stems were ousted by the *man*-stems. In Hittite the gen. sg. of neuter stems in *-mar* is in *-maš* (*arnummar* 'bringing', gen. sg. *arnummaš*). It is usually said that there has been assimilation of *mn* in such genitives, but this cannot be proved, and the alternative theory is possible that such genitives are formed from the unextended *m*-stem. Here we may compare certain Vedic instrumentals, *drāghmā́, raśmā́,* (*drāghmán-* 'length', *raśmán-* 'rein') which in the same way may well be formed from the simple *m*-stem and not from the extended stem in *-man*.

Thematic derivatives from *man*-stems frequently appear without the final element of this suffix : *priyádhāma-* 'fond of home', *viśvákarma-* 'accomplishing all' containing the stems *dhā́man-* and *kárman-* ; cf. also *dhárma-* masc. 'law' : *dhárman-* nt. 'id' ; *éma-* 'way, course' : *éman-* 'id' ; *tókma-* 'shoot, offspring' : *tókman-* 'id' ; *yákṣma-* 'disease' : *yákṣman-* 'id' ; *darmá-* 'destroyer' : *darmán-* 'id'. In these cases also there is no evidence to support the theory of a change *mn* to *m*, and the thematic type illustrated by these examples must have been based on the simple *m*-stem.

The suffix *-má* makes a fair number of adjectives and nouns of adjectival origin : *ajmá-* 'career, march' (Gk. ὄγμος ; *man*-stem in *ájman-*, Lat. *agmen*), *idhmá-* 'fuel', *grīṣmá-* 'summer' (*gr-īṣ-má-*, cf. *gurú-* 'heavy'), *gharmá-* 'heat' (originally adjectival, cf. Gk. θερμός, Lat. *formus* 'hot'), *jihmá-* 'athwart, oblique', *tigmá-* 'sharp' (Gk. στιγμός 'puncture', *n*-stem in στίγμα, nt.), *dasmá-* 'wonderful' (*dasmánt-* 'id'), *dhūmá-* 'smoke' (cf. *mar*-stem in *dhūmrá-*), *narmá-* 'sport, pastime' (also *nárman-* nt. 'id'), *yudhmá-* 'fighter', *rukmá-* 'ornament', *vāmá-* 'charming' ($\sqrt{}$*van-*), *śagma-* 'beneficial', *śyāmá-* 'black' (*śyāvá-*, with alternative suffix), *himá-* 'cold, frost'. The adjective *ū́ma-* 'helper' has anomalously the accent on the root, but the weak grade shows that this is not original. There are a number of thematic action nouns with the normal radical accent and masculine gender, presumably to avoid the repetition of *m* : *dhárma-* 'law', *bhā́ma-* 'illumination', *kṣéma-* 'residence; security', *śárma-* 'flowing', *sóma-* 'the pressed out juice of the *soma* plant' (Av. *haoma-*), *stóma-* 'hymn of praise', *hóma-* 'offering'. The customary alternation of accent between substantive and adjective appears in *srā́ma-* 'lameness' and *srāmá-* 'lame'.

The gradation *-amá* appears in *daśamá-* 'tenth' (i.e. *daśam-á-*, Lat. *decimus*; *dáśa*, *decem*), *saptamá* 'seventh' (after which *aṣṭamá-* 'eighth'), *madhyamá-* 'middlemost', *adhamá-* 'lowest' (Lat. *infimus*), *paramá-* 'furthest, highest'. From the ordinal *saptamá-* there is extracted *tama* which is applied to other numerals (*viṃśatitama-*, etc.). This is identical with the superlative suffix *-tama* which presumably arose in the same way: *ántama-* 'nearest, most intimate' (Av. *antəma-*, Lat. *intimus*), *uttamá-* 'highest', *ugrátama-* 'strongest', *mīḍhúṣṭama-* 'most gracious', *mātṛ́tama-* 'most motherly', *ratnadhā́tama-* 'most wealth-giving', etc., etc.

A compound suffix *-ima* appears rarely: *agrimá-* 'foremost', and in combination with other suffixes, *kṛtríma-* 'artificial', *bhidelima-* 'fragile', etc. Other combinations of suffixal *m* are *-mi*: (masc.) *ūrmí-* 'wave' (Av. *varəmi-*, AS. *wielm*), *raśmí-* 'rein, ray'; (fem.) *bhū́mi-* 'earth'; *-mī*, (fem.) *lakṣmī́* 'mark, sign', *sūrmī́* 'tube'; *-mā*: *hímā* 'cold season', *kṣumā́* 'flax'.

§16. The Suffixes *i* and *u*

These two suffixes, like the other suffixes, had in Indo-European a guṇated form, *ei̯*, *eu̯*, and a weak form, *i*, *u*, depending on the position of the accent. They could also be vṛddhied under the same circumstances as the other suffixes, and in general they develop on the same lines. The neuters were the most primitive type, and on the basis of these, adjectives could be formed by accenting the suffix, old neuters may be transferred to the masc.-fem. class, a process which is very common in the case of these suffixes; there are neuter thematic extensions, and adjectives are formed by adding the accented thematic vowel. They combine with other suffixes in the usual way; of these combinations the suffixes *-ira*, *-in*, *-ina*, *-ri*, *-ni*, *-var*, *-vara*, *-ura*, *-van*, *-vana*, *-una*, *-vant*, *-ru*, *-nu*, *-is*, *-us*, *-yas*, *-vas*, *-iṣa*, *-uṣa*, *-it*, *-ut*, *-vat*, *-ti*, *-tu*, *-ima*, *-mi* have already been mentioned.

Neuter nouns in *-i* are rare; it is a type that early tended to become extinct, largely by the transference of such stems to the masc.-fem. class. The few that remain are mainly defective. Of these *śámi* ' work ' is indeclinable ; *ásthi* ' bone ', *ákṣi* ' eye ', *sákthi* ' thigh ' and *dádhi* ' curd ' substitute an *n*-stem in declension (gen. sg. *asthnás, akṣṇás, sakthnás, dadhnás*) ; *vā́ri*, ' water ' adds *n* to the stem in the same circumstances (gen. sg. *vā́riṇas*, cf. the same thing with neuter *u*-stems, and occasionally elsewhere, e.g. *śíras, śīrṣṇás*) ; *hā́rdi* ' heart ' substitutes the root stem (gen. sg. *hṛdás*, etc.). There is one rare neuter with the compound suffix *-vi, sṛkvi* which inflects like *vā́ri*.

The neuters have not preserved an inflection in which the *i*-suffix is preserved throughout, in contradistinction to the neuter *u*-stems where such exists (*mádhu, mádhvas*). It can be traced however in the declension of *ávi-* ' sheep ', gen. sg. *ávyas*. This type of inflection contrasts strongly with the adjectival inflection (*agnés*, etc. ; in the end this becomes the only inflection), and when the similar opposition in the *u*-stems is considered (*mádhvas* ; *sūnós*) it becomes clear that this first type of declension is that proper to the neuter nouns, as opposed to the adjectives. The difference is due to the different accentuation of the two types of stem, corresponding to that which we have found elsewhere. The declension of *ávi-* indicates that it was originally a neuter ; it has been transferred, on account of natural gender, but has retained some of its old features in declension. Greek has the same inflection in this word, and retains the more ancient alternating accent : *ὄϊς, οἰός*.

There are occasional neuter *i*-stems which have come to be used as adverbs : *sáci* ' with ', *práti* ' against ' (*pr-ati, ti*-stem).

Often original neuter *i*-stems have been replaced by various extensions : *nábhya-* ' nave ' retains the old neuter gender of the *i*-stem which in *nā́bhi-* ' navel ' has been replaced by the feminine gender. An old neuter **mádhi* ' middle ' (in Av. *maiδyāirya-* ' belonging to the middle of the year ' for **madhi-yārya-*) is replaced by *mádhya-* nt. (originally *madhyam-, m*-stem, cf. above) ; likewise *krávi* ' raw flesh ' (*ákravihasta-*) is enlarged to *kravya-* (*kravyā́d-*, cf. Lith. *kraũjas*), and alternatively by addition of the *s*-suffix to *kravíṣ-*. Similarly the neuters *arcíṣ-* ' flame ', *rocíṣ-* ' light ' and *śocíṣ-* ' flame ' are *s*-extensions of old neuters in *-i*, but the *i*-stems *arcí-* masc., *śocí-* fem., *rúci-*, *rocí-* fem. have been transferred from the neuter to masculine or feminine gender.

This and similar evidence makes it quite clear that neuter

action nouns in *-i* were originally common. Further evidence comes from another quarter. At a time when these formations were readily made, the whole category of *i*-neuters was incorporated in the verbal conjugation, and served to form passive aorists of the third person singular. As such they are well represented in Indo-Aryan and Iranian: *tā́ri, jáni, darśi, pā́di, sā́di*; with augment *ákāri*, etc. Similarly Av. *srāvi* 'is heard', etc. The accent is on the root as regularly in the case of neuter stems.

Neuter *u*-stems remain more common than neuter *i*-stems. They are regularly accented on the root and not uncommonly have vṛddhi: *mádhu* 'honey' (Gk. μέθυ, AS. *medu*), *vásu* 'property', *ā́yu-* 'life' (RV. 1,89,9 and 3,49,2, restored from evidence of metre), *jā́nu-* 'knee' (Gk. γόνυ, Lat. *genu*, Hitt. *genu*), *dā́ru* 'wood' (Gk. δόρυ, Hitt. *taru*) *sā́nu* 'summit, top' (also masc.), *dā́nu* 'moisture' (also fem.), *páśu* 'domestic animal' (RV. 3. 53, 23, Goth. *faíhu*, Lat. *pecu*; elsewhere transferred to the masculine and accented on the suffix), *śmáśru* 'beard', *áśru* 'tear' (Toch. A. *ākru-nt* pl.), *játu* 'gum' (AS. *cwidu*), *játru* 'collar-bone' (also *jatrú-* masc.), *tā́lu* 'palate', *trápu* 'tin', *yā́śu* 'sexual embrace', *snā́yu* 'sinew', *títaü* 'sieve'.

The *u*-stem could serve throughout as the basis of inflection. This type of neuter inflection is seen in *mádhu* 'honey', gen. sg. *mádhvas* and *vásu* 'wealth' gen. sq. *vásvas*. The same type appears in Gk. γουνός, δουρός, with the more ancient terminational accent in the gen. sg. which Sanskrit has abandoned for the fixed radical accent as in other kinds of neuters (gen. sg. *nā́mnas, vácasas*, etc.). The old terminational accent is seen in gen. sg. *paśvás* but it has come to be associated with an altered type of stem. The old IE neuter *pék̑u* (Lat. *pecu*, etc.) is preserved in one instance in the *Ṛgveda* (see above) as *páśu*, showing that the change is of recent origin. The change of gender in the usual *paśú-* is due to natural gender. The change of accent which has also occurred is due to the old terminational accent of *paśvás* gen. sg., etc. Since the normal neuters have adopted the fixed radical accent, the only stems in which there is commonly alternation of accent from stem to suffix in declension are suffixally accented masculines with reduced grade of suffix in the weak cases: nom. sg. *pitā́*, dat. sg. *pitré*, nom. sg. *Pūṣā́*, gen. sg. *Pūṣṇás*, etc. On this analogy it is easy to see how a suffixally accented *paśvás* (after the style of the old neuters) still preserved at the time of the change of gender should bring about the suffixal accentuation of the new nom. sg. *paśús*. In the same way we may judge *pitú-* ' food ', gen. sg. *pitvás*, which from being an action noun and from having the neuter type inflection, may also be regarded as a transferred neuter. The stem *krátu-* ' intelligence ', old neuter for the same reasons, has on the other hand established radical accentuation throughout.

Alternatively neuter *u*-stems operate in the weakest cases with an extended suffix *-un-*(cf. *vā́riṇas* gen. sg.) : gen. sg. *mádhunas, vásunas, drúṇas* ; Loc. sg. *ā́yuni* (cf. Gk. αἰϝεν, loc. without ending), *sā́nuni* ; gen. loc. du. *jā́nunos* (cf. Toch. A. *kanweṃ* ' knees ' with strong form of same suffix appearing in dual). Greek, when extending the suffix in these cases, has the extra *t*-suffix as with other neuter *n*-stems : gen. sg. γούνατος, δούρατος.

In addition the Veda has some forms from these stems in which the adjectival type of inflection is employed : *drós, snós, mádhos*. This is not surprising since the adjectival type of inflection has become universal in *i*- and *u*-stems by the classical period, and the process was already far advanced in the earliest period, only a few of the old type being left.

Beside the neuter *i*- and *u*-stems there is a fair number of action nouns in *-i* and *-u* which appear as masculines or feminines. The action nouns in *-i* are normally feminine : *jálpi-* ' muttering ', *ráṃhi-* ' speed ', *ráji-* ' direction ' (Lat. *regiō* with additional *n*-suffix ; cf. the same feature in connection with the *ti*-stems, above), *rópi-* ' pain ', *dhrā́ji-* ' impulse, force ', *nā́bhi-* ' navel ' ; *tvíṣi-* ' splendour ', *rúci-* ' light ' ; with suffixal accent, *saní-* ' winning ', *ājí-* ' contest ', *kṛṣí-* ' ploughing ', *cití-* ' understanding ', *nṛtí-* ' dancing ', *bhují-* ' benefiting '. The few datives of *i*-stems classified as infinitives have likewise suffixal accent , *dṛśáye* ' to see ', *yudháye* ' to light ', etc. Masculines are rare: *arcí-* ' ray ', *dhvaní-* ' noise ', *rayí-* ' wealth '.

With the *i*-stems as with the *ti*-stems the old rules about accent and apophony have long been superseded. All possible types are represented (*jálpi-, saní-, tvíṣi-, kṛṣí-*) and the variations are of no grammatical significance. Obviously *ráji-* ' direction ', which has a connection in Lat. *regio* represents the oldest type. In *rayí-*, gen. sg. *rāyás* (for *ra*Hí-, *ra*Hyás, earlier *rá*Hi-, *ra*Hyás) we may recognise the same accent development as has taken place in *paśú, paśvás*. The differences in apophony between *dhvaní-* 'noise' and *dhúni-* 'roaring' are those that exist between action and agent nouns, but the accent position is reversed. Obviously very complicated changes, which cannot now be followed, have affected the *i*-stems to produce this complete lack of system. This is associated with the fact that in this type of stem the earliest mass transfers from the neuter of action nouns took place.

On the other hand the non-adjectival masculine and feminine *u*-stems have as a rule accent and guṇa of root: masc. *ásu-* 'life' (*as-* 'to be': Av. *aŋhu-*), *sváru-* 'stake, post', *mánu-* 'man', *bándhu-* 'relation'; fem. *jásu-* 'exhaustion', *dhánu-* 'sandbank', *párśu-* 'rib', *śáru-* 'dart', *hánu* 'jaw' (Gk. γένυς, Toch. A. *śanweṃ* du.). The words *aṃśú-* 'filament, ray' (Av. *ąsu-* 'shoot'), *reṇú-* 'dust' and *śaṅkú-* 'peg, stake' have final accent, but at the same time guṇa of root. The accent of *bāhú-* 'arm' disagrees with that of Gk. πῆχυς; the apophony shows the Greek to be original. The weak grade of the root in *íṣu-* masc. and fem. 'arrow' and *síndhu-* masc. and fem. 'river' is exceptional; they are probably of adjectival origin with the shift of accent seen frequently in nominalised adjectives.

There is a small number of neuters in *-ya* to be classified as thematic extensions of *i*-stems: *mádhya-* 'middle' (see above), *kravya°* 'raw flesh', *nábhya-* 'nave', *ā́jya-* 'clarified butter', *drávya-* 'substance', *rā́jya-* 'kingdom' (Ir. *rīge*). The formation is not uncommon in tatpuruṣa compounds of the type *havirádya-* 'eating the oblation', *hotṛvū́rya-* 'choosing a sacrificial priest', *brahmabhūya-* 'becoming Brahma'. In *sakhyá-* 'friendship' as opposed to *sákhi-* the normal accentual relation is reversed because *sakhyá-* is a secondary neuter, just as in the case of *hotrá-* nt.: *hótar-* masc. (see above, p. 137). In *hṛ́daya-* 'heart' the thematic extension is added to the guṇated suffix.

The neuter suffix *-ya* originating as a simple extension of *-i* has developed independently and on a very wide scale in the formation of secondary neuters, either with vṛddhi, as usually in the later language, *saúbhāgya-* 'welfare', etc., or in some cases without, *dūtyà-* 'embassy', etc.

As with the other neuter suffixes adjectives and nouns of adjectival type could be made from neuter *i* and *u* stems by shifting the accent to the suffix. For instance we have, with the oldest type of apophony, the IE neuter *pélu* (Goth. *filu* 'much') and with accentuation of suffix and reduction of root an adjectival stem *pleú-* which appears in Gk. πλέες (for *πλέϝ-ες). The system has undergone various modifications, and several different types of declension have emerged as a result.

(1) The first, and oldest type, is represented by *sákhi-*, nom. sg. *sákhā* 'friend'. This is characterised by vṛddhi of the nom. sg., and in declension it follows the general lines of the declension of the agent nouns in *r* and *n* (nom. acc. dat. sg. *sákhā, sákhāyam, sákhye* ; *svásā, svásāram, svásre*). This rare type is found also in *apratā́ RV.* 8, 32, 16 (*ná sómo apratā́ pape* 'soma is not drunk which gives not a return'), and in Av. *kavā* nom. sg. (*kavi-* title of kings, Skt. *kaví* 'wise man'). In Sanskrit this type has usually been replaced by that in which the nom. and acc. sg. terminate in *-is* and *-im*, but considerable traces remain to show that the formation was originally more widely used. The feminine derivatives *Agnā́yī* and *Manā́vī* are based on the old vṛddhied nominative singulars **Agnā́(y)* and **Manā́v*. An old vṛddhied nom. sg. forms the first member of the compounds *Agnā́viṣṇū* (cf. *mātā́pitarau*) and *kavāsakhá-* 'he who enjoys the friendship of the wise'. Above all the usual form of the loc. sg. of *i-* and *u-* stems (*agnā́*, later *agnaú, sūnaú*, etc.) can only be explained as a locative without ending equivalent to the old vṛddhied nom. sg. of adjectival stems.

(2) The few *u*-stems which have retained vṛddhi in the nom. sg. add the nominative *s* to this. The type is represented in Sanskrit nom. sg. *dyaús* 'sky, sky-god' (Gk. Ζεύς ; the meaning 'sky-god' is the original one, and this accounts for the adjectival form of the word) and in *gaús* 'cow'. It is somewhat more frequent in Iranian, examples being O. Pers. *dahyauš* 'land' and Av. *hiθāuš* 'companion' and *uzbāzauš* 'with uplifted arms'. In Avestan a tendency to differentiate adjectival and nominal declension is seen in the contrast between *uzbāzauš* and *bāzuš* 'arm' in the nom. sg. and between *darəgō-arštaēm* and *frādat̰-fšaom* as opposed to *arštim* 'spear' and *pasum* 'domestic animal' in the acc. sg. In Greek this type has become productive, and a distinction has been developed between agent nouns of the type βασιλεύς 'king' γονεύς 'parent' (: Skt. *janu-ṣ-* nt.) and the adjectives of the type πολύς.

The Vedic nom. sg. *vés* 'bird' is also of this type, but the guṇa instead of vṛddhi is unusual and unexplained. The corresponding Latin word *avis* conforms to the usual type of *i*-stems.

Gk. *ᾠόν* ' egg ' *(<*ṓwyom*) is a thematic extension of an old neuter **ṓwi* ' egg ' (with vṛddhi of root as frequently in *i-* and *u-* stems). Skt. *vés* is therefore a formation of adjectival type (' one connected with eggs, egg-bearer ') and the suffixal accent which is proper to adjectives has brought about the reduction and disappearance of the radical vowel.

(3) The usual adjectival type forms the nom. and acc. singular in *-is, -im, -us, -um.* Adjectives in accented *-u* are very common and frequently have corresponding forms in other IE languages: *tṛṣú-* ' thirsty ' (Goth. *þaúrsus* ' dry '), *ripú-* ' treacherous, enemy ' (Lith. *lipùs* ' sticky, slimy '), *pṛthú-* ' broad ' (Av. *pərəθu-* ' id ', Gk. *πλατύς* ' flat ', Lith. *platùs* ' broad '), *raghú-, laghú-* ' swift, light ' (Gk. *ἐλαχύς*), *gurú-* ' heavy ' (Gk. *βαρύς* Goth. *kaúrus*), *bahú-* ' much ' (Gk. *παχύς* ' thick '), *purú-, pulú-* ' many ' (Gk. *πολύς* ; the corresponding neuter in Goth. *filu*), *urú-* ' broad ' (Av. *vouru-*, Gk. *εὐρύς*), *tanú-* ' thin ' (Gk. *τανυ°*), *āśú-* ' swift ' (Av. *āsu-*, Gk. *ὠκύς*), *svādú-* ' sweet ' (Gk. *ἡδύς*), *aṃhú-* ' narrow ' (Goth. *aggwus*, O. Sl. *ązŭ-kŭ*), *ṛjú-* ' straight ' (Av. *ərəzu-*), *kṛdhú-* ' shortened, mutilated ' *jāyú-* ' victorious ', *dārú-* ' destroying ', *nṛtú-* ' dancer ', *pīyú-* ' spiteful ', *valgú-* ' handsome ', *vidhú-* ' solitary ', *śayú-* ' lying ', *sādhú-* ' good '.

The accent in *gurús* nom. sg., etc., is what is expected for adjectives, but it is in complete contradiction to the weak grade of the suffix which appears in the nom. acc. sg. It follows clearly that such a form of adjective cannot have remained unaltered from the beginning. We have seen that an older type is represented in a few archaic examples and that evidence exists that this was once more widely spread. The forms in *-us, -um* may therefore be regarded as substitutes for this older type, but they are very ancient substitutes because they occur not only in the languages represented in the examples quoted above, but also in Hittite: nom. sg. *aššuš* ' good ', *parkuš* ' high ', etc.

The strong form of suffix which should go with the accent, but which has been replaced in the nom. acc. sg. appears in the case of these stems in the dat. and gen. sg. Here the adjectival declension (*agnés, gurós*) is differentiated from what remains of the old neuter declension (*mádhvas*) in a way that accords with the position of the accent in the two types. The reduction of the termination of the gen. sg. to *-s* in accordance with the old rules of apophony shows that this form is very ancient. The same guṇa is found in Goth. *sunaus*, Lith. *sūnaũs* and, without reduction of the termination, in Gk. *ἡδέος* and Hitt. *aššawaš*. The distinction between neuter declension and adjectival declension appears elsewhere: Hitt. *genuwaš* as opposed to *aššawaš*, etc.

The extension of the guṇated suffix to the dat. and gen. sg. distinguishes these stems from the adjectival *n*- and *r*-stems. The latter are not normally distinguished in form in these cases from the neuter stems (*yaknás, ukṣṇás*), because the adjectival stems retain the terminational accent. But outside Sanskrit there is some evidence that even these stems shared to some extent the tendency, notably in the case of Av. *pitarš* gen. sg. which is parallel in every way to *agnés* and *sūnós*. On the other hand we have seen that *sákhā*, dat. *sákhye* follows the type of the adjectival *r*- and *n*-stems, showing that two alternative types of inflection existed for adjectival stems. One became predominant in *r*- and *n*-stems, the other in *i*- and *u*-stems, but to a certain extent both are represented in each of the two classes of stem.

The root in these adjectives has usually the weak form in accordance with the accentuation. In the case of *su*- 'good' as opposed to Hitt. *aššuš*, Gk. *ἐύς* the suffixal accent has resulted in the complete reduction of the radical vowel. Since the word has ceased to be used except in composition, there is no evidence as to its earlier inflection, but in Av. *hao-sravah*- the guṇated suffix which is in accordance with the adjectival accent is represented. The prefix *ku*- 'bad' appears to be of the same nature. The usual association of this with the interrogative pronoun can hardly be justified, so we may take it to be a *u*-adjective, similar in form and function to *su*.

There are a few instances where corresponding neuters exist beside adjectives in *-u*: *ā́yu*- 'length of life' (formed with simple *u*-suffix and vṛddhi from the IE root *ai*- 'to apportion, give', i.e. 'one's allotted span'): *āyú*- 'alive, mortal'; Gk. *πῶυ* 'herd, flock': Skt. *pāyú*- 'protector'. The plural *jatrávas* 'cartilages of the collar bones' differs in meaning from the radically accented neuter *jatru*- 'collar-bone' and is therefore likely to be an adjectival form. Earlier it may be presumed that such doublets were more regularly met with, and the interaction of the two types will account for radical guṇa or vṛddhi appearing in the suffixally accented adjectives. It is clear that the strong form of the radical element in *āyú-* derives from the neuter *ā́yu* where it is in accordance with the rules of apophony, and it may be assumed that similar mutual influence of the two contrasting types accounts for the form of such adjectives as *āśú-* 'swift', etc. The Hitt. nt. *aššu* is used as a noun in the sense of 'goods, property' (like Skt. *vásu*), and as such it must be regarded as continuing the primary neuter on which the adjective was built (*ésu* : (*e*)*seú-*). From this source comes the guṇa in Hitt. *aššuš*, Gk. ἐύς as opposed to the reduction of the root in Skt. *su-*. No doubt also the early prevalence of the form of the nom. acc. sg. in *-ús*, *-úm*, as opposed to the forms with strengthened suffix, was assisted by the coexistence of such neuters. Obviously an easy alternative for distinguishing the two types existed in the simple addition of the terminations *-s*, *-m* to the neuter stem in these cases. As a general rule this was done in conjunction with the retention of the adjectival accent. On the other hand radical accent appears in *áṇu-* 'fine, small', *mádhu-* 'sweet' and *vásu-* 'good'. The two latter stems occur more abundantly as neuter nouns, and their adaptation as adjectives with the minimum change of form appears to be comparatively late.

Adjectives and nouns of adjectival origin terminating in the *i*-suffix, and inflecting after the same pattern as the *u*-adjectives above, are fairly numerous: *agní-* 'fire' (Lat. *ignis*, etc.), *āpí* 'friend' (Gk. ἤπιος 'friendly, kind', thematic), *kapí-* 'monkey' (originally adj. of colour, cf. *kapilá-*), *kaví-* 'wise man' (older inflection in Avestan, cf. above), *kīrí-* 'singer', *krīḍí-* 'playing', *jāmí-* 'consanguineous, closely related' (cf. Lat. *gemi-nus* 'twin'), *nadí-* 'roarer', *svarí-* 'noisy', etc.; with radical accent *ŕ̥ṣi-* 'seer'. *kā́ri-* 'singing hymns', *gŕ̥bhi-* 'containing', *múni-* 'sage', *śúci-* 'shining, pure', *hári-* 'green', *tū́rvi-* 'overcoming', *plúṣi-* 'flea' (cf. Alb. *pl'ešt*, Arm. *lu*, etc.; √*plu* 'hop, jump').

As with the action nouns in *-i* there is complete absence of rule in the matter of accent and apophony. For this reason it is not always possible to decide to which class a noun originally belongs, e.g. *así-* 'sword' (Lat. *ensis*), *girí-* 'mountain' (Av. *gairi-*), *áhi-* 'snake' (Gk. ἔχις, ὄφις), *maṇí-* 'jewel', etc. The original system, however, has left its mark in declension (*agnés* as opposed to *ávyas*; cf. Hitt. *šallaiaš* : *ḫalkiaš*), in the same way as in the *u*-declension. As with the *u*-stems the adjectival declension has spread at the expense of the nominal, and to an even greater extent.

As with the suffixes previously dealt with, thematic adjectives could be made on the basis of *i*- and *u*-stems, and this served as an alternative to the type with accented suffix. Thus Lat. *socius* ' ally ' bears the same relation to Skt. *sákhi*-, nom. sg. *sákhā* ' friend ' (cf. the old neuter stem preserved as adverb, *sáci*), as Hitt. *veštaraš* to Av. *vāstar*- or Gk. *ἰατρός* to *ἰατήρ*.

The suffix *-ya* is very frequent and at an early period in Indo-European it developed widely as an independent suffix, so that the connection with *i*-stems has for the most part ceased to exist. The way the suffix originated is made clear by such examples in Sanskrit as *ū́rmya*- ' undulating ', *sṛ́ṇya*- ' furnished with a sickle ', *kavyá*- ' wise ', *ávya*- ' coming from a sheep ', *bhūmyá*- ' terrestrial ', *yonyá*- ' forming a receptacle ', *aryá*- ' kind, devoted, pious ', which have corresponding *i*-stems (*ūrmí*-, *sṛ́ṇi*-, *kaví*-, *ávi*-, *bhū́mi*-, *yóni*-, *arí*-). The suffix, originating in this way, became widespread at an early period producing adjectives meaning ' belonging to . . . , connected with '. In the case of thematic stems the suffix is substituted for the thematic suffix. In the case of a word like *ajryà*- ' belonging to the plain ' (Gk. *ἄγριος* ' wild ') the derivative could have been formed on the old neuter *r*-stem (*ager*) from which *ájra*- and Gk. *ἀγρός* are themselves derived. It is in some such way that this type of substitution must have been evolved.

In the case of the derivative *-ya* the accent in Sanskrit may appear either on the suffix or on the root : (a) *agryá*-, *agriyá*- ' foremost ', *divyá*- ' heavenly ' (cf. Gk. *δῖος*), *satyá*- ' true ', *grāmyá*- ' of the village ', *somyá*- ' relating to Soma ', *rājyá*- ' regal ' (Lat. *rēgius*), ; (b) *áṅgya*- ' of the limbs ', *gávya*- ' bovine ', *nárya*- ' manly ', *jámbhya*- ' an incisor tooth ' (Gk. *γόμφιος*), *kṣámya*- ' terrestrial ' (Gk. *χθόνιος*), *pítrya*- ' paternal ' (Gk. *πάτριος*, Lat. *patrius*), *sū́rya*- ' sun ' (Gk. *ἠέλιος*, *ἥλιος*), *ványa*- ' belonging to the forest ', etc.

This suffix, associated with accented root, is commonly used to produce adjectives from verbal roots which function as gerundives : *gúhya* ' to be hidden ', *ī́ḍya*- ' to be worshipped ', *yódhya*- ' to be fought ', *hávya*- ' to be invoked ', *jáyya*-, *jéya*- ' to be conquered ', *vā́cya*- ' to be spoken ', etc.

Vṛddhied derivatives appear abundantly from the earliest

period : *ādityá-* ' descendant of Aditi ', *graívya-* ' relating to the neck ', *prājāpatyá-* ' relating to Prajāpati ', *pā́ñcajanya-* ' relating to the five peoples ', etc.

In the Sanskrit suffix *-ya* two suffixes have been confounded. These are distinguishable in the Veda by means of the metre which shows that there is a monosyllabic *-ya* appearing in such words as *kavyá-* ' wise ', *ávya-* ' belonging to a sheep ', *ványa-* ' of the forest ', etc., and a disyllabic suffix *-iya* appearing in *dámiya-* ' belonging to the house ', *ráthiya-* ' relating to a chariot ', *jániya-* ' relating to the people ', *viśíya-* ' belonging to the community ', *udaníya-* ' watery ', etc. Of these *-ya* is the suffix discussed above, and it was formed on the basis of the suffix *-i* by the addition of the thematic vowel. On the other hand the suffix *-iya* represents earlier *-iHa* and it was formed on the basis of the suffix *-iH*>*ī*. These formations are therefore dealt with in the next section in connection with that suffix.

A small number of thematic formations have the *i*-suffix in the guṇa grade. Such are : *śaśayá-* ' abundant, frequent ' (cf. *śáśīyas-* ' more numerous ' and *śáśvant-*), *śuṣmáya-* ' strengthening ', *gavayá-* ' Bos gavaeus ', *sánaya-*, *sanáya-* ' old ', *tánaya-* ' offspring, son ', *kúpaya-* ' seething ', *dáśataya-* ' tenfold ' (: *daśati-* ' decade ') ; also a couple of double formations *hiraṇyáya-* ' golden ', *gavyáya-* ' bovine '. The same type of suffix is found in other IE languages : Gk. *χρύσεος* ' golden ', Lat. *aureus, igneus*, etc.

Though the adjectival suffix *-va* is not uncommon, it never received anything like the extension of *-ya*, and its connection with the *u*-suffix, or other derivatives from it, remains in most cases evident. Examples with final accentuation are *ṛṣvá-* ' lofty ' (Av. *ərəšva-* ' upright, exalted '), *ūrvá-* ' enclosure ' (*vṝ-* ' to surround, cover ', originally adj. ' enclosed '), *hrasvá-* ' short ', *ūrdhvá-* ' erect ' (Av. *ərəδwa-*, Lat. *arduus*), *takvá-* ' speedy ' (beside *táku-*), *yahvá-* ' young, youngest ' (Av. *yezivī* fem. ; beside *yahú-* ' id '), *ṛkvá-* ' singing hymns ' (beside *ṛ́kvan-*, *ṛ́kvant-*, ' id '), *dhruvá-* ' firm ' (Av. *drva-*, O. Pers. *duruva-* ' sound, healthy '), *malvá-* ' foolish ', *śyāvá-* ' dark ' (Av. *syāva-* ; beside *śyāmá-* with *m*-suffix), *raṇvá-* ' joyful, enjoyable ' (beside *ráṇvan-*), *jīvá-* ' alive, living being ' (O. Sl. *živŭ*, Lith. *gývas*, Lat. *vīvus*, Osc. *bivus* nom. pl.), *pakvá-* ' cooked, ripe ' (adapted as past participle), *śarvá-* n. of a deity (Av. *saourva-*, lit. ' one armed with a *śáru-*, ' dart '), *sruvá-* ' ladle ', *śikvá* ' skilful ' (beside *śíkvan-* ' id '), *kharvá-* ' mutilated ' (Av. *kaurva-* ' id '). In these, the most numerous examples, the original adjectival accent is preserved. A small number have radical accent: *áśva-* ' horse ' (Lat. *equus*, Goth. *aíhva°-*, etc.; cf. *āśú-* ' swift '), *sárva-* ' all ' (Av. *haurva-*, Gk. ὅλος, οὖλος, etc.), *pū́rva-* ' former ' (O. Sl. *prŭvŭ*), *pī́va-* ' fat ' (beside *pī́van-* ' id '). The stem *kulva-* ' bald ' (Lat. *calvus*) appears only in the cpd. *atikulva-*.

The *u*-suffix appears with guṇa in *arṇavá-* ' waving; flood, ocean ', *keśavá-* ' long-haired ' (cf. Av. *gaēsav-* ' hair '), *pávīrava-* ' having a metallic share ' (*pávīru-*), *vidhávā* ' widow ' (Lat. *vidua*, etc.; cf. *vidhú-* ' solitary ').

In some cases *-va* has acquired the character of a secondary suffix: *añjivá-* ' slippery ', *śantivá-* ' beneficial ', *śraddhivá-* ' credible ', *rājīva-* ' striped, streaked; blue lotus ', *saciva-* ' companion, minister '.

Stems in *-u* are occasionally enlarged by the addition of the suffix *-i*: *ghṛ́ṣvi-* ' lively, joyful ' beside *ghṛ́ṣu-* ' id '; other *vi*-stems are *dhrúvi-* ' firm ', *dárvi-* fem. ' ladle ', *jā́gṛvi-* ' wakeful *dā́dhṛvi-* ' sustaining ', *dī́divi-* ' shining ', *súśiśvi-* ' swelling or growing well (in the womb) ', cf. *śíśu-* ' child '. This addition appears also in other IE languages, notably in Latin, where all the old adjectival *u*-stems are supplanted by *vi*-stems: *levis* ' light ' (Skt. *laghú-*), *mollis* ' soft ' (Skt. *mṛdú*), *brevis*, *gravis*, etc.

Conversely *-u* is added to the suffix *-i* producing the compound suffix *yu*: *yájyu* ' pious ', *śundhyú-* ' pure ', *sáhyu-* ' strong ', *manyú-* masc. ' anger ', *mṛtyú* masc. ' death ' (Av. *mərəθyu-*), *dásyu-* ' barbarian ', *bhujyú-* ' wealthy '. In Sanskrit this has developed chiefly as a secondary suffix: *duvasyú-* ' worshipping ', *udanyú-* ' irrigating ', *adhvaryú-* ' a kind of priest '. It has come to be specially connected with the denominative verbal base, *devayú-* ' pious ': *devayáti* ' he is pious ', etc., and it tends to acquire a desiderative meaning, *vasūyú-* ' desiring wealth ', etc. The formation is very productive in the Veda, but disappears almost completely in the later language.

§ 17. The Suffix *i* as Union-Vowel

It was noticed above that the suffix *t* acquired under certain circumstances the character of an augment or special insertion between root and suffix (*kṛ-t-ya-* ' to be done ', etc.). The suffix *i* also functions in this way in Sanskrit on an extensive scale.

The use of *i* as a connecting link between root and suffix or between root and termination is particularly common in the verbal formation. The Indian grammarians call the *i* so used *iṭ*, and according to their terminology the forms which take this *i* are called *seṭ* (with *iṭ*) and those that do not are called *aniṭ* (without *iṭ*). The two types of conjugation may be illustrated by the following examples :

I. Present, root-class, *íśiṣe, īśidhve, īśire* ; future, *patiṣyáti, bhaviṣyáti, vardhiṣyáti* ; aorist, *-iṣ, árociṣam, ájīviṣam* ; desiderative, *jíjīviṣāmi* ; perfect, 1 pl. oct. *bubudhimá, tenimá*, 3 pl. mid. *bubudhiré, teniré* ; pass. part. *śaṅkitá-, lajjitá-* ; gerund. *patitvā́, yācitvā́* ; infin. *várdhitum, yā́citum.*

II. Present, root-class, *átsi, vitsé, śeṣe* ; future, *vakṣyáti, chetsyati* ; aorist, *-s, ácchaitsam, ádrākṣam* ; desiderative, *dídṛkṣati, vívitsati* ; perfect 1 pl. act. *cakṛmá, jagṛbhmá*, 3 pl. mid. *yuyujre, vividre* ; pass. part. *kṛtá-, dṛṣṭá-* ; gerund, *chittvā́, kṛtvā́* ; infin. *kártum, dráṣṭum.*

This *i* is also found in nominal derivatives other than the participial and infinitival forms illustrated above. In the agent nouns in *-tar* it appears mostly in agreement with the forms of the infinitive and gerund: *yācitár-, vardhitár-*, etc., as opposed to *kartár-, draṣṭár-*, etc. Examples in the case of other suffixes are: *prathimán-* 'breadth', *khanítra-* 'shovel', *rociṣṇú-* 'shining', *várivas-* 'wide space', *átithi-* 'guest' (as opposed to Av. *asti-*), *dravitnú-* 'running', etc.

It is not possible to formulate any simple general rule governing the presence or absence of this *i* in the verbal conjugation and elsewhere, but a general tendency is observed to use the *seṭ*-forms where inconvenient consonant groups would result (*paptimá*, etc.). The use of *-i-* is more predominant in the later language than in the Veda. For instance the Vedic language has both *-re* and *-ire* in the 3 pl. mid. of the perfect, but the classical language knows only *-ire* ; in later Sanskrit the stems in *-iṣya* account for three-quarters of the futures, while in the earlier language the larger proportion (five-ninths) are still formed with simple *-sya-*. This continues a process which had been going on in pre-Vedic times. Old Iranian, close as it is to Sanskrit, shows very few formations of this nature, which makes it clear that in the main the great extension of the use of *-i-* in the verbal conjugation is a special development of Indo-Aryan. Its adoption on such a large scale is clearly connected with characteristic tendency of Indo-Aryan, observable from the very beginning, to get rid of consonant groups.

To begin with the *i* in verbal and nominal derivation must, in such cases where it existed, have had etymological justification, that is to say it must have been the suffix *i* compounded with other suffixes in the usual way. A number of such suffixes containing *i* have already been enumerated, *-iṣ*, *-iṣa*, *-ira*, etc., formed on the basis of the *i*-suffix in the same way as *-uṣ*, *-uṣa*, *-ura*, etc., are formed on the basis of the *u*-suffix. The suffixes forming the verbal stem are the same as those of the corresponding nominal stems. For instance the stem of the *-iṣ* aorist *árociṣam* appears also in the noun *rocíṣ-* ' light '. Since *rocíṣ-* ' light ' is an extension of the simpler *i*-stem in *rocí-*, *ruci-*, the verbal stem also is originally built up from the *i*-stem. Similarly in the future the suffix *syá* is formed from the *s*-stem with the addition of the denominative *yá*, (the stems, *vakṣyá-ti*, etc., differ only in apophony from denominatives of the type *namasyáti*). In the same way the future in *-iṣya* was to begin with based on the *iṣ*-stem. As regards the form of the stem *bhaviṣyá-*, etc., are exactly parallel to the denominatives in *-uṣyá* (*uruṣyáti*, *vanuṣyáti*), and in the *Ṛgveda* a number of such formations are clearly to be classed as denominatives. Such are *aviṣyáti*, *saniṣyáti*, which have beside them nominal forms (*aviṣyā́*, *aviṣyú-*, *saniṣyú-*) which are commonly associated with the denominative but never with the future.

Those participles in *-ita* where the *i* may be considered to be original have incorporated an *i*-suffix which appears elsewhere in the inflection of the root. This is the case for instance in *sitá* ' bound ' (*sā-* ' to bind ') where the suffix *i* is so frequently associated with the root that the simple root (aor. *ásāt*) has become comparatively rare ; e.g. *s-yáti* ' binds ', *s-é-tave* ' to bind ', *siṣā́ya* ' bound ', etc. The *-ita* of the participles from other roots in *-ā* (*śitá-* ' sharp ', *ditá-* ' bound ', *sthitá* ' stood ', etc.) originates in the same way. The participle of causative and tenth class verbs (*gamitá-* : *gamáyati*, etc.) includes the suffix which is used in the formation of the present, and comparative evidence shows that this practice is old (cf. Goth. *gatarhiþs* : *gatarhjan* ; *wasiþs* : *wasjan*, etc.). The same connection is seen between participles in *-ita* and presents of the fourth class (*kupitá* : *kúpyati*, cf. Lat. *cupio*, *cupītus*) or presents in athematic *i* (*stanitá-* : *stanihí*, cf. further *stanayitnú-*, *tanyatú-*, O. Sl. *stenjǫ*, etc., for the prevalence of the *i*-suffix in connection with this root). A similar incorporation of suffixal *u* is seen in *ádbhuta-* and *ánatidbhuta-* from the root *dabh-* (pres. *dabh-n-ó-ti*).

In the same way we may account for *-itar* beside *-tar* in the agent nouns: *mar̥ḍitár-* 'forgiver', cf. *mr̥ḍáyati, mr̥ḍayā́ku-, mr̥ḍīká-* (Av. *mərəždika-*), *panitár-* 'praiser', cf. *panáyati, panāyáti, paniṣṭa,* aor., *panayā́yya, pániṣṭi-*); likewise *vardhitár-: vardháya-, coditár-* : *codáya-*, etc. The process is illustrated by a similar development occasionally in connection with the *u*-suffix. The agent nouns *tarutár-* 'conqueror', *dhanutár-* 'running swiftly' and *sánutar-* 'winning' incorporate the *u*-suffix which appears in the present tense (*tarute, tū́rvati* ; *dhánvati* ; *sanóti*) and elsewhere (*táruṣa-* etc.).

From these instances it is clear that the *i* in a fair number of verbal forms and nominal derivatives was etymologically justified, and the analysis in such cases does not differ from that of any other forms containing compound suffixes. What Indo-Aryan has done is, on the basis of a modest number of such forms to extend the use of *i* in the verbal derivation on a vast scale. The analogical *i* which then comes to be so abundantly used, ceases to be subject to the usual analysis and acquires the character of a union vowel or euphonic augment.

The *i* which appears in the alternative form of certain terminations (*papt-imá* beside *cakr̥-má*, etc.) was also in origin suffixal. There are some non-thematic presents in *-i* (*svápiti, śvásiti,ániti, jakṣiti*, etc.) with parallels elsewhere (Lat. *capiō, capis, capit*, etc.). They are defective, and since they no longer form a complete present system, they have been attached to the root class, the *i* being treated as union vowel. There are also some scattered preterite forms (*ajayit, bādhithās, atārima, avādiran, asth-ithās, asthiran*, etc.) which have become attached to the *iṣ*-aorist. This type of conjugation is based on the *i*-stem, just as Vedic *tarute* is based on a *u*-stem, so that in origin the *i* here is not different from suffixal *i* elsewhere. But it came to have the character of an addition to the termination and this enabled this type of termination to be transferred to the perfect. The perfect stem is based only on the root, so the *i* in the perfect terminations can only be accounted for as a borrowing from the present and preterite forms of the above type where its presence is etymologically justified (*bubudhimá, dadimá* ; *bubudhiré, dadhiré*, etc., after *atārima, ī́śire*, etc.).

§18. The Suffixes *ā, ī, ū*

The suffix *-ā* has two functions. On the one hand it forms the feminine of adjectives in *-a* (*bāla-* masc. 'boy', *bālā* fem. 'girl'), and on the other hand it appears as an independent suffix of derivation, producing action nouns, abstract nouns, and the like. In having the two functions, adjectival and non-adjectival, it resembles the suffixes previously discussed, but it differs from them in that its adjectival use is confined to the formation of feminines. This was the result of specialisation since the feminine gender was not present in the earliest Indo-European, and as a result of this development of adjectival *-ā*, the action nouns too, which to begin with did not differ from the ordinary neuters (*ā*, i.e. *-a*H, like *-as*, *-ar*, etc.), have acquired the feminine gender.

The following are examples of action nouns and the like terminating in the suffix *-ā* in Sanskrit: *krīḍā́* 'play', *dayā́* 'pity', *nindā́* 'blame', *śaṅkā́* 'doubt', *hiṃsā* 'injury', *kṣamā* 'patience', *bhāṣā* 'speech', *sevā* 'service', *spṛhā* 'desire', *śā́khā* 'branch', *śíphā* 'whip' (cf. Av. *sif-* 'to strike with a whip'), *ā́śā* 'direction', *ukhā́* 'pot', *ulkā́* 'meteor', *venā́* 'longing', *kṣapā́* 'night', *chāyā́* 'shadow' (cf. Gk. *σκιά*), *jarā́* 'old age', *doṣā́* 'evening', *rasā́* 'moisture' (O. Sl. *rosa*, Lith. *rasà* 'dew'). There is no consistent rule about the accentuation of such words, but final accentuation is the commoner; in the corresponding forms in Greek (*γονή*, etc.) final accentuation is the rule. The old general rule about the distribution of accent has obviously long ceased to have any relevance to this class.

The suffix *-ā* is added to the other primary suffixes in the usual manner, producing a series of compound suffixes:

-nā: *tṛ́ṣṇā* 'thirst', *ū́rṇā* 'wool' (Av. *varənā*, Lith. *vìlna*, etc.); *-anā*: *jaraṇā́* 'old age', *arhádṇā* 'worth', *kapanā́* 'caterpillar' (cf. Gk. *κάμπη* 'id'); *-rā*, *súrā* 'strong liquor', *támisrā* 'darkness'; *-sā*, *manīṣā́* 'thought, wisdom'; *-vā*, *jihvā́* 'tongue' (Av. *hizvā*), *grīvā́* 'neck' (O. Sl. *griva* 'mane'), *ámīvā* 'disease', *apvā́* 'a kind of disease', *dū́rvā* 'a kind of grass'; *-yā*, *jāyā́* 'wife', *māyā́* 'magical, supernatural power', *ityā́* 'course', *vidyā́* 'knowledge', *kriyā* 'action', *samajyā* 'assembly', etc.; *-tā*, *kṛṣṇatā* 'blackness', etc., etc.

The suffix *-ī* likewise is predominantly used for making feminines of adjectives, preferably from consonantal stems. In addition there are a small number of primary action nouns and the like. Such are :

(a) *Devī*-declension : *śácī* ' power ', *śámī* ' holy work ', *táviṣī* ' strength ', *āsandī́* ' stool '.

(b) *Vṛkī*-declension : *nadī́* ' river ', *dehī́-* ' wall, embankment ', *starī́-* ' barren cow ' (Gk. στεῖρα), *sūrmī́* ' tube ', *sṛṇī́-* ' sickle ', *palālī́-* ' straw ', *sphigī́-* ' hip ', *nāndī́-* ' joy ', *atharī́-* ' flame ', *oṇī́-* ' breast ', *kṣoṇī́-* ' flood ', *khārī́-* ' a measure ', *cakrī́-* ' wheel ', *tandrī́-* ' sloth, lassitude ', *tapanī́-* ' heat ', *lakṣmī́-* ' mark, auspicious mark, good fortune ', *tarī́-* ' raft ', *tantrī-* ' string '.

The suffix *-ū* is used for making feminines to stems in *-u* (alternatively *-vī* is used, or the unaltered stem functions as feminine), e.g. *tanū́-* ' thin ', *phalgū́-* ' reddish ', *babhrū́-* 'brown', corresponding to masculines *tanú-*, *phalgú-*, *babhrú-*. It also forms a small number of independent nouns, *camū́-* ' dish ', *tanū́-* ' body ', *vadhū́-* ' bride ', *kadrū́-* ' soma-vessel ', *jatū́-* ' bat ', *dhanū́-* ' sandbank ', *nabhanū́-* ' well ', *śvaśrū́-* ' mother-in-law ' (O. Sl. *svekry*, Lat. *socrus*).

Sanskrit *-ā* in this suffix resolves itself ultimately in Indo-European into the thematic vowel + H. Similarly *ī* and *ū* represent *-i*-H and *-u*-H. In this form the parallelism of these three suffixes to the three *s*-suffixes *-as, -is, -us*, becomes clear. The simple suffix is *-a*H, which like neuter *-as* appears with guṇa, and in the compound suffixes *-i*H and *-u*H, old neuter *i-* and *u-* stems are extended by suffixal -H, in the same way as they are extended by *s* in the compound suffixes *-is* and *-us*. Thus *śámī* fem. is an extension of *śámi* nt. (indecl.) (cf. the relation of *arcí-* and *arcíṣ-*, etc.) and *dhanū́* fem. ' sandbank ' along with *dhánvan-* nt. and *dhanuṣ-* nt. are alternative extensions of *dhánu-* ' id ' (fem., originally nt.) The two compound suffixes sometimes appear with guṇa (*vātyā* ' whirlwind ', *jihvā́* ' tongue'), as is alternatively the case with other compound neuter suffixes, *várivas*, etc. The close similarity in function between the H- and *s*- suffixes in making primary action nouns is seen from the frequent instances in which the two are found side by side in words of the same meaning : *tánā*, *tánas* ' offspring ', *jarā́*, *jarás-* ' old age ', *tanū́*, *tánuṣ-* ' body ', *dhanū́-*, *dhánuṣ*, etc. Like the other primary neuter suffixes this *-ā* has no specific meaning and stems in *-ā* frequently occur side by side with root nouns, the extension adding nothing to the meaning : *kṣáp-*, *kṣapā́* 'night', *tán-*, *tánā* 'offspring', *díś-*, *diśā́* 'direction', etc.

The action nouns in *-ā, ī, ū*, are formed in precisely the same way as the neuter action nouns made with other suffixes, but differ from them in being feminine in gender. Since the feminine gender is a comparatively late development in Indo-European, it is to be expected that these stems were originally neuter. Direct evidence of this is provided by the neuter plurals of the type *yugā́*. This *-ā* is the same as the *ā*-suffix, which was used (like some of the other neuter suffixes) as a collective, and eventually as a plural. In this use the suffix still retains the indifference to the distinction between nominative and accusative which characterises neuter stems. The reason for the feminine gender of these action nouns is that these suffixes in their adjectival use became specialised as feminines, and the action nouns on account of similarity of form eventually followed suit.

We have seen that the normal accent of neuter action nouns was on the root. Little trace of the general system remains in the formation of these stems. The accent of the *ā*-stems is variable, showing the same complete absence of rule which was observed in the *i*-stems. The nouns in *ī* and *ū* have a regular accent; on the final. This accent is in complete contradiction to the general rule, but the apophony, with weak suffix, and usually guṇa of root (*tanū́-*, *dehī́*) shows that this is not originally; only radical accentuation will account for such forms, IE *ténu*H, etc. A parallel shift of accent was observed in the neuter stems in *-iṣ, havíṣ-*, etc.

There is a tendency with the other neuter suffixes for the suffix *n* either to replace or to be added to the other suffixes. There are some traces of that system here. Corresponding to *kanyā̀* 'girl', Av. *kainyā*, there is in Avestan a genitive singular *kainīnō* which is related to it in the same way as Skt. *śīrṣṇás* to *śíras*. In Sanskrit this form of the stem appears in the Vedic genitive plural *kanī́nām*. The *-n-* is normal in the genitive plural and the agreement between Sanskrit and Germanic (OHG. *gebōno*, ON. *runōno*), shows that its presence in *ā*-stems goes back to Indo-European. It appears that this *-n-* is the heteroclitic *n*-suffix, which has been generalised in the genitive plural, but abandoned elsewhere, though Av. *kainīno* shows that it could originally appear in other cases.

Stems in *-ā* are used to form a number of adverbs, in the same way as is done with the neuter suffixes above. Such are : *sádā* ' always ', *purā́* ' formerly ', *dvitā́* ' doubly so ', *mṛṣā́* ' falsely ', *sácā* ' with ', *devátā* ' among the gods ', *sasvártā* ' secretly '. In this class are the absolutives in *-tvā́* and *-tvī́* (see above, p. 171).

In their adjectival function these suffixes are principally used to make the feminine stem of adjectives, etc. : *návā* ' new ', *devī́* ' goddess ', *madhū́* ' sweet ', etc. This is the result of specialisation in the later Indo-European period. Originally, it must be assumed, adjectival *-ā, -ī, -ū* were on a par with other suffixes used adjectivally, indifferent to gender, and having the usual relation to the corresponding action nouns. Traces of the more general use of *ā*-stems as agent nouns survive in a number of languages which still have some masculine agent nouns in *-ā* : Lat. *scriba, agricola, nauta*, Gk. *ναύτης, πολίτης*, O. Sl. *sluga* ' servant ', etc. Stems of this kind have totally disappeared from Indo-Iranian, but there remain in the Vedic language a number of masculine stems in *-ī*, of which the commonest is *rathī́-* ' charioteer ' as well as two rare and obscure masculines in *-ū* (*prāśū́-, kṛkadāśū́-*). These are the remnants of an older system in which adjectives and agent nouns of a general type could be made with these suffixes in the same way as with other suffixes.

Some evidence that there originally existed a formal distinction between the action nouns and adjectives of this class is provided by the existence of two types of declension of *ī*-stems in the Vedic language. One type is represented in the declension of *rathī́-*, nom. sg. *rathī́s*, gen. sg. *rathíyas* and the other in that of *devī́*, nom. sg. *devī́*, gen. sg. *devyā́s*. This distinction corresponds exactly to that between the two types of *i*- and *u*-stems (gen. sg. *ávyas, mádhvas* : *agnés, bahós*). In the case of the *i*- and *u*-stems there was evidence enough to show that one type was the declension proper to the neuter action nouns and that the other was the special adjectival declension. It is likely therefore that the same is the cause of the different declensions of the *ī*-stems. The bulk of the feminines formed from adjectives and agent nouns (*devī́* ' goddess ', *pṛthvī́* ' broad ', *adatī́* ' eating ', *jagmúṣī* ' having gone ', *návīyasī* ' newer ', *avitrī́* ' helper ', *dhenumátī* ' possessing cows ', *ámavatī* ' strong ', *saṃrā́jñī* ' sovereign ', *ṛtā́varī* ' pious ' and *ápatihgnī* ' not slaying her husband ', illustrate the various types) inflect in what according to this theory is the adjectival declension. The weak stem in the nom. acc. sg. is parallel to that of the *i*- and *u*-stems. The origin of the variation is not clear, but as with the *i*- and *u*-stems, it appears that a more original form of the adjectival stem is preserved in the gen. sg., etc.

Stems of the *vṛkī́* type comprise both action nouns and agent nouns together with some miscellaneous feminines. The declension of this type (*rathī́*-, gen. sg. *rathíyas*) and its accentuation is closely analagous to that of the adjectives in *-in* (*balī́*, *balínas*). In the case of the latter type it was observed that the generalisation of the weak stem (from gen. sg., etc., which were originally suffixally accented) was secondary, and that comparative evidence indicated original vṛddhied nominatives of the usual type. The same type of generalisation of the weak stem is likely to have happened in the case of *rathī́*, *vṛkī́*, etc., and in Avestan some traces of an older type of declension are preserved. The Avestan word for tongue is declined as follows: nom. sg. *hizva*, acc. sg. *hizvąm*, instr. sg. *hizvā*, gen. sg. *hizvō*, loc. sg. *hizvō*, instr. pl. *hizubiš*. This is clearly the same type of declension as is found in *dātā*, dat. sg. *dātré*, *sákhā*, dat. sg. *sákhye*, *ukṣán*-, gen. sg. *ukṣṇás*, etc., with weak form of suffix in the oblique cases. As remarked above there are two forms of adjectival declension, one with the weak cases having the same form as the neuters (*dātré*, etc.), and another with strong form of suffix and weak form of the gen. sg. termination in these cases (Av. *pitarš*, Skt. *agnés*, etc.). Both types are found among *i*-stems (*sákhye* : *agnáye*) and among the *ī*-stems they are represented by *vṛkī́*- (gen. sg. *vṛkíyas*) and *devī́* (gen. sg. *devyā́s*) respectively. The oldest type of inflection is that which appears in the *vā/ū* stem *hizvā/ū* in Avestan. Leaving aside the heteroclitic *-n-* the same type of inflection appears in Av. *kainya*, gen. sg. *kainīnō* and in Skt. *kanyà*, gen. pl. *kanī́nām*. Elsewhere the weak stem is generalised as in *balī́*, *balínas*. Alternatively the strong form was generalised in which case there was a transfer to the *ā*- declension: *jihvā́*, *jihvā́yās*.

The adjective *mahā́* ' great ' remains in Sanskrit the only non-feminine adjectival *ā*-stem, and it is defective. Apart from compounds where it remains in use in classical Sanskrit, it appears only in the Veda in the acc. sg. masc. *mahā́m*. The gen. sg., etc., appear as *mahás*, etc. The other IE languages show *g* in this root (Gk. μέγας) and the *h* (<*ĝh*) of Sanskrit is due to a combination and the H which originally belonged to the suffix. The original genitive was therefore *meĝ*-H-*és* with terminational accent and weakening of the suffix of the adjective (cf. *ukṣṇás*, etc.). This is the only place outside the thematic and other derivatives to be mentioned below, where the *ā*, i.e. *a*H of the suffix appears in its weak form. Elsewhere the strong form is generalised in both action nouns and adjectives, between which no formal differences exist. In the neuter sg. of this adjective a stem *máhi* with an extra suffix -*i* is used (*meĝ*-H-*i*, cf. Hitt. *mekki*-).

The thematic vowel and other vocalic suffixes could be added to the suffix -*a*H (*ā*) and the latter, being unaccented was weakened to H. This H remains in Sanskrit in the form of the aspiration of a preceding occlusive. Thus *caturthá*- 'fourth' may be explained as **caturtā* (<°*a*H) 'fourness, group of four' +adjectival -*á*, i.e. 'one connected with four, fourness', Similarly *rátha*- 'chariot' is formed by the addition of the thematic suffix to **rota*H> Lat. *rota* 'wheel'. Originally an adjective 'wheeled' it has had the accent thrown back on to the root, in common with many other nominalised adjectives (*vṛ́ka*- 'wolf', etc.). The compound suffix -*tha* out of -*t*-H-*a* is not uncommon: *ártha*- nt. 'object, aim', *várūtha*- nt. 'protection'; *yajátha*- 'worshipping', *vakṣátha*- m. 'growth', *śapátha*- m. 'curse', *sacátha*- m. 'companionship', *sravátha*- m. 'flowing', *ucátha*- nt. 'utterance', *vidátha*- nt. 'worship'; with final accent, *gāthá*- m. 'song', *bhṛthá*- 'offering'; (neut.) *ukthá*- 'utterance', *tīrthá*- 'ford', *yūthá*- 'herd', *rikthá*- 'inheritance'. Most of these forms seem to belong to the class of thematically extended action nouns formed in exactly the same way as *nákṣatra*-, *pátatra*-, *vádhatra*-, etc., above. Those finally accented are presumably adjectival in origin, e.g. *rikthá*- 'that which is left'. The *th* in the suffixes -*thi* (*átithi*- 'guest', etc.) and -*thu* (*vepáthu*- 'quivering', etc.) is in the same way a combination of the suffixes *t* and H; cf. -*tri*, -*tru*.

Other examples of aspirates concerning this suffix are: *sákhi*- 'friend' from *sac*- 'to associate (simple *a*H> *ā* suffix in *sácā* 'with'); *makhá*- 'happy, exulting' from a **maka*H to be compared with Gk. μάκαρ (old neuter adapted as adjective) with variant *r*-suffix; *nakhá*- 'nail', where ultimately both *k* and H are suffixal since other languages have a variant *g* (Lat. *unguis*, etc.), *śaṅkhá*- 'shell', Gk. κόγχος (adjectival accent, original meaning ' curved, coiled ', *śaphá-* ' hoof ' (' striker ', cf. Gk. κόπτω and Sl. *kopyto*), *síndhu-* ' river ' for *sind*-H-*u*-, cf. *syand-* ' to flow ' ; *sádhiṣ-* ' seat, abode ' for *sad*-H-*is*- : *sad-* ' to sit ' ; *aghá-* ' wicked ' perhaps from an **ágaH* side by side with *ā́gas*, Gk. ἄγος ' sin '.

§ 19. Other Suffixes

Of the remaining suffixes the most important is the suffix *-ka*. In other IE languages the element *k* may appear as a non-thematic suffix : Lat. *senex* ' old man ', Gk. μεῖραξ ' lad, lass '. This state of affairs has disappeared in Sanskrit, which has corresponding to these forms the thematic stems *sanaká-* ' old ' and *maryaká-* ' young man '. The suffix rarely appears in primary formations in Sanskrit ; such cases are *śúṣka-* ' dry ' (Av. *huška-*), *ślóka-* ' call ; fame ; verse ' (: *śru-* ' to hear ') and *átka-* ' garment ' (Av. *aδka-*). Normally it is added after vocalic suffixes, in particular after the thematic vowel. The latter type is rare in other IE languages but in Sanskrit it is exceedingly frequent. Examples are *dūraká-* ' distant ', *vamraká-* ' ant ', *arbhaká-* ' small ', *kumāraká-* ' little boy ', *putraká-* ' little son '. It is often simply an extension which adds nothing to the meaning, but also it has in some cases a diminutive sense seen in the last two examples. More rarely it is used to form adjectives from nouns : *ántaka-* ' making an end ', *rūpaká-* ' having an assumed form '. Other vocalic suffixes are likewise extended : *avikā́* ' sheep ' (O. Sl. *ovĭca*), *mṛḍīká-* nt. ' grace ', *dhénukā* ' cow ', *ghā́tuka-* ' killing ', *jatūkā* ' bat '. It is more rarely added to consonantal suffixes : *aṇīyaská-* ' thinner ', *mastíṣka-* ' brain ', *vikṣiṇatka-* ' destroying '. The feminine of the combination *-ika* is extended beyond its original field (*avikā́*, etc.) and it comes to function as the feminine to masculines in *-aka* : *kumāraká-* ' little boy ', *kumārikā́* ' little girl ', etc.

Suffixal *k* is followed by *i* and therefore palatalised in *márīci-* ' ray of light ' and *śvitīcí-* ' bright '. It is followed by *-u* in a few formations like *pṛ́dāku-* ' water-snake ' and *yuvā́ku-* ' belonging to you two '.

The corresponding suffix in the *centum*-languages is *k* to which in Sanskrit *ś* is the most frequent corresponding sound. But in the case of this suffix such *ś* appears only rarely, e.g. *yuvaśá-* ' young ' (Lat. *iuvencus*), *romaśá-* ' hairy ', *babhruśá-* ' brown ', *kapiśa-* ' tawny '.

The voiced guttural, palatalised to *j* appears in the following athematic formations: *dhṛṣáj-* 'bold', *sanáj-* 'old', *bhiṣáj-* 'physician' (cf. Av. °*biš*, *bišaz-*) *sráj-* 'garland' (cf. *pratisara-* and Lat. *sero*), *tṛṣṇáj-* 'thirsty', *ásvapnaj-* 'not sleeping'; (with weak form of suffix) *uśíj-* 'a kind of priest' (Av. *usig-*), *vaṇíj-* 'merchant', *bhuríj-* 'shears', *sphíj-* 'hip' (: cf. *sphyá-* 'flat ladle'). In the nominal forms *tṛṣṇáj-* and *ásvapnaj-* we have the same suffixal combination as is used in the formation of the seventh class of verbs.

A thematic *-ga* appears rarely, e.g. in *śŕṅga-* nt. 'horn' (cf. Lat. *cornu*, etc.), *váṃsaga-* 'bull' (of uncertain etymology), *pataga*, *pataṅgá-* 'bird'.

Suffixal *d* appears in a small number of athematic formations: *dṛṣád-* 'stone' (cf. Gk. δειράς), *darad-* 'cliff, ravine' (themat. *darada-* 'Dard'), *śarád-* 'autumn' (cf. Av. *sarəd-* 'year'), *bhasád-* 'posterior, rump', *vanád-* 'desire', *kakúd-* 'summit' (cf. *kaku-bh-* with different suffix). It appears compounded with *n* in *sadandi-* 'permanent' (cf. the *-nd-* of the Lat. gerundive).

The suffix *gh/h* is likewise extremely rare. It occurs in *dīrghá* 'long' (cf. Gk. δολιχός, Hitt. *dalugaš*; note that it is preceded by three different suffixes in the three languages, Hitt. *u*, Gk. *i*, Skt. H, i.e. *dḷ-H-ghó-*). The root appears without this suffix in O. Sl. *dlina* 'length'. Other cases are *varāhá-* 'boar' (: Av. *varāza-*; the root in Lat. *verrēs*, etc.), *sarágh-* 'bee', and compounded with *r* it appears in *śīghrá-* 'swift' (: *śībham* adv. 'quickly' with different suffix).

Suffixal *dh* appears in a number of combinations. The suffix *-dhra* appears in *várdhra-* 'thong' (: *varatrā* 'id'); it is common in certain other IE languages. The combination *-dhya-* appears in infinitives like *gámadhyai* 'to go', *bháradhyai* 'to bear', *sáhadhyai* 'to overcome' and the like (some thirty-five instances).

A suffix *-pa* appears in a few rare instances like *yū́pa-* 'sacrificial post' (*yu-* 'to attach, join', cf. *yūthá-* 'herd' for *ū*) and *stū́pa-* 'top-knot' (cf. °*stu* and *stúkā* 'id').

Non-thematic *-bh* appears in *kakubh-* 'summit' (cf. *kaku-d-* above), and thematic *-bha* in a small number of nouns, mostly animal names: *vṛṣabhá-* and *ṛṣabhá-* 'bull', *gardabhá-* 'donkey', *rāsabhá-* 'id', *śalabhá-* 'locust', *sthūlabhá-* 'big'. The specialisation of this suffix in animal names is known also in other IE languages: Gk. ἔλαφος 'stag', O. Sl. *golǫbĭ* 'dove', etc.

This completes the list of Sanskrit and IE suffixes. As will be seen all IE consonants were capable of being used as elements in the suffixal system.

§20. Vṛddhi in Derivation

In its use of vṛddhi Sanskrit has developed a system of derivation which was totally unknown in the parent IE language. It is used in connection with a number of suffixes, which may also function without being associated with vṛddhi, and as such have already been treated. Its use is a speciality of the secondary as opposed to the primary derivation. In the earlier language alternative forms without vṛddhi occur. Thus the suffix *-a* (normally accented) which makes adjectives on the basis of the old neuter suffixes, may be associated with vṛddhi, e.g. *mā́nuṣa-* 'connected with men; man' beside *mánuṣa-* 'man', and *vāpuṣá-* beside *vápuṣa-* 'beautiful' from *vapuṣ-*. This type of formation may be illustrated by a few examples classified according to the various suffixes.

Suffix *-a*: *āṅgirasá-* 'descended from Aṅgiras', *mā́ruta-* 'relating to the Maruts', *mānavá-* 'human; man', *jaítra-* 'victorious', *auśijá-* 'connected with the priests called *uśíj-*, *mārḍīká-* nt. 'mercy'.

Suffix *-ya*: *daívya-* 'divine', *saumyá-* 'relating to Soma', *vāyavyá-* 'belonging to the wind'; neuter abstracts, *pā́litya-* 'greyness', *ā́rtvijya-* 'priestly office'.

Suffix *-i*: *Ā́gniveśi-* 'a descendant of Agniveśa-', *Paúrukutsi-* 'a descendant of Purukutsa'. This type is almost entirely confined to patronymics.

Suffix *-āyana*: patronymics, *Kāṇvāyana-*, *Dākṣāyaṇa-*, etc.

Suffix *-īya*: *pārvatīya-* 'of the mountains'. This type is practically confined to the later language.

Suffix *-ka*: *māmaká-* 'mine', *āvaśyaka-* 'necessary', *vā́santika-* 'of the spring time', *dhārmika-* 'religious', etc.; this type is mainly confined to the later language and few Vedic examples are quoted.

Suffix *-eya*: *ārṣeyá-* 'descendant of a sage', *Jānaśruteyá-* 'son of Janaśruti', *vā́steya-* 'of the bladder' (*vasti-*), *paúruṣeya-* 'relating to man', etc.

Derivational vṛddhi with other suffixes is exceedingly rare;

such cases are *ā́gnīdhra-* ' belonging to the fire-kindler ' (*agnī́dh-*) and *āśvīna-* ' a day's journey on horseback '.

The exact details of the development of this use of vṛddhi are somewhat obscure, but the material enables a number of observations about it to be made. The process began in the late Indo-Iranian period, developed rapidly in the pre-Vedic period of Indo-Aryan and continued to extend during the historical development of Sanskrit. The complete absence of any such formations in IE languages outside Indo-Iranian, makes it clear that it was a development confined to those languages, and the fact that in early Iranian examples of this vṛddhi are exceedingly rare, shows that this type of formation was only in its beginning at the time of the separation of Indo-Aryan and Iranian. Iranian examples are O. Pers. *mārgava-* ' inhabitant of Margiana ', from *margu-* ' Margiana ', Av. *āhūiri-* ' belonging to Ahura- ', *āhūirya-* ' son of a prince ', from *ahura-*, *māzdayasni-* ' belonging to the Mazdayasnian religion ', *xštāvaenya-* ' descendant of Xštavi. The three suffixes *-a*, *-i* and *-ya* which occur in connection with vṛddhi in these Iranian examples are the ones that most frequently occur in this connection in Sanskrit, and the suffix of the patronymic *xštāvaēnya* is related to the *-āyana* which makes patronymics in Sanskrit.

The point of departure of this derivational vṛddhi must be sought in the old IE phonetic vṛddhi, which, as instanced from time to time above, is found sporadically in the radical syllable of nouns of primary derivation. Instances quoted are *rā́jan-* ' king ', *bhā́rman-* ' burden ', *vā́sas-* ' garment ', *dā́ru* ' wood ', *sā́nu-* ' top ', *grā́hi-* ' seizure ', and the like. Examining some of the older cases of derivational vṛddhi it can be seen that *mānavá-* ' man ', *kāvyá-* ' one having the qualities of a *kavi-*, wise man ', *ā́rya-* ' Aryan ', and *nādyá-* ' born from a river ' and similar forms which from the point of view of Sanskrit show the vṛddhi of secondary derivation, are not essentially different in form from words like *dānavá-* ' demon ', *bhāvyá-* ' which is to be ', *vā́rya-* ' to be chosen ' and *ādyà-* ' to be eaten ' which are either classified as primary formations, or (in the case of *dānavá-*, etc.) are derived from primary formations with phonetic vṛddhi. Likewise Skt. *vāsará-* ' matutinal ; day ', would appear to have derivational vṛddhi (cf. *vasar°*), but elsewhere in Indo-European a long vowel is seen in the primary neuter (Gk. ἔἰαρ <**wēsṛ*, etc.). It may be assumed that primary formations with vṛddhi of the type *dā́ru-*, *nā́bhi-*, were originally more general, and that forms of the type **mā́nu-* existed in paradigmatic alternation with *mánu-*, etc.; and that when the guṇa grade, *mánu-*, etc., was eventually generalised in the majority of the simple formations, there remained a class of thematic derivatives formed on the basis of obsolete vṛddhied stems, i.e. *mānavá-* beside *mánu-*. This nucleus showing the alternation guṇa in the primary and vṛddhi in the secondary derivative, would then be the starting point of the system in which vṛddhi came to be widely used in the formation of secondary derivatives.

This means that derivational vṛddhi must have appeared first in the case of the vowel *ā*, and that the use of *ai* and *au* in these formations must be due to analogy, for the reason that *ai* and *au* do not occur in primary nominal derivation. There is evidence that this was the case, since in Iranian, which reflects this process in its early beginnings, *ā* is the only vṛddhied vowel which appears in this type of derivative. Forms such as *θraētaona-* n. pr. (cf. Skt. *traitānā́-*) and *haomanaŋha-* 'kindness' (cf. Skt. *saumanasá-*) which have been quoted as parallels to the Sanskrit *ai* and *au* vṛddhi, contain not vṛddhi but guṇa. Since the words from which they are derived had by nature a guṇa as well as a weak grade (*trai-/tri-* '3'; (*a*)*sau-*/(*a*)*su-* 'good') there is no reason why the above formations should not be straight derivatives from this (like *trétā* 'triad'). It is in accordance with secondary origin of the *ai* and *au* vṛddhi that cases of derivational vṛddhi with these vowels are much rarer in the *Ṛgveda* than those containing *ā*.

On the whole the system has been fully built up by the time of the *Ṛgveda*. The main types are in existence, but examples do not occur with the same frequency as in the later language. There exist also a greater number of formations of the older type, in which the secondary suffixes are added without vṛddhi, e.g. *vápuṣa-* beside *vāpuṣá-* and *viśyà-* beside *vaíśya-*. In the later period the popularity of the vṛddhied forms rapidly increases, and it develops into one of the most characteristic features of the Sanskrit language.

§21. Grammatical Gender

In common with the other IE languages all Sanskrit nouns are classified according to the three genders, Masculine, Feminine, and Neuter. This classification corresponds only partly to the natural order of things, that is to say in so far as the nouns or adjectives apply to human beings and to certain of the larger animals. For the rest of the language the choice of gender is arbitrary and without any logical foundation. In spite of this the system has proved remarkably tenacious in the majority of IE languages ; in the modern Indo-Aryan languages, for instance, where traces of the old IE grammatical system have been reduced to a minimum, the system of grammatical gender remains in operation. Languages such as English or Persian which have abolished the distinction remain a minority even now among the descendants of Indo-European.

A study of the evidence provided by the comparison of the IE languages particularly of those which are recorded at an early period, enables some insight to be gained into the origin of this system. This is because grammatical gender was, at the period of Indo-European which can be reached by comparison, a comparatively recent innovation, and evidence enough can be gathered from the main existing languages, to understand the nature of its development.

Two stages can be traced in this development. At the earliest stage there were two classes of nouns, on the one hand a ' common gender ' later differentiated into masculines and feminines, and on the other hand the ' neuters '. This state of affairs is faithfully reflected in Hittite, which is distinguished from all other IE languages by the absence of a special feminine gender. The next stage sees the development of the feminine, and it is only at this period that it is proper to speak of gender in the true sense.

The existence of an earlier dual system is attested not only by Hittite, but also by abundant evidence gathered from the remaining languages. Meillet and others had adopted it on the basis of this latter evidence before anything much was known about Hittite, and the discovery of Hittite has gone further to confirm the theory. Attempts have been made to explain the dual system of Hittite as due to the loss of the feminine gender in that language, but no satisfactory evidence has been adduced for this. The fact is that the evidence of the other languages points unambiguously to the pre-existence of a dual system, and since such a system is to be found in Hittite, which in other respects preserves archaic features not known to the remaining languages, there is no reason why the Hittite evidence should not be taken at its face value. The evidence from Sanskrit and the other languages is briefly that (1) the bulk of the masculine suffixes is also to be found in feminine nouns, and (2) that the specifically feminine suffixes *ā, ī* are used also in masculine derivatives.

(1) The suffix *-tár* forms mainly agent nouns which are masculine. For the feminine the suffix *ī* is added (*dātrī́*) and a similar differentiation appears in other languages (Gk. δοτεῖρα, Lat. *dātrīx*). On the other hand in the ancient group of nouns in *-tar* expressing family relationships the undifferentiated suffix is used for masculine (*pitár-*) and feminine (*mātár-, yā́tar-*) nouns. This conservative type preserves the older system which has been abandoned in the ordinary agent nouns in favour of a system in which masculine and feminine are distinguished.

The suffix *-sar* which appears in *svásar-* ' sister ', also in *tisrás, cátasras,* Lat. *uxor* and thematised in Hitt. *išḫaššaraš* ' lady ' functions adjectivally in the same way as *-tar* (both being opposed to the neuter *-sar, -tar*), but it tended at an early period to be specialised in feminine formations. The eventual adoption of H-suffix as the normal means of expressing the feminine checked this development, and only these few survivals remain.

The adjectival suffix *-man* is normally masculine (*brahmán-*, etc.), but in bahuvrīhi compounds it remains indifferent to gender according to the earlier system. Vedic examples of this are *purúśarmā* (*Áditis*), *dyutádyāmānam* (*uṣásam*), *sutármānam* (*nā́vam*), acc. pl. *śúcijanmanas* (*uṣásas*), instr. pl. *vā́jabharmabhis* (*ūtíbhis*). The Atharva-veda first begins to show special feminine forms in compounds containing the word *nā́man-* ' name ' : *páñcanāmnī* ' having five names ', etc.

The feminine suffix is added to the present participle in Sanskrit and in Greek (*bhárantī*, φέρουσα), but in Latin the older undistinguished type is used for both masculine and feminine (*ferens, ferentem*).

The non-neuter (i.e. accented) suffix *-as* functions in both masculine and feminine nouns, e.g. *apás-* ' active ' masc. and fem. as opposed to *ápas-* neut. ' work ' ; likewise in bahuvrīhi compounds, *sumánās* nom. sg. masc. and fem. ' well-disposed '. The same state of affairs appears in Greek, ἀληθής, εὐμενής, etc. The compound suffix *-yas*, functioning in a comparative sense, adds the feminine *-ī* in Sanskrit (*bhū́yasī*, etc.) but Latin preserves the undifferentiated usage (*maiōr*, masc. and fem.).

Non-neuter nouns in *-i* and *-u* are both masculine and feminine. The adjectives in *i* do not distinguish a masculine and feminine stem (*śúcis* nom. sg. masc. and fem.) and those in *-u* optionally follow the same system (*cā́rus* masc. and fem.). The latter may optionally form feminines in two ways (*bahvī́* 'much' *tanū́* 'thin'), but the fact that this still remains optional shows that it is a comparatively recent innovation.

The thematic suffix *-a*, accented and forming adjectives was originally in the same way indifferent to the distinction between masculine and feminine. This state of affairs has become altogether extinct in Sanskrit, but in addition to its being preserved in full force in Hittite, it has left considerable traces in Greek and Latin. It is preserved in Greek in compounds (ῥοδοδάκτυλος ἠώς, etc.) and in both Greek and Latin in a number of individual formations. A good illustration is provided by the word for daughter-in-law which appears with the thematic suffix in Greek and Latin (νυός, *nurus*) as opposed to the specifically feminine *ā*-suffix which appears in Sanskrit (*snuṣā́*) and Slavonic (Russ. *snoxá*). There is no doubt that the form preserved in Greek and Latin is the more original, and that the form as it appears in Sanskrit and Slavonic is an innovation due to the growth of the system of grammatical gender; IE *snus-ó-* was formed at a time when the accented thematic vowel was used simply to make adjectives on the basis of neuter stems in the way amply illustrated above (*udrá-* : ὕδωρ, etc.) and was, as still in Hittite, indifferent to gender. The word is based on an obsolete neuter in *-us*, and etymologically this *sn-u-s-* is to be connected with *sn-eu-bh-* in Lat. *nūbo*, etc.

(2) Instances in the reverse direction are quotable from a variety of IE languages. In dealing with the suffix *-ā* (*-a*H) it was pointed out that it could appear with two functions, one originally neuter forming verbal abstracts, etc., and the other adjectival; also that, since the usual variations in accent and apophony between the two types were mainly eliminated in these stems, there is no formal difference between the two. The feminine gender developed with the specialisation of this suffix, in its adjectival function, as a feminine suffix, but there are still preserved a number of masculine adjectival formations with this suffix. Examples of such masculines are seen in Lat. *scriba*,

nauta, *agricola*, etc., O. Sl. *sluga* 'servant', *vojevoda* 'army commander' which are in no way formally differentiated from feminines. Greek also has such masculine *ā*-stems, but has differentiated them on its own by adding *-s* in the nom. sg. (ποιητής, etc.). In Sanskrit this type has become obsolete like that of the feminine *o*-stems. On the other hand there remain a number of masculines formed with the compound suffix *-ī* (*-i*-H) which functions side by side with *ā* in the formation of feminines. Skt. *rathī́-* 'charioteer' is a survival from the time when adjectival *-ī* was indifferent to gender, before it became specialised as a feminine suffix. In Italic and Celtic this adjectival *-ī*, by an easy change of syntactical function, was adapted to form the genitive singular of *o*-stems (*equī* stands to *equus* as *rathī́-* to *rátha-*).

The existence of these common masc.-fem. formations so abundantly in Sanskrit and other IE languages, together with the twofold system of Hittite which shows no trace of a feminine gender, is capable of only one explanation. An older dual system has been replaced by a threefold classification into genders. The old system is preserved in its entirety in Hittite; in Sanskrit and other languages it is still partly preserved, as the above examples show, but in the main it has been replaced by the threefold system.

The process of this development cannot be followed in detail since it lies in the prehistory of the languages concerned. All that can be said is that at some period of later Indo-European the suffix *ā* (*-a*H) together with the compound suffixes *ī* (*-i*-H) and *ū* (*-u*-H) came to be specialised as feminine suffixes. This must have applied first to these suffixes in their adjectival use beginning possibly with a small nucleus of words which happened to possess this suffix and were feminine by meaning (e.g. Skt. *gnā́*, Gk. γυνή). The suffixes so used are either an addition to the primary adjectival suffix (*rājñī*) or in the case of thematic stems a substitution for it (*néwos*/*néwā*).

The nature of the earlier dual system has been made sufficiently clear in dealing with the individual suffixes above. The words of 'common gender' from which masculine and feminine nouns eventually derive are in origin adjectives or, what from the point of view of early Indo-European is the same thing, agent nouns. The fundamental division is the one represented on the one hand by Gk. ὕδωρ 'water', Hitt. *arkuwar* 'prayer', Skt. *yáśas-* 'fame', *bráhma* 'prayer', *sthā́tar 'stability', and on the other hand by Skt. *udrá-* 'water-animal, otter', *ŕ̥kvan-* 'worshipping, worshipper', *yaśás-* 'famous', *brahmán-* 'priest', and *sthātár-* 'stander', and in other examples copiously quoted above. It is therefore misleading to speak of an 'animate' and 'inanimate' gender as if the twofold classification were in origin the expression of such a distinction. It is clear enough from the evidence that the origin of the system was primarily grammatical and not due to any psychological classification of objects in the external world. The so-called nouns of 'common gender' or 'animate gender' are in origin agent nouns, and they are predominantly 'animate' (and in the main designative of human beings), because it is natural that the agent type of noun is most frequently applied to persons. It is not however exclusively so, and this may be illustrated by a number of Greek formations in -τηρ, e.g. ἀορτήρ 'sword-belt', λαμπτήρ 'lamp-stand', κρατήρ 'mixing-bowl', τριπτήρ 'pestle', ζευκτήρ 'yoke-strap', etc. These represent an ancient type, better preserved in Greek than elsewhere, and show how in origin the adjective/agent-noun class of stem had nothing to do with the distinction between animate and inanimate. We have seen that these suffixally accented formations are originally based on a class of neuters which are well represented by the Hittite formations in *-tar*. The latter are in the main verbal abstracts or nouns of a similar type. The adjectival type with suffixal accent means somebody or something connected with the meaning of the primary neuter, and could originally apply to things as well as to persons. Because in practice such formations were most frequently applied to persons, the tendency was to eliminate their use as inanimates, so that in the case of nouns in *-tēr* for instance such usage is rare outside this Greek type.

Another type of archaism is preserved in the Vedic language. This is the occasional use of the masculine form of adjectives, in the case of consonantal stems, in agreement with neuter nouns. As examples of this we may quote *vácaḥ . . . dvibárhāḥ* RV. 7. 8. 6, *śárdho . . . anarvā́ṇam* 1. 37. 1, *visarmā́ṇam kr̥ṇuhi vittám* 5, 54, 9, *śárdho mā́rutam . . . satyáśravasam ŕ̥bhvasam* 5. 52. 8, *tád rāṣṭrám ojasvī́ bhavati* MS 4, p. 47,4. These reflect an early state of affairs when the formations with accented suffix and vr̥ddhied nominative were purely adjectival, unconnected with gender, and could therefore be used in agreement with any noun. With the growth of the gender system a new type of adjectival neuter was created, e.g. *purú* beside *purús* 'much', and traces like the above were eventually eliminated. The process is still to be seen in the course of development in Sanskrit in the case of the agent nouns in *-tṛ*; the neuter formation *kartṛ́-* 'doer' (gen. sg. *kartṛ́ṇas*) is unknown in the earliest texts and is a later analogical development. The older neuter forms of adjectives, though of early origin, were to begin with innovations of the same type.

The foundation of the non-neuter class lies in the adjectival formations, but it was early augmented by transferences which introduced a growing number of action nouns. These have been classified separately in the above pages and are illustrated by such examples as *bhārá-* masc. 'burden', *jigīṣā́* 'desire of conquest', *vā́c-* fem. 'speech', *ojmán-* masc. 'strength', *bhiyás-* fem. 'fear', *matí-* fem. 'intelligence', and *tántu-* masc. 'thread'. The nature of this transference seems to have been mainly mechanical. Personification plays a certain part but this is strictly subsidiary. It is understandable that a stem like *uṣás-* should appear as feminine for this reason in view of the place of *uṣás-* in the Vedic pantheon; or that *omán-* 'assistance' and *dāmán-* 'liberality' which are invoked as divine attributes of the gods should be masculine rather than neuter. But no such consideration can apply to the majority of such nouns. For instance, while it is quite clear that *vā́c-* fem. 'speech' is in Sanskrit usage quite definitely personified as opposed to the neuter *vácas-*, it cannot be said that it owes its feminine gender to this. On the other hand it is capable of being personified because for other reasons it has acquired the feminine (derived from the originally common) gender. Stems terminating in occlusives in all IE languages take the nominative *s* and distinguish between nominative and accusative. In this they are distinguished from the mass of neuter action nouns and agree with the adjectival and agent noun type. It is clear also from the absence of cases to the contrary that this must have been the case from a very early period. There is no logical basis for this; all that can be said is that there is a general rule that all stems of this type inflect in this way, that *vā́k(s)*, *vā́cam* is so inflected because it is a radical stem ending in an occlusive. The fact that it is inflected in this way, and thereby acquires a non neuter, eventually feminine gender, enables it to be personified. In the same way we may judge the relationship between *ā́pas*, nom. pl. fem. and *udakam*, *udan-* (Gk. ὕδωρ, etc.) ' water '. There is nothing about radical action nouns as such, from the point of view of their meaning which should cause them to become masculines or feminines ; only the mechanical development which caused them to inflect in the same way as the adjectival type of noun which formed the basis of the ' animate ' gender is responsible for their becoming such.

In the same way other action noun stems ending in occlusives early inflected in this way (Hitt. *kartimmiyat-* ' anger ', etc.). The neuter *i*-stems were eliminated except for small remnants, and a similar tendency, though on a smaller scale is observable among the action nouns in *-u*. The thematic action nouns are extensions of root stems which were originally common gender, and this characteristic they retained ; when the common gender split into masculine and feminine they naturally became masculines because this is the masculine adjectival suffix. In the same way the action nouns in *-ā* are feminine because this is the feminine adjectival suffix.

An essential part is played in the development of the IE system of gender by the system prevailing in these languages by which an adjective must be inflected in the case, number and gender of the noun with which it is in agreement. This is one of the most characteristic features of Indo-European, as grammatical congruence on this scale is hardly to be found elsewhere. Traces of an earlier system, in which the simple adjectival stem could function in attributive use, survive in nominal composition, indicating that the full system was only gradually built up, but it is none the less of ancient origin. It is fully developed in Hittite and applies there to gender in so far as the ' common gender ' and the ' neuter ' are distinguished, that is to say in the nominative and the accusative. With the growth of the feminine gender, which is the final stage in the development of the system, the system of congruence was correspondingly extended.

§ 22. Nominal Composition

The capacity to combine independent words into compound words is inherited by Sanskrit from Indo-European, and similar formations are found in other IE languages. Sanskrit differs from the other IE languages in the enormous development which the system has undergone, which is unparalleled elsewhere. This development, however, is characteristic only of the classical language, and in the Vedic language the use made of nominal composition is much more restricted. It is estimated that in the *Ṛgveda* the role it plays is not more important than in Homeric Greek. From the point of view of comparative philology it is mainly the Vedic language that has to be considered. The unlimited development of nominal composition in the later classical literature is artificial and not based on spoken usage.

The main features of a compound, though not invariably present, are (1) the appearance of the first member in its stem form, without the inflectional endings with which, except in the vocative, it is associated in independent use, and (2) the uniting of the two elements under one accent. The first feature is of great interest from the point of view of early Indo-European morphology, since it points to a time when the simple stem of a noun or adjective could appear in syntactical relation to other words of the sentence, without the case terminations which later became obligatory for the expression of such relationships. A compound comes into existence when two words appear so regularly and frequently together that they become to all intents and purposes a single expression, a process which is normally associated with the development of a specialised meaning. In the case of inflected groups this leads to compounds like *Bṛ́haspáti-* proper name of a divinity ('lord of prayer'). On the other hand a compound like *viśpáti-* 'chief of a clan' can only derive, as a type, from a state of affairs in which the relationship which is later expressed by the genitive case, could be expressed by the simple juxtaposition of two nouns in a certain order (*vík póti-s*). The compounds as a system are the fossilised remains of an earlier state of Indo-European which has long been supplanted by the consistently inflected type which appears in Sanskrit and the classical languages.

Four main classes of compound were recognised by the Indian grammarians, *Tatpuruṣa* (with a special subdivision *Karmadhāraya*) *Bahuvrīhi*, *Dvandva* and *Avyayībhāva*, terms which will be defined below. Of these the last two are in the main specifically Indian developments; the types inherited from Indo-European are those classified as tatpuruṣa and bahuvrīhi.

For the purpose of this brief exposition the inherited types may be divided into two major classes, namely I. those which function as nouns and II. those which function as adjectives. These are followed by III. Dvandva and IV. Avyayībhāva.

The first class falls into two main divisions according to whether the first member is (a) an adjective or noun in apposition with the second member or (b) a noun standing in such relationship to the second member as would normally be expressed by a case termination. Conversely the adjectival type can conveniently be divided into two classes according to whether the final member is adjective or noun. Of the two major classes, nominal and adjectival, the former are rare in the early language, and this is the case elsewhere in Indo-European. On the other hand the various types of adjectival compound are abundantly represented, as elsewhere, particularly in Greek. We shall see that there is very good reason for this disparity and that it is of significance for understanding how the system evolved.

I. A. Compounds in which the two members stand in apposition to each other are named Karmadhāraya by the Indian grammarians. The main class consists of an adjective followed by a noun. The type is rare in the Saṃhitās, but becomes more frequent in the later Vedic prose texts. Examples are *candrá-mā̆s-* '(bright) moon', *pūrṇámāsa-* 'full-moon', *ekavīrá-* 'unique hero', *kṛṣṇaśakuní-* 'raven', *mahāgrāmá-* 'great host', *mahāvīrá-* 'great hero', *mahādhaná-* 'great wealth', *nīlotpalá-* 'blue lotus', *rajatapātrá-* 'silver vessel', *dakṣiṇāgní-* 'southern fire', *adharahanú-* 'lower jaw', *tṛtīyasavaná-* '3rd pressing', *navadāvá-* 'land newly burnt for cultivation', *kṛṣṇasarpa-* 'cobra'. Such compounds possess frequently specialised meanings, which would not automatically be expressed by the simple combination of the meanings of the adjective and the noun. The word *kṛṣṇaśakuní* literally 'black bird', means more specifically 'raven'; 'black bird' would be expressed by the uncompounded noun and adjective. Similarly *nīlotpalá-* means not merely 'a blue lotus', but a particular botanical species (*Nymphaea cyanea*). It is only in the later language that such compounds show a tendency to be used as simple equivalents of the combination adjective + noun.

In a smaller class the first member is a noun in a relation of apposition to the second member. Such are *puruṣamṛgá-*

'male antelope', *ú́lūkayātu-* 'owl demon', *vṛṣā́kapi* 'man-ape', *rājarṣi-* 'royal sage', *dhenuṣṭarī́* 'barren cow', *ukṣavehát-* 'an impotent bull'.

The karmadhāraya is represented in other IE languages by such examples as Gk. *ἀκρόπολις, μεσόγαια, ἀγριάμπελος*, Lat. *angiportus*, etc., and the second type can be compared with formations like Gk. *ἰατρόμαντις* 'physician-seer'. But just as in the earliest Sanskrit these formations are rare. This is natural in view of the origin of these compounds and their place in the grammatical structure of Indo-European in its various stages. They are the remains of a time when the adjective, when used attributively, took no inflections for gender, number and case. Such a state of affairs came early to be replaced in Indo-European by one in which the attributive adjective was inflected in agreement with its noun in all cases, genders and numbers, but there remained a few expressions which were so grown together in usage that they continued as relics of the old system. These could then serve as models for the creation of new examples of the same type.

B. Tatpuruṣas with an ordinary substantive as their first member are in the earliest language somewhat more numerous than compounds of the karmadhāraya type, but they are still distinctly rare in comparison with Bahuvrīhis and other adjectival types. They are rarest in the earliest part of the *Ṛgveda* and become gradually more important in the succesive stages of Vedic literature. Examples are *rājaputrá-* 'king's son', *mṛtyubándhu-* 'companion of death', *viśpáti-* 'lord of the tribe', *drupadá-* 'post of wood', *hiraṇyarathá-* 'car of gold', *devakilbiṣá-* 'offence against the gods', *indrasenā́* 'Indra's army', *camasā́dhvaryu-* 'the priest connected with the cups', *drughaṇá-* 'mace of wood', *ācāryajāyā́* 'teacher's wife', *puruṣarājá-* 'king of men', *ajalomá-* 'goat's hair', *aśvavālá-* 'hair (from the tail) of a horse', *udapātrá-* 'bowl of water'. The relationship between the two members is most frequently that expressed by the genitive case, but being very general it can in various examples be transcribed by all cases, and the Indian grammarians have classified them on these lines: Dative, *yūpadāru* 'wood for a sacrificial post' (*yūpāya dāru*), ablative, *caurabhaya-* 'fear of thieves' (*caurebhyo bhayam*), locative *grāmavāsa-* 'dwelling in a village', accusative *videśagamana* 'going abroad'.

Compounds of which the last member is a verbal action noun in *-ti* form a special class. Such are *dhánasāti-* 'winning of wealth', *deváhūti-* 'invocation of the gods', *sómasuti-* 'pressing of soma' and *deváhiti-* 'ordinance of the gods'. These have accent of the first member as opposed to the tatpuruṣas above and in this respect go with the adjective compounds whose final member is a participle in *-ta* (*vīrájāta-*, etc.). They are also abundantly formed in the earliest language, a characteristic which is usually reserved for adjective compounds. A few instances where the final member in *-ti* has acquired a concrete sense are to be classed with the examples above, e.g. *devahetí* 'weapon of the gods'.

The corresponding type appears in other IE languages in such examples as Gk. *μητροπάτωρ* 'mother's father', *πατράδελφος* 'father's brother', *οἰκοδεσπότης* 'master of a house', Lat. *muscerda* 'mouse dung', Goth. *þiudangardi-* 'king's house', O. Sl. *vodotokŭ* 'watercourse'.

Besides these there exists in the Vedic language a new type of compound in which the first member retains its genitive ending, and, most frequently, its accent. These are commonest with *páti-* as the last member: *vánaspáti-* 'lord of the wood, tree', *gnā́spáti-* 'husband of a divine woman', *bṛ́haspáti-* 'lord of devotion', etc.; with one accent *aṃhasaspatí-* 'lord of distress', name of an intercalary month. Other examples appear rarely: *dívodāsa-* 'servant of heaven', *rā́yaspóṣa-* 'increase of wealth'; later, *góṣpada-* 'cow's footprint, small puddle', *dāsyāḥputra-* 'slave-girl's son (term of abuse)'. Compare Gk. *Διόσκουροι*, etc. This is the type of compound an inflected language might be expected to form. Its emergence in the Vedic language is to be viewed in connection with the comparative rarity of the ordinary type. As in Greek, etc., these had come to play only a small part in the language, and were in comparison with other kinds of compound, unproductive. Later the reverse process sets in; the frequency of the true tatpuruṣa increases and the development of the new inflected type is checked.

II. Compounds functioning as adjectives may be divided into two classes according as to whether the latter member is an adjective or noun.

A. (1) (a) *Compounds with verbal adjective as second member.* In these the first member most frequently stands in the accusative relationship to the verbal adjective which forms the second member. They may be classified according to the various types of stem that appear in the second member.

Root-stems: *havirád-* 'eating the oblation', *aśvavíd-* 'knowing horses', *vṛtrahán-* 'slaying enemies'. Roots in *i*, *u*, *ṛ* may not appear as root nouns and add the augment *-t*: *dhanajít-* 'conquering wealth', *somasút-* 'pressing soma', *jyotiṣkṛ́t-* 'making light'. Such compounds with root stems have sometimes a passive meaning: *manoyúj-* 'yoked by the will', *hṛdayāvídh-* 'pierced to the heart'. The type is familiar in other IE languages, cf. Gk. *βουπλήξ*, Lat. *fidicen*, *artifex*, etc.

Thematic suffix: *annādá-* 'food-eating', *goghná-* 'killing cows', *devavandá-* 'god-praising', *karmakara-* 'workman'. A newer type in which the first member takes the accusative (or occasionally some other) termination is common in connection with this suffix: *dhanañjayá-* 'conquering wealth', *purandará-* 'destroying cities', *talpeśayá-* 'lying on a bed'. The thematic type is familiar in other IE languages: Av. *hašidava-* 'betraying a friend', Gk. *θυμοφθόρος*, *δρυτόμος*, Lat. *causidicus*, *magnificus*, Russ. *vodonós* 'water-carrier', etc.

Suffix *-ana*: *keśavárdhana-* 'cutting hair', *amitradámbhana-* 'deceiving enemies', *devayájana-* 'worshipping the gods'.

Suffix *-in*: *ukthaśaṃsín-* 'singing hymns', *vratacārín-* 'performing a vow', *satyavādín-* 'speaking the truth'.

Suffix *-i*: *pathirákṣi-* 'protecting the road', *sahobhári-* 'bearing strength'.

Suffixes *-van* and *-man*: *somapā́van-* 'drinking soma', *baladā́van-* 'giving strength', *svādukṣádman-* 'sharing out sweet things'. Cf. Gk. *πολυδέγμων*.

Other suffixes - *rāṣṭradipsú-* 'injuring the kingdom', *lokakṛtnú-* 'world making', *nṛpātṛ́-* 'men-protecting'.

Among formations of this kind there is a considerable class in which the form of the last member is modelled on the present stem taken by the root in question. Such are stems ending in:

-ya (4th class): *punarmanyá-* 'again thinking of', *akṛṣṭapacyá-* 'ripening without ploughing', *asūryampaśyá-* 'not seeing the sun'.

-aya (10th class and causatives): *anilayá-* 'not resting', *janamejayá-* 'rousing the people', *dharmadhāraya-* 'maintaining the law'. Cf. Av. *narō vaēpaya-*.

-nva: *viśvaminvá* 'stimulating all', *dhiyaṃjinvá-*, *dānupinvá-*.

-na: *duradabhná-*, *kulampuná-*, *sadāpṛṇá-*. Cf. Gk. μίσθαρνος, πολυδάμνης.

Infixed nasal: *agnimindhá-*, *śalyakṛntá-*, *govinda-*. Cf. Av. *yimō·kərənta-*.

Reduplicated formations: *śardhañjaha-*, *manojighra-*, *iḍādadha-*. Cf. Av. *azrō·daδa-*.

(b) Compounds with a past participle passive as second member differ from these in the syntactical relation of their members, and also in having their accent normally on the first member. For this reason they may be treated as a separate sub-class. They are a very productive type: *hástakṛta-* 'made by hand', *vīrájāta-* 'born of a hero', *devátta-* 'given by the gods', *prajā́patisṛṣṭa-* 'created by P.', *ulkā́bhihata-* 'struck by a thunder bolt'; *indrotá-* 'helped by Indra'. This is an old Indo-European type which is also represented in related languages: Av. *ahura-δāta-*, Gk. θεόδμητος, ἱππήλατος, etc.

The type of compound instanced under (a) is characterised by the fact that the second member is very frequently, in the case of some classes almost invariably, a stem that cannot appear in independent use. Compounds like *goghná-* may be formed at will but a simple *ghná-* does not exist. The same feature is shared by the related languages and goes back to the Indo-European period. The origin of this type of compound goes back to an earlier phase of Indo-European with a different and simpler structure to that prevailing in the historical period and the period immediately preceding it. What in the historical period are compounds were to begin with constructions of a type which are familiar in languages with a less developed inflection than Indo-European. The relative participles known in Dravidian and certain other linguistic groups are instances of this type of construction. In Indo-European the growth of inflection led to the disuse of such simple constructions but this type of compound, based on them, continued to flourish.

(2) Compounds having as their last member an ordinary adjective are comparatively few. Such are: *tanū́śubhra-* 'shining in body', *yajñádhīra-* 'versed in the sacrifice', *sā́mavipra-* 'skilled in Sāma chants', *tilámiśra-* 'mixed with sesamum'; with case termination of the first member, *máderaghu-* 'quick in exhilaration', *vidmanā́pas-* 'working with wisdom'.

B. (1) *Bahuvrīhi-*. The bahuvrīhi or possessive compounds contain the same elements and in the same order as the karmadhāraya and tatpuruṣa compounds but differ in meaning in that the compound functions as an adjective qualifying some other concept. They also differ in accentuation from the karmadhāraya and tatpuruṣa types, being characterised normally by the retention of the accent of the first member of the compound. The distinction between the two opposing types is illustrated by such cases as *rā́japutra-* 'having kings as sons' as opposed to *rājaputrá-* 'son of a king' and *sū́ryatejas-* 'having the brightness of the sun' as opposed to *sūryatejás-* 'the sun's brightness'. The following will serve as typical examples of the bahuvrīhi type: *bahúvrīhi-* 'having much rice' (after which the class is named), *màyū́raroman-* 'having the plumes of a peacock', *índraśatru-* 'whose foe is Indra', *ugrábāhu-* 'having powerful arms', *dīrghā́śmaśru-* 'long-bearded', *jīvā́putra-* 'having living sons', *iddhā́gni-* 'whose fire is kindled', *práyatadakṣiṇa-* 'who has presented sacrificial gifts', *chinnápakṣa-* 'whose wing is severed', *śucádratha-* 'having a shining chariot', *páñcāṅguri-* 'five-fingered', *mádhujihva-* 'honey-tongued', *maṇigrīvá-* 'having a necklace on the neck', *pā́trahasta-* 'having a vessel in the hand', *vájrabāhu-* 'armed with the vájra', *kharamukha-* 'donkey-faced'. In the Vedic language there are occasional examples with inflected first member: *krátvāmagha-* 'constituting a reward gained by intelligence', *āsánniṣu-* 'having arrows in the mouth', *divíyoni-* 'whose origin is in heaven'.

The type is widely distributed in the IE languages. Gk. λευκώλενος 'white-armed', ῥοδοδάκτυλος 'rose-fingered', Lat. *magnanimus* 'great-souled', *capricornus* 'having the horns of a goat', Goth. *hrainya-hairts* 'pure-hearted', O. Sl. *crĭnovlasŭ* 'black-haired'.

The bahuvrīhi likewise originated in the earlier, less inflected period of Indo-European, and it remained after the system of declining adjective and noun in apposition was developed. That development was, as we have seen, unfavourable to the growth of a large class of karmadhāraya compounds, since in the simple collocations of adjective and noun the inflected forms were used. On the other hand the bahuvrīhi construction could not be so simply transformed, since a substitute could only be found by clumsy periphrases. Consequently it survived in the more developed inflectional stage in the form of these compounds.

Though the latter member of these compounds is always a noun, it does, in the case of consonantal stems always have an adjectival form, e.g. *súyaśas-* ' of good fame '. From *(*a*)*su yáśas-* ' good fame ' (cf. Hitt. *aššu-* ' good ') an adjective, nom. sg. *súyaśās* is formed in the same way as *yaśā́s* from simple *yáśas*, since the apophony indicates that the accent was originally on the last syllable of the compound too. The same applies to the *n*-stems : nom. sg. *purúnāmā* ' having many names ', etc. Adjectival *-á* is frequently used in the same way as with simple nouns : *anudrá-* ' without water ', *urūṇasá-* ' having a broad nose ', *trivatsá-* ' three years old ', *sarvavedasá-* ' (sacrifice) in which all property is given away '. Other adjectival suffixes are frequently appended, e.g. *-ka* : *jīvapitṛka-* ' whose father is alive ', *púṇyalakṣmīka-* ' having auspicious marks ' ; *-ya* : *híraṇyakeśya-* ' golden haired ', *mádhuhastya-* ' having sweetness in the hand ' ; *-in* : *mahāhastín-* ' having a large hand ', *śatagvín-* ' having a hundred cows '.

(2) Adjectival compounds are formed on the basis of the combination preposition + noun. Corresponding to *áty áṃhas* ' beyond distress ' there exists the compound *átyaṃhas-* ' one who is beyond the reach of distress '. Similarly *ánuvrata-* ' obedient ', *abhídyu-* ' directed to heaven ', *upakakṣá-* ' reaching to the shoulder ', *ūrdhvánabhas-* ' being above the clouds ', *parihastá* ' something put round the hand, amulet '. These compounds frequently take the adjectival suffixes which have been noted above in the case of bahuvrīhis : *ājarasá-* 'reaching to old age ', *ā́pathi-* ' being in the way ', *paripanthín-* ' waylayer ', *upatṛṇya-* ' lurking in the grass '.

(3) An archaic class, confined entirely to the Vedic language, is composed of a participial first member governing the second member. Examples : *vidádvasu-* ' winning wealth ', *bharádvāja-* ' carrying off prizes ', *taráddveṣa-* ' overcoming hostility ', *mandayátsakha-* ' rejoicing friends '. The same type is established in Old Iranian : Av. *vanat·pəšana-* ' winning battles ', etc. Sporadically other verbal noun stems are used in the same way : *Trasádasyu-* ' making enemies tremble ', *radāvasu-* ' opening up wealth ', *dā́tivāra-* ' giving choice things '. Similar governing compounds are familiar in Greek : φερέοικος ' carrying his house ', ἑλκεσίπεπλος ' dragging robes '.

Adjective compounds used as adverbs

Compound adjectives may be used adverbially in the same way as simple adjectives, and as such normally appear in the accusative singular neuter. This is common with bahuvrīhis and in the classical literature long conglomerations of this nature are frequently so used. It is also common with the compounds having a preposition or other indeclinable as first member, thus *atimātram* adv. ' excessively ' from *atimātra-* adj. ' excessive '. Such adverbial compounds are considered by the Hindu grammarians to be a separate class of compound and they are termed *avyayībhāva-*. The reason for this lies in the fact that in the later language there is a considerable class of such adverbs without actual adjectives corresponding to them. This class is represented by such examples as *uparājam* ' near the king ', *upanadam* ' near the river ', *pratyagni* ' facing the fire ' and *pratiniśam* ' nightly '. A productive class of indeclinables is formed by those compounds, which have a relative adverb as prior member: *yathākāmam* ' according to wish ', *yāvajjīvam* ' as long as one lives ', etc.

III. *Dvandva Compounds.*

This type has nothing exactly corresponding to it in the related languages and has developed mainly within the historical period of Sanskrit itself. The earliest type which is common to Sanskrit and Avestan consists of two duals, each retaining its own accents, which are juxtaposed in such a way that $a+b$ is expressed by $2a+2b$: *Mitrā́-Váruṇau* ' M. and V.', *dyāvā-pṛthivī́* ' heaven and earth ', *uṣā́sā-náktā* ' dawn and night '; cf. Av. *pasu vira* ' beast and man ', gen. *pasvå vīrayå*. Sometimes elliptic duals may be used in place of this construction: *Mitrā́* ' M. and V.', *pitárā* ' parents ', *dyā́vā* ' heaven and earth '.

This represents the oldest state of affairs. Out of such constructions, which are not in the proper sense of the term compounds, the Sanskrit system of dvandva compounds developed and some of the intermediate stages may be observed in the early literature. Thus (1) the form of the nom. acc. dual is retained in the first member in cases other than nom. acc.: *mitrā́-váruṇayoḥ* instead of *mitráyor váruṇayoḥ*; (2) in a small number of instances in the RV., and in a somewhat larger number in the later Saṃhitās, the first member of such a combination loses its accent: *indrāpūṣṇóḥ, somārudráyoḥ.* The final stage appears when the first member appears in its simple stem form: *indravāyū́* (only example in RV.) *vāyu-savitṛ́bhyām, dakṣakratū́,* etc.

Because the ending of the agent nouns, etc., in *-tar* in the nom. sg. coincides with that of the first member of the dual dvandva, this form is chosen in dvandva compounds having such a stem as first member: *pitāputraú* 'father and son', *hotā́dhvaryū,* etc.

Plural dvandvas are exceedingly rare in the earliest language. Of the few examples *indrāmarutaḥ* (voc.) and *pitāputrāḥ* 'father and sons' are modelled, as far as their first member is concerned, on the dual dvandvas. An example of the normal type, with simple stem of first member, appears in a late hymn of the *Ṛgveda*: *ajāváyaḥ* 'sheep and goats'. In the later Vedic literature such examples become more common: *devamanuṣyāḥ* 'gods and men', *bhadrapāpāḥ* 'good and bad'. In this period also dvandva compounds with more than two members begin to appear: *prāṇāpānodāneṣu.*

Feminine nouns are not found employed in the oldest type of dvandva in the Veda, though such are known from Avestan: *āpa urvaire* 'water and crops'. They appear in the later Vedic period in the fully developed type of compound: *jāyāpatī́* 'wife and husband'.

A few neuter dvandvas of the fully developed type appear even in the *Ṛgveda*: *satyānṛté* 'truth and falsehood', *ahorātrā́ṇi* 'days and nights'. There are also a few older types: *idhmā́-barhíṣ-* with two accents and *iṣṭāpūrtá-* with the first member modelled on the old type of masculine dvandva. In the plural dvandvas *áṅgāpárūṃṣi* 'limbs and joints' (two accents) and *ukthāśastrā́ṇi* 'hymns and praises' the form of the first member may be interpreted as the old form of the nom. acc. pl. neut.

At an early period there was created a type of neuter dvandva which functions as a singular collective stem: *kṛtākṛtá-* 'what has been done and what has not been done', *tṛṇodaká-* 'grass and water', *kaśipūpabarhaṇá-* 'pillow and bolster'. In the examples both members are neuters. The same type also appears early in cases where one member is neuter, whether it be the last member as in *keśaśmasrú-* 'hair and beard' and in *klomahṛdayá-* 'lungs and heart', or the first member as in *ahorātrá-* 'a day and a night', *śirogrīvá-* 'head and neck' and in *yugaśamyá-* 'yoke and the attaching pin'. Finally the stage is reached (in the Brāhmaṇas) when two non-neuters are combined to form a singular collective dvandva : *oṣadhivanaspatí-* ' plants and trees ', *candratārakā́-* ' moon and stars ', *uṣṭrakhara-* ' camels and asses '.

Adjectival dvandvas are formed by the combination of two adjectives applying to the same noun, and such occur from the *Ṛgveda* onwards : *nīlalohitá-* ' dark blue and red ', *tāmradhūmrá-* ' dusky copper-coloured ', *aruṇábabhru-* ' red brown ', *kṛṣṇa-śabala-* ' speckled black ', *śītoṣṇa-* ' lukewarm ', etc. There are parallels to these in other IE languages (e.g. Gk. λευκόπυρρος, λευκόφαιος, γλυκύπικρος) and it is likely that in contradistinction to the nominal dvandvas the type is inherited from Indo-European.

CHAPTER V

THE DECLENSION OF NOUNS

§ 1. Accent and Apophony

The IE declensional system was characterised by a shift of accent from the stem in the strong cases (nom. acc. sg. and du., nom. pl.) to the termination in the weak cases, that is to say in the majority of the oblique cases. This shift of accent entailed apophonic changes affecting stem and suffix. The system was already in decay in the late IE period, and tending to be replaced by a system of fixed accent. In Vedic the shift of accent is best maintained in monosyllabic stems, but considerable traces of it are found in the case of other types of stem, both radically accented neuters (*yákṛt, yaknás*) and suffixally accented masc.-fem. types.

The three grades of apophony associated with this accent shift are clearly seen in the declension of *vṛtrahán-* : nom. sg. *vṛtrahā́*, acc. sg. *vṛtrahánam*, gen. sg. *vṛtraghnás*. It is seen also in the suffixally accented *r-* and *n-*stems of the type *pitā́*, *pitáram, pitré, ukṣā́* 'bull', *ukṣáṇam, ukṣṇás*. Elsewhere it has been modified and simplified in various ways. The vṛddhi of the nom. sg. tends to be extended to the acc. sg. and nom. pl., e.g. *pā́t* 'foot', *pā́dam, pā́das*, as opposed to Gk. πόδα, πόδες. The accent shift may remain while the vowel gradation is abandoned, e.g. *dík* 'direction', gen. sg. *diśás* for what must originally have been **deíks* : *dikés*. Conversely the accent may be stabilised but the vowel gradation retained, e.g. *paśumā́n* 'possessing cows', *paśumántam, paśumátas*.

The system of accent shift is best preserved in radical consonantal stems. In these the accent regularly appears on the termination outside the strong cases. On the other hand the accompanying vowel gradation is only partially preserved. The three grades appear in the declension of *kṣám-* 'earth' : nom. du. *kṣā́mā* with vṛddhi, loc. sg. *kṣámi* with guṇa, gen. sg. *kṣmás, jmás, gmás* with zero grade of root. Elsewhere the zero grade is rare in alternating stems : cf. *vṛtraghnás* already mentioned, *havyaúhā* instr. sg. of *havyavā́h-* ' carrying the oblation ', *dúras* (once *durás* RV. 2. 2. 7.) acc. pl. of *dvā́ras* ' doors '. In other stems there is only alternation between vṛddhi and guṇa, e.g. nom. sg. *pā́t* ' foot ', gen. sg. *padás, ā́pas* nom. pl. ' water ', acc. pl. *apás, nā́sā* nom. acc. du. ' nostrils ', gen. loc *nasós*. The vṛddhi grade is generalised in *vā́c-* ' speech ' (nom. sg. *vā́k*, gen. sg. *vā́cas*) as also in Lat. *vōx, vōcis*, in contradistinction to the guṇa grade in Gk. *ὄψ, ὄπα*. The guṇa grade is generalised in such nouns as *kṣáp-* ' night ', instr. sg. *kṣapā́, spáś-* ' spy ', etc.

Root nouns having *i, u,* or *ṛ* as the radical vowel have generalised the weak grade in all cases : *dík* nom. sg. ' direction ', gen. sg. *diśás*, instr. pl. *digbhís*, similarly from *ṛ́c-* ' hymn ', *ṛ́k, ṛcás, ṛgbhís*, and so on without exception. With these belong root nouns originally ending in H, namely radical stems in *-ī* and *-ū*, e.g. *dhī́-* ' thought ' (*dhī́s, dhíyam, dhiyás*) and *bhū́-* ' earth ' (*bhū́s, bhúvam, bhuvás*).

Accent alternation has been abandoned as a general rule in the case of those root stems which appear at the end of compounds, e.g. *trivṛ́t-* ' threefold ', gen. sg. *trivṛ́tas*. The older alternating system is only preserved in *vṛtraghnás* because the vowel of the root had been elided. In the alternating stem *anaḍvā́h-* gen. sg. *anaḍúhas* the apophony indicates that there was originally a shifting accent which has been replaced by a fixed accent. An exception to the general tendency is found in the various formations in *-añc* (*pratyáñc-*, etc.) which are originally compounds of prepositions with the root of *ákṣi* ' eye '. Here the accent appears on the termination in the weakest cases (gen. sg. *pratīcás*) but it is shifted back in the middle cases with a corresponding difference of grades (*pratyágbhis*).

The movable accent was originally characteristic of the neuter nouns formed with the various suffixes classified above. The tendency was from the late IE period for this to be given up and replaced by a fixed radical accent. Nevertheless there remain in Sanskrit, as also in Greek, various survivals from this system. The accent shift is usually preserved in the archaic neuters with alternating *r/n* stem : *ásṛk, asnás* ' blood ', *yákṛt, yaknás* ' liver ', *śákṛt, śaknás* ' dung ' ; likewise in the stems in *i/n* : *ákṣi, akṣṇás* ' eye ', *ásthi, asthnás* ' bone ', *dádhi, dadhnás* ' curd '. Similar terminational accent appears also in *āsnás* gen. sg. (*āsyà-* ' mouth '), likewise in *doṣṇás, yūṣṇás, udnás* and *śīrṣṇás* (gen. sg. to *dós* ' forearm ', *yū́ṣ-* ' broth ', *udaká-* ' water ', and *śíras* ' head '). The terminational accent in the oblique cases entails in some instances a reduction of the root, e.g. *udnás* as compared with Engl. *water*, etc. It is seen also in gen. sg. *usrás* ' of the dawn ' compared with the strong stem *vasar*° which appears in compounds. In two cases fixed accent has been applied to nouns of the old *r/n* declension : *áhar, áhnas* ' day ', *ū́dhar, ū́dhnas* ' udder '.

In the masc. and fem. *r*- and *n*-stems the accent shift to the termination is preserved in the weakest cases where the vowel of the suffix is lost : *pitā́, pitré*, cf. Gk. *πατήρ, πατρός, mūrdhā́* ' head ', gen. *mūrdhnás, ukṣā́* ' bull ', *ukṣṇás*, cf. Gk. *ἀρήν, Ϝαρήν* ' lamb ', gen. *ἀρνός*. In the middle cases where the *n* and *r* of the suffix were vocalised on the loss of the guṇa vowel the accent is retracted to the suffix : *pitṛ́bhis, mūrdhábhis*. In certain cases the apophony indicates that the accent was originally of the alternating variety although it has become fixed : *śvā́* ' dog ', gen. *śúnas* (original accent in Gk. *κυνός*), *yuvā́* ' young man ', gen. *yū́nas, maghávā, maghónas*.

With *as*-stems traces of this accent shift are exceedingly rare. The instr. sg. *bhīṣā́* (*bhiyás*- ' fear ') and the gen. sg. *uṣás* (for *uṣ-s-as*) show both the terminational accent and the corresponding weak form of suffix and root. Otherwise these stems have been normalised.

This accent was originally characteristic of the *i*- and *u*-stems, and traces remain notably in Greek : *οἶς* ' sheep ', gen. *οἰός, γόνυ* ' knee ', *γουνός, δόρυ* ' spear ', *δουρός*. Sanskrit in general has stabilised the accent (*ávyas, mádhvas*) though occasionally the apophony indicates original accent of the termination, e.g. in *drúṇas* (<*druṇás*) gen. of *dā́ru* ' wood '. The nom. sg. *páśu* nt. and the gen. sg. *paśvás* (masc. but originally neuter) represent the original IE inflection, but they no longer belong together, since the forms classed with *páśu* have acquired a normal radical accent, and a masc. *paśús* has come into being, to which the gen. sg. *paśvás* is attached. Elsewhere terminational accent appears in a small number of suffixally accented nouns which take the gen. sg. termination *-as* : *arís* : *aryás* ; *rayís* : *rāyás* ; *pitús* : *pitvás*.

The accent shift remains in the case of those participles in *-ant* which are accented on the suffix : nom. sg. *adán* ' eating ' : instr. sg. *adatā́* ; *yuñján* ' joining ' : *yuñjatā́* ; *sunván* ' pressing ' : *sunvatā́*, etc. ; but this does not apply to the middle cases where the accent is on the suffix and not the termination.

These are the main cases where shift of accent appears in declension in Sanskrit. Elsewhere, and these form the majority of stems, the accent has been stabilised either on the root or on the suffix. Fixed accent on the root becomes the normal accentuation of neuter nouns in Sanskrit : *dhánva* ' bow ', *dhánvanas* ; *nā́ma* ' name ', *nā́mnas* ; *bráhma* ' prayer ', *bráhmaṇas* ; *áṃhas* ' distress ', *áṃhasas* ; *mádhu* ' honey ', *mádhvas, mádhunas* ; *vā́ri* ' water ', *vā́riṇas*. Fixed radical accent is likewise the rule in those masculine and feminine nouns which are accented on the root : *bhrā́tā* ' brother ', instr. *bhrā́trā* ; *rā́jā* ' king ', gen. *rā́jñas* ; *bhávan* ' being ', *bhávatas* ; *gómān* ' possessing cows ', *gómatas* ; *ávis* ' sheep ', *ávyas* ; *pátis* ' lord ', *pátes, pátyus* (husband) ; *krátus* ' wisdom ', *krátvas* ; *śátrus* ' enemy ', *śátros*.

Thematic stems, both those accented on the root and those accented on the suffix, have invariably fixed accent both in Sanskrit and Greek. The same applies to verbal thematic stems. The evidence is that in Indo-European such stems were characterised by fixed accent from the beginning.

Fixed suffixal accent in the case of non-thematic stems appears in a number of types. It is rare in Sanskrit in the *r*- and *n*-stems, though not uncommon in Greek (ποιμήν ποιμένος, and with vṛddhi carried through, δοτήρ, δοτῆρος). Such accent only appears in Sanskrit in those *n*-stems in which the suffixal vowel is not elided in the weak cases : *brahmā́, brahmáṇas*.

On the other hand this type of accentuation has assumed great importance in the case of the *i*- and *u*-stems, where it produced a special inflection of the suffixally accented type (adjective and agent noun), which was eventually applied to all masculine and feminine nouns however accented. Inflection of the type *pitā́* : *pitré* is found only in the stem *sákhi*-' friend ', nom. sg. *sákhā*, dat. sg. *sákhye*, but there has been a secondary shift of accent to the root which must have originally been the same in the two cases. Elsewhere in the normal type (*agnís, agnés*) there is fixed radical accent, and this type must be very ancient because accent and apophony are in agreement in the gen. sg., etc. The accent causes the retention of the guṇa grade of the suffix in the genitive, dative (*agnáye*) and nom. pl. (*agnáyas*), and the reduction of the gen. sg. termination to -*s* (*agné-s*). Likewise in the case of *u*-stems the inflection of the type *vāyús* ' wind ', gen. sg. *vāyós* arises from the fixation of the accent on the suffix of suffixally accented agent nouns and adjectives. This type of declension eventually ousts the alternative type, which was originally exclusively used with neuter nouns (*mádhvas, paśvás* originally neuter) and optionally in the agent noun-adjective type (*sákhye* with secondary radical accent). The decline of the neuter as opposed to the masc.-fem. types is largely responsible for this development.

Fixed accent on the suffix is to be found also in masc. and fem. stems in *-as* : nom. *rakṣā́s*, gen. *rakṣásas* and in the stems in *-mant* and *-vant* in so far as they are accented on the suffix : *paśumā́n, paśumátas*. In the latter case the apophony indicates an original shifting accent. It does so also in the perfect participles whose fixed accent must be of secondary origin : *cakṛvā́n, cakrúṣas*.

The accent of certain infinitival forms calls for mention since it differs from any of the types listed so far. This appears in certain dative infinitives which are accented on the suffix. This is most commonly found in infinitives formed from *s*-stems, e.g. *ṛcáse* 'to praise', *caráse* 'to move', *spūrdháse* 'to strive', *bhojáse* 'to enjoy'. Some examples are also found from *man-* and *van*-stems : *vidmáne* 'to know' *dāváne* 'to give', *turváṇe* 'to overcome'. This accent cannot be original since suffixal accent is proper to the adjective and agent-noun type, whereas the neuter action nouns, to which these infinitives belong, are accented on the root. It is also hardly possible that this type of accentuation should have supplanted a radical accentuation, since that has become the normal type, and the reverse would be expected. The accent normal to neuter nouns does sometimes occur in these infinitives, rarely in those with suffix -as (*áyase* 'to go', *dhā́yase* 'to cherish'), more preponderantly elsewhere (*dā́mane* 'to give', *dhū́rvaṇe* 'to injure'. Since it is unlikely that this normal type would be supplanted, the infinitival accent on the suffix must be explained as a substitution for older terminational accent (**ṛcasé*, etc.). The cause of this change is not altogether clear but it may be associated with the tendency observed elsewhere to avoid final accentuation in forms of more than two syllables : cf. *trivṛ́tas* as opposed to *ṛcás*, and *akṣábhis* as opposed to *akṣṇā́*. It may also be due partly to influence of locative infinitives where the regular accent was on the suffix.

A few action nouns in *-as* have also acquired suffixal accent, notably *bhiyás-* 'fear', instr. *bhiyásā* beside older *bhīṣā́* (p. 159). When the neuter nouns had substituted fixed radical accent for the shift of the accent to the suffix in the oblique cases, the only type where it normally took place were masculine stems in which the vowel of the suffix was elided in these cases: *ukṣā́*, *ukṣṇás*. On this analogy the few remaining neuter stems which retained oblique cases with terminational accent received suffixal accent in nom. acc. (acc. *bhiyásam* corresponding to *bhīṣā́* like *ukṣáṇam* to *ukṣṇā́*; later *bhiyásā* is created by stabilisation of the new accent). In this noun the feminine gender results from its changed accent.

Suffixal accent has become normal in the majority of the neuter nouns in *-iṣ*: *arcíṣ-* 'flame', gen. sg. *arcíṣas*, etc., as opposed to the rarer type *jyótiṣ-* 'light'. The anomalous nature of this accent is clear from the weak grade of the syllable on which it is placed, and also from a comparison with the related *-as* and *-uṣ* stems. The same type of accent appears in the *ī*-stems of the *vṛkī́-* type and in *ū*-stems (originally *-i*H and *-u*H stems). The system here is more complicated inasmuch as these classes contain both action-noun types (*dehī́* 'rampart', *tanū́* 'body') and agent-noun/adjective types (*vṛkī́-* 'she-wolf', *agrū́-* 'maid'). The accent of the former type is exactly parallel to that of *arcíṣ-*, etc. An exact parallel to the latter type is found in the adjectives in *-in*: *balī́*, *balínas*. In both these adjectival types the suffixal accent is regular, but its weak grade is to be explained out of forms in which the accent was originally on the suffix (**vṛkiyás*, **balinás*). The weak grade associated with the latter forms has been generalised, but also the suffixal accent of the nom. acc. where originally the strong grade of the suffix must have prevailed. The action nouns of the (*vṛkī*) *ī*- and *ū*-stems have fallen together with the adjective/agent-noun type in accent as in other respects.

The same kind of development seems to have taken place in a number of originally neuter *i*- and *u*-stems. This is clearest in the case of the stem *paśú-* 'domestic animal'. A neuter *páśu* is preserved in one instance and comparative evidence shows that this form with its radical accent is original (cf. Lat. *pecu*, Goth. *faíhu*, O. Pruss. *pecku*: IE *pḗku*). The old form of the gen. sg. to this, with its terminational accent is preserved in Sanskrit (*paśvás*), but by the analogy of the masc. stems mentioned above this form is the cause of the creation of a new. masculine, nom. sg. *paśús*. The same seems to have occurred with *pitús* ' food ', gen. sg. *pitvás*, since this by its meaning is an action noun, and among *i*-stems with *rayís* : *rāyás* ' wealth ' (for **ráHis* : *raHyás*). Possibly also some masc. *n*-stems which are not of the adjective/agent-noun type arose in this way, e.g. *mūrdhā́*, gen. sg. *mūrdhnás* ' head '.

§2. Heteroclitic Declension

The mutual relation of the *r*- and *n*-stems has been dealt with at some length in the section dealing with the formation of nouns, and may be briefly summarised here. The neuter *r*-stems that remain in Sanskrit are normally not declined outside the nom. acc. sg., *n*-stems being used in the remaining cases : *áhar/áhnas* ' day ', *yákṛt/yaknás* ' liver ', etc. This type of inflection is found elsewhere in Indo-European, but always, outside Hittite, as an archaic survival, and not as a productive formation. In Hittite, on the other hand, this type of alternation is exceedingly common, and appears regularly in the inflection of neuters in *r/n*, and in the compound suffixes *-mar, war, šar, tar/n*. It was therefore at an earlier period of Indo-European much commoner than later, and its decline is due partly to the decline of the old neuter types in general, and partly to the extension of the *n*-stem to the nom. acc. sg. This system arose too early for it to be possible now to say how precisely it came into being. It does not however appear that the neuter *r*-stems were from the beginning incapable of inflection, since such examples occur in all languages (Skt. *svàr/sū́ras* ; *vasar°/usrás* ; Gk. ἔαρ/ἔαρος; Hitt. *kurur/kururaš*, etc.), and there is no reason to believe that this type is not ancient. Nor can it be said that the *n*-suffix is in origin either a case termination or a formative making an oblique case. It is a suffix in its own right, on a par with the others, and it appears like them in the nom. acc. sg. in many ancient examples (e.g. Skt. *nā́ma* ' name ', Lat. *nōmen*, Hitt. *lāman*, etc.). It is therefore difficult to say how exactly these two stems so often combined to form a single paradigm, but this took place in the early period of Indo-European, and though the system was beginning to become obsolete in the final stages of the parent language, it persists as an archaic survival in several of the existing languages.

In the same way the few neuters in *-i* substitute an *n*-stem outside the nom. acc. sg. : *ásthi* : *asthnás* ' bone ', etc. Besides these the instr. pl. *naktábhis* may correspond to an old neuter *nákti* ' night ' which has been replaced by a feminine (nom. sg. *náktis*). In the case of *vā́ri* ' water ' the *n*-suffix is added to n instead of being substituted for the *i*-suffix (gen. sg. *vā́riṇas*). This process appears commonly in neuter *u*-stems : *dā́ru drúṇas*, *mádhu* ' honey ', *mádhunas*, etc., and its antiquity is guaranteed by similar formations elsewhere : Gk. δόρυ, δόρατος (**dorwn̥tos*, with the additional *t*-suffix characteristic of Greek). In the Vedic language this is only one means of inflecting the neuters (the alternatives are *mádhvas* and *mádhos*, the latter an innovation borrowed from the masc.), but it becomes the general rule in the classical language. This *n*-extension in the oblique cases is found occasionally with other suffixes : e.g. the *as*-stem *śíras* ' head ', gen. sg. *śīrṣṇás*, and the *yā*-stem *kanyā̀*, gen. *kanī́nām*, Av. also gen. sg. *kainīnō*. The use of this *n* is much extended in certain cases, e.g. instr. sg. of masc. *i*- and *u*-stems (*agnínā*, *vāyúnā*) ; in the gen. pl. it has been introduced in the case of all vocalic stems : *devā́nām*, *agnīnā́m*, *pitṝṇā́m*, etc.

Certain defective neuter *n*- and *m*-stems appear in the Veda mainly as instrumentals, and have become attached to the corresponding *man*-stems : *bhūnā́*, *mahnā́*, *preṇā́*, *prathinā́*, *mahinā́*, *variṇā́* (*bhūmán*- ' abundance ', etc., *prathimán*- ' width ', etc.). It has been noted above that it is unnecessary in these cases to assume a change of *-mn-* to *-n-*.

An alternative *uṣ/van* similar to the *r/n* alternation appears in the Vedic declension of *dhánuṣ*- ' bow '. The *uṣ*-stem appears in the nom. sg., while elsewhere the stem *dhánvan*- is used. It is probable that the two stems *páruṣ*- and *párvan*- ' joint ' were originally distributed in the same way. This combination of *n*- and *s*-stems is found also in the corresponding masculines. The voc. sg. of certain *van*-stems in the Veda is in *-vas* : *r̥tāvas*, *eva-yāvas*, *vibhāvas*, *mātariśvas* from *r̥tā́van*- ' righteous ', etc. There are also doublets like *ŕ̥bhvan*-, *ŕ̥bhvas*- ; *śíkvan*-, *śíkvas*- (both meaning ' skilled ') in which the two suffixes alternate without any apparent rule. This voc. *-vas* appears also, and more regularly, in the stems in *-vant*, which is a *t*-extension of the *van*-suffix, and in the parallel stems in *-mant* : *r̥ṣīvas*, *gnāvas*, *patnīvas*, *tuviṣmas*, *bhānumas*, *śuciṣmas*. In the case of these stems the *s*-forms are more extensively used in Iranian, since Avestan has nominatives of this kind attached to stems in *-vant* : *amavå* (*amavant-*).

On analysis the Sanskrit forms of the nom. sg. are derived from this (*námasvān, paśumā́n*, etc.). The nominative formed from the *vant-* and *mant*-stems would have appeared as °*van* and °*man* (like °*an* in the *ant*-stems). The nominatives in *-vān, -mān* are derived from **-vāns, -māns* (*-vāṃs, māṃs*) which have replaced **-vās*, **-mās* by analogical extension of nasalisation to the nom. sg. This phenomenon is found elsewhere in Sanskrit in *s*-stems, and since it does not appear in Iranian, it is to be taken as a special Indian development. The alternation of nasalised forms in the strong cases with forms without nasal in the weak cases in such classes as the present participles (*adán, adántam, adatā́*, etc.), which is due to the change of the sonant nasal to *a*, led to the extension of *n* to the strong cases of other classes where the nasal does not originally belong. This is found notably in the comparatives in *yas* (*śréyān* ' better ', *śréyāṃsam, śréyasas*) and in the perfect participles in *-vas* (*vidvā́n, vidvā́ṃsam, vidúṣas*). It is found also, in the declension of *puṃs-* ' man ' : *pumā́n, pumā́ṃsam, puṃsás*. This is a masc. *-ás*-stem, but one which in contradistinction to the normalised type (*rakṣā́s, rakṣásam, rakṣásas*) has preserved some archaic features. These are (1) the weakening of the radical vowel as a result of the accentuation of the suffix, (2) the old terminational accent of the oblique cases as in *pitré, ukṣṇás*, etc., and (3) the consequent weakening of the suffix in these cases. In addition the inflection is complicated by the introduction of the nasal into the nom. acc. sg. (replacing **pumā́s*, **pumā́sam*).[1] There is one other example of this nasalisation among the masc. *as*-stems, namely *svávān*, nom. sg. of *svávas-* ' helpful '.

The introduction of *-n-* into the heteroclitic nom. sg. of the *vant-* and *mant*-stems follows this general principle, and it was further facilitated by the existence of *-n-* regularly in the acc. sg. which was formed with the *vant*-stem. The distribution of the two stems corresponds to that of the neuter *uṣ* and *van* in *dhánuṣ-*/*dhánvan* above except that in the masculine the acc. sg.

[1] The masc. *pumás-* would correspond to a neuter **peúmos-* ' pubes '. The Lat. words *pūbēs, pūber*, have different suffixes. Since the final root here is likely to be that which appears also in Lat. *pu-d-ōr*, *b* and *m* may also be varying suffixal elements, alternatively *b* in Latin may be for *m* before *r* in *pūber* as in *hibernus, tuber* (: *tumōr*).

has a form different from the nom. sg. and this form follows the analogy of the majority of cases.

The *vant*-suffix is built on the *van*-suffix and though no nom. sg. in *-vās* is recorded for the latter type of stem, the vocatives in *-vas* are an indication that the nom. sg. may once have been so formed.

In some stems the suffixes *van-* and *vant-* are combined heteroclitically. The stem *maghávan-* (nom. sg. *maghávā*, gen. sg. *maghónas* uses the *vant*-stem before terminations beginning with a consonant (instr. pl. *maghávadbhis*). An instr. sg. *ṛ́kvatā* appears beside the usual stem *ṛ́kvan-* ' praising '. The stems *árvan-* and *árvant-* ' steed ' are interchangeable. The stem *yúvan-*, *yū́n-* makes its neut. sg. *yúvat*, and this extended stem is the basis of the fem. *yuvatí-*.

The perfect participle is formed mainly with the stem in *-vāṃs-/uṣ*, but before the terminations beginning with a consonant, there appears a stem in *vat* (*vidvádbhis* instr. pl.). This suffix reappears in Greek, where it forms the normal basis of the declension (εἰδώς, εἰδότος) and it is attested also in Gothic (*weitwōd-* ' witness '). The comparative evidence shows it to be different from the *vat* (*wn̥t*) which is the weak form of the *vant*-suffix, since it has no nasal.

The word for ' path, way ' declines with a variety of stems. The strong form in the *Ṛgveda* appears as nom. sg. *pánthās*, acc. sg. *pánthām*, nom. pl. *pánthās*, to which correspond Av. *pantå*, *pantąm*. In the weak cases the stem appears as *path-* (instr. sg. *pathā́*, etc.). The relation of these two stems is one of apophony : strong form of suffix *a*H (> *ā*), weak form H. The weak form of the suffix, H, aspirates the preceding *t*, and this aspiration is then extended to the nom. sg., etc. The same development occurs in the case of the strong and weak stems *mahā-*, *mah-* ' great ' (*mege*H_2*-/meg*H_2). In the middle cases of *path-* an *i*-stem is used, which occurs elsewhere (O. Sl. *pǫtĭ*, O. Pruss. *pintis*) : instr. pl. *pathíbhis*, etc. (on the other hand Av. has *padəbiš* without *-i-*). In the same way *mahā/mah-* has a supplementary *i*-stem, in this case in the neut. sg. (*máhi* ; in Av. also in the instr. pl. *mazibiš*). After the *Ṛgveda* there appears another strong stem of *path-*, an *n*-stem (acc. sg. *pánthānam*, nom. pl. *pánthānas*). This is also ancient since the same formation appears in Avestan : *pantānəm*, *pantānō*. The same kind of inflection is laid down by the grammarians for *ṛbhukṣ-* ' n. of a divine being ' and *math-* ' churning-stick '.

§ 3. The Case-terminations

Nominative Singular, Masc. and Fem. The nominative singular of masculine and feminine nouns is formed in three ways, (1) by vṛddhi of the suffix, (2) by the termination *s*, (3) by the simple stem uncharacterised in any way. The basis of the first method has been dealt with at length in the section dealing with the formation of nouns. There it was seen that adjectives and agent nouns were formed on the basis of the various types of neuter stem by the transference of the accent to the suffix, and that for phonetic reasons which are not now clear, this led to the vṛddhi of the suffix in the nom. sg. Associated with this vṛddhi there is a tendency for the final semivowel of a suffix to be elided : *pitā́, brahmā́*. The vṛddhied type of nom. sg. appears regularly in the case of masc. *r*-, *n*- and *s*-stems (*dātā́*, cf. Gk. δοτήρ ; *brahmā́*, cf. Gk. ποιμήν ; *rakṣā́s, sumánās*, cf. Gk. ψευδής, εὐμενής), rarely in the case of *i*-stems (*sákhā*). A similar vṛddhied nom. sg. originally existed in the case of *u*-stems of this type, but in all cases where such vṛddhi is preserved it has secondarily acquired the addition of -*s* : Skt. *dyaús*, Av. *uzbāzauš*, Gk. βασιλεύς (for -ηύς), etc.

The termination -*s* appears in Sanskrit, which in this respect is in close agreement with the related languages, in the masculine *a*-stems (*devás*, Lat. *deus*) in masc. and fem. *i*- and *u*-stems, both of the action-noun (*matís, krátus*, Gk. βάσις, πῆχυς, etc.) and adjectival type (*śúcis, purús* ; Gk. ἴδρις, πολύς, etc.), in *ī*-stems of the *vṛkī́*-type and *ū*-stems, in consonantal stems (action-noun or agent), including the monosyllabic stems originally ending in -H (*dhī́s, bhū́s*).

It is clear that there is no common principle uniting these various formations, and distinguishing them from those classes in which the nom. sg. masc. and fem. is formed differently. It is also clear that the range of *s*-nominatives has extended at the expense of other types. This has already been observed in the case of the vṛddhied nominatives in -*aus*. It is also clear that the feminines in -*ī* of the *vṛkī́* class, and those in -*ū* (*tanū́s*) have acquired their -*s* from the radical stems in -*ī* and -*ū* which elsewhere are declined like them. The feminines in -*ā* and those in -*ī* of the *devī́* class preserve the uncharacterised nominative which was original to the stems in -H. Furthermore it is doubtful whether the *s*-nominative was originally attached to the *i*- and *u*-stems, though it must have extended to them at a very early period. The reason for this is that the action nouns of these classes would be expected, according to the general analogy, to have been originally neuters, and this is borne out by the existence of survivals of the type ; on the other hand in the case of the agent-noun/adjective types there is evidence of a vṛddhied treatment parallel to that of the *r*-, *n*- and *s*-stems, and though this is rare in the historical period, it can be shown to have been much commoner earlier. The probability is that the nominative *s* was originally proper to the adjectival thematic stems, since they are definitely a class apart. Its extension to the *i*- and *u*-stems is not difficult to understand, since like the thematic stems they are vocalic stems. In this process the morphological distinction and agent-noun/adjective appears to have counted very little, and the *s* of the nominative (and with it the distinction between nom. and acc.) became early attached even to the action nouns of these classes. In this way the majority of such nouns acquired the masc. or fem. (earlier, common) gender. Historically they do not take *s* in the nom. sg. because they have gender, but rather they have acquired gender as a result of taking *-s*. In the same way stems in occlusives were from an early period characterised by *s* in the nom. sg., and this regardless of whether they were action or agent nouns. In monosyllabic stems the *s* was also added after consonants other than occlusives (nasals, Gk. εἶς, κτείς ; H, Skt. *dhī́s*, *bhū́s*).

The feminines in *-ā* and those in *-ī* of the *devī́* class have no special sign for the nom. sg. To this extent they agree with the neuters. The action nouns ending in these suffixes originally were neuters, and in the case of this suffix the adjectival type, which was specialised as a fem. formation was always less clearly distinguished from the action noun type than was the case with other suffixes.

Accusative Singular, Masc. and Fem. The accusative singular masc. and fem. shows no such variation. The termination appears as *-m* after vocalic stems (*áśvam*, Lat. *equum* ; *agním*, Lat. *ignem*, etc.) and *-am* after consonantal stems (*pā́dam*, *rā́jānam*, *pitáram*, etc.). In the latter case Greek has α out of *m̥* (πόδα, πατέρα) and, this is the form which would be expected phonetically, but Indo-Iranian substitutes the fuller form which has the advantage of greater clarity. In some languages (Gk., Celt., Germ.) this final *-m* changes to *-n*, as it also does in the nom. acc. sg. neut. (Gk. λύκον, πέδον), and it is certainly wrong to assume, as is sometimes done, that the latter is the more original form.

Nom.-Acc. Sg. Neuter. Apart from *a*-stems neuter nouns have no endings in these cases : *ū́dhar*, Gk. οὖθαρ ; *mádhu*, Gk. μέθυ ; *nā́ma*, Lat. *nōmen*, Hitt. *lāman*, etc.). In thematic neuters the termination in both cases is *-m*. It has been suggested above that the *-m* of the old neuters of this class was originally the suffix *-m* (*yugám* : *yugmá-*, etc.) and as a result of these forms coinciding with the acc. sg. of thematic adjectival stems, a neuter thematic type was developed.

Instrumental Singular. The instrumental singular shows no united formation in Indo-European. Forms corresponding to the *-ā* which is the regular ending in Indo-Iranian, appear only in certain languages, and there only in certain classes of stem. In addition there appear the endings *-bhi* (Gk. θεόφι, Arm. *mardov*) and *-mi* (O. Sl. *vlŭkomĭ*, Lith. *sūnumì*). The former element is that which appears in the instr. pl. in Sanskrit (*-bhi-s*). In Greek it is used indifferently either as singular or plural, and further in a wide sense, covering instr. loc. and abl. Hittite has a different formation of its own (*-ēt*) which is not to be reconciled with any of the other forms in Indo-European. It appears that the instrumental with its various forms is a comparatively new case, and consequently has no common form covering the whole of Indo-European.

The Sanskrit form is normally *-ā*, i.e. *-a*H : *padā́*, *pitrā́*, *rā́jñā*, etc. But it may also appear in the zero grade, -H, notably in the case of feminine *i*-stems : *cíttī* (Av. *čisti*), *ūtī́*, *júṣṭī*, etc. In Avestan this form is also attested for *u*-stems : *mainyū*, *xratū*, etc. It must further be assumed for thematic stems (*vṛ́kā*, Av. *vəhrkā*, etc.), since the acute accent which appears elsewhere (Lith. *vilkù*, *gerů-ju*, and cf. the Gk. adv. ἐπισχερώ which is interpreted as an old instrumental) speaks against contraction (IE therefore *wḷkʷo*-H, not *wḷkʷo-o*H/*e*H). The quality of the long vowel that developed from this varied between *-ō* (Lith. *vilkù*, OHG. *wolfu* with *u* <*ō*) and *-ē* (Goth. *ƕammē-h*, *ƕē*, Skt. (adverbs) *paścā́*, *uccā́* with palatalisation indicating *-ē*. This implies an original IE metaphony eH_1/oH_1.

Dative Singular. The termination is *-e*, Av. *-e*, *ōi*, Indo-Ir. *-ai* : *padé*, *pitré*, *śúne*, *mánase* ; Av. *bərəzaite*, *vīse*, *piθre*, *paiθyaē-ča*. *ərəžəjyōi*, etc. The IE ending *-ei* is preserved in

Oscan (*paterei, regaturei, leginei*) and Phrygian (Ϝανακτει). Elsewhere phonetic developments have obscured it (Lat. *mātrī*, O. Sl. *materi*, etc.). There has been some dispute about the original form of the dative ending, since alternatively the Greek infinitives in -αι have been compared (δόμεναι, δοϜεναι, δοῦναι, etc.). But the existence in Greek of certain traces of the dative in *-ei* (ΔιϜειφιλος), shows that, whatever the explanation of these infinitives, they should be discounted in settling the form of the IE dative.

Ablative Singular. A special form for the ablative singular, which elsewhere has the same form as the gen. sg., is found only in the declension of thematic stems: *-āt* (*-ād*) in *vṛkāt*, etc., Lat. *lupō(d)*. This represents the IE state of affairs. In certain languages, notably in Italic and the later Avestan, this form is extended to other classes (Osc. *toutad* ' civitate ', Lat. *magistratud*, Av. *āθrat̰, garoit̰*, etc.). In Slavonic this termination serves both for the ablative and the genitive of the thematic declension (O. Sl. *vlŭka*). It is not possible to determine whether the final consonant was originally *d* or *t*. The vowel was *ō* in ordinary nominal declension alternating with *ē* in adverbial forms (Lat. *facillumēd*). In the latter type the termination was accented (Skt. *paścā́t, sanā́t*). The vowel was of circumflex quality (Lith. *tõ*, Gk. (dial.) τῶδε ' from here ') indicating contraction (*-ōd* <*-o-od*), and this is reflected by occasional disyllabic scansion in the Veda.

Genitive-Ablative Singular. The termination, which outside the thematic class combines the functions of the ablative and the genitive, is *-as* representing IE *-es* and *-os*. The difference between the two depended on accentuation, *-es* occurring in connection with the original terminational accent, *-os* in those cases (Gk. σώματος, etc.) where the accent had become fixed on the root. This distinction is nowhere preserved, since in the various languages one or other form is generalised, e.g. *-os* in Gk. (σώματος, ποδός) and *-es* (>*is*) in Latin (*corporis, pedis*, but O. Lat. *regus*, etc.). In addition there exists a reduced termination *-s* which appears in conjunction with adjective and agent noun types with accented suffix. This appears in Sanskrit in connection with *i-* and *u*-stems (*agnés, sūnós*), in Avestan also in some *r-stems* (*pitarš*). In the *i-* and *u*-stems the form has spread from the adjectival type to which it properly belongs, to the majority of action nouns (*matés, étos*). Only a few examples remain in the Veda of the alternative type (*ávyas, mádhvas*).

Locative Singular. Three types of locative singular are found in Sanskrit, illustrated by the alternative forms of locative of the word for 'eye': *akṣán, akṣáṇi, akṣṇí.* Their chronology appears to be in this order. The type *akṣṇí* is the latest. According to the grammarians the locative of *n*-stems may be in *-ani* or *-ni* (*rā́jani, rā́jñi*; *sakthā́ni, sakthní*), but in the language of the *Ṛgveda* the latter type does not appear, and is therefore clearly an innovation. It is due to an analogical tendency to put the loc. sg. on the same footing as the other oblique cases by accenting the termination and weakening the suffix. In many of the consonantal stems this tendency had already become general in the pre-Vedic period (*adatí, bhágavati, vidúṣi*, etc.), but the older type with accent and guṇa of suffix is preserved in the *an*-stems, in *r*-stems (*svásari, pitári*), to which certain monosyllabic stems can be added: *kṣámi, dyávi* (beside *diví*).

The oldest form, the locative without ending, appears in *n*-stems (*áhan, mūrdhán, śīrṣán*; cf. Gk. αἰέν 'always', and infinitives like δόμεν, etc.), and in the vṛddhied forms of the *i*- and *u*-stems. It also appears sporadically elsewhere, e.g. in *parút* 'last year' as opposed to Gk. πέρυσι, πέρυτι, a compound whose last member (*-út*) is the weak form of the *wet* that appears in Hitt. *wett-*, Gk. Ϝέτος 'year'. In Avestan there appears a locative without ending from a root noun *man-* 'mind' in the phrase *mə̄n ča daidyāi* 'and to put in the mind, remember'.

The locative in *-i* is based on the older locative without ending, to which a suffix or particle *-i* has been added. This produces a clearer form which tends to oust the earlier form without ending, but the process is not yet complete by the Vedic period. To a large extent this form of locative preserves the accent and guṇa of the suffix which characterised the form without ending, and it is thus sharply differentiated from the genitive and dative singular with their accented termination. At the same time analogy has tended to adapt the loc. sg. to their type, in some cases in the prehistoric period (*adatí*, etc.) and in other cases during the history of Sanskrit itself (*rā́jñi*, etc.). The suffixal accent of the old locatives without ending is parallel to that which has been observed to occur in adverbs based on neuter stems (*prātár*, etc.).

Vocative Singular. The vocative singular consists of the simple uninflected stem, and it is therefore a survival from the time when the inflection of the noun had not been built up to the degree which appears later. In this respect it points to the same conclusion as the system of nominal composition, indicating an early period of IE in which the bare stem could function as a word. In thematic stems the vocative is formed simply by dropping the *-s* which characterises the nominative : *vṛka*, Gk. λύκε, Lat. *lupe*. The various languages agree in having the *e*-grade of the suffix in this case instead of the usual *o* (λύκος, etc.). Stems which take vṛddhi in the nom. sg. substitute guṇa in the vocative (*śvan*, *pitar* as opposed to *śvā́*, *pitā́*, etc.), and this characteristic is found also in related languages (Gk. κύον, πάτερ). This guṇa appears also in *i*- and *u*-stems (*ágne*, *sū́no*) since the formation of adjectival *i*- and *u*-stems was originally parallel to that of the adjectival *r*- and *n*-stems. The feminines in *-ī* and *-u* substitute the short vowels *i* and *u* and this is probably to be regarded as the regular development of *-i*H and *-u*H when followed by a pause. Compare the similar development of *-a*H to *ă* in Greek vocatives like νύμφα, συβώτα. The vocative of the *ā*-stem is anomalous (*bāle*, voc. of *bālā* ' girl ') and is perhaps due to the addition of an enclitic particle *i* (*-e* for *-a*H*-i*). The vocative is unaccented in Sanskrit, except when it appears at the beginning of a sentence or pāda, and in these conditions it has a special accent of its own, namely on the first syllable, regardless of the normal position of the accent in the word. There are traces of this latter type of accentuation elsewhere (Gk. πάτερ, ἄδελφε, as opposed to πατήρ, ἀδελφός in the nom. sg.), but nowhere to the extent that is found in Sanskrit. The system cannot be very ancient, otherwise there would not be regular guṇa of the suffix, which is due to the suffixal accentuation which characterises these types normally.

Nominative Plural, Masc. and Fem. The Sanskrit *-as* (*pā́das* ' feet ') corresponds to IE *-es* which is preserved elsewhere (Gk. πόδες). The termination always appears in the full grade though it is never accented. It is associated with the strong stem in stems of varying grades, and this may be either guṇa (*pitáras*, *ukṣáṇas*, *agnáyas*) or vṛddhi (*dātā́ras*, *rā́jānas*). As in the accusative singular the latter type is due to extension from the nominative singular.

An *s* appears in most of the plural cases, e.g. acc. *-ns*, instr.

-bhiṣ, dat. abl. *-bhyas*, loc. *-su*. It is possible, but not certain that this *s* is identical with that of the nom. pl. The IE plural system is complicated by two unusual features. On the one hand if this *s* is the sign of the plural it is distinguished from the type found in most linguistic families by being added after instead of appearing before the case terminations. In the second place the terminations of the plural are for the most part different from those that appear in the singular and this appears to be quite an unusual phenomenon. A further problem is presented by Hittite. In this language the nominative plural has a form of its own, and likewise the accusative (*ḫumantēš*, *ḫumanduš* 'all') but for the gen. dat. there appears normally a form identical with the gen. sg., and otherwise the inflection is undeveloped. It is uncertain to what extent this is due to Hittite innovation, but it may be an indication that the plural inflection in IE is a later development than the singular.

Accusative Plural, Masc. and Fem. The ending in IE was *-ns* after vocalic stems, *-n̥s* after consonantal stems. This is preserved in Gothic and certain Greek dialects, notably Cretan (Gk. ἐλευθέρονς, υἰύνς, Goth. *wulfans*, *gastins*, *brōþruns*). In Sanskrit the accusative plural of masc. vocalic stems (*-ān*, *-īn*, *-ūn*, *-ṝn*) preserves this *-s* in sandhi (*-āṃs*, etc., before *t-*). In the Veda its effect is seen also before a vowel (*-āṃ*, *īṃr*). The long vowel in Sanskrit is not original but arises in thematic stems from the analogy of the nom. pl. (*-ās* with long vowel whence acc. *-āns* for *-ans*). From this declension the long vowel has spread to the stems in *-i*, *-u* and *-ṛ*. The ending *-n̥s* after consonantal stems becomes regularly *-as* in Sanskrit as in Greek (*padás*, πόδας). The acc. pl. is a weak case in Sanskrit, that is to say the termination may be accented and the stem appears in its weak form. This is in contradiction with the fact that the termination itself appears in the weak grade and it is therefore in all probability an innovation. If IE *-ns* in this case is derived from *-ms* the form can have arisen by the addition of the plural sign *-s* to the acc. sg.

The feminine vocalic stems show no trace of *n* in Sanskrit (*-ās*, *-īs*, *-ūs*, *ṝs*). This absence of *n* is shown to be IE in the case of stems in *-ā* by the agreement of Indo-Iranian (*Skt. kanyā̀s*, Av. *urvarå*) and Germanic (Goth. *gibōs*). Non-distinction of nominative and accusative, which characterises neuters was originally characteristic of *-ā* (*-a*H) stems when these had not become differentiated from the other neuters. It is preserved in the *ā*-formation which serves to provide the plural of neuter thematic stems (nom. acc. pl. *yugā́*). The normal feminines have acquired the plural -*s* of the non-neuter classes but they still retain in the plural the absence of distinction between nom. and acc. From the *ā*-stems the type spreads to the fem. *i*-, *u*- and *ṛ*-stems which did not originally in IE have a form distinct from that of the corresponding masculines (Gk. (dial.) ὄϝις 'sheep'.).

Nominative-Accusative Plural Neuter. (1) The neuter plural appears still in the Vedic language in some cases undifferentiated from the singular: e.g. in *ū́dhar divyā́ni* 'divine udders', *víśvāni vásu* 'all goods', *yójanā purú* 'many leagues', *sám aranta párva* 'the joints came together'. This is a survival from an early stage when the inflectional system was less developed. (2) There exists in Iranian, beside this type, a series of neuter plurals characterised by vṛddhi of the suffix: Av. *ayārə* 'days', *vačā̊* 'words', *nāmąn* 'names', etc. This type is ancient since examples are also quotable from Hittite, e.g. *widār*, pl. of *watar* 'water'. In Greek on the other hand such vṛddhied neuter forms appear merely as singulars: ὕδωρ, τέκμωρ, etc. These may be old plural forms utilised as singulars after the type had died out as a plural formation. Sanskrit has in the main replaced this type by that which is extended by the suffix -*i* (*nā́māni* 'names') but the Vedic language still retains it (beside the alternative form) in the case of neuter *n*-stems (*bhū́mā* 'beings', *áhā* 'days', *śīrṣā́* 'heads') in which the *n* of the suffix is elided as elsewhere in connection with vṛddhi (*rā́jā*, etc.). (3) The neuter plurals which are made by suffixing *i* to these vṛddhied forms appear also in Avestan (*nāmə̄ni* 'names', *sāxᵛə̄nī* 'teachings', *varəčāhī* 'energies') as an alternative to the plurals with simple vṛddhi. A neuter plural suffix -*i* is found in Hittite (*kururi* pl. of *kurur* nt. 'hostility'), which testifies to its antiquity in Indo-European as a method of forming the neuter plural. The *i* is apparently identical with the suffix -*i* which appears in the formation of neuter nouns. Other IE languages have mainly the suffix *a* or *ā* which originates from the thematic stems (Gk. ὀνόματα like ζυγά, etc.). In Vedic the *i*-form of the plural has been much extended in comparison with the Indo-Iranian state of affairs which can be deduced from the comparison of Avestan. The formations with simple vṛddhi have disappeared in the case of most types of stem. In addition the nasal of the *n*- and -*nt*-stems (*nā́māni*, *ghṛtávānti*) has been analogically introduced into other types of stem, e.g. *mánāṃsi* 'minds' for *mánās-i*, similarly *havī́ṃṣi* 'ablations', *cákṣūṃṣi* 'eyes', etc. A non-nasalised form remains only in the case of *catvā́ri* 'four'. The process is continued further in the post-Ṛgvedic period by the creation of nasalised *i*-plurals for consonantal root-stems, e.g. °*śaṅki* from °*śak*- 'able', °*bundhi* from °*budh*- 'understanding'. In addition, on the analogy of the neuter *n*-stems like *nā́māni* there is created a new type of neuter plural for *a*-, *i*- and *u*-stems: *bhúvanāni* 'worlds', *śúcīni* 'bright', *vásūni* 'riches'. In the Vedic language these forms occur in competition with the older forms (*bhúvanā, śúcī̆, vásū̆*), but in the later language they are exclusively used. Furthermore, on this analogy the later language creates a neut. pl. -*tṝṇi* for stems in -*tṛ*. (4) The inherited neuter plural of thematic stems is in -*ā* (*yugā́*, Gk. *ζυγά*, Lat. *iuga*, Goth. *juka*, O. Sl. *iga*). This -*ā* is identical with the suffix -*ā* which in the historical period forms feminines. As already pointed out this *ā* (<*a*H) was not originally distinct from the usual type of neuter suffix. These plurals were originally singular neuter collectives, and in Greek they retain this character to the extent that they are still construed with a singular verb (*τὰ ζῷα τρέχει*). In this function the suffix -*ā* retains its primitive characteristic of being indifferent to the distinction between nominative and accusative. The variation in the IE languages between *ā* and *ă* appears to be due to different sandhi developments of IE -*a*H (-*ă* before vowels or a pause, otherwise -*ā*) and it is paralleled by a similar fluctuation in the case of feminines in -*ā*. The neuter stems in -*i* and -*u* also make plurals by lengthening the vowel of the stem, and if these forms are not simply made on the analogy of the thematic neuters, they can be analysed -*i*-H and -*u*-H with the weak form of the suffix added to the stem. In the Vedic language they exist side by side with forms undifferentiated from the singular and with the innovating type -*īni*, -*ūni* which later becomes the rule.

Instrumental Plural. The ending of the instrumental plural -*bhis* (Av. -*biš*) contains an element -*bhi*- which according to the evidence of Greek (*θεόφι, ἀγέληφι, ἶφι, ναῦφι, ἐρέβεσφι*, etc.) was at an earlier period of IE of much vaguer and wider application, being used both in the singular and the plural, and covering the meanings of instrumental, locative and ablative. In Indo-Iranian, as opposed to Greek and Armenian (*gailov*, pl. *gailovk'* : *gail* ' wolf ') this formative appears only in the plural, the instrumental singular being formed in quite a different manner. The final *-s* may be interpreted as the *-s* of the plural added to this element, or possibly in view of such adverbial forms like Gk. λικριφίς ' crosswise ' and Av. *mazibiš* ' greatly ' may be merely some adverbial suffix (cf. ἀμφί: ἀμφίς, etc.), which in view of the regular occurrence of *-s* in the plural led to its being understood as such. As elsewhere Balto-Slavonic and Germanic have *-m-* in this case (Lith. *sūnumìs*, etc.) which it is not possible phonetically to relate to the *-bh-* of the other languages.

Dative-Ablative Plural. Anomalously the ablative which in the singular has mainly the same form as the genitive, has in the plural a form identical with that of the dative. The ending is *-bhyas*, Av. *byō*. The western IE languages have a form similar to this going back to original *-bhos* (Lat. *-bus*, Osc. *fs*, *ss*, Venet. *-bos*, Gallic *-βo*). It is possible but not certain that this *-bhos* has developed out of *-bhyos* through the sporadic loss of post-consonantal *-y-*, easily understood in a weakly stressed termination. The analysis of the form is indicated by the comparison of the datives of the personal pronouns. Beside the usual forms *túbhyam*, *asmábhyam* the Vedic language preserves also a form without *-m*, whose antiquity is attested by Iranian (Av. *maibyā*). The *-bhyas* of the dat.-abl. plural can be interpreted as this *-bhya* followed by the *-s* which characterises the plural. In this way the case would originally be a dative, and its use also as ablative can naturally be explained by the fact that the *-as* which comes at the end of the termination is similar in form to the *-as* of the gen.-abl. sg.

Genitive Plural. The termination of the genitive plural is distinguished from the majority of the plural cases by the absence of *s* (with the exception of the pronominal forms *téṣām*, *tā́sām*). The termination is *-ām* which is frequently scanned as disyllabic in the Veda, and this in conjunction with the circumflex accent in Gk. *-ῶν*, points to an original contraction of *-o-om*. This can only have come about in thematic stems, and it must be assumed that the original termination *-om* has elsewhere been replaced by the long contracted *-ō̃m* which arose in this class. The shorter termination *-om* has been generalized in Slavonic (> *ŭ, māterŭ, imenŭ*), and also probably in Latin (*hominum*), where it appears unnecessary to assume that *-um* has developed out of an earlier form with a long vowel. A variant *e*-grade of this formative appears in Gothic only (*wulfē, suniwē*). The Sanskrit vocalic stems are characterised by an *-n-* inserted before the termination, and the Avestan declension agrees with this system with the exception of the stems in *-ṛ*. The only agreement elsewhere is in Germanic, in the *ā*-stems (OHG. *gebōno* ' of the gifts ') and it is likely that the inserted *-n-* began in this class and from there spread to the other vocalic classes.

Locative Plural. The Sanskrit termination *-su* (*patsú*) appears also in Iranian, Slavonic (*-chŭ*<*su*) and dialectically in Lithuanian. In Greek on the other hand the termination is *-σι* (*ποσσί*, etc.). This variation indicates that the termination is analysable into two elements, on the one hand *s* + *u* and on the other hand *s* + *i*. The *s* can be identified as the plural *s* which appears in other cases, to which the further elements *i* and *u* are added in the two types. The *-i* of Greek is apparently to be identified with the *-i* of the locative singular, and the *-u* of the other languages in an alternative suffix performing the same function. The case would thus originally be formed by the addition of plural *-s* to the endingless form of the loc. sg. (in thematic stems to the loc. sg. in *-oi*), and the addition of *i* and *u* is secondary, just as is the addition of *-i* in the loc. sg.

Nom. Voc. Acc. Dual. This case was made by various formatives in IE, according to the type of stem. The ending *-au*, *-ā* of Sanskrit was originally, from the evidence of the related languages, confined to the thematic stems (Gk. *λύκω*, Lith. *vilkù*, O. Sl. *vlŭka*) from which in Sanskrit it has been extended to other types of stem (*pā́dau, pitárau*, etc.). In these latter classes Greek and Lithuanian have an ending *-e* (*μητέρε, áuguse*). It has been suggested that this termination, elsewhere replaced by *-au* in Sanskrit, is preserved in the dual dvandva *mātarā-pitarau* ' parents ' which the grammarians quote as a northern form. The termination is regularly *-au* in classical Sanskrit, but in the Vedic language it varies between *-au* and *ā*. As a general rule *-au* is used before vowels, becoming *-āv*, elsewhere *ā*. Some such variation must go back to the IE period, and it is the latter form which has been generalised in the related languages.

The feminines in *-ā* and the neuters take the termination *-ī*. This agreement is another sign of the close relations existing between the feminine *ā*-stems and the neuters. Examples from neuter consonantal stems are: *vácasī, cákṣuṣī, nā́mnī, bṛhatī́*. In the thematic neuters and the feminines in *-ā* this *-ī* combines with the vowel of the stem to form the diphthong *-e*: *yugé, śṛ́ṅge*; *áśve, séne*. This *-ī* is found also in Old Slavonic, though rarely (*imeni, tělesi*), and Slavonic shows the same diphthong in *o*- and *ā*-stems (*selě, rọcě*) a form which then spreads to consonantal stems (*imeně* 'two names'). The *i*- and *u*-stems make the dual by lengthening the vowel of the stem: *pátī, sūnū́*, and with them are to be classed the feminines in *-ī* of the *devī́* type in the Vedic declension (du. *devī́*, later *devyaù*). This type is ancient, appearing also in Avestan (*gairi, mainyu*), Slavonic (O. Sl. *pọti, syny*) and Lithuanian (*naktì, sū́nu*).

Instr. Dat. Abl. Dual. The termination that serves for all the three cases is *-bhyām*, and it contains the same element *-bhi-* that occurs in the dat.-abl. and instr. pl. A corresponding *-byąm* appears only once in Avestan (*brvaṯbyąm* from *brvat-* 'brow'). Elsewhere it has *-byā̆* and O. Pers. has *-biyā*, which makes it clear that *-m* is an element secondarily added, as elsewhere (cf. *tubhya, tubhyam*, etc.). The Balto-Slavonic languages have, as in the plural, *-m-* instead of *-bh-* here (O. Sl. *očima*, etc.). The termination is ordinarily added to the normal stem, but in the earlier language sometimes to the form that serves as nom. acc. du., e.g. *akṣī́bhyām*, cf. *akṣī́* 'the two eyes' (cf. O. Sl. *očima* : *oči* 'the two eyes'). This has become the normal form in the case of thematic stems: *vṛ́kābhyām*, cf. *vṛ́kā(u)*, etc.

Genitive-Locative Dual. The termination common to these two cases is *-os*: *padós, pitrós*, etc., which is added to the weak form of the stem. Avestan on the other hand has two separate terminations, *-ō* (*zastayō*) for the locative and *-å* (*nāirikayå*) for the genitive. The ending *-ō* is derived from *-au* and is equivalent to the Sanskrit ending minus the final *-s*. The genitive *-å* (<*-ās*) is peculiar to Avestan. Slavonic has a termination *-u* which could represent either *-ou* (Av. *-ō*) or *-ous* (Skt. *-os*). Lithuanian which keeps this inflection only in some adverbial forms has both *-au* and *-aus*: *dvějau, dvějaus* 'in twos, as a pair', cf. Skt. *dváyos*. The *-ay-* which in Sanskrit appears before the termination in *a* and *ā*-stems has spread from the declension of the pronouns and the numeral 'two' (*táyos, dváyos*). It remains confined to these cases in Slavonic: *toju, dvoju,* but *vlŭku, igu, rǫku.*

§4. The Declension Classes

The complication of the Sanskrit declension consists not so much in the system of terminations thus briefly described, as in the combination of these with the various types of stem, and the alternation of the stem itself in respect of accent and apophony. The classification of the stem types and the declensions based on them falls naturally into five main divisions: (1) consonantal stems, (2) stems in *-ṛ*, (3) stems in *i, u*, (4) stems in *ā, ī, ū*, (5) stems in *-a* (thematic stems). After the practice of the grammar of the classical languages, and also for reasons of convenience, the descriptive grammars normally deal with these classes in the reverse order to that given here. Since however the normal scheme of terminations as described above appears most clearly in the consonantal declension, and since the thematic declension is the most aberrant from this, having adopted a variety of special declensional forms from the pronouns, it is more convenient from the point of view of comparative grammar to proceed in this order.

§5. Consonantal Stems

The consonantal stems consist of the root stems (*pad-*, etc.) and derivative stems in *-n, -nt, -s*, etc. The latter fall into two classes, neuters and masculine-feminines. The particulars of their formation, and the mutual relation of the two classes have already been dealt with. The inflection of the neuters and non-neuters is distinguished only in the nom. and acc. In this respect the consonantal stems differ from the stems in *i* and *u* (*mádhvas* : *sūnós*), and also from the practice of certain other languages with consonantal stems (Gk. *οὔθατος, ὀνόματος*, neut.: *φέροντος, ποιμένος*, masc.). The declension of these stems calls for little extra comment. The normal endings are added with little modification throughout this declension. The special development of Sanskrit phonetics cause some complication (e.g. *viś-* 'settlement': nom. *víṭ*, acc. *víśam*, instr. pl. *viḍbhís*, loc. pl. (vedic) *vikṣu*) but this aspect of the problem belongs more properly to phonetics than to morphology. For the rest the complications that occur in this class have already been described under the headings of (1) Accent and Apophony (*pāt* : *padás*, etc.) and (2) Heteroclitic Declension (*ū́dhar*, *ū́dhnas*, etc.). The strong tendency of Sanskrit to nasalise the stem in the strong cases has also been noted (*vidvā́n*, *vidvā́ṃsam*, *vidúṣas*). It spreads by analogy from those cases where it is historically justified (*bhávan*, *bhávantam*, *bhávatas*, etc.) and it is paralleled by a similar development in the neuter plural.

§6. Stems in *ṛ*

Sing. Nom. *pitā́*, acc. *pitáram*, *dātā́ram*, instr. *pitrā́*, dat. *pitré*, gen.-abl. *pitúr*, loc. *pitári*, voc. *pítar*. Du. N.A.V. *pitárau*, *dātā́rau*, I.D. Ab. *pitṛ́bhyām*, G.L. *pitrós*; Pl. N. *pitáras*, *dātā́ras*, Acc. *pitṝ́n*, *mātṝ́s*, I. *pitṛ́bhis*, D. Ab. *pitṛ́bhyas*, G. *pitṝṇā́m*, L. *pitṛ́ṣu*.

The fact that the stems in *ṛ* are classed in Sanskrit as vocalic stems rather than consonant stems is due to certain developments of Sanskrit which have tended to enhance their vocalic character. This appears particularly in the acc. and gen. plur., forms which are Sanskrit innovations. On the analogy of the consonantal stems the acc. plur. would have been *pitrás*, but this is replaced by a new form in *-ṝn*, based on the analogy of *-ān*, *-īn*, *-ūn*. By this process Sanskrit creates a new long vowel *ṝ* which has no phonetic basis among the inherited IE sounds. The old type of gen. pl. appears in Av. *dugədrąm*, etc. In Sanskrit it is preserved occasionally in the Veda, e.g. *nárām* (: Osc. *nerum*), gen. pl. of *nár-* ' man ', and once *svásrām*. Elsewhere it has been replaced by the innovation *-ṝṇām*, created by the same type of analogy on the pattern of *-ānām*, *-īnām*, *-ūnām*.

In the vṛddhied nom. sing. the *r* is elided in the same way as the *-n* of *n*-stems (*pitā́* : *rā́jā*). This elision appears also in Iranian (Av. *māta*, etc.), Baltic (Lith. *motė̃*, *sesuõ*) and Slavonic (O. Sl. *mati*). In other languages the *-r* of the stem is preserved (Gk. μήτηρ, etc.). The acc. sg. has guṇa of the suffix in most of the names of family relationship (*mātáram*, *duhitáram*, etc.), but in *svásṛ-* ' sister ', and in the agent nouns in *-tṛ* vṛddhi appears which has been introduced from the analogy of the nom. sg. The same distinction appears in the nom. acc. du. and nom. pl. In the weakest cases the old type of inflection, with transference of the accent to the termination is normally preserved. Elsewhere in IE this type is found in the conservative names of relationship (Gk. πατρός, πατρί, Lat. *patris*, etc.), beside which there is found an alternative type with guṇa of suffix (Gk. μητέρος beside μητρός, cf. ποιμένος, Osc. *patereí*, O. Sl. *materi*, cf. *agnáye*). Indo-Iranian alone preserves the primitive type in the case of the agent nouns in *-tṛ*. Elsewhere this has been replaced by innovating forms with guṇa or vṛddhi of suffix in these cases (Gk. δοτῆρος, δώτορος, Lat. *datōris*, etc.). In Sanskrit guṇa of the stem appears in the declension of *nar-* ' man ' (D. *náre*, G. *náras*) as opposed to the older type of inflection seen in Greek (ἀνδρός, ἀνδρί).

In this respect the Sanskrit *ṛ*-stems differ markedly from the adjectival *i*- and *u*-stems which keep the guṇa and accent of the suffix in the dat. and gen. sg. (*agnáye*, *agnés*). The difference between the two classes becomes less when the nature of the gen. sg. of *ṛ*-stems is examined. To agree with the form of the dative this would normally have been in *-ás* with accented termination, and such forms are in fact found in Iranian (Av *brāθrō*, *dāθrō*) as well as in other IE languages (Gk. πατρός, etc.) The form which actually occurs (*-ur*, *-us*, *-uḥ*) goes back on the evidence of Iranian (Av. *nərəš*) to *-ṛš* (**pitṛ́š*). Such a form with weak grade of both suffix and termination cannot be origina and it must therefore be regarded as an innovation which ha replaced something else. There is no way by which it could hav developed from **pitrás* if that had been the only form, and it origin is therefore to be sought in yet another type of gen. sg which Iranian preserves: *narš*, *zaotarš*, *sāstarš*. This type, wit which we may compare Lith. *moteȓs* is of exactly the same for mation as the gen. sg. of adjectival *i*- and *u*-stems (*agné-s*). It ha arisen by the same process, i.e. by the extension of the accent an guṇa of suffix proper to adjectival stems to the gen. sg. and sinc it involves a reduction of the termination it must be ancient. I Sanskrit and partly in Avestan the *-arš* has been replaced by *-ṛ* (> Skt. *-ur*). The reason for this is that elsewhere in the wea and middle cases the suffix appears in its weak form (*pitr*, *pitṛ́bhis*, *pitṛ́ṣu*), and this grade has been analogically extende to the genitive singular.

No forms of the loc. sg. without ending are preserved, thoug such presumably existed at one time. This case always retai the guṇa of the suffix which is proper to it, in contradiction other stems (*rā́jñi*, etc.) and the practice of other IE languag in nouns of this class (Gk. πατρί, etc.).

Of the old neuter nouns in *-r* such few as remain infle

heteroclitically, and they have lost connection with the masc.-fem. *r*- (*ṛ*-) stems. On the other hand Sanskrit creates a new adjectival type of neuter in -*ṛ* which has no prototype in IE. This differs from the masc.-fem. in the nom.-acc. as usual (*dhātṛ́*, *dhātṝ́ṇi*, *dhātṛ́ṇi*), and also in the weak cases by inserting -*n*- after the style of the neuters in *i* and *u* (*dhātṛṇā*, etc.). It is not of frequent use.

§7. STEMS IN *i* AND *u*

Sing. N. *agnís*, *sūnús* ; *vā́ri*, *mádhu*, Acc. *agním*, *sūnúm*, I. *agnínā*, *sūnúnā* ; *gátyā*, *dhenvā́*, D. *agnáye*, *sūnáve* ; *pátye*, *paśvé* ; *vā́riṇe*, *mádhune* ; *gátyai*, *dhenvaí* ; Ab. G. *agnés*, *sūnós* ; *ávyas*, *mádhvas* ; *vā́riṇas*, *mádhunas* ; *gátyās*, *dhenvā́s*, L. *agnaú*, *sūnaú* ; *sā́no*, *sā́navi*, *sā́nuni* ; *gátyām*, *dhenvā́m* ; V. *ágne*, *sū́no*. Du. N.A. *agnī́*, *sūnū́*, I. D. Ab. *agníbhyām*, *sūnúbhyām*, G. L. *agnyós*, *sūnvós* ; *vā́riṇos*, *mádhunos*. Pl. N. *agnáyas*, *sūnávas* ; *aryás* ; *śúcī(ni)*, *purū́(ṇi)*. Ac. *agnī́n*, *sūnū́n* ; *gátīs*, *dhenū́s* ; *aryás*, *paśvás*, I. *agníbhis*, *sūnúbhis*, D. Ab. *agníbhyas*, *sūnúbhyas*, G. *agnīnā́m*, *sūnūnā́m*, L. *agníṣu*, *sūnúṣu*.

The most ancient and fundamental division of these stems is between the neuters on the one hand and the masculine-feminines on the other. The latter two classes were originally identical in declension and the distinction between them which is observed in Sanskrit is a secondary development. On the other hand the distinction between the neuter and masc.-fem. types (*mádhvas* : *agnés*) which is caused by variation of accent goes back to an ancient period of Indo-European.

The inflection of the neuters was effected by the addition of the normal endings, which in the weak cases originally bore the accent (Gk. *δουρός*, *γουνός*), and in this respect it did not in principle differ from that of the consonantal stems. This type of declension was not originally confined to the neuters (see below, *sákhye*, etc.), but the special type developed by the masc.-fem. class as a result of their suffixal accentuation (*agnáye*, *agnés*) was foreign to them. In Sanskrit the accent has become fixed on the root throughout the declension, *mádhvas* gen. replacing **madhvás*, as in other neuter stems. A few traces remain. The IE declension of the neuter *u*-stem meaning ' domestic animal ' was of the type *péku*, *pekwés*. Corresponding to these forms Sanskrit has a neuter *páśu* (once in RV.) and a gen. sg.

paśvás which directly continue the old type, but *paśvás* has become the gen. sg. of an analogically created nom. *paśús*, while corresponding to *páśu* there has been created a dat. sg. *páśve* by the usual levelling process.

As a result of the stabilising of the accent on the root in the normal type of neuters, the only type remaining in which the accent normally changed from the stem to the termination in declension consisted of those suffixally accented masculines and feminines in which the vowel of the suffix was elided in the weak cases (*mūrdhā́* : *mūrdhnás*, etc.). The result was that in certain cases, where an old neuter noun had preserved the terminational accent in the gen. sg., a new suffixally accented stem was created on this analogy, and with this change of accent was associated a change of gender : *paśús* masc. for *páśu* neut. Of the same type is *pitús* : *pitvás* 'food'.

The number of stems inflecting in this way in the Vedic language is very small, and in addition to neuters it includes some masc. and fem. nouns : *ávis*, *ávyas* 'sheep', *krátus*, *krátvas* 'intelligence', cf. Av. *xratuš*, *xraθwō*. These may be regarded as transferred neuters. Such a development is easily understandable in the case of *ávi-* on account of its animate nature. The action nouns in *-i* and *-u* were originally, in accordance with their meaning, of the neuter type, but in general they have been transferred to the masculine and feminine classes. In doing this they have normally adopted the adjectival type of declension (*matís* : *matés*, etc.) but the neuter type has remained in a few cases as an indication of their originally neuter class. The masculines of this type use sometimes special forms of the nom. acc. plur. (nom. Av. *pasvas* 'cattle', *ərəzvō* 'fingers', acc. Skt. *paśvás*) but also those of the normal type (*paśávas*, *paśū́n*).

The Vedic declension of the stem *rayí-/rāy-* is of this type (n. *rayís* : g. *rāyás*, etc.). It represents earlier **raHí-s/raHyás*. It is a transferred neuter of the *ávi-* type, and the terminational accent of the gen. sg. has effected a change of accent from root to suffix in the nom. sg., just as has happened in the case of *paśú-*. Besides this there exists a root stem *rā-* corresponding to Latin *rēs*. In the classical declension this is combined with the *rāy-* form of the *i*-stem. Similar is the declension of *naús*, *nāvás* 'ship' (Gk. ναῦς, νηός) for **naHu-s*, **naHvás*. In the only place where the nom. sg. occurs in the *Ṛgveda* it is pronounced as a dissyllable : *naüs* (*navús*) and in this respect it can be compared directly with *rayís*. The long diphthong is a later contraction of these vowels in hiatus. The acc. sg. is an innovation like the *rā́yam* which supplants *rayím*.

The stem *arí-* in which two different words have been confused (*arí-* ' pious ', **alí-* ' alien, hostile ') inflects according to this type, although adjectival in sense. Since there are found elsewhere in IE examples of old neuters being adapted to this use without the usual modification of the stem, its characteristic inflection (gen. sg. *aryás*, etc.) might be explained by its being an old neuter of this type transferred to the masculine. If it were originally an adjective it would have to be assumed that it inflected originally like *sákhi* (I. *sákhyā*, D. *sákhye*) and that from these weak forms the type of inflection characteristic of this class has spread to the nom. pl. (*aryás* like *paśvás*). On the whole the absence of any trace of the strong form of the suffix makes the first explanation more probable.

The same doubt exists in the case of *páti-*. In the meaning ' lord ' this word follows the normal inflection (type *agní-*), but in the meaning ' husband ' it forms cases after this style (dat. *pátye*). The accent and the *-n-* of the derivative *pátnī* ' wife ' might be held to indicate an old alternating neuter ; on the other hand the nom. pl. is always normal and weak cases of this type are shown also by the adjectival *sákhi-*. The stem *jáni-* ' woman ' has a gen. sg. *jányus* with a termination *-us* which appears also in *sákhyus*, *pátyus* and which is clearly borrowed from the nouns of relationship (*pitus*, etc.). In all three cases the normal gen. ending *-as* has been replaced. Avestan has *ǰanyōiš*, a compromise form replacing **ǰanyas*. This type of genitive inflection indicates that the stem is an old neuter transferred to the feminine.

There existed an alternative way of inflecting the neuters of this class in IE, by the employment of the heteroclitic *n*-suffix In the few neuter *i*-stems that remain this *n* replaces the *i*-suffix (*ákṣi*, *akṣṇás*), so that these stems are in the main removed from this declension. On the other hand the neuter stems in *-u* add this *-n-* to the stem before the vocalic weak terminations : dat. sg. *mádhune*, gen.-abl. *mádhunas*, *sā́nunas*, *drúṇas*, loc. *mádhuni*, *vā́stuni*, nom. acc. du. *jā́nunī* ' knees ', gen. loc. du. *jā́nunos*. Similar forms in other languages show that this practice is ancient (Gk. gen. sg. γόνατος for **gónwn̥tos*,

Toch. du. *kanweṃ* 'knees'). It is probable that originally a corresponding extension *-r* could be added in the nom. acc. sg. whence the two types of suffix *-ura/una-* in derivative adjectival stems. In the early language these endings are, with very rare exceptions, used only with neuter nouns. In adjectives the neuter is not normally distinguished in form outside the nom.-acc. In the classical language the *n*-forms are the rule for neuter substantives, but optional in the case of adjectives. The *-n-* has already in the earliest language spread to the instrumental singular of the masculines (*sūnúnā*).

Examples of this kind of inflection in neuter *i*-stems are exceedingly rare (*akṣiṇī* 'eyes') and the only common neuter that inflects in this way, *vā́ri* 'water', gen. sg. *vā́riṇas*, does not appear in the earliest language. This is to be expected in view of the rarity of such stems, the existence of an alternative type of heteroclitic declension (*ásthi/asthnás*), and the fact that the adjectival *i*-stems do not, any more than the corresponding *u*-stems, distinguish the neuter in these cases in the early language (gen. sg. nt. *bhū́res*). Nevertheless it may be assumed to be old from the existence of the alternating suffixes *-ira-/ina-* and the fact that this *-n-* has already in the earliest language spread to the instr. sg. of the masculines.

In the Veda the neuter nouns in *-u* may as a third alternative inflect according to the normal masculine type: gen. sg. *mádhos, drós, snós*, etc. This is an innovation which is eliminated in the classical grammar.

The neuter type of declension shows three types of loc. sg. in the *u*-stems which differ from the normal type of the masculine stems (*sūnaú*). (1) A locative without ending appears in *sā́no, vásto*. This type appears also in Iranian (Av. *pərətō*, O. Pers. *Bābirauv, gāθav-ā*), and it corresponds to similar formations from *n*-stems (*akṣán*), except that the characteristic accentuation of the loc. sg. has been eliminated. In *sā́navi* this formation is extended by the addition of locatival *-i* as has happened in *akṣáṇi*, etc. In the Vedic language this type has been extended to a small number of masculines (*ánavi, dásyavi*, etc.). (3) The locative may be made on the basis of the stem extended by *-n-*: *sā́nuni, vā́stuni*. This becomes the regular inflection in the classical language.

The common masc.-fem. type, consisting originally of adjectives and agent nouns, but at an early period enriched by wholesale transfers of action-nouns from the neuter, was differentiated in IE from the corresponding neuters by its suffixal accent: *pélu* nt. subst. ' much ' (Goth. *filu*), *pleú-* adj. ' much, many ' (Gk. πλέες). On the basis of this adjectival stem there could be formed a vṛddhied nom. sg., uncharacterised by the termination *-s*, on the same pattern as in the *n-*, *r-* and *s*-stems: *sákhā* ' friend ' (stem. *sákhi-*) like *pitā́, rā́jā*. In Sanskrit this word, in which the accent may be presumed to have been secondarily transferred to the root, remains the only example of this type of formation from an *i*-stem. As a general rule the forms *-is, -im* and *-us, -um* are substituted in the nominative and accusative, forms which go back to an early period in Indo-European. The vṛddhi which appears in the acc. sg. and nom. pl. (*sákhāyam, sákhāyas*) is as elsewhere (*dātā́ram*, etc.) an extension of the form of the nom. sg. Guṇa was originally proper to these cases. Some forms of the acc. sg. with guṇa are preserved in Avestan (*kavaēm, frādaṯ-fšaom*). Sanskrit has no such forms but it preserves the regular guṇa in the nom. pl. of the ordinary declension (*agnáyas, sūnávas*). The accented and guṇated suffix could also appear in the dat. and gen. sg. (*agnáye, agnés*) and this type has become the normal one in Sanskrit for masculines and feminines. Alternatively, on the analogy of *pitré*, etc., the accent could appear on the termination in stems of adjectival type, so that in these cases their declension is not distinguished from that of the neuters. Apart from the shift of accent this type is preserved in the dat. *sákhye*, and also in *pátye* if this word is of adjectival origin. The Avestan declension of *haxā* ' friend ' corresponds in general to that of *sákhā* (nom. s. *haxā*, acc. *haxāim*, dat. *hašе*, etc.) thus establishing it as Indo-Iranian. In the gen. sg. this stem has been influenced by the names of relationship of the *ṛ*-declension (*sákhyus* after *pitús*). The old endingless locative has been replaced by one in which the *-y-* of the dat. sg., etc., has been introduced (*sákhyau*). A similar form appears in the case of *páti-* ' husband ' (*pátyau*).

Although the vṛddhied nom. sg. which appears in *sákhā* is isolated in Sanskrit, signs are not wanting that it was originally more common in the *i-* and *u*-stems of the adjectival and agent-noun type. In Avestan the stem *kavi-* which has been normalised in Sanskrit still inflects in this way: nom. sg. *kavā*. In the acc. sg. this word has the original guṇa (*kavaēm*, i.e., *kavayam*, cf. *pitáram*), as opposed to the vṛddhi in Skt. *sákhāyam*, Av. *haxāim*. In the gen. sg. in Avestan the guṇated suffix normally appears, but once apparently it is inflected on the analogy of the heteroclitic neuters (*kəvīnō*, cf. *vā́riṇas*).

A vṛddhied nom. sg. in *-āuš* appears in Iranian in the case of some *u*-stems: Av. *hiθāuš* 'associate', *uzbāzāuš* 'with arms aloft' (and *uγra°*), O. Pers. *dahyāuš*. These have developed from the asigmatic vṛddhied nom. sg. by the secondary addition of the nom. sg. *-s*. The adjectival nature of this form of termination emerges clearly from the juxtaposition of *uzbāzāuš* and *bāzuš* 'arm'. In the acc. sg. we may have the old guṇa grade preserved (Av. *daiṅhaom*) or vṛddhi extended from the nom. sg. (O. Pers. *dahyāum*, Av. *nasāum* 'spirit of the corpse'). The contrast between the acc. sg. *pasum* 'domestic animal' and *frādat̰fšaom* 'increasing cattle' illustrates the adjectival nature of this kind of inflection. A similar variation appears between *arštim* 'spear' and *darəγō · arštaēm* 'having a long spear'. In the gen. sg. these stems have either the old type of inflection undifferentiated from the neuter (*uzbāzvō*), the normal type with guṇa (*daiŋ́hə̄uš*), or by later innovation forms with vṛddhi (*nasāvō*).

In Greek the adjectives and agent nouns have separated into two types in the case of *u*-stems. The adjectives have, as in Sanskrit, adopted the endings *-us*, *-um* (-υν) in the nom. acc. sg. πολύς : *purús*), at the same time preserving the original suffixal accent. On the other hand the agent-noun type (βασιλεύς, γονεύς, φονεύς, etc.), have developed on the basis of the old vṛddhied nom. sg. to which *-s* has been secondarily added as in Iranian (-εύς for -ηύς). The vṛddhi is carried through the declension as in the case of certain other types of stem (βασιλῆ(Ϝ)ος, cf. δοτῆρος).

To return to Sanskrit there is possibly one example of a formation parallel to *sákhā*: *apratā́* in RV. viii, 32, 16, *ná sómo apratā́ pape* 'Soma is not drunk without recompense' (*prati-*, cf. Lat. *pretium*). This is usually interpreted as loc. sg., but as non-adjectival compounds with *a-* are against the normal usage of the Vedic language, it is probably better taken as a nom. sg. interpreting the compound as a bahuvrīhi

The inflectional type of which Avestan preserves traces in examples like *uzbāzāuš* is preserved in Skt. *dyaús* 'sky'. This is conventionally classed as a diphthongal stem, but, as elsewhere this classification is unsound. On the one hand the normal *i*- and *u*-stems are themselves partly diphthongal (*agnés, sūnós*), and on the other hand this word is in part of its inflection not diphthongal (gen. sg. *di-v-as*, cf. *madh-v-as*). It is an adjectival *u/eu* stem *dy-eú-* with accent and guṇa or vṛddhi of suffix according to the general rule. The addition of *-s* in the nom. sg. is secondary but of IE date (*dyaús* : Ζεύς). In the oblique cases of the singular there appears most commonly the undifferentiated type with accented termination (*divás* : Gk. Διός) but also the special adjectival type with accent and guṇa of suffix (*dyós* : Av. *dyaoš*). With this must be classed *gaús* ' cow ' (dat. *gáve*, gen. *gós*) whose accent and declension show it to have this adjectival suffix (*g-ó-*, i.e. $g^{w}\text{H}_3$*-eú*, cf. Gk. βόσκω). It inflects only according to the adjectival type and goes further than other *u/o*-stems in introducing the guṇa into the cases of the plural (instr. *góbhis*, etc.). In the acc. sg. the forms *dyā́m, gā́m* appear to be from **dyaum, *gaum*, with vṛddhi from the analogy of the nom. sg. and elision of the final element of the diphthong before *-m*.

The stem *ví-* ' bird ' is an adjectival formation based on an old IE neuter **ōwi* ' egg ' (whence with thematic extension Gk. ᾠόν) and the accentuation of the suffix has resulted in the total elision of the radical vowel (as opposed to Lat. *avis*). In the RV. it has a nom. sg. *vés* with guṇa and nom. *s*. There is no parallel to this formation.

An old nominative *agnā́(i)* is traceable from the derivative *Agnā́yī* ' wife of Agni ', and it appears also in the compound *Agnā́viṣṇū* ' Agni and Viṣṇu ' (cf. *mātā́pitarau*). Similarly *Manā́vī* ' Manu's wife ' is based on an old nominative **Manaú*. More important than this the vṛddhied nominative of the adjectival type is preserved intact in the form that appears in the locative singular : *agnā́(u), sūnaú*. These forms are a special adjectival type of the locative without ending, being identical in every respect with the forms that originally served as the nom. sg. In that function they have normally been replaced by the termination *-is, -us*, but in their locatival function they have been retained.

The terminations *-is, -im, -us, -um* are therefore innovations in IE, and this accounts for the association of the accent with the weak grade of the suffix (*purús*). Nevertheless they are of considerable antiquity, and they have become the normal type in the various languages (Hitt. *šalliš* ' great ', *aššuš* ' good ', Gk. *πολύς* ' much ', Lith. *lipùs* ' sticky ', Goth *kaúrus* ' heavy ', etc.). Their origin is to be sought in the fact that in the masculine and feminine *i*- and *u*-stems two classes have coalesced. To the adjectival class consisting of adjectives proper (*purú*-, etc.) and nouns of adjectival type (*sūnú*-, etc.) there has been added a large class of action nouns (*gáti*-, *sétu*-, etc.) which were transferred at an early period from the neuter class. This involved the adding of the case terminations *-s*, *-m* in the nom. acc. sg. on the analogy of the thematic stems, thus producing a type ending in *-is, -im, -us, -um*. In the amalgamation of the two classes in a common masc.-fem. declension, this type of formation in the nom.-acc. is generalised, but in the dat. and gen. sg. the formation proper to the adjectival type is generalised (*gátes* after *agnés*, etc.).

The type of inflection prevalent in *i*- and *u*-stems in Sanskrit appears also in other IE languages : cf. gen. sg. Goth. *anstais, sunaus*, Lith. *naktẽs, sūnaũs*, dat. sg. O. Sl. *synovi*. In Hittite and Greek the forms of the gen. sg. with non-reduced termination (Hitt. *šallaiaš, aššawaš*, Gk. *ὄφεος, ἡδέος*) may be regarded as innovations replacing this type.

In the locative singular the *-au* of the *u*-stems (*sūnaú*) has been introduced into the *i*-stems (*agnaú*), but the Vedic language also has *agnā́* (i.e. *agnā́*(*i*)). The locative without ending appears also in other IE languages (Goth. *anstai, sunau*, O. Sl. *synu*, etc.), but it is not possible to determine whether a long or short diphthong is represented in these cases.

The special feminine terminations in the dat., gen.-abl. and loc. sg. (*gátyāi, -ās, -ām* ; *dhenvā́i, -ās, -ām*) are adapted from the *ī*-declension. They are still rare in the RV. but become very common in the later pre-classical literature. The grammarians allow optionally in the case of feminine nouns either these terminations (*gátyai*, etc.) or the common masc.-fem. terminations (*gátaye*, etc.).

§ 8. Stems in *ā, ī, ū*

-ā : Sg. N. *sénā*, A. *sénām*, I. *sénayā*, D. *sénāyai*, G. Ab. *sénāyās*, L. *sénāyām*, V. *séne* ; Du. N.A.V. *séne*, I.D. Abl. *sénābhyām*, G.L. *sénayos*, Pl. N.A.V. *sénās*, I. *sénābhis*, D. Ab. *sénābhyas*, G. *sénānām*, L. *sénāsu*.

-ī : (A) Sg. N. *vṛkī́s*, A. *vṛkyàm*, I. *vṛkyā̀*, D. *vṛkyè*, Ab. G.

vṛkyàs, Loc. *gaurī́* ; Du. N.A.V. *vṛkyā̀(u)*, I.D. Ab. *vṛkī́bhyām*, G.L. *vṛkyòs* ; Pl. N.A.V. *vṛkyàs*, I. *vṛkī́bhis*, D. Ab. *vṛkī́bhyas*, G. *vṛkī́ṇām*, L. *vṛkī́ṣu*.

(B) Sg. N. *devī́*, A. *devī́m*, I. *devyā́*, D. *devyaí*, Ab. G. *devyā́s*, L. *devyā́m*, V. *dévi* ; Du. N.A. *devī* [*devyàu*], I.D. Ab. *devī́bhyām*, G.L. *devyòs* ; Pl. N. *devī́s* [*devyàs*], A. *devī́s*, I. *devī́bhis*, D. Ab. *devī́bhyas*, G. *devī́nām*, L. *devī́ṣu*.

-ū : Sg. N. *tanū́s*, A. *tanvàm*, I. *tanvā̀*, D. *tanvè*, Ab. G. *tanvàs*, L. *tanvì*, V. *tanu* ; D. N.A.V. *tanvā̀u*, I.D. Ab. *tanū́bhyām*, G.L. *tanvòs* ; Pl. N.A. *tanvàs*, I. *tanū́bhis*, D. Ab. *tanū́bhyas*, G. *tanū́nām*, L. *tanū́ṣu*.

The nouns of these classes have in common an IE suffix -H (-*a*H, -*i*-H, -*u*-H> *ā*, *ī*, *ū*). With this suffix action nouns could be formed which originally did not differ from the usual neuter types (cf. the neuters in *-as*, *-is*, *-us*), and also adjectives which came eventually to be specialised as feminines. The dual type of inflection which appears in the *ī*-stems is traceable to the distinction of these two types, since whereas the *vṛkī́* type inflects according to a system which may appear in both neuter and adjectival types, the *devī́* declension contains inflections (*devyā́-s*, etc.) of a specifically adjectival nature, in which the strong form of the suffix is due to the original adjectival accent.

The stems of the *vṛkī́* type consist of both action nouns (*dehī́* ' rampart ') and nouns of adjectival type, masculine and feminine (*rathī́-* ' charioteer ', *vṛkī́* ' she-wolf '). In the former the accent has been shifted to the suffix, where it remains throughout the declension, in the same way as has happened in the stems in *-iṣ* (*havís*, *havíṣas*, similarly -*í*H, -*i̯*H*os*). In the adjectival class the strong form of the stem (**vṛkyā́*), whose original existence is to be assumed on the basis of the accentuation and of the general system (*pitā́*, etc.), has been replaced by the weak form, a process for which a parallel is to be found in the *in*-stems (*balī́*, *balínas*). As a result of these processes, and because of the acquisition of feminine gender by action nouns with suffix -H, the two classes become completely fused together in declension.

The same two types are found among the *ū*-stems ((1) *tanū́-* ' body ', (2) *śvaśrū́-* ' mother-in-law ') and their fusion has proceeded in the same way.

Since the *-s* of the nom. sg. was originally not characteristic of the H-stems. from which it remains absent elsewhere, its existence in these two classes must be regarded as an importation from the root stems in *ī* and *ū* which are declined in the same way (*dhī́s, dhiyás, bhū́s, bhuvás*). For the rest the declension is of the normal consonantal type calling for little comment. The stem and ending are pronounced as separate syllables in the Veda (*tanúvam*, etc.) although written according to the later system (*tanvàm*, etc.). The normal type of loc. sg. appears in *camvì, tanvì*, etc., the endingless variety in *camū́*, etc. The few locatives in *-ī* of the *ī*-stems could either be the result of contraction (<**iyi* <**i*H*i*) or be locatives without ending. In the gen. pl. *-n-* has been introduced on the general analogy of the vocalic stems.

The *devī́* type is the one that normally appears in the feminine of non-thematic and some thematic stems (*rājñī, dātrī, pṛthvī, kalyāṇī*). It is thus predominantly an adjectival suffix, and although the accent of stems of this type has become variable in Sanskrit, the suffixal accent which frequently appears may be considered to be the more original type. The strong forms of the suffix, which are to be explained by this adjectival accent, appear in the dat., abl.-gen. and loc. sg. In the nom.-acc. the weak form of the suffix appears, so that there exists an alternation here parallel to that which appears in the *i*- and *u*-stems. Theoretical considerations indicate that the weak form of the nom.-acc. sg. (and of the nom. pl. following suit) are innovations, just as the similar formations in the adjectival *i*- and *u*-stems, and the related languages provide some evidence that this is so. This is clearest in the case of the acc. sg. which for phonological reasons cannot be original, since these stems were originally consonantal and *-*i*H*am* could only produce *-iyam* (*-yam*). In Balto-Slavonic and Germanic the strong form appears in the acc. sg. (Lith. *nešusią*, O. Sl. *nesušą*, Goth. *bandja*, etc.) and there is no reason to believe that these forms are innovations. On the other hand these languages have the weak stem in the nom. sg. (Goth. *frijondi*, Lith. *vežanti*, O. Sl. *veząšti*) a fact which indicates that the weak form was earliest established in the nom. sg. Greek on the other hand has *-*ya* in the nom. sg. (πότνια, φέρουσα, μία), and this cannot be phonetically equated with the *ī* of the other languages since IE -*i*H- develops into *ī* in Gk. as elsewhere. The final -*ă* here as elsewhere (νυμφᾰ, etc.) represents IE -*a*H and the short vowel, as opposed to the long *ā* elsewhere, arises from the pre-vocalic sandhi of this combination. It is clear that the accent of *μία* is not original since it rests on a weakened syllable and it follows that the accent of the oblique cases (*μιᾶς*) must have originally prevailed in the nom. sg. also (**smiáH*).

The distinction between the two types of declension of the *ī*-stems, which is strictly observed in the Vedic language, is not retained in later Sanskrit. The *devī́* inflection is preserved at the expense of the *vṛkī* inflection, but it adopts the inflections of the latter class in the nom.-acc. du. and nom. pl.: *devyaù*, *devyàs*. Among the *ū*-stems inflection of a type parallel to that of the *devī́* stems is exceedingly rare in the RV. In the later language it becomes the normal type: *vadhvaí*, *vadhvā́s*, *vadhvā́m*, the development running parallel to that of the *ī*-stems.

The fusion of the termination and suffix in certain cases (*devyaí*, *devyā́s*) produces the special feminine terminations which are later applied to the feminine *i*- and *u*-stems. The loc. sg. has a special termination *-m*. This *-m* is absent in Iranian (O. Pers. *harauvatiyā*), which shows that the loc. was originally without termination. The secondary addition of *-m* is paralleled elsewhere: *túbhya*: *túbhyam*; instr.-dat.-abl. du. *-bhyām*: Av. *-byā*.

The stems in *-ā* have been influenced in declension by the stems in *-ī*. The cases of the singular from the dative onward are formed by the addition of *-yai*, *-yās*, *-yām* which have been abstracted from the *devī́* declension. This peculiarity is shared by Iranian: Av. dat. sg. *daēnayāi*, etc. The older IE endings are preserved elsewhere: gen. sg. Gk. *χώρᾱς*, O. Lat. *viās*, Goth. *gibōs*, etc.

§ 9. Stems in *-a*

Sg. N. *devás*, A. *devám*, I. *devéna*, D. *devā́ya*, Ab. *devā́t*, G. *devásya*, L. *devé*, V. *déva*; Du. N.A.V. *devaú*, I.D. Abl. *devā́bhyām*, G.L. *deváyos*; Pl. N. *devā́s*, A. *devā́n*, I. *devaís*, D. Ab. *devébhyas*, G. *devā́nām*, L. *devéṣu*.

Neuter N.A. *yugám*, Du. *yugé*, Pl. *yugā́ni*.

The stems in *-a* are the most numerous type in the language (45 per cent of all nominal stems in the *Ṛgveda*). They are characterised by the absence of any shift of accent in declension, and this seems always to have been the case. Thematic stems are either masculine or neuter, and these differ in declension only in the nominative and accusative. This declension contains some special features which may be briefly summarised. It has been considerably influenced by the pronominal declension. In the instr. sg. the termination *-ena* has been taken from that source. The older termination *-ā* still exists in the Vedic language, though it is a good deal less common than *-ena*. In Avestan only the ending *-ā* appears. The Indo-Iranian termination of the dat. sg. was *-āi*, a contraction of the stem vowel and the termination *-ai*, and this was inherited from Indo-European (*-o* + *ei*): Av. *haomāi*, Gk. *ἵππῳ*, etc. To this a postposition *ā̆* might optionally be added as in Av. *ahurāi ā* and in Skt. this element has become permanently attached, producing the extended termination *-āya*. The ablative sg. which is distinguished from the gen. sg. in this declension alone, is inherited directly from IE (O. Lat. *-ōd*, etc.).

There exists no common IE form of the gen. sg. In Balto-Slavonic the old abl. sg. functions also as gen. sg. and in view of the identity of the two cases elsewhere this could be ancient. Italic and Celtic have an ending *-ī*, which is the adjectival suffix *-ī* substituted for the thematic suffix. This *ī* appears in Sanskrit in constructions of the type *samī-kṛ* 'to make even'. In Hitt. the gen. sg. of the thematic class is equivalent to the nom. sg. There exists in the Veda a small number of compounds like *rathaspáti* which possibly contain such a form of gen. sg. A form corresponding to the Sanskrit termination appears in Greek and Armenian (Gk. *οιο*, Arm. *-oy*). A similar formation, but without the *-y-* appears elsewhere: Goth. *wulfis* (<°*eso*), O. Sl. *česo* 'whose'. These terminations may be presumed to have originated in the pronominal declension, as has happened elsewhere. The elements *-so* and *-syo* which are thus added to the stem appear to be demonstrative pronouns of that form.

The loc. sg. is analysable into the stem vowel and the normal termination *-i*: cf. Gk. *οἴκοι*, etc. The nom. pl. *-ās* (*a* + *as*) appears in a similar form elsewhere (Goth. *wulfōs*, Osc. *núvlanús*), but in its place an ending *-oi*, derived from the pronouns is also frequent (Gk. *λύκοι*, Lat. *lupī*, Lith. *vilkaĩ*, Toch. B. *yakwi*). The ending *-ās* is in the Vedic language sometimes pleonastically extended to *-āsas*, a feature which is also observed in Iranian (Av. *-å̊ŋhō*). This innovation is again abolished in classical Sanskrit, but it lives on in some early Pali forms (*paṇḍitāse*, etc.). The acc. pl. has acquired its long vowel from the nom. pl. (original form in Gk. (dial.) λυκονς, etc.). The gen. pl. has acquired its *-n-* from other classes, the innovation being common to Indo-Aryan and Iranian (Av. *mašyanąm*, O. Pers. *bagānām*). The original termination is preserved only in the phrase *devā́ñ jánma* ' the race of gods ' ; cf. Av. *staorąm*, Gk. θεῶν, Lat. *deum*, etc.

Two forms of the instr. pl. appear in the Vedic language, in *-ais* and in *-ebhis*. In Iranian Avestan has *-āiš*, O. Persian *-aibiš*. Elsewhere there exist only forms corresponding to *-ais* : Gk. λύκοις, Lat. *lupīs*, Osc. *núvlanúís*, Lith. *vilkaīs*. This form of the case has the appearance of being a pluralisation of the form that appears in the singular as dative. If so it must go back to a time when the cases were less differentiated than they became later. The ending *-ebhis* is an Indo-Iranian innovation after the pronominal declension. The innovation is later eliminated in classical Sanskrit, but it is the basis of the Middle Indo-Aryan forms of this case (: Pali *-ehi*, Pkt. *-ehi*(*ṃ*)). The *-e-* which appears here is from the form of the pronominal stem which appears in most of the cases of the plural (nom. pl. *té*, etc.). It also appears in the dat.-abl. and loc. pl. of this declension (*-ebhyas*, *-eṣu*).

CHAPTER VI

NUMERALS, PRONOUNS, INDECLINABLES

§ 1. NUMERALS

The Sanskrit numerals from 1-1000 are inherited from Indo-European. They are constructed on the decimal system, the numerals 1-10 being the foundation of the whole series. The numerals from 1-10 are adjectives, as also 11-19 which are compounded with *dáśa* ' ten '. The higher numbers are properly collective nouns, though a tendency to treat them as adjectives appears as the language develops. The numbers from 1-4 are fully inflected in the three genders ; those from 6-10 are defective and appear originally to have been uninflected.

1. Two roots appear as the basis of the numeral 1 in Indo-European, of which the one (*oi-*) appears to have had the meaning of ' alone ', the other (*sem-*) that of ' together '. In Sanskrit *éka-* ' one ' is formed from the first root with the suffix *-ka*, and it is declined according to the pronominal declension. The only form exactly corresponding is the Aryan *aika-* which is found in the Hittite documents. Elsewhere different suffixes appear : Av. *aēva-*, Gk. οἶος ' alone ' ; Lat. *ūnus*, O. Ir. *óin*, Goth. *ains*. The root *sem-* provides this numeral in Greek (εἷς, μία : **séms*, **smía*) and Tocharian (A. *sas*, B. *ṣeme*). This root appears in Sanskrit in its reduced form (*sm̥-*) in *sakŕ̥t* ' once ' (: Av. *hakərət̰*), and in compounds of the type *sámanas-* ' of one mind, the same mind '. The adjectives *samá-*, *samāná-* ' same ' are derived from it.

2. The numeral *dvaú* (: Gk. δύω, Lat. *duo*, O. Sl. *dva*, etc.) is like the normal dual of an *a*-stem : N.A. nt. *dvé* (: O. Sl. *dvě*), I.D. Ab. *dvā́bhyām*, G.L. *dváyos* (: O. Sl. *dvoju*). The uninflected thematic stem appears in the Gk. variant δύο. There is an alternative stem formed by means of the suffix *-i*, which appears in compounds (*dvipád-* ' two-footed ', Gk. δίπους, Lat. *bipes*) and in various derivatives (*dvitī́ya-* ' second ', etc.). Beside the numeral proper there is a stem *ubhá-* ' both ' which inflects in the same way. The exact nature of its relation to Gk. ἄμφω,

Lat. *ambō*, O. Sl. *oba*, Lith. *abù*, Goth. *bai*, Engl. *both*, etc., is not altogether clear.

3. The stem *trí-* contains a suffix *-i* which is absent in the ordinal *tṛtī́ya-*. It is inflected like a normal adjective in *-i* (nom. pl. *tráyas* : Gk. τρεῖς, etc.), except in the gen. pl. where *tráyāṇām* has replaced an earlier *tráyām* (: Av. *θrayąm*, with guṇa from the nom. pl. as opposed to Gk. τριῶν, etc.). It preserves the alternation of accent in declension : instr. pl. *tribhís* as opposed to *víbhis* ' with birds '.

4. This numeral is formed on the basis of a root *k*ʷ*et-* which seems originally to have meant something like ' angle ' (cf. Lat. *triquetrus* ' triangular '), whence ' square ' and from that ' four '. In the masc. and neut. (*catvā́ras*, *catvā́ri*, Lat. *quattuor*, etc.) the stem is formed by means of the suffix *-var*, with adjectival accent and vṛddhi in the nominative. In the other cases (acc. *catúras*, etc.) the suffix has the weak form according to the general rule. A neuter noun **cátvar*, or its IE prototype, is presupposed by the thematic extension *catvara-* ' square, crossroads '. Elsewhere the simple *r*-suffix may appear (Gk. Dor. τέτορες, Lat. *quater*), or the elements of the suffix may be reversed (Av. *čaθru-*).

The feminine of these two numerals (nom. acc. *tisrás*, *cátasras* : Av. *tišrō*, *čataŋrō*) is made by means of the suffix *-sar*, which elsewhere (see p. 141) shows a tendency to become a specifically feminine suffix. In *tisrás* the *-r-* of *tri-* has disappeared through dissimilation. The common form of the nom. acc. is in origin accusative. The original forms of the nom. to be assumed for IE, **tisores*, **k*ʷ*etesores*, are continued in Celtic : O. Ir. *teoir*, *cetheoir*.

The numerals from 5-10 have a less developed system of inflection than the preceding ones. With the exception of the dual ending of *aṣṭaú* ' eight ', they do not inflect in the nom. acc. In the Vedic language they may appear uninflected also in the other cases : *páñca kṣitíṣu* ' in the five tribes ', *saptá hótṛbhiḥ* ' with seven priests ', etc. In Greek and Latin the corresponding words are uninflected, also in Germanic when used attributively. This is the oldest state of affairs. The beginnings of inflection may be put in the late IE period, the uninflected type surviving by the side of the new inflected type down to Vedic times.

5. In *páñca* (: Gk. πέντε, Lat. *quinque*, etc.), representing IE

péŋkʷe, we find an uninflected thematic stem. As such are to be assumed, from the evidence of compounds, etc., to have existed freely at an early stage of IE, this is an interesting archaism. The root *peŋkʷ-* is in all probability that which appears in Engl. *finger* (**peŋkʷró-*) and *fist* (<**pŋkʷsti-*, cf. O. Sl. *pęstĭ* 'id'). The derivative *paṅktí-* (: O. Sl. *pętĭ* 'five') means from the *Ṛgveda* on, not only 'group of five', but more generally 'group, series'.

6. Skt. *ṣaṭ* (<**ṣaṭṣ*<*saṭṣ* with assimilation of initial) represents IE **seḱs* : cf. Lat. *sex*, Goth. *saíhs*, etc. The forms of this word in Indo-European are rather complicated, since there also exist forms beginning with *sw-* (Welsh *chwech*), *ks-* (Gk. ξέστριξ 'in rows of six', O. Sl. *šestĭ* 'six'), *ksw-* (Av. *xšvaš*) and simple *w-* (Arm. *veç*, O. Pruss. *uschts* 'sixth'). The original initial consonant group has been simplified variously in the different languages. Middle Indo-Aryan *cha* goes back to an original differing from the Sanskrit form, and beginning with *kṣ-*.

7. The final *-a* of *saptá* (: Gk. ἑπτά) represents IE *-m̥*, as is clear not only from Lat. *septem* but also from the ordinal *saptamá-*. The agreement between Greek and Sanskrit shows that the final accentuation existed already in IE (*septm̥ ́*), but it cannot be original since it appears on a reduced syllable.

8. In *aṣṭaú* (: Gk. ὀκτώ, Lat. *octō*, Goth. *ahtau*, etc.) there appears the termination of the dual. The meaning of the stem *oḱtó-* of which this is the dual may be inferred from a related *i*-stem, *ašti-*, which is found in Avestan. This is a measure of length meaning 'the width of four fingers', from which it may be inferred that the dual **oḱtṓ(u)* meant originally 'two groups of four fingers'. In classical Sanskrit there exists beside this a form *aṣṭa* with short *a* from the surrounding numerals.

9. The *-a* of *náva* 'nine' (: Gk. ἐν-νέα) may go back to *-m̥* (cf. *navamá-*, Lat. *novem*) or possibly *-n̥* (cf. Lat. *nōnus* 'ninth'). The word has been considered to be related to IE *néwos* 'new', which in view of the formation of the preceding numeral is not without plausibility.

10. The primary series closes with *dáśa* 'ten' (: Gk. δέκα, Lat. *decem*, Goth. *taíhun*, etc.) representing IE *déḱm̥*, about the etymology of which no likely suggestions exist.

11-19. These are dvandva compounds of 1-9 with 10: *dvā́daśa* '12', *tráyodaśa* '13', *cáturdaśa* '14', *ṣóḍaśa* '16', etc.; cf. Gk. δώδεκα, Lat. *duodecim*, etc. The long vowel of *ékādaśa* ' 11 ' is from *dvā́daśa*. The numeral 19 may alternatively be expressed *ekonaviṃśati* ' 20 less 1 '.

The tens from 20-90 are feminine substantives and as such decline properly in the singular, with the gen. pl. of the things enumerated : *navatím nāvyànām* ' 90 navigable streams ', etc. But they may also be construed either (1) agreeing in case, but not in number, with the noun enumerated, *viṃśatyā́ háribhiḥ* ' with 20 bay horses ', or even (2) adjectivally, agreeing also in number with it : *pañcāśadbhir bāṇaiḥ* ' with 50 arrows '. The intervening numerals are constructed like those from 11-19 : *tráyastriṃśat-* ' 33 ', *cátuḥṣaṣṭi* ' 64 ', etc.

20-50 : *viṃśatí-* : cf. Av. *vīsaiti*, Gk. εἴκοσι, Lat. *vīgintī*, etc.

triṃśát : cf. A. *θrisąs*, acc. sg. *θrisatəm*, Lat. *trīgintā*, etc.

catvāriṃśát : cf. Av. *caθwarəsatəm* (acc. sg.), Gk. τετταράκοντα, Lat. *quadrāginta*, etc.

pañcāśát- : cf. Av. *pančāsat-*, Gk. πεντήκοντα, Lat. *quinquāginta*, etc.

The element *-śat-* which appears in these four numerals is out of *-k̂m̥t-*, which further stands for *dkm̥t-*, a reduced form of the numeral 10, with the *t*-suffix that appears in Skt. *daśát-* ' decade '. The reduced form belongs properly to the weak cases, since Av. *θrisąs* ' 30 ', and *visąs* ' 20 ', show that the strong stem (*-śant-*) was originally used in the nom. sg. This stem was originally neuter and could be inflected as such along with the preceding numeral (Gk. τετταρά-κοντα ' 4 tens ', etc.). In Sanskrit the neuter pl. inflection appears in the first member in *catvāri-m̥-śát* and *pañcā-śát-*. Its absence from the second member is explained by the fact that this inflection could be optionally omitted (cf. *víśvāni vásu*, etc., p. 237). The *i*-stem *viṃśatí-* was originally a dual **vī̆ śatī̆* ' 2 tens '. The *vī̆* which appears here in the sense of ' 2 ' is the normal word in Tocharian in place of the usual *dvaú*, etc. (A. *wu*, *we* (fem.), B. *wi*). It may be identified with the prefix *vi-* ' apart, separate '. The presence of the nasal at the end of the first member is unexplained, and outside Indo-Aryan it appears only in Oss. *insäi* ' 20 '.

60-90. *ṣaṣṭí*, *saptatí-*, *aśītí-*, *navatí-*. These are formed in a manner quite different from the preceding. They are abstract or collective nouns formed by means of the suffix *-ti*, meaning primarily ' hexad ', etc. The primary meaning is retained in the similarly formed *paṅktí-* ' group of 5 ', and O. Sl. *šestĭ*, which corresponds in form to Skt. *ṣaṣṭí-*, means simply ' 6 '. The specialisation of these forms as names of the tens is common to Indo-Aryan and Iranian, cf. Av. *xšvašti-*, *haptāiti-*, *aštāiti-*, *navaiti-*. The form of the numeral 80 in Sanskrit is an independent formation from the root which is not paralleled elsewhere but which is obviously ancient. It has been replaced in Iranian by a normalised form based on *aštā*.

100. The original form of *śatám* (Av. *satəm*, Gk. ἑ-κατόν, Lat. *centum*, etc.) was **kṃtóm*, as is clear from Lith *šim̃tas*. In view of this, and in view of the fact that the *-śat-* in *triṃśát*, etc., means ' ten ', the IE original is derived from *dkṃtóm*, a neuter collective noun meaning ' a decad (of tens) '.

1000. *sahásra-* (: Av. *hazaŋra-*) is connected with Gk. χίλιοι, χείλιοι, χέλλιοι (*χέσλιοι), and the initial element *sa-* is identified with IE *sṃ-* ' one, together '.

These two numerals are neuter substantives, but the same variations of construction are found as with the tens. The numerals above a thousand are purely Indian : *ayúta-* '10,000', *lakṣá-* ' 100,000 ', *prayúta-* ' 1,000,000 ', *koṭi-* ' 10,000,000 ', etc. The series is carried to great lengths, particularly among the Jains and Buddhists (*asaṃkhyeya-* $= 10^{140}$), but among the higher numbers there is little agreement in the names between the various texts.

Ordinals : 1 *prathamá-* (Av. *fratəma-*), 2 *dvitī́ya-* (: Av. *daibitya-*, *bitya-*, O. Pers. *duvitiya-*), 3 *tṛtī́ya-* (Av. *θritya-*, Lat. *tertius*, etc.), 4 (a) *caturthá-* (Gk. τέταρτος, Lith. *ketvir̃tas*, etc.), (b) *turī́ya-*, *turya-* (Av. *tūirya-*), 5 (a) *pakthá-* RV. 10, 61, 1 (Av. *puxδa-*, OHG. *funfto* from *pŋkʷt(h)ó-* : Gk. πέμπτος, Lith. *peñktas*, etc., from *peŋkʷto-*), (b) *pañcathá-*, Kāṭh. (: Gall. *pimpetos*, O. Welsh *pimphet*), (c) normally *pañcamá-* (Pahl. *panǰum*, Oss. *pänǰäm*), 6 *ṣaṣṭhá-* (Gk. ἕκτος, Lat. *sextus*), 7 (a) *saptathá-*, RV. (Av. *haptaθa-*), (b) normally *saptamá-* (Pers. *haftum*, Gk. ἕβδομος, Lat. *septimus*, etc.), 8 *aṣṭamá-* (Av. *aštəma-*), 9 *navamá-* (Av. *naoma-*, O. Pers. *navama-*), 10 *daśamá* (Av. *dasəma*, Lat. *decimus*, etc.).

The simplest type of ordinal is made by adding the accented thematic vowel to the numeral in its usual adjectival function : *saptam-á-*, *daśam-á*. From these ordinals the formation is further extended to cases where it did not originally belong : *aṣṭamá-*, as opposed to the more original Gk. ὄγδοος, Lat. *octāvus* ; *navamá-* as opposed to Lat. *nōnus*. The suffix *-thá*, i.e. *-t-*H*-á-* must have originally arisen through the addition of the accented thematic vowel to a collective or abstract derivative in *-tā*, i.e. *-ta*H (**caturtā + á> caturthá-*). There is no evidence of an H outside Indo-Iranian : Gk. *πέμπτος*, etc., are formed on the basis of the simple *t*-stem.

The first ordinal differs in the various languages (Gk. *πρῶτος*, Lat. *prīmus*, Lith. *pìrmas*, etc.), but they agree in deriving it from the same root meaning ' in front ', and not from the corresponding cardinal. The ordinals from 11-19 are thematic formations with accentuation of suffix : *dvādaśá-*, etc., cf. Av. *dvādasa-*, etc. The suffix *-tama* which serves also as a superlative suffix is used to form ordinals from the tens, 100 and 1000 : *triṃśattama-* (Av. *θrisastəma-*, Lat. *trice(n)simus*) '30th'), *ṣaṣṭitama-* ' 60th ', *śatatama-* ' 100th ', *sahasratama-* ' 1000th ' (Av. *hazaŋrō · təma-*). Alternatively there exists for 20-50 the type *viṃśá-*, *triṃśá-*, *catvāriṃśa-*, *pañcāśa-*, to which nothing corresponds outside Indo-Aryan. They are formed analogically on the pattern of *ekādaśá-*, etc.

Of adjectival derivatives other than ordinals *dvayá-* (Gk. *δοιός*, O. Sl. *dvojĭ*) and *trayá-* (O. Sl. *trojĭ*), meaning ' of two (three) sorts, parts ' are inherited. Sanskrit has created by means of the suffix *-taya* a series *ékataya-*, *cátuṣṭaya-*, etc., used in the same sense. Old adverbial derivatives are *dvís* (Av. *biš*, Gk. *δίς*, Lat. *bis*) and *trịs* (Av. *θriš*, Gk. *τρίς*) ' twice, three times '. It is not certain whether *catúḥ* ' four times ' is the simple stem *catur* used adverbially, or whether it is from **catur-ṣ*, with the addition of this adverbial *-s*. Av. *caθruš* ' four times ' has such an *-s* (though the elements of the suffix are arranged in different order), but it is not necessary to assume its original presence in Lat. *quater*. Elsewhere this meaning is expressed by the use of *kŕ̥tvas* ' times ' : *pañca kŕ̥tvaḥ* ' 5 times, etc.'. The root of this word appears in the compound *sakŕ̥t* ' once ', and in Lith. *kar̃tas*, O. Sl. *kratŭ*. Other adverbial formations are made by means of the suffixes *-dhā* (*trídhā* ' in 3 parts ', etc.) and *-śas* (*śataśás* ' in hundreds '), etc.

§ 2. PRONOUNS

Personal Pronouns

1. Sg. N. *ahám*, A. *mā́m*, *mā*, I. *máyā*, D. *máhyam*, *me*, Ab. *mát*, G. *máma*, *me*, Loc. *máyi*.

Du. N.A.V. *āvā́m*, I.D. Ab. *āvā́bhyām*, G.L. *āváyos*, and A.D.G. *nau*.

Pl. N. *vayám*, A. *asmā́n*, *nas*, I. *asmā́bhis*, D. *asmábhyam*, *nas*, Ab. *asmát*, G. *asmā́kam*, *nas*, L. *asmā́su*.

2. Sg. N. *tvám*, A. *tvā́m*, *tvā*, I. *tváyā*, D. *túbhyam*, *te*, Ab. *tvát*, G. *táva*, *te*, L. *tváyi*.

Du. N.A.V. *yuvā́m*, I.D. Ab. *yuvā́bhyām*, G.L. *yuváyos*, and A.D.G. *vām*.

Pl. N. *yūyám*, A. *yuṣmā́n*, *vas*, I. *yuṣmā́bhis*, D. *yuṣmábhyam*, *vas*, Ab. *yuṣmát*, G. *yuṣmā́kam*, *vas*, L. *yuṣmā́su*.

The inflection of the pronouns differs in many respects from that of the nouns, and this difference is most marked in the personal pronouns. (1) These pronouns show no difference of gender, which is in accordance with the earliest IE practice, and contrasts with the practice of other language families (e.g. Semitic) in which gender is distinguished. Only an isolated *yuṣmā́s* acc. pl. fem. is quotable from the Vedic texts. (2) The distinctions of number are expressed by the use of different stems, which contain different radical elements. (3) The same distinction appears in the first person between the nom. sg. and the other cases. (4) The terminations of the plural are partly identical with those of the singular, and this was much more marked in the prehistoric period. (5) The individual terminations differ widely from those of the noun.

The nom. sg. *ahám* (Av. *azəm*) contains a suffix *-am* which is elsewhere prevalent in the declension of the personal pronouns. The form is found also in Slavonic (O. Sl. *azŭ* with *ŭ* <*-om*). Elsewhere there appear forms without ending (Lith. *eš*, *aš*) and forms terminating in *-ō* (Gk. ἐγώ, Lat. *ego*). The latter form was originally *egó*H, and the aspiration in Sanskrit shows that it was to this form that the *-ám* has been added (*ego*H + *óm* > *eg*H*-óm*). The *-am* of *tvám* (Av. *twə̄m*, *tū̆m*) is not found outside Indo-Iranian and is therefore of more recent origin. The other languages have *tū̆* which also survives in Iranian, and possibly also in the Vedic particle *tu* (cf. RV. 8, 13, 14 *ā́ tū́ gahi*, *prá tú drava*). In the other cases of the first person there appears a stem beginning with *m-*, before which on the evidence of Greek (ἐμέ acc. sg.) and Hittite (*ammuk* acc. dat. sg.) a vowel has been lost in most of the IE languages. On the other hand the pronoun of the second person does not differ radically in these cases. The base *tĕ̄* which appears elsewhere (O. Sl. *tę* = Skt. *tvā́m*, etc.) may have arisen out of **twĕ̄* by sporadic loss of *-w-* after initial *t-*. The final *-m* in the acc. sg. forms *mā́m*, *tvā́m*

(: Av. *mąm, θwąm*) is found outside Indo-Iranian only in Slavonic (O. Sl. *mę, tę*). It is an innovation replacing the older forms which are preserved only as enclitics : *mā, tvā* (: Av. *mā, θwā*). The relation of these forms with long vowel to the forms with short vowel like Gk. ἐμέ, με, σέ, σε is not clear.

The enclitic forms *me, te* (: O. Pers. *maiy, taiy*, Av. *mōi, me, tōi, te*, Gk. μοι, σοι, Lith. *mi, ti*) are forms of stem and contain no case ending. As such they are more ancient than the accented forms which have evolved a full case system. It is also an ancient feature that their use is much wider than that of a normal case form. They are used regularly in the sense of both genitive and dative, and occasionally even more widely. Originally there must have been corresponding accented forms with similar wide use. The growth of a full system of inflection for the accented personal pronouns has abolished these, but the older undeveloped system is preserved in the enclitics.

The lateness of the fully inflected case forms is shown by the fact that a number of them have no exact correspondences in other IE languages. Such is the case with the instr. sg. *máyā*. This is formed on the basis of the stem form preserved in the enclitic *me*. On the other hand the original form of the instr. sg. of the second person was *tvā́*, as is shown by the agreement of this rare Vedic form with Av. *θwā*. It is replaced by *tváyā* formed on the pattern of *máyā*. The same form of stem is the basis of the loc. sg. *máyi*. The original loc. sg. of the second person is *tvé* which appears in the RV. It is replaced from the AV. on by the analogical *tváyi*. In the absence of Iranian evidence it is not possible to say anything about the earlier history of this case.

The forms of the abl. sg. *mát, tvát* (: Av. *mat̰, θwat̰*, cf. O. Lat. *mēd, tēd*) are formed with the same element that appears in the declension of thematic stems. A form *mámat*, influenced by the gen. sg. appears in the RV., and later the extended forms *mattáḥ, tvattás*, formed with the ablatival suffix *-tas*, come to be frequently used. The forms of the dat. sg. are *máhyam, túbhyam*, but *túbhya* is attested in the RV., and both *máhya* and *túbhya* are frequently required by the metre. These are the earliest forms and the *-m* is a secondary addition of Sanskrit, as elsewhere. The *-m* is absent in Iranian : Av. *maibyā, maibyō, taibyā, taibyō*. The final element *ă* found in Indo-Iranian is absent elsewhere (Lat. *mihi*, *tibi*, Umbr. *mehe*, *tefe*, O. Sl. *tebě*, O. Pruss. *tebbei*), and it is therefore to be regarded as a postposition which has become attached to the original case form. The *h* (<*ĝh*) in Skt. *máhyam*) is shown to be original as opposed to the -*b*- in the Avestan form, because it appears also in Italic. The -*u*- of *túbhyam* is peculiar to Sanskrit : all the other languages have forms derived from original *te*-. The gen. sg. *táva* (: Av. *táva*) representing IE **téwo* is an uninflected thematic adjectival stem, and therefore an isolated survival of archaic IE usage. Elsewhere this stem is found inflected as a full adjective : Gk. τεός, Lat. *tuus*. On this analogy *máma* may be explained as a substitute for **áma*, the initial *m*- being introduced from the rest of the paradigm. This **áma* would correspond to the stem of Gk. ἐμός ' my ' in the same way as *táva* to τεός. Such an IE form of gen. sg. is represented in Armenian *im*. The gen. sg. in Iranian (Av. *mana*, O. Pers. *manā*) which corresponds exactly to that of Slavonic (O. Sl. *mene*) is a different formation, containing an *n*-suffix which in Germanic is attached to the diphthongal base (Goth. *meina*).

The nom. pl. *vayám* (: Av. *vaēm*) contains the same additional element -*am* that appears in the nom. sg. It points to an original IE *wei* which appears in Gothic with the secondary addition of the plural -*s* (*weis*, cf. also Hitt. *weš*). This -*s* appears also in the nom. pl. of the second person in Av. *yūš*, Goth. *jus*, Lith. *jũs*. A second form *yūžəm* exists in Avestan with the addition of the common pronominal termination -*am*. In Sanskrit *yūyám* the -*am* is added to the stem without -*s*, with the intervention of a -*y*- taken from *vayám*.

The cases of the plural from the accusative on are made from the bases *asmá*- and *yuṣmá*- to which corespond exactly Gk. (Aeol.) ἄμμε and ὔμμε. The *as*- of the first person is for *n̥s*- (=Goth. *uns*) which is explained as the weak grade of the form of the pronoun which is used as an enclitic, *nas*. It is possible that in *yuṣmá*- the initial *y* has been secondarily introduced from the nom. pl., and that an original **us*- was in the same way the weak form of *vas*. The stem extension resembles that in the masc. sg. of the demonstrative pronouns (*tásmāt*, etc.). These bases originally took the inflections of the singular, and the introduction of the plural termination is of comparatively recent origin. The old state of affairs is still preserved in the dative and ablative : *asmábhyam* (: Av. *ahmaibyā*), *yuṣmá*-

bhyam (: Av. *yūšmaibyā*) ; *asmát* (: Av. *ahmaṯ*), *yuṣmát* (: Av. *yūšmaṯ*, *xšmaṯ*).

For the accusative the simple uninflected base was originally used as in the Greek forms quoted above and in Avestan *ə̄hmā*, *ahma*. The introduction of the termination *-ān* is an innovation of Sanskrit. The original (singular) ending of the instr. pl. is preserved in Av. *xšmā*, and also in Vedic in a few compounds, like *yuṣmā́-datta-* 'given by you'. The long *-ā́-* of *asmā́bhis*, *yuṣmā́bhis* is derived from this form of instrumental, and from here it has been introduced into the loc. pl. : *asmā́su*, *yuṣmā́su*. The forms of the gen. pl., *asmā́kam*, *yuṣmā́kam* (: Av. *ahmākəm*, O. Pers. *amāxam* ; Av. *yušmākəm*) are based on the adjectival stems *asmā́ka-* and *yuṣmā́ka-* which still function as such in the RV. The original form, which still occurs occasionally in the Vedic language, was the uninflected stem as in *táva*, and the *-m* as elsewhere is a later addition.

An earlier form of the locative, *asmé*, *yuṣmé* appears in the Vedic texts, with the peculiarity that it can be used also as dative and genitive. This archaic characteristic of combining the meanings of several cases indicates that the forms are ancient, though nothing exactly parallel is quotable elsewhere.

Only one form of enclitic appears in the plural, *nas*, *vas*, which serves as acc. dat. gen. In Avestan the corresponding *nə̄*, *nō*, *və̄*, *vō*, serve only as dat.-gen. while for the acc. there appear forms with a long vowel, *nå*, *vå*. These correspond in form to Lat. *nōs*, *vōs* and O. Sl. *ny*, *vy*.

In classical Sanskrit three case-forms are distinguished in the dual of the personal pronouns, as elsewhere. In the Vedic language more numerous distinctions are found. The nominative *āvám*, *yuvám* are distinguished from the accusative *āvā́m*, *yuvā́m*. The ablative forms *āvát* and *yuvát* appear. A separate instrumental is attested by compounds of the type *yuvā́-datta-* 'given by you two'. The uninflected adjectival stem *yuvā́ku* is found functioning as gen. du. In Avestan there exists a gen. du. *yavākəm* more closely parallel to the forms of the plural. The forms of the dative and locative, *yuvábhyām*, *yuvós* are replaced by more regularised forms in the classical language : *yuvā́bhyām*, *yuváyos*.

The nom. du. *yuvám* is formed from the same radical element as the nom. pl. The unextended form is seen in Lith. *jù-du* 'you two'. For the first person a nom. du. *vā́m* is attested once in the RV. (6. 55. 1). This corresponds to Av. *vā*, the *-m* being obviously a secondary addition of Sanskrit. Av. *vā* corresponds exactly to O. Sl. *vě*, and from these forms Goth. *wi-t* and Lith. *vè-du* differ in having a short vowel. All these forms contain the same radical element as the nom. pl. A form corresponding to *āvā́m* is found only in Av. *ə̄əāvā* (acc.), and there is nothing similar in the rest of IE. The most plausible explanation of this formation peculiar to Indo-Iranian is that a dual *ā* of the pronominal stem *a-* has been prefixed to the original *vā*, *va* (IE *wē*, *we*).

The enclitic forms of the dual, whose usage corresponds to that of the plural enclitics, are *nau*, *vām*. Forms corresponding to *nau* appear in Av. *nā* (gen.), O. Sl. *na* (acc.) and Gk. *νώ* (nom. acc.). It is clear, particularly from Greek, that this formation was not originally confined to enclitic use. A form of the second person without *-m* appears once in the RV. (4. 41. 2), and a comparison with Av. *vā* (acc.) shows this form to be original. In O. Sl. the corresponding form *va* is an accented form used as both nom. and acc.

There existed in IE a reflexive pronoun which inflected after the fashion of the personal pronouns (Lat. *sē*, *sibi*, etc.). The initial varied between *sv-* and *s-* in the same way as that of the second personal pronoun. There are some remnants of this inflection in Avestan (dat. sg. *hvāvōya*, i.e. **hvawya*), but it does not remain in Sanskrit. The stem *sva-* ' self ' is used in compounds (*sva-yúj-* ' yoking oneself ', etc.), in the adverbial *svatas* ' from oneself ', and in certain derivatives (*svatvá-*, etc.). Apart from these cases the stem *svá-* is a possessive adjective corresponding to Lat. *suus*, etc. There is also an indeclinable *svayám* ' self ', which is formed by adding the usual pronominal increment *-am* to a base **svai-* (*sve-*, cf. *me*, *te*). As an enclitic this base appears with initial *s-* in Av. *hōi*, *hē*, *šē*, O. Pers. *šaiy*, functioning in the same way as *me*, *te*. It has been thought that this enclitic pronoun is represented in Pkt. *se*, but the latter is more likely to be of secondary origin. The Vedic enclitic *sīm* (acc.) appears to be radically related to this group, though differing widely in formation. In Iranian there are corresponding forms of the dual (Av. *hī*) and plural (Av. *hiš*, O. Pers. *šiš*).

The old possessive adjectives based on the first and second personal pronouns (cf. Lat. *meus*, *tuus*, etc.) have been lost in Sanskrit, although they are preserved in Iranian (Av. *ma-* ' my ', *θwa-* ' thy '). It is pointed out above how the stem of such adjectives is adapted as a gen. sg. In their place there are some fresh creations of Sanskrit, e.g. *māmaká-*, *tāvaká-* with vṛddhi, based on the gen. sg.; *māmakīna-*, etc.; *madīya*, *tvadīya-*, *asmadīya-*, *yuṣmadīya-*, based on the compositional stem; *matka-* ' mine ', etc.

Substitution of some honorific term for the singular of the second personal pronoun is a characteristic shared by Sanskrit with many languages. To some extent the plural serves this purpose, as in English, etc. (*yūyam me guravaḥ* ' you are my teacher '), but the normal substitute is *bhavān* (stem *bhavant-*) ' your honour ' with the third person singular of the verb. The word is an irregular contraction of *bhágavān* ' the fortunate, blessed one ', which is itself used in this way. The vocative *bhos* (<*bhagavas*) which is still further contracted, preserves the old Vedic form of the vocative.

Substitutes for the old, reflexive pronoun are provided by the nouns *tanū́-* ' body ' and *ātmán-* ' soul '. The former is so used in the Vedic language (*sū́ra upāké tanvàm dádhānaḥ* ' placing himself near the sun ') and the usage is paralleled in Avestan. It disappears in this usage in the classical language, but derivatives of it appear in later dialects of the North-West (N.W. Prakrit *tanuvaka-*, *tanuvaǵa-* ' one's own ', Torwali *tanu* ' id ', etc.). The classical alternative *ātmán-* appears also in the RV., and supersedes the other word from the early prose onwards.

Demonstrative, Interrogative and Relative Pronouns

Sg. N. m. *sá-s*, f. *sā́*, n. *tád*, A. m. *tám*, f. *tā́m*, n. *tád*, I. m. n. *téna*, f. *táyā*; D. m. n. *tásmai*, f. *tásyai*, Ab. m. n. *tásmāt*, f. *tásyās*, G. m. n. *tásya*, f. *tásyās*, L. m. n. *tásmin*, f. *tásyām*.

Du. N.A. m. *taú*, f. n. *té*, I.D. Ab. m. f. n. *tā́bhyām*, G.L. m. f. n. *táyos*.

Pl. N. m. *té*, f. *tā́s*, n. *tā́*, *tā́ni*, A. m. *tā́n*, f. *tā́s*, n. *tā́*, *tā́ni*, I. m. n. *taís*, *tébhis*, f. *tā́bhis*, D. Ab. m. n. *tébhyas*, f. *tā́bhyas*, G. m. n. *téṣām*, f. *tā́sām*, L. m. n. *téṣu*, f. *tā́su*.

Those demonstrative, interrogative and relative pronouns whose stem ends in the thematic vowel inflect according to the above pattern. The masculine and neuter pronouns inflect partly in agreement with the nominal *a*-stems and the feminines partly in agreement with the *ā*-stems. In addition they have forms of inflection which are not shared by the nominal stems. These are as follows :

The nom. sg. in the pronouns *sa, eṣa* and *sya* appear without final *-s* when followed by a word beginning with a consonant : *sa dadarśa* ' he saw ', but *so 'bravīt* ' he said ', *puruṣa eṣaḥ* ' this man '. Forms without the nominative *-s* appear also in the corresponding Gk. ὁ, Goth. *sa.*

The nom. acc. sg. nt. ends in *d/t* : *tát* (: Av. *taṯ*, Gk. τό <**tod*, Lat. *is-tud*), *etát* (: Av. *aētaṯ*), *tyát, yát* (: Av. *yaṯ*, Gk. ὅτ-τι), *kát* RV. (: Av. *kaṯ*, Lat. *quod*), *tvat, enat.* The Sanskrit sandhi does not allow any decision as to whether the original consonant is *-d* or *-t*, but it is clear that the final consonant was originally *-d* both from the evidence of other languages (Lat. *quod*, Goth. *þat-a*) and from forms in Sanskrit where a further suffix is added to this stem : *tadā́, idám*, etc.

The instr. sg. masc. nt. is in the classical language identical in noun and pronoun. In the Vedic language the noun has also the termination *-ā*, which is not used in the pronoun with the exception of *enā* (classical *enena*) and the adverbial *anā́* ' thus '. It is clear that *-ena* is the termination proper to the pronoun and that this has been transferred to the noun. The form is based on the diphthongal stem (*ke-*, etc.) which elsewhere is confined to plural use. The *-n-* appears to be of the same nature as the *-n-* which appears in the instr. sg. of masc. and neut. *i-* and *u*-stems. As opposed to classical *-ena*, the Vedic language has both *-ena* and *-enā*, due to different developments in sandhi of final *-a*H (> *-ǎ* before vowel). No forms corresponding exactly to these are found outside Indo-Aryan. In Iranian there are some forms with the intrusive *-n-*, but they are formed on the ordinary thematic, not on the diphthongal stem : Av. *kana*, O. Pers. *tyanā, avanā*. The instr. sg. fem. (*táyā*, etc.) is likewise based on the diphthongal stem, without the *-n-*. It has likewise been adopted by the nominal declension (*sénayā*).

In the dat. abl. loc. sg. the stem of the pronoun is enlarged by an element *-sm(a)-*. This element is fairly widespread in IE : Umbr. *esmei pusme*, Goth. *imma, þamma* (*-mm-* <*-sm-*), O. Pruss. *stesmu*, etc. It is not altogether clear whether the simple *-m-* which appears in O. Sl. *tomu*, etc., is a development out of this or stands for an originally variant form. If *-sm-* only is original it could perhaps be connected with the root of *samá-*, so that *tásmai*, for instance, would mean originally ' to that same '.

The dat. sg. preserves the old termination of the thematic stems, which in the noun has been replaced by the extended *-āya*. The *-in* which forms the termination of the loc. sg. appears nowhere else. In Iranian there are forms with simple *-i*: Av. *ahmī, kahmi, čahmi, yahmī*. These forms are clearly more original, and the *-n* of Sanskrit must be regarded as a secondary addition, whatever its origin. There is also absence of nasalisation in some of the middle IA forms : Pa. *tamhi*, Pkt. *taṃsi*, as opposed to Pkt. *tassiṃ*. These may be connected directly with the Iranian forms, and they point to a dialect variant **tásmi*, etc., in Old Indo-Aryan, existing beside *tásmin*, etc., adopted by the literary language.

In the dat. gen. abl. loc. sg. fem. an element *-sy-* appears before the termination. This is found also in Iranian (Av. *ahyāi, aiŋhāi, aiŋhå*, etc.) and in Old Prussian (dat. sg. *stessiei*, gen. sg. *stessias*). In Germanic there appears in these cases simple *-s-* (Goth. dat. sg. *þizai*, gen. sg. *þizōs*). The most plausible explanation of these forms is that they are based on the gen. sg. *tásya*, etc., which were originally common to both genders, the feminine being eventually discriminated by the addition of the termination *-ās*. From this starting the rest of the cases could easily be formed on the analogy of the noun.

The terminations of the dual are the same as those of the noun. In the gen.-loc. this is due to the transference of the pronominal forms to the noun, as can be seen from the opposition of two types of formation in Slavonic (*vlŭku, toju*). A few forms with simple *-os* appear in the Vedic language (*avós, enos*).

The nom. pl. masc. is formed by the diphthongal stem : *té, ké*, etc. Similarly in other IE languages : Gk. *τοί*, Goth. *þai*, Lith. *tiẽ*, O. Sl. *ti*, etc. Since in O. Lat. *quoi* (gen. *quoius*, dat. *quoiei*) we find such a form of stem used in the singular, and since in Sanskrit it appears in certain cases outside the plural (instr. sg. *té-n-a*, fem. *táy-ā*, gen. loc. du. *táy-os*), it must be assumed that this form of stem was not originally exclusively plural, and that it gradually became specialised as such. The form of stem that appears in the nom. pl. forms the basis of the other cases (*tébhis*, etc.) with the exception of the acc. pl. which is in all probability borrowed from the nominal declension. In the RV. the only forms of the instr. pl. that occur are of the type *tébhis*, and the nominal declension shows a tendency to borrow this type. Later the pronominal form of the case is not only excluded from the noun, but also in the pronoun it is replaced by the nominal form (*taís*). The only exception is the stem *a-* which preserves the old form of instrumental in the later language (*ebhís* : Av. *aēibiš*).

In the gen. pl. both in the masc.-neut. and in the feminine an *-s-* appears between the stem and the termination. The same *-s-* appears elsewhere : masc. Av. *aēšąm*, O. Pers. *avaišām*, O. Sl. *těchŭ*, O. Pruss. *steison* ; fem. Av. *å̊ŋhąm*, Gk. *τάων*, Lat. *istārum*, Osc. *eizazun-c*. Allowing for the fact that in Germanic (AS. *ðāra*) and Slavonic (*těchŭ*) the masculine forms have replaced the feminine in this case, the *-s-* forms are clearly more widespread in the feminine than in the masculine (e.g. Gk. *τάων* but *τῶν*). This may well indicate that the formation is more original in the feminine, and if so the *-s-* would be the *-s* of the nom. pl. *tā́s*, to which the gen. pl. termination is added. Apart from the gen. pl. the inflection of the feminine does not differ from that of the nouns in the plural.

The thematic pronominal stems that appear in Sanskrit are *sá/tá-* ' that ; he, she , it ', *eṣá/etá-* ' this ', *syá/tyá-* ' that ', *ena-* ' him, her, it ', *áma-* ' this ', *avá-* ' that ', *tva-* ' one, one . . . the other ', *ká-* ' who, which ? ', *yá-* ' who (relative) ', *sama-* ' any, every ', *simá-* ' self ', *néma-* ' a certain ', *a-*, *ana-* and *imá-* ' this '.

The stems *sá-* and *tá-* combine together to make one paradigm, and they are divided so that *sa-* appears in the nom. sg. masc. and fem., and *tá-* elsewhere. In this respect Sanskrit is in agreement with Iranian (Av. *hā*, *hō*, *hā*, *taṯ*, etc.), Greek (ὁ, ἡ, τό, etc.) and Germanic (Goth. *sa*, *sō*, *þata*, etc.). This continues the IE state of affairs, and where *t-* appears in these two cases (Lith. *tàs*, *tà*, O. Sl. *tŭ*, *ta*) it is an innovation. The absence of the *s*-termination in the nom. sg. masc. was also an original characteristic of this pronoun. In Sanskrit the pronoun has this termination (*saḥ*) when it appears at the end of a sentence, and in sandhi before vowels it is treated as if it were *sás* (*sa āha*, *so 'dya*). Greek also has a form *ὅς* ' he ', which appears predominantly at the end of a clause, which suggests that this variant form of the nom. sg. goes back to the IE period. For the rest of the paradigm *tá-* follows the regular form of the declension of these pronouns, with the possible exception of RV. *sásmin*, loc. sg. Since however the meaning of this in some contexts appears to be ' the same, one ', it should perhaps be connected with the IE root *sem-* ' one ', rather than with this pronoun.

The stems *eṣá-/etá-* and *syá/tyá-* alternate in the same way as *sa/ta-*. The former of these is compounded *e-*, which is the *ay-* of the *ayám*-pronoun, and the above stem *sa/ta-*. The combination appears also in Avestan (nom. sg. masc. *aēša, aēšō*, fem. *aēša*, nt. *aētaṯ*) but not elsewhere in IE. The pronoun *syá/tyá-* appears mainly in the RV. There are a small number of occurrences in the later preclassical literature, and even in early Pali texts (Jāt. *tyamhi, tyāsu*), but it is not used in the classical language, although it is recognised by the grammarians. Outside Indo-Aryan the only corresponding forms are O. Pers. *hya/tya-*, used as a relative pronoun in place of Skt. Av. *yá-*.

The interrogative pronoun *ká-* ' who ? ' is declined regularly according to the pronominal declension with the exception of the nom. acc. sg. nt. *kím*, beside which the RV. has also *kát* (: Av. *kaṯ*, Lat. *quod*, Goth. *ƕa*) formed regularly from the *a*-stem. In Indo-European there existed both an *a*-stem (Skt. *ká-s*, Av. *kō*, Lith. *kàs*, Goth. *ƕas*, etc.) and an *i*-stem (Gk. *τίς*, Lat. *quis*, Hitt. *kwiš*). Indo-Iranian had likewise both forms of stem, and this state of affairs is continued in Iranian : Av. nom. sg. *čiš*, acc. sg. *čim* nom. pl. *čayo*, etc. The tendency in Sanskrit has been to eliminate this form of the pronoun. An isolated interrogative *kís* is quoted once from the RV., elsewhere this form only occurs in the combinations *ná-kis* and *mā́-kis* ' no one ' (: Av. *naē-čiš, mā-čiš*). A particle *kīm* of the same formation as *īm, sīm*, which occurs in combinations like *ná-kīm, mā́-kīm* (cf. Av. *naē-čīm, mā-čim*) also belongs here. The only *ki-* form which maintains itself in the regular paradigm is nom. acc. sg. nt. *kím*. This form does not correspond to that found in other IE languages, which has the normal pronominal *-d* of the neuter (Hitt. *kwit*, Lat. *quid*, Av. *čiṯ*, etc.). This form is preserved in Sanskrit in the enclitic particle *cit* (*káścit* ' anybody '), from which the existence of an interrogative **cíd* may be inferred at an earlier stage of the language. How the final *-m* should be explained is not quite clear, but the existence of the Avestan particle *čīm* would seem to indicate that it is at least of Indo-Iranian date, and further connections with the Latin adverbial termination in *inter-im, ōlim*, and of Skt. *kíṃcit* with Arm. *in-č* ' something ' have been suggested. The restoration, by analogy, of the *k*- before the palatalising vowel is a common feature of Sanskrit in contradistinction to early Iranian. It has also taken place in certain of the thematic stems which originally contained the vowel *e*, e.g. gen. sg. *kásya*, Av. *čahyā*, Gk. *τέο*, O. Sl. *česo*.

There is a variety of adjectival and adverbial derivatives from this pronoun based on the three stems *ka*-, *ki*- and *ku*-.

ka- : *katará*- 'which of two' (: Av. *katāra*-, Gk. *πότερος*, Goth. *ƕaþar*), *katamá*- 'which of many' (: Av. *katāma*-), *káti* 'how many' (: Av. *čaiti*, Lat. *quot*), *kathā́*, *katthám* 'how' (: Av. *kaθā̆*) *kadā́* 'when' (: Av. *kadā*, *kaδa*), *kárhi* 'when'.

ki- : *kī́vant*- 'how much' (: Av. *čvant*-) *kíyant*- 'id'.

ku- : *kū* in *kū́cit* 'everywhere', *kuv-ít* particle of interrogation (: Av. *kū* 'where'), *kvà* 'where', *kúha* 'id' (: Av. *kudā*, O. Sl. *kŭde*), *kútra* 'id', *kútas* 'whence'.

The relative pronoun *yá*- is paralleled in Iranian (Av. *ya*-) Greek (*ὅς*) and Phrygian (*ios*), and in various derivatives elsewhere. Its declension is of the normal pronominal type (*yás*, *yā́*, *yád*, etc.) and calls for no further comment. Among the various derivatives from it mention may be made of *yatará*- 'which of two' (: Av. *yatāra*-), *yáti* 'how many', *yā́vant*- 'how big' (: Av. *yavant*-), *yáthā* 'how' (: Av. *yaθā̆*), *yátra* 'where' (: Av. *yaθrā̆*), *yadā́* 'when' (: Av. *yadā̆*), *yádi* 'if' (Av. *yeδi*, *yeiδi*, O. Pers. *yadiy*).

The enclitic pronoun *ena*- 'him, her, it' is used only in the acc. of all numbers, in the instrumental singular, and in the gen. loc. du. In other cases unaccented forms of the *ayám* pronoun are used with the same syntactical function (*asya*, *asmai*, etc.). No pronoun which can be compared with this is found in Old Iranian, nor in the rest of IE, but possibly M. Pers. *ēn*, Mod. Pers. *īn* go back to the same source.

The pronominal stem *avá*- is nearly extinct already in the Vedic language, being confined to three occurrences in the gen. loc. du. (*avós*). In Iranian on the other hand it remained in common use (Av. O. Pers. *ava*-) and a corresponding pronoun is found also in Slavonic (O. Sl. *ovŭ*).

The unaccented pronoun *tva*- 'a certain one, many a one' (when repeated 'one . . . another') occurs in the Veda but is absent from the later language. Outside Indo-Aryan it is possible to compare Av. *θwa̰t*, nt. sg. used adverbially (as also is Skt. *tvat*). Avestan has also a pronoun *hvō* 'he', which suggests that there was originally an alternating stem **sva/tva-* after the fashion of *sya/tya-*.

The pronoun *áma-* ' this one ' appears only in one ritual phrase. Elsewhere the stem appears only in the O. Pers. adverb *amata* ' from there ', and possibly in the Vedic adverb *amā́* ' at home '.

The Vedic pronoun *néma-* ' a certain one, many a one ' is used in much the same sense as the pronoun *tva-*, and may be combined with it in phrases like *néma u tva āha* ' one or the other said '. It is the stem of Skt. *néma-* ' half ', Av. *naēma-* ' half, side ' used adjectivally, ' he, they on the one side '.

The unaccented *sama-* ' any, every ' is likewise confined to the earliest language. It corresponds to Av. *hama-* ' every ', Goth. *sums* ' a certain one ', and it is ultimately derived from the IE root *sem-* ' one '. An adverb *samaha* ' somewhere, somehow ' is derived from it.

The pronoun *simá-* ' oneself ', which is also confined to the Vedic language, has nothing exactly corresponding to it outside Sanskrit. In structure it can be compared to the pronominal stem *imá-*, *simá-* having the same relation to *sīm*, for instance, as *imá-* to *īm*.

The stems *á-*, *aná-* and *imá* form part of the *ayám* declension, and are treated below.

This form of declension is followed by a variety of adjectival stems, consisting partly of pronominal derivatives, and partly of certain other adjectives. The full pronominal declension with nom. acc. sg. nt. in *-at* is taken by *anyá-* ' other ' (*anyát*, cf. Gk. *ἄλλο*, Lat. *aliud*) and such pronominal derivatives as *katará-*, *katamá-*, *yatará-*, *yatamá-*, and *ítara-* ' other '. Pronominal inflection, but with nom. acc. sg. nt. in *-am* is taken by such stems as *víśva-* ' all ' (nom. pl. masc. *víśve*, gen. pl. masc. neut. *víśveṣām*, etc. : Av. *vīspe*, *vīspaēšąm*), *sárva-* ' all ' (Indo-Aryan development on the analogy of *víśva-*), *éka-* ' one ' (cf. Av. *aēvahmāṯ*, etc., from *aēva-* ' one '). Other adjectives which show declension of this type are certain comparatives and superlatives such as *ádhara-*, *adhamá-*, *ántara-*, *ántama-*, *ápara-*, *apamá-* and the like, and a few other adjectives such as *pū́rva-* ' prior, east ', *dákṣiṇa* ' right, south ' and *ubháya-* ' of both kinds '. In this latter class there is considerable fluctuation of usage ; in some cases pronominal inflection is optional, and in others pronominal inflection only occurs in specific senses.

The Pronouns ayám and asaú

Paradigms :

(1) Sg. N. m. *ayám*, f. *iyám*, n. *idám*, A. m. *imám*, f. *imā́m*, nt. *idám*, I. m. n. *anéna*, f. *anáyā*, D. m. n. *asmaí*, f. *asyaí*, Ab. m. n. *asmā́t*, f. *asyā́s*, G. m. n. *asyá*, f. *asyā́s*, L. m. n. *asmín*, f. *asyā́m*.

Du. N.A. m. *imaú*, f. n. *imé*, I.D. Ab. *ābhyā́m*, GL. *anáyos*.

Pl. N. m. *imé*, f. *imā́s*, n. *imā́ni*, A. m. *imā́n*, f. *imā́s*, n. *imā́ni*, I. m. n. *ebhís*, f. *ābhís*, D. Ab. m. n. *ebhyás*, f. *ābhyás*, G. m. n. *eṣā́m*, f. *āsā́m*, L. m. n. *eṣú*, f. *āsú*.

(2) Sg. N. m. f. *asaú*, n. *adás*, A. m. *amúm*, f. *amū́m*, n. *adás*, I. m. n. *amúnā*, f. *amúyā*, D. m. n. *amúṣmai*, f. *amúṣyai*, Ab. m. n. *amúṣmāt*, f. *amúṣyās*, G. m. n. *amúṣya*, f. *amúṣyās*, L. m. n. *amúṣmin*, f. *amúṣyām*.

Du. N.A. *amū́*, I.D. Ab. *amū́bhyām*, GL. *amúyos*.

Pl. N. m. *amī́*, f. *amū́s*, n. *amū́ni*, A. m. *amū́n*, f. *amū́s*, n. *amū́ni*, I. m. n. *amī́bhis*, f. *amū́bhis*, D. Ab. m. n. *amī́bhyas*, f. *amū́bhyas*, G. m. n. *amī́ṣām*, f. *amū́ṣām*, L. m. n. *amī́ṣu*, f. *amū́ṣu*.

These two pronouns may be classed together as being in many ways aberrant from the normal pronominal declension. The *ayám* pronoun is distinguished by the number of different stems that combine to form the paradigm. The fundamental stems are *ay-(e-)/i* and *a-*. The nom. sg. masc. *ayám* (: Av. *aēm*) is made by the addition of the common pronominal *-ám* (cf. *ahám*, etc.) to the guṇated form of the first stem. The nom. sg. fem. *iyám* (Av. *īm* for **iyəm*, O. Pers. *iyam* both masc. and fem.) is a similar extension of *ī-*<*i-*H. In the same way the nom. acc. sg. nt. is an extension of *íd* (: Lat. *id*) which remains in use as a particle. Latin has the same extension in *idem* ' the same ', with a specialised sense that is absent in Sanskrit. The same extension applied to an acc. sg. masc. **im* (Gk. ἴν · αὐτόν, Lat. *im* ' eum ') has produced *imám* (: Av. *iməm*, O. Pers. *imam*), from which a new stem *imá-* is abstracted and extended to the acc. sg. fem. *imā́m* (: Av. *imąm*, O. Pers. *imām*), nom. acc. du. masc. *imaú* (: Av. *ima*), fem. nt. *imé*, nom. pl. masc. *imé* (: Av. *ime*, O. Pers. *imaiy*), acc. pl. masc. *imā́n* (: Av. *imą*), nom. acc. pl. fem. *imā́s* (Av. *imå(s)*, O. Pers. *imā*) nt. *imā́(ni)* (Av. *imā*). The stem is occasionally extended to other cases in the Vedic (but never in the classical) language : *imásya*, *imásmai* ; similarly in Iranian (Av. nom. acc. sg. nt. *imaṯ*,

O. Pers. gen. pl. *imaišām*), Middle Indo-Aryan (Pa. *imassa*, etc.), and in Buddhist and other incorrect forms of Sanskrit (*imeṣu*, etc.).

The stem *a-* appears in the D.G. Ab. L. sg., in accordance with Avestan (*ahmāi*, *ahmat̰*, *ahyā/ahe*, *ahmi*, fem. *aŋhyāi*, etc.) with the normal corresponding forms in the instr. pl. etc. (*ebhís* : Av. *aēibiš* ; fem. *ābhís*, : Av. *ābiš*, etc.). In the Vedic language the instr. sg. appears as *enā́*, fem. *ayā́*, and the gen. loc. du. as *ayós*. These are (allowing for the alternation *-a/ā* in *kéna*, etc., as opposed to *enā́*) the normal thematic endings, and the stem therefore is *a-*. On the other hand in the classical language these are replaced by *anéna*, *anáyā*, *anáyos*. In Avestan there is an instr. sg. *anā̆*, formed like *kana*, etc., from the stem *a-*, and corresponding to it there is a Vedic adverb *anā́* ' therefore '. It seems that the stem *ana-*, on which the above Sanskrit forms and the Av. instr. pl. *anāiš* are made, originated in this form *anā́*. On the other hand there is in Slavonic a pronoun *onŭ* which can be compared. It is possible that the Slavonic pronoun has arisen by the generalisation of a stem which arose in the same way as Indo-Iranian *ana-*.

There is a difference of accentuation between this pronoun and the corresponding forms of the normal pronominal declension (*asyá* as opposed to *tásya*, etc.), which is apparently due to a generalisation of the final accentuation of *ayám*. As an anaphoric pronoun (*asmai* ' to him ', etc.) the cases of the *a*-stem are unaccented.

A variety of adverbial forms are made, on the basis of the pronominal stems *a-* and *i-* : *átra* ' there ' (: Av. *aθrā̆*), *átas* ' from there ', *idā́* (: Av. *iδa*), *idā́nīm* ' now ', *ihá* ' here ' (Av. *ida*, *iδa*, O. Pers. *ida*), *itthám* ' thus ', etc.

The only part of the *asaú* pronoun for which anything corresponding can be found in another language is the nom. sg. *asaú*. Corresponding to this Iranian has Av. *hāu*, O. Pers. *hauv*, but in the other cases it uses the stem *ava-*, which has become almost extinct in Sanskrit. The most likely explanation of **sāu* is that it consists of the pronouns, *sa*, *sā* and a particle *-au* indicating distance. In the same way the acc. *amúm* may be explained as replacing *am-ú*, with a variant grade of the same particle. The *am-* would originally be the acc. sg. of the pronominal stem *a-*, the specific sense of the pronoun (' that over there ') being provided by the added element *-u*. Once this is interpreted as a stem, and the acc. sg. termination added it naturally forms the basis of a fully inflected pronoun declined on the analogy of the other pronominal stems. If it had been an older stem with suffix *-u*, inflection after the style of the *u*-stems would be expected. The fact that in contradistinction to all other *u*-stems it inflects according to the thematic type (in its pronominal variety) indicates that it is a late creation peculiar to Sanskrit which has arisen in some such way as described above.

The Sanskrit nom. sg. masc. fem. has an initial *a-* which is absent from Iranian *hāu*. It is clear that this has arisen from the analogy of the *amú*-stem, and that Iranian *hāu*, representing Indo-Ir. **sāu* is the more original form. The nom. acc. sg. nt. *adás* is a form for which no analogy appears elsewhere. The most likely interpretation of this form is that it was really *adó* misinterpreted as being for *adás* in those sandhi contexts where *-as* becomes *-o*. In support of this explanation one instance of *adó* before initial *p-* can be cited from the RV. The nom. pl. *amī́* and the remaining cases based on this stem are not easy to explain. It is suggested, but without any degree of certainty that an analogical diphthongal form *amui* was created corresponding to the diphthongal plural stems of the thematic pronouns (*té*<*tai*<*toi*, etc.) and that since this combination was new and unfamiliar (inherited *u*+*i* becoming *vi-*), it was unstable and became changed to *-ī*.

§ 3. Indeclinables

Some of the oldest types of adverb have been mentioned already in connection with the formation of nominal stems. It was observed that adverbs of the type *prātár* 'early' are formed by means of suffixes that were originally used in the formation of neuter stems. Adverbs of this type have most commonly accent on the suffix which also appears in the endingless locatives, with which they are identical in formation. There is also a type with radical accent (*ánti*, etc.) having the form of an unaltered neuter stem. The following is a list of adverbs of these types arranged according to suffix:

Neuter stems without suffix: *yugapad* 'simultaneously', *ānuṣák* 'in order'.

-ar: *avár* 'down', *púnar* 'again'. *-tar*: *prātár* 'early', *sanutár* 'away, apart', *antár* 'inside'; *-tur*: *sanitúr* 'away,

apart'; *-var*: *sasvár* 'secretly'; *-ur*: *múhur* 'suddenly'; *-i*: *sāmí* 'half' (usually in compounds, cf. Gk. ἡμι-, Lat. *sēmi-*), *pári* 'around'; *-ti*: *ánti* 'near', *práti* 'opposite, towards'; *-u*: *míthu* 'falsely', *makṣú* 'immediately' (cf. Lat. *mox*), *múhu* 'suddenly' (cf. Av. *mərəzu°-* 'short', Gk. βραχύς), *anuṣṭhú* 'at once'; *-as*: *mithás* 'falsely', *hyás* 'yesterday' (: Gk. χθές, Lat. *herī* with additional suffix), *śvás* 'tomorrow' (as opposed to *r*-stem in Av. *sūr-* 'morning'), *avás* 'down', *adhás* 'id', *prāyas* 'generally', *sadyás, sadívas* 'today, immediately', *tirás* 'across', *parás* 'beyond', *purás* 'before'; *-is*: *āvís* 'openly', *bahís* 'outside'; *-us*: *anyedyús* 'on the following day', *prādús* 'forth to view'; *-at*: *dravát* 'quickly', *drahyát* 'stoutly' (RV. once), *īṣát* 'a little'; *-it*: *pradakṣiṇít* 'so as to keep something to the right', *cikitvít*; *-ad*: *smát, sumát* 'with' (: Av. *mat̰*); *-k*: *jyók* 'for a long time' (cf. Lat. *diū*).

A number of adverbs functioning as verbal prefixes have the form of uninflected thematic stems, namely *áva* 'down', *ápa* 'away from' (: Gk. ἄπο), *úpa* 'up to, near' (: Gk. ὕπο 'under'), and *prá* 'forth' (Gk. πρό, etc.). Since the thematic suffix was originally used for the formation of adjectives, words of this type may be regarded as fossilized adjectival stems without inflection which have acquired the function of prepositions and verbal prefixes.

The above adverbs are formed on the same lines as the corresponding nominal stems. Other adverbs contain specifically adverbial suffixes. The more important of these are as follows:

-tas: This suffix makes adverbs which have in general an ablatival sense: *itás* 'from here', *tátas* 'from there', *anyátas* 'from another place', *dakṣiṇatás* 'from the right, on the right', *hṛttás* 'from the heart', etc. In some cases such forms function like forms of the ablative case: *sarvato bhayāt* 'from all fear', *kutaś cid deśād āgatya* 'coming from some district or other'. It has already been pointed out that this formation may be explained as deriving from the gen.-abl. of old *t*-stems. When simple *t*-formations became rare forms of the type *dakṣiṇat-ás* were reinterpreted as *dakṣiṇa-tás*, etc., and a new adverbial suffix created. Corresponding formations appear in other IE languages: Av. *x*^{v}*atō* 'of oneself', *aiwitō* 'around', O. Pers. *hača paruviyata* 'from of old', *amata* 'from there', Gk. ἐκτός 'outside', Lat. *funditus, caelitus*, etc.

-tāt : This formation which arises from a contamination of the above with the ablative termination *-āt* appears in such adverbs as *údaktāt* 'from above', *prā́ktāt* 'from in front', *adhástāt* '(from) below', *purástāt* 'from or in the front' and the like. There are no parallels in other languages.

-tră : With this suffix are formed adverbs with a locatival sense from noun stems (in the Veda only) and from pronominal stems : *devatrā́* 'among the gods', *puruṣatrā́* 'among men', *śayutrā́* 'on a couch', *dakṣiṇatrā́* 'on the right side', *atră* 'here', *tátra* 'there', *kútra* 'where', etc. The forms (compare those in *-tas*) are occasionally used as substitutes for the locative case : *hásta ā́ dakṣiṇatrā́* 'in the right hand'. Similar formations in Iranian are Av. *vaŋhaθra* 'at the place of dwelling', *iθra* 'here', *aθră* 'there', *kuθră* 'where', etc. As already indicated these adverbs are based on the extinct class of neuters in *-tar* (**śayutar* 'couch', **vasatar* 'dwelling-place'), of which they are instrumentals, with the locatival sense which instrumental forms always have when used adverbially. The fluctuation between *ă* and *ā* is due to variant treatment in sandhi of final *-ā*<*a*H, of which examples are noted elsewhere.

-thā, -tham : The suffix *-thā* forms adverbs of manner : *ṛtuthā́* 'regularly', *pratnáthā* 'as of old', *viśváthā* 'in every way', *anyáthā* 'otherwise', *táthā* 'so', *kathā́* 'how', *itthā́* 'thus', etc. More rarely *-tham* appears in the same sense : *kathám* 'how', *itthám* 'thus'. A similar formative appears only in Iranian : Av. *kaθa, kuθa* 'how', *avaθa* 'thus', *hamaθa* 'in the same way', etc.

-dā, -dānīm, -di : The suffix *-dā* in *kadā́* 'when', *tadā́* 'then', *idā́* 'now', *sarvadā́* 'always' contains clearly as its first element the *-d* of the neuter pronouns (*tad*, etc.). Similar formations appear in Iranian (Av. *kaδa, taδa*, etc.), and Lithuanian (*kadà, tadà* ; *visadà* 'always'). These forms may be extended by the addition of an element *-nīm* of obscure origin : *idā́nīm, tadā́nīm* ; *viśvadānīm* 'always'. The same pronominal *-d* appears in the *-di* of *yádi* 'if' (: O. Pers. *yadiy*, Av. *yeiδi*).

-dhā : This suffix meaning 'in so many parts' appears in such words as *trídhā* 'triply', *caturdhā́* 'four fold', *katidhā́* 'in how many parts', *bahudhā́* 'in many ways', *viśvádhā* 'in every way', *bahirdhā́* 'outside', *mitradhā́* 'in a friendly manner'. The *-dhā* is not in origin suffixal, but the root *dhā* forming a compound with the previous member (cf. *tridhā́tu* 'consisting

of 3 parts' beside *trídhā*), but it has come to function exactly like a suffix.

-dha, -ha: A suffix *-dha* appears occasionally, e.g. Vedic *sadha-* 'with' (in certain compounds; usually it is weakened to *-ha*: *sahá* 'with'). The same suffix with the same weakening appears in *ihá* 'here' (Pa. *idha*, Av. *iδa*), *kúha* 'where' (Av. *kudā*, O. Sl. *kŭde*), *viśváha* 'always' (O. Sl. *vĭsĭde* 'everywhere') and *samaha* 'in some way or other'.

-śas: This suffix makes distributive adverbs from numerals and other words: *dviśás* 'in twos, two by two', *śataśás* 'by hundreds', *sahasraśás* 'in thousands', *śreṇiśás* 'in rows', *devaśás* 'to each of the gods', etc.; cf. Av. *navasō* 'in nines'. The corresponding suffix in Greek is -κας, in ἑκάς 'by oneself' and ἀνδρακάς 'man by man'. The ultimate analysis of this element is not certain.

-rhi: *kárhi* 'when?', *tárhi* 'then', *etárhi* 'now', *yarhi* 'where (rel.)', *amúrhi* 'there'. The first element of this double suffix appears independently in various IE languages to make adverbial derivatives from pronominal stems: Lat. *cur* 'why', Goth. *þar* 'there', Lith. *kur̃* 'where', *visur̃* 'everywhere', etc. The second element is best explained as a weakening of *-dhi* (cf. *-ha* above) and this *-dhi* may be compared with the -θι which appears in Greek in such words as πόθι 'where', τόθι 'there'.

Adverbially Used Case Forms. It has been pointed out that a large number of the adverbs dealt with above are, in their ultimate analysis, case forms of nominal stems, e.g. the simple neuter stem which elsewhere functions as nom. acc. sg. nt. (*jā́tu*), endingless locative (*prātár*), instrumental (*śayutrā́*). In principle such adverbs are formed in the same way as those below, but the stems on which they are based no longer exist apart from the adverbs concerned. The following list consists of adverbs formed from stems which are used also as substantives or adjectives.

The most common case form used in the making of adjectives is the nom.-acc. sg. nt. By this means adverbs are formed, occasionally from nouns, copiously from adjectives, including all compounds which are adjectives. Typical examples are *purú* 'abundantly', *urú* 'widely', *máhi* 'greatly', *bhū́yas* 'more, again', *ráhas* 'secretly', *nyàk* 'downwards', *nā́ma* 'by name', *súkham* 'happily', *bálavat* 'strongly', *dhṛṣṇú* 'boldly', *satyám* 'truly', *nítyam* 'continually', *cirám* 'for a long time', *sādaram* 'respectfully', *nānārathám* 'on different chariots', *pradāna-pūrvam* 'accompanied by a gift'. Those compounds which have a preposition as their first member are classed by the grammarians as *avyayībhāva*. Such are *pratyagni* 'towards the fire', *anuṣvadhám* 'by one's own will', *pratidoṣám* 'towards evening', and the like.

Adverbs meaning 'like —' are formed by means of the suffix *-vát* in its nom. acc. sg. nt. form, the accent being on the suffix (as opposed to *bálavat*, etc.): *manuṣvát* 'like Manu', *purāṇavát* 'as of old', etc.

The acc. sg. is occasionally so used in the case of masculine and feminine nouns: *kā́mam* 'at will, if you will', *náktam* 'by night', *vaśam* 'freely, as one wills'. The feminine accusative functions adverbially in certain cases where the suffixes *-tara* and *-tama* are added to adverbs: *uccaistarā́m* 'higher', *śanaistarām* 'more gradually', etc. These suffixes are allowed by the grammarians to be added even to finite verbs—*sīdate-tarām*, etc., thoqgh no trace of such usage appears in the earlier language. From the adverbial accusative there develops a special form of gerund in *-am*: *abhikrā́maṃ juhoti* 'approaching (the fire) he offers', *viparyā́sam avagū́hati* 'he buries it upside down'. These formations are common in the *Brāhmaṇas*, but rare earlier. In the later language only a repeated variety is used: *madhukarāṇāṃ kvaṇitāni śrāvaṃ-śrāvaṃ paribabhrāma* 'constantly hearing the humming of bees he wandered about'.

The adverbial use of the instrumental may be illustrated by such examples as *sáhasā* 'suddenly', *áñjasā* 'suddenly', *diṣṭyā* 'fortunately', *aśeṣeṇa* 'completely', *dakṣiṇena* 'to the south', *śánakais* 'slowly', *uccaís* 'on high', *nīcaís* 'below'. A number of adverbial instrumentals in *-ā* have a locative rather than an instrumental sense: *dívā* 'by day', *doṣā́* 'in the evening', etc. Shift of accent sometimes characterises the form as an adverb: so in *dívā*, *madhyā́* 'in the middle', *dakṣiṇā́* 'to the right'. In the Vedic language there occur adverbs in *-ayā́* such as *naktayā́* 'by night', *ṛtayā́* 'in the right way', *sumnayā́* 'piously', *svapnayā́* 'in a dream'. Avestan has similar formations, *angrayā* 'evilly', *ašaya* 'rightly', etc. These have the appearance of instrumental singulars of feminine *ā*-stems, but no such *ā*-stems occur. Possibly they have developed out of the locative singular with postposition *-ā* of the type O. Pers. *dastayā* 'in the hand'. On the other hand a similar formation appears (also confined to the Vedic language) in connection with stems in *-u* : *raghuyā́* 'quickly', *dhṛṣṇuyā́* 'boldly', etc. ; cf. Av. *āsuya* 'quickly'. A satisfactory explanation to account for both types is difficult to find.

Examples of other cases used adverbially are : dat. (rare) *aparā́ya* 'for the future', *cirā́ya* 'for long', *ahnāya* 'presently'; abl. *paścā́t* 'behind', *sākṣā́t* 'evidently', *sanā́t* 'from of old' (with changed accent), *adharā́t* 'below' ; gen. (rare) *aktós* 'by night', *vástos* 'by day' ; loc. *dūré* 'afar', *ráhasi* 'secretly', *sthāne* 'suitably', *sapadi* 'immediately'.

Miscellaneous Adverbs and Particles. In addition to the adverbs classified above, mention may be made of the following. The particle *evá* 'only' is possibly to be identified with the stem of that form of the word for one which appears in Iranian and Greek (Av. *aēva-*, Gk. *οἶος*), and *evám* 'so' is probably the neut. sg. of the same word. Of the particles of comparison *iva* 'like' appears to be based on the pronominal base *i-* and its formation may be compared with that of the stem *ava-*. In the Vedic language a particle *ná*, homophonous with the negative particle is used in this sense : *gauró ná tṛṣitáḥ piba* 'drink like a thirsty bison', etc. A comparable form elsewhere appears only as an enclitic particle in certain combinations : Av. *yaθanā̆*, *čiθənā*, Lat. *quidne*. This enclitic may be seen also in Skt. *cana* (*káścana* 'anybody').

The negative *ná* is a common IE base : cf. Av. *na-*, O. Sl. *ne*, Lith. *nè*, Lat. *ne-*, Goth. *ni*, etc. As the first member of compounds it appears in a weakened form, *a-* (<*n̥-*), before vowels *an-* ; similarly Av. O. Pers. *a-*, *an-*, Gk. *α-*, *αν-*, Lat. *in-*, Ir. *an-*, Goth. *un-*.

The adverbs *nú*, *nū́*, *nūnám* 'now' belong to a family well represented in Indo-European : Av. *nū*, *nūrəm*, Mod. Pers. *nūn*, Oss. *nur*, O. Sl. *nyně*, Lith. *nù*, Gk. *νύ*, *νύν*, *νῦν*, Lat. *nun-c*, Engl. *now*, etc. The radical element is that which appears in the adjective *náva-* 'new'. Formed directly on the adverb Sanskrit has *nū́tana-*, *nū́tna-* 'new, belonging to the present time'. From a comparison of Greek it appears that the form *nūnám* is to be analysed *nūn-ám*, and that it contains the same strengthening affix which was frequently met with in the pronominal formations. The *n/r* alternation between Skt. *nūnám* and Av. *nūrəm* is of the same origin as that of the nominal formations (cf. Gk. νεαρός : νεᾱνιας, etc.).

The adverb *nā́nā* 'variously' (the Veda has also an extended form *nānānám*) is of unknown derivation.

The conjunction *ca* 'and' (Av. *ča*, Gk. τε, Lat. *que*, Goth. *-h*) is enclitic, as in all the languages. The same applies to *vā* 'or', cf. Lat. *ve*. A non-enclitic in the former sense is *utá* 'and, also' (Av. O. Pers. *uta* 'and').

Of miscellaneous particles of asseveration, etc., mention may be made of *aṅgá* 'verily' *hánta* (expressive of incitement), *kíla* 'forsooth', *khálu* 'indeed', *tú* 'but', *hí* 'for' (Av. *zī*), *gha, ha* 'indeed' (the latter a weakened form of the former; cf. O. Sl. *že*), *vā́í* 'verily', *vā́vá* 'id' (with two accents that have not been explained), *u, áha, sma, bhala*. The particle *sma* used in conjunction with a present tense gives it an imperfect value. In the later language particles are less frequent than in the earlier, and those that remain tend to lose their significance, and serve in poetry simply as devices for filling out the metre.

A few interjections may be merely listed: *ā, hā, ahaha, he, ayi, aye, aho, baṭ, bata, dhik*. Some noun and adjective forms have acquired this function; *re, are* (voc. of *arí-* 'enemy'), *bhos* (for *bhavas*, voc. of *bhavant-* 'your honour'), *kaṣṭam* 'woe is me!', *svasti* 'hail!', *suṣṭhu, sādhu* 'good, excellent!', etc.

Prepositions and Postpositions

In contradistinction to other IE languages Sanskrit has not a developed series of prepositions. Furthermore those adverbial formations which are used to define more closely the case-relationship are normally placed after the noun used in this case, and not before it as in other IE languages. In comparison with the Vedic language later Sanskrit is noticeably poorer in words of this type, so that the distinction between it and the usual type of IE language is partly due to regression. On the other hand the system as it appears in the Vedic language, with freer order and looser connection of such words with the nouns they govern, is clearly more primitive than that found in Greek, Latin, etc., and is closer to the IE beginnings of the development of the prepositional system.

Of the words so used in the Veda the most important class, as elsewhere, consists of those words which are also used as verbal prefixes (see below). The majority of these can be so used, but *ud, ni, parā, pra, ava* and *vi* are exceptions. Their use, mainly postpositional, may be illustrated by a few examples :

áti : *yó devó mártyān áti* ' the god who is beyond mortals '.

ádhi : *pṛthivyā́m ádhy óṣadhīḥ* ' the plants upon the earth '.

ápi : *yā́ apā́m ápi vraté* ' who are in the domain of the waters'.

ánu : *máma cittám ánu cittébhir éta* ' follow after my mind with your minds '.

abhí : *yā́ḥ pradíśo abhí sū́ryo vicáṣṭe* ' what quarters the sun looks abroad to '.

ā́ : *mártyeṣu ā́* ' among mortals '.

upa : *amū́r yā́ úpa sū́rye* ' those who are near the sun '.

pári : *jātó himávatas pári* ' born from the Himalaya '.

práti : *ábodhy agníḥ práty āyatī́m uṣā́sam* ' Agni has been awakened to meet the approaching dawn '.

sám : *te sumatíbhiḥ sám pátnībhir ná vṛ́ṣaṇo nasīmahi* ' may we be united with thy favours as males with their spouses '.

The use of the last one is rare, and in its place the radically related *sahá* commonly appears as a postposition with the instrumental in the earlier and later language. Of the other words listed above the only ones so used in the later language are *ánu, prati* and *ā*. The first two are used as postpositions, the latter as a preposition with the ablative meaning ' up to ', *ā samudrāt* ' up to the ocean '.

In addition a variety of adverbs, both the old inherited type and the newer adverbially used case-forms, are used to define more closely the relation expressed by a case affix or in conjunction with it to express a relation which cannot be expressed by a case-termination alone. Such are :

With accusative : *tirás* ' through ', *antár, antarā́* ' between ', *avareṇa* ' below ', *páreṇa* ' beyond ', *úttareṇa* ' to the north of ', *dakṣiṇena* ' to the south of ', *nikaṣā* ' near ' ; e.g. *yé 'vareṇâdityam, yé pareṇâdityam* ' those who are below the sun, those who are beyond the sun ', *dákṣiṇena védim* ' to the south of the altar ', *nikaṣā Yamunām* ' close to the Jumna '.

With instrumental : Mainly words meaning ' with ', e.g. *saha* (above), *sākám, sārdhám, samám, samáyā, sarátham,* but also *vinā* ' without ' which follows the analogy of the words of contrasting meaning.

The dative is the only case which is not used in conjunction with words of prepositional character. Nevertheless, as noted above, the form of the dative of *a*-stems (*-āya*) can only be explained by the incorporation of what was originally an independent postposition.

With ablative : *bahís* ' outside of ' *purás* ' in front of ', *avás*, *adhás* ' below ', *purā́* ' before ', *parás* ' beyond '. *vinā* ' without ' (also instrumental), *arvā́k* ' this side of ', *paścā́t* ' behind ', *ūrdhvám* ' above ', *ṛté* ' without ', etc.

With genitive : mostly case-forms of nouns or adjectives which take this case by virtue of retaining their nominal character. Such are *agre* ' in front of ', *abhyāśe*, *samīpe* ' near ', *arthe*, *kṛte* ' for the sake of ', *madhye* ' in the midst of '. Words of more purely adverbial character used with the genitive are *upari* ' above ', *parástāt* ' beyond ', *purastāt* ' before ', etc.

With locative : *antár*, *antarā́* ' inside ', *sácā* ' with '.

Verbal Prefixes. A widespread feature of Indo-European is the compounding of verbs with prepositional prefixes. It is normally the same words which appear in use as the common prepositions which are compounded with the verbs. In Sanskrit, it has been noted, the system of prepositions (or postpositions) used in conjunction with nouns is much less developed than in the related languages. On the other hand the use of the same class of words as verbal prefixes is as fully developed in Sanskrit as in the other IE languages.

The common prefixes so used are as follows : *áti* ' across, beyond ' (Av. *aiti*, O. Pers. *atiy* ; Gk. ἔτι ' also, still ', Lat. *et* ' and ' which are used differently), *ádhi* ' above, on, on to ' (Av. *aidī*, *aiδi*, O. Pers. *adiy*) *ánu* ' after, along, towards ' (Av. *anu*, O. Pers. *anuv* ; Gk. ἀνά with variant suffix), *antár* ' within ' (Av. *antarə*, O. Pers. *antar*, Lat. *inter*), *ápa* ' away, from ' (Av. O. Pers. *apa*, Gk. ἄπο, Lat. *ab* ; Hitt. *appa* ' back, behind '), *ápi* ' unto, upon ' (Av. *aipi*, O. Pers. *apiy*, Gk. ἐπί ; in Sanskrit used rarely in this way but mostly as a conjunction ' also ', cf. Gk. ἔτι, Lat. *et* above), *abhí* ' to, towards, against ' (Av. *aiwi*, O. Pers. *abiy*, O. Sl. *obŭ*, *obĭ*, Lat. *ob*), *áva* ' down, off ' (Av. O. Pers. *ava*, O. Pruss. *au-*, O. Sl. *u-*, Lat. *au-*), *ā́* ' to, up to, at ' (Av. O. Pers. *ā*), *úd* ' up, forth, out ' (Av. *us-*, *uz-*, O. Pers. *ud-*, Ir. *ud-*, *od-*, Goth. *ūt* ' out '), *úpa* ' to, toward, near ' (Av. *úpa*, O. Pers. *upā*, Gk. ὑπό, Goth. *uf*), *ní* ' down ' (Av. *ni-*, O. Pers. *niy-*), *nís* ' out, forth ' (Av. *niš-*), *párā* ' forth, away ' (O. Pers. *parā*). *pári* ' around ' (Av. *pairi*, O. Pers. *pariy*, Gk. περί), *prá* ' forward, forth ' (Av. O. Pers. *fra-* O. Sl. *pro*,

Lith. *pra*, Gk. πρό, Lat. *pro-*) ; *práti* ' against, back, in return ' (Gk. πρότι, προτί, προς, O. Sl. *protivŭ*, etc.), *ví* ' apart, asunder, away ' (Av. O. Pers. *vi-* ; cf. Toch. *wi* ' two ', etc., above, p. 260), *sám* ' together, with ' (Av. O. Pers. *ham-*, O. Sl. *sǫ, su*, Lith. *są-, sù*).

These are the regular and normal prefixes. In addition there are a few of more restricted application. In the Veda *ácchā̆* ' to, towards ' is fairly common, but it dies out later. Others occur, in the Veda and later, only in connection with a restricted number of roots : *āvís* ' forth to sight, in view ' (with *bhū*, *as* and *kṛ*), *prādús* ' id ' (with the same roots), *tirás* ' through, across, out of sight ' (with *kṛ, dhā, bhū*) *purás* ' in front ' (with *kṛ, dhā, i* and a few others.

More than one prefix can be combined with a verb (as in Greek, etc.). Combinations of two are common, of three, not unusual, but more than three are very rarely found. There are no particular rules as to the order in which they may appear, but the prefix *ā* is practically never separated from the verb.

All these prefixes were to begin with independent adverbs. In the language of the Veda they partly retain this character and it is only in the later language that they become inseparably combined with the verbal stem. A similar difference is to be observed between Homeric and later Greek, which makes it clear that the development of the full system of verbal composition is largely a parallel development in the various languages.

In the Veda, a prefix most frequently stands immediately before the verb (*ā́ gamat* ' may he come ') but it may be separated from it by another word (*ā́ tvā viśantu* ' may they enter thee ') and it may even follow the verb (*Índro gā́ avṛṇod ápa* ' Indra disclosed the cows '). Whatever its position, in a principal clause the preposition is regularly accented, and the verb, according to the general rule, is unaccented. When two prefixes are used both are accented normally in the RV. (*úpa prá yāhi* ' come forth here ') a fact which emphasises their status as independent words. But besides this there is a system, showing the transition to a closer form of union, according to which the second only of two prefixes is accented when they immediately precede the verb : *áthâśtaṃ vipáretana* ' then scatter ye away to your home '. In subordinate clauses the process of composition has preceded further, the preposition generally appearing compounded, and since the verb in these cases is accented, the prefix is without accent : e.g. *yád . . . niṣī́dathaḥ* ' when ye two sit down '. Even here, however, it may appear separate from the verb and accented (*ví yó mamé rájasī* ' who measured out the two spaces '), while occasionally it is treated as a separate word and accented even when it immediately precedes the verb : *yá ā́hutim pári védā námobhiḥ* ' who fully knows the offering with devotion '.

In the preclassical prose texts the prefix is still to some extent separated from the verb, but on a much more limited scale. By the classical period its independence is totally lost, and except for the few that continue to function as postpositions, the verbal prefixes have ceased to exist as independent words.

In combination with the nominal derivatives of verbal root the verbal prefixes appear fully compounded from the beginning : *adhivāsá-* ' garment ', *ápaciti-* ' retribution ' (Gk. ἀπότισις), *abhidrúh-* ' treacherous ', *avapā́na-* ' drinking place ' ; *udáyana-* ' rising (of the sun) ', *úpaśruti* ' overhearing ', *nidhí-* ' deposit, treasure ', *niráyaṇa-* ' going out ' ; *prabhaṅgín-* ' crushing ', etc. In such cases the general rule is that the prefix loses its accent in favour of the second member of the compound but in some cases it is regularly accented, namely (1) in combination with the past passive participle, *páreta-* ' gone forth ', *antárhita-* ' concealed ', *ávapanna-* ' fallen down ', etc. ; (2) with the verbal action nouns in *-ti*, *ápaciti*, etc. In both these cases there is agreement in the matter of accent between Sanskrit and Greek (ἀπόβλητος, ἀνάβλησις, etc.) ; (3) with the infinitival forms based on the *tu*-suffix : *sáṃhartum* ' to collect ', *ápidhātave* ' to cover up ' ; *ávagantos* ' of descending '.

CHAPTER VII

THE VERB

§ 1. The Verbal Root

The roots of the Sanskrit language as enumerated by the Hindu grammarians comprise a list of some two thousand. Something like half of these are not attested in actual use, and since it is unlikely that many of them will ever turn up they may for all practical purposes be neglected. Of the rest a considerable number may be dismissed as being either reduplications (*dīdhī-*), stem forms (*ūrṇu-*), denominatives (*arth-*, etc.) or in some other respect not primitive. When allowance is made for these there remain somewhat over eight hundred roots, which form the basis not only of the verbal system, but also the larger part of the inherited nominal stems of the language.

Chiefly owing to its antiquity the Sanskrit language is more readily analysable, and its roots more easily separable from accretionary elements than is the case with any other IE language. This is because the suffixes with which the present and aorist stems are formed, are normally kept out of the other forms of the finite verb, and from nominal derivatives : *sunóti* ' presses out ' : perf. *suṣā́va, suṣumá*, fut. *sóṣyati*, part. pass. *sutá-*. Nevertheless even Sanskrit is not wanting in cases where suffixes whose primary function is the formation of the present stem, have become permanently attached to the root, and consequently appear throughout the conjugation of the verb. For instance from the present *pṛccháti* ' asks ', formed with the IE suffix *-sk̑e-* an extended root *pṛch-/prach-* is made which appears in the perf. *paprā́ccha* and elsewhere. Similarly Latin has *poscō, poposcī* (<*pṛk̑sk̑ō*). The simpler form of the root appears in Lat. *precem* (acc. sg.), *procus* and in Skt. *praśná-* ' question '. The root *kṣṇu-* ' to sharpen ' contains the *nu*-suffix which elsewhere forms the fifth present class. From a number of presents in which this suffix enlarged by the thematic vowel appears, extended root forms ending in *-nv* develop : *pinv-* ' to fatten ', pres. *pínvati*, perf. 2 du. *pipinváthus* (beside simple root *pi-*

in *páyate*, etc.). Similar extended roots are *inv-* 'to send' (: *i-*) and *jinv-* 'to quicken' (: *ji-*). From present stems in *-va* a number of roots ending in *-v* are created: *jīv-* 'to live', pres. *jī́vati* (: simple root in *gáya-* 'livelihood, belongings'), *dhūrv-* 'to injure' (: *dhvṛ-*), *tūrv-* 'to overcome' (: *tṝ-*) and *bharv-* 'to chew' for which no simpler form exists.

Accretions of this type are of comparatively recent origin, and it is quite clear how they have arisen from particular stem forms that are current in the verbal conjugation. Besides them there exists another class of extended roots, of much more ancient date, containing accretions whose functions it is for the most part no longer possible to discern. These elements are fairly easily recognisable, either through the coexistence of a simpler form of the root, or by the existence of synonymous roots which differ only in the final element. They are identical with the individual suffixes which have been enumerated in treating of the formation of nouns, and may conveniently be enumerated in the same order:

-ar/ṛ: *dhar-* (*dhṛ-*) 'to hold' (i.e. *dh-ar-*, cf. *dhā-*), *svar-* 'to sound' (: cf. *svan-* 'id' with alternating *-n*).

-an: *kṣan-* 'to wound' (: *śas-* 'to cut': Gk. κτείνω for **kstenvō* has compound suffix *-ten-* alternating with *-ter-* in κτέρες· νεκροί), *svan-* 'to sound' (see above), *khan-* 'to dig' (i.e. *k*H*-an-*: cf. *khā-* without *n*-suffix, likewise *ākhú-* 'mole' and *ākhará-* masc. 'hole' with alternating *r*).

-as/s: *tras-* 'to fear', Gk. τρέω (: Lat. *tremō*), *bhyas-* 'to fear' (: *bhī-* 'id'), *gras-* 'to devour' (*gṝ-* 'to swallow'), *dhvas-* 'to scatter' (*dhū-* 'to shake'), *śruṣ-* 'to hear', O. Sl. *slyšati*, Toch. *klyos-*, etc. (: normally *śru-* 'id', Gk. κλυ-, etc.), *akṣ-*, *nakṣ-* 'to attain' (: *aś-*, *naś-* 'id'), *uks-* 'to sprinkle' (: Gk. ὑγρός 'wet', etc.), *nikṣ-* 'to pierce' (: O. Sl. *vŭ-nizą* 'id'), *bhakṣ-* 'to partake of, eat' (: *bhaj-* 'to divide, share'), *mikṣ-* 'to mix' (: *miśrá-* 'mixed'), *mṛkṣ-* 'to rub' (: *mṛj-* 'wipe', Gk. ὀμόργνῡμι, etc.), *rakṣ-* 'to protect', Gk. ἀλέξω 'to ward off' (: Gk. ἀλαλκεῖν 'id', AS. *ealgian* 'to protect'); *vakṣ-* 'to increase', Gk. ἀέξω (: Lat. *augeō* 'id', etc.,) *hās-* 'to go forth' (: *hā-* 'id'). In contrast with most of the extensions the suffix *s* plays a considerable part in the conjugation of the verb, and this no doubt accounts for the comparative frequency of such forms.

-am: *dram-* 'to run', Gk. ἔδραμον (: *drā-*, Gk. διδράσκω; *dru-* 'id'), *gam-* 'to go', Goth. *qiman*, etc. (: *gā-* 'id', Gk. ἔβᾱ;

Gk. *βαίνω*, Lat. *veniō* from *gʷ-en-*), *kṣam-* 'to endure', by metathesis for **zgham-*, cf. *Paštō zγaməl* 'id' (: *sagh-* 'to be equal to, endure'), *bhram-* 'to revolve, wander' (: *bhur-* 'to be in uneasy motion'.).

-*i*: *jri-*, *jráyati*, 'to move', *jrayasānā́-* 'extending': *jar-* 'to move', Ir. *zar-* 'id'; *kṣi-*, *kṣáyati* 'to rule', as opposed to *kṣatrá-* 'sovereignty' and Gk. *κτάομαι* 'possess'; *śri-*, *śráyati* 'to lean', Gk. *κλίνω*, etc. (:Lith. *atsikal̃ti* 'to lean against', Russ. *klon* 'inclination', etc.). Alternative forms of root appear in the conjugation of *śvi-*, *śū-* 'to swell', *si* (<sHi-), *sā-* 'to bind', and *śi-*, *sā-* 'to sharpen'. It has not in these cases become completely incorporated, but it shows a tendency in the direction.

-*u*: *śru-* 'to hear': the unextended form of the root appears in the Skt. present, *śṛ-ṇó-ti*; elsewhere the *u/o*, which appears as part of the suffixal complex in this form, is permanently attached to the root. Other examples are *dru-* 'to run' (: *dram-*, *drā-* above) and *sru-* 'to flow' (*sar-* 'to move, flow', cf. *sarít-* 'river').

-*a*H/H: *gā-* 'to go' (: *gam-* above), *yā-* 'to go' (: *i-* 'id'), *psā-* 'to devour', Gk. *ψώω* 'chew' (: *bhas-* 'to devour'), *drā-* 'to run' (: *dram-*, etc.), *mnā-* 'to note' (: *man-* 'to think'), *trā-* 'to rescue' (: *tṝ-* 'to cross'), *pyā-* 'to swell (udder)' (: *pi-* 'id'), *pī-* (*pīy-*) 'to abuse' (i.e. *pi*-H-: *piś-* in *píśuna-* 'malicious, tale-bearing', Gk. *πικρός*, etc.). A series of roots belonging to the ninth class contain this enlargement. The simple form of the root appears in the present tense, where the *a*H/H suffix is separated from it by the intervening *n*-suffix with which it is combined: e.g. *pṛṇā́ti* 'fills' for *pl̥-n-é*H-*ti* as opposed to *pūrṇá-* 'full' for *pl̥*-H-*nó-*. Similar cases are *jū-* 'to be swift' (*junā́ti*, *jūtá-*), *pū-* 'to purify' (*punā́ti*, *pūtá-*), *stṝ-* 'to strew' (*stṛṇā́ti*, *stīrṇá-*) and so on. The enlargement tends to be introduced into the present tense, so that from *mī-* 'to damage' for instance there appear both *minā́ti* and *mīnā́ti*. In some cases the root appears only with the enlargement in the present tense, e.g. *bhrīṇā́ti*, Av. *brīnənti* 'cut' and *krīṇā́ti* 'buys' though in the latter case the metre of the *Ṛgveda* indicates a pronunciation *krĭṇā́ti*.

-*t*: *kṛt-* 'to cut' (: Gk. *κείρω*), *cit-* 'to perceive' (*ci-* 'id'); in combination with *i*, *mrit-* 'to fall in pieces' (*mṝ-* 'to crush', *mṛd-* 'id'), *śvit-* 'to be bright' (: *śuc-* 'to gleam', *śubh-*

'to be bright'), with *u*, *dyut-* 'to shine' (*di-* in *dína-* 'day', etc.).

-th (i.e. *t*-H-): *prath-* 'to extend' (: Hitt. *palḫiš* 'wide', Lat. *plānus*, etc.), *vyath-* 'to be unsteady' (*vij-* 'to tremble', *vip-* 'id'), *śnath-* 'to pierce' (: simple root in *śiśná-* 'organ of generation', cf. Gk. *κεντέω* 'pierce' with guṇa of root and simple *t*-suffix); similarly *śrath-* 'to loosen', *grath-* 'to tie', *mith-* 'to alternate' (*mi-* 'to exchange').

-d: *kṣad-* 'to divide' (: *śas-* 'to cut', cf. *kṣan-* above), *chid-* 'to cut', Lat. *scindo*, etc. (: cf. *chā-*, *chi-* 'id'), *rud-* 'to weep', Lat. *rudo*, AS. *rēotan*, etc. (: *ru-* 'to cry', O. Sl. *rjuvǫ*, etc.), *mṛd-* 'to rub, crush' (: *mṝ-* 'to crush'), *pīḍ-* 'to press' (<**piẓḍ-* : *piṣ* 'to crush'); in combination with *n*, *syand-* 'to flow' (: *sic-* 'to pour', Toch. *sik-*, etc.), *krand-*, *kland-* 'to cry out', cf. Gk. *κέλαδος* 'cry, shout' (: Gk. *καλέω* 'call', etc.).

-dh: *mṛdh-* 'to neglect, be careless', cf. Gk. *μαλθακός* 'soft', etc. (: Gk. *ἀμαλός* 'soft', etc.), *edh-* 'to prosper', cf. Av. *azdya-* 'thriving, fatness', Gk. *ἐσθλός* 'good' (: IE *es-* in Gk. *ἐύς* 'good', Hitt. *aššu-*, Skt. *su-*), *spṛdh-* 'to contend', Av. *sparəd-*, cf. Goth. *spaúrds* 'race-course' (: *spṛ-* 'to win', *spṛh-* 'to be eager', Gk. *σπέρχομαι*, etc.); combined with *u*-suffix, *kṣudh-* 'to be hungry' (: Hitt. *kašt-*, Toch A. *kašt*, B. *kest*, with guṇa of root and dental suffix whose exact nature cannot be specified).

-p: *dīp-* 'to shine' (: cf. *di-*, *dyut-* above), *mlup-* '(sun) to set' (: *mruc-*, *mluc-* 'id'), *rip-*, *lip-* 'to smear' (: *lī-* 'to cleave to', Lat. *lino*, etc.), *rup-*, 'to break', Lat. *rumpo* (: *ru-* 'to break', Lat. *ruo*; *ruj-* 'to break'), *vip-* 'to tremble' (: cf. *vyath-*, *vij-* above), *svap-* 'to sleep', AS. *swefan* (: Gk. *εὕδω* 'id' <*seu-d*).

-bh: *śubh-* 'to be bright' (: *śuc-* 'to gleam', etc., above) *stubh-* 'to praise' (: *stu-* 'id').

-c: *mluc-* 'to set' (: *mlup-*), *yāc-* 'to ask' (: Av. *yās-* with different enlargement), *ruc-* 'to shine' (*rúśant* 'bright'), *sic-* 'to pour' (: *syand-* above).

-j: *tarj-* 'to threaten' (cf. *tras-*, etc., above, Lat. *terreo*), *yuj-* 'to join' (: *yu-* 'id'), *ruj-* 'to break', *vij-* 'to tremble' (*rup*, *vip-*).

-h: *spṛh-* 'to be eager' (: *spṛdh-*, etc., above), *druh-* 'to injure' (: *dhru-* 'id').

The identity of these elements with the suffixes enumerated

in dealing with the formation of nouns is evident, and it is in accordance with the fact that nominal and verbal stems are formed fundamentally on the same principles. The enlargements of the verbal roots are simply incorporated suffixes, and do not require, as is sometimes considered, a separate morphological classification. All the IE consonants and semivowels can appear in this function, just as they can in the formation of nouns. In the latter case those so used with any frequency are, as has been seen, necessarily limited in number. In the case of the enlargements the distribution is more even, and with the exception of *s* and H, which had a considerable part to play in the IE conjugation, the common nominal suffixes do not appear correspondingly frequently as enlargements. The suffixes *n* and *r*, for instance, which are of very great importance in nominal stem formation, appear only rarely as enlargements. This would suggest that, on the whole, the enlargements of the verbal root reflect a comparatively early stage of IE stem-formation, that is to say a period when the emphasis on a comparatively few suffixes out of the large number available had not developed to the extent with which we are familiar later. It is also clear that the growing clarity of the distinction between verb and noun, which evolved in the later pre-history of Indo-European, tended to prevent the incorporation of such suffixes (e.g. *r* and *n*) which were felt as predominantly nominal.

In their guṇa grade such roots may appear in two forms, on the one hand that which appears in *cet-* ' perceive ', *sec-* ' pour ', *rod-* ' weep ', etc., and on the other hand that which is seen in *tras-* ' fear ', *kṣad-* ' divide ', *śro-* ' hear ', etc. That is to say, either the root or the enlargement may have the guṇa, but, in accordance with the principles of IE apophony, it is not possible that both should have it. The difference between the two types of guṇa form is without any significance as far as the meaning of the roots is concerned, or their conjugation. It is only in connection with nominal stems that this kind of distinction is significant. There it provides the distinction between neuter action nouns and adjectives or agent-nouns. Since these roots were originally stems, and in the early period, when noun and verb were less clearly distinguished, as much nominal as verbal, it is reasonable to assume that the distinction in form between the two types of extended root, was originally the same as that which is fundamental in the formation of nouns.

That is to say a root form **trés-* (Skt. *trásati*) would originally be a nominal stem meaning ' fearing, one who fears ', and the alternative form **térs-* (Lat. *terreo*) would be a stem meaning ' fear '.

In these cases when the ultimate root has been reached by analysis it is seen never to consist of more than two consonants and the guṇa vowel (*ter-*, etc.), or if the root begins with a vowel, of this vowel and a following consonant (*ed-*, *es-*). The number of roots which can be so reduced is sufficiently great to justify the extension of this principle to other roots of three consonants, even where shorter or variant forms are not preserved. There is little reason to doubt that the third consonant of all roots which have it is to be regarded as an incorporated suffix.

§2. System of the Finite Verb

Voice. The Sanskrit verb contains two voices, Active and Middle, which are distinguished by means of two sets of personal terminations throughout the conjugation. The difference in meaning between the two is expressed by the names given to them by the Sanskrit grammarians, *parasmai padam* ' a word for another ' and *ātmane padam* ' a word for oneself '. The middle is used when the subject is in some way or other specially implicated in the result of the action ; when this is not so the active is used. For instance *kaṭam karoti* ' he makes a mat ' would be used of the workman employed in the trade of mat-making who makes a mat for another, while the middle *kaṭam kurute* would be used of one who makes a mat for his own use. The same distinction is seen between *pacati* ' (the cook) cooks ' and *pacate* ' he cooks (a meal for himself) ' and between *yajati* ' (the priest) sacrifices (on behalf of another) ' and *yajate* ' (the householder) sacrifices (on behalf of himself) '. Again the special sense of the middle is seen in those cases where the direct object of the verb is a member of one's own body : *nakhāni nikṛntate* ' he cuts his nails ', *dato dhāvate* ' he cleans his teeth '. In another class of roots there appears a distinction of a different nature, that between transitive (active) and intransitive (middle) : *dṛṃhati* ' makes firm ', *dṛṃhate* ' becomes firm ', *vardhati* ' increases, makes bigger ', *vardhate* ' increases (intr.), becomes bigger ', *vahati* ' (chariot) carries (man) ', *vahate* ' (man) rides (in chariot) '. From this the development is not far to the distinction between active and passive, and the use of the middle to express a passive sense becomes common in the perfect and the future, which possess no other means of expressing the passive. One sense that the middle does not normally express is that of a direct reflexive, which is expressed by means of the accusative *ātmānam* ' self '. Not all verbs are capable of appearing in both voices. Some are used only in the active, e.g. *ad-* ' to eat ', *as-* ' to be ', *kṣudh-* ' to be hungry ', *bhuj-* ' to bend ', *sarp-* ' to creep ', etc. ; others only in the middle, e.g., *ās-* ' to sit ', *kṣam-* ' to endure ', *labh-* ' to receive ', *vas-* ' to wear (clothes) ', *sac-* ' to accompany '. Occasionally a different voice appears in different tenses of the same verb, the most usual alternation being that of active perfect and middle present: *vartate* : *vavarta*.

The distinction between active and middle is inherited from Indo-European (cf. the equation *sácate*, Gk. *ἕπεται*, Lat. *sequitur*), and outside Indo-Iranian the language which shows the greatest similarity to Sanskrit in form and usage is Greek. In later Indo-Aryan the distinction dies out, and this is reflected in the Epic and other less correct forms of Sanskrit.

Tense. The Sanskrit verb has four tense stems: Present, Future, Aorist and Perfect. The present stem forms the basis of a preterite, the so-called Imperfect, in addition to the present tense. In the same way there is formed a preterite of the future which functions as a conditional. In the Vedic language a form of preterite is formed on the basis of the perfect stem. These pluperfect forms are rare even in the earlier language, and disappear later. The aorist stem forms only a preterite.

The clearest division to be found in this somewhat complicated system is that between the perfect on the one hand and the other three systems on the other. The perfect is distinguished from the other tenses not only in stem-formation, but also in the fact that it possesses a special series of personal endings. Between the perfect and the rest of the conjugation we have clearly the most ancient and fundamental division in the Indo-European system. On the other hand when we examine the future and the aorist in their relation to the present system it is clear that they are in origin only special modifications of the same type of formation. The future for instance is only one subdivision of the class of present stems in *ya* in which are included the verbs of the fourth class and the various types of denominative. The close relation between the aorist and present systems is seen by the fact that certain types of aorist stem are identical in form with certain types of present stem. This is so with the root aorist (*ákar*, etc.) which is formed like the imperfect of the root class (*áhan*, etc.), and the *a*-aorist (*áruhat*, etc.) which resembles the imperfect of the sixth class (*átudat*, etc.). The aorist or imperfect character of these two types of formation is determined not by the form itself but by the existence or non-existence of a present from the same stem. In other cases there is evidence for the one time existence of presents from those forms of stem which in Sanskrit are used exclusively as aorists. Thus corresponding to the reduplicated aorist *ájījanat*, Avestan has a present *zīzanənti* ' they give birth '. Even in the case of the *s*-aorist, which is most clearly marked off from the present system, the existence of presents like Av. *nāismi* ' I insult ' demonstrates that such formations were not always exclusively aoristic.

The relation of the present-imperfect on the one hand, and the aorist on the other, can be discussed only in view of the meaning of the three tenses. In Sanskrit this is not at all complicated. The present indicates simply present time, and the imperfect past time in contradistinction to this, no more and no less: *hánti* ' he slays ', *áhan* ' he slew ', etc. There exists no trace of an ' imperfect ' sense in the Sanskrit tense of that name, and such a sense, if it is needed, is expressed by the present tense with the addition of the particle *sma*. The aorist in contradistinction to the imperfect expresses a special kind of past time, inasmuch as it is used for describing an action which has just recently been completed: *úd asaú sū́ryo agāt* ' yonder sun has risen ', etc.

This clear distinction of meaning between the aorist and present stem is found only in the case of the indicative, in these two kinds of preterite. There exist also various moods—injunctive, subjunctive, imperative and optative—and also participles, active and middle, which may be formed alternatively from the present or aorist stems. But in all these latter types of formation no serious distinction of meaning can be found in the Vedic language between those formed from the present and those formed from the aorist stem, e.g. *kárat* subj. ' he will do ' does not differ in any demonstrable sense from *kṛṇávat* ' id ' from the present stem.

The absence of distinction of meaning in all these types of formation between the present and aorist stem, in contradistinction to the clear distinction between the two types of preterite, points to the conclusion that it was specifically in these preterite forms that the aorist developed as a special grammatical category. It appears that originally Indo-European distinguished in the indicative simply between present and preterite, the forms of which could be made from a wide variety of stems. This state of affairs is continued in Hittite, which shows no sign of ever having had a tense corresponding to the aorist of other languages. The next stage of development is the evolution of a double set of preterite forms, one with a corresponding present (imperfect) and one detached from the present tense (aorist) and having a special sense. This stage is represented in Indo-Iranian. In Greek the distinction between the present and aorist systems is carried further, and applied to moods, participles and infinitives derived from the two stems. The two stems in all formations express different modes of action, namely punctual (aorist) and durative (present). Consequently the preterite of the present acquires an 'imperfect' sense which is absent from it in Hittite and in the corresponding formations in Sanskrit.

The perfect is independent in formation from the present/aorist system, and is also characterised by the possession of a special series of personal endings. It appears to be one of the more ancient IE verbal formations, and to bear some relation to the conjugation of the Hittite verbs in *-ḫi*. In that language there are two conjugations of verbs, one making the 1st person singular in *-mi* (like Skt. *ásmi*, etc.) and the other in *-ḫi*. The relation between the two is not at all that which exists between the present and perfect in other IE languages, but the endings of the *-ḫi* conjugation are comparable in some ways to the perfect endings of Sanskrit, Greek, etc., so that while the detailed relation of the two formations remains obscure, there is general agreement that some definite connection exists between them.

The fundamental meaning of the perfect, as it emerges from a comparison of Sanskrit and Greek, and is confirmed by the evidence of the other IE languages, is that of state as opposed to process which is expressed by the present: e.g. *bibhāya* 'he is afraid' as opposed to *bhayate* 'he becomes afraid'; *ciketa* 'he is aware of, knows': *cetati* 'he becomes aware of, notices';

tasthau 'stands' (permanently): *tiṣṭhati* 'takes his stand', etc. Closely related is the meaning of continuous action seen in such examples as: *ná śrāmyanti ná ví muñcanti éte váyo ná paptuḥ* 'They do not become weary or stop, they fly (continually) like birds'. The perfect is thus in origin a special kind of present tense, not a preterite form, and in such cases it is normally to be translated by the English present. Its development to a preterite takes place in two stages, both of which are represented in the Vedic language. The first stage is the development of a sense which is rendered in translation by the English perfect. Since a state is normally the result of a preceding process, it was natural that the perfect should be used to express the fact that such an action had already taken place. As examples of this use we may quote: *yát sīm ā́gaś cakṛmā́ tát sú mṛḷatu* 'whatever sin we have committed, let him forgive that', and *yáthā jaghántha dhṛṣatā́ purā́ cid evā́ jahi śátrum asmā́kam indra* 'as thou hast boldly slain (enemies) in the past, so slay our foe now, O Indra'. The difference in meaning between this use of the perfect and the aorist remains clear, because the aorist is confined to those actions which have taken place in the immediate past, while the perfect indicates completion of the action regardless of the precise time. The final step takes place when the preterital sense acquired by the perfect in contexts like these becomes the predominant sense, with the result that the perfect becomes a tense of narrative with a meaning that does not differ materially from that of the imperfect. The last usage has already become quite common in the *Ṛgveda*: *áhan áhim ánv apás tatarda*, '(Indra) slew the dragon, he penetrated to the waters'. The same usage has developed widely in other sections of Indo-European, notably in Italic, Celtic and Germanic.

The pluperfect, the augmented preterite of the perfect, is rare even in the *Ṛgveda*, and it quickly dies out. It appears to have no specific meaning proper to itself, being used as a rule in sense of the imperfect (narrative), occasionally in that of the aorist.

Mood. Five moods are enumerated in Sanskrit grammar, the Injunctive, the Imperative, the Subjunctive, the Optative and the Precative. In the older language modal forms may be made from all three types of stem, present, aorist and perfect, without any apparent difference of meaning. In the classical language injunctive forms are confined to the aorist stem, imperative and optative forms to the present stem, while the subjunctive, except for such forms of it as are incorporated in the imperative, dies out. The precative is in the later language connected with the root aorist in the active and with the *iṣ*-aorist in the middle. Earlier, while confined to the aorist it appears associated with a greater number of forms.

Injunctive. The so-called injunctive is not strictly speaking a separate morphological category at all. In form the injunctives are unaugmented aorists and imperfects: *dhāt, vṛṇak*, etc., but forms of this nature may also be used as simple preterites of the indicative, in the same way as the augmented forms. Comparative study of the languages makes it clear that the augment was originally an optional prefix in the formation of these preterites, and that the unaugmented forms are the most ancient. The fact that these forms can also be used in an 'injunctive' sense, that is to say as futures, imperatives and in the expression of a wish, takes us back to an extraordinarily primitive state of the language when owing to the undeveloped nature of the verbal system one form had perforce to serve in many meanings.

The three main meanings of the injunctive may be briefly illustrated by a few examples: (1) as future: *kó no mahyā́ áditaye púnar dāt* 'who will give us back to the great Aditi', *índrasya nú vīryā̀ṇi prá vocam* 'I will now proclaim the manly deeds of Indra'; (2) as imperative: *gárbham ā́ dhāḥ* 'deposit the embryo', *pári tveṣásya durmatír mahī́ gāt* 'let the great malevolence of the impetuous one avoid us'. Where special forms of the imperative do not exist, in the 2nd person plural, etc., the injunctive remains the only way of expressing the imperative, and such forms are incorporated into the imperative system. The injunctive is used exclusively with *mā́* to express prohibitions: *mā́ gāḥ* 'do not go', etc. This construction remains in the classical language where it is the only type of injunctive (except for those forms incorporated in the imperative) which continues to exist; (3) in the expression of a wish: *agním hinvantu no dhíyas téna jeṣma dhánam-dhanam* 'let our prayers urge Agni; may we continually win wealth through him'.

Imperative. The imperative possesses distinct forms only in a certain number of persons and numbers, namely in the 2. 3.

singular and 3. plural. Of these the forms of the 3. sing. and plur. have originally evolved from injunctive forms by the addition to such forms of a particle *-u* : *váhatu* from *vahat + u*. The forms of the 2. 3. dual and 2. plural are unaltered injunctive forms. The forms of the first person in the later language are subjunctives which have been incorporated in the imperative system ; they do not belong to this system in the earlier language. The imperative expresses commands just as the injunctive may do, but it is not used in the other senses which the injunctive has. It is also used more commonly in this sense than the injunctive.

Subjunctive. Morphologically the subjunctive arises by the evolution of a particular kind of injunctive. It is natural therefore that its sphere of meaning should correspond in general to that of the injunctive. Like the injunctive the subjunctive may be used (1) simply in a future sense : *prá nú vocā sutéṣu vām* 'I will now praise you two at the libations', *uvā́sa uṣā́ ucchā́c ca nú* 'Dawn has shone forth (in the past) and she will shine forth now' ; (2) equivalent to an imperative : *ā́ vām vahantu . . . áśvāḥ, pibātho asmé mádhūni* 'let your horses bring you here and drink ye draughts of mead with us' ; (3) in the expression of a wish : *pári ṇo héḷo váruṇasya vṛjyāḥ, urúṃ na índraḥ kṛṇavad u lokám* 'may the wrath of Varuna avoid us, may Indra procure for us a wide space'. While the sphere of the subjunctive coincides with that of the injunctive, there is a difference of emphasis inasmuch as the future meaning is much more prominent in the case of the subjunctive. The subjunctive is, in fact, the normal means of expressing the future in the Vedic language. There are also certain important syntactical differences between the use of the two moods. The injunctive for instance is alone used to express prohibitions in connection with *mā́*. Another important difference is that the injunctive is rarely used in subordinate clauses (relative, conditional, etc.). On the other hand the use of the subjunctive is very widely developed in this connection, and even more distinctively so in the related languages, whence the name of the mood.

Optative. The optative differs from the moods so far described in that it is formed on the basis of a special stem formed by the suffix *yā/ī*. Its original meaning appears to have been the expression of a wish (from which its name is derived) and this meaning is well preserved in Sanskrit : *vayám syāma pátayo rayīṇā́m* 'may we be lords of riches'. From this there arises a potential meaning (the mood is sometimes so called) which from the testimony of the various languages was already well established in the Indo-European period : *yád agne syā́m ahám tvám, tvám vā ghā syā́ ahám, syúṣ ṭe satyā́ ihāśíṣaḥ,* 'if, Agni, I were you or you were me, then your prayers would come true'. A usage widely developed in Sanskrit is that of the prescriptive optative, which appears largely in law books and similar texts : *sāṃvatsarikam āptaiś ca rāṣṭrād āhārayed balim,* 'he should have the annual tax collected from the kingdom by suitable officials'.

Precative. The precative is formed on the basis of the optative stem by the addition of *s* to the optative suffix, producing the combination *yās/īṣ*. Its use is in all cases confined to the expression of a wish : *bhágo me agne sakhyé ná mṛdhyāḥ* 'may my good fortune, O Agni, not relax in (thy) friendship'; *yó no dvéṣṭi ádharaḥ sás padīṣṭa* 'may he who hates us fall down'.

§ 3. The Verbal Stem

The foregoing analysis of the root shows how from the earliest period the verb could be built optionally on the root itself, or the root already provided with suffixes. These suffixes are in all cases identifiable with the corresponding suffixes which appear in the formation of nouns. In these formations of the oldest type the suffixes are completely incorporated and new, fuller roots are created. Besides these suffixes there exists a series used only to form the present stem but excluded from the other verbal formations. These are likewise identifiable with corresponding nominal suffixes, e.g. *dhṛṣṇó/u* of the fifth class, from *dhṛṣ-* 'to be bold', with the adjectival stem *dhṛṣṇú-* 'bold'. The general structure of nominal and verbal stems runs closely parallel. Both may be based either on the simple root or on the root provided with suffix. The suffixes may be simple or compound and the compound suffixes arise always by the addition of one suffix to another. The formations are divided into non-thematic and thematic classes, the latter in both cases progressively increasing in importance. Verbal stems may be accented on the root or the suffix, e.g. in the case of non-thematic stems *vámiti, jéṣma* as opposed to *śṛṇóti, pṛṇā́ti,* and in the case of thematic stems, *bhávati* as opposed to *tudáti.* The fact that such accentual difference corresponds to no difference of meaning in the verbal system, but clearly does so in the nominal system, may be held to indicate that these stems are primarily nominal in origin.

In the classical language the present stem of a verb is normally made according to one only of the ten different types. In the Vedic language greater latitude is observable. While in general the distribution of the roots among the ten present classes corresponds to that of the later language, a large number of roots is found which form their present tense according to two, three, or even more different types. Such cases are illustrated by *kṛṣ-* 'to plough', I *karṣati*, VI *kṛṣáti*; *jṝ-* 'to grow old', I *járati*, IV *jīryati*; *dā-* 'to divide', II *dā́ti*, IV *dyáti*; *dhū-* 'to shake', V *dhunóti*, VI *dhuváti*; *pṝ-* 'to fill', III *pipárti*, IX *pṛṇā́ti*; *bhī-* 'to fear', I *bháyate*, III *bibhéti*; *ṛdh-* 'to prosper', IV *ṛ́dhyati*, V *ṛdhnóti*, VII subj. *ṛṇádhat*; *tṝ-* 'to cross, overcome', I *tarati*, III ptc. *titrat-*, VI *tiráti*, VIII *tarute*. To a large extent this variation of stem is not associated with any difference of meaning, but sometimes the difference between transitive and intransitive is connected with the use of alternative stems; *jávate* 'hastens, is quick', *junā́ti* 'speeds, urges on', *tápati* 'heats', *tápyati* 'becomes hot', *pácati* 'cooks, ripens (trans.)', *pácyate* 'becomes ripe'. In particular an intransitive sense tends to be associated with stems of the fourth class.

It is clear from the comparative study of the IE languages that this variability of stem formation was even greater in the prehistoric period. Avestan shows in some respects even greater variety than the language of the Veda. Furthermore the discrepancies in stem formation between the various IE languages (Skt. *riṇákti*: Gk. λείπω, etc., etc.) shows that in the earlier IE period the greatest freedom prevailed in the formation of present stems. In all this variety of stem formations no inherent difference of meaning was attached to the various types, just as in Sanskrit the ten present classes are equivalent in function. At the same time there arose early in Indo-European a tendency for certain of these formations to acquire a special meaning and function. The suffix *-sco-* for instance acquired an inchoative meaning which is represented in a variety of languages. In Hittite formations in *-nu-* (corresponding to the Skt. fifth class) acquired a special function as causatives, a development which is not shown by the other languages. In Sanskrit those present formations which acquired a special meaning became the foundation of what is called secondary conjugation, namely causatives with stems in *-áya*, desideratives with reduplicated stems in *sa,* intensives with strong reduplication and radical stem or stem in *ya*. These were originally conjugated in the present system only and it is a special development of Sanskrit which allows them to be inflected in other parts of the verbal system. With these must be classified the passive which is a special development of the fourth class and which arises from a tendency of stems of that class to specialise as intransitives.

§ 4. Accent and Apophony of Verbal Stems

By a rule peculiar to Sanskrit, the like of which is not traceable in other IE languages, the verb is unaccented in an independent clause, except at the beginning of such a clause and under certain special conditions; it retains its accent in dependent clauses. When accented the verbal stem has an unchangeable accent in the case of thematic formations, which in this respect agree entirely with the nominal thematic formations. In the non-thematic formations the accent varies between stem and personal ending, and this variation corresponds to a variation between the guṇa (occasionally vṛddhi) grade of the stem and the zero grade. The general rule is that in the indicative the stem has the accent and the guṇa grade in the three persons of the singular active, and that in the dual and plural of the active and in the whole of the middle the accent is on the termination and the stem appears in its weak form: *dvéṣṭi* 'hates', 3 pl. *dviṣánti*, 3 sg. mid. *dviṣṭé*, *yunákti* 'joins', 3 pl. *yuñjánti*, 3 sg. mid. *yuṅkté*. Exceptions to the rule (e.g. in the *s*-aorist) are comparatively rare. This old IE system appears also in other languages (e.g. Gk. εἶμι ἴμεν), though nowhere so clearly and consistently as in Sanskrit.

§ 5. Augment and Reduplication

In addition to a large variety of suffixation Indo-European made use of two types of prefixation in the formation of tense stems, Augment and Reduplication.

The augment (IE *e-*, Skt. *a-*) is prefixed to the various preterites (imperfect, aorist, pluperfect, conditional) to indicate past time. It is found in Indo-Iranian (Skt. *ábharat*), Greek (ἔφερε), Armenian (*eber*), and Phrygian (ἐδαες 'constructed'), but it is absent in the rest of Indo-European. It is thus an important feature in connection with the dialectal divisions of Indo-European, since it is clearly of late origin, and has established itself over only part of the IE linguistic area, among dialects which for other reasons also may be held to have been contiguous. Even where it established itself it existed originally only as an optional formation, augmented and unaugmented forms being optionally used. The unaugmented forms were of course alone used in an injunctive sense, but they could be also used as preterites just like the augmented forms. The coexistence of augmented and unaugmented preterites is a characteristic both of the earliest Greek and the earliest Sanskrit. It is only in the later stage of both languages that the augment ceases to be optional and becomes obligatory. In Iranian the augment is regularly used in Old Persian, but only rarely in Avestan, where the unaugmented type of preterite has mainly prevailed. In the early stage of Middle Indo-Aryan, which still preserves an old preterite made up of imperfect and aorist forms, the old Vedic freedom of usage is maintained, but the unaugmented instead of the augmented forms become the most common.

The augment seems in origin to have been a separate word, namely a particle *é* meaning 'there, then' which came to be compounded with the verb. It invariably bears the acute accent whenever the verb is accented. When the verb is compounded with a preposition, it always appears between the preposition and the verb: *samábharat*, etc., and likewise in Greek. An irregular sandhi appears when it is combined with a root beginning with *i*, *u* or *ṛ* (*aícchat* 'wished', *aúrṇot* 'covered' *ā́rdhnot* 'thrived' from *iccháti*, *ūrṇóti*, *ṛdhnóti*, with vṛddhi instead of the expected guṇa, and this indicates that up to a late period it was pronounced as a separate syllable with hiatus (*aïcchat*, etc.). On the other hand its coalescence with initial *a* (IE *e*, *a*, *o*) appears to be ancient, judging by parallels between Greek and Sanskrit (Skt. *ā́s* 'was', Gk. Dor. ἦς, Skt. *ā́jat* 'drove', Gk. Dor. ἆγε). Before roots beginning with *v*, *y*, *n* and *r* the augment may appear as long *ā* in the Vedic language (*ā́vṛṇak*, *ā́yunak*, etc.). The reason for this is not very clear but a parallel phenomenon in the case of initial *v*- is found in Greek (Hom. ἠ-[F]είδη, Att. ᾔδει).

Reduplication consists normally of the repetition of the initial consonant of a root with a vowel which may or may not be the same as the radical vowel. It appears in one class of present (the third class), in the reduplicated aorist, in the perfect, in the desiderative and in the intensive. The main varieties which will be detailed below under the separate formations are as follows :

(1) Reduplication with the vowel *a* (IE *e*) : *dadhā́ti* ' places ', *tatāna* ' stretched ', cf. Gk. γέγονε, Lat. *pepigī*, etc.

(2) Reduplication with long *ā* : *jāgarti*, *jāgā́ra* ' is awake ', cf. Gk. δηδέχαται ' they welcome ', etc.

(3) Reduplication with the vowel *i* when that is not the vowel of the root : *tíṣṭhati* ' stands ', *dídṛkṣate* ' desires to see ', cf. Gk. ἵστημι, γίγνομαι, Lat. *sisto*, etc.

(4) Similar reduplication with long *ī* : *ájījanat*, ' gave birth to ', cf. Av. *zīzanənti*.

(5) Reduplication with weak form of vowel of roots in diphthongs : *juhóti* ' sacrifices ', *bibhéda* ' split ', cf. Lat. *pupugī*, *scicidī*.

(6) Intensive reduplication with guṇa vowel of such roots and similar reduplication with repeated final *r*, *n*, etc. : *nenikté* ' washes ', *dédiṣṭe* ' points out ', *várvṛtati* ' they turn (continually) ' ; cf. Av. *naēnižaiti*, *daēdōišt*, etc. This involves the complete repetition of roots containing only two consonants : *nónāva* ' roars mightily ', *jaṅghanti* ' smites violently '.

(7) Such intensive reduplication with *ĭ* suffixed to the reduplicating syllable : *bhárībharti* 3 sg., *bháribhrati* 3 pl. This type alternates with one in which the *ĭ* is suffixed after the root : *jóhavīti* ' calls loudly ', etc.

(8) Initial *a* may be reduplicated producing *ā* (*āsa* ' was ') or some more complicated process may appear.

In the case of roots beginning with two consonants the first is reduplicated with the exception of the combination *s* + occlusive : *śuśrā́va* ' heard ', cf. Av. *susruma*, Gk. κέκλυτε, *śiśriyé* ' rested on ', cf. Gk. κέκλιται, *sasmā́ra* ' remembered ', *sasnau* ' bathed ', etc. When the root begins with the group *s* + occlusive, the occlusive is repeated in Sanskrit : *tíṣṭhati* ' stands ', *caskánda* ' sprung ', *paspárśa* ' touched '. On the other hand, *s* (> *h*) appears in the reduplicating syllable in such cases both in Iranian and Greek. The same type of reduplication appears also in Lat. *sisto* and in Celtic (Ir. *-sescaind* from *skinnim* ' jump out ', cf. Skt. *skand-*). Yet other varieties of reduplication in the case of these groups appear (a) in Lat. perfects of the type *stetī, scicidī, spopondī,* which preserve the consonant group in the reduplicative syllable but simplify it in the root, (b) in Gothic where the full group appears in both root and reduplication: *skaískaiþ* (*skaidan* 'cut'). In view of this variety it is unlikely that there was any universally consistent usage in the IE period.

Certain sound changes have affected the reduplicated forms in Sanskrit. By the rule which prevents a succession of two aspirated consonants, a non-aspirate is substituted in reduplication for an aspirate: *dádhāti*, etc. In the case of *h* <IE *ĝh* the non-aspirated form appears as *j*: *jahā́ra.* Since *a* in a reduplicating syllable was originally *e*, the old velar series is palatalised before it: *cakā́ra, jagā́ma, jaghā́na.* The same treatment appears regularly when the vowel of the reduplicating syllable is *i* (*cíkīrṣati*) and it is applied analogically in the case of *u*: *cukópa.*

§ 6. Personal Terminations

Sanskrit, like the parent Indo-European, has two sets of personal terminations, one for the active and one for the middle voice. These two sets embrace further subdivisions which appear in different parts of the verbal conjugation. In the present-aorist system the so-called *primary* endings appear in the present and future, while a different series, the *secondary* endings, appear in the imperfect, aorist and optative. The subjunctive has optionally either. The perfect endings, where they differ from the above, do so more fundamentally than the primary and secondary endings differ from each other. The imperative has special endings only in the 2 singular and in the 3 singular and plural. The subjunctive has a separate termination in the 1 singular, which is old, and some special middle endings which are an Indian innovation. The primary, secondary and perfect endings are listed in the following table:[1]

A. Primary

	Active			Middle		
	s.	d.	pl.	s.	d.	pl.
1	*mi*	*vas*	*mas*	*e*	*vahe*	*mahe*
2	*si*	*thas*	*tha*	*se*	*āthe*	*dhve*
3	*ti*	*tas*	*anti*	*te*	*āte*	*ante, ate*

[1] For table of imperative and subjunctive endings see under the respective sections.

B. Secondary

I	*am, m*	*va*	*ma*	*i, a*	*vahi*	*mahi*
2	*s*	*tam*	*ta*	*thas*	*āthām*	*dhvam*
3	*t*	*tām*	*an, ur*	*ta*	*ātām*	*anta, ata, ran*

C. Perfect

I	*a*	*va*	*ma*	*e*	*vahe*	*mahe*
2	*tha*	*athus*	*a*	*se*	*āthe*	*dhve*
3	*a*	*atus*	*ur*	*e*	*āte*	*re*

Active Terminations:

I *Sing.* P. Skt. *ásmi* ' I am ', Gk. *εἰμί*, Lith. *esmì*, Hitt. *ešmi*; *émi* ' I go ', Gk. *εἶμι*, *dádāmi* ' I give ', Gk. *δίδωμι*, etc. This ending was originally confined to the non-thematic classes, and a different ending -*ō* (-oн) appeared in the thematic classes: Gk. *φέρω*, Lat. *fero*, Goth. *baíra*. Some such forms are preserved in Iranian (Av. *spasyā*: Lat. *specio*), but usually in Iranian, and always in Sanskrit, *mi* from the non-thematic verbs is added to the older form: Skt. *bharāmi*, Av. *barāmi*. S. *ábharam*, Gk. *ἔφερον*, *ágām*, Gk. *ἔβην*, *syā́m* ' sim ', O. Lat. *siem*. Non-thematic verbs have the fuller ending -*am*, *ā́sam* ' I was ', O. Pers. *āham*, as opposed to Gk. *a*<*m̥* in Hom. *ἦα*. A similar difference between the two languages was observed in the case of the acc. sg. of non-thematic stems. Pf. Skt. *véda*, Gk. *οἶδα*; *dadárśa*, Gk. *δέδορκα*. Sbj. The Vedic language has either *ā* or *āni*, *bravā* ' I will speak ', *bharāṇi* ' I will bear '. In the classical language, where these formations have entered the imperative system, only the fuller ending *āni* is used. The ending -*ā* is identical with the -*ō* which in other languages appears in the present indicative of thematic verbs as well as in the subjunctive: Gk. *ἄγω*, *φέρω*, etc. The extension -*ni* appears only in Indo-Iranian and is of uncertain origin.

2 *Sing.* P. *éṣi* ' you go ', Lith. *eisì*, *bharasi* ' you bear ', Av. *barahi*; cf. O. Russ. *velišĭ* ' you command ', Hitt. *iyaši* ' you do '. S. *ásthās*, Gk. *ἔστης*, *ábharas*, Gk. *ἔφερες*, *bháres* Gk. *φέροις*, Goth. *baírais*. Pf. *véttha*, Gk. *οἶσθα*, Goth. *waist*, *dadātha*, Av. *dadāθā*. Impv. *ihí* ' go ' (<**idhí*), Av. *idī*, Gk. *ἴθι*, *jahí* ' slay ' (*han*-), Av. *jaiδi*, *viddhí* ' know ', Gk. *ἴσθι*. In thematic verbs the simple stem serves as the second person singular of the imperative: *bhara*, Gk. *φέρε*, Goth. *baír*; Lat. *ege*, etc.

3 *Sing.* P. *ásti,* Lith. *ẽsti,* Gk. ἔστι, Hitt. *ešzi,* (*zi*<*ti*); *hánti* 'slays', Av. *jainti,* Hitt. *kuenzi*; *bhárati,* Av. *baraiti,* O. Sl. *beretĭ* (beside *beretŭ*). S. *ábharat, syāt,* cf. Av. *barat̰,* Gk. (with loss of *-t*) ἔφερε, φέροι, Lat. *erat, sīt* (O. Lat. *sied*), etc. Pf. *dadárśa,* Gk. δέδορκε. Impv. *ástu,* Hitt. *eštu, étu* 'let him go', *bharatu,* O. Pers. *baratu.* An alternative ending *-tōd* appears in Greek and Latin (ἔστω, *estō*(*d*)). Forms corresponding to this are found in Sanskrit, e.g. *vittā́t* (=Gk. ἴστω) but they are used for both the second and third persons, and for all numbers.

A different kind of inflection in the primary endings of the 2, 3 sing. appears in Gk. thematic verbs: 2 ἄγεις, 3 ἄγει. A comparison with Lith. *vedì* 'take: you take' shows that the *s* of the 2 sing. is a later addition, and that the two persons were originally identical. They contain no personal terminations, only an appended *i* indicating present time. Such an *i*, unassociated with a personal ending, is found in Hittite verbs of the *-ḫi* class: *aki* 'dies', *dāi* 'takes'. Sanskrit has innovated here by applying the endings of the *mi*-conjugation, just as in the 1 sing., but in this case the innovation is more widely shared by other IE languages, Lat. *agis, agit,* Goth. *baíris, baíriþ,* etc.

1 *Plur.* P. (a) *imás* 'we go', *bhárāmas* 'we bear', cf. Gk. Dor. ἵμες, φέρομες, Lat. *īmus, ferimus,* O. Sl. *damŭ, nesemŭ,* etc., (b) *smási* 'we are', O. Pers. *amahi, bhárāmasi,* Av. *barāmahi,* cf. O. Ir. *ammi* 'sumus', *bermai, bermi* 'we bear'. S. and Pf. *ábharāma, syā́ma,* Av. *hyāmā, vidmá* 'we know', Goth. *witum.* Forms with long vowel which appear in the Vedic language, particularly in the perfect (*vidmā́,* etc.) appear to be ancient, and not merely metrical lengthening, on account of the occurrence of similar formations in other languages: Lith. *sukomė-s* (reflexive), Goth. *baíraima* opt. (out of °*mē* or °*mō*).

The variations between IE-*mes* and *-mos* were due to differences of accentuation, like the similar phenomenon in the genitive singular: originally **imés* but **bhéromos.* The alternative ending *-masi* appears in the Vedic language beside *mas,* but it is disused in the classical language. In Iranian the corresponding *mahi* has come to be exclusively used as the primary ending. In Greek there is an alternative termination -μεν, used both as a primary and secondary ending. It was customary to regard the final-ν of this form as ephelcystic, and to equate the Gk. ending with the Skt. secondary ending, but it is now clear from

Hittite that this is not so. The Hittite terminations are: P. *weni, meni* (with *i* appended as in Skt. *masi*), S. *wen, men*. The variety with *w-* is related to the dual endings of other IE languages; the forms with *m-* appear after *u* (*arnummeni* 'we bring', etc.) and the secondary form *-men* corresponds exactly with the Greek ending. In Indo-Iranian this form of ending is traceable in Khotanese: *hämāmane* 'we may become' (subj. mid.).

2 *Plur.* P. (a) *bháratha*, cf. Av. *xšayaθā*, (b) *vádathana* 'you speak'. S. (a) *ábharata* (impf.), *bhárata* (impv.), cf. Gk. φέρετε, Lat. *ferte* (impv.), Goth. *baíriþ*, O. Sl. *berete*, (b) *ájahātana* 'you abandoned', *hantana* 'slay' (impv.), cf. Hitt. *kuenten* pret. and impv. (*kuen-* 'slay'). Pf. *cakrá* (*kṛ-* 'to do'), *vidá*. The primary endings with aspiration (*-tha* <tHe) do not appear outside Indo-Iranian. The other languages have normally one form which serves as both primary and secondary ending, and this corresponds to the secondary ending of Indo-Iranian. Hittite has evolved a distinction between primary and secondary ending here in quite a different way (P. *teni*, S. *ten*). The longer forms were analysed as *tha-na* and *ta-na*, the *na* being regarded as an appended particle, and the whole form as a Sanskrit innovation. In view of Hitt. *-ten* we should analyse rather *-tan-a* of which *tan* corresponds exactly to Hitt. *-ten*, and the *a* is simply a thematic enlargement such as is found elsewhere in the formation of words. The perfect form is properly without termination and nothing like it is found outside Indo-Iranian.

3 *Plur.* P. *bháranti*, Gk. Dor. φέροντι, *sánti*, Gk. Dor. ἐντί, Lat. *sunt*, Goth. *sind*, O. Sl. *sǫtĭ* (beside *sǫtŭ*), Hitt. *ašanzi*; *ghnánti* 'they slay', Hitt. *kunanzi*; *dádati* 'they give', cf. Gk. (Delph.) καθεστᾰκᾰτι, (Hom.) λελόγχᾱσι. S. (a) *ábharan*, Av. *barən*, Gk. ἔφερον; (b) *ádadur* (impf.), *ádhur* (aor.), *syur* (opt.). Cf. Av. *ādarə* 'they made', *hyārə* 'they might be', *ǰamyārəš* 'they might come', Hitt. *wekir* 'they wished', *ekuer* 'they drank'. Pf. *āsúr* 'they were', cf. Av. *āŋharə*, *cikitúr* 'they are aware of', cf. Av. *čikōitərəš*. Impv. *bhárantu*, cf. Hitt. *iyandu*.

The full form of the ending varied between *-onti* and *-enti* according to accentuation, like the variation between *-mes* and *-mos* in the 1 plur. Also due to accent is the weakening to *-n̥ti* > *ati* which appears in Sanskrit and Greek. A corresponding weak form of the secondary ending, *-at* < *n̥t*, appears in Iranian: Av. *dadaṯ*, *ǰīgərəzaṯ*. In such cases Sanskrit always has the alternative ending *-ur*. The secondary ending was originally *-ant* which has been reduced to *-an* by the normal cause of phonetic development in Sanskrit as in most of the related languages (Gk. -ον <οντ, etc.).

The alternative secondary ending *-ur* appears in the imperfect of the reduplicating class (*ádadur*), in the imperfect of root stems ending in *-ā* (*áyur* : *yā́ti* 'goes'), in non-thematic aorist stems and in the perfect. Outside Indo-Iranian *r*-endings of the 3 plur. appear in Hittite, Latin (*dixere*) and Tocharian (*kātkar* 'they arose', *mrasar* 'they forgot'). In Iranian this *r* may be enlarged by an additional element *s* (*čikōitərəš*, etc.). The form of the Sanskrit ending shows that it also originally contained this enlargement, since *-ur* has developed out of *-r̥š* here in the same way as it has done in *pitúr* <**pitŕ̥š*. Of the various types of *r*-formation which Iranian preserves, one has been generalised in Sanskrit at the expense of the rest.

1 *Dual.* P. *bhárāvas*, cf. Goth. *baírōs* (<**bherōwes*), *svás* 'we two are'. The corresponding ending in Iranian is an extended *-vahi* (cf. *masi* beside *mas*): Av. *usvahi* 'we two wish'; a form *-vasi* after the style of *masi* does not appear in Skt. S. and Pf.; impf. *ábharāva*, opt. *bháreva*, pf. *vidvá*, cf. Av. *ǰvāva* 'we two lived', Lith. pret. *sùkova*, *-vō-s*, O. Sl. pres. *jesvě*, *vezevě*, Aor. *vezově*, Goth. opt. *bindaiwa*. As in the 1 plur. only Indo-Iranian distinguishes between primary and secondary terminations. The variation between the long and short vowel (Skt. *va* : Sl. *vě*) was noticed also in the plural. The first person of the dual is found only in Indo-Iranian, Balto-Slavonic and Germanic. Hittite contains a termination which is related to these forms, P. *weni*, S. *wen*, but it is used as a plural side by side with the rarer *-meni/men*. The most satisfactory explanation of this is that there existed originally in IE parallel formations beginning with *w* or *m* which were optionally used as 1 plur. ending. Hittite has preserved this state of affairs but restricted the use of the *men-* termination to stems in *u*. The above-mentioned languages have kept both types of ending but specialised as duals the *w*-variety. About the remaining IE languages it is not possible to say anything owing to lack of evidence.

2, 3 *Dual.* P. 2 *bhárathas*, 3 *bháratas*, cf. Av. *yūidyaθō*, *baratō*- Goth. *baírats*. In Avestan no 2 dual is found; the terminations *tō* and *-θō* are used promiscuously as endings, of the 3 dual, the two forms having been confused. The Gothic form is used only for the 2 dual. S. 2 *ábharatam*, Gk. ἐφέρετον, 3 *ábharatām*, Gk. ἐφερέτην. Pf. 2 *cakráthur*, 3 *cakrátur*, cf. Av. *yaētatarə*.

With the primary terminations of the 2, 3 dual it is possible to compare the *-tis* (<*-tes*) of Lat. *legitis*, etc., which is used as 2 plur. As in the first person the dual endings seem to have arisen by the specialisation in dual usage of a variant form of the plural ending. It is also noteworthy that the variation between *t* and *th* serves quite a different purpose in the two numbers, to distinguish 2 from 3 in the dual, and to distinguish primary from secondary in the plural. Secondary adaptation in both cases would account for this difference. The 3 dual is not of independent origin but merely a variant in form of the 2 dual. The same form may appear for both as in the Gk. primary ending (φέρετον). In Balto-Slavonic there appears an ending in *-tā* which in Lithuanian appears only in the second person (*sùkata, sùkato-s*) in Slavonic in both (O. Sl. 2, 3 *vezeta*). It corresponds to the secondary ending of the third person in Sanskrit (*-tām* : Gk. -την, Dor. -τᾱν) to which *-m* is a secondary addition. The perfect endings are an Indo-Iranian creation with *-ur* (Ir. *ar*) introduced from the 3 plur.

Middle Endings

1 *Sing*. P. *bruvé* 'I speak', Av. *-mruye, yáje* 'I worship', Av. *yaze*. A different formation with *-m-* as in the active of *mi*-verbs appears in Greek: φέρομαι, etc. S. non-thematic, *áduhi* 'I milked', *akri* 'I have done', Av. *aoǰī* (*aog-* 'to say'), *mə̄nghī*=Skt. (*á*)*maṃsi* (*man-* 'to think', *s*-aor.). Thematic stems have *-e* as in the primary system, *ábhave*, etc. Greek has a quite different ending: ἐφερόμην, Dor. °μᾱν. Pf. *śuśruvé*, Av. *susruye* with same ending as primary system. Sbj. *máṃsai*, Av. *mə̄nghāi*, *yájai*, Av. *yazāi*. Opt. *tanvīyá*, Av. *tanuya*.

2 *Sing*. P. *bhárase*, cf. Av. *pərəsahe* 'you ask', Gk. φέρεαι φέρῃ, Goth. *baíraza*; *datsé* 'you give', Gk. δίδοσαι. S. *ákṛthās*, *ádhatthās*, etc. In contradistinction to Sanskrit, Iranian and Greek both agree in having forms representing IE *-so*: Av. *-zayaŋha*, Gk. ἐφέρεο, ἐφέρου. These bear the same relation to the primary ending *-sai* as the 3 sing. secondary *-to* to primary *-tai*. Pf. same as primary, *ririkṣé, dadhiṣé*, cf. Gk. λέλειψαι, δέδοσαι. Impv. *bhárasva*, Av. *baraŋuha*.

3 *Sing*. P. *bhárate*, Gk. φέρεται, Goth. *baírada*, *ā́ste* 'sits',

Gk. ἧσται. In the Vedic language there occur some forms without the *-t-*, the termination being identical with that of the first person as in the perfect : *duhé, śáye, śṛṇvé*, etc. In view of the Hittite middle formations of the third person of the type *eša, kiša* (cf. *aduha* below), this type must be regarded as ancient and not as an importation from the perfect system. S. *ábharata*, Gk. ἐφέρετο, opt. *bháreta*, Gk. φέροιτο. The *-ta* which appears in Hittite as primary ending *arta* ' stands up ', *kitta* ' lies ' beside *artari, kittari*) is equivalent to the Sanskrit secondary ending. Rare forms without *t* corresponding to the presents *duhé*, etc., are *aiśa* and *aduha* (*īś-* ' to rule ', *duh-* ' to milk '), cf. Hitt. primary *eša, kiša*, etc. Pf. *dadhé, cakré*, etc. On the other hand Gk. has *-t-* as in the present, δέδοται, etc. Impv. *bháratām, dhattām*, cf. Av. *vərəzyatąm*. This form and the corresponding plural *antām/atām* are without parallel outside Indo-Iranian. A form without *-t-*, corresponding to the indicative endings P. *-e*, S. *-a*, appears occasionally in the Veda : *duhām*.

1 *Plur*. P. Pf. *yájāmahe*, Av. *yazamaide, brūmáhe* ' we say ', Av. *mrūmaide, cakṛmáhe*, etc. S. *ábharāmahi*, cf. Av. *varəmaidi* (*var-* ' to choose '), etc. Sanskrit *-h-* is from *-dh-*, as in the imperative *-hi*, etc., the original Indo-Iranian terminations being **-madhai* and *-madhi*. Closely related to these forms but differing in the matter of the final vowel is Gk. -μεθα <**medha*, which serves as both primary and secondary ending : φερόμεθα, ἐφερόμεθα. Greek has also a fuller ending -μεσθα, with which Hitt. *-wašta* is to be compared, there being the same alternation of *m* and *w* as appears in the active (*men/wen*).

2 *Plur*. P. Pf. *bháradhve, dadidhvé*, cf. Av. *mərəngəduyē* (*marək-* ' to destroy '). S. *ábharadhvam*, cf. Av. *dārayaδwəm*, etc. The Greek ending -σθε (primary and secondary) may be related presuming it is out of *-zdhwe*, and more closely the dual ending -σθον (<*zdhwom*) the dual use of which is, as elsewhere, a secondary adaptation. The Hittite termination, primary *duma* (*paḫḫašduma* ' you protect '), S. *dumat* is more obviously connected, *-dum-* being the weak grade corresponding to *-dhvam*.

3 *Plur*. P. (a) *bhárante*, Gk. φέρονται, *ā́sate* ' they sit ', Gk. Hom. ἥαται (<**ēsn̥tai*) ; (b) *śére* ' they lie ', Av. *sōire, saēre, duhré, sunviré*, with the same endings as the perfect. A combination of *a* and *b* appears in *śérate, duhrate*. S. (a) *ábharanta*, Gk. ἐφέροντο, *ā́sata* ' they sat ', Gk. Hom. ἥατο ; (b) Three

varieties of *r*-ending appear: (1) *-ra*: *áduhra,* (2) *-ran*: *áduhran, áśeran,* opt. *ā́sīran, bhā́reran,* (3) *-ram*: *asasr̥gram,* cf. Av. *vaozirəm* (*vaz-* 'to carry'). The types (2) and (3) are clearly enlargements of type (1) which must be regarded as most original. By combination of (a) and (b) arise the terminations *-ranta* and *-rata*: *ávavr̥tranta* (*vr̥t-* 'to turn'), *bhárerata.* Outside the optatives in *-eran, -īran,* the *r*-endings are comparatively rare and archaic formations in the Vedic language beside the normal *nt*-formations. They are almost completely discarded in the classical language. It will be observed that the *r* is identical with the *r* which appears in the third plural of the active, and it is the elements added to it which characterise the terminations as middle (*-e* in *duhré,* etc., *-a* in *aduhra*). Pf. Exclusively *r*-endings: *duduhré, cakriré,* etc., cf. Av. *čāxrare* (variant *-arai* which does not occur in Skt., cf. Av. *-arə* active which is likewise missing in Skt.).

1 *Dual.* P. Pf. *bhárāvahe, cakr̥váhe,* S. *ábharāvahi.* Avestan has only *-vaidi*: *dvaidī* (*dav-,* i.e. *du-vaidi*). The Hitt. plural ending *-wašta* has formally the same relationship to Indo-Iranian *-vadhi* as Gk. -μεσθα to *-madhi.*

2, 3 *Dual.* P. Pf. thematic 2 *bhárethe, cárethe,* cf. Av. 3 dual *čarōiθe,* 3 *bhárete,* cf. Av. *vīsaēte*; non-thematic 2 *bruvā́the, mamnā́the,* 3 *bruvā́te, mamnā́te.* S. thematic 2 *ábharethām,* 3 *ábharetām,* cf. Av. *jasaētəm* (with short vowel of termination as opposed to long vowel in Sanskrit); non-thematic 2 *áśruvāthām* (*śru-* 'to hear'), 3 *áśruvātām,* Av. *asrvātəm.* The variation between Iranian *-tam* and Skt. *-tām* in the third person corresponds to a similar difference in the active (Av. *jasatəm,* Skt. *ágacchatām*). No corresponding endings appear outside Indo-Iranian. The Greek terminations, P. 2, 3 -σθον, S. 2 -σθον, 3 -σθην are connected with the second plural of the middle. On the other hand the Indo-Iranian forms are connected with the corresponding active terminations of the dual. The same variation between *th* and *t* appears between the two persons in the primary endings, and in the middle this is introduced also into the secondary endings. The final *-e* of the primary endings is the same *-e* characterising the middle which appears throughout the primary system. The influence of this *-e* of the middle is responsible for the substitution of *e* for the *a* of thematic stems (*ábhavetām* as opposed to active *ábhavatām,* Av. *jasaētəm* beside *jasatəm*). Non-thematic verbs are distinguished by an *ā* of the middle ending, but examples like Av. *dazde* 3 du. pf. and Skt. *cikéthe* indicate that this is an innovation. It can only have come from formations of roots in *ā* like *dadā́the, dadā́te* where the *ā* is originally part of the root as in 2 sg. *dadā́tha* (beside *dadithá*) and 2 pl. *dádhātana* (beside *dhattana*).

§ 7. Structure and Origin of the Terminational System

A comparison of the primary and secondary endings shows that from the historical point of view they are incorrectly named. It is the 'secondary' endings that are primary, and vice versa. The relation of the series *-m, -s, -t, -an*(*t*) with the primary *-mi, -si, -ti, -anti* can only be explained by the assumption that in the latter series a particle *-i* indicating present time has been secondarily added. In the same way in the imperative endings *-tu, -antu,* a particle *-u* is added to the same basic terminations. This is made clear, among other things, by the fact that these same elements *-i* and *-u* may appear by themselves in formations that have no personal termination, e.g. in Gk. φέρει (φερε + ι), Hitt. *śakki* 'knows' and in Hittite imperatives of the *-ḫi* class: *aku, dāu* (*ak-* 'to die', *dā-* 'to take'). This addition of *-i* to *-t*, etc., implies an earlier period when secondary terminations alone existed; the 'primary' system, and therefore the present tense is formed on the basis of the 'secondary' system of the preterites. The unaugmented preterite and the 'injunctive' form the primary basis of the IE present-aorist system.

It does not seem that the distinction between primary and secondary terminations was fully worked out in the IE period. For instance in the 1 plur. and in the 2 plur. Greek makes no distinction (P. S. -μεν), and this indifference is shared by other languages (O. Sl. *nesemŭ, nesomŭ,* Goth. *bindam, witum, -budum*). The distinction appears in Hittite and Indo-Iranian, but it is effected by quite different means. In Hittite *-weni, -meni* beside *-wen, -men* is clearly a private innovation modelled on the three persons of the present and the 3 plur. In Indo-Iranian the distinction is effected by the choice of two different forms of the suffix (*mas*/*ma*, similarly du. *vas*/*va*) and there is no evidence to show that this variation was connected with the distinction between secondary and primary in the IE period.

Possibly *-ma* was originally the perfect ending in view of the frequency of final *-a* in forms of that tense (*véda, véttha, véda,* 2 pl. *vidá*). The innovation Skt. *-masi*, Av. *-mahi*, Av. *-vahi* resembles the Hittite development, but it is quite independent, and expresses no such distinction (P. *mas* and *masi* as opposed to Hitt. P. *-meni, -weni*, S. *men/wen*). Hittite treats the 2 pl. in the same way (*ten/teni*) and here again Sanskrit expresses the difference in quite a different way (*-ta/tha*). In all other languages the distinction does not exist. Apart from lack of support from other languages, the fact that the distinction between *t* and *th* is used in the related dual endings for a totally different purpose (2 *-thas*, 3 *-tas*) makes it altogether unlikely that the difference between the two forms of suffix was from the beginning connected with the distinction between primary and secondary ending.

In the middle the priority of the secondary endings is no less clear. The primary endings all terminate in *-e*, and the comparative evidence shows that the extension of this *-e* to all the primary persons of the middle is a special Indo-Iranian development. In Greek, which is closest to Indo-Iranian in its verbal inflection, a corresponding -αι is found only in the three persons of the singular and in the 3 plural. Elsewhere (-σθον, -μεθα, -σθε) the endings are not characterised by this element, the same ending functioning as both primary and secondary. It is certain that in this respect Greek represents the more original state of affairs, and that in Sanskrit *-mahe* and *-dhve* (and the same applies to the dual endings) are new formations on the basis of *mahi* and *dhvam* which originally functioned indifferently as primary and secondary endings. Comparison between Sanskrit and Hittite confirms this. Hittite differs from Sanskrit more than Greek does, and it shares with Italic, Celtic and Tocharian an element *r* in the middle endings which Greek and Sanskrit agree in ignoring. Nevertheless there exist forms in the two languages which can be directly compared, and these are invariably secondary endings in Sanskrit: Hitt. 3 sg. pr. *arta*: cf. Skt. *ákṛta*; 3 pl. *aranta*: Skt. *aranta*; 3 sg. *eša*: cf. Skt. *áduha*; 2 pl. *paḫḫašduma*: cf. Skt. *ábharadhvam*. The Hittite terminations all belong to the present (primary) system, as opposed to the identical forms in Sanskrit which belong to the secondary system.

The formation of the middle endings, as is clear from a survey of the Sanskrit forms, is remarkably heterogeneous, and its study is made more complicated by the existence in Indo-European of two distinct types, one (Hittite, Italic, Celtic, Tocharian) which makes extensive use of an element *r* in its formation, and another (Indo-Iranian, Greek, Germanic) which ignores this element. At the same time there is a nucleus of forms, as instanced above, which bridge the gap between the two types. Among the oldest forms we can observe several types. (1) In the 3rd person a thematic variation of the same suffix serves as the middle ending : *ákar*(*t*) : *ákṛta* ; *ábharan*(*t*) : *ábharanta* ; *duhúr* : *áduhra*. (2) In the 1st person dual and plural the middle ending is formed by the addition of particles (Skt. *-hi* <**dhi*, Gk. *θα* <**dha*) to a form of the active ending. The Greek alternation -*μεθα*/-*μεσθα*, which contains as its first element two variant forms of the active ending (cf. Skt. *-mas* and *-ma*), makes this quite clear. Hitt. *-wašta*, with the *-w-* that elsewhere appears in the dual, but in Hitt. in the plural, is naturally to be explained in the same way as Gk. -*μεσθα*.)3) In the 2nd plur. an ending which is quite different from the active ending is used. The 2nd sg. *-thās* is likewise quite different from the active *-s* but it is clearly connected with the perfect active ending *-tha*. The final *s* may be explained as a secondary addition, since *-s* characterises the 2nd person elsewhere. The relation between **-thā* and *-tha* is apparently the same as that between *mā* and *ma* (IE *mē*/*me*) of the 1st person plural.

The simplest form of the 1st person middle termination in Hittite is *-ḫa* (*zaḫḫiyaḫḫa*) which occurs rarely beside the more usual *-ḫari*, *ḫaḫari*. This ending is represented in Sanskrit in the 1st person middle of the optative (*bháveya*). Elsewhere there is a secondary ending *-i* (*áduhi*, *ákri*) for which there are no parallels outside Indo-Iranian (Av. *aoǰī*, *mǝnghī*).

It is clear from the agreements between Sanskrit and Hittite that the oldest nucleus of middle endings is common IE property. Further developments based on this show remarkable divergence, since Hittite shares with Italic, Celtic and Tocharian an element *r* which is not known to Sanskrit and Greek. In Hitt. this *r*, which appears with the addition of the primary *-i* of the present, is optional, e.g. 3 sg. *arta* and *artari*, 3 pl. *aranta* and *arantari*. It is clear that it must have been in the same way optional in Indo-European, and that in the further course of development it became established as a necessary element in Italo-Celtic and Tocharian, and on the other hand went out of use in that dialectal area of Indo-European from which Indo-Iranian and Greek derive.

The primary middle endings of Sanskrit arise in the first place, as in the active, from the addition of *-i* to the secondary endings : *bhárata + i > bhárate*. Corresponding to the *-e*, Greek has *-αι*. This vocalism is most simply explained as due to the ending of the 1st person (-H*a* + *i* > *ai*) from which it spread by analogy to the other persons. In Sanskrit this final *-e* appears in all the primary forms, but its presence in the dual and in the first and second persons of the plural is due entirely to analogy, and these are to be regarded as the latest parts of the system.

The active endings of the perfect are in the singular identical with the oldest forms of the middle endings : (1) -H*a* > *a*, *véda*, cf. *bháveya* ; (2) *-tha*, cf. *-thā-s*, Hitt. *-ta* ; (3) *-a* (IE *-e*), *veda*, cf. *aduha*, Hitt. *eša*. That this is no accident is clear from the frequent cases in which active perfects with intransitive sense appear by the side of middle forms in the other tenses, e.g. Skt. *vártate* : *vavárta*, Gk. *γίγνομαι* : *γέγονα*, etc. Originally, it seems, the perfect had no distinction of the two voices, and both in form and sense it was closer to the middle than to the active. The development of separate middle forms may be regarded as a late Indo-European feature. In Sanskrit these perfect terminations are identical with those of the present, and these, as already observed, are later formations than the corresponding secondary endings.

As to the nature of the personal endings it is quite clear that they have nothing to do with the corresponding personal pronouns. The theory that these endings are of the nature of suffixed pronouns has often enough been put forward in the course of IE studies, but concrete evidence in the form of detailed comparisons is lacking. It is possible to find an *-m-* in the ending of the 1 sg., and a *t* in the 3 sg., which are letters that occur in the corresponding pronouns (acc. sg. *mā* : *ta-*), but beyond this there is practically nothing. Since no theory can be based on the comparison of one or two single letters, the attempt at explaining the personal endings as suffixed pronouns has to be abandoned. When this is done, and the terminations are analysed in such detail as the comparative evidence will permit, it becomes clear that the elements of which the system is constructed are in the main identical with the suffixes of derivation which are met with in the formation of nouns. This is clearly so in the purely thematic formations which have no ending in the proper sense: 2 sg. impv. *ája*, 3 sg. impf. mid. *áduha*, 2 pl. pf. *vidá*. Such formations are in no way to be distinguished from ordinary thematic nominal stems. The same correspondence is generally seen between the ending of the 3 pl. (Skt. *-an(t)/anti*, IE *-ent/-ont*) and the suffix which forms present participles (Skt. *bhárant-*, Lat. *ferens*). In addition it has been pointed out that the relation of the two kinds of ending in the 3 pl., the above and that consisting of or containing an element *r*, is reminiscent of the alternation found in nominal stems between *r* and *n/nt*: Gk. *ὕδωρ*, *ὕδατος*, etc. Elsewhere too there are features about the verbal terminations which recall those of the nominal suffixes. There appears to exist the same relation between the terminations of the active and middle of the 3 sg. ((*á*)*kar*(*t*), (*á*)*kṛta*) as is found in the nominal suffixes in *kṛt-*: *kṛtá-*. The suffix of the 2 pl. contains also a *-ta* which may be equated with the corresponding nominal suffix (*bhárata*, cf. the nominal stem *bharatá-*). In Indo-Iranian alone there exists a variant ending *-tha* which functions as primary ending. It is probably no coincidence that Indo-Iranian is also the only branch which shows a suffix *-tha* beside *-ta* in the formation of nouns (*yajátha-* 'worship': *yajatá-* 'to be worshipped').

The behaviour of the suffix of the 1 pl. is in several ways reminiscent of the corresponding nominal suffix. In the first place the coexistence of two forms, one beginning with *w* and one with *m*, which is seen in Hittite, is matched by a similar duality in the infinitival forms containing the same elements: *tiyawar*, *tiyawanzi*; *tarnummar*, *tarnummanzi*. In Sanskrit the suffixes *-vant* and *-mant* are found in the same way side by side with similar function. Another similarity between the verbal and nominal forms is seen in the variation of the latter part of the suffix: IE *wen/wes*, *men/mes*. This is paralleled by the variations in nominal declension, e.g. in the vocatives *ṛtāvas*, *patnīvas*, *tuviṣmas* from the stems *ṛtā̆van-*, *pátnīvant-* and *túviṣmant-*.

Correspondences of this kind make clear the original nature of a considerable section of the verbal terminations. By some process of adaptation, the course of which it is not now possible to follow, certain nominal formations became associated with particular persons and numbers, and at least a fair proportion of the existing personal terminations came into being in this way.

§8. The Ten Present Classes

The roots of the Sanskrit language are arranged by the Hindu grammarians in ten classes, according to the way in which they form the present system, and named after a verb taken as typical of its class. The order in which these classes are placed corresponds to no discoverable grammatical principle, and for convenience of exposition it needs to be rearranged. The verbs are divided into two major types, (a) non-thematic (classes 2, 3, 5, 7, 8, 9) and (b) thematic (classes 1, 4, 6, 10).

A. *Non-thematic Presents*

Root Class (Second or *ad-* class)

Paradigm : (*dviṣ-* ' to hate ').

Present, Active, S. 1 *dvéṣmi*, 2 *dvékṣi*, 3 *dvéṣṭi*, D. 1 *dviṣvás*, 2 *dviṣṭhás*, 3 *dviṣṭás*, P. 1 *dviṣmás*, 2 *dviṣṭhá*, 3 *dviṣánti*.

Middle, S. 1 *dviṣé*, 2 *dvikṣé*, 3 *dviṣṭé*, D. 1 *dviṣváhe*, 2 *dviṣā́the*, 3 *dviṣā́te*, P. 1 *dviṣmáhe*, 2 *dviḍḍhvé*, 3 *dviṣáte*.

Imperfect, Active, S. 1 *ádveṣam*, 2 *ádveṭ*, 3 *ádveṭ*, D. *ádviṣva*, 2 *ádviṣṭam*, 3 *ádviṣṭām*, P. 1 *ádviṣma*, 2 *ádviṣṭa*, 3 *ádviṣan*.

Middle, S. 1 *ádviṣi*, 2 *ádviṣṭhās*, 2 *ádviṣṭa*, D. 1 *ádviṣvahi*, 2 *ádviṣāthām*, 3 *ádviṣātām*, P. 1 *ádviṣmahi*, 2 *ádviḍḍhvam*, 3 *ádviṣata*.

Inflection of this type in Sanskrit is made from nearly 130 roots. In most other IE languages it has largely died out, its place being taken by thematic formations. Consequently direct comparisons with forms of other languages are confined to a few common roots : *ásti* ' is ', Gk. ἔστι, Lat. *est*, etc. ; *émi* ' I go ', *imás* ' we go ', Gk. εἶμι, ἴμεν, Lith. *eimì*, etc. ; *átti*, ' eats ', Lat. *est*, Russ. *jest'* ; *ā́ste* ' sits ', Gk. ἧσται ; *śéte* ' lies ', Gk. κεῖται, Hitt. *kitta*, *kittari*. Hittite is the only language beside Sanskrit in which this type of formation is well preserved, and here further parallels are available : *hánti* ' he slays ', *ghnánti* ' they slay ', Hitt. *kuenzi*, *kunanzi* ; *vaṣṭi* ' he wishes ' (*vaś-*) Hitt. *wekzi* (Gk. only ptc. ἑκών) ; *sásti* ' sleeps ', Hitt. *šešzi*.

Beside the regular endings given above there exists a variant type : active, 3 pl. impf. *cakṣur, duhur* ; middle, 3 sg. pres. *íśe, cité, duhe, bruve, śáye, vidé,* 3 pl. *duhré, śére* ; *duhrate, śérate* ; impf. 3 sg. *aiśa, aduha,* 3 pl. *aduhra* ; *aduhran, áśeran* ; *áśerata* ; impv. 3 sg. *duhā́m, vidām, śayām,* 3 pl. *duhrām* ; *duhratām, śeratām.* These forms (for which see above, § 6) are confined to the Vedic language with the exception of the root *śī-* ' to lie ' which preserves such inflection in the classical language (3 pl. *śérate*). This series is important because it shows that there were originally two types of conjugation in the case of root stems, corresponding to the Hittite *-mi* and *-ḫi* conjugations. Sanskrit has generalised the *mi-* type in the active, but in the middle the Vedic language preserves these traces of the old dual system.

With certain exceptions the normal system of accent and apophony prevails in this class, that is to say the root has accent and guṇa in the three persons of the active, while elsewhere it appears in its weak form and the accent is on the termination : *hánti* : *ghnánti* ; *váśmi* : *uśmási* ; *ásmi* : *smás,* etc. Roots in *-u* followed by endings beginning with a consonant, take vṛddhi instead of guṇa in the strong forms : *staúti,* ' praises ', *yaúti* ' joins ' ; also certain others, e.g. *mā́rṣṭi* ' rubs ' ; 3 pl. *mṛjánti.* A number of roots retain accent and guṇa throughout for reasons which are not clear : e.g. *śéte* ' lies ', *váste* ' wears clothes '. Certain roots with long vowels where this applies, e.g. *ā́ste* ' sits ', *ī́ṣṭe* ' rules ' have perhaps been adapted from the perfect system (*ās-* originally perfect stem of *as-* ' to be '). In the Vedic language the strong form of the root is optional in the 2 pl. : pres. *nethá,* impv. *stota,* impf. *ábravīta.* The weak form of the 3 pl. mid. termination (*dviṣáte* as opposed to *dviṣánti*) indicates original final accent which is preserved ocassionally in the Veda : *duhaté, rihaté.* The root *śās-* has the weak termination also in the active (*śā́sati* 3 pl.) which accords with its radical accent.

The conjugation of this class is complicated by changes due to internal sandhi. As this is a matter of phonology rather than morphology, a few examples will suffice : *duh-* ' to milk ', *doh + si > dhokṣi, doh + ti > dogdhi* ; *lih-* ' to lick ', *leh + ti > leḍhi*; *śās- + dhi > śādhi.* Analogy is responsible for the 3 sg. impf. *áśāt* (instead of **aśās* < **aśāst*) and in the same way for *áleṭ.* Different formations are occasionally substituted where the operation of phonetic laws would leave a form too short or obscure : 3 sg. impf. *ā́dat* with thematic vowel from *ad-* 'to eat' *ā́sīt* with *-ī-* beside Vedic *ā́s* from *as-* 'to be'.

Some of the roots of this class contain enlargements, e.g. *trā-* 'to save, protect', *śā-s-* 'to command', *v-as-* 'to clothe', which means that originally they did not belong to the root class. Such roots tend to be irregular in the matter of accent and apophony. Some reduplicated formations have come to be classed here, e.g. *jakṣ-* (1) 'to laugh' (*has-*), (2) 'to eat' (*ghas-*) which retains some features of reduplicated inflection (3 pl. act. *jákṣati*), and *niṃs-* 'to touch closely, kiss' (*nas-*); likewise certain intensive formations which are treated as roots by the grammarians: *jāgarti* 'is awake', *daridrāti* 'runs about, is poor', *dīdeti* 'shines'.

Here are classified certain roots making a stem by means of the suffix *i*, namely, in the classical language, *rud-* 'to weep', *svap-* 'to sleep', *an-* 'to breathe', *śvas-* 'to breathe' and *jakṣ-* 'to eat': 3 sg. pres. *roditi, svapiti*, etc. Further examples are found in the Vedic language: *vámiti* 'vomits', *janiṣva* 'be born', *vásiṣva* 'wear', *śnathihi* 'smash', *stanihi* 'roar', and the M.Bh. has *śocimi*. This formation corresponds to the Latin 3rd conjugation verbs of the type *capio* (*capis, capit . . . capiunt*). Like the other non-thematic classes it shows changes in accent and apophony (1 pl. *rudimás*), but it had originally nothing to do with the root class, being an independent formation. But it is a formation which from the earliest period of the language is on the way to obsolescence. Most of the forms quoted are isolated and not parts of complete paradigms. Even in the most stable group which the classical language preserves, the *i*-suffix is absent before endings beginning with a vowel (3 pl. *rudánti*) and in the 2 and 3 sg. impf. it is replaced either by long *ī* (*ā́nīt*), or by a thematic formation (*ā́nat*). The type has ceased to form a full separate class, and by interpreting the suffix as the union vowel *i* (*iṭ*), and attaching it to the root class, the grammarians were able to account for most of its characteristics.

A suffix *ī* appears in the conjugation of *brū-* 'to speak', but only in the strong forms before terminations beginning with a consonant (*brávīti, ábravīt*; *ábravam, bruvánti*). In the corresponding Avestan verb it does not appear at all: 3 sg. *mraoiti*, impf. *mraoṯ*. The suffix has importance elsewhere in the formation of verbal stems, namely in Latin (*audīre*) and Slavonic

(O. Sl. *supitŭ* ' sleeps ' *mluvitŭ* ' mutters '). Like the short *i* above it is obsolescent in Sanskrit, and in addition to *brū-* only a few roots are found to take it in the Vedic language : *ámīti* (*am-* ' to injure '), *tavīti* (*tū-* ' to be strong '), *śamīṣva* (*śam-* ' to labour ').

The Reduplicating Class (3rd or *hu-* class)

Paradigm : (*hu-* ' to sacrifice ').

Present, Active, S. 1 *juhómi*, 2 *juhóṣi*, 3 *juhóti*, D. 1 *juhuvás*, 2 *juhuthás*, 3 *juhutás*, P. 1 *juhumás*, 2 *juhuthá*, 3 *júhvati*.

Middle, S. 1 *júhve*, 2 *juhuṣé*, 3 *juhuté*, D. 1 *juhuváhe*, 2 *júhvāthe*, 3 *júhvāte*, P. 1 *juhumáhe*, 2 *juhudhvé*, 3 *júhvate*.

Imperfect, Active, S. 1 *ájuhavam*, 2 *ájuhos*, 3 *ájuhot*, D. 1 *ájuhuva*, 2 *ájuhutam*, 3 *ájuhutām*, P. 1 *ájuhuma*, 2 *ájuhuta*, 3 *ájuhavur*.

Middle, S. 1 *ájuhvi*, 2 *ájuhuthās*, 3 *ájuhuta*, D. 1 *ájuhuvahi*, 2 *ájuhvāthām*, 3 *ájuhvātām*, P. 1 *ájuhumahi*, 2 *ájuhudhvam*, 3 *ájuhvata*.

Forms according to this class are made from some 50 roots all told, but only from 16 in the classical language. The formation is well represented also in Greek : πί(μ)πλημι, πί(μ)πλαμεν ' I, we fill ', Skt. *píparmi*, *piprmás* ; εἰσπιφράναι ' to introduce ', cf. Skt. *bíbharmi*, *bibhr̥más* ; δίδωμι, Skt. *dádāmi* ; τίθημι, Skt. *dádhāmi* ; ἵστημι, Skt. *tiṣṭhāmi* (transferred to thematic class). Elsewhere it has become comparatively rare.

The vowel of reduplication corresponds to the radical vowel in the case of roots containing the vowels *i* and *u* : *cikéti* ' observes ', *jihréti* ' is ashamed ', *viveṣṭi* ' is active ', *bibhéti* ' fears ', *ninikta* 2 pl. impv. ' wash ' ; *yuyoti* ' separates '. In other roots it is sometimes *i* and sometimes *a*.

(a) *jigharti* ' sprinkles ', *píparti* ' fills ', *bibhárti* ' bears ', *jigāti* ' goes ', *mímāti* ' bellows ', *śiśāti* ' sharpens ', *síṣakti* ' cleaves to ' (*saj-*).

(b) *dádāti* ' gives ', *dádhāti* ' places ', *jahāti* ' leaves ', *bábhasti* ' eats ', *vavartti* ' turns ', *sásasti* ' sleeps ', *saścati* ' they accompany '.

This is in contradistinction to Greek which has almost exclusively *-i-* in the reduplicating syllable.

The accent of verbs of this class is somewhat unstable. It may appear on the root in the strong forms (*juhóti*, etc.) which is in accordance with the guṇa of the root, or in the case of certain verbs on the reduplication (*dádhāti*, etc.). The latter type is most prevalent in the Vedic language, appearing often when the later language has radical accent (*bíbharti* : *bibhárti*). Greek has also accent of the reduplication (δίδωμι, etc.), but the apophony indicates that radical accent must be original in the three persons of the singular active. On the other hand accent of the reduplication appears to be ancient in the 3 pl. active, where both root and ending appear in weakened form : *dádati*, *sáścati*. In the weak forms the normal accentuation of the terminations is found, with the exception that the accent is thrown back on to the reduplicating syllable when the termination begins with a vowel (*júhve*, *bíbhre*, etc.). This develops in the post-Vedic period (V. *juhvé*) from the analogy of the 3rd person plural.

The weakening of the radical vowel results in samprasāraṇa in the case of *vyac-* (*viviktás*) and *hvar-* (*juhūrthās*), and in loss of syllable in *sac-* and *bhas-* (3 pl. *sáścati*, *bapsati*). Roots in long *ā* are treated variously. In the commonest, *dā-* and *dhā-*, the root is fully reduced and the vowel elided : *dadvás*, *dadmás* ; *dadhvás*, *dadhmás*, etc. In the case of other roots this type is superseded by one in which the vowel *-i-*, or more usually *-ī-* is inserted between the reduced form of the root and the termination. The short appears in some forms from the root *hā-* 'to leave' : *jah-i-mas*, *jahihi*, etc. This reduplicated formation may be compared to the type *svapiti* of the root class. Normally however the vowel is long : *śiś-ī-hi* (*śā-* 'to sharpen'), *mímīte* (*mā-* 'to measure'), *rarīthās* (*rā-* 'to bestow'), etc. The prevalence of the long vowel is due to rhythmical reasons, and the suffixal *ī* balances the *ā* of the root in such a way that the two have acquired the appearance of being the strong and weak forms of the root.

The nu- and u- Classes (Fifth and Eighth, *su-* and *tan-* classes)

Present, Active, S. 1 *sunómi*, 2 *sunóṣi*, 3 *sunóti*, D. 1 *sunuvás*, etc. . . . P. 3 *sunvánti*, Middle, S. 1 *sunvé*, 2 *sunuṣé*. . . . P. 3 *sunváte*.

Imperfect, Active, S. 1 *ásunavam*, 2 *ásunos*, 3 *ásunot*, D. 1 *ásunuva*. . . . P. 3 *ásunvan*, Middle, S. 1 *ásunvi*, 2 *ásunuthās*, 3 *ásunuta*, D. 1 *ásunuvahi*. . . . P. 3 *ásunvata*.

About 50 roots make presents according to this class. Typical examples are : *ṛṇóti* 'rises' (cf. Gk. ὄρνῡμι), *stṛṇóti* 'strews' (cf. Gk. στόρνῡμι), *kṣiṇóti* 'destroys' (cf. Gk. φθίνω, *φθινύθω*) *minóti* 'harms, lessens' (cf. Lat. *minuo*), *dhūnóti* 'shakes' (cf. Gk. *θῦνω* 'rage'), *tṛpṇóti* 'is satisfied', *ṛdhnóti* 'thrives', *āpnóti* 'reaches, obtains', *aśnóti* 'obtains', etc. This suffix, which is compounded of *n* and *u*, appears also in the formation of nouns, frequently from the same roots, e.g. *dhṛṣṇú-* 'bold' beside *dhṛṣṇóti* 'is bold'. In a series of roots the alternative suffix *nā* (ninth class) appears side by side with *no/nu* : *vṛṇóti* : *vṛṇāti* ; *stṛṇóti* : *stṛṇāti* ; *kṣiṇóti* : *kṣiṇā́ti*.

A simple suffix *u*, without the *n*, often appears in related formations : *ṛṇóti*, cf. Gk. *ὀρούω* ; *stṛṇóti*, cf. Goth. *straujan* ; *vṛṇóti* 'covers', cf. *várutra-* ; *dhṛṣṇóti* 'is bold', cf Gk. *θρασύς* ; *dabhnóti* 'injures, deceives', cf. *ádbhuta-* '(that cannot be hurt, divine) wonderful' ; *jinóti* 'enlivens', cf. *jīvá-* 'alive' ; *sādhnóti* 'accomplishes', cf. *sādhú-* 'straight, good'. The same relation exists between *kṣurá-* 'razor' and *kṣṇáuti* 'sharpens', which the complete incorporation of the suffix has caused to be transferred to the root class. In *śru-* 'to hear' (partc. *śrutá-*, Gk. *κλυτός*, etc.) this *u* has been incorporated in the root everywhere except in the present tense (*śṛṇóti* : IE **kḷ-n-eu-ti*). In Iranian, by later substitution it appears even here (Av. *surunaoiti*).

Verbal classes corresponding to this appear in Greek (*ὄρνῡμι* etc.) and Hittite, where the formation has developed a special causative sense (*arnummi*, etc.), but in neither case is the old apophony seen in Sanskrit preserved intact. Elsewhere formations of this type have been replaced by thematic formations (Ir. *ro cluinethar* 'hears', etc.). Thematic formations based on this suffix are found : *pínvati* 'fattens' (cf. *pinute*, Av. *pinaoiti*), *invati* 'drives, attacks' (cf. *inóti*), *hínvati* 'impels' (cf. *hi nóti*) *jínvati* 'enlivens' (cf. *jinóti*).

In accent and apophony this class conforms to the normal type, with the usual Vedic irregularities, e.g. strong form of suffix in 2 pl. (*ákṛṇota*(*na*)) and final accentuation of 3 pl. middle (*kṛṇvaté*, *vṛṇvaté*, etc.). Concerning the form of the endings it may be noted that the *u* of the suffix may optionally be omitted in the 1 du. and pl. (*sunvás*, *sunmás* ; this starts of course in the 1 du.), and that before vocalic terminations *-nuv-* appears instead of *-nv-* after roots ending in a consonant (*śaknuvánti* 'they are able'). The terminations *-é* of the 3 sg. middle (*śṛṇvé* 'is heard', *sunvé* 'is pressed') and *-ré* of the 3 pl. (*śṛṇviré*, *sunviré* etc.) appear sporadically in the Veda, the latter being always associated with the union vowel *-i-*. This union vowel is found also in Vedic *śṛṇviṣé* 2 sg. middle.

Under the eighth class are classified certain roots formed by the simple suffix *o/u* instead of *no/nu*. These consist of a number of roots terminating in *n*: *tan-* 'to stretch', 3 sg. *tanóti*, similarly *sanóti* 'wins' (cf. Gk. ἄνυμι 'achieve'), *vanóti* 'wins', *manuté* 'thinks', *kṣaṇóti* 'wounds', and the root *kṛ-* 'to do': 3 sg. *karóti*. There is some uncertainty in interpreting the forms from the roots in *-n*, since it is possible to argue that here the suffix is really *no/nu* before which *a* stands for *n̥* appearing in the reduced form of the root (*tn̥-neu-ti*). On the whole it seems preferable to adopt the simpler theory, and evidence for it may be seen in the existence of Vedic *tarute* which appears to be exactly parallel to *manuté*.

The other important root classed here, namely *kṛ-* 'to do' (*karóti, kuruté*) also presents a problem because both the Vedic language and Iranian agree in inflecting it as a *nu*-verb (V. *kṛṇóti, kṛṇuté*, Av. *kərənaoiti*, O. Pers. *akunavam* <*akṛnavam*). This might suggest that the classical forms are 'prakritisms', but this is rendered implausible by the fact that a phonetic development of *ṛṇ* to *ar/ur* is wholly anomalous in Middle Indo-Aryan (cf. *tṛ́ṇa-* 'grass' > *táṇa-, tiṇa*, etc., and Pkt. *kuṇaï* from the Vedic form of the verb). The formation must therefore be regarded as a genuine and ancient dialect variant formed, like *tarute*, with the simple suffix *u*, which also appears in the Vedic noun *karúṇa-* nt. 'action'. The weak form of the root presents some complication since normally either complete reduction (*kr-*) or restoration of guṇa as in *tarute* might be expected. Since suffixal H which produces the combination *-ur-* in the weak grade elsewhere (*gurú-*, etc.) is here out of the question, the only theory that remains to explain the form of the weak grade is the assumption that the root originally began with a labio-velar. The form *kur-* may then be classed with those survivals where this labial element is found to function as a vowel (Gk. γυνή, Hitt. *kunanzi*, etc., see p. 74). As to the etymology it seems that the IE root *kʷel-* diverged in Indo-Iranian, consequent on the second palatalisation, to produce two roots, on the one hand an intransitive *car-* 'to move, go', and on the other hand a transitive *kṛ-* 'to do, make'.

The *u* of the suffix of this verb is always omitted in those cases where such omission is optional in the *nu*-verbs (*kurmás*, etc.). It is also omitted in the active of the optative : *kuryā́m* as opposed to *kurvīyá*. These may be radical formations incorporated in this conjugation.

The nā- Class (Ninth or *krī-* class)

Present, Active, S. 1 *krīṇā́mi*, 2 *krīṇā́si*, 3 *krīṇā́ti*, D. 1 *krīṇīvás*, 2 *krīṇīthás*, 3 *krīṇītás*, P. 1 *krīṇīmás*, 2 *krīṇīthá*, 3 *krīṇánti*.

Middle, P. 1 *krīṇé*, 2 *krīṇīṣé*, 3 *krīṇīté*, D. 1 *krīṇīváhe*, 2 *krīṇā́the*, 3 *krīṇā́te*, P. 1 *krīṇīmáhe*, 2 *krīṇīdhvé*, 3 *krīṇáte*.

Imperfect, Active, S. 1 *ákrīṇām*, 2 *ákrīṇās*, 3 *ákrīṇāt*, D. 1 *ákrīṇīva*, 2 *ákrīṇītam*, 3 *ákrīṇītam*, P. 1 *ákrīṇīma*, 2 *ákrīṇīta*, 3 *ákrīṇan*.

Middle, S. 1 *ákrīṇi*, 2 *ákrīṇīthās*, 3 *ákrīṇīta*, D. 1 *ákrīṇīvahi*, 2 *ákrīṇāthām*, 3 *ákrīṇātām*, P. 1 *ákrīṇīmahi*, 2 *ákrīṇīdhvam*, 3 *ákrīṇata*.

Some fifty roots all told make presents according to this class. Typical examples are : *krīṇā́ti* 'buys' (cf. Ir. *crenaid*), *linā́ti* 'sticks, adheres to' (cf. Ir. *lenaid* 'id'), *śṛṇā́ti* 'smashes' (cf. Ir. *ara·chrinat* 3 pl. 'collapse'), *jinā́ti* 'inflicts loss', *mṛṇā́ti* 'crushes', *pṛṇā́ti* 'fills', etc.

The suffix is compounded of *n* and *ā* (-*a*H-), and these elements often appear separately in related formations. The *n* which appears in *iṣṇā́ti* appears in connection with other elements in *iṣaṇat* and *iṣaṇyáti*. The *ā*-suffix without *n* appears in a number of parallel formations in -*āya*- : *gṛbhāyáti*, *mathāyáti*, *skabhāyáti* beside *gṛbhṇā́ti*, etc. The *ā* is often partially incorporated in the roots, e.g. in *jyā-* 'to inflict loss' and *prā-* 'to fill' beside the presents *jinā́ti*, *pṛṇā́ti* ; cf. the same process, though more complete, in *śru-/śro* beside *śṛṇóti*. With the addition of the weak form of the suffix roots in *i*, *u* and *ṛ* become roots in *ī*, *ū*, and *ṝ*. This is how they are normally given and how they normally appear outside the present system : *prītá-* 'pleased', *pūtá-* 'purified' (: *punā́ti*), *pūrṇá-* 'full' (: *pṛṇā́ti*). In the tense there are two kinds of treatment : (a) the unextended form of the root appears before -*nā*-, e.g. *jinā́ti*, *punā́ti*, *mṛṇā́ti* ; (b) the extended form of the root is introduced even into this formation, e.g. *prīṇā́ti*, *bhrīṇā́ti*, a process which is found only in the case of roots in *i*. The root *vlī-* 'to press down' makes both types and Pali has *kiṇāti* 'buys' (corresponding to the Celtic form) as opposed to Skt. *krīṇā́ti*.

The alternation between the strong form of the suffix *-nā-* with *-nī-* in the weak cases is not found outside Sanskrit. In Greek there is alternation between long and short vowel, *δάμνημι, δαμνᾰμεν*. In Avestan complete loss of *ā* in the weak grade, which is the regular Indo-Iranian phonetic development, is found: 3 sg. mid. *vərəntē, °stərəntē*. In Sanskrit this type is replaced by one containing an extra suffix *-ī-*, in a way similar to that observed in the third class, e.g. *vṛṇīté* having the same relation to Av. *vərəntē* as Skt. *mimīté*, etc., to *datté*. This *ī* is only introduced before the consonantal terminations; before vowels the simple reduced form of the suffix is found: *jānáte*, cf. A. *zānaitē*.

Nasal-infixing Class (Seventh, *rudh-* class)

Present, Active, S. 1 *yunájmi*, 2 *yunákṣi*, 3 *yunákti*, D. 1 *yuñjvás*, 2 *yuṅkthás*, 3 *yuṅktás*, P. 1 *yuñjmás*, 2 *yuṅkthá*, 3 *yuñjánti*.

Middle, S. 1 *yuñjé*, 2 *yuṅkṣé*, etc. ... P. 2 *yuṅgdhvé*, 3 *yuñjáte*.

Imperfect, Active, S. 1 *áyunajam*, 2 *áyunak*, 3 *áyunak*, D. 1 *áyuñjva*, etc. ... P. 3 *áyuñjan*.

Middle, S. 1 *áyuñji*, 2 *áyuṅkthās*, etc. ... P. 3 *áyuñjata*.

About thirty roots inflect in this manner. Common examples are: *riṇákti* 'leaves' (Lat. *linquo*), *chid-* 'cut', *chinatti* (Lat. *scindo*), *bhid-* 'split', *bhinatti* (Lat. *findo*), *piṣ-* 'crush', *piṇaṣṭi* (Lat. *pinso*), *añj-* 'anoint', *anákti* (Lat. *unguo*), *bhuj-*, *bhunákti* 'benefits', *bhuṅkté* 'enjoys' (Lat. *fungor*).

In most languages outside Indo-Iranian the strong forms have been replaced by the weak forms, and the whole type transferred to the thematic class. The same tendency is seen in Skt. *vindáti* finds as opposed to Av. *vinasti*, and in the later history of Indo-Aryan such forms completely replace the older type (Pa. *yuñjati*, etc.). In Hittite the corresponding class has a double nasal infix and no apophony, e.g. *ḫarnink-* 'to destroy'; both these features are special developments of Hittite, out of the regular IE type which Sanskrit preserves.

This type appears superficially to be different from the two preceding types, the present stem being made by infixation instead of suffixation. Ultimately they are not really different, since in most of the roots of this class, the final consonant can be interpreted as an extension, that is to say originally a suffix which in course of time has become incorporated in the root.

Beside the root *yuj-* 'to join' for instance there is also a simpler root *yu-* (*yáuti*) with the same meaning. Evidence of the same kind is available in the case of a number of roots: e.g. *chid-* 'to cut', cf. *chyáti* 'cuts', *chitá-* 'cut'; *ric-* 'to leave', *riṇákti*, cf. *riṇā́ti* 'lets flow'; *tṛd-* 'to pierce', *tṛṇátti*, cf. *tṛ́ṇa-* 'grass', Engl. *thorn*; *kṛt-* 'to spin', *kṛṇátti*, cf. Lat. *colus* 'distaff'. In such cases the analysis of the forms of this class is the same as of those of the other two nasal classes: 5 *kḷ-n-éw-ti* (*śṛṇóti*), 9 *pḷ-n-é*H*-ti* (*pṛṇā́ti*), 7 *yu-n-ég-ti* (*yunákti*).

At the same time not all forms can be explained in this way, e.g. *anákti* 'anoints'. Once the infixing class was established through the incorporation of the second suffix, it attracted a certain number of other roots which did not belong to the original nucleus.

B. *Thematic Presents*

Radically Accented Class (First or *bhu-* class)

Present, Active, S. 1 *bhávāmi*, 2 *bhávasi*, 3 *bhávati*, D. 1 *bhávāvas*, 2 *bhávathas*, 3 *bhávatas*, P. 1 *bhávāmas*, 2 *bhávatha*, 3 *bhávanti*.

Middle, S. 1 *bháve*, 2 *bhávase*, 3 *bhávate*, D. 1 *bhávāvahe*, 2 *bhávethe*, 3 *bhávete*, P. 1 *bhávāmahe*, 2 *bhávadhve*, 3 *bhávante*.

Imperfect, Active, S. 1 *ábhavam*, 2 *ábhavas*, 3 *ábhavat*, D. 1 *ábhavāva*, 2 *ábhavatam*, 3 *ábhavatām*, P. 1 *ábhavāma*, 2 *ábhavata*, 3 *ábhavan*.

Middle, S. 1 *ábhave*, 2 *ábhavathās*, 3 *ábhavata*, D. 1 *ábhavāvahi*, 2 *ábhavethām*, 3 *ábhavetām*, P. 1 *ábhavāmahi*, 2 *ábhavadhvam*, 3 *ábhavanta*.

This is the commonest of all the present classes in Sanskrit, being formed by nearly half of the verbal roots in the language. The predominance of thematic formations is paralleled in the nominal stems, and it recurs in other IE languages. Direct equations between Sanskrit and other languages, attesting IE forms, are commoner in this class than anywhere. Examples are: *plávate*, *právate* 'floats', Gk. πλέ(Ϝ)ω; *srávati* 'flows', Gk. ῥέει; *svánati* 'sounds', O. Lat. *sonit*; *stánati* 'roars', Gk. στένει; *bhárati* 'bears', Gk. φέρω, Lat. *fero*, Goth. *baíriþ*, Ir. *berid*, O. Sl. *beretŭ*; *cárati* 'goes', Gk. πέλομαι, Lat. *colo*; *bódhati* 'understands', Gk. πεύθομαι; *jóṣate* 'enjoys', Gk. γεύομαι 'taste', Goth. *kiusiþ* 'tests, chooses'; *ródhati*, *róhati* 'grows', Goth. *liudiþ*; *óṣati* 'burns', Gk. εὔω, Lat. *ūro*;

vártate 'turns', Lat. *vertitur*; *párdate* 'breaks wind', Gk. πέρδεται; *sárpati* 'creeps', Gk. ἕρπει, Lat. *serpit*; *yásati* 'seethes', Gk. ζέω; *váhati* 'carries', Gk. Pamph. Ϝέχω, Lat. *vehit*, O. Sl. *vezetŭ*; *vásati* 'dwells', Goth. *wisiþ* 'is'; *násate* 'resorts to', Gk. νέομαι 'return', Goth. *ganisiþ* 'is saved'; *májjati* 'plunges', Lat. *mergit*; *trásati* 'trembles', Gk. τρέω; *pátati* 'flies', Gk. πέτομαι; *sthágati* 'covers', Gk. στέγει, Lat. *tegit*; *sácate* 'associates with', Gk. ἕπεται 'follows', Lat. *sequitur* 'id'; *dáhati* 'burns', Lith. *degù*; *pácati* 'cooks', Lat. *coquit*, O. Sl. *pečetŭ*; *tákṣati* '(carpenter) joins, constructs; hews', Lat. *texit* 'weaves'; *hávate* 'calls', Av. *zavaiti*, O. Sl. *zovetŭ*; *ájati* 'drives', Gk. ἄγει, Lat. *agit*, Ir. *ad·aig*; *ánati* 'breathes' (beside *ániti*), Goth. *uzaniþ* 'breathes out, expires'.

The majority of roots conform to the normal type, the stem consisting of the accented and guṇated root followed by the thematic vowel. In a small number of verbs vṛddhi instead of guṇa is found: *bā́dhate* 'repels', *bhrā́jate* 'shines', *dhā́vati* 'runs' (Gk. θέω with guṇa grade), *krā́mati* 'strides' (beside middle *krámate*), *ācāmati* 'sips'. The class is augmented by a number of varied thematic formations with accent on the root or first syllable which did not originally belong here: e.g. (1) a form with infixed nasal, *níndati* 'blames' (cf. *níd-* 'contempt, insult', Gk. ὄνειδος); formations of this type are commoner in the sixth class; (2) forms with a suffix *-va*: *jī́vati* 'lives', *tū́rvati* 'overcomes', etc.; in such cases it can be seen from the apophony that the initial accent is not original; (3) stems containing the IE inchoative suffix *-ske/sko-* (> *ccha-*) with secondary radical accent: *gácchati* 'goes' (cf. Gk. βάσκε, impv.) *yácchati* 'holds'; (4) reduplicated thematic formations: *tíṣṭhati* 'stands' (*sthā-*), cf. Lat. *sistit*, *píbati* 'drinks' (*pā-*), Ir. *ibid*, *jíghrati* 'smells' (*ghrā-*); in *sī́dati* 'sits', Lat. *sīdo* (IE *sizd-* from *sed-*) the normal phonetic development would have given *ḍ* in Sanskrit, but *d* appears here through the influence of other parts of the conjugation.

Suffixally Accented Class (Sixth or *tud-* class)

This and the following two classes are conjugated in exactly the same way as the preceding. The sixth class is fairly common, something like 150 roots being conjugated in this way. Typical examples: *rujáti* 'breaks', *viśáti* 'enters', *tudáti* 'pushes', *diśáti* 'points out', *mṛśáti* 'strokes', *spṛśáti* 'touches', *suváti* 'drives', *kiráti* 'scatters', *sṛjáti* 'lets go'. In contrast to Sanskrit this type is rare in most of the IE languages, because the preceding class has become normal for thematic verbs. In Greek this type of stem is found usually only in aoristic use, where its contrasts in apophony with the normal thematic presents, *φεύγω* : *ἔφυγον*. In such presents of this type as can be found the accent has been transferred to the root (*γλύφω*).

A fairly common sub-class here is formed by roots taking an infixed nasal: *siñcáti* 'sprinkles', *muñcáti* 'releases', *vindáti* 'finds', *kṛntáti* 'cuts', *lumpáti* 'breaks', *limpáti* 'smears'. Some are obvious transfers from the seventh class, e.g. *undáti*, *yuñjáti* beside *unátti*, *yunákti*, and it is possible that the whole series arose in this way.

The accented suffix *-cchá-* (IE *-ske-*) appears in *icchátí* 'wishes', *ucchátí* 'shines', *ṛcchátí* 'goes' (roots *iṣ-*, *vas-*, *ṛ*). In *pṛcchátí* 'asks' (Lat. *poscit*) it has been incorporated into the root (pf. *papráccha*), but the unextended root appears occasionally in nominal derivatives: *praśná-* 'question'.

Ya- Class (Fourth or *div-* class)

The fourth class contains some 130 roots which form their present by means of the suffix *ya*: e.g. *kúpyati* 'is angry', *krúdhyati* 'id', *túṣyati* 'is pleased', *yúdhyati* 'fights', *vídhyati* 'pierces' (*vyadh-*), *dī́vyati* 'plays', *hṛ́ṣyati* 'rejoices', *tápyate* 'is hot', *páśyati* 'sees', *náhyati* 'ties'. This suffix is also used in the formation of denominative verbs, and the form of the passive differs from the middle of this class only in having suffixal accent. The formation is found in Hittite (*wemiezzi* 'finds', *zaḫḫiezi* 'fights') and Greek (*μαίνεται* 'is mad', cf. Skt. *mányate* 'thinks', *βαίνω*, *στίζω*, etc.). In Latin on the other hand non-thematic stems in *-i* appear instead of this type (*cupio*, *cupit* as opposed to Skt. *kúpyati*). In Sanskrit the existence of a present *stányati* 'thunders' (O. Sl. *stenjǫ*) beside the non-thematic *stanihi* illustrates how the formation may arise by the thematic enlargement of an *i-stem* in the same way as in nominal stems (°*kravi*° : *kravya-*, etc.). The apophony of the majority of forms indicates original suffixal accent, such as is found in the passive. On the other hand there are certain forms with vṛddhied root, e.g.

mādyati 'becomes intoxicated', *śrā́myati* 'becomes tired', which must have had radical accent from the beginning, which makes it appear that there were originally two types combined in this class.

Certain roots in *ā* which belong here, e.g. *gā-* 'to sing' (*gā́yati*), *glā-* 'to be weary' (*glā́yati*), *trā-* 'to save' (*trā́yate*) and *dhyā-* 'to think' (*dhyā́yati*), are by the grammarians attached to the first class by the wholly unnecessary assumption of roots of the form *gāi-*, etc. Since the roots are certainly to be set up as *gā-*, etc., these presents must be attached to this class, in which their form and accent are regular.

There are a number of roots in *ā* which lose this vowel before the accented suffix *-yá-* : *dā-* 'to bind' (*d-yáti*), *chā-* 'to cut' (*chyáti*), *śā-* 'to sharpen' (*śyáti*) and *sā-* 'to bind' (*syáti* : cf. Hitt. *išḫiya-* 'bind'). They retain what must have been, as noted above, the original accent of this class, because the complete reduction of the radical syllable made impossible any shift of accent to the root.

The Tenth Class (*cur-* class)

The suffix is *-áya-*. This has normally been specialised in the formation of causative verbs, but it is not exclusively used for this purpose, and a nucleus of forms remain which belong to the primary rather than the secondary conjugation. In the language of the Veda there is a fairly clear distinction between presents in *áya* which do not have strengthening of the root (guṇa or vṛddhi) in which a causative sense is usually absent, and those in which it is so strengthened which are normally causative. Examples of the former are : *citáya-* 'notice, observe', *iṣáya-* 'flourish', *turáya-* 'hasten, speed', *dyutáya-* 'shine', *rucáya-* 'id', *śubháya-* 'be splendid', *mṛḍáya-* 'pardon', *spṛháya-* 'desire', *patáya-* 'fly about'. Here belong originally such presents as *hváyati* 'calls', *śváyati* 'swells' and *dh-áyati* 'sucks', which the grammarians have attached to the first class by the assumption of the root forms *śvi-*, *hve-*, *dhe-*.

In the classical language the verbs classified here are more miscellaneous and they include a variety of formations of denominative or causative origin : e.g. *kāmáyate* 'desires', *coráyati* 'steals', *chādáyati* 'covers', *avalokayati* 'looks upon', *dūṣáyati* 'spoils', *bhūṣáyati* 'adorns', *tāḍáyati* 'beats', etc.

§9. The Future

The stem of the future is formed by means of the suffix *-syá-*, or, with connecting vowel *-i-*, *-iṣya-* added to the guṇated root, and it is inflected in precisely the same way as the thematic presents: *dāsyáti* 'he will give', *dhokṣyáti* 'he will milk', *bhaviṣyáti* 'he will be', *kariṣyáti* 'he will do', etc. There are no simple rules by which the distribution of the two forms can be stated. In Iranian there exists a corresponding formation in *-sya-* (Av. *vaxšyā* 'I will say'), but none corresponding to *-iṣya-*. The same formation appears in Lithuanian: *dúosiu* 'I will give'. On the other hand the Greek future (δείξω, etc.) appears to be based on a simple *so*-stem. In the early period of the Sanskrit language the future tense is comparatively rare, as it is in the *Avesta*, the sense of the future being most usually expressed by the subjunctive, but it rapidly becomes more common.

The future is a specialised type of present stem and it belongs with the various denominative formations in *-yá-*. It is capable of forming a preterite in the same way as the present stems proper. This formation functions as a conditional: *yad evam nâvakṣyo mūrdhā te vyapatiṣyat* 'If you had not spoken in this way, your head would have fallen off'. Only one example of the conditional is found in the *Ṛgveda* and it is never very common during any period of the language.

In addition to the ordinary future Sanskrit created a second or periphrastic future based on the agent nouns in *-tar*. In the third person the nom. sg., du. and pl. of such nouns functions as the second future without any addition: *kartā́*, *kartā́rau*, *kartā́ras*. In the first and second persons forms of the verb 'to be' are added to the nom. sg. of agent noun, in the dual and plural as well as in the singular: *kartā́smi*, *kartā́si*; *kartā́svas*; *kartā́smas*. The function of the second future is to express the future in connection with some specified time: *śvó vraṣṭā́* 'it will rain tomorrow', etc. This type of future first begins to appear in the Brāhmaṇa period, and its use continues later, though it is never anything like as common as the first future. There was created also a corresponding middle, which, however, is exceedingly rare, since it appears to have been current in the living language for only a very limited period. The special middle forms, which exist only for the first and second persons, are as follows: S. 1 *kartā́he*, 2 *kartā́se*, D. 1 *kartā́svahe*, 2 *kartā́sāthe*, P. 1 *kartā́smahe*, 2 *kartā́dhve*.

§ 10. The Aorist

The aorist is formed by seven different types of stem which fall clearly into two classes, non-sigmatic and sigmatic. Of the non-sigmatic types the root aorist (*ádhāt*) and the *a*-aor. (*áruhat*) do not differ in their formation from the imperfects of the corresponding present classes (*áyāt, átudat*). It has been pointed out that the two types of preterite, imperfect and aorist, have arisen by specialisation out of a system with undifferentiated preterite, and the continued existence of forms common to the two remains as an indication of this. The difference in function depends on whether a corresponding present exists or not. The reduplicating aorist is less closely connected with corresponding present stems and it has undergone special developments of its own, but it cannot be separated in origin from the reduplicating type of present. On the other hand the various aorist *s*-stems are formations which are confined to this use, with the rarest exceptions (Av. *nāismi* is a present from an *s*-aor. stem.)

The Root-Aorist

The root-aorist is abundantly represented in the Vedic language. The apophony differs from that which is regular in the imperfect in that guṇa of the root appears normally in all the persons of the active with the exception of the third person plural. The normal weak form of the root appears in the middle. Typical forms are: S. 1 *áśravam, agām, ákaram*, 2 *ágās, áśres, akar* (for *ákars*), 3 *áśrot, ásthāt, ákar* (for *ákart*, cf. Av. *čōrət̰*), D. 2 *agātam, ábhūtam* 3 *ákartām, ádhātām*, P. 1 *ákarma, ádāma, áhema*, 2 *ákarta, ágāta, áhetana*, 3 (a) *ákran, ákṣan* (*ghas-*), *ágman*, (b) *ádhur, ásthur, ákramur*.

Middle: S. 1 *ákri, áyuji*, 2 *ákṛthās, agathās, ayukthās*, 3 *ákṛta, ámata* (*man-*), *áyukta*, D. 1 *ganvahi* (*gam-*), P. 1 *ágan-mahi, ámanmahi* (with strong form of root), *ayujmahi, áhūmahi*, 2 *acidhvam, ayugdhvam*, 3 (a) *akrata, ágmata*, (b) *ádṛśran, abudhran*, (c) *ádṛśram, ábudhram*.

The root aorist of the root *bhū-* (which is conjugated only in the active) is anomalous in having the weak grade throughout: *ábhūvam, ábhūs, ábhūt, . . . ábhūta, ábhūvan*.

Certain root aorists are attested as Indo-European by such correspondences as Skt. *ásthāt*, Gk. ἔστη; *ágāt*, Gk. ἔβη; *ágamam, ágan, ágata*, etc., cf. Arm. *ekn* 3 sg., Gk. βάτην 3 du.; 3 sg. mid. *akṣata*, Gk. ἔκτατο; impv. *kṣidhí* 'destroy', cf. Gk. ἔφθιτο, φθίμενος. The anomalous form of the root aorist of *bhū-* reappears in Greek, 3 sg. ἔφυ, etc. Occasionally what appears as root aorist in one language appears as imperfect in another, showing that the distribution of these radical stems between the two tenses was not completely settled in the IE period: Skt. *áhata* 3 sg. mid. impf., cf. Gk. ἄπεφατο : ἀπέθανεν (aor.); *kṣéti* 'dwells', Gk. κτίμενος (aorist stem); conversely Skt. *ávṛta*, aor. compared with Lat. *vult*, present.

The Greek aorists of roots in long vowel that belong here show the weak form of the root in the plural of the active (ἔδομεν, ἔθεμεν) which is in contradistinction to Sanskrit (*ádāma, ádhāma*), but, since it conforms to the general pattern of verbal apophony, doubtless more original. The weak forms that appear in the middle (ἔδοτο, ἔθετο) are in accordance with the Sanskrit practice, but in the case of roots in *ā* Sanskrit has, in accordance with its common practice, introduced the union vowel *-i-* into the middle forms to help out the conjugation: *a-dh-i-thās, adhita*; *adithās, adita*; *ásthithās, asthita, asthiran*. In some cases the union vowel appears as *ī* (cf. *-ī-* in the present, *brav-ī-ti* and elsewhere): *a-dh-ī-mahi, adīmahi* (*dā-* 'to cut'), *á-ś-ī-ta* (*śā-* 'to sharpen'). It seems necessary also to assume such an *-i-* after such roots, in this case after the strong forms, in the optatives (active) of the root aorist: *dheyām, deyām, stheyāma*, etc. (*sta*H*-i-yā-*, etc.), otherwise the roots should appear with *ā* (as *yāyām*, etc., of the present).

The phonetic tendencies which brought about the reduction of final consonant groups in the earliest Indo-Aryan strongly affected the 2 and 3 sg. active of the root aorist, producing forms which ceased to be grammatically clear and unambiguous: e.g. *akar*, or in the appropriate sandhis, *akaḥ*, etc.; *ānaṭ* for *-naś+s* and *-naś+t*; *aghas* 2 and 3 sg.; *skan* for *skand-t*, etc. In addition when the root terminates with an occlusive and the termination begins with one (*abhakta*, etc.) it is not possible to tell from the form itself the difference between root aorist and *s*-aorist, on account of the elision of *s* in such position. In the post-Vedic period the root aorist undergoes a rapid decline, and there is little doubt that this phonetic mutilation and the consequent ambiguities were largely responsible for the development. All that remains of the root aorist in the classical language is the active inflection of certain roots in *ā* (*ádāt*, etc.) and of *bhū-* (*ábhūt*).

In addition there are certain forms of the 2 and 3 middle of the root aorist (where the root terminates in a short vowel according to the grammarians) which in the later history of the language became heteroclitically attached to the *s*-aorist, e.g. we find 2 sg. *ávṛthās* and 3 sg. *ávṛta* forming part of the same paradigm with 1 sg. *ávṛṣi* and 3 pl. *ávṛṣata*, etc. In the same way the middle forms quoted above from the roots *dā-*, *dhā-*, *sthā-* with connecting vowel *-i-* are combined with *-iṣ-* aorist forms to produce a series like sg. 1 *a-sth-iṣ-i*, 2 *á-sth-i-thās*, 3 *ásthita*.

The a- Aorist

The form and conjugation of the *a*-aorist agrees with the imperfect accented *a*-class: *ásicam*, *ásicas*, *ásicat*, etc., cf. *átudam*, *átudas*, *átudat*, etc. The stems agree in apophony, and also in accent, in the comparatively rare instances where the unaugmented aorist forms bear the accent: S. 1 *ruhám*, 2 *vidás*, 3 *dhṛṣát*, *vidát*, P. 3 *dhvasán*, *vidán*, *tṛpán*; regularly in the participle *tṛpánt-* *dhṛṣánt-*, *śucánt-*, etc., middle, *śucámāna-*, etc.

Correspondences with other languages attest the IE date of a number of such formations: *ávidat*, Gk. *ἴδον*, inf. *ἰδεῖν*, Arm. *egit*; *dṛśan*, Gk. *ἔδρακον*; *áricat*, cf. Gk. *ἔλιπον*, Arm. *elikʻ*; *budhanta*, cf. Gk. *ἐπύθοντο*. At the same time there is sometimes disagreement between languages in the assignment of a form to imperfect or aorist: Skt. *ádaśat* impf.: Gk. *ἔδακον* aor.; Skt. *ábhujat* impf.: Gk. *ἔφυγε* aor. The suffixal accent is retained in Greek in participles and infinitives (*λιπών*, *λιπεῖν*).

In addition to the regular type there are a number of *a*-aorists in Sanskrit whose form agrees rather with imperfects of the first class rather than of the sixth class since they have guṇa of root: e.g. *áśakam*, *ásanam*, *ásaram*, *ákaras*, *ágamat*, *atanat*, *ásadat*. This is the normal form of the *a*-aorist for roots consisting of two consonants and the thematic vowel. Furthermore where accent occurs these forms are accented like stems of the first present class. Examples of this are *káras*, *sánat*, *sárat*, *dárśam* (= the Gk. present stem *δέρκομαι*), *gáman*, *sádatam, sádatam*, and the participles *sádant-, sánant* (these have also contaminated the regular type above to some extent, so that forms accented like *rúhat* occur occasionally).

A number of the stems listed here are probably thematisations of root aorists, and not ancient. For instance the *a*-aorist *ágamat* appears later in the history of the language than the root aorist *agan*. On the other hand some are clearly old (e.g. *ásadat*), and since the type appears also in Greek (ἐγένετο, γένεσθαι) it must be referred to Indo-European.

The *a*-aorist has attracted a number of reduplicated forms which did not originally belong to it, namely *ápaptat* (*pat-* ' to fall '), *ávocat* (for *avavc-, vac-* ' to speak ') and, with what in the perfect becomes a substitute for reduplication, *neśat* (*naś-* ' to perish ').

Reduplicated Aorist

Active, S. 1 *ájījanam*, 2 *ájījanas*, 3 *ájījanat*. . . . P. 3 *ájījanan*. Middle, S. 1 *ájījane*, 2 *ájījanathās*, 3 *ajījanata*. . . . P. 3 *ájījananta*. The typical reduplicating vowel of this is *ī* but the reduplication is subject to the following modifications: (1) If the root begins with two consonants short *i* is employed in reduplication: *acikṣipat, apispṛśat*. (2) If the root vowel is *u* the reduplicating vowel is *ū* or *u* under the same circumstances: *abūbudhat, acukrudhat*. (3) If the root is a heavy syllable two processes are found: (a) the root is unaltered and the reduplication is short: *adidīkṣam, abubhūṣam*; where the radical vowel is *a* followed by two consonants or long *ā* the reduplicating vowel is *a*: *adadakṣam, adadhāvam*; (b) in order to preserve the rhythm favoured in this aorist heavy roots may be weakened: *avīvaśam* (*vāś-*), *acikradat* (*krand-*). It is in accordance with this principle that roots appear either with guṇa or in the weak form: *ajījanat* but *avīvṛdhat*. Verbs which make a causative stem in *-āp-* substitute *-ip-* in the reduplicated aorist: *atiṣṭhipat* (*sthāpayati*). (4) Roots beginning with a vowel are found either to repeat the whole root (*āmamat*) or, later, to repeat the last consonant with *i* (*ārpipat*).

In the Vedic language there are a number of non-thematic forms attached to the reduplicated aorist: *ajīgar, aśiśnat, dīdhar*, etc. These represent an alternative type of the reduplicated aorist which was early abandoned owing to the prevalence of the thematic type.

The reduplicated aorist stands out from the other forms of aorist because it is attached not to the simple verb but to the causative; *ájījanat* is the aorist of *janáyati*, *ávīvṛdhat* of *vardháyati* and so forth. Such an aorist is therefore made from all roots which have causatives, in addition to their normal aorists. This arrangement is essentially a development of Indo-Aryan, though its roots go back to Indo-Iranian. The other IE languages have nothing which can strictly be compared. In form the stem of the reduplicated aorist is related to the reduplicating present (*bíbharti*), and more closely to the thematic variety of the same (*tíṣṭhati*; Gk. *γίγνομαι*; Lat. *gignit, sistit*) but it has developed features of its own, namely the length of the reduplication and the guṇa of the root in certain forms (*ajījanat*). The transitive sense which is observable in some of the related stems with this type of reduplication (Lat. *gignit*, etc.) has been generalised and eventually developed into a full causative.

Related Iranian forms provide some interesting information about the history of this formation, because it has also present stems formed in the same way: *zīzanənti* 3 pl., etc. (also non-thematic *zīzənti* 3 sg., cf. the Skt. type *ajīgar*). From this it is possible to conclude that originally this was a type of stem forming both present and preterite in the manner of the various formations of the present system. The aorist, it has been observed, came about by the specialisation of certain preterite formations, and this is a case in point. To begin with we may assume two pairs **jījanati* : *ájījanat* and *janáyati* : *ájanayat* having essentially the same sense. In the further development *janáyati* comes to be exclusively used in the present and *ájījanat* originally simple preterite (= imperfect) becomes when isolated integrated into the aorist system.

There are a few roots in the classical language which take this aorist as part of their primary conjugation, e.g. *aśiśriyat* and *adudruvat* from *śri-* 'to resort' and *dru-* 'to run'. There are further examples in the Veda (e.g. *ácikradat* from *krand-* 'to roar') and also some non-thematic forms which are made exactly like imperfects of the reduplicating class: *áśiśret, ádudrot*. Certain reduplicated stems which became attached to the *a*-aorist have already been mentioned. These continue the IE usage which had reduplicated aorists in primary function and none that were specifically causative: cf. Gk. ἔπεφνον, ἐκέκλετο, etc.

The s- Aorist

Active, S. 1 *ánaiṣam*, 2 *ánaiṣīs*, 3 *ánaiṣīt*, D. 1 *ánaiṣva*, 2 *ánaiṣṭam*, 3 *ánaiṣṭām*, P. 1 *ánaiṣma*, 2 *ánaiṣṭa*, 3 *ánaiṣur*.

Middle, S. 1 *áneṣi*, 2 *áneṣṭhās*, 3 *áneṣṭa*, D. 1 *áneṣvahi*, 2 *áneṣāthām*, 3 *áneṣātām*, P. 1 *áneṣmahi*, 2 *ánedhvam*, 3 *áneṣata*.

The s-aorist stem differs from other verbal stems in having the vṛddhi grade throughout the active, in the dual and plural as well as in the singular. In the middle roots with medial vowel *i*, *u*, *ṛ* appear in the weak form (*acchitsi*, *árutsi*, *ásṛkṣi*); also roots in final *ṛ* (*ákṛṣi*) and in the Veda certain roots with final nasal, e.g. *ágasmahi* from *gam*- and *masīya* opt. 1 sg. from *man*- (cf. Av. *māhmaidī*). Elsewhere there is guṇa. The subjunctive takes guṇa in both active and middle (*stoṣāni*, etc.) and this is extended to certain injunctive formṡ (*jeṣma*).

Before terminations beginning with occlusive when the root ends in such the s of this aorist is elided according to the usual phonetic rule : *araudh-s-ta* becomes *arauddha*, etc. This leads to some confusion between this aorist and the root aorist, but this is largely eliminated in the post-Vedic period by the disuse of the root aorist except in connection with very few roots. Phonetic decay also strongly affected the 2 and 3 sg. active, with the result that both the tense sign s and the terminations frequently disappear : *abhār* for *abhār-s-t* and *abhār-s-s*, similarly *araik*, *aśvait*, etc. In the post-Vedic period these inconvenient and ambiguous forms are abandoned and their place is taken by new formations taking the connecting vowel -*ī*- : *ánaiṣīt*, *ácchaitsīt*, etc.

The s-aorist and the other forms of sigmatic aorist are sharply distinguished from the other classes of aorist in that there are no present-imperfect stems formed in the same way. There are indeed in the Veda certain isolated forms of the present made in this way (*stuṣé*, *hiṣé*, *kṛṣe*) as well as some anomalous formations containing s which cannot be referred to the s-aorist stem (i *arcase*, *ṛñjase*, ii *gṛṇīṣé*, *puniṣé*) but these have the appearance of being tentative formations which never developed very far rather than relics of an earlier system.

The s-aorist is found in Greek (ἔζευξα, ἔδειξα, etc.) and Slavonic (*věsŭ*, *sluchŭ*, etc.). In Latin s-aorist forms have coalesced with perfect forms to make one tense (perf. *dīxī*, *dūxī*, etc.). In Irish injunctive and subjunctive forms of the *s*-aorist are retained (the *s*-subjunctive). No trace of it appears in Germanic. Radical vṛddhi is attested for the vowel *e* by Latin and Slavonic (Lat. *vēxī*, O. Sl. *věsŭ* : Skt. *ávākṣam* from *vah-*) ; for roots in diphthongs there is no clear evidence. In Hittite there is no *s*-aorist any more than any other kind of aorist, but there are certain preterite forms in the 2 and 3 singular which have final *-š* : 2 sg. *da-a-aš* ' you took ', *tarna-a-š* ' you put in ', *da-iš* ' you placed ', *pa-iš* ' you gave ' ; 3 sg. *da-a-aš* ' he took ', *da-a-iš* ' he placed ', *ag-ga-aš* ' he died ', etc. These forms consist of the verbal stem enlarged by the suffix *-s* and have no personal ending proper, and beside them there are forms to which the personal terminations have been secondarily added : 2 sg. *da-iš-ta* beside *da-iš*, 3 sg. *na-iš-ta* ' lead ' beside *na-i-iš*. These forms are compared to the *s*-aorist of other IE languages, but it seems unlikely that they are simply remains of a fully developed IE *s*-aorist system. In the first place we have seen reason to believe that the aorist in general has arisen by specialisation out of an undifferentiated preterite, and in this respect Hittite should represent an earlier state of affairs. Furthermore there is some agreement between Hittite and Tocharian on this point, since the latter language has also a certain type of preterite using an *s*-stem in the 3 sg. : A. *präkäs*, B. *preksa* ' he asked ', and this coincidence does not seem to be fortuitous. Bearing these considerations in mind we may perhaps rather explain the IE *s*-aorist to be a post-Hittite formation based on the extension to the whole paradigm of an *s*-suffix which was originally restricted to the preterite of certain persons (notably the 3 sg.) of one class of verbs.

The iṣ-Aorist

Active, S. 1 *ápāviṣam*, 2 *ápāvīs*, 3 *ápāvīt*, D. 1 *ápāviṣva*. . . . Pl. 3 *ápāviṣur* ; Middle S. 1 *ápaviṣi*, etc. . . . P. 3 *ápaviṣata*.

This aorist has in the active vṛddhi of the root if it terminates in a vowel (*ápāviṣam*, *átāriṣam*, *áśāyiṣam*) and guṇa in the case of medial *i*, *u*, *ṛ* (*árociṣam*, etc.). Both types occur from roots with medial *a* : *ákāniṣam* ; *ávadhīt*. In the middle the root has normally guṇa, but occasional forms with weak root occur : *nudiṣṭhās*, (opt.) *ruciṣīya* beside *rociṣīya*, *gmiṣīya*, *idhiṣīmahi*.

Just as the *s*-aorist is founded on certain *s*-stems which functioned as finite verbal forms, so the *iṣ*- aorist is formed on stems in the compound suffix *-i-s*, cf. *arociṣṭa* beside *rocíṣ-*

'light'. To judge by the small number of such forms in Iranian (*xšnəvīšā* 'I will satisfy', *čəvīšī* 'I expect') it was not to begin with very frequent, but it became more common in Indo-Aryan in accordance with the tendency that is observable everywhere with *seṭ* forms of the verb. Several different but closely related types of formation have come to be associated with the *iṣ*-aorist. (1) The suffix *-īṣ-* (as opposed to *-iṣ-* with short *-i-*) is used in the case of the root *grabh-* 'to seize': *agrabhīṣma*. (2) Non-sigmatic formations in *-ī-* (compare *abravīt*, etc., of the present system) appear: *agrabhīm, avadhīm, agṛhītām, agṛhīthās*. The normal 2 and 3 sg. of the *iṣ*-aorist is adapted from this formation, since *-is-s* and *-is-t* cannot phonetically produce *-īs* and *-īt*. (3) Some preterite stems in short *-i-* (compare presents of the type *vamiti*) have been incorporated in this aorist: *atārima, avādiran, bādhithās, avitá*, etc.

The isolated and anomalous *vanuṣanta* of the RV. is interesting because it is formed on the bases of an *-uṣ-* stem in the same way as this aorist is founded on *-iṣ-* stems, but unlike the *iṣ*-aorist it has never developed to form a system.

The aorist forms *stheṣam, stheṣur, deṣma, jñeṣam, khyeṣam*, etc., from roots in *ā* are best interpreted as regular *iṣ*-aorist forms (*sta*H*-is-*, etc.). There are corresponding middle forms with weak root as in the examples quoted above: *asth-iṣ-i, asthiṣata*, etc. With these are associated certain non-sigmatic forms which were mentioned in connection with the root aorist: *asth-i-ta*, etc.

The siṣ- Aorist

This aorist, which is inflected exactly like the preceding (*áyāsiṣam, áyāsīs, áyāsīt*, etc.) arises from a mixture of the two preceding. It is an innovation of Indo-Aryan, unknown to Iranian, and in the RV. it can be quoted only from two roots (*gā-* 'sing', *yā* 'go'). More examples are found later but it is never very common. In the classical language it is allowed to be made, in the active only, from roots in *ā* and *nam-* 'bow', *yam-* 'hold', *ram-* 'be content'.

The sa- Aorist

The *sa-* aorist has the normal thematic inflection and the weak root. The accent on unaugmented forms, when it occurs, is on the suffix (*dhukṣán*) which is in accordance with the apophony. It is made only from roots containing a medial vowel *i, u, ṛ* and a final consonant which combines with the *s* of the suffix to produce *-kṣ-* e.g. *ádikṣat, ámṛkṣat, amṛkṣanta, avṛkṣam, adukṣat* later *adhukṣat* from *diś-* ' point ', *mṛś-* ' touch ', *mṛj-* ' wipe ', *vṛh-* ' tear ', *duh-* ' milk '. It is rare in RV. (examples from 7 roots), which may suggest that it is an innovation, though from Iranian (O. Pers. *niyapišam* ' I wrote down ') it appears to be of at least Indo-Iranian date. Nothing that can be exactly compared is found in the other IE languages.

The Passive Aorist in -i

There exists a passive aorist in *-i*, used only in the 3rd person singular, which is independent of any of the foregoing aorist stems: *ájñāyi* ' was known ', *ádarśi* ' was seen ', etc. Unaugmented forms (which appear in both indicative and injunctive use) are always accented on the root syllable: *śrávi, pā́di*, etc. Roots having *i, u, ṛ* as medial vowel appear in the guṇa grade (*aceti, ábodhi, asarji*); elsewhere there is normally vṛddhi (*ágāmi, ákāri, ástāvi, aśrāyi*), more rarely guṇa (*ajani, avadhi*). The formation is taken by some 40 roots in the RV., to which others are added later. It appears also in Iranian (Av. *srāvī*, O. Pers. *adāriy* = Skt. *śrāvi, ádhāri*), but not elsewhere in Indo-European.

Neglecting the augment, which was a secondary and optional addition to preterite formations in Indo-European, it is clear that these forms are nothing more than old neuter *i*-stems, without any termination, which have been adapted to the verbal conjugation.

§ 11. The Perfect

Active, S. 1 *cakára, cakā́ra*, 2 *cakártha*, 3 *cakāra*, D. 1 *cakṛvá*, 2 *cakrathur*, 3 *cakratur*, P. 1 *cakṛma*, 2 *cakra*, 3 *cakrur*.

Middle, S. 1 *cakré*, 2 *cakṛṣé*, 3 *cakré*, D. 1 *cakṛváhe*, 2 *cakrā́the*, 3 *cakrā́te*, P. 1 *cakṛmáhe*, 2 *cakṛdhvé*, 3 *cakriré*.

The perfect is formed from the root stem but this is characterised by (1) reduplication and (2) a special series of endings. The general principles of reduplication have already been detailed (§ 5). Of the types there enumerated the one adopted for the perfect is that which uses the vowel *a* (IE *e*) in the reduplicating syllable, with the proviso that in Sanskrit (as opposed to Greek, etc.) *i* and *u* are substituted before roots which contain such a vowel (*tatā́na* : *pipéṣa, bubhója*). Special features of the perfect reduplication, in addition to those mentioned above are as follows: (1) There is a class of roots in the Veda which reduplicate with a long vowel: *ā́dhāra, jāgā́ra, māmṛjé, pīpā́ya, tūtā́va*. This is mainly intensive reduplication, but in some cases the *a* of the normal reduplication has coalesced with an element elsewhere lost before the beginning of the root, e.g. in the perfects of *gṛ-* 'to awake' and *mṛj-* 'to wipe'; cf. Gk. ἐγείρω, ὀμόργνυμι. (2) Two roots in *ū* reduplicate with *a* instead of the usual *u* and in both this is associated with irregular weak form of root in the singular active: *babhūva, sasū́va* from *bhū-* 'to be' and *sū-* 'to give birth'. (3) Roots beginning with *a* normally have *ā-* (*a* + *a*) in the perfect, e.g., *āda, āsa* from *ad-* 'to eat' and *as-* 'to be'. A different type appears in the perfect of *añj-* 'to anoint' and *aś-* 'to attain' (variant root forms *aṃś-, naś-*) where an *n* which forms part of the root is repeated in the reduplication: *ānáñja, ānajé; ānáṃśa, ānaśé* (cf. Ir. *t-ān-aic* 'he came'). This spreads by analogy to other roots including a number beginning with *ṛ-*: *ānárca, ānṛcé* from *ṛc-* or *arc-* to praise. (4) Roots beginning with *i* or *u* reduplicate with these vowels which in the strong forms of the active are prefixed to the guṇa grade of the roots with intervening *-y-* and *-v-* and in the weak grade coalesce with the radical vowels to form *ī* and *ū*: *iyéṣa, īṣé, uvóca, ūcé* from *iṣ-* 'to seek' and *uc-* 'to be accustomed'. (5) A similar type of reduplication appears in the case of one root beginning with *ya-* and a number beginning with *va-* which reduplicate with *i* and *u*. These coalesce with *i-* and *u-* in the weak forms of the root to produce *ī* and *ū*: *iyā́ja, ījé* from *yaj-* 'to sacrifice' (weak form *ij-* in pass. *ijyáte*, etc.), *uvā́ca, ūcé* from *vac-* 'to speak' (weak form *uc-* in *ucyáte, uktá-*, etc.); similar forms from *vap-* 'sow', *vad-* 'speak', *vas-* 'dwell' and *vah-* 'carry'. (6) Roots having a medial *a* before a single consonant, and beginning with a consonant that is unchanged in reduplication have the normal reduplication only in the strong forms: *tatāna, papā́ta* from *tan-* 'stretch' and *pat-* 'fall'; the weak forms of the perfect are made by substituting *-e-* for the *a* of the root: *tené, tenúr, pecé, pecúr*. This is an innovation of Sanskrit which is by no means complete in the Vedic period; the more original forms which occur are V. *paptima, tatne, mamnāte*, etc. The type originated in certain roots which acquired such form through normal phonetic development, notably *sad-* 'to sit' where *sedúr* stands regularly for earlier **sazdur* (cf. Av. *hazdyāt̰* pf. opt.) and roots beginning with *y-* (*yemur* for **yaymur*). (7) The root *vid-* ' know ' has no reduplication, and this is in accordance with the related languages: Skt. *véda*, Gk. *οἶδα*, Goth. *wait*, etc. There are a few other sporadic cases of unreduplicated perfect forms in the Veda, e.g. *takṣathur, takṣur, skambhathur, skambhur*, and three perfect participles formed without reduplication: *dāśvás-* ' pious ', *mīḍhvás-* ' liberal ' and *sāhvás-* ' overpowering '.

In apophony the perfect follows the normal type of verbal inflection, that is to say the strong form of the root appears in the three singular persons of the active, the weak form elsewhere. Normally the strong grade is guṇa (*vavarta, ciketa, bubodha*) but wherever in the strong stem medial *a* appears before a single consonant (1 sg. act. *tatápa, bibháya, cakára*, etc.) vṛddhi is substituted in the 3rd person sg., and in the later language optionally in the 1st: *tatā́pa, bibhā́ya, cakā́ra*, etc. This feature does not appear outside Indo-Iranian; the majority of the languages show guṇa only, and by general agreement the *o*-grade of the root: Gk. *γέγονε*, etc. Original *o*-grade is attested also by Sanskrit, since certain roots which have undergone the second palatalisation retain the original guttural in these perfect forms: *cikā́ya, cikéta, jigā́ya, jaghā́na* from *ci-* ' gather ', *cit-* ' observe ', *ji-* ' conquer ' and *han-* ' slay '.

The weak forms of the root are the normal ones that result from the loss of the guṇa vowel: *cakré, jaghné, jagmúr, bubudhe*, etc. Roots in *ā* lose this vowel altogether in the weak forms as generally (*da-dh-ur*), but before consonantal endings invariably insert the union vowel *i* (*dadh-i-ré*) in contradistinction to the present. Samprasāraṇa appears in such roots as *vyadh-* ' to pierce ' and *svap-* ' to sleep ' (*vividhúr, suṣupur*; their reduplicating vowel goes with this form). In some roots having nasal in the strong form the weak form is marked by the absence of this nasal: *cakradé* from *krand-* ' to roar '. On weak stems of the type *ten-* see above.

For the personal terminations see § 6. There are not many complications. Instead of the normal endings roots in *ā* terminate in *-au* in the 1 and 3 sg. of the active: *dadaú, dadhaú, tasthāú, jajñāú* from *dā-* ' to give ', *dhā-* ' to place ', *sthā-* ' to stand ', *jñā-* ' to know ' (for IE **dedōH-u*, etc., with vṛddhi before laryngeal). The final *u-* element, which appears here in place of a personal termination, is found also in Latin, incorporated into certain perfect forms: *nōvit* 'knew', cf. Skt. *jajñaú*; *plēvit* 'filled', cf. *paprāú*.

A feature of the perfect conjugation is the frequency with which the connecting vowel *-i-* appears before the terminations that begin with a consonant: 2 sg. *bubódhitha*, 1 du. *bubudhivá*, 1 pl. *bubudhimá*, . . . 3 pl. mid. *bubudhiré*, etc. In the later language the *-ré* of the 3 pl. mid. has it always. Before other consonantal endings except the 2 sg. act. it is taken by the vast majority of verbs. In the 2 sg. act. the *aniṭ* forms allowed are more numerous, and a number of roots take optionally either form, e.g. *ninétha, nináyitha*. Roots in *ā* have this option, but when taking *-i-* they appear in the weak form and the accent is transferred to the ending: *dadā́tha, dadithá*. In the Veda the use of the union vowel is less extensive than in the classical language. As a general rule it appears after roots ending in a consonant provided the last syllable of the stem is a heavy one: *vivéditha, ūcimá, paptimá*, etc., as opposed to *tatántha, yuyujmá*, etc. It is also taken by roots in *-ā* (*dadimá, dadhimá*) but the type *dadithá* of the 2 sg. is unknown to the early usage. In Iranian the use of the auxiliary vowel is exceedingly rare which makes it clear that in the main its employment in the perfect (as elsewhere in the verbal system) is an innovation of Indo-Aryan.

The perfect tense is widely represented in Indo-European, having been dropped only in Armenian and Balto-Slavonic. Perfects common to Sanskrit and other languages may be illustrated by such examples as the following: *jajā́na* (*jan-* 'to beget'): Gk. γέγονε; *dadárśa* (*dṛś-* 'to see'): Gk. δέδορκε; *cicchéda, cicchidé* (*chid-* 'to split'): Lat. *scicidī*, Goth. *skaískaiþ*; *didéśa, didiśé* (*diś-* 'to point out'): Gk. δέδειχα, δέδειγμαι, Goth. *ga-taih*; *riréca, riricé* (*ric-* 'to leave'), Gk. λέλοιπα, Lat. *līquī*, Goth. *laiƕ*; *nineja, ninije* (*nij-* 'to wash'), Ir. *-nenaig*; *tutóda, tutudúr* (*tud-* 'to push'), Lat. *tutudī*, Goth. *staístaut*; *vavárta* (*vṛt-* 'to turn'), Lat. *vortī, vertī*, Goth. *warþ*; *dadhárṣa* (*dhṛṣ-* 'to be bold'), Goth. *ga-dars*; *jaghā́na* (*han-* 'to slay'), Ir. 1 sg. *-gegon*, 3 sg. *-gegoin*.

In some languages, notably Latin and Germanic, the reduplication is not an essential part of the perfect formation. It occurs with certain roots and is absent in the case of others. This corresponds more nearly to the original state of affairs in IE. The reduplication was, to begin with, no more an essential part of the perfect formation than was the augment of the aorist and imperfect. Its generalisation in Greek and Indo-Iranian is one of the many isoglosses that unite those two branches within the IE family. Even they preserve in *véda* 'knows' the older type of non-reduplicating perfect.

Here, as elsewhere, Hittite shows greater divergence from the normal IE type. Hittite has no perfect, but a special type of present conjugation, the *ḫi-* conjugation, which has been compared with, and has certain features in common with, the normal IE perfect. At the same time the gap is not easy to bridge, since we have on the one hand a special tense with a sense of its own (state, result) which is made by most roots in addition to the present tense, and on the other hand a variant form of the present taken by certain roots. It is probable that in this matter Hittite is the major innovator, but it is not possible simply to derive the Hitt. *ḫi*-conjugation from a system corresponding to the IE perfect, because there are outside Hittite also certain present formations which go with it: notably (1) Skt. formations of the type *áduha* enumerated above, (2) the Gk. conjugation of thematic verbs (λέγω, λέγεις, λέγει).

The perfect in Sanskrit and Greek conjugates in both active and middle. There is reason to believe that this is a secondary arrangement. In Sanskrit the middle endings of the perfect are in the main obvious imitations of the present, in marked contrast to the active endings which differ so markedly from those of the present. Furthermore it has already been pointed out that an active perfect not infrequently corresponds to a middle present, and that the endings of the active are more closely related to certain middle endings than to other active endings. All these indications lead us to believe that the existence of two voices in the perfect is of later origin than in other parts of the verbal system.

The evidence also points to the conclusion that the perfect did not to begin with have a corresponding preterite. Such forms of this kind as exist in several languages are to be classed as independent innovations. This applies both to Sanskrit and to Greek, and to a greater extent in the former, since while Greek did eventually develop a pluperfect with a meaning of its own, the forms classified as such in Sanskrit are in the main isolated and unstable formations which appear in the Vedic language but are not used later. Such are sg. 1 *ajagrabham*, 3 *ájagan*, du. 2 *amumuktam*, pl. 3 *ábībhayur*, mid. pl. 3 *ajagmiran*. The distinction between these forms and the imperfect of the reduplicating class is not very clearly to be drawn. Their sense is normally that of simple preterites.

§ 12. Injunctive and Subjunctive

The so-called injunctive is no separate morphological category, but the term is applied to those unaugmented forms of the imperfect or aorist which are used with the force of subjunctive or imperative (§ 2). In the RV. the augmentless forms are more than half as common as the augmented and they may appear indifferently in preterite or injunctive use. Such forms occur from both imperfect and aorist stems, more frequently from the latter. In the later Atharvaveda the proportion of such forms occurring is noticeably less, and of those that do occur a greater part are formed from the aorist stem. In post-Vedic Sanskrit the injunctive disappears except in one construction. Prohibitions continue to be expressed by the use of *mā* in connection with unaugmented aorist forms : *mā bhaiṣīḥ* ' do not be afraid ', *mā gāḥ* ' do not go ', etc.

The subjunctive stem is formed by the addition of the vowel *a* to the indicative tense stem, the guṇated form of such a stem being employed if it exists : *dóha-*, *juháva-*, *yunája-*, etc., from the tense stems *dóh-*, *juhó-*, *yunáj-*. This *a* combines with the *a* of thematic stems to form long *ā* : *bhávā-*, *tudā́-*, *ucyā́-*. The inflection of the subjunctive from non-thematic verbal stems is illustrated by the following paradigms :

Active, S. 1 *áyāni*, *áyā*, 2 *áyasi*, *áyas*, 3 *áyati*, *áyat*, D. 1 *ayāva*, 2 *áyathas*, 3 *áyatas*, P. 1 *áyāma*, 2 *áyatha*, 3 *áyan*.

Middle, S. 1 *ā́sai*, 2 *ā́sase*, *ā́sāsai*, 3 *ā́sate*, *ā́sātai*, D. 1 *ā́sāvahai*, *ā́sāvahe*, 2 *ā́saithe*, 3 *āsaite*, P. 1 *ā́sāmahai*, *ā́sāmahe*, 2 *ā́sadhve*, *ā́sādhvai*, 3 *ā́sante*, *ā́santa*, *ā́sāntai*.

It will be observed that the endings of the subjunctive are partly secondary and partly primary. In 1 du., 1 pl. and 3 pl. of the active secondary endings are employed ; in 2 and 3 du. and 2 pl. primary endings ; in 2 and 3 sg. either primary or secondary endings are used. In the middle forms with secondary endings are rare, appearing normally only in the 3 pl.

The 1 sg. active has a special ending of its own, *-āni*, beside which in the earlier language simple *-ā* appears which is to be compared to the -*ō* which appears in Greek in the subjunctive as well as in the active of the 1 sg. of thematic verbs (ἄγω). The 1 sg. middle ending -*ai* arises from the contraction of the *a* of the subjunctive stem with the -*e* of the termination. This -*ai* is then extended to other parts of the middle inflection and such eventually become the normal forms. This type of termination is preceded by the vowel *ā* even in subjunctives of non-thematic verbs.

The conjugation of subjunctives from thematic stems is the same as the above but based on a stem in *ā* arising from the combination of the *a* of the tense stem and the subjunctive *a* :

Active, S. 1 *bhávāni*, 2 *bhávāsi*, *bhávās*, 3 *bhávāti*, *bhávāt*, D. 1 *bhávāva*, 2 *bhávāthas*, 3 *bhávātas*, P. 1 *bhávāma*, 2 *bhávātha*, 3 *bhavān*.

Middle, S. 1 *bhávai*, 2 *bhávāse*, *bhávāsai*, 3 *bhávāte*, *bhávātai*, D. 1 *bhávāvahai*, 2 *bhávaithe*, 3 *bhávaite*, P. 1 *bhávāmahai*, 2 *bhávādhvai*, 3 *bhávāntai*.

The subjunctive can be formed in the Vedic language from all three tense stems, present, aorist and perfect. This variety of formation is not matched by any variety of meaning, e.g. *śṛṇávat*, *śravat* and *śuśravat* all mean ' he will hear ' or ' let him hear ' and no sort of difference related to the tense stem appears between them. Aorist subjunctives are commonest from the root aorist (*karat*, *gamat*, *yamat*, *varat* ; *karati*, *jóṣati*, *bhédati*, etc.) and from the *s*-aorist (*jéṣat*, *néṣat*, *matsat* ; *neṣati*, *parṣati*, etc.) ; none are found from the *sa*-aorist. Examples of subjunctives from the perfect stem are *jaghánat*, *jújoṣat*, *paspárśat* ; *jújoṣati*, *dídeśati*, *búbodhati*, etc.

The subjunctive remained in use during the later Vedic period (Brāhmaṇas and Upaniṣads), but, apart from the first persons which were incorporated in the imperative, it is extinct in the classical language.

A subjunctive corresponding in form and meaning to that of Sanskrit appears in Greek. Here the primary endings are exclusively used and the forms with long vowel associated with thematic stems have become predominant. The quality of this vowel (where Sanskrit has *ā*) varies in accordance with the variation in the indicative (ἄγωμεν, ἄγητε). Some old short vowel subjunctives are preserved as futures (ἔδομαι, πίομαι) and the simplest explanation of the *s*-future is that it is the subjunctive of the *s*-aorist. The Latin future *erit* corresponds to the Skt. subjunctive *ásat(i)* and both Italic and Celtic have forms deriving from the *s*-aorist subjunctive (Lat. *faxō*, Osc. *deivast*, Ir. 1 sg. *-tias*, 3 pl. *-tiassat* from *tiagu* 'go'). These two groups have also an *ā*-subjunctive which does not appear in Greek or Sanskrit.

The subjunctive is absent over a considerable part of Indo-European, and has the appearance of being a comparatively late formation. It can be plausibly explained as having grown out of the injunctive, certain forms of which developed into an independent system. The hesitation between primary and secondary endings in Sanskrit represents a transition from an earlier system in which the endings were secondary (as in the injunctive) and a new one in which primary endings are applied as being more appropriate to its predominantly future meaning. This transition has been completed in Greek. Of the short and long vowel subjunctives the former is the earlier and more original. The addition of the thematic suffix to a stem already provided with such is without parallel elsewhere in IE stem formation, and its presence here is due to the analogy which created *bhavā-*, etc., having the same relation to *bhava-* as *asa-* to *as-*. The short vowel subjunctives with secondary endings (*kárat, gámat*) have a form which cannot in itself be distinguished from injunctives (augmentless preterites) of thematic stems. That they are subjunctives depends not on the nature of the stem itself, since such stems are commonly used in the formation of present/imperfects, but in their relation to other forms in the system. The absence of any distinctive formative in the most original type of subjunctive is a clear indication of its secondary origin.

§13. The Imperative

Active, S. 1 *bhávāni, áyāni*, 2 *bháva, ihí*, 3 *bhávatu, étu*, D. 1 *bhávāva, áyāva*, 2 *bhávatam, itám*, 3 *bhávatām, itā́m*, P. 1 *bhávāma, áyāma*, 2 *bhávata, itá*, 3 *bhávantu, yántu*.

Middle, S. 1 *bhávai, ā́sai*, 2 *bhávasva, ā́ssva*, 3 *bhávatām, ā́stām*, D. 1 *bhávāvahai, ā́sāvahai*, 2 *bhávethām, ā́sāthām*, 3 *bhávetām, ā́sātām*, P. 1 *bhávāmahai, ā́sāmahai*, 2 *bhávadhvam, ā́ddhvam*, 3 *bhávantām, ā́satām*.

This paradigm is composite. The first persons in the three numbers are properly subjunctive forms. Injunctive forms are employed in 2 and 3 du. and 2 pl. Specific imperative forms occur in 2 sg. and 3 sg. and pl. In the 2 sg. the stem of thematic verbs functions as imperative without any addition in Sanskrit as in the related languages: *bhára*, Av. *bara*, Gk. *φερε*, Arm. *ber*, Goth. *baír*, Ir. *beir*; *pṛcchá* 'ask', Lat. *posce*; *ája* 'drive', Gk. *ἄγε*, Lat. *age*, etc. With non-thematic verbs the ending is *-hi*, originally *-dhi*: *ihí* 'go', Av. *idī*, Gk. *ἴθι*. The original *-dhi* appears in Sanskrit after consonantal stems (*viddhí* 'know', Gk. *ἴσθι*, *dugdhí* 'milk', etc.) and occasionally elsewhere, *edhí* for **azdhí* (cf. Av. *zdī*) from *as-* 'to be', *juhudhí* from *hu-* 'to sacrifice'. The Veda has further examples: *śṛṇudhí* 'hear', *gadhi* 'go', *vṛdhi* 'cover'.

The forms of the 3 sg. and pl. are made by the addition of a particle *-u* to the secondary endings: *bhávat-u*, etc. Corresponding forms occur in Hittite: 3 sg. *eštu*: Skt. *ástu*, *kuendu*, Skt. *hántu*; 3 pl. *ašandu*, Skt. *sántu*; *kunandu*, Skt. *ghnántu*, etc. In the *ḫi*-verbs which have no *t*-ending in the 3 sg. present, this element *u* appears alone in the 3 sg. impv.: *aku*, *aru* from *ak-* 'to die', *ar-* 'to arrive', 3 sg. pres. *aki*, *ari*.

In the middle the termination of the 2 sg. is *-sva*. A corresponding formation is found only in Iranian: *baraŋuha*, Skt. *bhárasva*; *kərəšvā*, Skt. *kṛṣvá*, etc. This *-sva* is considered to be the stem of the reflexive pronoun. The 3 sg. and pl. are made by the addition of *-ām* to the secondary endings and here too corresponding forms are found only in Iranian, *vərəzyatąm*, *xraosəntąm*. The few verbs which have inflections without *t* in the 3 sg. active (e.g. *duhé*, *áduha*) keep this feature in the 3 sg. impv.: *duhām*, *śayām*. In the 3 pl. they have *-rām* with *r* as in the indicative: *duhrā́m*, cf. 3 pl. mid. *duhré*. Compromise forms are *duhratām* and *śératām*.

Beside the normal endings above there appears, particularly in the earlier language an ending *-tāt*. This is indifferent to the distinction between active and middle and it appears most frequently used as 2 sg.: *brūtāt* 'say', *dhattāt* 'put', *dhāvatāt* 'run', *vittā́t* 'know', etc. It may also be used for other persons and numbers: 1 sg. *jāgṛtād ahám* 'let me keep awake', 3 sg. *rā́jā mūrdhā́nam ví pātayatāt* 'let the king cause his head to fall off', 2 pl. *ā́paḥ . . . devéṣu naḥ sukṛ́to brūtāt* 'O waters, announce us to the gods as well-doers'. In the later language the use as 3 sg. tends to preponderate, but the total of examples as compared with the earlier language is small.

This form of imperative appears also in Greek (as 3 sg.) and in Latin (as 2, 3 sg.) : ἴστω 'let him know', Skt. *vittā́t*, δότω, ἴτω, ἔστω, etc. ; Lat. *vehitō*, Skt. *váhatāt*, *poscitō*, *habētō*, *estō*, etc., O. Lat. *estōd*, etc., cf. Osc. *líkítud*, *estud*.

In the Veda there are certain 2 sg. forms in *-si* with imperative value : *dhákṣi* 'burn', *yákṣi* 'worship', *párṣi* 'cross', *prā́si* 'fill', *śróṣi* 'hear', etc. The termination is identical with that of the 2 sg. indic. pres., but these imperatives are quite clearly distinguished because the presents are differently formed (*dáhasi*, *śṛṇóṣi*, etc.). One corresponding form is quoted from Avestan: *dōišī* 'show' from *daēs-*.

In the classical language the imperative forms are from the present stem. In the Vedic language imperatives may be made from all three stems, present, aorist and perfect, and, as in the case of the other moods, no difference of meaning appears between them. Examples of aorist imperatives are : *kṛdhí*, *śrudhí*, *gahi*, *gantu*, *yukṣvá* ; *sada*, *sána*, *sadatu* ; *vocatāt*, *vocatu* ; of perfect imperatives, *cikiddhi*, *mumugdhí*, *śaśādhi*, *dídeṣṭu*, *vavṛtsva*. It should be noted that imperatives are not normally made from the *s*-aorist. There are a few formations such as 2 sg. *neṣa*, 3 sg. *neṣatu* and 3 sg. mid. *rāsatām* which are all thematic formations and therefore cannot properly be attached to the *s*-aorist.

§14. Optative and Precative

Non-thematic :

Active, S. 1 *duhyā́m*, 2 *duhyā́s*, 3 *duhyā́t*, D. 1 *duhyā́va*, 2 *duhyā́tam*, 3 *duhyā́tām*, P. 1 *duhyā́ma*, 2 *duhyā́ta*, 3 *duhyúr*.

Middle, S. 1 *duhīyá*, 2 *duhīthā́s*, 3 *duhītá*, D. 1 *duhīváhi*, 2 *duhīyā́thām*, 3 *duhīyā́tām*, P. 1 *duhīmáhi*, 2 *duhīdhvám*, 3 *duhīrán*.

Thematic :

Active, S. 1 *bháveyam*, 2 *bháves*, 3 *bhávet*, D. 1 *bhávema*, 2 *bhávetam*, 3 *bhávetām*, P. 1 *bhávema*, 2 *bháveta*, 3 *bháveyur*.

Middle, S. 1 *bháveya*, 2 *bhávethās*, 3 *bháveta*, D. 1 *bhávevahi*, 2 *bháveyāthām*, 3 *bháveyātām*, P. 1 *bhávemahi*, 2 *bhávedhvam*, 3 *bháveran*.

The non-thematic inflection of the optative differs in apophony from the usual system. The strong form of the suffix is not confined to the three singular persons of the active, but extended to all the active with the exception of the 3 pl. That this is an innovation is clear from Latin which preserves two grades in the case of the verb ' to be ': O. Lat. *siem, siet* for later *sim, sit* beside *sīmus*. A similar extension of the strong forms was observed in the case of roots in *-ā*: 1 pl. pres. *yāmas* ' we go ', aor. *ádhāma* ' we placed '. In the thematic classes the diphthongal stem of the optative (*bháres, bháret*, etc. = Gk. *φέροις, φέροι*, Goth. *baírais, baírai*) is formed by contraction of the thematic suffix and the weak form of the optative suffix (*o* + *ī*).

The terminations of the optative are mainly the normal secondary terminations. The 1 sg. middle has a special ending which has been noticed (§ 6), and the *-ran* of the 3 pl. appears in a minority of preterite forms (*áduhran*, etc.). The anomalous Vedic 3 sg. *duhīyát* (after which 3 pl. *duhīyán*) seems to be based on **duhīyá* formed without *-t-* after the fashion of the indicative (*duhé, áduha*).

In the classical language the optative is formed from the present stem. In the Vedic language it is formed from all three stems, present, aorist and perfect, and, as with the subjunctive, no difference of meaning is attached to this difference of formation. Root aorist optatives are fairly common: *aśyā́m, ṛdhyām, gamyās, bhūyāt*, middle *aśīya*, etc. They are rarer in the *a*-aorist and reduplicated aorist. From the sigmatic aorists optatives are formed only in the middle and the 2 and 3 sg. take invariably the precative *s*: *masīya* (*man-* ' to think '), *maṃsīṣṭhā́s, maṃsīṣṭa, gmiṣīya, janiṣīṣṭa, yāsiṣīṣṭhās*, etc. The perfect optative is common: *jagamyām, riricyām, vavṛtyās, ninīyāt, papatyāt, vavṛtīya, cakṣamīthās, jagrasīta*, etc.

The oldest type of optative is that attached to root stems, present or aorist. Here the suffix is attached to the root in the same way as in the various present stems, and the normal secondary endings are added to it: *gam-yā-m* like *krī-ṇā-m*. This stem developed on its own lines on account of the special meaning which became associated with it. The main developments which produced the optative in its final form were (1) the incorporation of the optative in the present system (*aśnuyā́t* replacing *aśyā́t*, etc.) and (2) the creation of optative forms to thematic stems by combining with them the weak form of the optative suffix. The first process is still incomplete in the Veda. On this theory the optative was to begin with a quite independent stem and its association with the various tense stems secondary. The perfect optatives should be regarded from the same point of view. Reduplication in early IE was a feature liable to turn up in many parts of the verbal system, and on the other hand though it came to be especially associated with the perfect it was not to begin with an essential feature of that system. Bearing this in mind it is clear that a reduplicated optative is not in its origin connected with the perfect system. We have an optative stem (*gamyā-m*) originally independent of the tense stems, and beside it a reduplicated optative stem (*jagamyā-m*) originally equally independent. With the incorporation of the optative into the various tense stems these reduplicated optatives became formally attached to the perfect, but in meaning they never acquired any of the characteristics of the perfect. The dying out in the later language of all forms of the optative except those belonging to the present system, resulted naturally from the absence of any distinction of meaning between the different forms.

The forms of the Precative in the classical language are as follows:

Active, S. 1 *bhūyā́sam*, 2 *bhūyā́s*, 3 *bhūyā́t*, D. 1 *bhūyā́sva* 2 *bhūyā́stam*, 3 *bhūyā́stām*, P. 1 *bhūyā́sma*, 2 *bhūyā́sta*, 3 *bhūyā́sur*.

Middle, S. 1 *bhaviṣīyá*, 2 *bhaviṣīṣṭhā́s*, 3 *bhaviṣīṣṭá*, D. 1 *bhaviṣīváhi*, 2 *bhaviṣīyā́sthām*, 3 *bhaviṣīyā́stām*, P. 1 *bhaviṣīmáhi*, 2 *bhaviṣīḍhvám*, 3 *bhaviṣīrán*.

The active forms are always made directly from the root by the addition of the optative suffix extended by *s*. The older form of the 3 sg. act. was *bhūyā́s*, which is preserved in the Vedic language. The middle forms are formed from the stem of the sigmatic aorist, and the precative *s* is absent in the first persons and in the 3 pl. The precative is the only modal form from a non-present stem retained by the classical language.

The use of the precative is not common in the classical language and knowledge of its inflection is based on the statements of the grammarians. In the pre-classical language most of the active forms as given by the grammarians are attested with the exception that the older form of the 3 sg. is used. In the middle there is no distinction in the Veda between optative and precative. The optative of the sigmatic aorist invariably inserts the precative *s* in the 2 and 3 sg. and this *s* is employed nowhere else in the conjugation. Such optative forms with precative *s* are occasionally formed in the Veda from other stems : root-aorist, *padīṣṭá*, *mucīṣṭa*, *a*-aorist, *videṣṭa*, reduplicated aorist, *rīriṣīṣṭa*, perfect, *sāsahīṣṭhās*.

In the *Ṛgveda*, as opposed to the later Vedic literature, very nearly the same state of affairs prevails in the active. Precative forms from the root aorist are numerous in the 2 sg. (which cannot in this case be distinguished from the ordinary optative) and in the 3 sg. In the 3 sg. no non-precative forms are recorded. Outside these two persons there occur only 1 sg. *bhūyāsam* and 1 pl. *kriyāsma* (once each). Otherwise forms in *-yā* only appear outside the 2 and 3 sg. It is clear that the two first person precatives are innovations of the later RV. period and that in the original inflection *s* was proper only to the 2 and 3 sg., and there always used, as in the middle. The inflection may therefore be compared to that of the Hittite verbs mentioned above (§ 10, S. 1 *tarnaḫun*, 2 *tarnaš*, 3 *tarnaš*, P. 1 *tarnumen*, 2 *tarnatin*, 3 *tarnir*) in which *s* functions as the common termination of the 2, 3 sg. but does not appear in the other persons. In its earliest form the Sanskrit precative, which is not to be distinguished from the optative of the root aorist, or in the middle from that of the sigmatic aorist, preserves this ancient characteristic of one class of secondary endings. On the other hand, in the rest of the conjugation, the optative has adopted the normal secondary endings in these two persons. The precative is thus one of the most archaic formations in Sanskrit grammar.

§ 15. Secondary Conjugation

Under secondary conjugation are classified certain forms of present stem which differ from the ordinary series of present stems because (1) they have acquired a special meaning and (2) they are normally taken by roots in addition to their ordinary presents. The four types of secondary conjugation are (1) passive, (2) intensive, (3) causative and (4) desiderative. They are all essentially present formations, and with certain exceptions their inflection in other systems consists of more or less sporadic innovations.

I. *The Passive*

The formation of the passive is closely connected with that of the fourth present class. It differs from the middle of that class only in the position of the accent. In the passive this is on the suffix *yá* whereas in the fourth class it is on the root: *mányate* 'thinks', but *badhyáte* 'is bound'. This distinction is secondary since roots in the fourth class appear in their weak form (*íṣyati, íṣyate*) and this indicates original suffixal accent. Furthermore there are a few old intransitives (not passives) which are suffixally accented: *mriyáte* 'dies', *dhriyáte* 'is steadfast'. There is also fluctuation of accent in some passive and intransitive forms, *múcyate* and *mucyáte* 'is released', *kṣī́yate* and *kṣīyáte* 'is destroyed', *jī́yate* and *jīyáte* 'suffers loss', *pácyate* and *pacyáte* 'is cooked'.

The passive in this form is found also in Iranian (Av. *kiryeintē* = *kriyante*), but not elsewhere. It is an Indo-Iranian innovation based on the fourth present class, and its origin was due to the frequency of intransitive verbs in that class, particularly with middle inflection: *jā́yate* 'is born', *pácyate* 'becomes ripe, cooked', *tápyate* 'becomes hot', etc. Since a number of these verbs had differently formed transitive presents beside them (*tápati* 'heats', etc.) they could easily form the nucleus from which the passive system developed. Differentiation was made by the retention in the passive of the old accent, for which in the fourth class presents radical accent has been substituted. The examples above in which there is variation of accent are mainly old intransitives which have been adopted as passives (*múcyate* 'gets loose', etc.). The middle inflection is universal in Sanskrit (except for some late and incorrect Epic forms, *dṛśyati* 'is seen', etc.), but active forms are not uncommon in Iranian: Av. *bairyeiti* 'is carried', O. Pers. *θahyāmahy* 'we are called', etc. Probably to begin with the usage was uncertain and the exclusive use of the middle later generalised in Indo-Aryan.

The passive is inflected only in the present system. In the perfect and future the middle voice frequently functions as passive: *cakré* 'was done', *kariṣyáte* 'will be done'. In the aorist there is a passive 3 sg. of independent formation (*ákāri*) which has already been described. In the immediate pre-classical period there was a tendency, which did not go very far, to extend this by adding other forms. None are found in the Vedic literature, but the grammarians lay down, for roots ending in vowels and *grah-*, *dṛś-*, *han-*, special passive aorist forms based on the above, e.g. 1 sg. *ádāyiṣi*, 3 pl. *ánāyiṣata*, etc.: 3 sg.

ádāyi, ánāyi. This type of stem was further extended to the future : 1 sg. *dāyiṣye,* 3 sg. *ghāniṣyate,* etc. Such forms occur very rarely in classical Sanskrit, and they are all learned formations taken from the grammar.

In addition to finite verbal forms the passive meaning could be expressed by the passive participles in *-ta* and the future passive participle in *-tavya.* In the later history of Indo-Aryan, in the Prakrit period, all forms of active preterite were lost, and their place was taken by passive constructions with the participle in *-ta.* This process is reflected in the later Sanskrit literature ; the usual construction becomes *mayā brāhmaṇo dṛṣṭaḥ* 'the brahman was seen by me' instead of *aham brāhmaṇam apaśyam* 'I saw the brahman'. Associated with this is the increasing use of the impersonal passive : *iha sthīyatām* 'stay here' (lit. 'let it be stayed here'), *tena bhavitavyam* 'it must be him', etc. This type of later Sanskrit is largely Prakrit in disguise. By such devices the wealth of the Pāniṇean verbal morphology can be mostly ignored, and this simplified Sanskrit was understandably popular.

II. *The Intensive*

The intensive is a form of present stem which expresses intensification or repetition of the sense expressed by the root. It is of common occurrence in the Vedic language, being attested from over 90 roots. In the classical language, though allowed by the grammarians to be made from every root, it is of infrequent occurrence. The stem consists of the root preceded by strong reduplication. In the case of roots containing *i* or *u* this reduplication has the corresponding guṇa vowel : 3 sg. act. *nenekti, vevetti,* mid. *nenikté, dediṣṭé* (*nij-* 'wash', *vid-* 'know', *diś-* 'point out') ; 3 sg. act. *jóhavīti, nónavīti,* 1 pl. *nonumas* (*hū-* 'call', *nu-* 'roar'). Where the vowel is *a* the corresponding long vowel appears in the reduplication : 3 sg. *cākaśīti, pāpatīti,* 3 pl. *nānadati* (*kāś-* 'appear', *pat-* 'fall', *nad-* 'roar'). When roots contain or terminate in *r* (*l*) or a nasal, this consonant is repeated in reduplication : 1 sg. *carkarmi,* 2 sg. *dardarṣi,* 3 sg. *jaṅghanti, calcalīti,* (with dissimilation) *alarti,* 3 mid. *nannate* (*kṝ-* 'to commemorate', *dṝ-* 'to split', *han-* 'slay', *cal-* 'move', *ar-* 'rise, go', *nam-* 'bend'). As an alternative reduplication with long *ā* is sometimes used with roots of this form : *jāgarti* 'is awake', etc. An *ī* is frequently inserted between the strong reduplication and the root: 3 sg. *varīvarti, kanikranti, ganīganti,* 3 pl. *davidyutati, bharibhrati* (*vṛt-* 'turn', *krand-* 'shout', *gam-* 'go', *dyut-* 'shine', *bhṛ-* 'carry'). The apophony of the root follows the usual system; it is strong in the three persons of the active, elsewhere weak: 3 sg. act. *nenekti,* pl. *nenijati,* 3 sg. mid. *nenikté.* When *ī* is inserted after the root in the singular active, the root only has guṇa where this does not produce a long syllable: *jóhavīti* but *vévidīti.* The accent is on the reduplication in the strong forms and in the 3 pl. (*vévetti, vévidati*); elsewhere on the terminations according to the classical grammar (*vevidmás,* etc.), but the Vedic usage fluctuates: 3 sg. mid. *nenikté,* etc., beside *tétikte,* etc.

The terminations are the normal ones (with *-ati* in the 3 pl. as in the reduplicating class). A common feature is the use of the connecting vowel *ī*. This was observed also in the root class (*brávīti,* etc.), but it is much more common in the intensive: *johavīti, tartarīti, dardarīti,* etc. It is never used when the same kind of *ī* appears after the reduplication. It is employed in the three singular persons and once in the dual (*tartarīthas*). In the 3 sg. mid. the ending *-e* occurs about as frequently as the ending *-te*: *cékite, jóguve, yoyuve,* etc. The 2 and 3 sg. of the imperfect suffer the usual phonetic mutilation: *ádardar* for 2 sg. **ádardar-s* and 3* *ádardar-t,* etc. The connecting vowel *-ī-* appears in the imperfect in the 3 sg. (*ájohavīt*) and once in the 3 du. (*ávāvaśītām*). The termination of the 3 pl. act. is *-ur* as in the reduplicating class: *ájohavur.*

The intensive forms subjunctives commonly, but almost exclusively with secondary endings. The root has guṇa only when this does not make a long vowel: 3 sg. *jaṅghanat, bobhavat*; *carkṛṣat, davidyutat.* Imperatives are not uncommon: 2 sg. *dardṛhi, carkṛdhi,* 3 sg. *vevestu, dadhartu,* 2 pl. *jāgṛtá*; with *-tāt,* 2 sg. *carkṛtāt, jāgṛtāt.* There are a few forms with the auxiliary vowel *ī*: *jaṅghanīhi, johavītu.* The optative is exceedingly rare (*veviṣyāt* AV.).

There exist a few intensives with perfect inflections. These are not perfects to the above, but an alternative type of present, in accordance with the old sense of the perfect. Such are *davidhāva, nonāva, dodrāva, lelāya* with the ordinary meaning of the intensive present.

There exists a second type of intensive formation which reduplicates in the same way as the above, but forms its stem by the addition of the accented *-yá-* suffix and inflects exclusively in the middle: *marmṛjyáte, dedīpyáte, dodhūyáte*, etc. (*mṛj-* 'wipe', *dīp-* 'shine', *dhū-* 'shake'). This is rare in the Vedic language, but in the classical language it is commoner than the basic type.

Intensive formations corresponding to the Sanskrit basic type were common in Old Iranian: cf. Av. *zaozaomi, čarəkərəmahi*, (opt.) *dardairyāṯ, daēdōišt*, (thematic) *naēnižaiti*, corresponding to the Sanskrit intensive bases *johav-, carkar-, dardar-, dediś* and *nenij-*. Though not recorded outside Indo-Iranian the formation is evidently ancient in Indo-European. The fact that it does not appear elsewhere is due to the general abandonment of non-thematic verbal inflection in the majority of IE languages. In contradistinction the second type of intensive formation (*dedīpyáte*), though rare in early Sanskrit, has parallels elsewhere, particularly in Greek: πορφῦρω 'be in uneasy motion' (Skt. *bhur-*), παμφαίνω 'shine brightly', δαρδάπτω 'tear asunder', μαρμαίρω 'glitter', etc.

III. *The Causative*

The causative is the most productive of the secondary conjugations from the early period onwards. The stem is formed by the addition of the suffix *-áya-* to the root, which normally appears in its strengthened form, and it is identical with the stem of the tenth class of verbs. There are a considerable number of verbal formations in *-áya-*, particularly in the early language which have no causative function. Some have a frequentative sense (*patáyati* 'flies about', etc.) which from the comparative evidence is ancient (Gk. ποτέομαι). The causative is only one of the uses attached to the *áya-* stem, but in course of time it becomes the predominant one. There is in the earlier language a distinction between causatives with strengthened root and non-causatives with weak root: *dyutáya-, rucáya-* 'shine': *dyotáya-, rocáya-* 'illuminate', etc.; similarly between guṇa and vṛddhi in *patáya-* 'fly about', *pātáya-* 'cause to fall'. The distinction is not absolute since there are formations with weak root having a causative sense (*dṛṃháya-* 'make firm') and conversely formations with strengthened root having a non-causative sense (*mādáya-* 'get intoxicated'). In the later language the bulk of the non-causative forms die out, and what remain are combined with formations of a more denominative character to form the tenth present class.

In the causative the root always has guṇa where this produces a long syllable: *tarpáyati, vardháyati, kalpáyati, bodháyati, cetáyati* from *tṛp-* 'to be satisfied', *vṛdh-* 'to increase', *kḷp-* 'to arrange', *budh-* 'to be aware' and *cit-* 'to observe'. Roots which in their strong form insert a nasal have this in association with guṇa in the causative: *mandáyati* 'gladdens', *sraṃsáyati* 'causes to fall', etc. Where the guṇa form produces a short syllable (*kar-*, etc.) vṛddhi is most commonly employed in the causatives: *kāráyati* 'causes to do', *trāsáyati* 'terrifies', *nāśáyati* 'destroys', *cyāváyati* 'causes to fall', etc. But a number of such roots retain guṇa: *gamáyati* 'causes to go', *tvaráyati* 'makes to hasten', *namáyati* 'causes to bend', etc. The non-strengthened form of the root appears normally only with roots that have no other form (*gūháyati* from *guh-* 'to conceal'), only rarely elsewhere (*giráyati, sphuráyati*). In *dūṣáyati* 'spoils' (intr. *duṣyati*, sb. *doṣa-*) the long vowel serves as a substitute for the normal strengthening. The anomalous *pūráyati* 'fills' is influenced by the form of the past participle passive (*pūrṇá-*).

Roots in *ā* commonly insert *-p-* before the causative suffix: *dāpáyati, sthāpáyati, māpáyati*, etc., from *dā-* 'to give', *sthā-* 'to stand', *mā-* 'to measure', etc. This *-p-* is an old suffix or enlargement which is known from comparative evidence to have been associated with certain of such roots (Lith. *stapýtis* 'to stand still'), and it has been extended to the whole class in the causative. It is further applied to the root *ṛ-* (*arpáyati*) and to a number of roots in *-i*: *adhyāpayati* from *adhi+i* 'to study', etc. In *ropáyati* 'plants' (*ruh-* 'to grow') it replaces the final consonant of the root. In Middle Indo-Aryan the popularity of this form of causative grew until it replaced the normal kind. A number of such Prakritic formations appear in later Sanskrit (*krīḍāpayati* 'causes to play', *jīvāpayati* 'causes to live', etc.).

There are a few other miscellaneous insertions before the causative suffix, namely *-l-*: *pālayati* 'protects' (*pā-*), *-n-* in *prīṇayati* 'pleases' (*prī-, prīṇāti*), *-s-* in *bhīṣayate* 'frightens', *-t-* in *ghātayati* 'has slain' (*han-*).

Formations outside the present system are made more commonly from the causative than from the other forms of secondary conjugation. The future (*vardhayiṣyati*, etc.) appears only very rarely in the *Ṛgveda*, but later is regularly made. For the aorist, as already observed, the reduplicated aorist has been adapted to serve for the causative. Besides this a few sporadic *iṣ*-aorist forms occur in the early language (*avādayiṣṭhās*, etc.). For the perfect the periphrastic form is used : *gamayāṃ cakāra*, *gamayām āsa*. The passive is made by suffixing the passive *yá* directly to the form of the root as it appears in the causative : *kāryáte*, *sthāpyáte*, etc. (simple passive *kriyáte*, *sthīyáte*). Nominal forms from the causative are : participle in *-tá*, *kāritá-*, gerundive, *kārayitavya-*, *kārya-*, *kāraṇīya-*, infinitive, *kārayitum*, gerund, *kārayitvā*. The suffix of the gerund in *-ya* is added directly to the root when this is strengthened in the causative (*-kārya*), otherwise to the *ay* of the causative suffix (*-gamayya*).

The present formations in *-aya* are closely related to the nominal *i*-stems (*roci-*/*rocay-* : *rocáyati*). The causative stem consists of a thematic enlargement of this suffix, of a type which occurs, though very rarely, in the nominal formations. The formation, since it contains a series of guṇa vowels, is not likely to be very ancient in Indo-European, but it occurs fairly widely : Gk. *τροπέω*, *στροφέω* (*τρέπω*, *στρέφω*), Lat. *spondeo* (: Gk. *σπένδω*), *moneo*, Goth. *nasjan*, *drausjan* (*ga-nisan*, *driusan*), etc. The meaning is frequentative, as usually in Greek, or causative. The latter meaning is normal in Germanic (*nasjan* ' to save ', *ga-nisan* ' to be saved ') and in Slavonic. Where Verner's law operates Germanic confirms the position of the accent on the suffix, as in Sanskrit : *wairþan* : *frawardjan*. It has also participial forms corresponding to the Sanskrit participles in *-itá* (*frawardiþs*) which are thus shown to be ancient. In Slavonic there is a series of causatives with vṛddhi as in Sanskrit, and this is one of the special features which connects the two families with Indo-European : O. Sl. *saditi* ' to plant ', cf. Skt. *sādáyati* ' makes to sit, settles ', *slaviti* ' to praise ', cf. Skt. *śrāváyati* ' makes to hear, be heard '.

IV. *The Desiderative*

The desiderative stem is formed by means of the suffix *-sa* associated with reduplication. The vowel of the reduplicating syllable is normally *i* but *u* is employed when that vowel occurs in the root : *bíbhitsati*, *títṛpsati*, but *yúyutsati* (*bhid-* ' to split ', *tṛp-* ' be satisfied ', *yudh-* ' to fight '). Long *ī* occurs in a very few cases: *mīmāṃsate* 'investigates' (*man-* 'to think'). The accent rests always on the reduplication.

The root appears normally in its weak form, but a final *i* and *u* are lengthened: *jígīṣati* 'desires to conquer' (*ji-*), *júhūṣati* 'desires to sacrifice' (*hu-*). Final *ṛ* of a root becomes *īr* or *ūr* before the desiderative *-sa*: *cíkīrṣati* 'desires to do', *títīrṣati* 'desires to cross', *múmūrṣati* 'is about to die'. This is phonetically justifiable only in the case of roots in *-ṝ*, i.e. those originally having final H (*tṝ-*, *tar*(H)- : *títīrṣati*) and from these it is extended to the rest.

A number of roots form an abbreviated stem in the desiderative in which the reduplication and the root are contracted into one syllable. An example is *dípsati* from *dabh-* 'to injure'. Corresponding to this Av. has *diwžaidyai* (inf.), and from a comparison of the two an Indo-Iranian stem *dibžha-* emerges. This represents a simplification of the original consonant group which occurred when the vowel of the root was elided in its weak form, i.e. *di-dbh-sa-*, a regularly formed desiderative. In the same way *śikṣa-* and *sīkṣa-* appear from *śak-* and *sah-*, later *dhīkṣa-*, *ripsa-*, *lipsa-*, etc. (*dah-*, *rabh-*, *labh-*); to these are added *īpsa-* and *īrtsa-* from roots beginning with a vowel (*āp-* 'to obtain', *ṛdh-* 'to prosper'). The roots *dā* and *dhā* make respectively *ditsa-* and *dhitsa-* in which the *ā* of the root has regularly disappeared in the weak form (*di-d-sa-*, *di-dh-sa-*).

The roots *van-* 'to win' and *san-* 'to gain' make the desiderative stems *vivāsa-* and *siṣāsa-* with *ā* out of *-n̥H-* as in other derivatives.

Roots in *ā*, apart from those mentioned above, generally keep the strong form in the desiderative: *yíyāsa-*, *pipāsa-*, from *yā-* 'to go', *pā-* 'to drink'. This, like the other forms with strong root below, is a Sanskrit innovation, as is clear from the preservation of ancient stems like *ditsa-* and the existence of Vedic *pi-p-ī-ṣa-* beside *pipāsa*. Anomalous strong forms appear from certain roots terminating in a nasal: *jighāṃsa-*, *jigāṃsa-* (beside *jigamiṣa-*) from *han-*, *gam-*. When the desiderative suffix appears as *iṣa* with the union vowel a final *i*, *u*, *ṛ* of a root necessarily and a medial *i*, *u*, *ṛ* optionally appear in the guṇa grade: *śiśayiṣa-*, *ninartiṣa-*, etc., but also *rurudiṣa-*. These and similar forms are laid down by the grammarians, but they do not occur in the earlier language.

Like other verbal formations the desiderative *sa* may be augmented by the union vowel *i* and appear as *-iṣa-*. In the early language there occurs only *didh-i-ṣa-* (*dhā-*, beside *dhitsa-*) ; also *ī* in certain cases where this enlargement has produced what is in practice an alternative form of the root (*pīpīṣa-*, *jihīṣa-*). The numerous classical formations in *iṣa* (which have normally guṇa of root as noted above) are complete innovations.

From the desiderative there are made, though not in the earliest language : a future in *iṣya* : *títikṣiṣye*, an *iṣ-* aorist, *ácikīrṣiṣam* and a periphrastic perfect, *īpsām cakāra/āsa*. Nominal derivatives from the desiderative stem occur earlier ; the most common are an adjective in *-u* (*titikṣú-*) and an abstract noun in *ā* (*mīmāṃsā́*).

In most desiderative stems the meaning (' wish to do something ') is straightforward and clear, though sometimes it is rather ' to be about to do something ' (*múmūrṣati*). In the case of a few roots the desiderative stem has developed a special meaning : *cikitsa-* ' cure ', *jugupsa-* ' despise ', *titikṣa-* ' endure ', *bībhatsa-* (*bādh-*) ' abhor ', *mīmāṃsa-* ' investigate ', *śuśrūṣa-* ' obey '.

The antiquity of the desiderative in Indo-European is attested by the reduced forms (*ditsa-*, *dipsa-*) which have been affected by the old apophony. Nevertheless it is not widely represented, a fact which must be due to loss in the individual languages. The only branch of Indo-European outside Indo-Iranian where a comparable formation occurs is Celtic. Since there are no close relations between these two members of the family this is itself an indication that the formation is ancient. The Celtic formation to be compared is the Old Irish reduplicated *s*-future : 1 sg. *-ninus* <**niniksō* (*nigid* ' washes ', cf. Skt. *nij-*, des. *níniкṣati*), 2 sg. *-riris* (*con-rig* ' binds '), 3 pl. *lilsit* from *ligid* ' licks ' (Skt. *lih-*, des. *lilikṣati*).

§ 16. Denominative Verbs

Denominative verbs are those that are formed on the basis of a noun stem. Ultimately, as already observed, all verbal stems are not to be distinguished from the corresponding noun stems, but they have acquired independence. The denominative proper is a formation by which verbal stems continue to be made from the nouns existing in the language. The suffix employed in making denominatives is accented *-yá-*, the same suffix which forms one of the primary verbal classes (*dī́vyati*).

The only difference is that the denominatives preserve the original accent of the suffix which in the primary verbs has been replaced by radical accent. The denominative is of IE origin and among the other languages it is particularly well represented in Greek: τεκμαίρω 'determine' (for *-aryō* from the neut. noun τέκμαρ) ἐχθαίρω 'hate', ὀνομαίνω 'name', σαλπίζω 'trumpet' (σάλπιγξ), κηρύσσω 'proclaim' (κῆρυξ), etc., etc. Similar formations in other languages are Lat. *custōdio, fīnio* (*custōs, fīnis*), Goth. *glitmunjan* 'glitter', *lauhatjan* 'shine', etc. They are also common in Hittite, which gives a greater antiquity to the denominative formation than might otherwise have been expected: *irmaliya-* 'to be ill' (*irmalaš* 'ill'), *kušaniya-* 'hire' (*kušan* 'pay'), *lamniya-* 'to name' (*lāman* 'name', cf. Gk. ὀνομαίνω), etc.

Denominatives in *-yá-* are formed from all the various nominal stems and they may conveniently be classified accordingly.

Stems in r: *vadharyáti* 'hurls a weapon', cf. *vádhar* 'weapon'. This type of nominal stem is practically obsolete, and the result is that there are a number of such denominatives where the corresponding nouns-stem has been lost: *śratharyáti* 'becomes loose', *saparyáti* 'attends to, worships', *rathharyáti* 'rides in a chariot', *adhvaryáti* 'performs a sacrifice', *vithuryáti* 'staggers'.

Stems in n: Denominatives formed from *n*-stems are *kṛpaṇyáti* 'solicits', *turaṇyáti* 'is speedy', *damanyáti* 'subdues', *bhuraṇyáti* 'is active', *saraṇyáti* 'hastens', *dhiṣaṇyáti* 'pays attention', *ruvaṇyáti* 'roars', *huvanyáti* 'calls', etc. This type is based on the old neuter *n*-stems, likewise mainly extinct, and corresponding nominal stems are either non-existent or take the form of thematic derivatives: *kṛpaṇá-*, *turáṇa-*, etc.

Stems in s: These are well preserved and denominatives are frequent: *apasyáti* 'is active', *namasyáti* 'reverences', *canasyáti* 'is pleased', *manasyáti* 'is mindful of', etc. In some cases the corresponding *s*-stem is not preserved, e.g. *irasyáti* 'is jealous', *daśasyáti* 'renders service to'. In other cases *-asya-* is extended to become an independent suffix, with a desiderative meaning: *vṛṣasyáti* 'desires the male', *stanasyáti* 'desires the breast'. From the compound stems *iṣ* and *uṣ* are formed *aviṣyáti* 'is eager to help' (the identity of this form with the future in *-iṣya-* should be noticed), *taruṣyáti* ' strives to overcome ', etc.

Rare examples of denominatives formed from stems in occlusive appear in *bhiṣajyáti* ' acts the physician ' and (from a stem not otherwise preserved) *iṣudhyáti* ' implores ' (Av. *išūidya-*).

It will be observed from the examples quoted above that the denominatives in *yá* are normally from the neuter consonantal stems. Denominatives from the masculine (agent-noun) stems are rare: e.g. *vṛṣaṇyáti* ' acts like a male '. A few such formations are based on the nominative singulars: *rājāyáte* ' is kingly ', *vṛṣāyáte* ' acts like a bull ', *svāmīyáti* ' treats as master '.

Stems in i and ī: *janiyáti* ' seeks a wife ' (*jáni-*), *taviṣīyáte* ' is strong ' (*táviṣī*). The form with long *ī* is usually extended to stems in short *i* (*kavīyáti* ' acts like a wise man ', *sakhīyáti* ' desires friendship ', *arātīyáti* ' is inimical '), but such forms are shortened in the pada text. The suffix *-īya-* develops to some extent independently, with a desiderative sense, and is applied to other than *i*-stems: *putrīyáti* ' desires a son ', *māṃsīyáti* ' craves flesh ', etc.

Stems in u and ū: Here also the long form of the suffix is applied to both types of stem, though short *u* is restored in the pada text: *ṛjūyáti* ' is straight ', *vasūyáti* ' desires wealth ', etc. In some cases there is no noun-stem and *-ūya-* functions as an independent verbal suffix: *asūyáti* ' grumbles ', *aṅkūyáti* ' moves crookedly ', *stabhūyáti* ' stands firm '.

Stems in ā: *pṛtanāyáti* ' fights ', *ducchunāyáte* ' desires mischief ', *manāyáte* ' is well disposed '. Denominatives from *ā*-stems are an ancient IE type, though more frequently elsewhere formed without the addition of *ya*: Hitt. *newaḫḫun* ' I renewed ', Lat. *novāre*, Gk. *νεᾶν*. This type is found in Sanskrit only when *ā* is incorporated in the root (*trā́ti*), otherwise the *-ya-* denominative is used. The suffix *-āya-* early became an independent suffix, and there are a number of roots which inflect in this way without there being any corresponding *ā*-nouns: *mathāyáti* ' stirs ', *śrathāyáti* ' loosens ', *muṣāyáti* ' steals ', etc. These stems commonly alternate with stems of the ninth class: *mathnā́ti*, *śrathnā́ti*, *muṣṇā́ti*, etc. As a result of the close association of the two types the denominative *yá* is sometimes appended to ninth class stems: *hṛṇāyá-*, *hṛṇīyá-* ' be angry ',

In the Vedic language the denominative in *-āya-* is commonly extended beyond its proper field and it is used to form denominatives from thematic stems beside the regular forms in *-ayáti* : *aghāyáti* ' plans mischief ', *aśvāyáti* ' seeks for horses ', *priyāyáte* ' holds dear '.

Thematic Stems : *amitrayáti* ' acts like an enemy ', *devayáti* ' cultivates the gods, is pious ', *vasnayáti* ' bargains ', etc. This is the latest type of denominative formation. The addition of a further suffix to a final thematic suffix is against the principles of IE stem formation. It appears here in the denominative purely by analogy, *deva-yá-ti*, etc., being created after the pattern of *brahmaṇ-yá-ti*, etc. The resulting stem is similar to the causative, differing only in accent, but the origin and analysis are quite different. On the one hand we have an *i*-stem with thematic extension (analyse *vardháy-a-*), on the other hand a thematic stem with the mechanical and analogical addition of the denominative *-yá-* (analyse *deva-yá-*). The similarity of the two forms gave rise to some confusion, and there are stems, apparently denominative in origin which have the causative accent : *artháyate* ' desires ', *mantráyate* ' takes council ', *mṛgáyate* ' hunts ', etc. These are normally classified in the tenth present class.

In the later classical language most of the old denominatives made from consonant stems disappear. The thematic type remains living and takes two forms : (1) in the active the normal *-ayati* is used, *kaluṣayati* ' makes turbid ', *taruṇayati* ' rejuvenates ', (2) in the middle, with intransitive sense, *-āyate* is used, *kaluṣāyate* ' becomes turbid ', *taruṇāyate* ' is rejuvenated '. It was noted above that the *-āya*-stem, properly a derivative from the nominal *ā*-stem, was commonly used in the Veda to make denominatives from thematic stems, with the result that there are two alternative formations. In the later development of the language those two are specialised in different uses as just stated.

Forms outside the present system from denominative stems occur with the utmost rarity. There are a few isolated *iṣ*-aorist (*avṛṣāyiṣata*) and future forms (*kaṇḍūyiṣyati*). Participles in *-ta* (*kaṇḍūyitá-*, etc.) are somewhat more frequent. In the Vedic language abstract nouns in *ā* (*vasūyā́*) and adjectives in *-u* (*vasūyú-*), made like the similar formations from the desiderative stem, are common, but the type in general dies out later.

§ 17. Infinitives

The difference between Vedic and classical Sanskrit is nowhere more marked than in the infinitive. The classical language has only one form of infinitive, in *tum*, which is added to the guṇated root (*kártum*), and which, like other verbal formatives may be provided with the connecting vowel *i* (*bhávitum*). In the Vedic language this formation is exceedingly rare, but there exists a whole series of other forms classed as infinitives which do not survive in the later language. These Vedic infinitives consist of a variety of verbal action nouns inflected in various cases, namely :

(i) *Accusative*, from root stems and stems in *-tu* : *pratíram* ' to prolong ', *dā́tum* ' to give '. The former may be compared with the Oscan-Umbrian infinitives in *-om/um* : Umbr. *erom*, Osc. *ezum* ' to be ', Osc. *edum* ' to eat ', etc. The latter, which eventually becomes the sole form of infinitive, has parallels in the Latin supine (*datum*) and in Balto-Slavonic (Lith. *dė́tų*, O. Sl. *dětŭ* ' to place ').

(ii) *Dative*, much the most frequent type. These infinitives are made from root stems (*dṛśé* ' to see ', *bhujé* ' to enjoy '), from stems in *-as* (*áyase* ' to go ', *arháse* ' to be worthy of '), from stems in *-i* (*dṛśáye* ' to see ', *yudháye* ' to fight '), from stems in *-ti* (*vītáye* ' to enjoy ', *sātáye* ' to win '), from stems in *-tu* (*étave* ' to go ', *yáṣṭave* ' to sacrifice ') from stems in *-tava* (*étavaí* ' to go '), from stems in *dhya* (*duhádhyai* ' to milk ', *sáhadhyai* ' to overcome '), from stems in *man* (*dā́mane* ' to give ') and *van* (*dāváne* ' to give '). Of these the infinitive in *-tavai* is remarkable in having a double accent (a phenomenon which has not been explained), and in always being followed by the particle *u* (*étavā́ u*). This infinitive, and the one in *-dhyai* are also distinguished in being formed from stems which are not otherwise in active use, and also in preserving the older form of the dative singular which has been replaced by *-āya* in the declension of nouns.

(iii) *Ablative-Genitive*, from root stems and stems in *-tu* : *avapádas* ' falling down ', *sampṛcas* ' coming in contact ' ; *étos* ' going ', *nídhātos* ' putting down '.

(iv) *Locative*, from root stems (*saṃcakṣi* ' on beholding '), stems in *-san-* (*neṣáṇi* ' to lead '), in *-tar* - (*vi*)*dhartári* ' to support (bestow) ', *sótari* ' in the pressing '.

The Vedic language (with Old Iranian) represents most accurately the state of affairs in Indo-European. The infinitive as an independent category is not yet fully developed. The forms classed as infinitives are various cases of verbal action nouns, in which as a general rule the case has its normal force :

Acc. *váṣṭi ārábham* ' he desires to begin, wants a beginning '.

Dat. *āvís tanvàṃ kṛṇuṣe dṛśé kam* ' you reveal your body for seeing '.

Abl. *sá īṃ mahīṃ dhúnim étor aramṇāt* ' he stopped the great river from flowing '.

A curious feature of the Vedic language is that the noun which is logically the object of the infinitive is placed in the same case as the infinitive, so that for instance ' to see the sun ' is expressed *dṛśáye sū́ryāya*, lit. ' for seeing, for the sun ' ; similarly, with ablative, *trā́dhvam kartā́d avapádaḥ* ' save us from falling into a pit ', lit. ' save us from a pit, from falling down '.

In the normal usage of the Vedic infinitive there is not a great deal to distinguish it from an ordinary verbal noun inflected in an oblique case. One of the few things that places these formations in a special category is the fact that the majority of verbal noun stems which appear in this usage are not otherwise used, nor in other cases. Taking the neuter *s*-stems as an example, there are many regular nouns so formed (*yáśas* ' fame ', etc.), but there are in addition a large number which appear only in the dative case, in this infinitival use. Many such dative infinitives are also distinguished formally, since they are given an accent (*jīvásе*) which is different from that of the neuter nouns. The infinitives in the Veda which are most removed from ordinary nominal formation are those formed from stems which are no longer used in the formation of ordinary nouns. Such are the dative infinitives in *-dhyai* and the comparatively rare locative formations in *-sani* and *-tari*. Another feature differentiating infinitive from verbal noun, one only partially developed in the Vedic language, is that it governs the accusative like a verb instead of the genitive like a verbal noun, e.g. *máhi dāváne* ' to give something big ' as opposed to *gotrásya dāváne* ' for the giving of a herd '.

In the classical language where the infinitive in *-tum* has replaced all others, the infinitive has become quite independent of the nominal formation. It also takes over the sense of the dative infinitive (*avasthātuṃ sthānāntaram cintaya* ' think of another place to stay in ') so that its original force as the accusative of a verbal noun is obscured. In one respect it retains a trace of its nominal origin, because it can be compounded, like a noun-stem, with *kāma-* and *manas* : *yaṣṭukāma-* ' desirous of sacrificing ', *vaktumanas-* ' minded to speak '.

The Sanskrit infinitive, in its final form, is much less developed and integrated into the verbal system than the infinitives of Latin and Greek. The latter languages have developed special forms for various tenses (*esse, fuisse*) and for the voices (*agere, agī*), by a process of adaptation which took place independently in the two languages. Nothing of this kind appears in Sanskrit. There are in the Veda a few forms where the infinitive appears attached to special tense-stems (*puṣyáse* ' to flourish ', *gṛṇīṣáṇi* ' to praise ', *-pṛ́ccham* ' to ask ' ; from the perfect *vāvṛdhádhyai* ' to strengthen '), but these tentative formations came to nothing. The system by which the infinitive is formed only from the root prevailed, and the syntactical use of the infinitive is correspondingly wide. In particular it has to function not only as active and middle indiscriminately, but also, when the context demands it, as passive : *kartum ārabdhaḥ* ' began to be made ', etc. This usage is particularly frequent with the passive forms of *śak-* : *kartuṃ na śakyate* ' cannot be done ', etc.

§18. Active and Middle Participles

Like the infinitives these participles are in origin purely nominal forms and as such have been treated in the chapters concerning the formation and declension of nouns. They belong to the verb inasmuch as they have become integrated into the verbal system. This integration goes further than in the case of the infinitive in Sanskrit (though not as far as in Greek), and the process started earlier. The various participles are attached to particular tense stems, and they are divided, like the finite verb, into active and middle.

The active participle in *-ant-* is in Classical Sanskrit entirely, and in the Vedic language mainly, formed from the present stems of the verb. In the Vedic language there is a small number of such participles which are attached to the root aorist stem (*kránt-, gmánt-* from *kṛ-* ' do ', *gam-* ' go ') and to the *a*-aorist stem (*tṛpánt-, vṛdhánt-* from *tṛp-* ' be satisfied ' and *vṛdh-* 'grow '). This association is mainly superficial, since such formations are not different from typical adjective formations with accented suffix added straight to the root. Before their integration into the verbal system the *-ánt-* formations were ordinary adjectives (of which some examples remain, *bṛhánt-* 'tall', etc.), and the original type, derived straight from the root and having the adjectival accent, is preserved in these aorist participles.

The adaptation of *ant-* adjectives to make participles began early, since there are *ant-* participles also in Hittite. But at the time of the separation of Hittite the *ant-* participle had not settled down into its final role since in that language the *ant-* participles are used in a passive sense, as opposed to the active sense in the rest of Indo-European. The specialisation of the formation in *ant* as an active participle was followed by its transference to the present system. The radical formations were replaced by formations made from the various types of present stem (*kránt-* by *kṛṇvánt-*, etc.). In the Veda this process is almost complete and the number of aorist participles is already small. By the classical period the process is complete. In Greek the same process began but ended differently, since there the appearance of present participles (*φεύγων*) beside the older aoristic (i.e. suffixally accented type) *φυγών* led to the evolution of a twofold system in which these two types of participle, like the moods associated with the two tenses, express different kinds of action (punctual and durative). Greek has further extended the formation of this participle to the *s*-aorist stem, where it is to all intents and purposes non-existent in Sanskrit, as it was in Indo-European.

The association of the active participle with the present system had the result that its accent (originally on the final, as an adjective) came to correspond to that of the verbal stem to which it was attached. It appears on the suffix in the case of the suffixally accented thematic class (*tudánt-*) and in non-thematic verbs (*duhánt-*, *śṛṇvánt-*, etc.). On the other hand the radically accented thematic verbs keep this accent in the participle: *bhávant-*, etc. The reduplicating verbs have accent on the reduplicating syllable associated with weak form of the participial suffix even in the strong cases: nom. sg. *bíbhrat*, acc. sg. *bíbhratam*.

The formation and morphology of the active perfect participle in *-vas/uṣ* have already been detailed. The existence of a separate participle for the perfect is in accordance with the view already recorded that the difference between present/aorist and perfect is the most original division in the verbal tense system. The perfect participle has the perfect sense (as opposed to the aorist participle which has no aorist sense, and as opposed to the moods of the perfect), *cakṛvás-* ' one who has done ', etc. The accent is on the participial suffix and the perfect stem appears in its weak form. The union vowel *i* (*tenivás*, etc.) appears under much the same conditions as in the rest of the perfect.

In the middle the participle used is in *-amāna* for thematic verbs (*bhávamāna-*, *viśámāna-*, *cintáyamāna-*) and in *-āna* for non-thematic verbs (*duhāná-*, *sunvāná-*, *yuñjāná-*, etc. ; accent final except in the 3rd class and intensives : *júhvāna-*, *cékitāna-*, etc.). The adaptation of these formations as participles is probably later than that of the active participles in *-ant*, since comparable forms are not widely spread in Indo-European. Corresponding to *-amāna-* Iranian has *-amna-* and Greek *-όμενος*, the actual forms varying in each case. No other IE languages have such participles, and where similar formations appear (Lat. *alumnus*, etc.) they are purely nominal. The participle in *-āna* is found only in Indo-Iranian, and only rare formations in the nominal derivation can be compared to it elsewhere (Lat. *colōnus*, etc.). The middle usage of the participle is through adaptation, and it is certainly much later than the existence of middle forms in the finite verb. How the adaptation came about is no longer clear, since there is nothing about the related *men*-formations of the noun that is connected with the middle, and in particular the Greek infinitives in *-μεν(αι)*, which have also become part of the verbal morphology, have an active, not a middle sense.

What was said above about the integration of the active participle into the present system applies also to the middle participle. Like other derivatives based on the simple *n*-suffix and the compound *men*-suffix these were originally made from the root, and after their adaptation as participles the present stem came to be used instead. In the classical language the aorist formations (*dṛśāná-*, *vṛdhāná-*, *śucámāna-*) which incorporate what remains of the old radical formations are replaced in favour of the present tense. In contradistinction to the active there is no special participial suffix for the perfect in the middle and the form *-āna* of the non-thematic verbs is used: *cakrāṇá-*, *jajñāná-*, etc. This is in accordance with the fact, noted before, that the middle is later in the perfect than in the present-aorist system.

§ 19. The Past Participle Passive

This participle is most commonly made by the addition of the suffix *-tá* to the weak form of the root (*śrutá-* 'heard', etc.), and like other verbal derivatives it frequently employs the auxiliary vowel *-i-* (*patitá-* 'fallen', etc.). The meaning is passive except in the case of intransitive verbs (*gatá-* 'gone', etc.). The formation is ancient in Indo-European as is clear both from the fact that it appears in large proportion of the languages, and because it is subject to the old IE apophony. At the same time it does not appear to go back to the period when Hittite separated, since in that language the passive participle is expressed differently, by the suffix *-ant*. In contradistinction to the active and middle participles it is not associated with particular tense stems but formed directly from the root both in Sanskrit and other IE languages.

A minority of roots form their past passive participle in *ná* instead of *-tá*. This is particularly the case with roots in *-r̥̄* (*kīrṇá-* 'scattered', *gīrṇá* 'swallowed'), roots in *-ī* (*kṣīṇá-* 'wasted away'), roots in *-d* (*bhinná-* 'broken', *chinná-* 'cut') and it is found in a number of roots in *-j* (*bhugná-* 'bent', *bhagná-* 'broken'). Very occasionally other suffixes are so used, notably *pakvá-* 'cooked, ripe'. The details of these formations have been systematically treated in the section dealing with the formation of nouns, and need not be repeated here.

The importance of the past participle passive increases in the later language, and still more so in Prakrit, on account of the change that took place from active to passive construction. It becomes customary in later time to express past actions not by active preterites but by the past passive participle associated with the instrumental: *sa mayā dr̥ṣṭah* 'he (was) seen by me' for 'I saw him'. This resulted in middle Indo-Aryan in the elimination of the old preterites, and in modern Indo-Aryan all the tenses expressing the preterite are based on the old past participle passive.

The past participle passive could be extended by the addition of the possessive suffix *-vant*: *kṛtávant-* 'one who has something (or things) done', and this naturally assumes the functions of an active past participle. This is a creation of Indo-Aryan and the first purely participial formation of this character appears in the Atharva-veda: *aśitā́vaty átithau* 'one's guest having eaten'. Later the participle in *tavant* (*-navant-* when roots take *-na* in this participle) comes to be used independently, the copula being understood, in place of an active preterite: *na māṃ kaścid dṛṣṭavān* 'no one has seen (saw) me'. In the classical language this is the common usage and it forms another alternative to the use of the preterite tenses in addition to the passive construction mentioned above.

§ 20. Gerundives or Future Passive Participles

Classical Sanskrit has three verbal adjectives of identical function and having the sense of the Latin gerundive: *kārya-*, *kartavya-*, *karaṇīya-* 'to be done, faciendus'. Of these the first is the only one to be found in the *Ṛgveda*, where it is common. The suffix is normally to be pronounced *-iya*. Formations of this kind are found with all three grades of root: *gúhya-* 'to be hidden', *dvéṣya-* 'to be hated', *vā́cya-* 'to be said'. Final *ā* of a root coalesces with the suffix to produce *-eya*: *déya-* 'to be given'. Roots in *i*, *u*, *ṛ* commonly take the augment *-t-* before this suffix: *śrútya-* 'to be heard'. The accent is normally on the root, but there are some exceptions: *bhāvyá-*, *ādyà-*.

The formation in *-tavya* first appears in the *Atharvaveda* (*janitavyà-* 'to be born', *hiṃsitavyà-* 'to be injured'). It becomes commoner in the period of the Brāhmaṇas, and in the classical language it is freely formed from all roots. The accent of the above two examples is the only type that occurs in accented texts. The grammarians allow also acute accent of the penultimate. In origin the formation is a secondary adjectival derivative from the action nouns in *-tu*.

The gerundive in *-anī́ya* (a secondary adjectival derivative from the verbal nouns in *-ana*) is likewise first recorded in the Atharvaveda (*upajīvanī́ya*). It remains rare in the Brāhmaṇas, but is common in the classical language, though not as frequent as the type in *-tavya*.

In addition to the three types of gerundive that appear in the classical language there are several formations in the same function that appear only in the Veda :

(i) in *-tva* (normally pronounced as two syllables, *-tuva*) with accent and guṇa of root : *kártva-* ' to be done ', *jétva-*, *hántva-*, *váktva-*, etc.

(ii) in *-enya* (*-eniya-*) : *dṛśénya*, *yudhénya*, *vareṇya*, etc.

(iii) in *-āyya* (trisyllabic) : *panā́yya-* ' to be praised, praiseworthy ', *dakṣā́yya-*, *śravā́yya-*, etc.

§ 21. Gerund or Indeclinable Participle

This form of participle was analysed above as being a kind of adverbially used action noun. The type of participle is not familiar elsewhere in Indo-European and although the form is explicable through the normal IE processes of stem formation, its adoption in this particular syntactic use is in the main a development of Indo-Aryan.

In the classical language the gerund is formed by means of the suffix *-tvā* when the verbal root is uncompounded by preposition, otherwise by the suffix *-ya*. In the *Ṛgveda* the latter suffix is in the majority of instances long (*-yā*) and this no doubt is the more original form, the suffix *-yā* making verbal abstracts being used adverbially in the same way as *-tvā*. Other instances have been noted of final *-ā* (*-a*H) appearing as short *a* due to special circumstances of sentence sandhi (*atra*, etc.).

Beside *-tvā* the *Ṛgveda* also has a form *-tvā́ya* which appears to be a contamination of the two alternative forms just mentioned. It also has a form in *-tvī* (*hitvī́* ' having left ', etc.) terminating in the suffix *-ī*, which is used in the same conditions as the *-tvā* form and is commoner than it. This *tvī-* form though absent in Sanskrit, is continued in certain Middle Indo-Aryan dialects of the North-West and West, and was clearly a local dialectal feature of Old Indo-Aryan.

Extended gerund forms in *-tvānam* and *-tvīnam* are mentioned as Vedic by the grammarians but examples of them have not been found in the extant literature. Middle Indo-Aryan has a common gerund in *-tūna* (*gantūna*) which appears to contain the same elements as *-tvānam*, but with different apophony.

The accusative of verbal action nouns in *-a* is used adverbially in constructions that resemble the gerund : *imā́ny áṅgāni* *vyatyā́sam śete* 'he lies down changing the position of these limbs', etc. This usage does not occur in the earliest literature (RV., AV.), but it is common in the pre-classical prose. In the later classical prose it is comparatively rare, being used chiefly where the form is repeated: *darśam-darśam* 'continually seeing', *śrāvam-śrāvam* 'continually hearing'.

CHAPTER VIII

LOANWORDS IN SANSKRIT

§ 1. Non-Aryan Influence on Sanskirt

In the preceding chapters the history and development of the Sanskrit language has been described, from its remote Indo-European beginnings until it received final and definite form in India. The process was one of continual linguistic change, and when Sanskrit was artificially stabilised by the grammarians, this process was continued in the popular speech to produce first the Middle Indo-Aryan languages and finally the Modern Indo-Aryan languages. So far we have dealt only with developments that affected the inherited linguistic material which constitutes the basic texture of the language. But this is not all that has to be taken into consideration, since there are to be found in addition many elements in the language whose origin is to be sought elsewhere, namely in the influence of the various non-Aryan languages in contact with which Indo-Aryan developed.

Such influence affected mainly of course the vocabulary of the language. In more general terms such influence is seen in the phonetic development of a new series of occlusives, the so-called cerebrals. To begin with cerebrals appear in pure Aryan words as a result of phonetic changes affecting these (*nižda-*> *niẓḍa-*> *nīḍa-*) and although such a development is a part of the processes taking place within Indo-Aryan itself, it can hardly be an accident that it should occur in the only branch of Indo-European which was in contact with languages possessing such sounds. In grammar the rapid loss of the Indo-European grammar in the stages subsequent to Sanskrit was very likely accelerated by the acquisition of Aryan speech by peoples who spoke originally different languages. On the other hand foreign influence in matters of detail is always difficult to establish. One feature in Sanskrit which may perhaps be assigned to such influence is the use of the gerund or conjunctive participle. In form these adverbial participles are of course purely Indo-

European in origin, and their structure has been analysed above. On the other hand this type of formation is not used to make such participles elsewhere in Indo-European, and the employment of such adverbial forms to make a type of participle not familiar elsewhere is one of the special characteristics of Indo-Aryan. The same type of participle with the same kind of syntactic usage happens also to be a noteworthy feature of Dravidian. It may well be that the extensive use made of this formation in Sanskrit is partly due to the influence of Dravidian usage.

Although a few points of this kind may profitably be examined from the point of view of foreign influence, it is mainly in the vocabulary that detailed confirmation of such influence must be sought, and it is to an examination of this side of the problem that the present chapter is devoted. The basic vocabulary of Sanskrit is Indo-European, and it is this which has appeared in the preceding chapters, but in addition there exist large numbers of words which are without Indo-European etymology. In the very earliest language such words are few, but they progressively become more numerous. In the Middle Indo-Aryan period there is a further growth of new vocabulary, and again in the Modern Indo-Aryan languages there appears an abundance of words which are unknown to the earlier stages of the language.

The tendency to substitute new words for inherited IE words has been permanently active in Indo-Aryan. Among common examples in Sanskrit we may note *ghoṭaka-* 'horse' which appears beside *aśva-* in later Sanskrit and supplants it in the later history of Indo-Aryan. Similarly *śván-* 'dog' gives way to *kukkura-* and its derivatives. It is not unusual to find pairs of names in Sanskrit, used equally commonly, of which one is non-Aryan, e.g. *mārjāra-* 'cat' (*mṛj-*) beside *biḍāla-*, *vyāghrá-* 'tiger' beside *śārdūla-*, *ṛ́kṣa-* 'bear' beside *bhallūka-*. Sometimes the number of synonyms is much greater. The common word for elephant is *hastin-* ('possessed of a hand'), but beside it, all in common use, we find *gaja-*, *kuñjara-*, *ibha-*, *nāga-* and *mātaṅga-*. Similarly beside *mahiṣá-* 'buffalo' we find other terms such as *kāsara-*, *lulāya-*, *sairibha-* and *heramba-*. In such cases what are clearly local words, belonging originally to different languages have been adopted into Sanskrit, and the multiplicity of the Sanskrit vocabulary reflects an original linguistic complication in India which has receded before the advance of Indo-Aryan.

These few examples serve to illustrate the composite nature of the Sanskrit vocabulary, and the total number of such extraneous words is very large. Their source is mainly to be found in pre-Aryan languages of India. It is likely that there existed in India various linguistic groups which have been totally extinguished by the advance of Indo-Aryan, and in so far as Sanskrit has drawn words from such sources, their origin must remain for ever unknown. On the other hand those non-Aryan languages which have maintained their independent existence form a valuable source for the investigation of the extraneous elements in Sanskrit. It will therefore be convenient to enumerate the various groups involved, and to examine what contribution each has to make to the investigation of the problem.

On its northern and eastern frontiers Indo-Aryan is contiguous with Tibeto-Burman languages and a number of such dialects are spoken within the political frontiers of India. In spite of this contact no evidence of influence from this side on Indo-Aryan has been produced. This linguistic family has always remained essentially external to India proper. Furthermore it appears that on the Eastern frontiers of India these peoples have displaced earlier Austro-Asiatic populations and that their contact is not very ancient. It is possible that a few Sanskrit words may eventually be traced to this origin, but at present no satisfactory evidence of such influence is available.

In the extreme North-West of India there is found Burushaski, a language which so far stands on its own. A connection between Burushaski and certain of the Caucasian languages has been suggested, but not proved, though it is possible that further work in this direction might be fruitful. An earlier form of this language must have existed in this region before the Aryan invasion, and it is likely to have occupied a more extensive territory. Evidence that Sanskrit has been influenced from this source has not been produced. It is a border language and such influence would only have been possible in the very earliest period of Indo-Aryan, since from the Vedic period it must have existed much as it does now, an isolated unit in a remote mountain tract.

In Eastern India there is found a family of languages which

is of considerable importance from this and other points of view. The Muṇḍa or Kolarian languages as they are variously called, have in no instances achieved the status of literary languages but they are important scientifically firstly because there is definite evidence that Indo-Aryan had been influenced from this source, and secondly because of their connection with Mon, Khmer and other languages east of India. The most important centre of this family is the Chota Nagpur Plateau, where Santali, Mundari, and a number of fairly closely related dialects are spoken. In Orissa, not far from the above area occurs Juang, and further south, on the Orissa Madras border, Savara, Gadaba and two other dialects which form a special group within the Muṇḍa family. Of these Savara is particularly well preserved and less overlaid by Indo-Aryan than most members of the family. The most western Muṇḍa tribe is that of the Kurkus, who occupy the Satpura and Mahadeo hills in Madhya Pradesh.

The most important linguistic family in India outside Indo-Aryan is the Dravidian family. Four members of this family have achieved the status of literary languages—Tamil, Malayalam, Telugu, Kanarese, and in the case of Tamil the literary tradition goes back for at least two thousand years. Besides the major languages there are numerous minor non-literary Dravidian languages spoken in various parts of India, namely :

(i) Southern : Tulu, Coorg, Toda, Kota.

(ii) Central : (*a*) Kolami-Naiki, Parji, Dravidian Gadba ; (*b*) Gondi, Konda, Pengo, Kui, Kuvi.

(iii) Northern : (*a*) Kūrukh, Malto ; (*b*) Brahui.

The existence of the last member of the family in Baluchistan, far away from the main concentration of Dravidian is consistent with the theory that before the Aryan conquest Dravidian occupied a much greater area including considerably portions of Northern India. We shall see that the extensive influence of Dravidian on Sanskrit, beginning at an early period, also seems to point to this conclusion.

In addition to the above-mentioned linguistic groups it has recently been established that the Nahali language still spoken by a small number of people in the Nimar district of Madhya Pradesh constitutes a further independent unit, unconnected with any of the groups previously mentioned. This language was briefly treated in the Linguistic survey of India where it was wrongly assigned to the Muṇḍa or Kolanian family. Examination of the material provided by the Linguistic Survey itself rendered this assertion extremely doubtful, and recent field researches, by greatly increasing the material available, have made it clear that Nahali is the last surviving remnant of what must originally have been a quite independent family. Yet others may have existed of which nothing is now known, and the possibility that Sanskrit (and also later Indo-Aryan) has drawn on such sources is always to be borne in mind.

Remains of an ancient language of India have been unearthed in the Indus cities of the third millennium B.C. So far no serious progress has been made in its decipherment, since no key to the solution is available. There is at present no means of knowing what kind of language is represented in these documents, which might be connected with one of the linguistic groups known in India, or be something quite different. Nor is there any means of knowing whether or not Sanskrit may have been influenced from this. There is only the possibility that some day, with the discovery of further information, a new chapter may be contributed to the linguistic history of India.

From this brief survey it is clear that there are two practical sources where the origin of the non-Aryan element in Sanskrit may be sought, namely the Muṇḍa and Dravidian languages, and in both these directions progress has been made. As far as the Muṇḍa languages are concerned the main difficulty is that many of them have been inadequately explored. A necessary basis for the study of their influence on Sanskrit is a proper comparative study of the languages themselves, but this cannot be undertaken until adequate grammars and dictionaries exist for all the independent members. At present the most detailed information exists for the Northern group (Santali, Mundari, etc.) but this happens to be the one which has been most profoundly influenced by Indo-Aryan. Consequently in the absence of full comparative evidence it is often difficult to decide which way the borrowing has taken place. There is also the question of the relation of Muṇḍa and Mon-Khmer. The evidence of this is clear enough to be decisive, but it has not been worked out in proper detail. This will eventually be necessary both for the comparative study of the Muṇḍa languages themselves, and for the special question under discussion, their influence on Indo-Aryan.

The connection between Muṇḍa and Mon-Khmer, etc., as members of a larger Austro-Asiatic family, has normally been assumed by those who have investigated this section of the Sanskrit vocabulary. Such etymologies are in some cases only available from Austro-Asiatic languages outside India. For instance one of the words for elephant mentioned above, *mātaṅga-* has been explained as Austro-Asiatic for 'animal with a hand' (cf. *hastin-*), but the forms with which it may be compared (*tang* 'hand', *maintoṅg* 'elephant') are quoted not from India but from the Malay peninsula. The same is the case with Skt. *aṅganā* 'women' which is explained as containing a common Austro-Asiatic word for woman with prefix *aṅ-*: cf. Khmer kan, Mon *k'ṅā*, etc., with prefix *a-*, Bahnar *akan*, with prefix *en-*, Nicobar *enkāna̱*. The bird known in Sanskrit as *kuliṅga-* ('fork-tailed strike') has apparently an Austro-Asiatic name (Khasi *khlīṅ* 'kite, eagle', Khmer *khleṅ*, Stieng *kliṅ* 'kite'), but forms are not quoted from Muṇḍa. Common Austro-Asiatic words may have ceased to be current in Muṇḍa, or not known through defective documentation, and consequently etymologies based on languages outside India may be consistent with Sanskrit having acquired the words in India. In some cases the source of a word is definitely to be sought outside India, e.g. in the case of imported plants. Such is the case with *lavaṅga-* 'cloves', where the origin of the plant as well as the name (Javanese *lawaṅ*, etc.) is to be sought in Indonesia.

The following is a short list of words for which, with reasonable plausibility, a Muṇḍa, or more widely, Austro-Asiatic source has been claimed:

alābu 'bottle-gourd': cf. Malay *labu*, *labo*, Khmer *lbow*, Batak *labu*, etc.

unduru- 'rat': with prefix *un-*; cf. Khmer *kāndŏr* with different prefix, Savara *guntur-* 'rat', further Savara *ondreṅ-* 'rat'.

kadalī 'banana': cf. Sakai *telui*, *kelui*, Nicobar *talūi*, Khmer *tut taloi*, Palaong *kloai* 'plantain'; Savara *kin-tēn-* 'banana'.

karpāsa- 'cotton' (>Gk. κάρπασος): cf. Malayan *kapas*, etc. An unprefixed form appears in Črau *paç*, *baç*, Stieng *patic*, which may be reflected in Ta. *pañci*, Ka. *pañji* 'cotton', and possibly in Skt. *picu* 'id'.

jambāla- 'mud': cf. Santal *jo̱bo̱*, etc., 'damp'. Kharia

jobhi ' swampy ground ', *jubilā* ' a wet field ', Ho. *jobe* ' mud ', Savara *jobbā-* ' id '.

jim-, *jemati* ' to eat ' (late ; common in Mod. IA, Hi. *jevnā* ' to eat ', *jimānā* ' to feed ', Mar. *jevnẽ* ' to eat ', etc.) : cf. Santal *jām*, Kurku *jome*, Juang *jim*, Savara *jvm*, etc.

tāmbūla- ' betel ' : prefixed form ; cf. Alak *balu*, Khmer *mluo*, Bahnar *bölöu*, etc. ; various prefixes, Mon *ǰablu*, Halang *lamlu*, etc. No form is quoted corresponding exactly to Sanskrit, but the same radical element is shared by all.

marica- ' pepper ': cf. Mon *mrāk*, Khmer *mereć* ' id '. In the Munda languages there are some forms corresponding to Skt. *marica-*, but the opinion now is that these are loans from Sanskrit.

lāṅgala- ' plough ', Pa. *naṅgala* : cf., with varying prefixes, Khmer *aṅkăl*, Čam *laṅal*, *laṅar*, Khasi *ka-lynkor*, Malay *teṅgala*, *taṅgāla*, Batak *tiṅgala*, Makassar *naṅkala*. In Muṇḍa there is Santal *nahel*. This word is interesting because Dravidian has borrowed independently from the same source : Ta. *ñāñcil*, Ka. *nēgal*, etc. A non-prefixed form with the change *k*>*h* characteristic of the northern group of Muṇḍa languages, appears in Sanskrit as *hala-* ' plough '.

sarṣapa- ' mustard ': Pkt. *sāsava-*; cf. Malay *sesawi*, etc. Old Tamil *aiyavi*, if form **sasavi* also belongs here.

This short selection of words is sufficient to show the importance of Austro-Asiatic as a source of Sanskrit words. When the languages concerned have been properly studied and properly compared it is expected that more will be available, and that there will be greater certainty about the detailed history of the forms concerned. At present such studies are in their infancy, so that it is not possible to estimate how much of the Indo-Aryan vocabulary will eventually prove to be derived from this source.

The most important source of the foreign element in the Sanskrit vocabulary is to be found in the Dravidian languages. Although the comparative study of the Dravidian languages is still in its infancy, the position is much better than with the Muṇḍa languages. Full lexicographical material is available for the major literary languages, and although much work remains to be done in the first-hand study of the minor languages, more is known about them than about the majority of the Muṇḍa languages. More work has been done on the influence of Dravidian on Sanskrit and more abundant results have been achieved. It is now possible to draw up a considerable list of words in Sanskrit which can be traced either with certainty or with a high degree of probability to a Dravidian origin. This is illustrated by the following list:

aguru 'fragrant aloe wood': Ta. Ma. *akil*, Tu. *agilu̥* 'id'.

aṅkola- 'Alangium hexapetalum': Ta, *ariñcil*, Ma. *ariññil* 'id'.

anala- 'fire': Ta. *aṉal* 'fire; vb. to burn', Ma. *anal* 'fire' Ka. *analu* 'heat'.

arka- 'Calotropis gigantea': Ta. *erukku*, Ma. *erikku*, Ka. *erke*, *ekke* 'id..

ulapa- 'bush, shrub, a kind of soft grass, a creeper': Ta. *ulavai* 'green twig with leaves on it, branch of a tree, grove, n. of various shrubs'.

ulupin- 'porpoise: Ka. *uṇaci*, Te. *uluca*, *ulusa*.

ulūkhala- 'mortar': Ta. *ulakkai* 'pestle', Ma. *ulakka*, Ka. *olake* 'id', Te. *rõkali* 'a large wooden pestle'.

eḍa- 'sheep, ram, wild goat': Ta. *yāṭu*, *āṭu* 'goat, sheep', Ka. *āḍu* 'goat', Tu. *ēḍu̥* 'id', Te. *ēṭa* 'ram', Go. *ēṭī* 'she-goat', Brah. *hēṭ* 'id'.

kaṅka- 'heron': cf. Ta. Ma. Ka. *kokku* 'crane, stork, heron', Tu. *korṅgu* 'crane', Te. *koṅga*, Kuvi *koṅgi* 'id'.

kajjala- 'soot, lampblack': Ta. *karical* 'blackness'.

kaṭu- 'pungent, acrid, sharp': Ta. *kaṭu* 'severe, pungent, sharp', Ma. *kaṭu* 'extreme, impetuous, fierce', *kaṭukka* 'to grow hard, sharp', Ka. Te. Tu. *kaḍu* 'severe, intense', etc.

kaṭhina- 'hard, firm, stiff': Ta. *kaṭṭi* 'anything hardened, coagulated', Ka. *kaḍugu* 'to become hard', *gaṭṭi* 'firmness, hardness', Tu. *gaṭṭi* 'firm, hard', Te. *kaṭṭĭḍi* 'hard-hearted', *gaṭṭi* 'hard, firm'.

karīra- 'shoot of bamboo': cf. Ka. *kaṟile* 'bamboo shoot', Tu. *kaṉile*, Pa. *karri*, Kur. *k͟harrā* 'id', Brah. *k͟harring* 'to sprout'.

kāka- 'crow': Ta. *kākkai*, Ma. *kākka*, Ka. *kāke*, Pa. *kākal*, Kur. *k͟hāk͟hā*, Malt. *qāqe*, Brah. *k͟hāk͟hō* 'id'.

kāca-, *kāja-* 'carrying yoke': Ta. *kā* 'id', *kāvu* 'carry with yoke', Pa. *kācal* 'carrying yoke', *kāñ-* 'to carry with yoke', Kui *kāsa*, Kuvi *kāñju* 'carrying yoke'.

kāñcika-, *kāñjika-* 'rice-gruel': Ta. *kañci*, Ma. *kaññi*, Ka. Tu. Te. *gañji* 'id'.

kānana- ' forest ': Ta. *kā* ' forest ', *kān* ' id ', *kāṉam* ' woodland, grove ', *kāṉal* ' grove or forest on the seashore ', Ma. *kāvu* 'garden, grove ', *kānal* ' dry jungle ', Ka. *kā* ' forest '.

kāla- ' black ': Ta. *kāṟ* ' blackness ', Ka. *kāṟ* ' id ', *kaṟgu* ' to turn black '.

kuṭa- ' pot ': Ta. Ma. *kuṭam,* Ka. *koḍa,* Ko. *koṛm* ' id '.

kuṭi- ' hut, house ': Ta. Ma. *kuṭi,* Ka. Tu. Te. *guḍi* ' hut, house, temple ', Kui *kūṛi* ' hut '.

kuṭila- ' crooked ': Ta. *koṭu* ' crooked ', *kuṭa* ' curved, bent ' *kuṭavu* ' bend, curve ', Ma. *koṭu,* Ka. *kuḍu* ' crooked '.

kuṭṭ- ' to pound ': Ta. *kuṭṭ-* ' cuff, strike with the knuckles ', Ma. *kuṭṭuka* ' to pound, cuff ', Ka. *kuṭṭu* ' to beat, pound '.

kuṇḍa- ' hole in the ground, pit ': Ta. *kuṇṭu* ' hollow, pool, pit ', Ma. *kuṇṭu* ' hole, pit ', Ka. *kuṇṭe, kuṇḍa, guṇḍi* ' hole, pit ', etc.

kuṇḍala- ' ring, earring, coil of rope ': cf. Ka. *guṇḍa, guṇḍu* ' round ', Tu. *guṇḍu* ' anything round ', *guṇḍala* ' an ear ornament ', Te. *guṇḍrana* ' roundness ', *guṇḍrani* ' round '.

kuddāla- ' kind of spade or hoe ': Ka. *guddali* ' kind of pickaxe, hoe ', Tu. *guddoli,* Te. *guddali* ' id ', Ko. *kudāy* ' hoe ', Malt. *qodali* ' id ': cf. Ka. *guddu* ' strike, pound ', etc.

kuntala- ' hair of head ': Ta. Ma. *kūntal,* Ka. *kūdal* ' id '.

kurula- ' curl ': Ta. *kuruḷ* ' to curl; a curl ', Ma. *kuruḷ* ' curls ', Ka. *kuruḷ,* Te. *kurulu* ' id '.

kulattha- ' Dolichos uniflorus ': cf. Ta. *koḷ,* Ma. *koḷḷu,* Tu. *kuḍu,* Pa. *kol* ' id.'.

kuvalaya- ' lotus ': Ta. *kuvaḷai,* Ka. *kōmaḷe, kōvaḷ, kōḷe* ' id '.

kūpa- ' mast ': Ta. Ma. *kūmpu,* Tu. *kūvè, kuvè* ' id '.

ketaka- ' Pandanus odoratissimus ': Ta. *kaitai, kaital,* Ma. Ka. *kēdage,* Te. *gēdage* ' id '.

kemuka- (also *kevuka-, kecuka-, kacu-, kacvī*) ' Colocasia antiquorum ': Ta. Ma. *cēmpu,* Tu. *cēvu, tēvu,* Ka. *kesu, kesa, kesavu, kēsu, kēsave,* Te. *cēma* ' id '.

koṭara- ' hollow, cavity ': Ka. *goṭaru, goṭru* ' hollow, hole (in wall, tree, etc.), cf. *goḍagu* ' id '.

koṇa- ' corner ': Ta. *kōṇ* ' crookedness, corner, angle ', *kōṇu* ' to be bent, crooked ', Ma. *kōṇ* ' corner, angle ', *kōṇuka* ' to bend ', Ka. *kōṇ, kōṇe,* Tu. *kōṇe,* Te. *kōna* ' corner '.

kōraka- ' bud ', Ta. *kuṟai* ' sprout, shoot ', Kui *kōṛu* ' new shoot or bud ', Kur. *k͟hōrnā* ' to shoot out new leaves ', *khōr* ' leaf-bud, new leaves ', Malt. *qōroce* ' to sprout '.

khala- ' threshing-floor ': Ta. Ma. *kaḷam* ' threshing-floor, open space ', Ka. *kaḷa, kaṇa* ' threshing floor ', Te. *kalanu*, Pa. *kali*, Kui *klai* ' id '.

khala- ' a rogue ': Ta. *kaḷ* ' to steal ', *kaḷvan* ' thief ', *kaḷavu* ' theft, deception ', Ka. *kaḻḻa* ' thief ', Te. *kalla* ' deceit ', *kallari* ' a rogue ', etc.

gaṇḍa- ' lump, excrescence, boil ' Ka. *gaḍḍe* ' mass, lump, concretion ', Te. *gaḍḍa* ' lump, mass, clot, boil '.

guḍa- ' globe, ball ': Ka. *guḍasu* ' anything round ', *guḍḍu* ' eyeball, egg ', Te. *guḍḍu* ' id '

ghūka- ' owl ': Ta. *kūkai*, Ka. *gūgi, gūge, gūbi*, Te. *gūba, gūbi* ' id '.

candana- ' sandal wood ': Ta. *cāntu* ' paste, sandal paste ', *cāttu* ' daub, smear ', Ma. *cāntu* sandal paste ', Ka. *sādu* ' a fragrant substance ', Te. *cādu* ' to rub into a paste '.

capeṭā ' slap with the open hand ': Ka. *capparisu* ' to slap ', *cappaḷi* ' clapping the hands ', Te. *cappaṭa* ' a clap of the hands '.

cikkaṇa- ' unctuous, viscid ': Te. *cikkā-baḍu* ' to become thick or inspissated ', *cikkani* ' thick or inspissated ', Ka. *cigil jigil* ' to be viscous, glutinous '.

cumb- ' to kiss ': Ta. *cūppu* ' to suck ', *cūmpu* ' to suck, fondle with the lips ', Tu. *jumbuni* ' to suck ', etc.

cūḍā ' tuft of hair, crest: Ta. *cūṭu* to wear on the head '; hair tuft, crest '. Ma. *cūṭuka* ' to wear on the head ', *cūṭṭu* ' cock's comb ', Ka. *sūḍu*, etc.

talina- ' thin, fine, slender, meagre ': Ka. *teḷ* ' thinness fineness ', *teḻḻane, teḻḻanna* ' thin, delicate ', Te. *tellena* ' thinnish ', etc.

tāḍaka-, tāla-, tālaka- ' lock, bolt ': Ta. *tāṟ* ' bolt, bar ', *tāṟkkōl* ' id ', Ma. Ka. *tāṟ*, Tu. *tārkolu* ' id '.

tāmarasa- ' lotus ',: Ta. *tāmarai*, Ma. *tāmara* Ka. *tāmare*, Te. *tāmara*, Pa. *tāmar* ' id '.

tāla- palmyra palm ': Ka. *tāṟ*, Te. *tāḍu* ' id '.

tubarī ' Cajanus indicus ': Ta. *tuvarai*, Ma. *tuvara*, Ka. *togari, tovari*, Tu. *togari, togarè* ' id '.

tuvara- ' astringent ': Ta. *tuvar* ' to be astringent; astringency ', *tuvarppu* ' astringent taste ', Ka. *tuvara, tovara, togari, togaru* ' astringent ', Kui *torpa* ' to be astringent '.

tūla- ' cotton, down ': Ta. Ma. *tūval* ' feather, down ', etc.

nakra- ' alligator ': Ka. *negaṟ*, Tu. *negaṟu*, Te. *negaḍu* ' id '.

nirguṇḍī ' Vitex negundo ': cf. Ta. *nocci*, Tu. *nekki* Ka. *nekki, lekki, lakki* ' id '.

nīra- ' water ': Ta. Ma. Ka. *nīr*, Tu. *nīru̥*, Pa. *nīr* ' water ', Kui *nīru* ' juice, sap, essence ', Brah. *dīr* ' water '.

paṭola- ' Trichosanthes dioeca ': Ta. *puṭal*, *puṭalai*, Ma. *puṭṭal*, *piṭṭal*, Ka. Te. *poṭla* ' id '.

paṇḍa- ' eunuch, effeminate man ': Ta. *peṇ*, *peṇṭu* ' woman ', *peṭṭaiyan̲*, *pēṭi* ' hermaphrodite ', Ka. *peṇ*, *peṇḍa* ' woman ', Te. *peṇṭi* ' woman ', *pēḍi* ' eunuch ', etc.

pallī ' house lizard ': Ta. Ma. Ka. Tu. *palli* ' lizard ,' Te. *balli* ' id '.

pallī ' small village ': Ta. Ma. Ka. *paḷḷi* ' hamlet, settlement, small village ', Te. *palli*, *palliya* ' id '.

puṅkha- ' feathered part of arrow ': Ta. *pur̲uku* ' arrowhead ', Ka. *piḷuku*, *piḷku* ' feathered part of arrow '.

puttikā ' the white ant or termite ': cf. Ta. *pur̲r̲u*, Ka. *puttu*, Te. *puṭṭa*, Kur. *puttā*, Malt. *pute* ' white anthill '; This Drav. word also appears in Skt. as *puṭa-* in *pipīlikāpuṭa-* ' anthill '.

punnāga Calophyllum inophyllum ': Ta. *pun̲n̲ai*, Ma. *punna*, Ka. *ponne*, *punnike*, Tu. *ponne*, Te. *ponna* ' id '.

baka- ' crane ': Ta. *vakkā*, *vaṅkā* ' white stork ', Te. *vakku* ' crane '.

bala- ' strength ': Ta. *val* ' strong ', *valam* ' strength ', Ka. *bal* ' strong ', *balume*, *baluhu* ' strength ', Tu. *balu* ' big, powerful ', Te. *vali*, *valudu* ' id ', etc.

bila- ' hole, cave ': Ta. *viḷavu* ' cleft, crack ', *viḷ*, *viḷḷu* ' to crack, split ', Ma. *viḷḷu* ' to crack, burst open ', *viḷḷal* ' a hollow, rent ', *viḷḷu* ' a crack, aperture '.

bilva- ' Aegle marmelos ': Ta. *viḷā*, *viḷavu*, *ceḷḷil* ' Feronia elephantum ', Ma. *viḷā*, Ka. *beḷaval*. Te. *velãga* ' id '.

maṅku- ' confused, stupefied ' (Buddh. Skt. *madgu-*): cf. Ta. *makku* ' to become dull; dullness ', *maṅku* ' to grow dim, lose lustre ', Ma. *maṅṅuka* ' id ', Ka. *maṅku* dimness, obscurity ', *maggu* ' grow dim or faint '.

mayūra- ' peacock ': Ta. *maññai*, *mayil*, Ma. *mayil*, Tu. *mairu̥*, Pa. *mañil* ' id '.

mallikā ' jasmine ': Ma. *mullai*, Ma. *mulla*, Ka. *molle*, Te. *molla* ' id '.

maṣi- ' ink, lampblack ': Ta. *mai* ' blackness, ink, lampblack ', Ka. *masi* ' dirt, impurity, soot, ink ', Tu. *maji* ' coal, black powder, ink ' Te. *masi* blackness, soot, charcoal, ink '.

mālā ' wreath, garland ': Ta. *mālai*, Ka. *māle*, Ma. Te. *māla* garland ', Ta. *malai* ' to wear as a garland '.

mīna- ' fish ': Ta. *mīṉ*, Ka. *mīn*, Te. *mīnu*, Go. *mīn*, Malt. *mīnu* ' id '.

mukuṭa- ' crest, diadem ': Ta. Ma. *mukaṭu* ' top, highest part, head ', Ta. *mucci* ' crown of head ', Ma. *mukaḷ* ' top, summit, ridge of roof ', Ka. Te. *mogaḍu* ' rudge of roof ', Tu. *mugili* ' turret ', Go. *mukur* ' comb of cock '.

mukula- ' bud ': Ta. Ma. *mukiṟ* ' a bud ', Ta. *mukai* ' to bud; a bud ', Ta. *mokkuḷ* ' a bud ', Ka. *muguḷ* ' a bud; to bud ', *moggu, mogge* ' a bud ', Kui *mogo* ' bud '.

muktā ' pearl ': Ta. *muttu, muttam*, Ma. Ka. Tu. *muttu* ' id '.

muraja- ' drum ': Ta. *muracu* ' drum ', *mracam* ' id ', *mural* ' ton sound ', Ka. *more* ' to hum ', Te. *morayu* ' to sound '.

muruṅgī Moringa pterygosperma ': Ta. *muruṅkai*, Ma. *muriṅṅa*, Ka. *nuggi, nugge*, Tu. *nurige, nurge*, Te. *munaga*, Pa. *mulŋga* ' id ', etc.

lālā ' saliva, spittle ': Ma. *ñōḷa, nōḷa*, Tu. *ñōli, nōṇe*, Ka. *lōḷe* ' id '.

valaya- ' bracelet ': Ta. *vaḷai* ' circuit, bracelet ', vb. to bend, be round, surround ', Ka. *baḷe* ' bracelet ', *baḷasu* ' to go round, encircle, encompass '.

vallī ' creeper ': Ta. Ma. *vaḷḷi*, Ka. *baḷḷi*, Te. *valli* ' id '.

śakala- ' scales of fish; bark ': Ta. *cekiḷ* ' skin or rind of fruit '; ' fish-scales ', Tu. *caguḷi* ' rind of fruit ', Malt. *ceglo* ' shell of fruit '.

sīmikā 'ant ': Te. *cīma*, Kol. *sīma*, Kuvi *sīma* ' ant '.

hintāla- ' the marshy date tree ': Ta. *īntu* ' date pam ', *īñcu, īccam-paṉai* ' id ', Ma. *ītta, īttal*, Ka. *īcal, īcil*, Tu. *īñcilu, īcilu*, Te. *īdu, īdāḍu* ' id '.

huḍukka- ' small drum ': Ta. *uṭukku, uṭukkai* ' a small drum ', Ma. *uṭukka*, Tu. *uḍuku*, Te. *uḍuka* ' id '.

heramba- ' buffalo ': Ta. *erumai* ' buffalo ', Ma. *erima*, Ka. *emme*, Tu. *erme*, Go. *ermī, armī* ' id '.

Concerning the date when these words were taken into Sanskrit it may be observed that the majority are post-Vedic. On the other hand it is important to note that there is a small nucleus already found in the Rgveda. Such are: *ulūkhala-, kaṭuka-, kuṇḍa, khala-, bala-, bila-, mayūra-*. The number added in the later Saṃhitās (e.g. AV *tūla-, bilva-*, VS *kaṅka-*) and in the Brāhmaṇas (e.g. ŚB *arka-, maṅku-*) remains comparatively restricted. The large majority first appear in the classical language, but in its early stage, being first recorded in

Pāṇini, Patañjali, Mahabhārata, Śrautasutra, etc. The majority appear also in Pali, which is important for dating since these canonical texts take us back to a period from 500–300 B.C. The number that occur first only in later Sanskrit literature is again comparatively small. It is clear that as far as Sanskrit is concerned the active period of borrowing from Dravidian was well over before the Christian era. In Prakrit there are some new borrowings from Dravidian, but they are a good deal less numerous than those recorded above for the early Sanskrit period. They form only a small percentage of the new vocabulary of Prakrit. The common vocabulary of Modern Indo-Aryan has further new elements as opposed to Prakrit, but it is only rarely that any of these can be shown to be Dravidian.

It is evident from this survey that the main influence of Dravidian on Indo-Aryan was concentrated at a particular historical period, namely between the late Vedic period and the formation of the classical language. This is significant from the point of view of the locality where the influence took place. It is not possible that at this period such influence could have been exercised by the Dravidian languages of the South. There were no intensive contacts with South India before the Maurya period by which time the majority of these words had already been adopted by Indo-Aryan. If the influence took place in the North in the central Gangetic plain and the classical Madhyadeśa the assumption that the pre-Aryan population of this area contained a considerable element of Dravidian speakers would best account for the Dravidian words in Sanskrit. The Dravidian languages Kurukh and Malto are preserved even now in Northern India, and may be regarded as islands surviving from a once extensive Dravidian territory. The Dravidian words in the *Ṛgveda* attest the presence of Dravidian in North-Western India at that period. Brahui in Baluchistan remains as the modern representative of north-western Dravidian.

It follows that the problem of Dravidian loanwords in Sanskrit is somewhat different from what is usually met with in loanword studies, since the particular dialects or languages from which the borrowings took place have vanished leaving no record behind, and the major Dravidian languages of the South, with which mainly the comparisons must be made, are separated by great distances geographically and by anything up to a millenium or over in time. Fortunately the differences between the various Dravidian languages are not so great as to render dubious the reconstruction of the primitive form of the language and the form of words met with in the loanwords in Sanskrit does not differ materially from that which is arrived at by the comparative study of the existing Dravidian languages. It is a characteristic of the Dravidian languages that they have not evolved with the same rapidity as Indo-Aryan, and consequently the classical Dravidian languages and even the minor spoken languages recorded only in modern times can be used profitably to trace the Dravidian origin of Sanskrit words which were borrowed before any of these languages are themselves recorded, and from other ancient Dravidian dialects which have themselves disappeared.

§ 2. Loanwords from Greek and Iranian

The Sanskrit vocabulary acquired a limited number of Greek words, partly as a result of the rule of the Bactrian Greeks in North-West India in the second and first centuries B.C., and partly through contacts in respect of trade, etc. with the Graeco-Roman world. Words that can be ascribed to the Bactrian Greeks are *khalīna-* 'bridle' (χαλῖνός), *suruṅgā* 'underground passage' (σῦριγξ) and *paristoma-* 'coverlet, blanket' (περίστρωμα), and possibly *kunta-* 'lance' (κοντός). The Sanskrit lexica have preserved a word *keṇikā* 'tent' which can be explained as a Prakritic adaptation of Gk. σκηνή. In common with other Hellenistic rulers the Greeks of Bactria and India adopted the title σωτήρ 'saviour' (rendered *trātara-* in their coins). This title, not in its precise sense, but as an honorific epithet gained currency in the local Prakrits as *soṭīra-/soḍīra-*, and thence was adapted into Sanskrit as *śauṭīra-* 'hero, noble and generous man'.

Other words of Greek origin are better accounted for as having been acquired through trade, etc., e.g. *kastīra-* 'tin' (κασσίτερος) *melā* 'ink' (μέλαν), *marakata-* 'emerald' (μάραγδος, σμάραγδος) *kimpala-* 'kind of musical instrument' (κύμβαλον). Some words of Greek origin which only appear very late in Sanskrit have probably been taken in the first place from some intermediate language, e.g. *kalama-* 'pen' (κάλαμος) *dramma-* 'a coin' (δραχμή). The word *kramelaka-* 'camel' (κάμηλος) is also late, and disguised by popular etymology (as if from *kram-*).

It is possible that *harimantha-* ' chickpea ' has been similarly adapted from Gk. ἐρέβινθος, though if so it has been even more effectively disguised.

There is a special class of Greek words occurring as technical terms in astronomical literature. The development of Indian astronomy in the early centuries of the Christian era was profoundly affected by Greek astronomy and a considerable number of its technical terms were adopted. Such words are *heli-* ' sun ', *horā* ' hour ', *kendra-* ' centre of a circle ' *jāmitra-* ' diameter ' (Gk. ἥλιος, ὥρα, κέντρον, διάμετρον). Some of these also were distorted by popular etymology, e.g. *hṛdroga-* ' the zodiacal sign Aquarius ' (Gk. ὑδροχόος).

Contact with the Graeco-Roman world introduced one Latin word only into Sanskrit, namely *dīnāra-* ' name of a coin ' (<*denarius*).

Following on the Greek invasions the northwestern part of India was the scene of a series of invasions by Iranian tribes, Pahlavas, Śakas, Kuṣānas and finally Hūṇas. This state of affairs prevailed during most of the first six centuries of the Christian era, and resulted in the establishment of a number of powerful dynasties of such origin, principally in Northwestern and Western India, but sometimes extending their sway further afield. This resulted in the adoption of a number of Iranian terms, first into Prakrit (principally the North-Western Prakrit), and eventually into Sanskrit. Examples from Indian inscriptions in Kharoṣṭhī and Brāhmī scripts are *horaka-* ' donator ', and *bakanapati-* ' shrine attendant ' (Khot. *haur-*, *hor-* ' to give ', Sogdian *βγnpt*). In the North-Western Prakrit used in Central Asia these are quite frequent. In Sanskrit itself there are a not inconsiderable number which have entered the language at various periods. One of the earliest is *lipi* ' writing ' (occurring in Aśokan also in the form *dipi-*) from OPers. *dipi-*. This word was borrowed at the time writing was introduced into India. Later a word *divira-* ' scribe ' of the same origin was introduced, though it had restricted currency. The word *mudrā* ' seal ' is likewise attributable to Old Persian, although it happens not to be recorded in Iranian until later (Pahl. NPers. *muhr*), and *karṣa-* ' n. of a particular weight ' has been considered to derive from OPers. *karša-*.

Among the other Iranian loanwords the following may be listed: *kṣatrapa-* ' satrap ' used as a title by certain of the above mentioned Iranian rulers, *vārabāṇa-* ' armour, mail ' (OIr. **varopāna-* ' protecting the breast '), *khola-* ' helmet, a kind of hat ' (Av. *xaoδa-*, Pašt. *xōl*), *jagara-* ' armour ' (cf. Pašt. *zgara* ' armour '), *māḍhī* ' armour mail ' (MPers. *māδī*(k)), *tīrī* ' a kind of arrow ' (NPers. *tīr*) *paryāṇa-* ' saddle ' (Ir. **paridāna-* in NPers. *pālān* ' pack-saddle ', etc.), *pīlu-* ' elephant ' (NPers. *pīl*) *bandī* ' prisoner, captive ' (NPers. *bandah*), *gola-* ' ball ' (NPers. *gōy*<**gauda-*), *gañja-* ' treasury ' (NPers. *ganǰ*). As can be seen from this list the words borrowed from Iranian have mainly to do with military affairs and equipment, which is in accordance with their military superiority over many centuries. Of words not connected with war, mention may be made of *pustaka-* ' book ' ultimately derived from Iranian (Pers.) *pōst* ' skin ' and *mihira-* ' sun ' (Pers. *mihr* OIr. *miθra-*). Some Iranian loanwords are attested only in writers from Kashmir (e.g. *gañja-*, *divira-*) where they derive from the North-Western Prakrit. There are others which are found only in Buddhist Sanskrit, e.g. *kākhorda-* ' wizard ' (cf. Av. *kax^{v}arδa-*) *mocika-* ' shoemaker ' MPers. *mōčak*) whence Hindi *mocī* ' id '. These words are also derived through the North-Western Prakrit, since it was the Buddhist writers of the North-Western schools who were responsible for their adoption.

APPENDIX TO THE THIRD EDITION

Supplementary Notes and Bibliographical References

CHAPTER I

§ 1. For a detailed discussion of the term *árya-* and its cognates see H. W. Bailey, *Iranian arya and daha*, Transactions of the Philological Society, 1959, pp. 71–115. For *árya-* as applied to the language of the Indo-Aryans, cf. Śāṅkhāyana Āraṇyaka 8, 9: *yatrāryā vāg vadati*, and Aitareya Āraṇyaka 3, 2, 5: *yatra kva ca āryā vāco bhāṣante*. For similar usage in Buddhist Sanskrit, see Bailey, op. cit. p. 102. The term Saṃskṛta is late in appearing, and it is not used by Pāṇini or Patañjali. The earliest recorded occurrence is in Rāmāyaṇa, 3, 10, 54, after which it becomes quite common (Nāṭyaśāstra, Suśruta, Kāvyādarśa, etc).

§ 3. The mutual relations of the Indo-European languages, as well as the question of their original home, have continued to be the subject of active discussions. Among recent works dealing with these problems the following list is a selection: W. Porzig, *Die Gliederung des indogermanischen Sprachgebietes*, Heidelberg, 1954; P. Thieme, *Die Heimat der indogermanischen Gemeinsprache*, Mainz, 1953; H. Krahe, *Sprache und Vorzeit*, Heidelberg, 1954; H. Hencken, *Indo-European languages and archaeology* (American Anthropological Association, Memoir 84) 1955; P. Bosch-Gimpera. *Les Indoeuropéens: problèmes archéologiques*, Paris, 1961; G. Devoto, *Origine indoeuropee*, Firenze, 1961; M. Gimbutas, *The Indo-europeans; archaeological problems* (in American Anthropologist, 65, pp. 815 ff.), 1963; V. Georgiev, *Introduzione alla storia delle lingue indoeuropee*, Rome, 1966; G. Cardona, H. M. Hoenigswald and A. Senn (ed.), *Indo-European and Indo-Europeans*, Philadelphia, 1970; R. A. Crossland, *Invaders from the North* (in Cambridge

Ancient History, pp. 824–876), 1971. Opinions as to the original Indo-European homeland continue to differ; suggestions include the region south of the Baltic sea (Thieme), the steppes north of the Caucasus (Gimbutas) and the Danube basin and surrounding regions (Georgiev). The last alternative seems to fit in best with the historical distribution of the languages and dialects.

§ 4. The inportance of the connections between Indo-Iranian and Baltic in particular has been stressed by H. W. Bailey (BSOAS 21 (1958), pp. 42 ff.) in connection with such words as *návanīta-* 'butter', *netra-* 'churning string' (cf. Lett. *niju, nīt* 'to make a circular movement, churn'), *bī́ja-* 'seed' (with *b-*<*m-*; cf. Lith. *miežỹs* 'barley-corn', Lett. *miezis*), *ríp-* 'ascent, elevation' (Lith. *lìpti* 'to rise, ascend').

Further Baltic comparisons, to be added to the list given in this section are as follows: *tand-* 'to be weary, slothful', *tandrī́* 'sloth': Lith. *tandus* 'lazy, slothful'; *mūrkhá-* 'fool': Lith. *mùlkis*; *tviṣ-* 'to sparkle, glitter': Lith. *tviskė́ti* 'to lighten'; *śakala-* 'chip, fragment, splinter': Lith. *šakalỹs* 'chip of wood'; *pūla-* 'bunch, bundle': Lett. *pūlis* 'heap', *buli-* 'anus', Lith. *bulìs* *vā́la-* 'the hair of an animals tail (particularly a horse's tail)': Lith *vãlas* 'hair of horse's tail'.

§ 5. The Indo-Aryan (and Indo-European) loanwords in the Finno-Ugrian languages are listed by B. Collinder in *Fenno-ugric vocabulary; an etymological dictionary of the Uralic languages*, pp. 129–141, Stockholm, 1955.

§ 6. Since 1955 a small amount of new Aryan material from the Near East has turned up. The documents from Nuzi have revealed certain colour adjectives applied to horses, in Hurrian form *paprunnu/babrunnu, pinkarannu, paritannu*, corresponding to Sanskrit *babhrú- piṅgalá-* and *palitá-*. The change of original *-l-* to *-r-* in *parita-* and *pinkara-*, a change which had previously been noted in *Šuriaš*, is of considerable importance, since it shows that this change, characteristic of Iranian and the Ṛgvedic dialect of Old Indian had already taken place before 1500 B.C. Other words that have been noted in this connection are *makanni* 'gift', *maninnu* 'neck ornament', cf. Skt. *maṇí-*, *maghá-*, and possibly *urukmannu* corresponding to Skt. *rukmá-*

'bright ornament'. If the connection between *mištannu* 'reward' and Skt. *mīḍhá-* proposed by Mayrhofer is accepted, then we have a pre-Vedic Indo-Iranian form (**mižḍha-*) represented.

A complete bibliography to the end of 1965, and a summing up of the subject, is provided by M. Mayrhofer in *Die Indo-Arier im alten Vorderasien; mit einer analytischen Bibliographie*, Wiesbaden, 1966. There is also a detailed discussion of the subject by A. Kammenhuber in *Die Arier im vorderen Orient*, Heidelberg, 1968. The work contains valuable discussions, but carries scepticism too far (on which see M. Mayrhofer, *Die vorderasiatischen Arier*, Asiatische Studien (Études Asiatiques) XXIII, pp. 139–154), Bern, 1969.

The Aryan gods of the Mitanni treaties are discussed in an important article by P. Thieme in JAOS, 80, pp. 301–317, 1960.

CHAPTER II

§ 2. On the subject matter of this section see further: M. B. Emeneau, *The dialects of old Indo-Aryan*, in H. Birnbaum and J. Puhvel (ed.), *Ancient Indo-European dialects*, Berkeley and Los Angeles, 1966.

§ 3. The study of Pāṇini and the Sanskrit grammarians has been actively pursued during recent years. The following are the most important publications since 1955: P. Thieme, *Pāṇini and the Pāṇinīyas*, JAOS, 76, pp. 1–23, 1956; L. Renou, *Terminologie grammaticale du sanskrit* (2nd ed.), Paris, 1957; Y. Ojihara and L. Renou, *La Kāśikā-vṛtti* (Adhyāya I, Pāda 1), Paris, 1960–67; K. V. Abhyankar, *A dictionary of Sanskrit grammar*, Baroda, 1961; B. Shefts, *Grammatical method in Pāṇini: his treatment of Sanskrit present stems*, New Haven, 1961; K. Birwé, *Der Gaṇapāṭha zu den Adhyāyas IV and V der Grammatik Pāṇinis, Versuch einer Rekonstruktion*, Wiesbaden, 1961, and *Studien zu Adhyāya III der Aṣṭādhyāyī Pāṇinis*, Wiesbaden, 1966; V. N. Misra, *The descriptive technique of Pāṇini*, The Hague, 1966; R. Rocher, *La théorie des voix du verbe dans l'école pāṇininéenne*, Brussels, 1968; G. Cardona, *Studies in Indian grammarians, I: the method of description reflected in the Śivasutras*, Philadelphia, 1969.

§ 7 (p. 61). The use of mixed Sanskrit in inscriptions, particularly of the Kushanas, is discussed, and illustrated with examples by E. Lamotte in *Histoire de la Bouddhisme indienne*, pp. 640–41, Louvain, 1958.

On Buddhist Sanskrit see further H. W. Bailey, *Buddhist Sanskrit*, JRAS, 1955, pp. 13–24; J. Brough, *The language of the Buddhist Sanskrit texts*, BSOAS, 16, 357–375, 1954; V. Raghavan, *Buddhist Hybrid Sanskrit*, Indian Linguistics, 16, 313–322.

(pp. 61–2). The vocabulary of Jaina Sanskrit has now been dealt with by B. J. Sandesara and J. P. Thaker in *Lexicographical studies in Jaina Sanskrit*, Baroda, 1962.

§ 8. For Sanskrit in Indonesia see now J. Ensink and J. A. B. Buitenen, *Glossary of Sanskrit from Indonesia, Vāk*, no. 6, Poona, 1964.

CHAPTER III

§ 3. There is now a detailed study of the surd aspirates by R. Hiersche: *Untersuchungen zur Frage der tenues aspiratae im Indogermanischen*, Wiesbaden, 1964. Hiersche rejects the laryngeal explanations, and considers the aspiration to have developed mainly in combinations with sibilant (*sthágati*, as opposed to Gk. *στέγω*, etc., a phenomenon to which reference was made above, p. 72). Initial surd aspirates are explained by assuming loss of mobile *s*- (*phéna*-: OPruss. *spoayno*, etc.). Unfortunately Hiersche does not deal at all with those cases of sonant aspirates where such an explanation is impossible: e.g. *rátha*-, *śaphá*-, *śaṅkhá*-, *śā́khā*. For the opposing view see F. B. J. Kuiper, Indo-Iranian Journal, 9, pp. 218–227. It seems however that only a portion of the instances can be explained by the laryngeal theory, and that for others (e.g. *phéna*-) an explanation on the lines proposed by Hiersche is preferable.

§ 5. The statement (p. 75, l. 21) that the *satəm* languages have uniformly abandoned all trace of the labial element needs qualification in one respect as far as Sanskrit is concerned. As first pointed out by O. Szemerényi in a paper ' The problem of Indo-European labio-velars ' read to the Philological Society in March, 1952, roots in *r̥̄* have a weak form in *ur*/*ūr* when the original was a labio-velar, just as happens in the case of the labials, whereas when the initial was a pure velar the weak form is in *ir*/*īr*. This is seen most clearly in the derivatives from the root *gṝ-*/*gur* 'to welcome' (original labio-velar) on the one hand, and *gṝ-*/*gir-* 'to sing' on the other. See further my article *Sanskrit gṝ/gur- 'to welcome'* (BSOAS, 1957, pp. 133–144), and Szemerényi, *Einführung in die vergleichende Sprachwissenschaft*, pp. 60–61.

§ 10. The most recent comprehensive discussion of IE mobile *s* is by F. Edgerton, *IE s movable*, Language 34, pp. 445–453. He takes it to be a sandhi-phenomenon due to the great frequency of final *-s* in Indo-European.

§ 11. The subject matter of this section is dealt with in detail in my two articles, *On the phonological history of Sanskrit kṣám- 'earth', ṛ́kṣa- 'bear' and likṣā 'nit'*, and *Sanskrit kṣi-: Gk. φθὶνω*, in Journal of the American Oriental Society, 79, pp. 85–90 and 255–262, 1959. The subject is treated differently, but beginning from the same standpoint (IE *dheĝhom-* 'earth', etc.) by W. Merlingen in *Μνήμης χάριν* (Gedenkschrift Kretschmer) II, 49 ff. 1957, and Die Sprache, 8, pp. 74–76, 1962. See also O. Szemerényi, *Einführung in die vergleichende Sprachwissenschaft*, pp. 46–47.

§ 13. The literature on IE H and its varieties ('laryngeals') since 1955 is extensive. A useful survey and summing up is to be found in W. Winter (ed.) *Evidence for laryngeals*, The Hague, 1965; especially to be recommended is E. Polomé's introductory survey in this volume: *The laryngeal theory so far. A critical bibliographical survey* (pp. 9–78).

§ 17. On Fortunatov's law see my article *A reconsideration of Fortunatov's law*, BSOAS, 35, pp. 531–544, 1972, which contains a brief account of the disputes concerning this subject, as well as a defence of Fortunatov's theory.

As regards spontaneous cerebralisation it was made clear by H. W. Bailey in a series of articles from 1952 onwards that this has taken place to a much greater extent than previously recognised. I have discussed this subject, adding to Bailey's material, in my article *Spontaneous cerebrals in Sanskrit*, BSOAS, 35, pp. 538–559, 1971.

There are also some cases where the occurrence of cerebral *-ṣ-*

after *a* and *ā* can be accounted for by special reasons: see my articles, *Sanskrit jálāṣa* in W. B. Henning Memorial Volume, pp. 89–97, 19, 1970, and *Sanskrit śáṣpa- and bāṣpa-*, JRAS, 1969, pp. 112–117.

§ 18. Under miscellaneous changes reference should be made to H. W. Bailey's remarks on the alternation of *b* and *m* (Skt. *bīja-*: Ir. *mīz-*, Lith. *miežỹs*) in his articles *Iranian miṣṣa-, Indian bīja-*, BSOAS, 18, pp. 32–42, and *Miṣṣa suppletum, ibid.* 21, pp. 40–47. See also my article, *Sanskrit āmoda- 'fragrance, perfume'*, *Indological Studies in honour of W. Norman Brown*, pp. 23–27, New Haven, 1962.

§ 24. There have recently been some investigations into the rendering of the Vedic accents by traditional reciters of the Veda in S. India. See J. E. B. Gray, *An analysis of Nambudiri Ṛgvedic recitation and the nature of the Vedic accent*, BSOAS, 22, 499–430, and J. F. Staal, *Nambudiri Vedic Recitation*, The Hague, 1961.

CHAPTER IV

§ 5 (p. 131). On the IE suffix *-men-* (and the Sanskrit suffix *-man-*) see now J. Haudry, Le suffixe I.E. *-men*, BSL, 66, pp. 109–137, 1972.

§ 13. The Sanskrit *s*-suffixes have been studied in detail by J. Manessy-Guitton in a number of books and articles; *Les substantifs en -as dans la Ṛksaṃhitā; contribution a l'étude de la morphologie védique*, Dakar-Paris, 1961; *Recherches sur les derivés nominaux a bases sigmatiques en Sanskrit et en Latin*, Dakar, 1963; *Les adjectifṣ simples en -as du Ṛk-saṃhitā* IIJ, 7, 258–283; *Les noms Sanskrits en -nas*, IIj, 8, 171–196, 1965.

§ 14 (p. 168). On the Sanskrit stems in *-ti* see the detailed study by G. Liebert, *Das nominal suffix -ti im altindischen*, Göteborg-Lund, 1947.

(p. 173). On the Vedic abstract nouns in *-tāt* and *-tāti* see now L. Renou, *Les dérivés abstraits en -tāt et -tāti du Ṛgveda*, BSL, 55, 10–19, 1960.

CHAPTER V

§ 9 (p. 256). The instrumental singular termination *-ena* of the *a*-declension is the subject of a detailed study by C. Hauri: *Zur Vorgeschichte des Ausgangs -ena des Instr. Sing. der a-stamme des Altindischen*, Göttingen, 1963.

CHAPTER VI

§ 1. The most recent comprehensive study of the Indo-European numerals is by O. Szemerényi: *Studies in the Indo-European system of numerals*, Heidelberg, 1960.

§ 2 (p. 268, ll. 33–34). The question as to whether Prakrit *se* is to be directly compared with the Iranian words quoted in this section has long been a matter of dispute. The subject has recently been exhaustively discussed by M. Scheller: *Das mittelindische Enklitikum se*, KZ, 81, pp. 1–53. He comes to the conclusion that Pkt. *se* is a secondary development from unaccented *asya*.

CHAPTER VII

§ 2 (p. 298 ff.). On the Indo-European (and Sanskrit) moods, see J. Gonda, *The character of the Indo-European moods*, Wiesbaden, 1956.

(p. 299). The use of the Vedic Injunctive has been exhaustively examined and discussed by K. Hoffman: *Der Injunktiv im Veda*, Heidelberg, 1967.

§ 3 (p. 302). The question of multiple presents formed from Sanskrit roots has been discussed by J. Vekerdi: *On polymorphic presents in the Ṛgveda, Acta Orientalia Academiae Scientiarum Hungaricae* 12, pp. 249–287, Budapest, 1955.

§ 9. On the periphrastic future see now J. Gonda, *A critical survey of the publications on the periphrastic future in Sanskrit, Lingua*, 6, 158–179.

§ 10. The Sanskrit aorist has been studied by T. J. Elarizenkova, *Aorist v Rigvede*, Moscow, 1960, and the sigmatic aorist in particular, very fully and exhaustively, by J. Narten, *Die sigmatischen Aoristen im Veda*, Wiesbaden, 1964. Cf. further on the reduplicated aorist, M. Leumann, *Der altindische kausative Aorist ajījanat*, *Indological Studies in honour of W. Norman Brown*, pp. 152–159, New Haven, 1962, and on the *sa*-aorist, S. Insler, *The Sanskrit sa-Aorist*, *Münchener Studien zur Sprachwissenschaft*, 26, pp. 43–50, 1969.

§ 13 (p. 350). Concerning the imperatives in *-si*, it should be stated not only that they are not normally formed from roots having root presents, but also that in the majority of cases they are formed from roots which make an *s*-aorist. From this it is clear that these forms are to be attached to the *s*-aorist stem, and they may be most simply classified as *s*-aorist imperatives. This is the conclusion reached by G. Cardona in a recent study of this problem; *The Vedic imperatives in -si*, *Language*, 41, pp. 1–18, 1965. On the other hand O. Szemerényi (*Language*, 42, 1–6, 1966) prefers to regard them as syncopated forms of original subjunctives (*darṣasi*>*darṣi*). This appears to be less satisfactory, not only on account of the phonetic difficulties involved, but also because the primary and predominant use of these forms is as imperatives. The few cases, to which Cardona and Szemerényi draw attention, in which they are used in subordinate clauses, are probably to be accounted for as misuse by later poets of a form which had become obsolete.

§ 14 (p. 352). The termination *-s* of the third person singular active of the root aorist optative/precative is found also in Iranian, for which see my article *The Sanskrit Precative* in *Asiatica* (Festschrift Weller), pp. 35–42, 1954.

§ 15 I. On the passive see J. Gonda, *Remarks on the Sanskrit passive*, Leiden, 1951.

§ 17. The latest study of the Vedic infinitives is by P. Sgall, *Die Infinitive im Ṛgveda*, Orientalia Pragensia I, pp. 137–268, Prague, 1958.

CHAPTER VIII

§ 1 (p. 374). On Sanskrit *ghoṭaka*- 'horse' see now my observations in *International Journal of Dravidian Linguistics* I, pp.

20 ff. (1972) where it is argued that it is in origin a middle Indo-Aryan descriptive epithet.

(p. 380). On *marica-* in the Muṇḍa languages see now N. H. Zide, *Current Trends in Linguistics*, Vol. V, pp. 420–421. In the same paragraph he also queries the origin of the verb *jim-* from Muṇḍa, on the ground that the vowel is different in the Muṇḍa languages (Santali *jom-*, etc.), and further remarks that ' the identification of words in Indo-Aryan and Dravidian as Muṇḍa loans, even when this has been done by careful scholars, is not often convincing, particularly in the light of newer data '.

As regards *sarṣapa-* ' mustard ', the Austro-Asiatic origin of this word has now been rendered doubtful by an article by W. B. Henning (Istituto Orientale di Napoli, *Annali, Sezione Linguistica*, VI, 29–47, 1965), where he treats of the Iranian words for ' mustard ' going back to an original **sinšapa-*, and obviously related to the Sanskrit word. In view of this Malay *sesawi*, etc., should probably be regarded as loanwords from Indo-Aryan rather than vice-versa.

SELECT BIBLIOGRAPHY

ALLEN, W. S. *Phonetics in ancient India,* Oxford 1953.

—— *Sandhi; the theoretical, phonetic and historical bases of word-junction in Sanskrit,* 's-Gravenhage 1962.

ARNTZ, H. *Sprachliche Beziehungen zwischen arisch und Balto-slavisch,* Heidelberg 1933.

BENVENISTE, E. *Origines de la formation des noms en indo-européen,* I, Paris 1935.

BLOCH, J. *L'indo-aryen du Veda aux temps modernes,* Paris 1934.

BRUGMANN, H. *Grundriss der vergleichende Grammatik der indo-germanischen Sprachen,* 2nd ed., Strassburg 1897–1916 (Reprint, Berlin 1967).

—— *Kurze vergleichende Grammatik der indo-germanischen Sprachen,* Strassburg 1902–4 (reissue, Berlin 1922).

BÜHLER, J. G. *Indische Paläographie,* Strassburg 1896.

CHATTERJI, S. K. *Indo-Aryan and Hindi,* Ahmedabad 1942.

DELBRÜCK, B. *Altindische Syntax,* Halle 1888.

EDGERTON, F. *Buddhist Hybrid Sanskrit,* I Grammar, II Dictionary, Newhaven 1953.

FRIEDRICH, J. *Hethitisches Elementarbuch,* I, Heidelberg 1940.

GEIGER, W. *Pali Literatur und Sprache,* Strassburg 1916.

GHOSH, B. *Linguistic Introduction to Sanskrit,* Calcutta 1937.

GONDA, J. *Old Indian* (Handbuch der Orientalistik, II Abt. Bd. I, Abschnitt 1), Leiden/Köln 1971.

HENDRIKSEN, H. *Untersuchungen über die Bedeutung des Hethitischen für die Laryngaltheorie,* Copenhagen 1941.

JACOBSOHN, H. *Arier und Ugrofinnen,* Göttingen 1922.

KENT, R. G. *Old Persian Grammar, Texts, Lexicon,* Newhaven 1950.

KURYLOWICZ, J. *L'accentuation des langues indo-européennes,* Cracow 1952.

L'apophonie en indo-européen, Wroclaw 1956.

MACDONELL, A. A. *Vedic Grammar*, Strassburg 1910.

MANSION, J. *Esquisse d'une histoire de la langue sanskrite*, Paris 1931.

MAYRHOFER, M. *Kurzgefasstes etymologisches Wörterbuch des Altindischen* (in progress), Heidelberg 1953 ff.

—— *Sanskrit-Grammatik* (*mit sprachvergleichenden Erlaüterungen*), Berlin 1965.

MEILLET, A. *Les dialectes indo-européennes*, Paris 1908 (1922).

—— *Introduction a l'étude comparative des langues indo-européennes*, 8th ed., Paris 1937 (1949).

PEDERSEN, H. *Hettitisch und die anderen indoeuropäischen Sprachen*, Copenhagen 1938.

—— *Tocharisch von Gesichtspunkt der indoeuropäischen Sprachvergleichung*, Copenhagen 1941.

PISANI, V. *Grammatica del Antico Indiano* (incomplete), Rome 1930–33.

PISCHEL, R. *Grammatik der Prakrit-Sprachen*, Strassburg 1900.

POKORNY, J. *Indogermanisches etymologisches Wörterbuch*, Bern 1959.

REICHELT, H. *Avestisches Elementarbuch*, Heidelberg 1909.

RENOU, L. *Grammaire sanscrite*, Paris 1930.

—— *Grammaire de la langue védique*, Paris 1952.

—— *Histoire de la langue sanskrite*, Lyon and Paris 1956.

SPECHT, F. *Der Ursprung der indogermanischen Deklination*, Göttingen 1944 (1948).

SPEYER, J. *Sanskrit Syntax*, Leiden 1886.

—— *Vedische und Sanskrit-Syntax*, Strassburg 1896.

STURTEVANT, E. H. *The Indo-Hittite Laryngeals*, Baltimore 1942.

—— *A Comparative Grammar of the Hittite Language* (Revised Edition), I, New Haven 1951.

SZEMERÉNYI, O. *Einführung in die vergleichende Sprachwissenschaft*, Darmstadt 1970.

THUMB, A. *Handbuch des Sanskrit.* Dritte, stark umgearbeitete Auflage von Richard Hauschild; I Teil: Grammatik, Heidelberg 1958–59.

UHLENBECK, C. C. *Kurzgefasstes etymologisches Wörterbuch der altindischen Sprache*, Amsterdam 1898–99.

WACKERNAGEL, J. and DEBRUNNER, A. *Altindische Grammatik*, vols. I–III, Göttingen 1896–1954.

WALDE, A. *Vergleichendes Wörterbuch der indogermanischen Sprachen, herausgegeben und bearbeitet von J. Pokorny*, 3 vols., Berlin and Leipzig 1927–32.

WHITNEY, W. D. *A Sanskrit Grammar*, 5th ed., Leipzig 1924.

INDEX